INTELLIGENCE AND
MILITARY OPERATIONS

By the same author

Israel's Political-Military Doctrine (1973)
Weak States in the International System (1981)
The Diplomacy of Surprise (1981)
Clausewitz and Modern Strategy (ed.) (1986)
Strategic and Operational Deception in
the Second World War (ed.) (1987)
Leaders and Intelligence (ed.) (1988)
War, Strategy and Intelligence (1989)

INTELLIGENCE
AND
MILITARY
OPERATIONS

Edited by

MICHAEL I. HANDEL

FRANK CASS

First published 1990 in Great Britain by
FRANK CASS AND COMPANY LIMITED
Gainsborough House, 11 Gainsborough Road,
London E11 1RS, England

and in the United States of America by
FRANK CASS
International Specialized Book Services,
5602 NE Hassalo Street,
Portland OR 97213

Copyright © 1990 by Frank Cass & Co. Ltd.

British Library Cataloguing in Publication Data

Intelligence and military operations
   1. Military intelligence services,
   1915–1945
   I. Handel, Michael I.
355.3'432'0904

ISBN 0-7146-3331-3
ISBN 0-7146-4060-3 Pbk

Library of Congress Cataloging-in-Publication Data

Intelligence and military operations/edited by Michael I. Handel.
                                p. cm.
Papers presented at an international conference held at the
US Army War College, April 1986.
1. Military intelligence–History—20th century–Congresses.
2. Military history, Modern—20th century—Congresses. I. Handel,
Michael I.
UB250.I56 1990   355.3'432'0904—dc   1990-18883
                                                CIP

This group of studies first appeared in a Special Issue on Intelligence and Military Operations of the journal *Intelligence and National Security*, Vol. 5, No. 2 (April 1990), published by Frank Cass & Co. Ltd.

The views expressed in this book are those of the authors and do not reflect the official policy or position of the Department of Defense or the US government.

Printed and bound in Great Britain by
BPCC Wheatons Ltd, Exeter

Dedicated to
PATRICK BEESLY

Contents

Contents

Acknowledgements

This collection of essays is based on papers presented in four international conferences on intelligence and military operations held at the US Army War College from 1985 to 1988. I would like to thank in particular for his encouragement and support the commandant of the US Army War College, Major-General Paul G. Cerjan, and the director of the Strategic Studies Institute (SSI) of the US Army War College, Colonel Carl Robinson. I would also like to thank Dr Andrew Marshall of the Office of Net Assessment for the generous support given to the US Army War College 1988 conference on intelligence and military operations from which a number of the essays included in this volume originated.

This volume is the third in a series of textbooks devoted to the study of military intelligence. The first two are *Strategic and Operational Deception in the Second World War* (1987) and *Leaders and Intelligence* (1988). Others will follow.

M.I.H.

Notes on Contributors

Patrick Beesly served in the Admiralty's Operational Intelligence Centre during the Second World War. He published three books: *Very Special Intelligence* (1977), *Very Special Admiral* (1980, a biography of Rear Admiral John Godfrey, wartime director of Naval Intelligence, and *Room 40* (1982), a study of the Admiralty's First World War signals intelligence, before his death in 1986.

Ralph Bennett was a senior intelligence officer at Bletchley Park during the Second World War. He is the author of two books, *Ultra in the West* (1979) and *Ultra and Mediterranean Strategy* (1989), and a former President of Magdalene College, Cambridge.

Horst Boog is Senior Director of Research and Chief of the Second World War Research Project at the Militärgeschichtliche Forschungsamt in Freiburg, West Germany. His research work focuses in particular on aviation and air war history. He is the author of *Graf Ernst zu Reventlow, Die deutsche Luftwaffenführung*, and co-author of *Der Angriff auf die Sowjetunion, Verteidigung im Bündnis*, and of Vols. 6 and 7 of the MGFA Second World War series *Die Ausweitung zum Weltkrieg* (1989).

Alvin D. Coox is Professor of History and Director of the Japan Studies Institute at San Diego State University, California. He has written and reviewed widely on Japanese military and diplomatic history and the Pacific War, his most recent book being *Nomonhan: Japan against Russia, 1939*, 2 vols. (1986). In 1988 he was awarded the Samuel Eliot Morison Prize by the American Military Institute for his contributions to the field of military history.

Sebastian Cox is a member of the research staff of the Air Historical Branch of the British Ministry of Defence, and was previously on the staff of the Royal Air Force Museum, Hendon. He is currently engaged in writing a biography of Air Chief Marshal Sir Wilfrid Freeman.

Edward J. Drea is the Chief of the Staff Support Branch, US Army Center of Military History in Washington, D.C.

John Ferris is the author of *The Evolution of British Strategic Policy, 1919– 1926* (1989), and of numerous articles on the history of intelligence. He teaches at the University of Calgary.

Michael I. Handel is Professor of National Security and Strategy at the US Army War College, Pennsylvania, and joint founding editor with Christopher Andrew of *Intelligence and National Security*. As author or editor he has published *War, Strategy and Intelligence* (1989), *Clausewitz and Modern Strategy* (1986), *Strategic and Operational Deception in the Second World War* (1987), and *Leaders and Intelligence* (1988).

Jay Luvaas is Professor of Military History at the US Army War College, Pennsylvania. His publications include *The Military Legacy of the Civil War: The European Inheritance* (1959) and *The Education of an Army: British Military Thought, 1915–1940* (1964).

Richard Popplewell did a PhD at Corpus Christi College, Cambridge on British Imperialism and Intelligence during the First World War. He is currently engaged on turning his thesis into a book.

Yigal Sheffy is the Director of Documentation System at the Moshe Dayan Center for Middle Eastern and African Studies, Tel Aviv University, and a Lieutenant-Colonel (res.) in Israel Defence Forces. The author of *Deception in the Western Desert Campaign, 1940–1942* (1987), he is currently preparing a PhD dissertation on the intelligence dimension of the Palestine Campaign during the First World War.

Now if the estimates made in the temple before hostilities indicate victory it is because calculations show one's strength to be superior to that of his enemy; if they indicate defeat, it is because calculations show that one is inferior. With many calculations, one can win; with few one cannot. How much less chance of victory has one who makes none at all! By this means I examine the situation and the outcome will be clearly apparent.

Sun Tzu, *The Art of War*[1]

Therefore I say: 'Know the enemy and know yourself; in a hundred battles you will never be in peril.

'When you are ignorant of the enemy but know yourself, your chances of winning or losing are equal.

'If ignorant both of your enemy and of yourself, you are certain in every battle to be in peril.'

Li Ch'uan: Such people are called 'mad bandits'. What can they expect if not defeat?

Sun Tzu, *The Art of War*[2]

Uncertainty of All Information

Finally, the general unreliability of all information presents a special problem in war: all action takes place, so to speak, in a kind of twilight, which, like fog or moonlight, often tends to make things seem grotesque and larger than they really are.

Whatever is hidden from full view in this feeble light has to be guessed at by talent, or simply left to chance. So once again, for lack of objective knowledge, one has to trust to talent or to luck.

Clausewitz, *On War*[3]

With uncertainty in one scale, courage and self-confidence must be thrown into the other to correct the balance.

Clausewitz, *On War*[4]

Intelligence and Military Operations

MICHAEL I. HANDEL

SOME DEFINITIONS

When considering the past and potential roles of intelligence in war and military operations, one must begin by establishing the meaning of the basic terms involved. Although operational intelligence means many things to many people, Carl von Clausewitz captures its essence in his brief statement that it is '... every sort of information about the enemy and his country – the basis, in short, of our own plans and operations'.[5] In a more lengthy discussion, Donald MacLachlan defines it as '... quite simply, ... information about the enemy. Not just any old information, any scrap of gossip, or rumour, but relevant information which has been processed and made as accurate as it can be ... Intelligence ... is always trying to reduce the margin of ignorance, the element of risk, in the planning of any military operation and indeed of any civil operation'.[6] Elsewhere he makes the important observation that 'intelligence about the enemy is incomplete and ineffective without full knowledge of one's own ... operations and plans. *What the enemy is doing is significant only in relation to what one's own forces are doing or planning to do. Intelligence must be supplied to a total situation* ... and that is possible only if the fighting men and planners will reveal to the intelligence men what they are doing or intend to do, and if the intelligence men confide to the fighting men all that they know without necessarily revealing how they know it'.[7] Starting from the same premise, Dr R.V. Jones then rounds out our definition with his remarks on the purpose of intelligence: '*The ultimate objective of intelligence is to enable action to be optimized.* The individual or body which has to decide on action needs information about its opponent as an ingredient likely to be vital in determining its decision: and this information may suggest that action should be taken on a larger or smaller scale than that which would otherwise be taken, or even that a completely different course of action would be better'.[8] (My emphasis.)

Thus, operational intelligence is essentially up-to-date information about the enemy that has been processed and distilled by experts from the mass of raw data received; and in order for the collection and analysis of intelligence to be useful in support of military operations, these experts must, in turn, be kept well informed of all the latest developments concerning their *own* forces' operations and plans. The availability of intelligence under such conditions permits the achievement of better results on the battlefield at a lower cost: or, to use modern jargon, intelligence acts as a force multiplier.

The term 'military operations' is even broader and more difficult to define than operational intelligence. The lexical definition of the word 'operation' states that in the military context, it means 'a military or naval action, mission, or maneuver including its planning and execution'.[9] More recently in the United States, however, the word 'operations' has also been used to denote a specific level of military action falling somewhere between (but also overlapping with) the strategic level on the one hand and the tactical on the other. This concept of a *level* of military operations originated with Napoleon's estabishment of operationally self-contained corps that were powerful enough to hold their own against a rather formidable opponent for at least 24 hours. Subsequently, the systematic development of a doctrine for this level was introduced in Germany by Moltke, and has been employed by the Soviet Union since the Second World War (as a result of the need to deploy large military formations over an extended front).

For the commander, military operations represents a way of thinking that transcends the tactical level and focuses his attention on the contribution of his plans and actions on the battlefield to the overall strategic objectives of the war. A comparison of two official US Army definitions of the term 'operations' illustrates how this concept has expanded over the last decade. FM 100–5 *Operations* (1982) includes the following description:

> The operational level of war uses available military resources to attain strategic goals within a theater of war. Most simply, it is the theory of larger unit operations. It also involves planning and conducting campaigns. Campaigns are sustained operations designed to defeat an enemy force in a specified space and time with simultaneous and sequential battles. The disposition of forces, selection of objectives, and actions taken to weaken or to out-maneuver the enemy all set the terms of the next battle and exploit tactical gains. They are all part of the operational level of war.[10]

More recently, however, FM 100–5 *Operations* (1986) takes the level of operations for granted, and, following a definition similar to the one quoted above, emphasizes the operational art instead.

> Operational art thus involves fundamental decisions about when and where to fight and whether to accept or decline battle. Its essence is the identification of the enemy's operational center of gravity – his source of strength or balance – and the concentration of superior combat power against that point to achieve a decisive

success. No particular echelon of command is solely or uniquely concerned with operational art, but theater commanders and their chief subordinates usually plan and direct campaigns. Army groups and armies normally design the major ground operations of a campaign. And corps and divisions normally execute those major ground operations. Operational art requires broad vision, the ability to anticipate, a careful understanding of the relationship of means to ends, and effective joint and combined co-operation. Reduced to its essentials, operational art requires the commander to answer three questions:

   1 What military condition must be produced in the theater of war or operations to achieve the strategic goal?
   2 What sequence of actions is most likely to produce that condition?
   3 How should the resources of the force be applied to accomplish that sequence of actions?[11]

In this context, then, the study of 'intelligence and military operations' relates to the contribution – actual or potential – of intelligence to the military leader's decisions in battle on a level that is lower than the strategic but higher than the tactical; it includes an analysis of the demands military commanders make on intelligence and investigates the various ways in which they can and must compensate for the lack of intelligence. Given the enormous range and complexity of the subject, only a fraction of the issues relevant to the study of intelligence and military operations can be discussed in this essay. Many important topics, such as the different sources of intelligence and their value to military operations,[12] the relationship of intelligence to command, control and communications, basic intelligence,[13] and intelligence as it relates to deception,[14] are mentioned only tangentially.

INTELLIGENCE AND MILITARY OPERATIONS: A BRIEF HISTORICAL PERSPECTIVE

Clausewitz and Tolstoy warn against reliance on intelligence as an unjustified act of faith. Far from being a wellspring of timely, accurate information about the enemy, tactical and operational intelligence on the battlefield of the nineteenth century was, they believed, most often the source of conflicting, unreliable reports that were more misleading than helpful.[15] 'As Clausewitz observes in *On War*, a commander caught in the midst of battle would usually suffer from a dearth of accurate information on the performance, condition and position of his *own* troops, not to mention those of his enemy.[16]

Our uncertainty about the situation at a given moment is not limited to the conditions of the enemy only but of our own army as well. The latter can rarely be kept together to the extent that we are able to survey all its parts at any moment and if we are inclined to uneasiness, new doubts will arise. We shall want to wait, and a delay of our whole plan will be the inevitable result.[17]

Tolstoy's description of the Battle of Borodino in *War and Peace* bears out Clausewitz's observations:

From the battlefield, adjutants he had sent out, and orderlies from his marshals, kept galloping up to Napoleon with reports of the progress of the action, but all these reports were false, both because it was impossible in the heat of battle to say what was happening at any given moment and because many of the adjutants did not go to the actual place of conflict but reported what they had heard from others; and also because while an adjutant was riding more than a mile to Napoleon, circumstances changed and the news he brought was already becoming false. ... On the basis of these necessarily untrustworthy reports, Napoleon gave his orders, which had either been executed before he gave them or could not be and were not executed.[18]

And even though Michael Carver's description of the Battle of El Alamein concerns a military conflict that took place over a century later in the age of technology, it also has much in common with the comments of Clausewitz and Tolstoy.

That Montgomery on the one side and Rommel on the other were the decisive figures is never at any time in doubt. They decided every move; but their own power evaporated when it came to the execution of their decisions in the front line. There the decision lay at the level of the battalion or company commander. He could and did decide whether to struggle on and, if so, how: to stop or, occasionally, to go back. His superiors at brigade, division or corps, who had made the plan, allotted the objectives, arranged the support of tanks, artillery and engineers, and fixed the time, no longer had any say, and, in the case of infantry attacks, little power to control events. They were lucky if they even knew what had happened until several hours later, and then only in the broadest terms. Between the army commander and the commanding officer, brigadiers and generals could interpose in planning and could distort or delay in execution; but their power and freedom of action was at all times severely limited.[19]

From a comparison of the preceding excerpts and the analysis of Clausewitz's chapter, 'Intelligence in War', it becomes clear that the issue at hand extends beyond the problem of insufficent or unreliable intelligence to the more complex question of how intelligence and the management of uncertainty relate to command, control and communication (C^3I). Even the most accurate intelligence (assuming it exists at all on the battlefield) is worthless unless it can be communicated in time for the commander to make and implement the appropriate decisions.

Before the mid-nineteenth century, obtaining and making the proper use of intelligence on the battlefield (that is, reducing risks and uncertainty, or achieving better control over events as they unfolded) was chiefly a communications problem. The commanders' inability to procure timely, accurate information and quickly make their decisions known to subordinate units was clearly the most critical obstacle to be overcome.[20] With the rapid development of the telegraph, telephone, radio, and later radar and television, however, information from any point on the battlefield or within the extended theater of operations could be transmitted and reviewed instantaneously (that is, in 'real time'). These technological breakthroughs in the means of communication in turn radically changed the potential value of intelligence for those conducting military operations. In a telling statement, Donald McLachlan has observed that 'the operation it is most difficult to get intelligence about is the primitive one, in which the planning is done by word of mouth, by orders transmitted on scraps of paper that are eaten, by bonfires that are quickly extinguished from one hill to another and so on'.[21]

The development of real-time communication and the special military branches responsible for it was, not surprisingly, accompanied by the corresponding growth of specialized intelligence branches. The increased respectability and value accorded intelligence, particularly since the Second World War, is directly attributable to the revolution in communications.

This does not, however, mean that accurate information about events taking place on the battlefield can always be obtained when needed; that intelligence has become fully reliable; or that uncertainty, friction or chance in war have been eliminated or even reduced. All that can be said is that although the *nature* of uncertainty has changed – and perhaps moved to a higher and more complicated plateau – it nevertheless remains the very essence of war as in the past.

The problem of transmitting information in real time may have been solved, but the problem of ensuring its reliability has not. To begin with, the increased dispersal of military formations, as well as the greater attention given to camouflage and secrecy, may in many ways have made information more difficult to obtain. Furthermore, not all of the information received is correct nor can it always be decoded, analysed or interpreted in time. The ever-present possibility of deception also casts doubt upon all the data received, since no dependable method of exposing deception has been, or can be, devised.[22] The staggering increase in the volume of information obtained means that if anything, more, not less, time is needed for processing today; it means that this plethora of information may lead to a higher incidence of contradictory data and at times to the paralysis of command.[23] The collection, analysis and dissemination of intelligence in support of military operations also requires quantities of manpower and equipment as well as levels of expertise that may not be available. It must be remembered that even perfectly correct information transmitted in real time can still change very rapidly in the heat of battle as in Clausewitz's time. The conditions on any battlefield are fluid and the direction of movement can be changed faster than ever before, while the enemy can modify his objectives in mid-course or react to a countermove in an unanticipated way; and although intelligence and information can in theory (but not always in practice) be updated in real time, the physical, material movements of bringing in reinforcements and air support or concentrating troops can require substantial time for implementation. Who can blame some generals for their nostalgic yearning for the 'simpler' days of the past when 'Napoleon could still appraise at a glance, from a single vantage point, the close well-ordered enemy forces, while in our day everything appears dissolved in a haze'?[24]

INTELLIGENCE, UNCERTAINTY AND THE ART OF WAR

Insight into how uncertainty (that is, the lack of intelligence) pervades every facet of war can be gained by comparing warfare to a game of chess or cards. In chess, both sides begin with equal capabilities, and as the game progresses, each player remains fully informed as to his opponent's resources (that is, his chess pieces). The rules of the game are highly structured and accepted by both sides, while moves are sequential – not simultaneous as in war. The rules determine the amount of information (intelligence) that becomes available to both players on an equal basis, thus allowing them to make their moves or choose their strategies accordingly. The degree of uncertainty in chess is therefore *relatively limited* because it is basically confined to assessment of the opponent's intentions; but while 'intelligence' is equally available to both sides, the use they make of it is not. The most important dimensions of uncertainty in chess are the *experience* and *skill* of the opponent; and it is this that makes chess an art resembling the commander's mastery of the art of war as emphasized by Clausewitz. Card games such as poker or bridge involve a greater degree of uncertainty from the start, since the distribution of cards (that is, of capabilities) is only partly known. This of course compounds the difficulty of evaluating the opponent's intentions, and makes it clear why Clausewitz, when comparing war to a game of chance, preferred the analogy of card games to that of chess.

Possession of good intelligence in war can be to some extent compared to a game of cards in which one player can see some or all of his opponent's hand in a mirror. This gives him almost perfect information with the exception of that concerning his opponent's intentions. Still, there is no guarantee that he will win, for much depends on the cards dealt to him (that is, his own capabilities). Thus, until the British developed the capabilities necessary to exploit the first-rate intelligence they had long been receiving from Ultra, their extraordinary insight into German intentions and capabilities could not guarantee success.

Uncertainty in war is, of course, infinitely more complicated. To begin with, there are very few, if any, accepted rules and even those rules that do exist are likely to change unexpectedly. '... Now in war there may be one hundred changes in each step.'[25] Numerous moves are carried out simultaneously – not sequentially – while the opponent's capabilities are unknown and new capabilities can be developed and introduced at any time. New participants are added, others eliminated, new objectives chosen, and so on. The opponent's moves frequently remain unknown until after they have been implemented, and even the details of one's own troop movements are not always known with precision. Above all, opponents in war do their best to increase the imperfection of information (or uncertainty) for their adversaries.[26] The degree of complexity and uncertainty prevailing within the antagonistic, non-cooperative environment of war makes it immeasurably more difficult to conduct than any other human activity. Finally, it must be remembered that while a game can be played over and over again, the loser in war may not have another opportunity to compete.

Some large-scale military operations and battles can become so incomprehensible that even after they have occurred and despite the fact that there is no shortage of available evidence, the *intelligence in retrospect*' (or historical reconstruction) is riddled with contradictions. Only the results can be known with a greater degree of certainty, as John Connell notes in his summary of the Battle of Sidi Rezegh:

> ... 'Crusader', so meticulously planned and launched with such skill and such confidence, developed into the first phase of the Battle of Sidi Resegh. No single description can be more apt than that it was enveloped in the fog of war. It was a strange, bewildering battle to fight; with the aid of maps, the accounts of individual experiences (which are numerous and vivid), and the careful reconstructions of

unit historians, it remains an even more than difficult battle to describe lucidly and consecutively. The pattern imposed by the original plan – of itself probably too rigid – broke up rapidly and totally, and it became a dusty, smoky swirl of confusion, disaster, muddle, heroism and glory. What happened, incident by incident, engagement by engagement, can never be sorted out; its consequences became desolately clear immediately afterwards.[27]

Much the same can be said of many other large-scale battles in recent history. The fact that it is impossible to understand fully the conduct of such complex battles in retrospect enables us to recognize how challenging it is, even with the benefit of hindsight, to evaluate intelligence, transmit it to the appropriate units, and then follow up on its use and on troop movements even under the most favorable wartime conditions.

CLAUSEWITZ ON UNCERTAINTY IN WAR

Carl von Clausewitz is best known for his emphasis on the primacy of politics in providing the logic, objectives and direction of war, but his most important and original contribution to the study of war was his recognition of the critical roles played by uncertainty, chance and friction.[28] It is the attention he pays to the factor of uncertainty that makes his work so relevant to our own times. After all, the ultimate purpose of developing a theory of war and detailed military doctrines is to minimize the powerful influence of uncertainty on the battlefield. As mentioned earlier, this uncertainty – inevitable in any type of warfare – was in Clausewitz's day created largely by the lack of reliable means of communication; this, in turn, made it extremely difficult for military leaders to obtain good intelligence on the disposition of their own troops, let alone on the enemy's capabilities and direction of movement.[29] When effective command and control were simply not practicable, commanders on the battlefield had little choice but to heed the wisdom of Napoleon's words: 'On s'engage, et alors on voit' (You engage and then you wait and see).

> In war, as we have already pointed out, all action is aimed at probable rather than at certain success. The degree of certainty that is lacking must in every case be left to fate, chance or whatever you call it.[30]
>
> In war, more than anywhere else, things do not turn out as we expect.[31]
>
> In war, where imperfect intelligence, the threat of a catastrophe, and the number of accidents are incomparably greater than in any other human endeavor, the amount of missed opportunities, so to speak, is therefore also bound to be greater.[32]

The outcome of a particular battle or operation always involves a high degree of uncertainty. In an age when a single decisive battle could on occasion determine the fate of war, war itself remained a highly unpredictable enterprise. Nevertheless, even in Clausewitz's time, most wars were decided by a series of engagements, the cumulative effect of which determined the ultimate victor. To some extent, therefore, war on the higher strategic level was, and still is, more predictable.

> ... Just as a businessman cannot take the profit from a single transaction and put it into a separate account, so an isolated advantage gained in war cannot be assessed separately from the overall result. A businessman must work on the basis of his total assets, and in war the advantages and disadvantages of a single action could only be determined by the final balance.[33]
> ... Another view ... holds that war consists of separate successes each unrelated to the next, as in a match consisting of several games. The earlier games have no effect upon the later. All that counts is the total score, and each separate result makes its contribution to the total.[34]

Clausewitz is particularly interested in the effect of uncertainty on the behavior and role of the military leader. On many occasions, he observes that the lack of accurate intelligence generally makes military leaders overcautious and disposed to prefer the paralysis of worst-case analysis to the perceived hazards of calculated risks.[35] In richly evocative language, Clausewitz goes on to describe the unsettling impact of uncertainty:

> In viewing the whole array of factors a general must weigh before making his decision, we must remember that he can gauge the direction and value of the most important ones only by considering numerous other possibilities – some immediate, some remote. He must *guess*, so to speak: guess whether the first shock of battle will steel the enemy's resolve and stiffen his resistance, or whether, like a Bologna flask, it will shatter as soon as its surface is scratched; guess the extent of debilitation and paralysis that the drying up of particular sources of supply and the severing of certain lines of communication will cause in the enemy; guess whether the burning pain of the injury he has been dealt will make the enemy collapse with exhaustion or, like a wounded bull, arouse his rage; guess whether the other powers will be frightened or indignant, and whether and which political alliances will be dissolved or formed. When we realize that he must hit upon all this and much more by means of his discreet judgment, as a marksman hits a target, we must admit that such an accomplishment of the human mind is no small

achievement. Thousands of wrong turns running in all directions
tempt his perception; and if the range, confusion, and complexity of
the issues are not enough to overwhelm him, the dangers and
responsibilities may.

This is why the great majority of generals will prefer to stop well
short of their objective rather than risk approaching it too closely,
and why those with high courage and an enterprising spirit will often
overshoot it and so fail to attain their purpose. Only the man who can
achieve great results with limited means has really hit the mark.[36]

Hence, Clausewitz's repeated admonitions against succumbing to this
tendency to 'play it safe'. 'With uncertainty in one scale', he observes,
'courage and self-confidence must be thrown into the other to correct
the balance.'[37] Yet the other extreme of relying almost exclusively on
boldness and initiative to compensate for the lack of intelligence – as the
Wehrmacht did during the Second World War – is likely to prove a
dangerous remedy since its initial, often spectacular success conceals
fundamental flaws until it is too late.

Incomplete knowledge of the enemy's situation also provides
Clausewitz with a principal explanation for the discrepancy between war
in theory and in reality. He reasons that, theoretically speaking, military
activity should never be interrupted or suspended until one party has
emerged the victor.

> Like two incompatible elements, armies must continually destroy
> one another. Like fire and water they never find themselves in a state
> of equilibrium, but must keep on interacting until one of them has
> completely disappeared.[38]

In reality, however, Clausewitz knew very well that military action is often
suspended, and he attributed this to the inherent differences in strength
required to attack or defend. In other words, both sides might have
enough strength to defend themselves, but not enough to attack each
other; consequently, the war comes to a halt. A military conflict might
also be brought to a standstill because of the human tendency to favor
delay, fear and indecision. And although one of the sides might actually be
sufficiently powerful to go on the offensive, his flawed or non-existent
intelligence on the enemy's strength will quite often cause him to perceive
himself as too weak to take action. '... Unreliable intelligence ... [and]
partial ignorance of the situation is, generally speaking, a major factor in
delaying the progress of military action and in moderating the principle
that underlies it'.[39]

What are some ways in which military leaders can nevertheless
compensate for the lack of reliable intellience? The art of war is designed

to a large extent to overcome the problems generated by uncertainty, whatever its source may be. Therefore, the side that can continue to operate effectively while minimizing uncertainty or, even better, learning to exploit it relative to the opponent will perform well. (In the North African Campaign, for example, Rommel did not always possess superior intelligence, but was often more adept at dealing with uncertainty on the battlefield and was willing to take action despite its presence.)

In general, there are two ways of coping with uncertainty in war. The first, which historically precedes the second, includes a wide variety of measures based on different dimensions of the operational art of war or fighting power; the second is improved intelligence, which did not begin to provide more effective means of reducing uncertainty until the second half of the nineteenth century.

The almost infinite number of possible methods for reducing uncertainty from the operational standpoint can be classified in three interrelated categories: the first includes technical and material means; the second concerns the so-called art of war; and the third derives from the quality of leadership.

TECHNICAL AND MATERIAL MEANS OF COPING WITH UNCERTAINTY

Technological 'solutions' to the problems of uncertainty are mainly intended to improve command, control and communications as related to intelligence (C^3I). The development of the telegraph, telephone, radio and other means of communication made possible the very rapid and reliable collection of information and the real-time transmission of orders (i.e., control). In particular, air reconnaissance, radar, satellites and other technologies made ascertaining the location of enemy forces – whether on land, at sea or in the air – a far easier task. Computers and related technologies have made it possible to organize, quickly and efficiently, massive amounts of information. The ability to pinpoint the location of an adversary combined with increased and more accurate precision-guided firepower represent additional material and technical possibilities of minimizing the negative consequences of uncertainty.

'Sensor-collected' data from radars, technological means of locating enemy troops, and electronic command, control and communications systems are not included in my definition of intelligence although they are frequently classified as such. Certainly all levels of intelligence work overlap and relate to the obtaining of information, but for my purposes, such technological means are not considered part of operational-level intelligence for the following reasons: although they deal with often vital information, their operation and the collection of such material is not usually performed by intelligence experts; it does not involve clandestine means of collection; and most of the data are gathered 'automatically' without the use of established methods of intelligence work and analytical skills. Higher-level intelligence requires more *time* for analysis and corroboration while radar, for example, supplies real-time data that require relatively little corroboration with other sources and can be distributed with no (or minimum) delay; intelligence is a complex *process* of assessment consisting of a multi-phased expert analysis substantiated by numerous sources. The unprecedented refinement of sophisticated means of communication, location methods and electronic warfare in general may indeed have contributed to confusion between electronic warfare and tactical intelligence on the one hand, and the traditionally higher-level analytical intelligence skills on the other. The misconception that electronic warfare can largely replace intelligence work on the higher operational level may already have had a deleterious effect on the general appreciation of and demand for the traditional intelligence officer.

In part, this may be viewed as a question of level of analysis; that is, most such collection and transmission of information, like direct visual reconnaissance on the battlefield of the past, should be considered as tactical not operational intelligence. The blurring of distinctions between these two levels of analysis is dangerous because it has led to neglect of the art of intelligence on the operational levels. Today, while many mid-level officers are very skilled in the tactical use of C^3 technologies, far fewer are trained to deal with the higher aggregate level of information supplied in abundance by such technologies and other sources. Yet this higher level of aggregation and analysis is precisely what operational intelligence is all about. The current situation may have created an expectation (whether conscious or not) that technologies which provide 'automatic' or 'nearly automatic' answers on the tactical level will also be able to perform a similar function on the operational level.

On the 'material' side, significant numerical superiority in soldiers, firepower, and the like – in either absolute or relative terms – *at the decisive point* is likely to make the favorable outcome of a battle more certain and less dependent on the availability of reliable intelligence. When overwhelming material superiority is concentrated against an enemy, brute force can to some extent compensate for the lack of intelligence. 'When one force is a great deal stronger than the other, an estimate may be enough. There will be no fighting: the weaker side will yield at once.'[40] Although unquestionable material superiority can make the outcome of war more certain even without detailed intelligence, the superior side in this type of situation tends to lapse into arrogant complacency: he underestimates his weaker opponent, employs his forces less economically, ultimately pays a price that is higher than necessary; and perhaps risks a serious defeat or setback. Well-known examples of this are the Italian invasion of Greece in 1940; the Russian attack on Finland in 1940; the 'combined' Arab attack on Israel in 1948; and the US invasion of Grenada in 1983.

THE ART OF WAR AS A COMPENSATING FACTOR FOR UNCERTAINTY AND THE LACK OF INTELLIGENCE

Clausewitz repeatedly emphasizes that absolute superiority is one of the keys to victory 'so long as it is great enough to counterbalance all other contributing circumstances. It thus follows that as many troops as possible should be brought into the engagement at the decisive point ...'[41] The first rule, therefore, should be: put the largest possible army into the field. This may sound a platitude, but in reality it is not'.[42] In the case of absolute superiority, intelligence becomes a much less critical factor. Still, how does one side know that it is superior to the other without intelligence; and how does it know where to concentrate its forces, where the enemy is located, and so on?

Unfortunately, *absolute* numerical superiority is not always possible; hence, Clausewitz and other military theorists insist that it is imperative to achieve at least *relative* superiority at the 'decisive point' despite the handicap of absolute inferiority.[43]

> Relative superiority, that is, the skillful concentration of superior strength at the decisive point, is much more frequently based on the correct appraisal of this decisive point, on suitable planning from the start; which leads to appropriate disposition of the forces, and on the resolution needed to sacrifice non-essentials for the sake of essentials – that is, the courage to retain the major part of one's forces united.[44]

Like most other maxims concerning the art of war, which advise, for example, keeping one's own forces united while devising a strategy that would force the enemy to divide his,[45] and retaining ample reserves on or near the battlefield to exploit sudden opportunitites or provide help if necessary, the theoretical simplicity of achieving numerical superiority at the decisive point belies the difficulty experienced in all aspects of its implementation.

The implementation of these theoretically simple principles depends, with varying degrees of emphasis, on the availability of good intelligence and on the talent of the military genius, whose experience, intuition and character equip him to make prudent decisions even in an environment of rampant uncertainty. And because Clausewitz had concluded that it was practically impossible to obtain accurate and timely intelligence on the battlefield, he devoted considerable attention to the idea that the military genius or artistic intuition of the commander must be cultivated and ultimately relied upon to deal with the unknown and unsubstantiated. Yet Clausewitz does not explicitly recognize that even the most inspired and experienced military leader needs at least *some* sort of intelligence to support his intuition − and the more the better. The military genius' intuition cannot replace intelligence; it can only function when it exploits information more adroitly than others could. In the end, therefore, Clausewitz's central concept of the military genius is unsatisfactory; it raises numerous questions such as how to identify the military genius *before* the outbreak of war, and how to cultivate genius. From the standpoint of intelligence and military operations, this concept can even be counter-productive, if not dangerous, because it may encourage commanders to prefer their intuition to intelligence even when reliable intelligence is available. Thus, intelligence remains essential in some measure regardless of one's starting point.

Some other methods of coping with inadequate information and unanticipated situations include the meticulous preparation of contingency plans; the training of troops to deal with the unexpected through rehearsals and exercises; the adoption of a detailed, flexible doctrine; and the education of commanders to improvise under pressure.

> Constant practice leads to *brisk, precise, and reliable* leadership, reducing natural friction and easing the working of the machine. In short, routine will be more frequent and indispensable, the lower the level of action. As the level of action rises, its use will decrease to the point where, at the summit, it disappears completely.[46]

Most of the material solutions, military maxims and other methods that have been mentioned up to this point pertain to *one's own side*. Among those principles or methods intended to increase ambiguity or the fog of war for the *enemy* are secrecy and camouflage, movement at night, and deception − all of which hinder the enemy's efforts to obtain good intelligence. The objective of these measures is to lay the groundwork for achieving some form of surprise − but once again, however, their planning and execution depend upon the availability of reliable intelligence as well as upon such elements as adequate strength and time (without which even superb intelligence could not ensure success).

Another important and well-known bit of advice to the commander is to be aggressive and maintain the initiative whenever possible. Through continuous movement, speed and vigorous attack, the creative military genius can dictate the pace and direction of the battle, thereby shifting the balance of uncertainty in his favor;[47] he holds the initiative − he knows where he is going and can concentrate his strength accordingly. The defender in such a situation may lose valuable time trying to identify the axis or *Schwerpunkt* of the attack and will generally find it necessary to divide his forces to meet a number of possible threats.

THE MILITARY LEADER AND UNCERTAINTY IN WAR[48]

The ideal combination of perfect intelligence and superior military strength would make the life of every military commander far easier, reducing the need for his intuition and creativity. But in real life, as Churchill once remarked in a different context, 'Generals only enjoy such comforts in Heaven. And those who demand them do not always get there'.[49] As mentioned earlier, judicious application of the principles of the art of war is one way of coping with uncertainty and at times even turning it to one's own advantage. This assumes, however, that the military commander has the experience, intuition and creative genius to do so. Clausewitz vividly describes the interplay of pressures faced by the commander on the battlefield:

> Since all information and assumptions are open to doubt, and with chance at work everywhere, the commander continually finds that things are not as he expected. This is bound to influence his plans, or at least the assumptions underlying them. If this influence is sufficiently powerful to cause a change in his plans, he must usually work out new ones; but for these the necessary information may not be immediately available. During an operation decisions have usually to be made at once; there may be no time to review the situation or even to think it through. Usually, of course, new information and reevaluation are not enough to make us give up our intentions: they only call them into question. We now know more, but this makes us more, not less, uncertain. The latest reports do not arrive all at once: they merely trickle in. They continually impinge on our decisions, and our mind must be permanently armed, so to speak, to deal with them.
>
> If the mind is to emerge unscathed from this relentless struggle with the unforeseen, two qualities are indispensable: *first, an intellect that, even in the darkest hour, retains some glimmerings of the inner light which leads to truth; and second, the courage to follow this faint light wherever it may lead.* The first is described by the French term, *coup d'oeil*; the second is *determination.*[50]

In sum, Clausewitz's twofold prescription for dealing with the lack of intelligence is for the commander to rely on his intuition (or what he calls *coup d'oeil*) and his capacity for *maintenance of aim.* (A third way would be to improve one's intelligence capabilities as well as the available means of communication, a solution that Clausewitz considered impossible at the time he wrote *On War*.) Given the inevitability of confusion and uncertainty on the battlefield, the commander's experience and creative application of the principles of war were his only recourse.[51]

The 'non-dogmatic' application of the principles of war[52] calls for artistic intuition, a talent for grasping the essence of the problem without getting lost in the fuzziness of the details. The military genius 'need not be a learned historian or a pundit ... '.[53] Instead, he needs to have an instinct for the 'quick recognition of a truth that the mind would ordinarily miss or would receive after long study and reflection'.[54] 'When all is said and done, it really is the commander's *coup d' oeil*, his ability to see things simply, to identify the whole business of war completely with himself, that is the essence of good generalship'.[55]

As noted earlier, Clausewitz believed that 'boldness grows less common in the higher ranks';[56] that in the absence of sound intelligence most military leaders tend to overestimate the enemy's capabilities and err on the side of caution. 'Given the same amount of intelligence, timidity will do a thousand times more damage in war than audacity.'[57] The military genius is a courageous – but not reckless – leader who takes calculated risks that are intended to exacerbate his opponent's confusion and uncertainty. Boldness and risk-taking in war are therefore essential for overcoming unpredictability by increasing it for the enemy.

> Let us admit that boldness in war even has its own prerogatives. It must be granted a certain power over and above successful calculations involving space, time, and magnitude of forces, for wherever it is superior, it will take advantage of its opponent's weakness. In other words, it is a genuinely creative force. This fact is not difficult to prove even scientifically. Whenever boldness encounters timidity, it is likely to be the winner, because timidity in itself implies a loss of equilibrium. Boldness will be at a disadvantage only in an encounter with deliberate caution, which may be considered bold in its own right, and is certainly just as powerful and effective; but such cases are rare. Timidity is the root of prudence in the majority of men.[58] ... Boldness governed by superior intellect is the mark of a hero. This kind of boldness does not consist in defying the natural order of things and in crudely offending the laws of probability; it is rather a matter of energetically supporting that higher form of analysis by which genius arrives at a decision: rapid, only partly conscious weighing of the possibilities. Boldness can lend wings to intellect and insight; the stronger the wings then, the greater the heights, the wider the view, and the better the results – though a greater prize, of course, involves greater risks. ... In other words, a

distinguished commander without boldness is unthinkable. No man who is not born bold can play such a role, and therefore we consider this quality the first prerequisite of the great military leader. How much of this quality remains by the time he reaches senior rank, after training and experience have modified it, is another question. The greater the extent to which it is retained, the greater the range of his genius.[59]

Being 'above successful calculations', boldness and risk-taking cannot therefore be subjected to a purely rational analysis by either the initiator or his opponent, who must try to predict the risk-taker's most likely course of action. This explains why taking risks tends to increase the opponent's uncertainty and why the intuition of the military genius may be the only way to deal with it.

Clausewitz's assertion that the majority of generals err on the side of timidity, when combined with the inherent superiority of the defense over the offense, suggests that in most instances uncertainty can be overcome most safely through the deliberate avoidance of risks. The degree of caution to be employed will depend on such variables as the specific circumstances, weapons technologies, and relative numerical strength. So once again, in the end there is no foolproof, convenient formula for success in war. At times, an inferior force taking very high risks may succeed (for instance, MacArthur at Inchon; the British forces under O'Connor in the Western Desert in 1941), while on other occasions, a smaller force would be wiser to adhere to a more careful, deliberate defensive strategy.

Nevertheless, the wisdom of Clausewitz's preference for the daring military genius over the cautious military leader is this: since most generals are cautious, they will probably project their own assessments on to their opponents. If, however, their opponents play by a different set of rules which includes acceptance of very high risks, their actions will, *at least in the short run*, become unpredictable (e.g. Rommel's actions *vis-à-vis* the British in North Africa). As long as the commander knows when to 'shift gears' from a high- to low-risk strategy, his boldness will pay handsome dividends; but history demonstrates that most daring generals do not know when to change their approach. Their actions are a function more of character than of long-term rational calculations, while earlier successes have only served to blind them to the folly of pursuing the same strategy indefinitely.

Other qualities essential for the military genius are *'energy, firmness, staunchness, emotional balance, and strength of character ...* These products of a heroic nature could almost be treated as one and the same force – strength of will – which adjusts itself to circumstances; but though closely linked, they are not identical.'[60] This includes 'the ability to keep one's head at times of exceptional stress and violent emotion'.[61] 'This [presence of mind] must play a great role in war, the domain of the unexpected, since it is nothing but an increased capacity of dealing with the unexpected. We admire presence of mind in an apt repartee, as we admire quick thinking in the face of danger.'[62] In a description that illustrates the accuracy of Clausewitz's insight into behavior under pressure and conditions of uncertainty, Brigadier General C.F. Aspinall-Oglander recounts an incident in the early stages of the invasion of Gallipoli:

> Tired by their efforts in the early morning, and overwrought by the tension of the landing, the strangeness of the situation, and the heavy losses in officers, some of the units of the 29th Division who landed early in the day were in sore straits during the first afternoon. Had they but known it, the enemy in front of them were equally distressed, and this must be so in every hard-fought battle. Each side is prone to imagine that further progress is impossible, and the side with the more resolute leader, who insists on one further effort, will generally prove the victor. On the 25th April, the Turks in the southern zone were too weak to win a victory, but the resolution of their leader was to gain them important advantages.
>
> 'I am sending you a battalion,' wrote Colonel Sami Bey, the commander of the Turkish 9th Division, to the officer in command of the 26th Regiment. 'It is quite clear that the enemy is weak; drive him into the sea, and do not let me find an Englishman in the south when I arrive.' With this inspiring message he encouraged his troops. Throughout the night, the weak Turkish detachments at W and X prevented any advance by the British, while by 8a.m. on the 26th the regrettable evacuation of Y Beach was in full swing. The small Turkish garrison of Sedd el Bahr, who, despite the terrifying effect of their first experience of naval gun-fire, clung doggedly to their position throughout the 25th, rendered a service to the defence which it would be difficult to exaggerate.[63]

The conflicting nature of intelligence reports on the battlefield exerts very strong pressure on the commander to issue orders and counter-orders, to hesitate, to contradict himself, and to confuse himself and his subordinates. This is how Clausewitz assesses the situation and defines the role the military genius must play:

> Many intelligence reports in war are contradictory; even more are false, and most are uncertain. What one can reasonably ask of an officer is that he should possess a standard of judgment, which he can

gain only from knowledge of men and affairs and from common sense. He should be guided by the laws of probability. These are difficult enough to apply when plans are drafted in an office, far from the sphere of action; the task becomes infinitely harder in the thick of fighting itself, with reports streaming in. At such times, one is lucky if their contradictions cancel each other out, and leave a kind of balance to be critically assessed. It is much worse for the novice if chance does not help him in that way, and on the contrary one report tallies with another, confirms it, magnifies it, lends it color, till he has to make a quick decision – which is soon recognized to be mistaken, just as the reports turn out to be lies, exaggerations, errors, and so on. In short, most intelligence is false, and the effect of fear is to multiply lies and inaccuracies. As a rule most men would rather believe bad news than good, and rather tend to exaggerate the bad news. The dangers that are reported may soon, like waves, subside; but like waves they keep recurring, without apparent reason. The commander must trust his judgment and stand like a rock on which the waves break in vain. It is not an easy thing to do. If he does not have a buoyant disposition, if experience of war had not trained him and matured his judgment, he had better make it a rule to suppress his personal convictions and give his hopes and not his fears the benefit of the doubt. Only thus can he preserve a proper balance.[64]

The commander must resist the temptation to change his orders continually, thereby adding to the confusion. He should keep in mind the maxim that 'order, counter-order brings disorder'. During the Battle of Midway, for example, Admiral Nagumo kept changing his orders to arm, disarm and rearm his aircraft for various types of missions, each of which required different types of ammunition. Before long, he had exhausted his maintenance crews, wasted valuable time, and finally was caught in the middle of rearming his aircraft by a US dive-bomber attack. Admiral Sir Dudley Pound faced the same sort of dilemma when, under the pressure of uncertainty and ambiguous intelligence, he decided to disperse Convoy PQ 17 instead of having it continue on course. This only confirms the wisdom of Clausewitz's advice to 'stand like a rock on which the waves break in vain'. (See Patrick Beesly's contribution on Convoy PQ 17.) Once again, though, this advice seems far easier in theory than in practice, for as Clausewitz admits, there is a very fine line between strength of character and obstinacy (see the discussion on the commander's intuition above).

The 'military genius' is central to Clausewitz's theoretical structure in dealing with the unpredictable. Since accurate intelligence is the exception rather than the rule, and the principles of war that can

compensate for imperfect intelligence are difficult to implement, in the
end much, perhaps too much, of his theory rests on the *coup d'oeil* of
the military genius. The Clausewitzian concept of compensating for
uncertainty through courage, self-confidence, persistence and genius can
be a very dangerous practice, as was borne out by the German experience
in the Second World War. As far as the conduct of military operations was
concerned, the German generals performed very well indeed, but their
Achilles' heel was their failure to appreciate the potential of intelligence at
higher levels.

> The fact is that the Germans had all the wrong ideas about intel-
> ligence and hitherto had not felt the need of improvement. What-
> ever errors they might make about the forces opposing them,
> they had always been strong enough for these errors to make no
> difference. One result was that the operations branch tended to pay
> no attention to what their intelligence branch told them. The time
> was coming when this could be a serious handicap. What struck
> me most at the time was the cool certainty with which these
> appreciations were presented. Any British Intelligence Summary,
> even at a later and more self-confident period of the war, would
> undoubtedly have hedged with a few 'probablys'.[65]

As long as the Germans maintained the initiative, their reliance on
excellence in military operations as a substitute for intelligence went
unnoticed. By the time the tide had turned against them, it was too late
to change their outlook or build a more reliable intelligence system.
Ultimately, this latent weakness was one of the major causes of
Germany's defeat in the Second World War.

Although elegant in its conception, Clausewitz's theoretical structure
raises almost as many questions as it solves. How can the 'military genius'
be identified as such *before* a war breaks out, particularly in modern times,
where the number of opportunities for military commanders to acquire
experience and have their talents recognized is very small or non-existent?
Furthermore, as I have argued elsewhere, the experience gained in one
war may be irrelevant or even counter-productive for another in the age of
technology and rapid change.[66]

Surely one cannot expect that a suitable military genius will always
appear at the right moment in the right place in future wars. In view of the
revolutionary improvements in modern communications on the battlefield and the availability of much improved – although not perfect –
intelligence, it seems more advisable to rely less on the commander's
intuition and more on the proper use of intelligence. To put it another
way, the modern military genius should cultivate a new type of intuition or
creative genius: he will have to rely somewhat less on his creativity in

applying the 'principles of war' and more on his understanding and appreciation of intelligence. This will include learning more about what intelligence can and cannot do for him, how he can digest massive quantities of information most efficiently, and how he can better task his intelligence organizations. Such a trend could already be observed on the British side during the Second World War, when, for example, Wavell, Auchinleck and Montgomery achieved much of their success on the battlefield through the astute use of intelligence. In contrast to their German rivals, they showed much more respect for intelligence and came to depend on it extensively in the preparation and execution of military operations. American generals were quick to follow suit during the later stages of the war in Europe.

Despite this shift in the relative importance of intelligence compared with operational creativity, military organizations continue to stress the operational aspects of war in the education of officers while neglecting to provide thorough instruction in intelligence matters. The fallacy of the Clausewitzian and traditional military approach to dealing with uncertainty is that excellence in the art of command is to a large extent perceived as a substitute for intelligence. Only one step away from ignoring the value of intelligence, this attitude is perpetuated in the education of military officers and thus later reflected in their long-standing underestimation of its importance.

OPERATIONS VS. INTELLIGENCE; A TALE OF TWO CULTURES

> On the one hand, intelligence work was thought of as a professional backwater, suitable only for officers with a knowledge of foreign languages and for those who were not wanted for command. On the other hand, the activities of the many men of average or less than average professional competence who were thus detailed for intelligence confirmed the low estimate that had already been made of the value of intelligence work.[67]

> Let's go out and kill some Viet Cong, then we can worry about intelligence.[68]

> Intelligence is too important to be left to intelligence officers.
>   Anonymous[69]

To reduce an argument *ad absurdum*, it can be suggested that while waging war successfully without intelligence might be dangerous and expensive but still possible, attempting to do so with excellent intelligence but no army is impossible. It is therefore natural that intelligence, like logistics, should always play a supportive role; yet the word supportive as used here is *not* synonymous with secondary or unimportant. Even as the most successful military operation must come to a halt without petrol or ammunition, so the best army will pay an unnecessarily higher price and reduce its effectiveness without intelligence. With the traditional focus on operations in military education, however, giving intelligence its due recognition, and easing the natural 'tension' between intelligence and operations through greater co-operation and understanding will not be an easy task.

Each branch's professional functions and missions as well as methods and operational requirements are worlds apart if not completely contradictory. Inevitably, the operations branch will try to dominate or ignore intelligence. We have already seen that before the development of communications and intelligence, the military relied on material superiority, refinement of the art of war, and the cultivation of military genius to cope with uncertainty and its attendant problems; and even though intelligence finally came into its own in the mid-twentieth century, these traditional remedies for uncertainty continue to hold sway.

In *all* military organizations (to some degree) the most sought-after career has been that of a successful operations officer. All other positions – no matter how critical – have remained secondary. The most important and most senior officers have always been (and still are) in operations, as evidenced by the universal tendency of higher-ranking operations officers to dominate lower-ranking officers who play a supportive role. Given the traditionally hierarchical disciplinary nature of military organizations, those of higher rank naturally expect to be obeyed and begin to regard the deference they receive as an affirmation of their superior knowledge and judgment. The relationship of the German intelligence officer and his operational colleagues during the Second World War is an admittedly extreme example of the type of attitude that still exists in all military organizations today. In its post-war report on German military intelligence, the Military Intelligence Division of the US War Department summarized the problem as follows:

> The German intelligence service was almost exclusively in the hands of, and dominated by, German General Staff officers. These men were selected for their abilities from the ranks of regular officers early in their careers and were given extensive training in all staff work. The General Staff formed the core of the German army, and was the brains behind all questions of direction and organization. Yet the greatest ambition of General Staff officers was still to be troop commanders in the field or to be assistants to such commanders. None wanted to become specialists on matters of transport, munitions, intelligence, or other technical matters ...
>
> The specialist, therefore, appeared inferior and not a little suspect

to the commanding type of officer: the operations officer (G–3) or the chief of staff. The Ic (G–2) was a Cinderella, and his position was considered as little more than a preliminary to something better and more important. It was German doctrine that the G–2 had to be able to work with the G–3, he had to have a good understanding of tactical situations and details, but he did not need a detailed knowledge of the enemy forces, the enemy language, or any other skill that would be expected in other armies from a man whose mission it is to gather information about the enemy ...

We must not, however, fall into the other extreme of underrating German operational intelligence. The subordination of the G–2 to the G–3 had the advantage of keeping the study of the enemy situation on a strictly practical plane; by which the Germans avoided the academic approach so common in Allied armies. Intelligence was there for one purpose: to help the G–3 and the chief of staff to make the right operational decisions.[70]

When, in 1942, the tables were turned and the Germans were thrown more and more on the defensive, the Allies had by far outstripped the Germans in the development and application of operational intelligence. This was perhaps most obvious in the development and application of operational intelligence ... Being the organizers and directors and the brains of the German Army, they [the General Staff officers] were well selected and superbly trained, especially as expert tacticians. Their training was designed to enable them to find their place in any General Staff assignment without much preliminary introduction. This, though it worked well in many fields, was certainly not sufficient in such a specialised field as intelligence ...

Belatedly, when the need for additional specialized training became obvious, a semipermanent intelligence school was founded at Posen in 1943, where regular intelligence courses for officers were held. Field units were asked, on a quota basis, to send officers to these courses, but it was rare that the division commanders sent their ablest and best-suited men ...

From the point of view of selection and training, the state of affairs in the G–2's staff was equally, if not more, grave. The Germans were reluctant to entrust positions of military responsibility in intelligence to men who, in civilian life, had acquired a knowledge of a foreign country or language but otherwise had no military background. Men with such special qualifications were in most cases drafted into the army, often to end up as gunners or engineers on the eastern front, though they spoke English and French, or to be assigned to some unit in the West or in Africa despite their knowledge of Russian.[71]

Under the German system ... intelligence was more than usually condemned to a secondary position. At division, where the Germans had no chief of staff but where the G–3 performed the functions of chief of staff and operations staff officer, the G–2 was completely dominated. At higher levels, where the G–2 who was disagreeing with the G–3 could apply to the chief of staff for a decision, the G–3, with his higher rank and status as chief of the tactical group, usually forestalled him and brought the matter to the attention of the chief of staff or the commanding general without the presence of the G–2 being required.[72]

As Professor Hinsley shows, similar negative attitudes toward intelligence work in general also prevailed on the British side before the Second World War. The explanations he gives such as the anti-intellectualism of the officer corps, resentment against the influence of intelligence strictly outside the 'informational field', or dislike for the less gentlemanly aspects of intelligence explain the attitudes of all other military organizations at that time as well.[73] As the war progressed, the longstanding negative attitudes displayed toward intelligence slowly dissolved as a result of many factors that contributed greatly to British success but which were not present initially on the German side. Most importantly, the British were at first on the defensive following a series of defeats, which created a feeling of vulnerability and an openness to innovative solutions; they had a wiser policy of recruiting civilians, which allowed many scholars trained by the military to fill senior intelligence positions without posing the threat of competition for the positions of regular army officers after the war; they experienced a number of early – sometimes spectacular – intelligence successes, which generated confidence in intelligence; and they benefited from the generally positive attitude toward intelligence that emanated from the highest political echelons.

As history has shown, the tendency of some military leaders responsible for operations to dominate intelligence can indeed be very counterproductive. The misuse of intelligence by Admiral Oliver and his principal deputy, Captain Thomas Jackson, preceding and during the Battle of Jutland is well-known. Their misunderstanding of, and for that matter lack of interest in, the finer points of what intelligence could and could not do changed the Battle of Jutland from a potential Trafalgar into an indecisive draw;[74] and because the intelligence mistakes of this battle were not studied by most senior naval commanders, they were doomed to be repeated by Admiral Pound in the battle for Norway and over Convoy PQ 17.[75]

An extreme case is that of Admiral Turner, the US Navy Director of

War Plans (OP–12) in the period before Pearl Harbor, who gradually brought the naval intelligence community under his control. 'Although he had no experience in evaluation, the new director of war plans assumed his judgement was superior to the ONI staff's when it came to analysing and interpreting strategic information. He maintained that the officers in his division were "more experienced than the officers in naval intelligence who were generally more junior, and were trained rather [sic] for the collection and dissemination of information, rather than its application to a strategic situation"'.[76] In order to 'run the whole show', Turner began preparing his own intelligence estimates and transmitting them independent of ONI.[77] While the director of ONI, a Captain Kirk, argued that his office was responsible for preparing the part of a formal estimate called Enemy Intention, Turner maintained that his department alone should 'interpret and evaluate *all* information concerning possible hostile nations from *whatever* sources received', and further insisted that ONI's only mission was to collect and distribute intelligence in accordance with his instructions.[78]

> He [Turner] continued to harass Kirk as he tried to turn ONI into nothing more than an intelligence drop-box. By May 1941 the increasing interference of War Plans in what ONI officers regarded as their prerogative in intelligence matters caused deep resentment. One of the fortnightly summaries on which Kirk had handwritten 'In my view the Japs will jump pretty soon' had been returned from 'coordination' by War Plans with the bold scrawl, 'I don't think that the Japs are going to jump now or ever! R.M.T.'[79]

Admiral Turner's policy of dominating ONI and monopolizing intelligence was a major underlying cause of the failure to anticipate Japan's attack on Pearl Harbor. This painful experience serves as just one more sorry reminder that a military leader's senior rank and responsibility for carrying out operations do not automatically qualify him as an intelligence expert.

A principal problem senior military leaders face is that experience is normally the only way to acquire a proper education in the use of intelligence on the higher levels of command. This was particularly true in earlier periods, when the amount of published literature available for self-education was minimal. (To be sure, official after-action intelligence reports existed all along, but the incentive or time to read them were not always present.)

Part of the problem is, then, that in the typical military leader's career, the time spent rising through the ranks may not be very helpful in providing the experience necessary to deal with intelligence on the higher levels of command. Having spent most of their formative years learning

about intelligence on the tactical and lower operational levels, some
generals tend to apply what they know about the utility and relevance of
intelligence on these levels to the very different world of operational or
strategic intelligence on the upper echelons of command. (A glance at
Table I will show how intelligence on the lower levels differs from that on
the higher levels.)

Intelligence on the lower tactical levels can often be highly unreliable;
most information has only a very short life span because circumstances
change so rapidly. Quite frequently, the most reliable intelligence in this
type of situation is obtained through direct contact, while the rest is likely
to prove inaccurate and misleading. The result is that an officer who is
repeatedly disappointed by the quality and utility of intelligence at the
tactical level may always harbor a skeptical attitude toward intelligence in
general. And although problems on the lower echelons of the operational
level may resemble those on the tactical level, this is no longer true for the
higher operational levels. Nevertheless, it is possible in some extreme
cases to find commanders such as Rommel who still insist on taking part in
reconnaissance missions:

> As the situation was rather confused, I spent next day at the front
> again. It is of the utmost importance to the commander to have a
> good knowledge of the battlefield and his own and his enemy's
> positions on the ground. It is often not a question of which of the
> opposing commanders is the higher qualified mentally, or which has
> the greater experience, but which of them has the better grasp of the
> battlefield. This is particularly the case when a situation develops,
> the outcome of which cannot be estimated. Then the commander
> must go up to see for himself; reports received second-hand rarely
> give the information he needs for his decisions.[80]

What is imperative and useful on the tactical level may actually
be dysfunctional on the operational. The commander on the higher
operational level should seldom go on direct reconnaissance himself; if he
does he may not only risk his life unnecessarily but may also become
bogged down in too many details.[81] Instead, he must learn to rely on his
intelligence adviser (Ic or G–2); and while it is of the greatest importance,
building a relationship of mutual confidence and cooperation is by no
means easy.

In some ways, the intelligence officer has more in common with the
scholar in search of the truth than with the professional military man. He is
usually accustomed to a detailed, 'objective' and systematic analysis; he is
used to dealing with criticism and is therefore less inclined to take it
personally. With these factors in mind, Donald McLachlan concludes that
'intelligence for the fighting services should be directed as far as possible

TABLE 1

DIFFERENT LEVELS OF INTELLIGENCE WORK AND THEIR RELATION TO MILITARY OPERATIONS

	TACTICAL LEVEL	OPERATIONAL LEVEL	STRATEGIC LEVEL
MAJOR SOURCES OF INFORMATION	COMBAT RECONNAISSANCE AND DIRECT CONTACT WITH THE ENEMY; INTERROGATION OF POW's; RADIO TRANSMISSIONS en Clair ; RADAR; RDF	RECONNAISSANCE AND DIRECT CONTACT WITH ENEMY; POW; AIR PHOTO RECONNAISSANCE; (PR) CODED SIGINT INTERCEPTS DECODED IN FIELD AND IN THE REAR; RPV; DRONES; SATELLITES	HIGH LEVEL SIGINT INTERCEPTS; HUMAN INTELLIGENCE; SATELLITE; COOPERATION WITH ALLIES AND OPEN SOURCES
DEGREE OF RELIABILITY AND LIFE SPAN OF INFORMATION	VERY SHORT LIFE SPAN; MOSTLY FOR IMMEDIATE ACTION. RELIABILITY OF INFORMATION FOR ACTION VERY LOW TO MEDIUM	MOSTLY SHORT TIME SPAN; PRESSURE FOR ACTION IS HIGH TO VERY HIGH; RELIABILITY OF INFORMATION IN ACTION VERY LOW TO MEDIUM	MEDIUM TO LONG-RANGE LIFE SPAN; LESS PRESSURE FOR IMMEDIATE ACTION; MEDIUM TO VERY HIGH RELIABILITY
THE FOCUS OF INTELLIGENCE TASKING AND CAPABILITIES	PRIMARILY ENEMY'S CAPABILITIES TO BE ENGAGED AND HIS IMMEDIATE INTENTIONS	ANALYSIS AND INFORMATION OF BOTH CAPABILITIES AND INTENTIONS; THE ENEMY'S DOCTRINE, STYLE OF FIGHTING, HIS ALLIES' SUPPORT; HIS OWN INTELLIGENCE	BOTH MILITARY AND CIVILIAN; LONG-RANGE POLITICAL, ECONOMIC, AND FORMAL CAPABILITIES; HIS OBJECTIVES (INTENTIONS); HIS INTELLIGENCE
QUALITY OF COMMUNICATION	VERY DIFFICULT TO GOOD	VERY DIFFICULT TO GOOD	GOOD TO VERY GOOD
REQUIREMENTS FOR THE COORDINATION OF INTELLIGENCE	GENERALLY LOW	HIGH OR VERY HIGH	VERY HIGH.
CONSEQUENCES OF FAILURE IN ACTION	DEFEATS, SETBACKS CAN BE RETRIEVED. SENSITIVITY TO A SINGLE FAILURE IS NORMALLY LOW	A SETBACK CAN HAVE A VERY SERIOUS IMPACT EVEN ON THE STRATEGIC LEVEL DIFFICULT TO RETRIEVE FAILURE.	CRITICAL OR DISASTROUS; VERY DIFFICULT TO RETRIEVE

by civilians'.[82] By comparison, most military commanders are to some extent unaccustomed to dealing with and accepting criticism, especially when the suggestion that they might be wrong comes from an individual of lesser rank or experience. Indeed, it is human nature to acquire such an outlook when one is constantly catered to and agreed with on a daily basis – and when only an extremely rare individual would venture to voice a contradictory opinion despite the risk of incurring his superior's displeasure. Having been long insulated from criticism through habit and experience, such a leader will view intelligence contradictory to his established plans or cherished aspirations as a personal challenge or even a threat.[83] Elsewhere, I have discussed examples of military leaders who rejected very clear evidence because it contradicted plans to which they had already committed themselves. Obsessed with his plan to capture Tobruk between October and November 1941, Rommel ignored all evidence that the British might in the meantime launch a massive attack on his rear flank; similarly, Montgomery rejected unambiguous information reporting the presence of substantial German tank formations in Arnhem, simply because accepting it would have meant cancelling his planned attack.[84] Another example is that of Air Marshal 'Bomber' Harris, who stubbornly refused to consider intelligence that area night bombing in Germany was not achieving its objectives, and that shifting the attack to other targets would be much more effective.[85]

Clearly, the danger is that the commanding general and his staff will solicit only those reports that confirm their wishful thinking and well-laid plans.

> ... There is a constant temptation, in the sphere of staff work, where Intelligence and Operations meet, to give an impression of the enemy situation which fits in with other requirements. This is known, I believe, in contemporary jargon as 'situating the appreciation', the opposite of 'appreciating the situation'.[86]

How, then, should an intelligence officer approach the very delicate task of convincing his commander that an operation is inadvisable or that his plans should be modified in light of recent, unambiguous intelligence reports? Ideally, the senior intelligence office should endeavor to form a close relationship of mutual trust with the commander; and his first steps in building such a rapport should be to become very familiar with his commander's working habits, character and ambitions. Equipped with this knowledge, the intelligence officer may then be able to make 'unpleasant' information more palatable. Both General de Guingand and Brigadier Bill Williams, Field Marshal Montgomery's intelligence advisers, had to develop special 'showmanship techniques' – a sort of 'Monty language' that would enable them to provide him with accurate intelligence while making it more acceptable to him to authorize the necessary changes in his meticulously prepared operational plans.[87] This entailed presenting advice in such a way as to make the commander think it was his own idea. In his memoirs, de Guingand gives an instructive account of how intelligence was 'packaged' to suit Monty's taste and therefore receive his serious consideration.

> At the height of the Battle of Alamein, I spoke privately to Montgomery about new intelligence from our 'Y' services that indicated a change in enemy dispositions. By altering the direction of our proposed thrust we would take maximum advantage of the new situation. Montgomery didn't take long to agree. He not only altered the plan as commander; it became, in his own mind, his own decision, his own proposal, and was referred to as such in his diaries. In the same way, during the Battle of Mareth, I suggested an alteration in the conduct of the battle in private, and summoned the Corps Commanders in readiness. As soon as he acknowledged the soundness of my reasoning, Montgomery made his decision: a decision which then became his own in his diaries, in his campaign account, and in his memoirs! I did not feel any disappointment at this subsequent failure to give credit; I recognized from the beginning that this was the way his mind, his personality, worked. How many times would he turn down an idea one day, and announce to me the following morning: 'Now Freddie, I've been thinking about it and I have decided to do the following ...'! Such appropriation of ideas and designs is the very basis of command – at least the appropriation of the best ideas. It was my task, as I saw it, to know my Chief, to know how his mind worked so well that I could happily deputize for him in his absence, either in the field or at the conferences he so hated to attend; to know him so well that I might sense when to put forward a suggestion and when to bide my time; when to wake him or let him sleep. If there are those who feel this to be an idle or inconsequential matter, let me instance what happened when such an approach was not adopted. No sooner was 'Supercharge', the final thrust, achieved at the Battle of Alamein, than Air Marshal Tedder, Air C' in C' in the Middle East, began to champ at the bit. He had seen chance after chance squandered in the desert during his time there, and had rather an airman's view of the fluid battle, so that he could never understand why we British were so slow on the ground. Thinking of his elite flying crews, he could not perceive the realities of army life. Ignoring the feeble performance of the RAF in strafing Rommel's retreating Afrika Korps, he now dispatched a signal to Montgomery stressing the importance of sending a mobile force

across the Cyrenaican bulge to cut Rommel off. If anything decided Montgomery not to pursue such a possibility – at least in strength – it was this meddling airman's presumptuous message. How much wiser to have visited Montgomery, congratulated him on his victory, questioned him about the RAF's performance from the army's point of view, asked his needs and in privacy conversed about Montgomery's future proposals! Yet Tedder never learned his lesson – and caused a lasting rift in inter-Allied relations in the summer of 1944 by carping about Montgomery's slow Normandy performance behind his back (indeed during his replacement) on the very eve of the greatest single victory of the war to date.[88]

Undoubtedly, it is no small feat to predict what sort of 'chemistry' will evolve in the relationship between the military leader and his intelligence adviser.[89] One thing, however, is certain: their relationship is not only fragile – it is also crucial to the success of any military operation. In some cases such as those of Nimitz and his advisers Rochefort and Layton; Montgomery and de Guingand or Bill Williams; Patton and Koch; or Eisenhower and Strong, the level of rapport was outstanding, while between Oliver and Hope; Pound and Godfrey or Denning; and perhaps Rommel and Mellenthin, for example, it was more problematic.

In a thoughtful and detailed study of this relationship and of the commander's use of intelligence in general, Dr Harold Deutsch concludes that

... in the average intelligence situation one must assign about a third share to the intelligence community's tendency to tailor to measure. At least another such share must be allocated to whatever tendency to ignore, twist, elaborate or accept there may be at the top. It is probably optimistic to grant the remaining third to the content of the intelligence message itself.[90]

Dr Deutsch's conclusions are pessimistic but probably realistic. Even more discouraging is the fact that he reached these conclusions – at least as far as the Allies were concerned – about a war in which intelligence made a more dramatic contribution to the conduct of military operations than ever before; a war in which high-level commanders had enough time to observe how successful intelligence could be and learn how to use it in the most effective way. Circumstances that favorable are not likely to recur often in the future, nor will future wars necessarily be long enough to allow a new and inexperienced generation of commanders the luxury of time to exploit the potential of intelligence to the full.

All such conflicts between different personalities and conflicting ambitions, or between political and personal interests, can never be completely resolved, but the most plausible way of improving the relationships between commanders and their intelligence staffs will be to pay far more attention to the role of intelligence in support of military planning and operations. This must be the rule from the earliest stages of military education through the highest levels of a commander's career. A realistic introduction to the role of intelligence in war would help military leaders to avoid the two extremes of either expecting the impossible from it on the one hand or deriding it as an irrelevant intellectual exercise on the other. Such an education must familiarize the officer with the various sources and methods of intelligence work; analyse what it can and cannot do; explore the most productive ways of working with intelligence experts; and, perhaps most fundamentally, facilitate the analysis of historical case-studies that demonstrate the uses and value of intelligence. This type of education would prepare commanders not only to understand the supportive role of intelligence better but also to be more open-minded to the advice provided by it and to treat the intelligence expert with more respect.

In the education of the intelligence expert, priority should be given to better acquaintance or previous experience with the problems of command and the planning of military operations. Emphasis must also be placed on the development of more effective salesmanship techniques and other interpersonal communications skills. Certainly, the selection of intelligence officers should be based not only on their professional qualifications but also on their strength of character and ethical standards. Finally, recognition of the autonomy of intelligence officers, both professionally and by rank, would undoubtedly be helpful as well.

Of the thirteen 'lessons' or recommendations that Donald McLachlan distilled from his experiences in the Second World War, seven concern the difficulties stemming from the gap between the two cultures of intelligence and operations as discussed earlier:

1. Fighting commanders, technical experts, and political leaders are liable to ignore, under-rate, or even despise intelligence. Obsession and bias often begin at the top.
2. Intelligence for the fighting services should be directed as far as possible by civilians.
3. Intelligence is the voice of conscience to a staff. Wishful thinking is the original sin of men of power.
4. Intelligence judgements must be kept constantly under review and revision. Nothing must be taken for granted either in premises or deduction.
5. Intelligence departments must be fully informed about operations and plans, but operations and plans must not be

dominated by the facts and views of intelligence. Intelligence is the servant and not the master.

9. Intelligence is ineffective without showmanship in the presentation and argument.

10. The boss, whoever he is, cannot know best and should not claim that he does.[91]

INTELLIGENCE AND MILITARY OPERATIONS

If reliable intelligence was almost impossible to obtain and transmit before the development of modern communications systems, during the years from the First World War to the end of the Second, reliable intelligence on all levels not only became available, but could also be considered a major component of military strength. Whereas accurate, timely and well presented intelligence can be seen as an important *force multiplier*, the lack of it can be considered both literally and figuratively as a *force divider*. Up to a point, good intelligence compensates for material or numerical inferiority by enabling the weaker side to employ its forces more economically; waste less time and fewer resources in search of the enemy; repeatedly hit the enemy at its most vulnerable points; intercept and interfere with the enemy's operations; and concentrate relatively superior forces at the decisive points of engagement. Conversely, the inability to identify the opponent's key weaknesses because of the absence of good intelligence may result in the unnecessary dispersion of forces and the waste of critical resources. Intelligence on the strategic, operational and tactical levels must therefore be seen as an important factor in the assessment of military strength and the balance of power. It might even be possible to speak of a *balance of intelligence* as a distinct method of assessing the relative strength of nations. Unfortunately, this is rarely feasible. Like the catalyst in a chemical reaction, intelligence – with its intangible output – is known to be a vital constituent of the process it influences so critically, but its precise function is difficult to isolate and measure with accuracy. The effectiveness and quality of intelligence is one of the best concealed secrets of every nation. Even the most exacting studies of military balances fail to mention anything about intelligence (just as they neglect to mention morale and national character, the quality of equipment maintenance, logistical support, quality of leadership, military doctrine and the like). It is precisely these non-quantifiable elements of power that make the study of its use so challenging. The Pope has not a single division, yet he may wield substantial authority and influence. There were no divisions or battalions of intelligence experts on any side during the Second World War; and in most general military accounts of the war – until the disclosure of Ultra and more recently, the details of the allied deceptions operations – intelligence was barely mentioned. Even today, the most exhaustive military histories scarcely discuss the weighty contribution of intelligence activities. This, of course, does not detract from its importance: on the contrary, it could be argued that in no other occupation during the war did so few achieve so much and receive so little appreciation. (No one receives medals for preparing accurately cross-indexed cards of German units or signals.) Victories in modern warfare, however, are won as much in laboratories and code-breaking rooms as on the battlefield. It has been said that amateurs study strategy and professionals study logistics. It might also be said that amateurs study strategy, professionals study logistics, and those who really know study intelligence. After all, the results in military conflict are always determined by the weakest link in the chain, and war is a systemic, synergistic enterprise in which the maintenance of equilibrium among the contributing elements is essential.

Hence, the best intelligence alone is no panacea. As argued above, a very powerful army confronting a weak one can win (usually a more costly victory) without good intelligence, whereas a weaker army with first-rate intelligence cannot always emerge victorious. At times, even a stronger force with superior intelligence can still be defeated; however, a militarily weaker force with poor intelligence can be expected to fare worst of all. Good intelligence does not always bring about victory; at times it can only mitigate the costs of defeat. Figure 1 outlines a possible framework for relating strength, quality of intelligence, and the outcome of major military operations. (By weakness in military or operational strength, only quantitative inferiority is meant.)

My selection of case-studies is intended to support and expand upon the theoretical discussion presented above. A common methodological technique in the natural sciences is to learn about the special properties of a chemical element of a variable in physics through experimental isolation. The complexity of human affairs in general and war in particular usually makes such an approach impossible in the study of history and strategy.[92] This is one of the main reasons that it is so difficult to evaluate the contribution of intelligence or deception to the outcome of military operations.[93] My discussion will concentrate on those case-studies that fall within the lower left and lower right boxes of Figure 1, and will comment only briefly on the others.

When both sides are roughly equal in strength and quality of intelligence, their strong and weak points will often cancel each other out; and when each commits many retrievable mistakes, such as those that occurred during the prolonged campaign in the Western Desert between 1941 and July 1942, or on the Eastern Front between 1943 and 1945, it is indeed a very challenging task to try to ascertain the overall contribution

FIGURE 1

INTELLIGENCE AND MILITARY OPERATIONS:
DIFFERENT POSSIBLE COMBINATIONS

OPERATIONAL (MILITARY) STRENGTH*

		WEAK	STRONG
QUALITY OF INTELLIGENCE	POOR	• BRITISH IN NORWAY 1940	• GERMANS IN BATTLE OF BRITAIN • GERMANY INVADING RUSSIA (BARBAROSSA) • JAPAN IN BATTLE OF MIDWAY • GERMAN U-BOATS IN THE ATLANTIC FROM MID 1943 • GERMANS IN NORMANDY
	VERY GOOD	• BRITISH IN BATTLE OF SIDI BARRANI (COMPASS) • BRITISH IN GREECE 1940 AND CRETE 1941 • GERMAN U-BOAT IN THE ATLANTIC 1939-1941 • U.S. NAVY IN BATTLE OF MIDWAY	• BATTLE OF JUTLAND • BRITISH IN EL ALAMEIN • ALLIES IN SICILY • RUSSIANS AT THE BATTLE OF KURSK

*QUANTITATIVE (NUMERICAL) STRENGTH

of intelligence. An opportunity to 'isolate' the influence of intelligence on important military operations is, however, provided by the relatively rare instances in which one side has such overwhelmingly superior military might that the other, weaker side is certain to lose unless compensated by superior intelligence. Even more helpful in 'isolating' the intelligence factor are situations in which the much more powerful side is so confident of victory that it does not develop adequate intelligence to support its own operations (that is, the 'balance of intelligence' favors the weaker side). In the Battle of Midway and the battles for Greece and Crete, for example, the existence of superior intelligence on the weaker side of the equation can therefore be clearly indentified.

US NAVAL INTELLIGENCE AND THE BATTLE OF MIDWAY

After the indecisive Battle of the Coral Sea, the Japanese Imperial High Command decided to consolidate its gains from the preceding period of expansion by occupying the strategically located island of Midway. At that time, the Japanese enjoyed overwhelming naval superiority over the US Pacific Fleet, in addition to having better carrier-based aircraft, better torpedoes and more experienced carrier-based air crews.[94] Had the Japanese been able to surprise the Americans in their attack on Midway, they would undoubtedly have won the battle easily. The extent of US naval inferiority at this stage meant that precise knowledge of the next Japanese objective offered the only hope of concentrating the remaining US carriers for effective action. American Naval Sigint provided the US Navy with the almost complete and accurate knowledge of Japanese plans[95] that enabled Admiral Nimitz to send carriers to intercept the Japanese force in the nick of time. In contrast, the Japanese had no knowledge of the whereabouts of the US carriers; intoxicated by their earlier success, they expected to achieve an easy victory anyway. By early May US naval intelligence in Hawaii had identified Midway as the next possible Japanese target. On 10 May, Midway (referred to in Japanese signals as AF) was definitively identified, while on 14 May it was learned that a Japanese invasion force would also be included in the imminent operation. The complete order of battle of the Japanese task force was obtained on the 25th, and by the 27th, Captain Layton was able to furnish Nimitz with the exact date of attack as well as its direction and the time that US reconnaissance could be expected to locate the approaching Japanese fleet. By 4 June, the Japanese had managed to concentrate a vastly superior force as evidenced by the following data:[96]

TABLE 2
JAPANESE AND US NAVAL STRENGTH COMPARED

	Japan	United States
Heavy aircraft carriers	4	3
Light aircraft carriers	2	0
Battleships	11	0
Heavy cruisers	10	6
Light cruisers	6	1
Destroyers	53	17
TOTAL SURFACE FIGHTING SHIPS	86	27
Carrier-based aircraft	325	233
Land-based aircraft	0	115
TOTAL AIRCRAFT STRENGTH	325	348

The Japanese, whose plan depended on the achievement of surprise, instead found themselves the victim of an unanticipated turn of events. In spite of their impressive numerical superiority, the Japanese suffered a resounding defeat. This is clearly reflected in a comparison of their relative losses (see Table 3).[97]

As the first major American victory in the Pacific, Midway was one of the most important turning points of the Second World War. What would

TABLE 3
RELATIVE LOSSES COMPARED

	Japan	United States
Casualties	2,500	307
Carriers	4	1
Heavy cruisers	1	0
Destroyers	0	1
Aircraft	332	147

have been a hopeless situation without such outstanding intelligence was turned into a narrowly won but decisive victory. The most decisive factor in this battle (other than the quality of the intelligence obtained) was the complete trust Admiral Nimitz placed in the intelligence he received from Commander Joseph Rochefort, head of the Combat Intelligence Office ('Hypo') in Hawaii, and Captain Edwin T. Layton, the Fleet Intelligence Officer. Although Nimitz had little reason to put his faith in naval intelligence after the attack on Pearl Harbor, the contribution of Hypo to the Battle of the Coral Sea convinced him to '... trust Rochefort over and above the often conflicting assessments being made by naval intelligence in Washington'.[98] Rather than encouraging divisiveness or competition, Nimitz listened to all sides of an issue without giving the 'messengers' the feeling that he had already made up his mind in advance. 'But once he made his decision, he proceeded full speed ahead. For that, the United States owes him a tremendous debt.'[99] Despite the fact that he could, as Commander of the Pacific Fleet, 'like Jellicoe lose the war in an afternoon,'[100] Nimitz 'stood like a rock'. His openness to information and ability to resist immense pressure once he had made up his mind surely entitle him to be considered one of Clausewitz's rare military geniuses.

Pressures that would have caused a less secure individual to hesitate and vacillate abounded. Admiral King in Washington, who was known for his domineering personality, apparently believed that Japan's next move in the Pacific would be against US island bases in the South Pacific (e.g., New Caledonia, Port Morseby or Fiji). In its eagerness to please Admiral King, naval intelligence in Washington '... tended to feed him information that reinforced his convictions, and every officer in Washington knew that King was struggling to get more resources for the Pacific war. Raising the level of alarm about the Japanese threat to our lifelines to Australia evidently was more likely to evoke the support of General Marshall than asking for reinforcements for Midway or the Aleutians'.[101] It is not surprising, therefore, that relying on the same evidence available to Rochefort in Hawaii, the intelligence authorities in Washington initially concluded that the South Pacific Islands – not Midway – would be the next Japanese objective. Others in Washington and Hawaii, including the

Chief of Staff, George C. Marshall, were afraid that the supposedly impending attack on Midway was only part of a deception plan to divert attention from other targets.[102] Unable to understand why the Japanese would want to concentrate a large force against such an apparently 'insignificant' objective such as Midway, some intelligence analysts and high-level military leaders were convinced that the Japanese actually intended to attack Oahu or even the west coast of the United States.[103] (Naval intelligence in Washington put additional pressure on Nimitz by consulting with Lieutenant-General Delos C. Emmons, commander of the Hawaiian Department and military governor of Hawaii. Emmons had little doubt that the next Japanese target was going to be Oahu.)[104]

In an effort to convince the skeptics that Midway was indeed to be the object of the next Japanese attack, Rochefort decided to implement an ingenious but simple plan proposed by one of his assistants; he decided to set up a trap that would prove his theory in a most definitive manner. The Japanese had, in their radio intercepts, sometimes mentioned 'AF' – a place which Rochefort believed to be Midway, not Hawaii. With the blessings of Layton and Nimitz, Rochefort had Midway radio Oahu a 'plain-language' message that Midway was suffering from an emergency water shortage. This was followed up with an encoded message, the code being one that the Japanese were known to have captured earlier. The Japanese promptly took the bait, and shortly thereafter, the Americans intercepted Japanese messages announcing to their own commanders that 'AF' had a water shortage for which they should prepare accordingly. After Nimitz and Rochefort had convinced Washington that 'AF' must mean Midway, Nimitz still had to fight for the release of Halsey's two carriers from Admiral King's standing order that they should be kept in the southwest Pacific as well as to convince Washington that the Japanese N-day was on 4 June rather than on the 15th.[105]

When forced to choose between the conflicting intelligence estimates of his staff and Washington, Nimitz preferred his own staff's appreciation. Other senior commanders might have either bowed to Washington's authority or failed to trust their own staffs to the same extent. Today, it is less likely that an independent position of this sort could be taken by a commander in view of the increased concentration of intelligence and command in Washington, improved communications, and the greater deference given to political and bureaucratic considerations. Very few commanders in Nimitz's position would have been ready to accept the risks and responsibilities that he did.

The central lesson once again is that this type of success requires an open-minded leader who is ready to listen but at the same time is steadfast enough to resist the inevitable pressure to keep revising his plans once he has made up his mind. Conflicts over who is to control intelligence and influence leaders should be anticipated and faced with equanimity, since they are typical of the personal and organizational political considerations that permeate the intelligence process.[106] Unavoidably, the perceptions in Washington and Hawaii were as different as those between London and Cairo. If not for the Pearl Harbor disaster, which had shaken Naval Headquarters and Naval Intelligence, Nimitz and his intelligence advisers might not have enjoyed the same degree of success in asserting their views over those prevailing in Washington.

Although Nimitz, in Lewin's words, '... had more intimate knowledge of his enemy's strength and intentions than any other admiral in the whole previous history of sea warfare',[107] the battle was won by the narrowest of margins. For once the battle began, the still considerable Japanese superiority had to be reckoned with. Even the best intelligence support *before* battle cannot be relied upon to continue unabated during the course of the battle itself, which is, as we have seen, dominated by uncertainty. Here the Americans were aided as much by luck as they had been by intelligence before the battle began. Very few such conflicts have been won by the loss of so many 'nails' and 'horseshoes' in favor of one side; it was a battle of chance and mischance 'shot with luck'. As Sir Francis Bacon once advised '... if a man look sharply and attentively, he shall see fortune; for though she be blind, yet she is not invisible'.[108] The Americans proved once again that chance works in favor of the well-prepared.[109]

The Japanese fleet was discovered almost by chance when the pilot of a reconnaissance plane decided to extend his flight a few minutes beyond his sector. Had he not done so, the Japanese task force might not have been detected in time.

> The final debacle was due to a stroke of good luck on the United States side – the uncoordinated coordination of the dive bombers hitting three carriers at once while the torpedo strikes were still in progress. Except for those six short minutes, Nagumo would have been the victor, and all his decisions would have been accounted to him for righteousness. Timidity would have become prudence, vacillation due deliberation, rigidity attention to the voice of experience.[110]

Had the Japanese committed fewer errors they might still have won the battle despite their inferior intelligence, as the Germans did in Crete. One blunder after another, however, took them beyond the point of salvageable mistakes: their radio security was lax; they neglected reconnaissance; and their incomplete search plan before the battle delayed submarine and sea plane patrols near Hawaii. On the morning of the battle, the Japanese failure to send out sufficient aircraft on reconnaissance missions was compounded by bad luck, since a Japanese plane flew directly over one of the American carriers without identifying it as such. The Japanese plan was far too complicated and depended not only on surprise but also on best-case projections of American reactions. Its execution was faulty as well: Admiral Nagumo concentrated all his aircraft in one attack on Midway, and rather than immediately redirecting them to attack the US carriers when they had the opportunity, he preferred to rearm them at the worst possible time. Too much of the Japanese plan hinged on its flawless execution and too little margin for error was left to absorb the unexpected friction. While it is possible though inadvisable to make such assumptions in the opening phase of a war against an unsuspecting victim (as in the case of Pearl Harbor), it is practically suicidal to assume that any complex plan can be executed perfectly in an ongoing war.

Arrogance and a sense of invincibility blinded the Japanese, who did not consider their opponent worthy of much attention. On the other hand, the Americans, who had been humbled early in the war and who lacked both confidence and ships, knew that learning as much as possible about their enemy was imperative. There is no stronger incentive to encourage the appreciation of intelligence than fear and weakness (whether actual or perceived); conversely, victory and power reduce one's motivation to learn about the enemy, thus bringing about the conditions that may eventually cause defeat.

One final decision in the American victory at Midway should be noted. Following the battle, Admiral Spruance had to decide whether to pursue the retreating Japanese task force in an attempt to finish off the remaining Japanese ships, or to withdraw. Although he knew that his planes had hit four Japanese carriers and left them in flames, he had not yet received information as to their condition. Moreover, he did not know the whereabouts of the other Japanese carriers or of at least half a dozen Japanese battleships, cruisers or submarines. On the other hand, he did know that many of his own aircraft had been lost or damaged and that his flight and maintenance crews were exhausted. Since he was responsible for the safety of Midway and for the only two US carriers in the central Pacific, Admiral Spruance decided against pursuing a possibly superior Japanese force. 'It is likely that the Battle of Midway would have been turned from an American triumph to a Japanese victory and the capture of Midway if Spruance had done anything else ... [If Spruance had decided in favor of pursuit] he would have run into a light carrier, the fleet carrier *Jintsu*, two battleships, numerous heavy cruisers and destroyers *in addition to* Yamamoto's flagship *Yamato*, and the rest of his and Nagumo's forces: nine battleships in all. A clash would have been certain; the outcome catastrophic.'[111] By knowing when to be bold and when to avoid risks, Admiral Spruance consolidated and secured the fruits of victory at Midway.

THE BATTLES FOR GREECE AND CRETE

The battles for Greece and Crete in 1941 provide another outstanding example of the contribution that good intelligence can make to a weaker force on the defensive. Unlike the Americans in the battle of Midway, the British and Commonwealth troops were unable to translate the advantage of superior intelligence into a victory over the invading Germans. In Greece, the British managed to extricate themselves from a very adverse situation despite odds that heavily favored the Germans both on the land and in the air. In Crete, they inflicted such great losses on the German paratroopers that Hitler and the German High Command never again undertook such an operation even when the circumstances justified it and when it could have altered the course of the war in Germany's favor in the Western Desert and North Africa. It is one of the greatest ironies of the Second World War that two battles considered at first to be unmitigated disasters actually turned out to be strategic 'blessings' for the Allies.

The battles for Greece and Crete were immediately preceded by the first major fleet action fought since Jutland in 1916: the battle of Matapan. Bletchley Park, which had penetrated the Italian naval codes, provided Admiral Cunningham in Alexandria with an advance warning of Admiral Iachino's intention to intercept British convoys *en route* from Africa to Greece on the night of 29 March 1941. This foreknowledge enabled Admiral Cunningham to surprise the Italian task force, sink two cruisers (*Zara* and *Fiume*), and seriously damage the battleship *Vittorio Veneto*. As the first important operation in the Mediterranean to be based on Sigint, this intelligence coup established British naval hegemony in the eastern Mediterranean and became a pivotal factor in the battles for Greece and Crete that followed.[112]

For Operation Marita, the Germans concentrated ten divisions (three of which were armored) and about 1,000 aircraft against which the British and commonwealth forces could field some 50,000 poorly equipped troops with no air cover. Although Bletchley Park deciphered the Luftwaffe's codes on a daily basis and supplied the commanders in the field with advance warning of the forthcoming German attack as well as with astonishingly accurate information on the German order of battle every evening, the odds were such that the final outcome of the campaign could never have been in doubt. There was simply nothing with which to strike back.[113]

It is not surprising therefore that 'the British campaign on the mainland of Greece was from start to finish a withdrawal'.[114] Under the pressure of tremendous German superiority and the unrelenting threat that his defense lines might be outflanked, General Wilson, the commander of W

Force, had to issue orders to withdraw from the Aliakmon line first to the Olympus–Servia Pass then to the Thermopylae line, and eventually to the beaches to escape capture or destruction at the hands of the advancing Germans. In the end, the main forces of both sides never met in a direct engagement.[115] The British managed to avoid this through a series of 'extremely well-timed' withdrawals, some of which were based on Enigma appreciations received by General Wilson.[116] With the advantage of good intelligence, the British were thus able to evacuate most of the expeditionary force sent to Greece with relatively few losses of troops, although all of the equipment that had been sent with them was left behind. (Over 50,000 soldiers were evacuated from Greek beaches.)[117]

Intelligence available before and during the battle for Crete was even more accurate. In Churchill's words, 'At no moment in the war was our intelligence so truly and precisely informed ... In the last week of April we obtained from trustworthy sources good information about the next German strike ... All pointed to an impending attack on Crete both by air and sea'.[118]

If the intelligence available to Commander Freyberg in Crete was so accurate, why then was the battle lost despite the much better chances for success than in Greece? Indications that the Germans planned to make extensive use of airborne troops in Greece came from Enigma in late March 1941 before the campaign had begun.[119] Further information from mid-April onwards indicated that extensive preparations were being made for a large-scale airborne operation, but there was no definitive evidence that Crete was the target. By 22 April, the Chiefs of Staff assumed that Crete was the most likely objective, but the possibility that Cyprus might be desirable merely as a stepping stone to Iraq or Syria could not be entirely discounted. It was on 27 April, only two days after Hitler had given his final approval for Operation Merkur, that the Luftwaffe's Enigma first made a direct reference to Crete. Nevertheless, Wavell, the Commander in Chief in the Middle East, was still worried that the appearance of a German threat might be a cover plan for an attack on Cyprus or Syria. In view of his other far-reaching responsibilities in the Middle East, and the events in Syria and Iraq, his fear that the threat to Crete was only a diversion was understandable. It must also be remembered that because of Wavell's personal interest in and extensive use of deception, he was more sensitive to the possibility that it could also be used against him.[120] By 5 May, however, the JIC in London had ruled out Cyprus as a German objective. In the meantime, the pressure under which the Germans were working as well as disagreements in their Athens headquarters about the final shape of their plan of attack forced them to make unusually heavy use of wireless traffic. This afforded British intelligence a welcome opportunity to eavesdrop. On 6 May Enigma revealed that the projected date for completing preparations for the attack was 17 May. On the 11th, it revealed that the German Chief of Air staff had requested a 48-hour delay of the original date, and on the 19th, London informed the Middle East and Crete that the attack would take place the next day. When the invasion finally began on the morning of 20 May, the story is that Freyberg calmly remarked, 'They're dead on time.'[121] It is very rare in the annals of modern warfare that such a precise warning of the timing of an impending attack has been sounded so far in advance.[122]

The exact timing of the coming attack was, however, only one of the vital pieces of information provided to the defenders of Crete. The continuous flow of intelligence from London and Cairo to Freyberg's headquarters also gave him remarkably accurate data on the German plan of attack itself: it reported that the assault on the island would be preceded by several days of air attacks; that on the first day of the attack, the airfields of Heraklion, Retimo and Maleme would be the main objectives of the German paratroopers; and that after the capture of the airfields, the next phase of the attack would concentrate on the ports of Suda and Heraklion. It was indicated that the paratroopers would be dropped directly on the airfields or in their immediate vicinity, and that heavy Junkers 52 troop carriers might attempt to land on open fields. The intelligence further suggested that at a later phase the Germans also planned to land troops from the sea, but that this was only of secondary importance.[123] On 16 May, more details on the German order of battle were supplied, including the estimate that 25,000 to 30,000 airborne and 10,000 seaborne troops would take part. In fact, the actual number was only 15,750 airborne and 7,000 seaborne troops.[124] And of the 600 transport aircraft expected, only 520 participated in the attack. Earlier estimates (Whitehall, 27 April) of German airpower in general also included 285 long-range bombers, 270 single-engine fighters, 60 twin engine fighters, and 240 dive bombers. Again, the actual numbers were somewhat lower, with 280 long-range bombers, 90 single-engine fighters, 90 twin engine fighters, and 150 dive bombers.[125] In addition, intelligence on German airborne doctrine and methods as well as suggestions on how best to counter them were made available. All of this priceless information was passed on to every sector commander as early as 12 May in an intelligence appreciation prepared at Freyberg's headquarters.[126] The report made one thing abundantly clear: that the success of the German plan rested entirely on their ability to capture the targeted airfields early in the battle.

No commander could ever expect to receive better intelligence than Freyberg did. The defenders knew exactly when the attack would begin, were twice as strong as the attacking Germans, and had as great an advantage as a defender can have in terms of the difficulties and vulnerability so characteristic of all paratrooper attacks. Above all, the availability of excellent intelligence solved one of the most critical questions every defender must ask – where to concentrate his forces. Since they knew that the key German objectives were the three airfields, the defenders stood a very good chance of winning the battle if they efficiently used their forces to prevent the Germans from securing a foothold in these areas. Yet despite the optimistic expectations of the defenders and the fact the Germans had lost the critical element of surprise, the Germans won by the narrowest of margins. The explanation for this provides an excellent opportunity to illustrate why even the best intelligence can only be a necessary but not a sufficient condition for the success of a weaker side on the battlefield. Intelligence, perhaps even more so than other factors in war, is valuable only if many other conditions are met. These conditions were not present on the island of Crete in May 1941. The importance of Crete to the British strategy in the Mediterranean was never a matter of dispute. Unfortunately, the pressure on the commander responsible for the Middle East, and the urgent demands made upon his deplorably inadequate resources in the Western Desert, East Africa, Syria and Iraq as well as in Greece made it impossible to devote enough attention to the preparation for the defense of Crete.

There was no sense of urgency. In six months, the British had appointed six different military commanders in Crete. As the last of the six, General Freyberg was unexpectedly appointed to the position on 29 April at Churchill's request; he assumed command on 30 April, barely three weeks before the German attack. The conditions necessary for the organization and careful preparation of the defense of Crete simply never materialized.[127] The principal problem facing the 32,000 garrison troops on the island was the shortage of equipment and ammunition of all types.[128] All commentators agree that a relatively small addition of the most needed equipment would have meant certain victory for the defenders. The severe shortage of comunications and signals equipment was critical, for once the battle had begun, Freyberg found it practically impossible either to receive information or to transmit his orders because of the lack of wireless equipment. Consequently, he lost the ability to control effectively the troops under his command. This undoubtedly proved to be the weakest link in the British defense of Crete.

General Freyberg was aware of the shortage of signal equipment (as he made clear in a cable to Wavell in the Middle East Headquarters in Cairo), but he never really insisted upon the need for 'field wireless apparatus'.[129] Yet as Stewart points out in *The Struggle for Crete*, 'a single plane, flying if necessary direct from England via Gibraltar, could have brought enough wireless sets to equip every unit in the island down to the company level ... The truth is (according to one of Freyberg's staff officers after the war) that a hundred extra wireless sets could have saved Crete.'[130] Thus, while

Freyberg was supplied with the best possible intelligence *before* the battle, he was unable to obtain what he desperately needed *during* the battle itself. From his point of view, once the fighting had begun he was inundated with continuously changing rumors and counter-rumors much like those that besieged Clausewitz's commander or Napoleon at Borodino.

Although the problems of obtaining intelligence before and during the battle are very different, they deserve equal attention. Even the best intelligence before the battle becomes progressively less relevant as the fighting continues. Information is needed on the actual developments on the battlefield – information as much on the position and situation of one's own troops as on those of the enemy. This is why intelligence on the battlefield can never be studied, as discussed earlier, without reference to command, communication and control. Clearly, gathering information before the fighting begins is much simpler than doing so in the heat of battle.

Given the autonomous nature of each fighting sector on the island, the battle might still have been won without direction from a central command post had each sector been supplied with adequate weapons.[131] There was a pressing shortage of the guns that would have been used to cover all three airfields and to which the paratroopers had no suitable answer. 'The presence on Crete of sixty 25 pounders would have transformed the situation.'[132] There were only six obsolete tanks on the island. A dozen or so additional tanks of better quality that could have been diverted from the 'Tiger' convoy and which '... might have altered the scale of events in Crete, was never sent'.[133] On the entire island there were only 32 heavy and 36 light anti-aircraft guns.[134]

Furthermore, even fewer than the 64 Hurricanes it was hoped might miraculously arrive in time would have greatly aided the defenders,[135] but this was a remote possibility; to make matters worse, there was an acute deficit of the ammunition, fuel, engine maintenance facilities and other equipment needed to keep them flying. On the eve of the battle, the few remaining fighter aircraft in Crete (listed by Freyberg as six Hurricanes and 17 obsolete aircraft) were withdrawn to avoid the pointless sacrifice of pilots and machines that could be used to much greater effect elsewhere. Without radar and communications equpment, control of the anticipated intensive air battle was impossible. Many months would have been required to prepare for the proper maintenance of even one squadron of Hurricanes – which were in short supply and needed elsewhere anyway. Consequently, the Germans were allowed to enjoy total control of the air, which is where they secured their most important edge over the defenders. Despite the last-minute decision to evacuate the remaining fighters, Freyberg was ordered not to take the step of mining or otherwise obstructing the airfields so crucial for support of the German invasion; this alone could have made it impossible for the Germans to resupply their paratroopers.[136] (One reason for this was probably the hope that the Royal Air Force would return in greater numbers at a later stage.)[137]

Still, such missed opportunities and numerous shortages might have been made up for by the commander's intuition had Freyberg been able to assess the situation more accurately during the battle and then exploit the series of German mistakes that occurred. In the absence of reliable information, however, Freyberg's intuition was not up to the task. 'In any battle much of what happens is explicable only if we take into account not only the strength and plans of each side, but also what each side took to be the strength and plans of the other.'[138]

Whereas the defenders had outstanding intelligence before the attack but poor intelligence once the battle began, for the Germans the opposite was true. Before the attack, German pilots on reconnaissance reported that the island appeared lifeless; no infantry positions could be identified within the olive groves and little shipping was observed. Ironically enough, it was German air superiority that had forced the defenders to camouflage their positions and move primarily at night. As a result, the Germans greatly underestimated the number of troops on Crete (which they estimated to be at the strength of one division) and failed to identify the troop concentrations on the island. Their intelligence on the island's defenses was sketchy at best; only when the German paratroopers were descending from the sky did they discover that the defenders were indeed ready for them.[139] Moreover, the Germans conveniently assumed that the local Greek population would be friendly or at least neutral – a gross misunderstanding, to say the least.

Thus surprised by the defenders, the Germans sustained very heavy casualties on the first day of the invasion while failing to achieve their objectives. During the afternoon of the 21st, Sigint enabled a British reconnaissance aircraft to discover two German convoys of caiques en route to Crete: the first was attacked on the same day and its ships were either sunk or dispersed; the second had been ordered to return to Piraeus, but was attacked at dawn on the 22nd.[140] The immediate threat of a seaborne attack on Crete was therefore eliminated with dispatch, although it is not known whether Freyberg – who had no direct communication with the Navy – knew of this. In the meantime, the German paratroopers did not make any noticeable headway on the second day of their attack; rather than concentrating the bulk of the attacking forces against one airfield at a time, they attacked three simultaneously. To compound their errors, they failed to understand the obstacles and delays involved in the process of reinforcement by sea. Having committed almost all of their air landing troops on the first day, they had no reserves left to reinforce the attack at the decisive point.[141] 'These failures had opened a series of brilliant opportunities to the defense. Andrew, Leckie, Hargest and Freyberg had each held victory within his grasp only to allow his vital moment to pass and for the same essential reasons. At every level they had been betrayed by their communication.'[142] What proved fatal was the collapse of short-range communications on the island between the defending sectors and Freyberg's headquarters. This is where Freyberg's 'intuition' was found wanting.

Instead of focusing his attention exclusively on the three airfields so crucial to the outcome of the battle, Freyberg was distracted by the threat from the sea (which was well protected by the Royal Navy with which he had no direct communication) and by his unfounded fear that German transport aircraft might crash-land outside the area of the airfields under attack. As he told Churchill after the war, 'We, for our part were mostly preoccupied by sea landings, not by the threat of air landings'.[143] This preoccupation caused him to underestimate the vital importance of the airfields, particularly in Maleme, where he ordered the local commander (Puttick) to position his troops in such a way as to be able to meet a threat from the sea or land.[144] As a result, not all of the available troops in the area were concentrated at the airfield of Maleme itself, even after it should have become clear on the first day how closely the Germans were adhering to the intelligence predictions in making the airfields their main objectives.[145]

Ronald Lewin comments on Freyberg's intuition by comparing it with that of Montgomery:

> In so fine-run a battle, victory awaited the man who knew what it was actually about – not in the coarse sense of winning or losing the island, but in the strictly professional sense of calculating to a nicety what must be the supremely important piece of ground. Freyberg, in effect, misread the evidence. *De quoi s' agit-il*? [what is it all about?] is the question all generals should ask. With the same intelligence available, Montgomery's incisive mind would surely have fastened on the one thing that mattered, and so distributed his troops that Maleme might have been just long enough for the parachutists to have withered without support. Ultra was a shadow until the generals gave it substance.[146]

In his new book, *Ultra and Mediterranean Strategy*, Ralph Bennett contradicts the hitherto generally accepted idea that General Freyberg was never permitted to learn of the Ultra secret.[147] Bennett states that Wavell informed Freyberg of Ultra's existence at the time Freyberg was appointed to command Crete. (This evidence is based on an account given by Lord Freyberg, General Freyberg's son.) Although it does not fundamentally change the overall assessment presented above, this disclosure raises a few interesting questions. It appears that General Freyberg was introduced to Ultra only shortly before the battle of Crete began and therefore had no time to become familiar with its proper interpretation. This situation was exacerbated by the fact that 'he was forbidden to show it (the information derived from Ultra) to anyone or to discuss it with his intelligence staff.'[148] Moreover, tight security regulations prohibiting him from taking action on the basis of uncorroborated Ultra evidence limited its value. According to Bennett, Lord Freyberg 'has convincingly shown that General Freyberg would have strengthened the defense of Maleme had he not been expressly forbidden to do so'.[149] Perhaps. But this claim must be considered with caution since Bennett himself shows that earlier evidence from Ultra between 11 and 16 May diverted much of General Freyberg's attention away from the airfields to a possible larger threat from the sea that did not materialize in the end.[150] It remains unclear why the information provided to him by Ultra, if correctly interpreted, did not allow General Freyberg to send 'reinforcements' to Maleme soon *after* the battle had begun on the 'corroborated' basis of local intelligence reports.

In any event, the success of the defenders and their obvious state of preparedness in the face of the German attack should have at least caused the Germans to reconsider the security of their enciphered communications network. This suspicion could have been reinforced by the capture of British documents, some of which were too closely based on Ultra intercepts.[151] The fact that the Germans seemed to have no inkling of a breach in their communications security in this case owed more to their overconfidence than to the British successful protection of Ultra.

Hitler's approval of the attack on Crete was contingent on the assumption that the attackers would be able to achieve surprise. This was not unreasonable, since avoidance of strategic or operational surprise is so difficult that it is the exception for any intelligence organization. Yet excellent British intelligence was able to sound a timely warning for the defenders of Crete; it succeeded where the Germans failed time after time. One can only imagine what might have happened had German intelligence provided the *Wehrmacht* with this type of warning before the invasion of Sicily, Salerno, Anzio or Normandy. The *Wehrmacht* was a highly efficient and powerful war machine which started almost all of its important battles blindfolded. Therefore, most of the major battles of the *Wehrmacht* from 1943 onwards can be placed in the upper right-hand side of Figure 1 (i.e., strong military but poor intelligence).

Without the timely warning sounded by British intelligence as well as their own courage, the defenders would not have been able to exact such a heavy toll from the Germans; and there can be no doubt that without the accurate information continuously supplied to the defenders *before* the battle began, the Germans would have won another blitzkrieg-style victory. One can only speculate that had General Freyberg possessed adequate communications equipment and also accurate information during the course of the battle, they might still have prevailed despite their general shortage of equipment and Freyberg's misperception of German operational intentions and capabilities. Intelligence is as important during the battle as it is before, for combat effectiveness depends on the ability to communicate in the midst of fighting.

The Germans won a Pyrrhic victory.[152] At the time it occurred, the loss of Crete was perceived as a strategic disaster, but in the long run, the outcome could not have been better. In the words of the official British history, 'It may be that fortune in a strange guise was with the British at this moment, and the loss of Crete at such a high cost to the Germans was almost the best thing that could have happened ... Strategic success must sometimes be bought at the price of a tactical reverse'.[153] No intelligence at the time could have predicted that the costly German victory was to have lasting repercussions that ultimately worked to the advantage of the British. Indeed, as General Student, commander of the parachute and glider troops of Fliegerkorps XI put it, 'Crete was the grave of the German parachutist ...'.[154] Jolted by the heavy casualties, Hitler concluded that the use of paratroopers was no longer a viable option because the element of surprise upon which they depended had been lost.[155] Following the invasion, Student proposed the occupation of Cyprus, which he believed would serve as an excellent jumping-off point for an attack on the Suez Canal. Hitler rejected the idea outright and never approved this type of operation again. At the time of Student's suggestion, the British forces on Cyprus were far from adequate, but the Führer – 'once bitten twice shy' – had overlearned his lesson. Later in 1941 and 1942, when the swift occupation of Malta (Operation Hercules) by a similar operation could have brought them victory in the Western Desert, Hitler and the *Wehrmacht*'s commanders could not bring themselves to make the decision. Had the British emerged victorious in the battle of Crete, it is also unclear how they would have held the island and resupplied it given the complete German air superiority. The cost of holding the island might have ultimately proved to be more damaging to the British than that of losing it.

From the discussion so far, one might conclude that the combination of high-quality intelligence and a powerful army or navy (lower right-hand box in Figure 1) would almost always ensure victory. For a number of possible reasons, this is not necessarily true:

(a) Much depends on how well even superior intelligence is understood or used by military leaders.

(b) Other factors such as a shortage of adequate communications equipment to receive and transmit information reliably during a battle, inferior equipment and-or inflexible and unimaginative military leadership, and a flawed military doctrine can render the combination of a quantitative and intelligence advantage useless. In fact, a numerically inferior enemy may end up victorious because it is better equipped, better led, and more adroit in its use of intelligence. Two examples will clarify this point: the battle of Jutland (31 May 1916), and the campaign in the Western Desert between 1941 and 1942.[156]

THE BATTLE OF JUTLAND: AN ANOMALY

British naval intelligence managed to break German naval codes early in the First World War. With the information thus obtained from decrypts of German wireless communications, the British were able to deprive the German fleet of the ability to achieve surprise, which, given its overall inferiority, was its major asset. Nevertheless, poor use of intelligence, inefficient communication between British ships at sea, and bad luck robbed the British of victory during the Scarborough raid and the Dogger Bank Battle. Since the mistakes committed in these earlier battles were not duly noted and impressed upon the collective consciousness of the naval leadership, they were repeated – with the same result – during the battle of Jutland. Patrick Beesly, who carefully studied the operations of Room 40 and the battle of Jutland, came to the conclusion that Admiral Oliver, as Chief of the British Naval War Staff, must be held personally responsible for the misuse of intelligence that precluded a British victory.

Somewhat disdainful of intelligence, Oliver misused it on more than one occasion because he had no understanding of its potential. He was a workaholic who could not bring himself to delegate responsibility; he preferred to draft every important signal by himself, making little use of his own staff officers as a result. This was disastrous for the work of Room 40: as far as is known, Oliver never visited it, distrusted the 'civilian amateurs' who worked there, and insisted, despite his ignorance of intelligence matters, on acting as his own intelligence analyst.[157] Oliver apparently suspected that Room 40 was overstepping the bounds of its assigned duties and trying to encroach on his territory. Never free of misunderstanding, the relationship between these departments was doomed to remain cold.[158]

On the basis of its work in intercepting and decyphering naval signals as well as in traffic analysis, Room 40 concluded that the German High Seas Fleet was preparing for a major operation as early as 28 or 29 May 1916. By noon on 30 May, it was able to predict that the High Seas Fleet would probably put out to sea early the next day. This enabled the British to send the Grand Fleet out to sea a few hours ahead of their adversaries. The German plan, which was designed to lure one or two British squadrons into a submarine trap, depended completely upon the achievement of surprise, now made impossible by Room 40's timely warning. Admiral Sir John Jellicoe, Commander-in-Chief of the Grand Fleet, and Admiral Sir David Beatty, Commander of the Battle Cruiser Squadron, were supposed to meet and concentrate their forces some 100 miles east of Aberdeen. In the meantime, German intelligence was unaware that the Grand Fleet had put out to sea thanks to a *balance of intelligence* that clearly favored the Royal Navy. From that point onward, however, nothing went well for the British as far as the *use* of intelligence was concerned. The first and most damaging error was a message sent by Oliver at 12.30 p.m. on 31 May to Jellicoe and Beatty, informing them that the German *Hochseeflotte* was still in port at 11.10 a.m., whereas in fact it was already out at sea. This mistake originated from a direct and very narrowly phrased inquiry made at Room 40 by Captain Thomas Jackson, Oliver's Director of Operations. Captain Jackson had asked one wrong question without bothering to solicit more background information from the members of Room 40, who in fact possessed very accurate information on the whereabouts of the High Seas Fleet.

Instead of asking *where* the German CNC (Admiral Scheer) was at that time, Jackson very specifically asked for the *place of origin* of the call signal DK. Unknown to him but known to Room 40, it was the practice of the German High Seas Fleet to try to deceive British Naval Intelligence by continuing to send DK messages from port even when the High Seas Fleet had put out to sea. As part of the ruse, Admiral Scheer ceased to use the call sign DK whenever he left port. Like Oliver, Captain Jackson had little respect for the work of Room 40 and did not encourage – and in fact by his demeanor discouraged – any elaboration on the answer to his question. In short, the answer to his question was that DK referred to Wilhelmshaven, from which Jackson and Oliver, in their ignorance of the situation, inferred that Admiral Scheer and the High Seas Fleet were still in Wilhelmshaven. The answer to the more important but unasked question was that the *Hochseeflotte* was no longer in port. The unfortunate consequences of this incident were twofold. Since he no longer saw any need for haste, Jellicoe decided to save fuel by slowing the speed of his ships, which in turn caused him to lose critical time. This left a considerable and growing distance between the Grand Fleet under Jellicoe and the Battle Cruiser Squadron under Beatty by the time the main battle began. Second, and even more harmful in the long run, Jellicoe and Beatty completely lost confidence in the Admiralty's intelligence when Beatty unexpectedly ran into the German fleet less than three hours later. As pointed out earlier, a commander's belief in the credibility of the intelligence provided is probably the most essential factor in his readiness to make use of it.

The major problem in each phase of the battle was to identify the course and direction of the High Seas Fleet. At about 2:20 Beatty encountered and gave chase to the smaller advance force of the High Seas Fleet commanded by Admiral Franz von Hipper. This was what the Germans were hoping for, since Hipper's forces attempted to lead Beatty into a trap by heading in the direction of the *Hochseflotte* some 50 miles away. After having engaged in some serious fighting for about two hours, Beatty received word that the main German fleet had been sighted about twelve miles away. Room 40 continued its brilliant performance when, at 4:35p.m., it fixed the position of the German main force as steering northwest at 15 knots in pursuit of Beatty's battle cruisers. Now it was Beatty's turn to lure the Germans into the same type of trap that they had just tried to set for him. Within half an hour this information was communicated to Jellicoe. Another report sent to Oliver from Room 40, however, was not transmitted to Jellicoe and Beatty, while other important signals were either delayed unnecessarily or not passed on at all to the commander of the Grand Fleet.[159] An extremely important signal detailing the exact course chosen by Admiral Scheer for his withdrawal was passed on by Room 40 at 9:55 and sent out by Operations at 10:41p.m. The nature of the information in this signal would have enabled Jellicoe to intercept the weaker and badly mauled German fleet in its attempt to flee; but Jellicoe, who earlier the same day had learned that the Admiralty's messages could not always be taken at face value, probably believed that the signal was unreliable or misleading and decided to ignore it. Yet another message deciphered in Room 40 and passed on to Operations proved that the earlier information on the German course of withdrawal was indeed accurate, but this critical message was never even communicated to Jellicoe. Room 40 received no fewer than sixteen similar messages, but only three were sent out. Consequently, the opportunity for the British to renew the battle in highly favorable circumstances the next day was missed.

Room 40 made no mistakes. 'Jutland would have been a crushing victory if only the inestimable advantage of superior intelligence had not been so needlessly dissipated by a faulty system.'[160] A few general comments summarizing some of the observations made above emerge from a study of the battle of Jutland.

• Operations did not fully appreciate the work done at Room 40. Instead of promoting a professional relationship of mutual respect, Operations emphasized its superiority and authority, never genuinely tried to understand the problems of intelligence work, and therefore missed the opportunity to exploit the first-rate information to its advantage.

• Once the commanders' faith in the intelligence provided by the Admiralty had been shaken, it became *de facto* irrelevant to their decision-making process.

• Intelligence *before* the battle was accepted as reliable and useful (the battle of Jutland would never have taken place had it been otherwise), but as soon as hostilities began, the contribution of intelligence declined very rapidly and had no influence on the course of the conflict. In the battle itself, the British command, communication and control system functioned erratically. In a manner reminiscent of Clausewitz's description of the eighteenth-century battlefield, the information received was inaccurate and the movements of German ships that had been observed directly by British ships were often not reported to Jellicoe or Beatty. British attempts to transmit orders and data were hampered by poor visibility, gun smoke and smoke screens, and by the ponderousness of signalling with flags or lights. Instead of visual signalling, the Germans used low-power wireless – a method that proved far more effective.[161] Unquestionably, the inefficiency of British communications added enormously to the confusion and undermined the ability to control the Grand Fleet. (Similar communications fiascos had occurred in the Dogger Bank Battle in January 1915, but the appropriate lessons had never been learned.)

Modern radio and radar may have revolutionized command, communication and control and greatly facilitated the identification of friend or foe, but they can never alter the fact that uncertainty is a dominant characteristic of war. The degree of confusion and uncertainty prevailing during the battle of Midway was comparable with that of the battle of Jutland; and although radar and radio theoretically improved C^3I, in reality the possibility of interference through jamming and various other counter counter-electronic measures constantly being devised threatens the effectiveness and reliability of communication today and in the future.

• Jellicoe's actions confirmed Clausewitz's perceptive observation that under conditions of uncertainty, most commanders err on the side of caution. On a number of occasions, Jellicoe's overestimation of German readiness to engage in battle in spite of their inferiority; reluctance to engage the Germans at night; withdrawal when the German destroyers launched a torpedo attack; and fear of a German submarine threat that never appeared – all led him to make a worst-case analysis. 'Great consideration was given to possible ways in which the enemy might surprise us, such as using submarines with the fleet, minefields and long-range torpedoes, but less attention was given to how we might exploit surprise on the enemy. This attitude rather tended to surrender the initiative.'[162]

To be sure, the use and misuse of intelligence was not the only factor determining the outcome of the battle. Other factors that worked to the advantage of the Germans were the superior German fire control system, the evening light that silhouetted the Grand Fleet, the weakness of the British cruisers' side armor, the British lack of flash protection for their magazines, and better German shells.[163] All of these German advantages were more than offset, however, by the impressive British superiority in the number of capital ships.[164]

TABLE 4

BRITISH AND GERMAN NAVAL STRENGTH COMPARED

	German High Seas Fleet	British Grand Fleet
Dreadnoughts	16	28
Pre-Dreadnoughts	6	0
Battle Cruisers	5	9
Light Cruisers and Armoured Cruisers	11	26 + 8
Destroyers	61	78

The ratio of capital ships favored the British almost two to one, but the losses unmistakably favored the Germans: the British lost 14 ships of 111,000 tons while the Germans lost 11 ships of 62,000 tons.[165]

Had the British skillfully used the impressive intelligence at their disposal, they could have concentrated their superior forces at the outset and surprised the numerically inferior High Seas Fleet; and in spite of this failure, they could still have recouped their losses and reversed the outcome of the battle in their favor. Through discerning and expeditious use of the information from Room 40, they could have at one point intercepted and inflicted heavy damage upon the withdrawing German fleet. Uncertainty dogged both sides equally, but the British committed more mistakes and missed more opportunities despite their better intelligence and superior strength. In the end, Germany won on the operational level while the British came out on top strategically in the long run.

INTELLIGENCE AND THE BATTLE OF THE ATLANTIC

The largest naval battle in history, the battle of Jutland, lasted no more than a single day, and although the mistakes committed therein by the British could still have been compensated for by the proper use of intelligence on the morning of the next day, this final opportunity was also missed. It is therefore interesting to evaluate the influence of intelligence on the course of *prolonged* battles, in which there is enough time to learn and apply lessons learned from the use and misuse of intelligence in military operations. Two very different examples come to mind: the battle of the Atlantic, and the campaign in the Western Desert in 1941 and 1942.

Waged from the first day of the Second World War to the last, the battle of the Atlantic was decisively influenced by the successes and failures of intelligence on both sides. There is no doubt that this critical conflict could not have been won by the Allies without the contribution of intelligence on all levels, particularly in the breaking of the German U-boat codes by Hut 3 at Bletchley Park and the development and refinement of radio direction techniques.

Compared with war at sea or in the air, which is fought over wide but vast, empty spaces, war on land is slower and more difficult to control. The principal (though by no means only) problem of war at sea and in the air is to identify the *location* and *direction* of the enemy's movement in order to make interception possible. In seeking to accomplish this, navies and air forces were aided immeasurably on the tactical and operational levels by the invention of radar, the development of radio direction-finding techniques, air reconnaissance, satellites, and aircraft carrying complex radar and 'command, control and communication' equipment. Once the location and direction of movement of an approaching enemy convoy or bomber formations has been determined, the allocation and concentration of the forces necessary for their interception (assuming the forces are available) is a *relatively* straightforward problem. The number of aircraft, ships or submarines possessed by each side as well as their speed, endurance and other performance characteristics are on the whole well known. Hence, the size and type of forces that must be sent out for protection or interception can be estimated with a reasonable degree of accuracy, while problems related to command, control and communication are more manageable than those in land warfare. Although uncertainty will never cease to dominate *all* forms of warfare, it will be present to a lesser degree in *prolonged* air and sea battles where the overall contribution of intelligence to operations is easier to appreciate than in the cluttered land environment. This can be demonstrated quite convincingly by the battle of the Atlantic, where the pivotal but less apparent battle of wits that was fought behind the scenes is plainly reflected in the numbers of ships and U-boats sunk.[166]

Between 1939 and the spring of 1943, the German xB-Dienst managed to decrypt a large proportion of various British naval codes. This gave the Germans information of enviable quality on destinations, cargoes and escorts of Allied convoys. After learning belatedly from their own deciphering of German codes just how successful the Germans had been, the British, in mid-June 1943, introduced a new naval cipher that was responsible for a prolonged blackout on the German side. From that point onward, xB-Dienst never again regained its former level of success in breaking British naval codes.[167] For their part, the British had little success in penetrating Germans codes until mid-1941. In their war against the U-boats, they were forced to rely primarily on direction-finding methods and traffic analysis, which helped them to divert some convoys at the last minute and at least mitigate shipping losses. From June 1941 to the end of January 1942 and then from mid-1943 to the end of the war, however, Bletchley Park was able to decrypt the Atlantic U-boat traffic almost in real time.[168] This information on the successes and failures of each side in the intelligence war can then be correlated with the detailed statistics in Table 5 and Figure 2 on German U-boat operations from 1939 to 1945.[169]

From these data it is evident that although the German submarine fleet was numerically small until mid-1941, good intelligence enabled it to sink a relatively large number of Allied ships. (The highest ratio of ships sunk per U-boat during the war was achieved in the period from July to September 1940.) British success in deciphering the U-boat radio traffic between 1941 and January 1942 brought a corresponding drop in the number of Allied ships sunk. Jürgen Rohwer estimates that the Allies thus

TABLE 5

GERMAN U-BOAT OPERATIONS 1939-1945

Year	Quarter	Total Fleet	Daily Average Numbers Operational in Atlantic	Engaged in Atlantic	Sunk	Atlantic Theatre New U-Boats, Commissioned	Ships Sunk by U-Boats
1939	Sept-Dec	57	12	5	9	2	105
1940	Jan-Mar	51	11	5	6	4	80
	Apr-Jun	49	10	7	8	9	75
	Jul-Sept	56	10	8	5	15	150
	Oct-Dec	75	11	9	3	26	130
1941	Jan-Mar	102	20	12	5	31	100
	Apr-Jun	136	25	15	7	53	150
	Jul-Sept	182	30	17	6	70	90
	Oct-Dec	233	35	16	17	70	70
1942	Jan-Mar	272	45	13	11	49	225
	Apr-Jun	315	60	15	10	58'	240
	Jul-Sept	352	95	25	32	61	290
	Oct-Dec	382	100	40	34	70	260
1943	Jan-Mar	418	110	50	40	70	200
	Apr-Jun	424	90	40	73	69	120
	Jul-Sept	408	60	20	71	68	75
	Oct-Dec	425	70	25	53	83	40
1944	Jan-Mar	445	65	30	60	62	45
	Apr-Jun	437	50	20	68	53	20
	Jul-Sept	396	40	15	79	50	35
	Oct-Dec	398	35	20	32	67	17
1945	Jan-May	349	45	20	153	93	55

FIGURE 2

CODEBREAKING AND THE BATTLE OF THE ATLANTIC

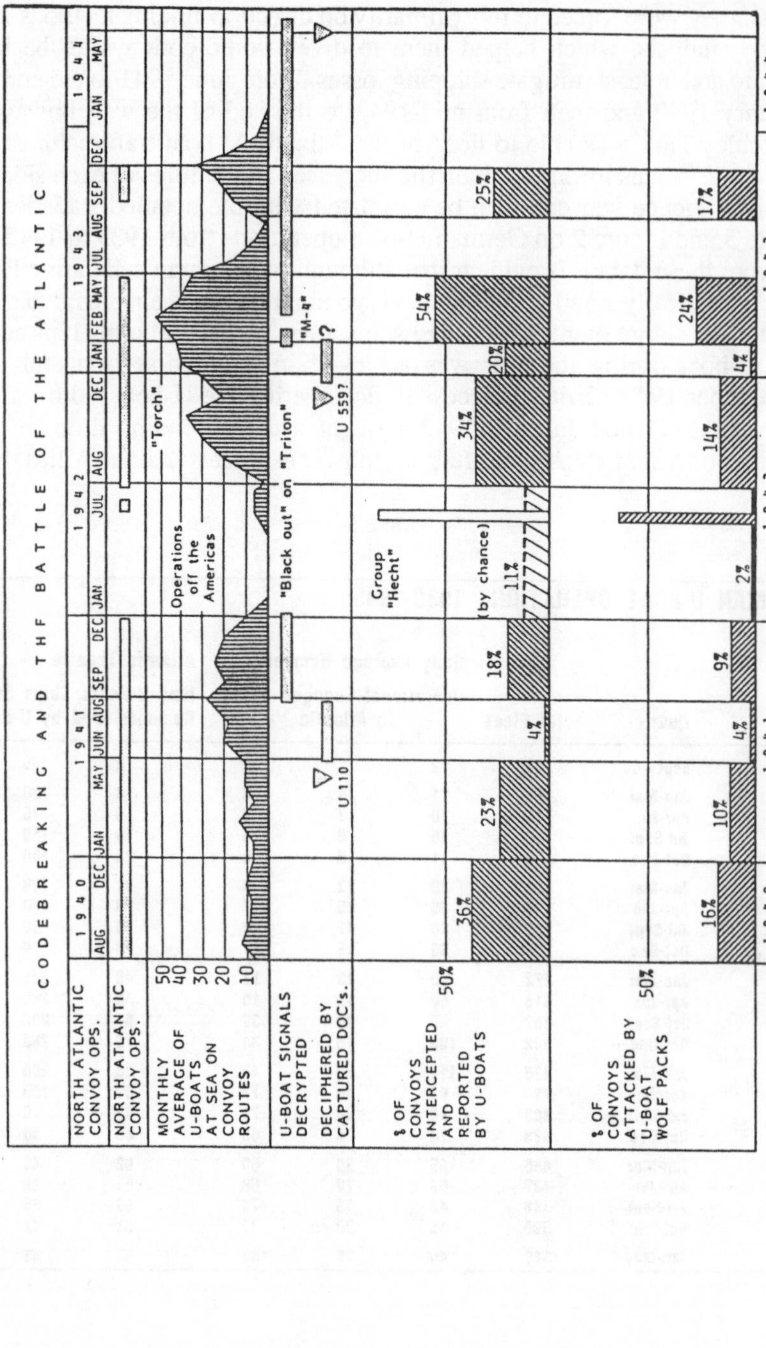
C O D E B R E A K I N G A N D T H E B A T T L E O F T H E A T L A N T I C
1 9 4 0
1 9 4 1
1 9 4 2
1 9 4 3
1 9 4 4
AUG
DEC
JAN
MAY
JUN
AUG
SEP
DEC
JAN
JUL
AUG
DEC
JAN
FEB
MAY
JUL
AUG
SEP
DEC
JAN
MAY
NORTH ATLANTIC CONVOY OPS.
NORTH ATLANTIC CONVOY OPS.
MONTHLY AVERAGE OF U-BOATS AT SEA ON CONVOY ROUTES
50
40
30
20
10
Operations off the Americas
"Torch"
U-BOAT SIGNALS DECRYPTED
DECIPHERED BY CAPTURED DOC's.
U 110
"Black out" on "Triton"
U 559?
"M-4"
?
% OF CONVOYS INTERCEPTED AND REPORTED BY U-BOATS
50%
36%
23%
4%
18%
Group "Hecht"
(by chance)
11%
34%
20%
54%
25%
% OF CONVOYS ATTACKED BY U-BOAT WOLF PACKS
50%
16%
10%
4%
9%
2%
14%
4%
24%
17%

Source: W.A.B. Douglas and Jurgen Rohwer, '"The Most Thankless Task" Revisited: Convoys, Escorts and Radio Intelligence in the Western Atlantic, 1941–43', p. 191, in James A. Boutilier, *The RCN in Retrospect, 1910–1968* (Vancouver, Canada: The University of British Columbia Press, 1982).

avoided shipping losses in the amount of 1.5 to 2.0 million gross tons during the second half of 1941;[170] he considers this the first serious setback suffered by the German U-boats, which is no less important than the losses inflicted on them from the spring of 1943 onward. The period of Allied blackout in the deciphering of German codes between January 1942 and mid-1943 is also the time during which the heaviest Allied ship losses occurred. This can be explained by a number of factors, the most important of which are:

(a) The blackout made it more difficult for the Allies to route, re-route and protect their convoys.

(b) This was also the greatest period of success the xB-Dienst had in deciphering British naval codes. With this advantage, the Germans were able to use their U-boats more efficiently while the Allies remained unaware of their intelligence coup.

(c) The US Navy's refusal to order ships in the Caribbean and along the US eastern coast to sail in convoys led to heavy and unnecessary losses.

After June 1943, the balance of intelligence clearly tipped in favor of the Allies, who were then able to decipher German codes regularly, while the introduction of more secure codes on their side created a blackout for the Germans. This shift in the balance of intelligence along with the introduction of new anti-submarine weapons, escort aircraft carriers, long-range anti-submarine aircraft and other weapons is accurately reflected in the information presented here. The Allies were now in a position not only to re-route their convoys but also to ambush the German U-boat wolfpacks. Furthermore, they managed to develop counter-measures to new German weapons (such as the acoustic torpedo) even before the weapons had been put into use; and once the counter-measures had been employed, the Allies could follow up on their performance through the U-boat reports.

Table 5 also helps to demonstrate one more point. In the period from mid-1943 to 1944, German production of U-boats and the number of U-boats constantly on patrol was higher than ever, yet the rate at which the now-blinded German submarines sank Allied ships declined rapidly. This would put the Germans on the upper right-hand corner of Figure 1 (i.e., a strong force or order of battle with poor intelligence). The fact that the xB-Dienst failed to obtain information on the whereabouts of Allied convoys and also remained ignorant of the Allied intelligence successes soon rendered the much larger U-boat fleet operationally impotent. Between July and September 1940, superior German intelligence enabled the smallest U-boat fleet of 56 submarines, of which only 10 were operational on average, to sink 150 British ships. Between January and March 1944, however, a U-boat fleet about eight times larger, with an average of 65 operational submarines, sank only 45 Allied ships. First-rate Allied intelligence, combined with new weaponry and electronic measures, had dealt a devastating blow to the largest submarine fleet ever assembled. Patrick Beesly summed up the contribution of the Naval Intelligence Division (NID) with the observation that '... NID was able to support, influence, and in effect, direct operations at sea to an extent that had never previously been the case ... It was a factor of the greatest importance in the Second Battle of the Atlantic'.[171] Rohwer concluded that '... while there were many factors which influenced the decisive Battle of the Atlantic, I could place "Ultra" on top of the list ...'..[172]

GENERAL REMARKS ON THE USE OF INTELLIGENCE IN THE WESTERN DESERT

Intelligence use during the prolonged campaign in the Western Desert was troubled by many of the same problems experienced in the battle of Crete. Of particular interest is the period between the arrival of Rommel and the Deutsches Afrika Korps in Tripoli in February 1941 and his defeat at El Alamein in November 1942. Although the campaign in the Western Desert is much too long and complex to be reviewed here even in the narrower context of operational intelligence, a number of useful general observations are in place.

The most basic lesson is that unlike the *relatively simpler* environment of naval warfare which at times permits isolation of the influence of intelligence on the course of a battle, the more complicated environment of a prolonged and fluid land maneuver encompasses too many variables the discrete effects of which are very difficult to assess. In the short run, measurable quantitative advantages, such as greater overall numerical strength, air superiority, better logistical support and good intelligence, can sometimes be offset by excellent, more experienced leadership, a more successful doctrine, the skillful use of combined arms, more advanced technology and communications procedures and, finally, better luck. Moreover, the difficulty of evaluating competing intelligence organizations – when, for example, one side has superior intelligence on the strategic level but is only equal or inferior on the lower operational and tactical levels – further complicates any attempt to gauge their overall contribution. And even if intelligence has clearly made a significant contribution to the planning and execution of an operation, how can one determine if it was put to the best possible use? How and under what conditions can an experienced military leader compensate for the lack of good intelligence?

A definitive answer to such questions is not possible, since it is derived mainly from a subjective interpretation of the evidence and the intuition of the historian or military expert. In complex land operations, therefore, we cannot isolate the direct contribution of intelligence even in retrospect, but we *can* identify circumstances that are generally favorable for its use and point out those aspects of its application that tend to erode its value. And as long as an accurate assessment of the contribution of intelligence remains elusive, we can at least increase the odds in our favor by learning the lessons of the past and creating an environment that promotes the best possible future use of intelligence. Such lessons can be learned in abundance from the campaign in the Western Desert.

A problem of particular interest is the disparity in perception that inevitably arises between the highest political and strategic level (in this case, Churchill and the British High Command) and the highest operational level of command in the region where the fighting is actually taking place (as personified by Wavell, Auchinleck and Montgomery). These often clashing perspectives are caused not only by differences in professional experience, decision-making style and sheer distance, but also by a situation in which those at the highest decision-making levels (such as Churchill in London) *possess more and, in some ways, better intelligence about the enemy than they do about their own forces in the region.* Encouraged by the information obtained from Ultra, Churchill was aware of the numerical inferiority of the Afrika Korps as well as of Rommel's persistent logistical problems. He also knew that the British forces in the Western Desert were numerically and logistically superior, and that in the most trying circumstances enormous efforts were being made to supply them from England. Equipped with this knowledge and compelled by the need to demonstrate the success of British arms under his leadership, Churchill continuously pressed Wavell, Auchinleck and Montgomery to launch premature offensives against their best judgment. In such circumstances, high-level political leaders tend to underestimate the strength of their opponents and overestimate the strength of their own troops. Churchill's estimates were too closely tied to a simplistic quantitative analysis; indeed, the British were able to maintain a significant edge in tanks, troops and supplies over the Germans (though not always over the Germans *and* Italians) for most of the campaign.[173] But this approach did not take into consideration the leadership ability and experience of the German's high-ranking field commander, the quality of their weapons, their communications systems or their military doctrine. For much of the campaign, Rommel's qualitative superiority in such areas more than compensated for his quantitative inferiority. As Lord Ismay notes, Churchill did not fully grasp the nature of modern mechanized warfare and the changes that had taken place on the battlefield since the First World War.[174] The combination of technological advances and innovative doctrines had sparked a revolution in the operational art of war which rendered intelligence assessments based on a simple bean count much less useful in the Second World War than in the First.

Paradoxically, it is often more difficult to obtain good information on one's own forces. In the first place, commanding officers are reluctant to admit that the training or morale of their troops and the quality of the doctrines they developed are inadequate for their assigned tasks. Even if commanders do acknowledge such shortcomings and are reluctant to take action until additional troops and supplies have arrived, political leaders are likely to attribute their reluctance to excessive caution, not to realism. Evaluation of the opposing forces is at times complicated by the contra- dictory assessments of field commanders and military bureaucrats, many of whom conceal or overlook the particular weaknesses of their own troops for which they are responsible. Whether conscious or not, this may lead to exaggeration of their own strength; at the same time, the reluctance to accept risks and the creeping paralysis that takes hold as they await the arrival of the supposedly crucial reinforcements may make the opponent seem more formidable than he really is. Thus, when Auchinleck requested a ratio of 50 per cent tanks in reserve to those in action before launching Crusader, and then after Crusader stipulated that a ratio of two to one was the minimum necessary to carry out a succssful offensive, Churchill found his recommendations neither credible nor acceptable.[175]

The phenomenon of being better informed about the opponent than about one's own forces is *universal*, for the process of 'net assessment' is considerably more sensitive than that of obtaining intelligence on the enemy's forces alone. After all, Churchill and his field commanders had better intelligence on the enemy than on their own forces, but inherent tensions between the different levels of command inevitably distorted the information received and prevented the correct correlation of forces or accurate net assessment. There is, therefore, no guarantee that even the most precise intelligence on the enemy will be put to the best use.

Nevertheless, immediate steps can be taken at least to minimize the distortion experienced in this very politically sensitive task. These include a realistic and detached assessment of one's own forces; a firm understanding that the quantitative comparison of opposing forces is not enough; a recognition of the unavoidable problems encountered in all quantitative analysis; and close co-operation between the intelligence officer, who knows more about the enemy, and the planner, who knows more about his own forces. It requires a systematic – not always popular – effort to go outside official channels in gathering information on the quality and performance of one's own troops (or on governmental policies that may affect military decisions). Numerous intelligence and operational disasters have occurred because intelligence analysts were well-informed about the enemy but ignorant of the problems or plans of their own army.[176]

During the campaign in the Western Desert, intelligence seems to have made its most significant contribution on the higher strategic level – primarily in enabling the British gradually to cut the flow of supplies from Germany and Italy to North Africa. Though not spectacular in the short run, the results were ultimately decisive.[177] Having thus limited Rommel's capacity to sustain prolonged military operations, the British left him a very narrow margin for error, which he ignored to his detriment on more than one occasion. Rommel's preference for commanding from the front and his habit of often disregarding logistical imperatives enabled him to achieve brilliant tactical and operational success at the cost of strategic failure. The very qualities that made him a great commander capable of compensating for his quantitative inferiority and inadequate intelligence blinded him to strategic considerations and hastened his downfall. Thus, superior British intelligence played a critical role in defeating Rommel's supply system, which in turn neutralized his excellent leadership and allowed the British to win by attrition.

It is one matter to exploit good intelligence on the strategic level and quite another to do so on the operational level. Accurate intelligence was frequently of immense value in predicting Rommel's intentions and direction of attack, but it did not always translate into adequate preparations and the proper disposition of the forces available (as in the battle of Gazala, for example). Once the battle began, inefficient command, control and communications systems (especially in the period up to the first battle of El Alamein) reduced the value of intelligence on the battlefield. While many causes of the failure to use intelligence properly on the battlefield were corrected during and following the first battle of El Alamein, the mistakes committed earlier are of great interest to the modern student of intelligence and military operations as they point to a multitude of problems that may exist today in every army that has not undertaken a major military operation for a long period of time. The problems encountered in making proper use of intelligence before the battle of Gazala and the first battle of El Alamein also provide us with an outstanding case-study that is very helpful in illustrating why good intelligence alone does not automatically guarantee success.[178]

The normally ephemeral 'life-span' of operational intelligence makes it much more dependent on certain prerequisites for its proper use. As in all military matters, there are many such variables: they include the quality of command, control, and communications (C^3I) and the military forces' capacity for adaptation to rapid changes in operational demands as well as the commander's character; flexibility; speed of reaction; familiarity with the potential value and limits of intelligence; readiness to take risks; and control over the forces at his disposal. In the period preceding the first

battle of El Alamein, the British experienced problems in a number of these areas:
• Evidence of foresight was conspicuously absent in the sluggish and unreliable British communications networks. 'Information was passed up and down chains of command with little or no provision for alternative routing in case of failure of one link in the chain. There was no means by which the 8th Army commander could communicate directly with forward troops if and when he needed to.'[179] When time-sensitive intelligence cannot be relayed quickly and reliably to those who need it most, it is of negligible value in the fast-paced environment of the modern battlefield. Success in solving this problem, which is as technical as it is organizational, requires meticulous planning and thorough testing. The Germans, who were much more experienced in mobile warfare, were able to build effective communications systems while the British were still engaged in a learning process.
• In contrast to the centralized German command and control system under Rommel, that of the British before the arrival of Montgomery was fragmented, poorly co-ordinated and loosely controlled by its commander-in-chief from the rear. Auchinleck in particular allowed field commanders to view his decisions as mere suggestions. Decision by correspondence – the practice between Auchinleck and Ritchie before Crusader[180] – left too many important decisions to field commanders who did not strictly adhere to a comprehensive plan. In combination with poor communication and faulty co-ordination from above, this gave rise to chaotic conditions that ended in loss of control which eventually forced Auchinleck to assume direct command in the field. This he did brilliantly. Here, Auchinleck's use of intelligence evinced a profound appreciation for and understanding of its potential. Similarly, before the battle of Gazala, Ritchie ignored Auchinleck's 'suggestion' (based on accurate Ultra intelligence) that his troops be positioned on Rommel's advancing flank. As a result, the British wasted superb intelligence and missed the opportunity to win a decisive defensive battle against an opponent who had overextended his lines of communication and resources.

When a desperate Rommel was almost ready to concede defeat at the 'Cauldron', British intelligence again provided the commander-in-chief and his field commanders with accurate information on his predicament. But instead of seizing the opportunity to attack Rommel's forces before they could regroup, the British field commanders became bogged down in a protracted debate and ended up squandering four precious days.[181] A quick reaction on the basis of incomplete intelligence or intuition alone would have been much more successful than a delayed response on the basis of perfect intelligence. This illustrates the wisdom of Clausewitz's emphasis on the need to compensate for insufficient intelligence through vigorous action, maintenance of the initiative and reliance on the commander's intuition. Once again, Auchinleck had to relieve Ritchie, the field commander, and assume direct control over the next phase of the battle. Having decided to direct the battle from a command post close to the front, Auchinleck proceeded to make very resourceful use of the intelligence supplied to him by Ultra and the 'Y' service and in the end won a defensive battle that had earlier appeared hopeless for the British.[182]

One other interesting question should be raised concerning the best location for the commander during the battle. There is no single ideal position because such depends on specific circumstances such as the quality of the communications system, technology, the temperament of the commander and his relationship with subordinates, and the anticipated shape of the battle.[183] A tentative conclusion is, however, that in order to make the optimal use of intelligence while co-ordinating a complex battle, the commander ought to place himself as close to the battlefield as is practical. This would give him a better grasp of the situation, allow him to use his intuition in co-ordination with the available intelligence, shorten the lines of communication, and accelerate the decision-making process so essential to the exploitation of fleeting opportunities.

Once the most critical phase of the battle is behind him or when future operational plans need to be considered, the senior military commander should move back to the rear where he is less likely to be swayed by tactical and operational considerations. Thus removed from the furore of the battle, the commander is in a position where his weighing of higher-level operational or strategic intelligence is more likely to result in a better estimate of the overall situation and a more carefully considered long-range view. While Rommel's presence on the front enabled him to use his intuition to make better use of intelligence, it also narrowed his view and caused him to subordinate strategic considerations to operational opportunism. For the British, the broader strategic responsibilities of their commander-in-chief (until Montgomery's arrival) reduced his direct involvement in the conduct of military operations; this left important decisions to less experienced commanders who were not as likely to make the best use of the available intelligence. As mentioned earlier, the commanders-in-chief were, on more than one occasion, compelled to intervene personally in critical situations and relieve commanders less practiced in the art of war.

Given the quality of modern communications systems and the abundance of information from numerous sources, the modern commander will be tempted to remain close to intelligence headquarters. One drawback of this practice is that it tends to remove high-level commanders from the front both physically and psychologically, thereby lulling them into a state of excessive dependence on intelligence. Faith in intelligence to such an unwarranted degree reinforces the existing tendency to avoid risks as described by Clausewitz. This, in turn, causes the commander's developing intuition to atrophy, leaving him without recourse when intelligence is unavailable. All in all, the modern commander must try to strike a balance between the increasing importance of intelligence and the fundamental need to hone his intution in preparation for coping with ambiguity.

The campaign in the Western Desert (as well as the Battle of Britain) also pointed to the growing importance of technological intelligence for military operations. The British did not begin to give much thought to this subject until after Crusader. While German scientific (and other) teams of experts were quick to assess the performance of British weaponry captured during the battle of France in 1940, the technical intelligence section of the Middle East Command – formed in 1940 – consisted of only a single officer. Soon after the arrival of Auchinleck, the size of the section doubled to include two officers and a truck.[184] This not surprisingly ended in the failure of British intelligence to collect sufficient data on German tanks and anti-tank guns – the dominant weapons which determined the outcome of most battles. The sorry state of British knowledge on this subject led to an inflated estimate of the relative quality of British weapons and overall British strength; the development of doctrines unsuitable for tank warfare; the formulation of unrealistic plans; and a gross misunderstanding of German tactics, combined arms operations and operational planning. In his book, *Military Errors of World War II*, Kenneth Macksey describes the problem as follows:

> Inevitably misleading technical information, which quite frequently was arrived at by guesswork instead of scientific investigation, impinged upon tactics. Although it had been known since May 1940 that the Germans had been using their powerful 88m anti-aircraft gun in a dual anti-tank role, for a long time there remained a delusion, due to inadequate testing, that it could not penetrate a heavy Matilda tank beyond 440 yards whereas, in fact, it could do so at 2,000! As a result, during the Battleaxe counterstroke launched by the British along the Egyptian frontier in June 1941, Matildas were confidently sent against 88s and were torn to pieces. Simultaneously, faster, lighter armoured AFVs, endeavouring to close to within the 500 yards at which, they were told, their 40 mm guns would penetrate the enemy tanks' armour, were sent to their doom since (a) they were unlikely to score hits on the move and (b) they were unlikely to penetrate when they did hit. Yet it was tactics such as these which conditioned the methods adopted during the major British Crusader

offensive of November 1941 in an endeavour to defeat enemy armour in battle, relieve besieged Trobuk, and clear Cyrenaica of the Axis forces.[185]

The disastrous consequences of this lack of technical intelligence were made clear during the first crucial battle of Operation Crusader. The British 30 Corps lost 400 out of 450 tanks (or close to 90 per cent in a two-day battle), while the Germans lost only 77.[186] The systematic collection of technical intelligence in the Western Desert remained very slow and amateurish for a long while. (It was not until March 1942 that someone took the trouble to investigate a German Panzer Mk IV that had been captured in April 1941 and discovered that it had hard-faced armor.)[187]

Before the outbreak of the war, technological questions were of much less interest to traditional officers in the British Army than to those in the RAF and the Royal Navy. Yet the value of familiarity with technological issues and the opponent's weapons transcended narrower tactical and purely technical issues and directly influenced such essential areas as the net intelligence assessment of the opposing force's strength, the planning of military operations, and the formulation of deployment doctrines. In this sense, technological intelligence cannot be separated from the study of the enemy's military doctrine and planning.

The British delay in learning the importance of technological intelligence in the Western Desert cost many lives and led to unnecessary setbacks on the battlefield, but at least the British had enough time ultimately to improve their performance in this area.[188] Today, military technology changes at a much faster pace and has assumed an even more significant role in warfare. There is no guarantee that modern conventional war will be of sufficient duration to allow for the gradual improvement of technological intelligence. While technological intelligence should be improved before the outbreak of war, the examination of captured enemy equipment must be performed on the battlefield as soon as possible so that the resulting technological intelligence can be put to immediate use while the battle is still being fought; and since the improvement of weapons or production of new equipment is a lengthy process, the only immediate response available for commanders in the field is improvisation in the doctrine of weapons deployment. Effective improvisation requires a considerable amount of thought and preparation before the outbeak of war as well as great flexibility.

CONCLUSIONS

Intelligence is of the utmost importance in war, but it is not a prerequisite for military conflict or even victory. The best intelligence is impotent without military strength, while military strength without intelligence can nevertheless accomplish its objectives though probably at a higher cost. Consequently, military organizations have traditionally viewed the operational branch, the fighting forces, as their central concern at all times. The seldom questioned perpetuation of this outlook has, however, brought many military organizations perilously close to or beyond the point at which benign neglect or misunderstanding of other branches such as intelligence or logistics has caused serious, self-inflicted damage. It is therefore essential that today's fighting forces recognize the importance of the non-combatant branches whose support is even more critical than in the past, when field commanders and their forces were to a large extent self-contained (for example, they could forage and feed themselves, and were responsible for their own reconnaissance). Modern armies have grown increasingly dependent on organizations outside their direct control for food, fuel, maintenance and intelligence. Good intelligence may not be absolutely essential for waging war, but it certainly allows for a more efficient and economical use of force.

While clearly important on all levels of war, intelligence is most valuable and identifiable on the strategic and higher operational levels. On the lower operational level, events today move so rapidly that even very accurate intelligence can often be too slow to have a timely influence on the course of a battle. Intelligence can make its greatest contribution *before* the fighting starts by providing the commander with the best possible data on his enemy's order of battle, intentions, weapons, performance, defense systems, morale and so on. Once the battle is joined, everything is in flux: events move extremely fast and by the time movements have been observed, the situation may have changed. And even when reports are accurate, they can still be misperceived or transmitted incorrectly. Furthermore, the commander cannot always ensure that his orders, based on the intelligence he has received, will be executed as he intended. (As described earlier, intelligence was critically important *before* the battles of Jutland, Crete or Midway, but once the fighting began, its relevance declined rapidly and the commander's 'feel' for the battle had to take over.)

There is no doubt that modern technology has made enormous progress in solving problems related to the transmission of intelligence and decisions, but it is still no panacea. Intuition remains indispensable on the battlefield, although its contribution may have declined relative to that of intelligence and it is called upon less frequently. But when there is little or no time for reflection and intelligence is unavailable, the military leader's *coup d'oeil* will still be as invaluable as it was in Clausewitz's time.

Uncertainty will always remain the essence of war on every level, though it is most prevalent on the lower operational level. Even when accurate intelligence exists at the opening phase of a battle, numerous elements such as friction, luck and chance increasingly come into play if a quick and decisive victory cannot be achieved. (In the 1967 Six Day War,for example, good intelligence led to the destruction of the Arab air forces on the ground, which was a major factor in the quick and decisive Israeli victory.) The effectiveness of accurate intelligence is always closely linked to other factors such as a leader's understanding of its value and objectives, and the quality of C^3 systems. It is not a coincidence that in Clausewitz's *On War*, the chapter on 'Intelligence' is immediately followed by one on 'Friction' (Book I, Chapters 6 and 7). And although intelligence provides one of the best potential means of reducing friction, Clausewitz makes it clear that friction will continue to remain an unavoidable part of military conflict.

It is far easier to identify the part played by intelligence on the higher strategic and operational levels where time is not as critical. Here there is enough time to learn to appreciate intelligence and make the best use of it by adapting military plans or developing suitable technologies and fighting doctrines. Shaped by the cumulative effect of many battles, strategy is more predictable than the course of a specific battle. While Clausewitz's skepticism concerning the relevance of intelligence is out-dated for the higher levels of warfare, his views are not without instructive value in the fluid and unpredictable environment of any large-scale battle where – despite all the technological changes that have taken place – the use of intelligence in field operations is much more problematic than on the higher strategic planes.

In the absence of intelligence, the intuition of the military commander may still be of the greatest importance on the lower levels of war where the time pressure is most acute. On the higher levels, however, the talent of the military genius lies in knowing how to integrate the available intelligence with the other elements in his decision-making process. He must be able to understand the potential and limitations of intelligence; he should strive to provide it with adequate tasks and make the best use of it *in combination* with his other qualities as a leader. These include creativity in operational planning, knowing when to take risks, and flexibility in the adaptation of means to objectives. Intelligence will always be a major means of enhancing the military leader's intuition – but never a substitute for it. The appreciation of intelligence is therefore only one of many qualities required of the modern military commander.

Since intelligence may be less useful on the tactical and lower operational levels, the modern military leader must learn to change his appreciation of intelligence as he advances in rank if he is to avoid the misapplication of irrelevant or counter-productive concepts to strategic or higher operational questions. In particular, the commander should remain alert to two possible pitfalls: first, his ambitions and operational plans should not be allowed to take precedence over his readiness to listen to his intelligence advisers (however unpleasant their reports); nor should such ambitions drive him to interfere in the intelligence process in order to obtain estimates that accord with his own wishes. Second, the commander should avoid viewing intelligence as the solution to all his problems. When intelligence is unavailable, inadequate or slow to arrive, he should be prepared to make timely, carefully weighed decisions in order to exploit short-lived opportunities. The dangerous habit of delaying action until definitive information has been received (and until risk and uncertainty have been eradicated) is reinforced by an environment in which the intelligence community promises to deliver more than it can, the myth of intelligence as panacea is allowed to persist, and commanders are *not allowed to make any mistakes*. More than in any other profession, learning from failure is essential in mastering the art of war. When errors are neither tolerated nor admitted, the fear of failure smothers the eagerness to take risks that is so essential to the achievement of victory. If the military intelligence community is equally reluctant to acknowledge failure or ignorance, it will be tempted to promise more than it can deliver, or to hedge its bets by relying on worst-case analyses and Delphic predictions. This is a certain prescription for failure.

In the future, the principles governing a military leader's proper use of intelligence will not change, but the circumstances in which they operate will. The tremendous increase in the quantity of information and intelligence (they are not identical) combined with the improvement of communications technologies may create increased pressure for commanders to stay close to intelligence headquarters. Reliance on such command 'by remote control' would then cause the commander to lose his 'feel' for what is happening on the battlefield. Better communications and more information can thus have their disadvantages. (Obviously there is a need, depending on the circumstances, to find the proper location for operational commanders somewhere between those who, like Rommel, are in the habit of getting too close to the front and those who prefer to control the battle from the rear. Once again the choice of the optimum position in each case can only be determined by the experience and intuition of the 'military genius'.)

The future commander will also have much less time to learn from experience, for the danger of nuclear escalation, high rates of attrition and other factors may limit the duration of wars. It is therefore increasingly important for commanders to learn all they can – in peacetime – about intelligence and its use in battle as well as about the need to consider the best position from which to command the problems of dealing with an over-abundance of information.

Intangible factors such as intelligence, leadership, morale, motivation, creativity, deception and surprise all play critical roles that are analytically difficult to isolate from the totality of qualitative and quantitative elements determining the resolution of a military conflict. Nevertheless, the difficulty involved in estimating the individual impact as well as interaction of these elements does not mean that this process should be ignored. Success in war requires that a proper balance be struck between all tangible and intangible, material and non-material factors. Excessive reliance on one dimension to the neglect of others may create serious vulnerabilities that can be exploited by the opponent. One such dimension is intelligence.

Nations that are powerful – or at least perceive themselves as such – are usually less motivated to improve their intelligence capabilities since they believe that they will be victorious in any event; conversely, those who feel vulnerable have a much stronger incentive to develop their intelligence organizations as rapidly as possible. Good intelligence will act as a force multiplier by facilitating a more focused and economical use of force. On the other hand, when all other things are equal, poor intelligence acts as a force divider by wasting and eroding strength. In the long run,therefore, the side with better intelligence will not only use its power more profitably but will also more effectively conserve it.

Modern warfare has taught us that superior power is often a short-lived illusion. The seeds of defeat are sown in many victories – in the inevitable overextension of resources and the steadily diminishing strength that accompany territorial expansion. In time, the euphoria of victory gives way to the psychological mechanisms underlying perceptions of greater strength and to the logic of the balance of power in the international system. It is for this reason that the use of military force must be guided by good intelligence. Admittedly, even the best intelligence will not solve every problem, but the use of military power without it is both wasteful and sterile.

* * *

In 'The Role of Intelligence in the Chancellorsville Campaign, 1863', and 'Lee at Gettysburg – A General Without Intelligence', Dr Jay Luvaas breaks new ground in his systematic analyses of intelligence and operations during the American Civil War. On a more general level, Dr Luvaas's essays raise questions related to the unique intelligence problems of civil wars. In contrast to other types of war, in civil wars the opposing sides speak the same language, and the officers on both sides are graduates of the same military academies; furthermore, while penetration of the opposing side is easier, a higher proportion of the information obtained is questionable owing to the unclear or highly volatile loyalties of the population.

From a technological point of view, the American Civil War was perhaps the first modern war. This becomes apparent from the widespread use of many new methods in intelligence work ranging from the tapping of telegraph lines and the use of balloons for observation to the extensive reliance on newspapers. As Luvaas explains, these new methods undeniably provided intelligence organizations with expanded opportunities but also created new security problems for field commanders and military organizations. Still, spies, deserters, scouts, cavalry used for reconnaissance, and other traditional methods remained the most important means of gathering intelligence before a battle. An interesting episode recounted by Luvaas concerns the Union's misuse of the information provided by their observation balloons. Observation balloons appear to have supplied the Union generals with accurate, timely intellignce on the operational and tactical levels. Indeed, Luvaas shows how worried the Confederate generals were about the Union's observation balloons and their own inability to acquire them as well. Nevertheless, in the aftermath of the Chancellorsville Campaign, Generals Hooker and Butterfield (counter to the evidence) blamed the observation balloons for being unable to provide them with reliable information and consequently recommended that their use be discontinued. In all likelihood, no one was misled by this attempt to use the observation balloons as a scapegoat, yet there were enough other 'interest groups' willing to see them go. If General Meade had had this method at his disposal during the Battle of Gettysburg, he might have been alerted to Longstreet's approach in time to implement counter-measures and achieve a more favorable outcome. While in their infancy, new military technologies must be protected and allowed sufficient time for integration with the more traditional and well-tested command and control systems. The temptation to attribute a defeat to a technological or intelligence scapegoat is rarely profitable and must be resisted now more than ever. Open-mindedness to newer technology, patience and the readiness to learn from failure are essential qualities for the modern commander.

Luvaas also shows that the availability of intelligence *per se* by no means guarantees success, as much depends on the commander's use of it during the operation. Luvaas concludes that General Hooker made poor use of the high-quality intelligence he possessed before the battle of Chancellorsville, while General Lee exploited his to the fullest. If anything, Hooker may have had too much rather than too little information – a problem even more accentuated today. Knowing what information to accept or reject, and knowing how to accept the intelligence relevant to the support of one's plans still requires mastery of the art of war. Combining superior intelligence with deception and his intuition, Lee was able to use intelligence to his advantage and win a brilliant victory, although his troops numbered 60,000 to the Union's 130,000. By the time Lee reached Gettysburg, though, the balance of intelligence had shifted in favor of his opponents. Hooker was replaced by Meade, and as Lee penetrated deeper into Union territory, he was increasingly deprived of the local population's co-operation. Over-confident following his victory at Chancellorsville, Lee felt that he could take action before he had received adequate information on his opponent's intentions and dispositions. At this stage, his intuition alone was not enough to compensate for the lack of intelligence and strength. 'Crippled for want of good intelligence', he could not concentrate his forces at the decisive point at the right time and lost the battle. The dearth of intelligence unacceptably narrowed Lee's options and did not allow him to use his numerically weaker forces as efficiently as before. In sum, good intelligence can help to compensate for numerical inferiority and make victory possible, while the combination of poor intelligence and weakness can only lead to defeat.

* * *

Part II of this volume includes two essays on intelligence and operations during the First World War on two different Middle Eastern fronts. One is a detailed summary of General Allenby's brilliant use of intelligence and deception in support of operations during the Palestine Campaign of 1917 and 1918; the other is a revealing study of how difficulties in obtaining and using intelligence in support of military operations led to the most humiliating British débâcle of the First World War – the Battle of Kut in April 1916.

Dr Yigal Sheffy's carefully documented and methodologically astute case study can be read with reference to my own essay on deception in general (which includes a much briefer look at Allenby's experiences). Published as the introduction to *Strategic and Operational Deception in the Second World War*, my essay provides a theoretical explanation for the importance of deception in support of military operations, and discusses such topics as the various types of deception and the problems encountered in assessing its effectiveness.

Deception can provide the military commander with excellent, almost always effective support in any operation: it facilitates the achievement of surprise in terms of the timing or direction; acts as a force multiplier by enabling the numerically weaker side to achieve superiority at the point of engagement through diversion of the enemy forces; is one of the very few ways for the attacker to compensate for the inherent superiority of the defense; and allows the achievement of more decisive results at a lower cost. Allenby's still unsurpassed use of intelligence and deception can be considered as an *ideal type* for all modern military deception operations: it included the extensive use of signal intelligence, camouflage and concealment, sophisticated baits and dummies – all of which were to be essential ingredients of the far more complex operations of the Second World War. Allenby was perhaps the first to institutionalize the use of deception, the success of which depended on thorough planning and preparation as well as such conditions as the denial of air superiority to the enemy and penetration of the enemy's intelligence system.

As Sheffy so elegantly shows, Allenby's use of deception was a perfect example of how to integrate intelligence and deception into all the planning phases of military operations. Deception, as argued earlier, should always play a supportive not independent role in the preparation of military operations, yet it must be an integral part of the planning process from the very beginning, and those charged with its implementation must be kept well informed of the commander's objectives and intentions if they are to give him the best possible support. Sheffy then goes on to explain why real troop movements should be closely co-ordinated with the deception plan – and why real and notional moves must reinforce one another whenever possible.

Perhaps the most important lesson to be learned from this case-study is that the commander's support is absolutely essential to the success of deception. The extent to which Allenby backed deception operations and fully exploited the opportunities they presented is unique. He is one of the very few commanders who encouraged deception even when the forces at his disposal were both quantitatively and qualitatively superior to those of the enemy. Furthermore, once deception enabled him to achieve surprise, Allenby capitalized on it to a degree greater than most commanders in the Second World War. His belief in the value of deception enabled him to prepare himself far enough in advance to make the most of it. It is not surprising, therefore, that the only First World War operation to approximate to a blitzkrieg type of campaign took place in the aftermath of the Battle of Megiddo.

Sheffy's meticulous reconstruction of Allenby's deception operations offers insight into many important dimensions of this aspect of intelligence work. For example, the most fundamental principle of successful deception plans is to reinforce the opponent's existing perceptions. In addition, the need to learn as much as possible about the enemy and to put oneself in his place should not be allowed to overshadow the need to be familiar with one's own dispositions and intelligence estimates. Security is extremely important, but the fact that the enemy knows he is a target of deception does not make it easier for him to identify or expose it. Finally, although deception is not costly, it may at times be labor-intensive.

Sheffy's conclusions are realistic and balanced. In his judgement, although deception was effective *overall*, it did not always have the desired impact nor could British success always be attributed to the deceivers' actions. Indeed, although the deceivers' actions were partially exposed (the Turks identified the true British order of battle) they still failed to change their plans; and for the British, it was difficult to distinguish between Turkish *self-deception* and their own deception activities (even without any deception at all, the Turks might have made the same decisions). On other occasions, the overall weakness of the Turkish intelligence and collection effort caused the Turks to misinterpret troop movements that were not even intended to trick them. Finally, Sheffy make the point that it is extremely difficult to separate the contribution of deception from that of myriad other factors – above all, Allenby's superior strength, which was enough to bring about a British victory in the Palestine campaign in any event. Nevertheless, the combined contributions of both deception and superior strength allowed Allenby to achieve quicker, more decisive and less costly victories in a period when all his predecessors and contemporaries had failed to do so. His atypically positive and open-minded attitude toward deception as well as his success in using it were not lost on one of his staff officers (and future biographer), Field Marshal Lord Wavell. Wavell carried on Allenby's tradition during the Second World War, where deception made an even more decisive contribution to the outcome of the war.

* * *

While Sheffy's essay is a study in the successful use of intelligence and deception on the battlefield, Dr Richard Popplewell's is a revealing examination of its failure. Popplewell – like Sheffy – is concerned with the problems experienced by the British in obtaining intelligence on the Turkish Army of the Ottoman Empire, but this is the limit of any similarity between the two. As Popplewell points out, the much larger area covered by the Mesopotamian front created more serious logistical and communications problems, a situation that was complicated by a terrain and climate that were much more difficult and less known than in Palestine. Serious obstacles were encountered – and never satisfactorily overcome – in securing even such basic intelligence as accurate maps. In Palestine, British intelligence could at least rely on the sympathy of some of the local population (for example, Jews and Christians) – but this was not true of the Arab population in Mesopotamia.

Popplewell devotes much of his essay to the organization of British intelligence against the Ottoman Empire and provides an incisive analysis of the unique aspects of collecting and preparing intelligence estimates on the Turkish Army. Of the few British military intelligence experts in

Mesopotamia, even fewer were fluent in Turkish, Arabic or Farsi. The intelligence received was further devalued by the illiteracy and lack of support of the local inhabitants. Adding to the confusion was the fact that the disorganized state of the Turkish Army made its nominal order of battle a sadly inadequate gauge for the assessment of its actual military strength: large Turkish military formations such as corps or divisions, unlike the standardized comparable units in Western Europe, varied widely in quality, performance and morale. Another problem faced by the intelligence analysts of the Indian Expeditionary Force (IEF) was that the central geographical position of the Turks enabled them to operate on shorter interior lines of communication; this made it possible to dispatch reinforcements from one region to another with relative speed. Since the IEF was a comparatively small force, the unanticipated appearance of even several Turkish divisions on this front could radically shift the balance of power in favor of the Turkish Army.

Nevertheless, the British defeat in the battle of Kut was not the result of faulty intelligence but rather of General Nixon's failure to believe the estimates that he did receive. Popplewell's account explains how General Nixon had been conditioned – until the battles of Ctesiphon and Kut – by earlier intelligence estimates that regularly overestimated the numerical strength, quality and morale of the Turkish Army. Since the British had experienced little difficulty in defeating the Turks up to that point in the campaign, General Nixon had developed a low regard for the quality of the intelligence he received, and decided that it was almost always going to be more misleading than helpful.

Though General Nixon's perceptions of past events were indeed accurate and his reasoning logical, his luck had run out. In an unprecedented move, the Turkish high command decided to send two high-quality, fully-equipped divisions to the defence of Mesopotamia. Following their success in the Gallipoli peninsula and on the Caucasian front against Russia, the Turks were able to release better units (with higher morale) for action in Mesopotamia. Furthermore, given the strategic importance of Baghdad, this should not have come as a surprise.

The outcomes of the campaigns described by Sheffy and Popplewell turned (as they always do) on the critical link of a military commander's attitude toward intelligence as much as on the quality of the intelligence itself. Allenby's early experience with intelligence work in the preparation and execution of the Palestine offensives was so positive that he relied increasingly on its counsel. In contrast, Nixon was provided with poor-quality intelligence from the beginning of the Mesopotamian campaign and therefore doubted the credibility of the improved estimates he received later on. Rather than automatically losing confidence in intelligence because of its past failures, military commanders should try to understand the reasons for such shortcomings and leave room for their correction. Under the extremely challenging conditions of intelligence work in Mesopotamia, the IEF's intelligence analysts needed more time and experience. General Nixon did not, however, give them another chance, preferring his own judgement to the collective wisdom of his intelligence officers.

* * *

Dr Alvin Coox's essay, 'Flawed Perception and its Effect upon Operational Thinking: The Case of the Japanese Army, 1937–41', differs from the others in this volume in that it does not focus on the contribution of intelligence to a specific military operation. The negative attitude of the Imperial Japanese Army officers toward intelligence did, however, determine the outcome of many operations and eventually, of the war itself. The Japanese military elite's markedly intolerant brand of ethno-centrism and arrogance was an extreme expression of attitudes that were also nurtured to a lesser degree by those in most other military organizations between the two world wars. More than in other armies, the Japanese military elite concentrated all of its energy on action, emphasizing the importance of the operations branch to the exclusion of intelligence and many other important elements of war. Most Japanese military leaders evinced no real interest in or curiosity about their actual or potential opponents, whom they viewed as undisciplined bandits or decadent amateurs. The complex psychological underpinnings of this attitude reflected, among other factors, the physically and mentally insular existence of the Japanese as well as subconscious feelings of insecurity that found expression in their conviction that they were racially and culturally superior. Unprovoked by the enemy's behavior, such 'pure aggression' requires denigration of the victim in order to avoid possible feelings of guilt and provide justification for his subjugation or annihilation.[188] The distorted Nazi perceptions of their victims – whether Slavic, Jewish, British or American – were very similar: in each case, the Germans felt only contempt for their decadent, inferior, materialistic opponents who supposedly harbored aggressive intentions. By virtue of their central European location and place in European history, the Germans could not, like the Japanese, attribute their actions to centuries of isolation from the mainstream of world history. As mentioned earlier, others such as the British and Americans were also stricken by a far less virulent strain of the same attitude.[189]

The Japanese high command was so action-oriented that this facet of their military activities took precedence over intelligence or long-range calculations. When it was not ignored, intelligence was viewed as the source of too many unpleasant, unconstructive questions that hindered or obstructed the planning and execution of military operations. As in the German Army, the status and influence of Japanese intelligence officers was far from enviable; in fact, 'the intelligence section was typically excluded from operations staff deliberations', an indignity that was spared its *Wehrmacht* counterpart. In one instance, the Southern Army Headquarters in 1942 completely did away with what little autonomy might have been left to the intelligence staff by 'combining [it] with operations after the successful first phase of campaigns of the Pacific War. The Southern Army simply assumed that the intelligence staff had lost any *raison d'être* by that time. This degradation of intelligence functions in the midst of a full scale war to the death is underscored by the fact that the Intelligence section of the Southern Army was not reactivitated until February 1944'.

Again as in the experience of Nazi Germany, the Japanese contempt for and lack of interest in the enemy was reinforced (and seemed to be vindicated by) their brilliant early victories which were achieved more by surprise, military skill and the ruthless application of brute force rather than by extensive intelligence preparations. By the time their early strategy began to fail, it was too late to change their deep-rooted negative conceptions and build an efficient intelligence organization from scratch. Having suffered the initial shock of surprise and defeat, the Allies in Europe and the Pacific had been impelled to learn as much as possible about their opponents. Their appreciation of the potential of intelligence combined with rational, steady efforts to improve their own intelligence capacity certainly made all the difference to the outcome of the war.

The Japanese and German approach to war was premised on irrational, sentimental thinking that *had* to ignore higher-level intelligence. As reflected in the reasoning of the German General Staff before the invasion of the Rhineland, the Munich Crisis, or the invasion of the West in May 1940, a rational analysis would have shown that winning a war on the scale envisaged by Hitler or the Japanese would be impossible in the long run. Since any intelligence officer with the temerity to present such a realistic, long-range intelligence estimate would have suffered the fate of the messenger bearing bad news, no such estimate was ever seriously prepared. War was launched in the hope that the enemy would conform to their distorted image and lose as expected. As the Japanese and Germans discovered, success in modern war depends on large bureaucracies as well as the intelligence, logistics, and industry that support them. It took total military defeat to move the Japanese to concentrate their energy in the fight for world markets – a competitive dimension in which intelligence is now seen as the basis of a rational strategy.[190]

* * *

The invention of radio revolutionized the transmission of information on the battlefield as well as from the battlefield to all levels of headquarters. For the first time, it had become possible to relay information reliably and in real time. Radio permeated every aspect of command and control in war. Commanders could make decisions on the battlefield or in the rear and immediately communicate them over long distances; this made possible the co-ordination and control of large formations over wide areas and accelerated the pace of battle. Like any other invention, it also generated new problems such as the inevitable tendency toward centralization in the control of war or command by remote control from the rear. It also created very serious security problems that had not existed in the past. Despite the revolutionary impact of radio and other communications methods on warfare, it seldom drew the interest of academics and was left almost exclusively to military professionals and communications experts. On the whole, scholars have rarely examined the consequences of improvements in communications on the events they describe. To date, no one has written a detailed account of radio and the evolution of modern warfare or of the influence of radio on the conduct of operations during the First or Second World Wars.

Dr John Ferris's essay, 'The British Army, Signals and Security in the Desert Campaign, 1940–42', stands out as a highly original first step in the detailed study of radio's impact on military operations in the Second World War. Ferris examines many relevant issues such as the fact that before the Second World War, British preparations in radio communications were inadequate in relation to the efforts made by the Germans in this field. Ferris discusses in some detail the influence of the different types of radio networks on the development of the British and German military doctrines, and analyses the various ways in which radio communications either expanded or limited each military organization's capacity to wage a fast-paced mobile war. He traces the further development of radio communications from the battle of France in May 1940 to the campaign in the Western Desert in 1941–42 – from Operation Battleaxe to Crusader and Gazala. This comparative study of British and German radio communications as they evolved in these two campaigns explicitly discusses for the first time the impact of radio communications on the operational performance of the two armies. Ferris correlates the state of each side's radio communications system with other factors such as military doctrine, the quality and style of command, and their relative security. The strong beginning made by this essay also points up the need for additional studies to analyse the same issues not only in greater depth but also in relationship to other military organizations such as those of the United States, the Japanese, Italians or Russians.

Ferris also provides the reader with valuable insight into the beginnings of a theory on the role of communications in modern warfare. The most interesting problem from the vantage point of intelligence and military operations is the tension between the need for security and the need for rapid transmission of all types of information and decisions during a battle. As Ferris shows, this problem is more critical and difficult on the operational level, where the life span of information can be measured in terms of hours or days but the pressure to act quickly is still very strong. In contrast, communication in plain language is both inevitable and less problematic on the tactical level, where decisions must be taken instantaneously and the life-span of all types of information is correspondingly short. And on the strategic level, where speed is not usually critical and where the life-span of information and decisions is the longest, it is much easier to opt for slower but more secure communications systems. As the worst of two worlds, operations requires a speed of decision-making that often approximates to that of the tactical level – while the extended life-span of value of the information being transmitted makes it essential to maintain the highest possible security.

Ferris describes how the Germans, notably under Rommel, exploited their superior command system, greater experience and initially better communications systems to impose a blitzkrieg type of war on the British. Indeed, until the battle of El Alamein, this caused the British command and communications systems to break down, thereby forcing the British commanders to speak *en clair*. At times, this in turn enabled Rommel to adapt his plans and improvise accordingly. As Ferris makes clear, the quality of communications and the quality of command are inseparable in war. From Crusader (November 1941) onward, the caliber of the British communications network and equipment improved tremendously, equalling if not surpassing that of the Germans – yet British commanders were still unable to take advantage of it because their weapons were inferior, their doctrine was weak, and they were less experienced.

Many of the problems Ferris describes would today be solved by advanced communications and encryption technologies. Growing automation and better equipment may make communications on contemporary and future battlefields faster and more secure. Nevertheless, one very important lesson in this essay for the modern military man is that all technical and organizational networks, personnel training, and testing of communications systems must be completed in peacetime. Unlike the Second World War, modern war may be too fast and unforgiving to allow for the gradual learning of lessons, the training of necessary personnel, and the procurement of essential equipment.

*   *   *

Patrick Beesly's essay, 'Convoy PQ 17: A Study of Intelligence and Decision-Making', was the last he wrote before his death. He had prepared it for presentation at an international conference at the US Army War College in April 1986, but was unable to present it in person because of ill health. Ralph Bennett presented it on his behalf. Beesly's death greatly saddened all who knew him and who will never forget his gentle manner, radiating kindness, and readiness to help. He will be remembered not only for his generosity but also for his superbly written pioneering work on naval intelligence in both World Wars, his exemplary scholarly research and his uncompromising quest for the truth. This volume is dedicated to his memory.

This essay on the fate of PQ 17 is an excellent example of the logical structure and succinct style that allowed him to study a very complex affair in depth despite limitations in space. It is a study in the dilemmas and inherent uncertainties of command in war as much as it is of intelligence. Beesly addresses the central themes of this book: namely, the interaction between intelligence and the conduct of military operations; and the problems created by leaders unfamiliar with the inner workings of the intelligence process – leaders who are not fully aware of its potential or limitations because they consider it to be either irrelevant or a panacea.

Beesly opens with a brief discussion of the strategic naval situation on the eve of the sailing of Convoy PQ17. After summarizing the organization of British naval intelligence, the relationship between naval intelligence and Bletchley Park, and the achievements and limitations of codebreaking as of June 1942, he makes it clear that it was the enigmatic personality of the First Sea Lord, Admiral of the Fleet Sir Dudley Pound, more than any other single factor that determined the tragic course of events. Like Admiral Oliver, who played a decisive and negative part in the British Admiralty's failure to make better use of accurate intelligence in the First World War, Admiral Pound monopolized both major and minor decisions. He often intervened in operational matters from his position in London which was too remote from the scene of the action to give him a precise grasp of the situation. Pound, as Beesly observes, 'was an officer of the old school' who had been 'brought up in the tradition of theirs not to reason why' – an attitude which seriously undermined the clarity of his orders and crippled his capacity to co-operate effectively with his intelligence advisers. Worse still, Admiral Pound, in Beesly's opinion, did not truly understand the world of intelligence; he rarely visited OIC and was not well acquainted with its top intelligence experts. Pound's poor health may have caused or at least exacerbated his pessimistic assessment, before the convoy had even sailed, of its chances for success as well as his haste in bringing the episode to a quick end. While there is no need to recapitulate here the events so brilliantly described by Beesly, it is useful to mention a few points directly related to earlier discussion.

One of the first concerns Clausewitz's observation that military commanders tend to opt for a worst-case analysis under conditions of uncertainty. On the German side, Admiral Raeder, under strict orders from Hitler not to endanger any major surface ships, was extremely reluctant to take unnecessary risks. The highest-level German naval commanders responsible for the attack on PQ 17 (Operation Rosselsprung – Knight's Move) suffered from uncertainty as much as, *if not more than*, their British counterparts. The Germans had difficulty in locating the convoy and identifying the task force protecting it. They wrongly suspected that a number of battleships, and perhaps even an aircraft carrier, were in close proximity to the convoy. It is unlikely that the German naval commanders would have ventured to risk the *Tirpitz* until they had received more definitive information on the British and American forces taking part in the operation. The Germans may have faced even more uncertainty than the British, because the successful British interception and deciphering of German signals made it clear that the Germans were gravely concerned about the possible presence of more than one British battleship. From this one could quite reasonably infer that the Germans would hesitate to send out the *Tirpitz* to attack PQ 17. By putting himself in the place of the German commanders, Captain Denning, the intelligence analyst, came to this conclusion, but was never given the opportunity to explain his reasoning to Admiral Pound. The predicament of the German commanders therefore went unnoticed by Admiral Pound, who had not attempted to penetrate the mindset of his adversaries. Faced with uncertainty, Admiral Raeder was more deliberate whereas Admiral Pound acted in haste. Although there was, as in all crises, great time pressure on all of the participating decision-makers, the need to take action was not as urgent as Pound felt. 'Pound's nerve certainly cracked before Raeder had to make a decision' and, in Admiral Tovey's words, gave the order to scatter the convoy prematurely.[191]

Pound, who did not fully appreciate the subtleties of the intelligence process, expected the OIC to give him a clear 'yes' or 'no' answer. In the heat of battle, it is indeed rare to receive such unequivocal answers. In this case, Denning's experience led him to conclude that the *Tirpitz* was in all probability still anchored at Alten Fjord, and that when she did put to sea there would be enough information to learn of it in advance. The co-ordination between Pound in Operations and those in Intelligence had failed. Pound did not encourage further discussion of the situation with OIC and Denning, while Denning was reluctant to offer his opinion without being asked. The lesson to be learned from this is deceptively simple: it is the duty of the commander to explore the available intelligence in depth and allow the intelligence analyst to present his case in detail, not just in terms of a simplistic and misleading 'yes' or 'no' response. The commander should encourage the intelligence analyst to approach him freely if the analyst has reached new conclusions or obtained additional information. In such a situation, it is also the moral duty of the intelligence officer to approach the commander in charge of the operation, even if this is disagreeable or difficult. Co-operation between these two must be in the form of an ongoing dialogue – not a one-way communication process that terminates after they meet.

From the operational point of view, Pound and his commanders had to choose between two evils: whether they decided to scatter or not, they were faced with almost equal dangers. Yet, as Captain Roskill suggests in the official history, the lessons learned until that point indicated that (all other things being equal) it was generally safer to run the convoy concentrated and maintain disciplined order rather than to disperse.[192] Given the degree of uncertainty involved and the fact that neither option was good, there was still enough time in hand at least to postpone the decision to scatter. The order to scatter was, after all, issued on the basis of the enemy's possible future intentions, not his actual movements. Commenting on Pound's frame of mind, Beesly states that he 'had virtually determined to scatter the convoy before it ever sailed and that his visits to OIC were merely to confirm that there was no incontrovertible evidence available which would compel him to make a different decision'. When decision-makers have thus made up their minds in advance, they view contradictory intelligence as an impediment. To a great extent, this is also unavoidable. Throughout their careers, military commanders are educated to take prompt action even if intelligence is ambiguous. This is one of the most fundamental dilemmas of command. when there is a 47 per cent chance that the surface ships (or enemy tanks, or divisions, etc.) will do X and a 53 per cent chance that they will do Y, the necessity of selecting a clear course of action often precludes compromise; despite the narrow margin, the decision must go one way or the other. This is where good or bad fortune comes into play. Admiral Pound may have made the wrong decision in this instance, but his performance as a commander should be judged on the basis of his entire record, not on one decision alone. In *On War*, Clausewitz argues that at times military decisions have to be judged not only by the result but by the logic and considerations behind them. Victories can be achived despite poor planning, and disasters can occur despite brilliant planning. If Admiral Pound failed, it was not so much in the decision itself as in the faulty process by which he arrived at it.

* * *

'Ultra Intelligence and General Douglas MacArthur's Leap to Hollandia: January–April 1944' by Edward J. Drea is the first detailed case-study on the use of Ultra and Sigint in land operations in the Pacific theater. It is a classic example of how to exploit excellent intelligence to the fullest in the preparation, planning and execution of a large-scale, complicated military operation. Ultra intelligence gave General MacArthur nearly perfect insight into the Japanese Eighteenth Army's order of battle, concentration of forces, vulnerabilities and intentions. So well-informed was MacArthur that he was persuaded to change his plans on relatively short notice; he decided to 'skip' a phase of the planned offensive in northern New Guinea which called for an attack on Hansa Bay and instead attack Hollandia, which was over 1000 miles away from his point of departure. By doing so he seemed to be taking an enormous risk. (Appropriately enough, the codeword for the Hollandia landing was *Reckless*.) Nevertheless, it can be argued that as in his landing at Inchon in November 1950 (said to be a 2000 to 1 risk), outstanding intelligence in fact reduced the risk to an acceptable level.

MacArthur knew from Ultra that the Japanese were concentrating the bulk of their forces in the Madang–Wewak area and preparing to defend Hansa Bay against an anticipated Allied attack. Furthermore, timely information concerning the timing and destinations of Japanese reinforcement convoys in late February and early March enabled US air and naval forces to intercept and destroy the convoys that were so critical for the Japanese defense of New Guinea. Accurate intelligence revealing the Japanese concentration of air power in Hollandia allowed Lt. General George Kenney, Commander of the Allied Air Force, to destroy the Japanese fighter and bomber force on the ground before MacArthur's invasion had begun. As Dr Drea demonstrates in some detail, Ultra also enabled the Allies to deceive the Japanese by reinforcing their appreciation that the Allies would attack in the area of Hansa Bay and Wewak.

MacArthur's landing on Hollandia and Aitape on 22 April 1944 at the rear of the Japanese Army facing Hansa Bay completely surprised the Japanese Eighteenth Army and eventually led to its destruction. Once again, though, intelligence alone was a necessary but not sufficient condition for this victory. MacArthur's readiness to accept the intelligence provided to him and rapidly revise his plans to take advantage of the 'windfall Ultra presented to him' was crucial. As Drea comments, 'lesser or more cautious commanders might have vacillated and let the chance slip from their hands'. Chance and luck also played a considerable role in this endeavor. MacArthur had begun to receive information of such incredible accuracy only a few months earlier, in January–February 1944. Furthermore, even the most reliable information would not have been of much use to MacArthur in 1943, before his command was reinforced with a sufficient number of landing craft including extended range and fighter cover. (The P–38 was equipped with external fuel tanks.)

It must, however, be emphasized that MacArthur's use of intelligence in Hollandia may have been the exception, not the rule, in his career. Before the landing in the Admiralty Islands on 29 February 1944, during the attack in Luzon and against Manila in January 1945, or during his advance on the Yalu in late 1950, he ignored reliable intelligence that did not suit his preconceived ideas and paid a heavy price each time.

* * *

An interesting comparison is afforded by 'German Air Intelligence in the Second World War' by Dr Horst Boog, and 'A Comparative Analysis of RAF and Luftwaffe Intelligence in the Battle of Britain' by Sebastian Cox. The story of the Luftwaffe's intelligence at the highest levels as told by Dr Boog is by and large a study in failure. Badly fragmented, the Luftwaffe's intelligence system was the center of a bureaucratic power struggle among multiple independent intelligence fiefdoms (at least a dozen by Boog's count) run by leaders who saw intelligence as their private source of power. Their reluctance to exchange information and co-ordinate the operation of their respective organizations impaired the ability of the Luftwaffe to produce accurate estimates based on material from *all* available sources. According to Cox, two of the strongest points of British air intelligence (and intelligence in general) were the outstanding co-ordination of all sources and limiting the number of independent organizations to the bare minimum.

German air intelligence was also undermined by the subordination of most intelligence work to the operations branch as discussed above; this practice inevitably led to the domination of short-range operational requirements over longer-range strategic and operational estimates and weakened the position of intelligence officers. The primacy of operations also led to the assignment of less qualified officers to intelligence duties or to the quick rotation of personnel which in turn prevented the Luftwaffe from ever developing a first-rate, permanent core of intelligence experts. Consequently, the professional standards of the German intelligence organizations were low in comparison with those of the British. Unlike the Luftwaffe, the RAF succeeded in recruiting a larger number of highly qualified civilians who developed invaluable expertise by serving in such positions throughout the war. Furthermore, Cox shows that British Air Intelligence was in a better position to influence the overall strategic and operational decision-making process because of its organizational independence (it was 'a separate directorate within the Chief of the Air

Staff's department in the Air Ministry, and its director was an Air Commodore *equal* in status to the Director of Plans ...').

Early in the war, the Germans showed relatively little interest in long-range intelligence; their quick and apparently decisive victories at the time reinforced their belief that victory was inevitable despite the paucity of intelligence on the enemy's war potential, order of battle, equipment, and trained manpower. Goering, for example, was convinced that RAF Fighter Command would be defeated in four days and before Barbarossa was optimistic that 'the Communist regime would collapse after fourteen days at the most, and that within four to six weeks at the most the River Volga or the Urals would be reached' (p. 384). The war potential of the British, Russians and Americans was cavalierly dismissed in the hope that rapid and decisive military success would render it irrelevant. As Cox shows, the British were much quicker in learning the lessons of war.

The most astonishing aspect of this attitude – best described by the Japanese as victory disease – was the inability of the Germans or Hitler to learn from experience. Having failed to vanquish Britain in a short period of time as they had expected, they later assumed that it would be possible to defeat the much more formidable Soviet Union in a short war; when the Germans and Soviets were locked in an intensive war of attrition (and the Soviet Union had not fallen before the German juggernaut), the war potential of the United States was considered limited and hardly relevant to the war in Europe. By the time the Germans had begun to see the merits of longer-range intelligence, it was too late for them to benefit from corrective action.

While the Germans for the most part grossly underestimated their opponents, the weaker and more vulnerable British at first consistently preferred worst-case analysis. Reflecting a conservative military tradition, the tendency of British air intelligence to operate on the basis of more pessimistic assumptions caused the British to accelerate their preparations for war and to husband their limited forces more efficiently; the perceived precariousness of their position left them almost no choice but to rely increasingly on intelligence as a force multiplier. On the other hand, the Germans enlarged the scope of the war without a commensurate increase in resources; and since the Luftwaffe was not very concerned about using intelligence to increase efficiency, the Germans wasted scarce resources by attacking the wrong targets or changing their strategy too often when victory was within their grasp.

Cox goes on to describe how, during the Battle of Britain, the Germans compounded their weakness in intelligence by committing the operational error of failing to maintain their aim. It is tempting to suggest that the Luftwaffe's poor intelligence caused it to snatch defeat out of the jaws of victory. Perhaps more than any other modern battle, the Battle of

Britain, which was fought by such evenly matched forces, was in the end won by intelligence. Superiority in intelligence as well as in command and control gave the British the needed edge.

German air intelligence was, however, crippled most by Hitler's personality. As Dr Boog makes clear, the Führer Principle as applied to intelligence can only lead to disaster. The Luftwaffe's elite, particularly Goering, were eager to provide selective information that justified Hitler's intuitive decisions. As is well known, this was not the case in Britain: when Marshal of the RAF Newall and Air Chief Marshal Dowding were convinced that certain squadrons were needed for the defense of Britain, they did not hesitate to resist Churchill's request that they be sent to France. Other decisions made by Churchill, in particular the support he gave Dr R.V. Jones against the majority of radio experts (which led to the effective interference with German radio navigation beams), were very positive.

In the end one can agree with Cox's conclusion that 'the structure of the intelligence organization is perhaps equally as important as the quality of the sources, and that such structures are likely to mirror the bureaucratic forms of the relevant state'. While the British political system tolerated the diversity and different opinions essential for good intelligence work, that of Nazi Germany could not.

* * *

In 'Intelligence and Strategy: Some Observations on the War in the Mediterranean 1941–45', Ralph Bennett points to the difficulty of making the best use of available intelligence (in this case, primarily Sigint and Ultra), which, as he notes, is a necessary but not sufficient condition for success in war. Bennett's analysis is based on his personal experience at Bletchley Park as well as on years of research for his recently published book, *Ultra and Mediterranean Strategy*. The degree to which intelligence is exploited depends upon how it is used by military commanders, as well as on the availability of military power and the presence of overriding political considerations. For example, both the intervention in Greece in 1941 and the launching of *Anvil* were political decisions taken contrary to the most rational military course of action as indicated by intelligence. Above all, Bennett shows that intelligence analysts and military leaders need time to learn how to draw the most reasonable conclusions from the intelligence they receive. At the beginning of a war, there are only amateurs in intelligence work. The transformation from amateur to professional is a slow and costly process of trial and error.

Emphasizing the numerous obstacles to be overcome in the use of intelligence on the strategic and operational levels, Bennett argues that while intelligence on the strategic level may be easier to appreciate, it also tends to be harder to obtain. Strategic intelligence is also more likely to be ignored because of political considerations. On the operational level, however, intelligence may be easier to appreciate but more difficult to use since it depends on so many other variables such as command and control, the availability of military might, and the commander's attitude. British intelligence in the Western Desert was, for example, of little help in 1941 and early 1942 as a result of the 'sluggish British command'. Once Montgomery arrived and fully appreciated the value of the intelligence he received, he was able to put it to better use from the battle of Alam Halfa onward. Yet Bennett is justifiably cautious in his conclusions. In the first place, he carefully notes that Monty appreciated the intelligence he received because it supported his earlier assessment of the situation. The reader is left asking what might have happened if the intelligence supplied to Monty before the battle of Alam Halfa had contradicted his own earlier assessments'. On later occasions, for instance before Arnhem, Monty did indeed ignore accurate intelligence which did not agree with his own estimates or plans. There were also instances when he did not fully exploit the benefits of outstanding intelligence (for example, his failure to pursue and annihilate Rommel's remaining forces immediately after the battle of El Alamein).

The contribution of intelligence to Monty's success at Alam Halfa is not easy to evaluate for other reasons, too. Not only did Montgomery have the most perfect intelligence since the battle of Crete concerning the enemy's intention to attack, he also had (unlike Freyberg in Crete) adequate equipment, air superiority, and enough time to prepare for battle. Intelligence – however valuable – was not the only condition for victory at Alam Halfa. As Bennett emphasizes, intelligence does not speak for itself. There is *the supreme need to interpose the judgement of a progress intelligence officer between the raw material and a commander's operational orders*. The failure of commanders to do so in the battle of Jutland and the battle for PQ 17 led to costly disasters that could have been avoided through better co-ordination between commanders and their intelligence advisers. Bennett also warns of the danger of forcing intelligence to fit one's preconceived ideas or political interests rather than examining it bit by bit in an objective way.

Ultimately it is the attitude of the 'consumer' – the military leader – that has the most powerful effect on the value of intelligence. As Bennett emphasizes, 'historians of intelligence have a special duty not to allow their vision to be distorted by their interests and to bear constantly in mind that the decisive factor is always the capacity to make use of intelligence. They should therefore be the first to point out that the early years of the Second World War saw examples of operational mistakes which could have been avoided by a better understanding of the value and use of intelligence, and to warn against the dangers which would follow a repetition'. Bennett is clearly warning the modern military leader that the gap between intelligence and operations must be bridged in peacetime with reference to past mistakes, for a future war may not always offer the time and opportunity necessary to learn from one's own experience.

NOTES

I would like to thank my wife Jill Handel for her professional editing of this essay, and my friend John Ferris of the University of Calgary for his advice and suggestions. I would also like to thank my friend Ralph Bennett for his perceptive and detailed suggestions, some of which unfortunately came too late to be incorporated. I must emphasize that since this essay is devoted to the study of the influence of intelligence on military operations, it does not include an in-depth appraisal of many other relevant factors such as the quality of planning, logistics and weapons technologies. I have discussed the effects of some of these other factors on the outcomes of battles elsewhere (see Michael I. Handel, *War, Strategy and Intelligence*, London, 1989).

1. Sun Tzu, *The Art of War*, trans. Samuel B. Griffith (New York, 1963), p.71.
2. Ibid., p.84. For a similar idea, see also p.129.
3. Carl von Clausewitz, *On War*, ed. and trans. Michael Howard and Peter Paret (Princeton, NJ, 1984), p.140. See also p.462.
4. Ibid., p.86.
5. Ibid., p.117.
6. Donald McLachlan, 'Intelligence: The Common Denominator', in Michael Eliot-Bateman (ed.), *The Fourth Dimension of Warfare: Vol.I: Intelligence, Subversion, Resistance*, (New York, 1970), pp.53–4. For a similar definition, see also Major General Joseph A. McChristian, *The Role of Military Intelligence 1965–1967* (Vietnam Studies) (Washington DC, 1979), p.3; pp.6–11; and p.157.
7. Donald McLachlan, *Room 39* (New York, 1968), p.30.
8. R.V. Jones, 'Intelligence and Command' in Michael I. Handel (ed.), *Leaders and Intelligence*, (London, 1988), p.288.
9. See *Webster's Third International New Dictionary Unabridged* (Springfield, Ma., 1981), p.1581.
10. FM 100–5 *Operations* (Washington DC: Headquarters, Department of the Army, 20 August 1982), pp.2–3.
11. FM 100–5 *Operations* (Washington DC: Headquarters, Department of the Army, 5 May 1986), p.10.
12. A good though somewhat outdated discussion of sources can be found in McLachlan, *Room 39*, pp.49–50.
13. Basic intelligence such as data on climate, demography and maps will not be discussed in this essay because it is usually possible to obtain this type of information from open sources under normal peacetime conditions. (A notable exception might be the Soviet Union, where until recently, even maps to be used by Soviet citizens were deliberately made to be inaccurate and misleading.) Sun Tzu devoted considerable attention to this subject:

> By weather I mean the interaction of natural forces; the effects of winter's cold and summer's heat and the conduct of military operations n accordance with the seasons ...
> Generally, the commander must thoroughly acquaint himself beforehand with the maps so that he knows dangerous places for chariots and carts, where the water is too deep for wagons; passes in famous mountains, the principal rivers, the locations of highlands and hills; where rushes forests, and reeds are luxuriant; the

road distances; the size of cities and towns; well-known cities and abandoned ones, and where there are flourishing orchards. All this must be known, as well as the way boundaries run in and out. All these facts the general must store in his mind; only then will he not lose the advantage of the ground. (Sun Tzu, *The Art of War*, p.64; pp.104–5. See also pp.105–6).

Basic intelligence was a major problem for all military organizations before the twentieth century, when maps, data on climate and so on were not readily available. At that time, military organizations had to dedicate most of their resources to the collection of basic intelligence and were, for the most part, mapping agencies.

This does not, however, mean that basic intelligence could be taken for granted during the present century. In *Room 39*, Donald McLachlan discusses in great detail the difficulties experienced in obtaining basic intelligence during the Second World War, a prime illustration of which was the arrival of British troops in Norway in 1940 without maps and other necessary knowledge of the area. (See pp.298–9.) In much the same way, the Germans invading the Soviet Union in 1941 had inadequate maps of Russian roads and, because of their previous complacency, arrived woefully unprepared for the harsh Russian climate. For an unusual paper on this subject, see Professor J. Neuman, 'Lack of Appreciation of Past Meteorological Data as an Important Factor in the Failure of the German Army in the Battle for Moskow', paper delivered at the Thirteenth International Colloquy on Military History, Helsinki, 31 May–6 June 1988), 15 pages. Neuman claims (p.13) that from 4 October 1941 to 30 April 1942, the German Army lost 100,000–110,000 men through frostbite (or 2/3 of those killed in action or missing). So much for the absence of basic intelligence.

Though no longer the central concern of military intelligence organizations, basic intelligence will always remain a critical and essential part of all military operations. Nothing is more foolhardy than believing that in the age of technology, basic intelligence has become irrelevant or of little consequence. See also Bernd Wegner, 'The Tottering Giant: German Perceptions of Soviet Military and Economic Strength in Preparation for Operation Blau (1942)' in Christopher Andrew and Jeremy Noaks (eds.), *Intelligence and International Relations 1900–1945* (Exeter, 1987), Exeter Studies in History, No.15, pp.293–311.

14. For a detailed look at the contribution and relationship of deception to military operations, see Michael I. Handel (ed.), *Strategic and Operational Deception in the Second World War*(London, 1987), in particular the introductory chapter, 'Strategic and Operational Deception in Historical Perspective', pp.1–91.

15. 'Many intelligence reports in war are contradictory; even more are false, and most are uncertain ...' Clausewitz, *On War*, p.117.

16. 'We hardly know accurately our own situation at any particular moment, while the enemy's, which is concealed from us, must be deduced from very little evidence.' Clausewitz, *On War*, p.217.

17. Carl von Clausewitz, *Principles of War*, trans. Hans W. Gatzke (Harrisburg, Pa., 1943), p.63.

18. Leo Tolstoy, *War and Peace* (New York: Simon and Schuster, 1952), pp.892–3. Similar accounts of such confusion on the modern battlefield abound. One of the most outstanding examples in modern history was the Battle of Sidi Rezegh (Operation Crusader) in November 1941. For comprehensive discussions see J.A.I. Agar-Hamilton and L.C.F. Turner, *The Sidi Rezeg Battles 1941* (Cape Town, 1957); and John Connell, *Auchinleck* (London, 1959), pp.329–61.

19. Michael Carver, *El Alamein* (London, 1962), p.203.

20. For a historical perspective on command and control, see Martin Van Creveld, *Command in War* (Cambridge, Ma., 1985).

21. McLachlan, 'Intelligence: The Common Denominator', p.58.

22. Handel (ed.), *Strategic and Operational Deception*, introductory chapter.

23. Handel (ed.), *Leaders and Intelligence*, p.20; also Jones, 'Intelligence and Command', op. cit., p.293.

24. Quoted from Lieutenant-General Günther Blumentritt's excellent study,

Reconnaissance (US Army War College Military History Institute, MS B–658, October 1947), p.19. For another relevant essay by the same author, see *Is the Enemy Defeated? Can the Situation be Exploited?* (MS B–660).

General Blumentritt's essays have been collected in one volume entitled *A Collection of the Military Essays of Günther Blumentritt* (in German) (MS C–096), 1202 pages. His wonderfully perceptive work covers subjects ranging from theory and practice in war, to the relevance of military history; interior and exterior lines in operations; the location of the commander during the conduct of militry operations (forward command or command from the rear); the *Schwerpunkt* in modern war; and Panzer tactics. It is a gold mine of untapped insights into the nature of modern war.

25. Sun Tzu, *The Art of War*, p.83.
26. See John McDonald, *Strategy in Poker, Business and War* (New York, 1950).
27. Connell, *Auchinleck*, pp.338–9.
28. 'Four elements make the climate of war: danger, exertion, uncertainty and chance.' Clausewitz, *On War*, p.104.
29. '... the very fact of interaction (i.e., battle) is bound to make [war] unpredictable.' Ibid., p.139.
30. Ibid., p.167.
31. Ibid., p.193.
32. Ibid., p.502.
33. Ibid., p.182.
34. Ibid., p.582.
35. 'Men are always inclined to match their estimate of the enemy's strength too high than too low, such is human nature.' Ibid., p.85.

   'As a rule most men would rather believe bad news than good, and rather tend to exaggerate the bad news.' Ibid., p.117.

   'With its mass of vivid impressions and doubts which characterize all information and opinion, there is no activity like war to rob men of confidence in themselves and in others, and to divert them from their original course of actions.' Ibid., p.108.
36. Ibid., pp.572–3.
37. Ibid., p.86.
38. Ibid., p.216.
39. Ibid., pp.84–5. On the problem of suspending action in war, see *On War*, Book 1, Ch.1, Sections 13–19, pp.82–5; and Book 3, Ch.16, pp.216–9.
40. Ibid., p.96.
41. Ibid., p.194–5.
42. Ibid., p.195. 'In tactics as in strategy, superiority of numbers is the most common element in victory.' Ibid., p.194.
43. 'To achieve strength at the decisive point depends on the strength of the army and on the skill with which this strength is employed.' Ibid., p.195.

   'The best strategy is always *to be very strong*; first in general, and then at the decisive point. Apart from the effort needed to create military strength, which does not always emanate from the general, there is no higher and simpler law of strategy than that of *keeping one's forces concentrated*.' Ibid., p.204.

   It must, however, be made clear that despite his stress on the need to achieve numerical superiority at the decisive point, Clausewitz did not consider this to be a panacea. '... To accept superiority of numbers as the one and only rule, to reduce the whole secret of the art of war to the formula of numerical superiority at *a certain time and in a certain place* was an oversimplification that would not have stood up for a moment against the realities of life.' (*On War*, p.135). Unlike Clausewitz, Liddell-Hart emphasized that modern warfare is dominated by *qualitative rather than by quantitative* trends, 'by firepower plus morality, rather than superiority in numbers ... The cult of numbers is the supreme fallacy of modern warfare. The way it persists is testimony to the tenacity of stupidity'. B.H. Liddell-Hart, *Thoughts on War* (London, 1944), pp.66; 69.

   Although the qualitative technological dimensions of warfare have grown in relative importance since Clausewitz's time, overemphasizing quality can have its own risks. Among the many reasons for this, two of the most important are that (a) when both sides are qualitatively matched at the point of engagement, the numerically superior side ought to win, all other things being equal; and (b) for the qualitatively inferior side, numbers may still be an important compensating factor. See Michael I. Handel, 'Numbers Do Count: The Question of Quality Versus Quantity', *Journal of Strategic Studies*, Vol.4 No.3 (September 1981): 225–60; and Michael I. Handel (ed.), *Clausewitz and Modern Strategy* (London, 1986), pp.51–95.

44. Clausewitz, *On War*, pp.196–7.
45. Sun Tzu, *The Art of War*, p.69; 80.
46. Clausewitz, *On War*, p.153.
47. Sun Tzu, *The Art of War*, p.134; 140.
48. For a discussion of leaders' use and misuse of intelligence, see Handel (ed.), *Leaders and Intelligence*.
49. Winston S. Churchill, *The Second World War: The Grand Alliance*, 6 vols. (Boston, 1951), Vol.3, p.399.
50. Clausewitz, *On War*, p.102.
51. 'Action can never be based on anything firmer than instinct, a sensing of the truth.' Ibid., p.108.
52. See ibid., p.152.
53. Ibid., p.146.
54. Ibid., p.102.
55. Ibid., p.578.
56. Ibid., p.191.
57. Ibid. Liddell-Hart's opinion of taking risks is diametrically opposite to that of Clausewitz: 'The habit if gambling contrary to reasonable calculations is a military vice which, as the pages of history reveal, has ruined more armies than any other cause. Rare have been generals who had the strength of will to resist this temptation.' Liddell-Hart, *Thoughts On War*, p.95.
58. Clausewitz, *On War*, p.190.
59. Ibid., p.192.
60. Ibid., p.104.
61. Ibid., p.105.
62. Ibid., p.103.
63. Brigadier General C.F. Aspinall-Oglander, *Gallipoli* (London, 1929), pp.254–5.
64. Clausewitz, *On War*, p.117.
65. Sir David Hunt, *A Don At War* (London, 1966), p.40. For a similar observation, see the US Army military intelligence report written after the war and reprinted by: Military Intelligence Division, US War Department, *German Military Intelligence 1939-1945* (Fredrick, MD:, 1984), particularly pp.273–95.
66. See Michael I. Handel, *War, Strategy and Intelligence* (London: Cass, 1989), the introductory chapter.
67. F.H. Hinsley, *British Intelligence in the Second World War: Its Influence on Strategy and Operations*, Vol.I (New York and London, 1979), p.10.
68. An anonymous US General quoted by Sir Robert Thompson in *Defeating Communist Insurgency: The Lessons of Malaya and Vietnam* (New York, 1966), p.84. The short chapter on intelligence is well worth reading (Chapter 7, pp.84–9.
69. Quoted in Herbert J. Boasso, Lt. Col. USAF, *Intelligence Support to Operations: The Role of Professional Military Education* (Maxwell Air Force Base, Alabama, October 1988), Research Report No. AN–ARI–88+1. It is not clear from the context whether or not the author approves of the statement he quotes.
70. Military Intelligence Division, US War Department, *German Military Intelligence: 1939-1945*, pp.273–74.
71. Ibid., pp.277–8.
72. Ibid., p.280.
73. Hinsley, *British Intelligence in the Second World War*, Vol.1, p.10.
74. See Patrick Beesly, *Room 40: British Naval Intelligence 1914–1918* (New York, 1982), pp.151–69; Arthur J. Marder, *From the Dreadnought to Scapa Flow*, Vol. III,

Jutland and After, second revised edition (Oxford, 1978), pp.172 ff.; Admiral Sir
Willian James, *The Eyes of the Navy* (London, 1955), pp.119–20.

75. Admiral Godfrey, Director of Naval Intelligence (DNI), recalled an incident which
demonstrates how little the First Sea Lord, Admiral Pound, must have understood
intelligence:

> Nor, unfortunately, does it seem to have been one of Sir Dudley Pound's favourite
> precepts. Three weeks before German airborne invasion of Crete, Special Intel-
> ligence revealed the enemy's intentions to the British. Naturally a signal
> was drafted in NID to inform the Naval Commander-in-Chief Mediterranean,
> Admiral Sir Andrew Cunningham. As it was so important, that draft signal was
> passed to the First Sea Lord to see and note before despatch. It read 'German
> airborne troops will attack Crete on 20 May …'. Next morning, when he saw the
> typed copy of the out signal, Godfrey was amazed to see that the word 'Crete' had
> been altered to 'Malta, Crete or Cyprus'. An element of untruth had been injected
> into a high grade intelligence report which, if discovered, would cast doubts on
> future reports from the same source. I pointed this out to Admiral Pound and he
> admitted that he had inserted the words 'Malta and Cyprus' to 'put people on their
> toes'. He realised that he had done wrong but would not admit it. In any event, it is
> unlikely that any harm was done because the correct version reached Wavell, and
> Freyberg in Crete, direct from BP but Pound's amendments may have shaken
> Cunningham's faith in the efficiency of NID in the same way that Captain Jackson's
> wretched signal to Jellicoe on the morning of the Battle of Jutland caused him to
> ignore subsequent accurate information sent him by Room 40.

Patrick Beesly, *Very Special Admiral* (London, 1980), pp.187–8.

76. Rear Admiral Edwin T. Layton (Ret.) with Captain Roger Pineau (Ret.) and John
Costello *And I Was There* (New York, 1985), p.97.

77. Ibid., p.98.

78. Ibid., p.99.

79. Ibid., p.100.

80. B.H. Liddell-Hart (ed.), *The Rommel Papers* (London, 1953), p.122.

81. Günther Blumentritt, 'Platz des hoheren militarisschen Fuhrers Wahrend der
Operations' in Günther Blumentritt, *A Collection of Military Essays of Günther
Blumentritt* (Historical Division, European Command, MS C–096), pp.769–85.

82. McLachlan, *Room 39*, p.365.

83. 'I have frequently discussed this question of the relationship between the Intelligence
Officer and his master with people who have experienced it and one thing that
they all agree on is that it is extremely difficult to get a commander who is well
advanced on an operation, or in the planning of an operation, to change his mind
in the light of intelligence. The fact that the enemy may have changed his dispositions,
or that the operation may, strictly speaking, be unnecessary or that it is untimely, is
something a commander cannot ignore; but the instinctive wish not to postpone
is extremely strong.' McLachlan, 'Intelligence: The Common Denominator',
p.70.
    For excellent insights into the different professional perspectives and roles of
the commander and his intelligence adviser, see Zvi Offer and Avi Kober
(eds.), *Intelligence and National Security* (Tel Aviv, 1987), particularly the chapter
by Brigadier General (Ret.) H. Ben Yemini, 'The Intelligence Officer and the
Commander', pp.557–85 (in Hebrew).

84. Handel (ed.), *Leaders and Intelligence*, pp.11–14.

85. See Sebastian Cox, 'The Sources and Organization of RAF Intelligence and its
Influence on Operations', unpublished paper, September 1988.

86. McLachlan, 'Intelligence: The Common Denomination', pp.72–3.

87. Ibid., pp.70; 74.

88. Major General Sir Francis de Guingand, *From Brass Hats to Bowler Hats* (South
Pomfret, VT.: Hamish Hamilton, 1979), pp.12–13.

89. Major General (Ret.) Shlomo Gazit, 'Intelligence Estimates and the Decision Maker'

in Handel (ed.), *Leaders and Intelligence*, pp.261–87.

90. Harold Deutsch, 'Commanding Generals and the Uses of Intelligence', in Handel (ed.), *Leaders and Intelligence*, p.254.
91. McLachlan, *Room 39*, pp.365–6.
92. Karl R. Popper, *The Poverty of Historicism* (New York, 1964), p.12.
93. For a discussion of this problem, see Handel (ed.), *Strategic and Operational Deception in the Second World War*, pp.58–82.
94. See Richard Hough, *The Longest Battle* (New York, 1986), pp.176–7.
95. For an in-depth analysis of the Battle of Midway, see Gordon W. Prange, *Miracle at Midway* (New York, 1982) and Samuel Eliot Morrison, *Coral Sea, Midway and Submarine Actions: May 1942–August 1942*, Vol.IV (Boston, 1950). For the most detailed analysis of the role of intelligence in the Battle of Midway, see Layton, *And I Was There*: and Ronald Lewin, *The American Magic* (New York, 1982).
96. Prange, *Miracle at Midway*, p.128. US inferiority in the number of ships involved in the battle was somewhat offset by the rough parity in aircraft numbers. The Japanese had some 325 carrier-based aircraft, while the United States had 233 carrier-based aircraft and 115 land-based aircraft for a total of 348. As Midway was the first major naval battle to be fought exclusively by carrier-based aircraft with no direct ship-to-ship engagements, air power was more significant than the type of naval power traditionally taken into account in naval battles. Ibid., p.129.
97. Ibid., p.396.
98. Layton, *And I Was There*, p.405.
99. Ibid., p.20; xiii.
100. Lewin, *American Magic*, p.91.
101. Layton, *And I Was There*, p.410.
102. The Japanese tried to implement an elaborate deception-cover plan for their operation in Midway by launching a diversionary attack against the Aleutian Islands. This ruse failed because US intelligence, as a result of its excellent Sigint work, managed to identify it as such at an early stage. This is one of the very rare instances in which an intricate deception operation was identified and exposed. See Layton, *And I Was There*, pp.433–6.
103. Prange, *Miracle At Midway*, p.38.
104. Ibid., pp.46–7; Layton, *And I Was There*, p.426.
105. The details of this elegant ruse are recounted in Layton, *And I Was There*, pp.421–2; and Prange, *Miracle at Midway*, pp.45–6. This ruse not only verified that 'AF' was indeed Midway as Rochefort had assumed all along – it also allowed US intelligence to identify the precise date of the attack. In order to make the evidence more credible to the naval intelligence authorities in Washington, Rochefort let the Belconnen Station in Melbourne, Australia transmit the intercepted message before he did. Layton, *And I Was There*, p.422. It is worth noting that when Nimitz recommended Rochefort to be decorated for his brilliant contribution to the Battle of Midway, Admiral King turned down his request. 'One is forced to the conclusion that in King's eyes, intelligence was good enough to win battles, but not quite respectable.' Prange, *Miracle at Midway*, p.384. As Patrick Beesly shows, Admiral Godfrey, head of British Naval Intelligence, was the only officer of his rank to receive no decoration whatsoever for his wartime success. See Beesly, *Very Special Admiral*; and also Patrick Beesly, 'British Naval Intelligence in Two World Wars' in Andrew and Noaks (eds.), *Intelligence and International Relations*, p.261.
106. Michael I. Handel, 'The Politics of Intelligence', *Intelligence and National Security*, Vol.2, No.4 (October 1987), pp.5–47.
107. Lewin, *American Magic*, p.96.
108. Sir Francis Bacon, *Francis Bacon's Essays* (London, 1958), p.121.
109. For a discussion of the role of chance and luck in intelligence work, see Michael I. Handel, 'Technological Surprise In War', *Intelligence and National Security*, Vol.1, No.1 (January 1987), appendix, pp.51–3.
110. Prange, *Miracle At Midway*, p.375.
111. Hough, *The Longest Battle*, pp.200–1.

112. See Hinsley, *British Intelligence in the Second World War*, Vol.I, pp.405–6; Ronald Lewin, *Ultra Goes To War* (New York, 1978), pp.196–200; and Antonio Bragadin, *The Italian Navy in World War II* (Annapolis, MD, 1957), pp.85–103. (Pages 98–103 include an interesting discussion of the Italian perspective on intelligence during the war.) See also S.W.C. Pack, *The Battle of Matapan* (New York, 1961); and Raymond de Belot, *The Struggle for the Mediterranean 1939–1945* (Princeton, 1951), pp.100–13; and John Winton, *Ultra at Sea* (London, 1988), pp.9–22.

113. Lewin, *Ultra Goes to War*, quoting C.M. Woodhouse, p.156.

114. Major General I.S.O. Playfair, *The Mediterranean and Middle East*, Vol.II (London, 1956), p.83.

115. Playfair, *The Mediterranean and Middle East*, p.84.

116. Hinsley, *British Intelligence, Vol.1*, p.409.

117. Playfair, *The Mediterranean and Middle East*, p.105.

118. Winston S. Churchill, *The Second World War*, Vol.IV (London, 1951), pp.270–71.

119. This discussion is based primarily on Hinsley, *British Intelligence, Vol.1*, pp.415–21.

120. See Handel, *Strategic and Operational Deception in the Second World War*, Introduction, pp.15–21.

121. Lewin, *Ultra Goes To War*, p.157.

122. On the difficulty of avoiding strategic surprise at the beginning of a war, see: Michael I. Handel, 'Intelligence and the Problem of Strategic Surprise', *Journal of Strategic Studies*, Vol.7 No.3 (September 1984), pp.229–81; and Richard K. Betts, *Surprise Attack: Lessons for Defense Planning* (Washington DC, 1982).

123. I. McD. Stewart, *The Struggle for Crete* (London, 1966), p.104.

124. Gavin Long, *Greece, Crete and Syria* (Canberra, 1953), p.219; and Hinsley, *British Intelligence*, Vol.1, p.419.

125. Hinsley, *British Intelligence*, Vol.1, p.41; and D.M. Davin, *Crete* (London, 1953), p.219.

126. Hinsley, *British Intelligence*, Vol.1, p.410; Davin, *Crete*, p.77; Stewart, *Struggle for Crete*, pp.102–6. Stewart strongly disagrees and maintains that very little information on the methods and doctrine of German paratroopers was distributed to the defending troops on the island.

127. Davin, *Crete*, p.457. Convinced that the preparations for the defence of Crete proceeded according to his suggestions, Churchill was, in the aftermath of the battle, surprised to learn that this had not been the case. He commented that '... the slowness in acting upon the precise intelligence with which they were furnished, and the general evidence of lack of drive and precision filled one with disquiet about this Middle East Staff'. Martin Gilbert, *Finest Hour: Winston Churchill 1939–1941*, Vol.6 (London, 1983), p.1110.

128. Stewart, *Struggle for Crete*, pp.96–102.

129. Ibid., pp.96–7.

130. Ibid., p.102; also p.481.

131. The autonomous nature of each of the sectors was imposed by the difficult terrain, the absence of roads, and the lack of transportation equipment.

132. Long *Greece, Crete and Syria*, p.216; Stewart, *Struggle for Crete*, p.101.

133. Alan Clark, *The Fall of Crete* (London, 1962), p.47; Stewart, *Struggle for Crete*, pp.98–100.

134. Playfair, *The Mediterranean and Middle East*, p.125.

135. Stewart, *Struggle for Crete*, p.1323; Playfair, *The Mediterranean and Middle East*, p.125.

136. Ibid., p.133. See also Davin, *Crete*, p.460.

137. Clark, *Fall of Crete*, p.44.

138. Davin, *Crete*, p.77.

139. Davin, *Crete*, P.461; Playfair, *The Mediterranean and Middle East*, pp.130–131; Stewart, *Struggle for Crete*, p.89. In *A Don At War*, Sir David Hunt reports that according to documents captured from the invading troops, the latest divisional intelligence summary issued on 19 May had estimated the strength of the garrison on Crete at no more than 5,000 men (pp.39–40).

140. Hinsley, *British Intelligence*, Vol.I, p.421; Playfair, *The Mediterranean and Middle East*, pp.136–40. In *A Don At War*, Sir David Hunt states that from Freyberg's headquarters, the burning German ships were visible along the horizon (p.42).
141. Stewart, *Struggle for Crete*, p.480.
142. Ibid.
143. Ibid., p.108.
144. Ibid., p.115.
145. 'For Freyberg the supreme moment of crisis had come at midnight on the 21st. Despite all vagaries of communication, he now knew that outline of the German plan and of its failure both at sea and in all the airborne landing, save that at Maleme. Interpreted with imagination and insight, here was enough for him to have sent out that night ... the orders that would have brought victory ... But he did not suspect the German dilemma. Intelligence had told him much. It had not told him enough. While remaining the victim of his prejudices about the capacity of powered aircraft to crash-land in open country, he did not know that the last of the parachutists had been committed. Thus he had failed to understand the total dependence of the Germans upon Maleme. Never daunted, but constantly bewildered, he was unable to grip the unique problem that faced him ... He had fallen under the spell of the omnipotent Luftwaffe, seeing things worse than they were, and becoming preoccupied with threats which never developed and with dangers that never existed. Stewart, *Struggle for Crete* pp.482–3.
146. Lewin, *Ultra Goes to War*, p.159.
147. According to Lewin in *Ultra Goes to War*, General Freyberg was told that the source of all the outstanding intelligence he received was a spy in the German Headquarters in Berlin. Later in the war, he reportedly asked Bill Williams, Montgomery's Chief Intelligence Officer, 'What happened to that Foreign Office chap we had working in Berlin?' (p.158). See also Geoffrey Cox, *A Tale of Two Battles* (London, 1987), p.51. Incidently, Stewart speculated in vain that the source was probably the head of the *Abwehr* himself. according to Hinsley, Freyberg received the Ultra material disguised as information supplied by an SIS agent in Athens: *British Intelligence*, Vol 1, p.417. Realizing the need to establish the credibility of the intelligence reports sent to Freyberg, Churchill recalled that at one point he wanted to send a special messenger to him with the original copies of the Enigma decrypts but ultimately decided against it. See Gilbert, *Finest Hour*, pp.1085–1086.
148. Ralph Bennett, *Ultra and Mediterranean Strategy* (London and New York, 1989), p.57.
149. Ibid., p.56, note 6.
150. Ibid., p.58.
151. Ibid., p.57, note 9.
152. The German casualties were 1,990 killed; 2,131 wounded; 1,995 missing (in other words, presumed dead) – a total of 6,116 (or close to half of all the German parachutist troops). Playfair, *The Mediterranean and Middle East*, p.147.
153. Ibid., pp.148; 150.
154. Davin, *Crete*, p.464.
155. Stewart, *Struggle for Crete*, pp.476–7.
156. Ibid.
157. For detailed accounts of the battle of Jutland, see Marder, *From the Dreadnought to Scapa Flow*, Vol.3; Beesly, *Room 40*, Ch.10; Richard Hough, *The Great War At Sea 1914–1918* (Oxford, 1986), Chs.13–16.
158. See Beesly, 'British Intelligence in Two World Wars' in Andrew and Noakes (eds.), *Intelligence and International Relations*, p.267; idem, *Room 40*.
159. Hough, *The Great War at Sea*, p.212.
160. Beesly, *Room 40*, pp.155–7.
161. Ibid., p.162.
162. Ibid., p.160.
163. Marder, *From the Dreadnought to Scapa Flow*, Vol.3, p.11.
164. Ibid., p.38.

165. Ibid., p.429.
166. For the role of intelligence in the battle of the Atlantic, see Patrick Beesly, *Very Special Intelligence* (Garden City, NJ, 1978); F.H. Hinsley, *British Intelligence in the Second World War*, 4 Vols. (New York and London, 1977–1988); Beesly, 'British Naval Intelligence in Two World Wars', pp.253–74 and Jürgen Rohwer, 'The Operational Use of Ultra in the Battle of the Atlantic', in Andrew and Noakes (eds.), *Intelligence and International Relations*, pp.275–92; R.V. Jones, *Most Secret War* (London, 1978); Patrick Beesly, 'Operational Intelligence and the Battle of the Atlantic: The Role of the Royal Navy's Submarine Tracking Room', and W.A.B. Douglas and Jürgen Rohwer, 'The "Most Thankless Task" Revisited: Convoys, Escorts and Radio Intelligence in the Western Atlantic, 1941–43', in James A. Boutelier, *The RCN in Retrospect, 1910–1968* (Vancouver, 1982), pp.175–86, 187–234.
167. Beesly, 'British Naval Intelligence in Two World Wars', p.265.
168. Ibid.
169. This table is from Terry Hughes and John Costello, *The Battle of the Atlantic* (New York, 1977), p.304.
170. Rohwer, 'The Operational Use of Ultra in the Battle of the Atlantic', p.284.
171. Beesly, 'British Naval Intellignce in Two World Wars', p.272.
172. Rohwer, 'The Operational Use of Ultra in the Battle of the Atlantic', p.292.
173. For a re-evaluation of the Italian part in the war, see James J. Sadhovich, 'Understanding Defeat: Reappraising Italy's Role in World War II', *Journal of Contemporary History*, Vol.24 (1989), p.27–61.
174. *The Memoirs of General the Lord Ismay* (London, 1960), p.270.
175. Connell, *Auchinleck*, p.257. 'I am reluctantly compelled to the conclusion that to meet German armoured forces with any reasonable hope of decisive success, our armoured forces as at present equipped, organized and led must have at least two to one superiority'. Ibid., p.446.
176. Bennett, *Ultra in the West*, p.16.
177. Hinsley, *British Intelligence*, Vol.2; and Bennett, *Ultra and the Mediterranean Strategy*.
178. See Hinsley; Bennett.
179. Gordon Welchman, *The Hut Six Story: Breaking the Enigma Codes* (New York, 1982), p.232.
180. See Connell, *Auchinleck*, in particular Book III, pp.237–653. See also Kenneth Macksey, *Military Errors of World War II* (London, 1988), pp.94–5.
181. For the details of this battle, see Correlli Barnett, *The Desert Generals*, second edition (London, 1983), Part 4, pp.121–77; Macksey, *Military Errors*, Ch.7; Hinsley, *British Intelligence*, Vol.II, pp.341–99; Bennett, *Ultra and Mediterranean Strategy*, p.109–38.
182. See note 81.
183. Tom Bower, *Paperclip Conspiracy* (London, 1987), pp.25–46.
184. Macksey, *Military Errors*, pp.80–81.
185. Bower, *Paperclip Conspiracy* (London, 1987), pp.25–46.
186. See Macksey, *Military Errors*, p.80; Bower, *Paperclip Conspiracy*, pp.25–6.
187. Hinsley, *British Intelligence*, Vol.II, Appendix 14, Technical Intelligence on Tanks and Anti-tank Weapons in North Africa, pp.705–18.
188. Ken Booth, *Strategy and Ethnocentrism* (New York, 1979).
189. John W. Dower, *War Without Mercy: Race in Power and the Pacific War* (New York, 1986).
190. Captain S.W. Roskill, *The War At Sea 1939–1945*, Vol.II, *The Period of Balance* (London, 1956), p.144.
191. Ibid., p.140.
192. There is some evidence that the symptoms of the Japanese victory disease have now been experienced in the economic sphere. Akio Morita and Shintaro Ishihara, 'The Japan that can say "No": The New US–Japanese Relations Card' (mimeo, 1989).

PART ONE

THE US CIVIL WAR

The Role of Intelligence in the Chancellorsville Campaign, April–May, 1863

JAY LUVAAS

After the bloody failure to storm Confederate positions at Fredericksburg on 13 December 1862, the Union Army of the Potomac returned to its old camps on the north side of the Rappahannock. It had lost nearly 13,000 men, most of them in vain assaults against enemy defenses at Marye's Heights, and with shattered morale and fading confidence in its commander, the army was 'all played out'. Six weeks later Major General Ambrose E. Burnside tried to retrieve the situation, but the entire country was an 'ocean of mud' and he was soon forced to abandon what became known officially – and derisively – as the 'Mud March'. On 25 January Burnside was relieved.

He was replaced by Major General Joseph Hooker, an experienced corps commander with a well-deserved reputation as an aggressive combat leader. In the weeks that followed, Hooker made many far-reaching changes. He abolished the 'Grand Divisions', each comprising two corps, that Burnside had introduced, and he created corps badges to be worn by officers and men to indicate the corps and division to which they belonged. He established the corps as a unit for the organization of his artillery, although he stripped his chief of artillery of all tactical functions and reduced him to his original purely administrative usefulness. He consolidated all of his cavalry into one corps, commanded by Major General George P. Stoneman, and he substituted pack-mules for army wagons on an extensive scale. Hooker also reorganized the Inspector-General's department to provide inspectors for his combat arms as well as for each brigade, and he improved the soldiers' fare while at the same time doing what he could to see that tobacco was regularly issued, that an occasional issue of whisky was made on return from extra duty, and that clothing was inspected and provided. More to the point, Hooker overhauled his intelligence service.[1]

In his official *Report* of the Chancellorsville campaign, the Confederate Commander, General Robert E. Lee, attributed his success at Chancellorsville 'to the skillful and efficient management of the artillery' and to the initiative and skill of his chief subordinates. Had it not been for the need to maintain secrecy, however, Lee surely would have given highest credit to his intelligence service, for as one of his division commanders later noted, 'every day Lee had information of Hooker's movements'. In contrast Hooker found himself frequently groping in the dark, unable to penetrate the designs of his enemy, sort out contradictory information, or even to get an accurate assessment of enemy numbers. In studying the Chancellorsville campaign, therefore, it is especially appropriate to look at the way in which each commander acquired and made use of intelligence, for, as the foremost authority on the campaign has observed, 'one of the most important qualifications of a commander is the ability to sift truth from conficting rumors and reports, and deduce therefrom the dispositions, movement, and intentions of the enemy'.[2]

The man responsible for acquiring military information for the Army of the Potomac had been Allan Pinkerton, who had come from Chicago in the wake of the fiasco at Bull Run in July 1861, accompanied by his entire detective force. Used initially to tighten security, Pinkerton arrested a number of people suspected of sending information secretly to Richmond, but soon his skilled operatives 'were traveling between Richmond and Washington', bringing 'valuable information' about enemy plans. 'Major Allan' as Pinkerton was then known, was in almost daily contact with the President, the Secretary of War, the provost-marshal general and the general in charge of the Union armies. He served as Major General G.B. McClellan's chief of intelligence in both the Peninsular and the Maryland campaigns. When McClellan was relieved from command a month after the battle of Antietam, Pinkerton became indignant at his treatment and refused to continue longer at Washington.[3]

According to one authority, the successful secret service agent must be 'keen-witted, observant, resourceful, and possessing a small degree of fear, yet realizing the danger and consequences of detection'.

> His work ... lay, in general, along three lines. In the first place all suspected persons must be found, their sentiments investigated and ascertained. The members of the secret service obtained access to houses, clubs, and places of resort, sometimes in the guise of guests, sometimes as domestics ... As the well-known and time-honored shadow detectives, they tracked footsteps and noted every action. Agents ... gained membership in hostile secret societies and reported their meetings, by which means many plans of the Southern leaders were ascertained. The most dangerous service was naturally that of entering the Confederate ranks for information as to the nature and strength of defenses and numbers of troops. Constant vigilance was maintained for the detection of Confederate spies, the

interception of mail-carriers, and the discovery of contraband goods. All spies, 'contrabands', deserters, refugees, and prisoners of war found in or brought into Federal territory were subjected to a searching examination and reports upon their testimony forwarded to the various authorities.[4]

When Hooker took over the Army of the Potomac, he could find no document of any kind at headquarters that contained information about the Confederate forces in his immediate front. 'There was no means, no organization, and no apparent effort, to obtain such information.[5] He immediately established an organization for that purpose, and soon he was able to acquire 'correct and proper' information of the strength and movements of the enemy. On 30 March he named Colonel G.H. Sharpe of the 120th New York Volunteers his new deputy provost-marshal-general, in which capacity he was placed in charge of the separate and special Bureau of Military Information. Sharpe remained at the head of this bureau for the rest of the war and supervised the secret service work in the East.[6]

Amid these organizational changes Hooker planned his campaign. His directive specified only that he assume the offensive without any unnecessary delay and that his operations should not uncover Washington. He thought first of crossing the river some distance to the south, where he could turn the Confederate right flank and possibly interpose his army between the Confederate forces under General Robert E. Lee and Richmond, but the rugged terrain, the expanding width of the river in that direction, and the ability of Lee's men to extend their breastworks as rapidly as his own troops could construct practicable roads caused him to set aside this plan in favor of a movement against the other flank. He would send his cavalry corps upstream to cross the rivers, then strike southward, with the primary object of cutting Confederate communications between Fredericksburg and Richmond. Then he would move three infantry corps 30 miles upstream to cross the Rappahannock at Kelly's Ford, with orders to descend the river and take Confederate fortifications at the United States and Banks' Fords in reverse. This would enable him to send two additional corps across the United States Ford to reinforce the marching column, and together they would move directly against the rear of Lee's lines at Fredericksburg. Lee would then either have to come out in the open to fight or retreat in the direction of Richmond. Hooker left two corps under Major General John Sedgwick to demonstrate against the Confederates at Fredericksburg, with orders to pursue the enemy 'with the utmost vigor' if he seemed to be falling back in the direction of Richmond.

The general tenor of the statements received make it appear that

Jackson's corps is left to guard the passage of the river. Ransom's division, of Longstreet's corps, is one mentioned as gone to Tennessee or South Carolina. Pickett's division is one gone to Charlestown.[8]

This disparity in the assessment of the size as well as the destination of enemy detachments and also in the time required for the news to filter back to headquarters was typical of most of the strategic intelligence that reached Lee and Hooker in the weeks ahead. With the departure of Longstreet, Lee had barely 60,000 men to guard the river line – his enemy could muster nearly 134,000.

A week after Longstreet's departure, Stonewall Jackson summoned his topographical engineer and gave him secret orders to prepare a map of the Shenandoah Valley 'extended to Harrisburg, Pa., and then on to Philadelphia – wishing the preparation to be *kept* a profound secret'.[9] On 9 April, Lee suggested to James A. Seddon, Secretary of War, that the enemy had probably decided to confine the operations of the Army of the Potomac and of forces south of the James to the defensive while reinforcing Union armies in the west: the recent transfer of Burnside's IX Corps to Kentucky raised this as a distinct possibility. 'Should General Hooker's army assume the defensive,' Lee suggested, 'the readiest method of relieving the pressure upon General Johnston and General Beauregard would be for this army to cross into Maryland.' For that he would require more provisions and suitable transportation. He would also need a pontoon bridge, and two days later he requested the Engineer Bureau to send a pontoon bridge train to Orange Court House, where it could be added to his army once he could seize the initiative and invade Pennsylvania.[10] The immediate problem, however, was to prevent Hooker from maneuvering him out of his lines and driving him back to the defense of Richmond.

'If I am able to determine the enemy's disposition while at the same time I conceal my own, then I can concentrate and he must divide'. These words are provided by Sun Tzu, but Lee made the thought his own.

* * *

The two armies went about gathering intelligence in much the same way. During the preparation for active operations, the chief source of information was probably a loose network of spies and scouts. The terms were often used interchangeably, but in the parlance of the day 'spies' were individuals located permanently within enemy lines or territory who were actively involved in collecting information valuable to their military leaders. Here the Confederacy had a natural advantage in that the border states, particularly Maryland, contained many southern sympathizers, and even in the North there were many who denied the right of the Federal Government to invade the south. This advantage was greater still in the occupied portion of the Confederacy, where nearly every inhabitant was a potential spy willing to provide military information to those fighting for southern independence. As the war went on, the use and number of Union spies were greatly increased, 'and in the last year the system reached a high degree of efficiency', with spies constantly at work in all the Confederate armies and in all the cities of the South. Only the names of a few 'have been rescued from obscurity'.[12]

To the Civil War soldier, however, most of what were loosely termed 'spies' would be considered 'scouts'. Scouts were organized under a chief who directed their movements, and their duties were to serve as couriers between the network of spies and their own military leaders. Because their duties involved bearing dispatches, locating enemy units, and acquiring precise information about the terrain that would facilitate the march of the army, it was inevitable that scouts would often function as spies. Scouts became 'the real eyes and ears of the army' as they probed forward as far as the enemy picket line and then used their trained powers of observation to find out what was happening on the other side. In the Confederate armies these men came primarily from the cavalry, while initially the Union commanders depended more upon civilian spies, detectives and deserters for information. After Sharpe became head of Hooker's Bureau of Military Information, he turned increasingly to scouts drafted from the army, although at the time of Chancellorsville Lee's intelligence system still enjoyed a decided edge. The *Official Records* contain few references to reports from Union scouts until Hooker's army was actually on the move, whereas Lee frequently received vital information from this source, as revealed in the following letter from Lee to President Jefferson Davis a month before the battle.

> All the reports from our scouts on the Potomac indicate that General Hooker's army has not been diminished, and is prepared to cross the Rappahannock as soon as the weather permits. Various days have been specified for him to advance, but that has been prevented by the occurrence of storms. The 17th ultimo was one of the days stated, and on the 22nd three days rations had been cooked and placed in the haversacks of the men.[13]

Two days later Lee heard from a scout he had sent into Maryland to watch the Baltimore and Ohio Railroad. This man confirmed what Lee had already heard from other reports, that Burnside's IX Corps was indeed being shipped west on the railroad. The scout had counted five divisions.

They were all infantry, transportation for the whole force requiring forty-seven trains. The troops had been encamped for several days in the neighborhood of Baltimore previous to their departure west, and he was able to converse with them at stopping places on the road. He reports that the men were unwilling to be transferred ... to the Western Department (and) that they were tired of the war. ...[14]

In contrast the reports Hooker received from his scouts often were misleading. In late February, for example, a Union scout named Yager reported from Fairfax Station that 'Jackson and his army are at Staunton, with the intention of making a raid in Maryland with the help of General Stuart'. A week later 'our scout' brought in information that 'Jackson was going up the Valley toward Strasburg' − information gleaned from a 'reliable' Confederate soldier who came from Warrenton.[15]

Both sides also used the Signal Corps to provide intelligence. The Confederate signal service was first in the field and gave timely warning of the Union advance upon the Confederate flank at the first battle of Bull Run. Meanwhile Major Albert Myer, a former surgeon who had been appointed Signal Officer for the Union Army a few weeks before the battle, conducted a signal camp of instruction in Georgetown for 17 officers selected for signal duty from the Pennsylvania Reserve Corps. Initially all officers except for Myer were simply acting signal officers on detached service from their regiments, but in March 1863 the Signal Corps was organized and it served Hooker well at Chancellorsville.

In both armies there were two kinds of signal stations − one with the primary mission of signal communication and the other to serve as an observation station from which enemy movements could be studied by trained personnel using a high-power telescope. When he later wrote the doctrine, Myer drew upon his Civil War experience.

If there is a commanding peak near where the enemy offer battle, signal officers should be hurried to it in advance of the army. The enemy are to be kept constantly in view ... (for) the knowledge to be gained by witnessing ... the formation of their forces, by estimating their strength ... and by witnessing early what preparations are made for the battle may be invaluable.

Signal officers were instructed to observe by what roads their ammunition and supply-trains came, to detect where the cavalry is posted, to note any unusual feature in the terrain, and to report upon enemy preparations or movements.[16] Because the Signal Corps operated often in exposed areas some distance from the field army it could be hazardous duty. The ratio of killed to wounded in the Signal Corps was 150 per cent compared with the ratio of 20 per cent in other branches of the service.[17]

To judge from messages published in the *Official Records*, Lee's signal corps seems to have rendered its greatest services at the operational level while Hooker's information from this source was limited primarily to movements about the battlefield. On 20 April, Confederate signal stations along the Potomac reported sailing ships and steamers descending the river in greater numbers than usual, although no troops were reported as having been seen on board. A week later a signal officer in Richmond forwarded a report from a special agent in Washington that confirmed previous reports to the effect that 'troops from the rear have been moved to the Rappahannock'. To Lee this meant that the campaign had begun, although he could not have known that that very day Hooker ordered the V, XI, and XII corps to start their turning movement.[18]

Newspapers were also helpful in estimating enemy intentions and capabilities. Both headquarters were frequently provided with the latest newspapers from Washington or Richmond.[19]

Since the Civil War was the first to be fully covered by the press, newspapers often revealed important military information. On 17 April, for example, the Washington *Morning Chronicle* published extracts from a letter by the medical director of the Army of the Potomac to Hooker, revealing the sanitary condition of the army by providing the number of sick soldiers and including the ratio of sickness per thousand men. This is all that Lee needed to compute the size of Hooker's forces, and since Lee later referred to these figures in his own correspondence there is every likelihood that he did so.[20] Several days later a circular was published for the Cavalry Corps stating 'if there is in this command such a person as the correspondent of the Philadelphia *Inquirer*, he will, by direction of the commanding general of the Army of the Potomac, be immediately sent out of the lines of the army, never to return.' The following day Hooker demanded that the New York *Times* and the Philadelphia *Inquirer* be called upon to name their correspondents who had furnished the information on a story about an alleged submarine cable in use by the Confederates between Falmouth and Fredericksburg, and threatened to suppress the circulation of both papers in the army and exclude their correspondents from his lines if the names were not supplied. And finally Hooker's headquarters issued a general order requiring all correspondents to publish their communications over their own signatures, which would at least identify those responsible for a serious breach in security.[21]

Although Union generals had frequent access to Southern papers, there is little evidence in the published reports to indicate that this was a source of much useful information. A study of newspapers and the problem of maintaining military secrecy during the war suggests that the Southern press perhaps exercised greater discretion and also was under stricter control, while the logic of the situation would suggest that the

southern press was less active in the field because resources were much
more limited.[22]

Perhaps it was the Confederate generals – who as a group were far less
active in politics – who acted with greater discretion. One of Jackson's
staff officers recorded in April 1863 how Jackson, after agonizing over
writing his after-action reports, would cross out entire passages, 'saying
that it would not do to publish to the enemy the reason that induced one to
do certain things and thus enable them to learn your mode of doing'.[23] In
sharp contrast we find the Secretary of War writing to Hooker scarcely a
month later to complain of an officer who had recently been assigned to his
staff:

> We cannot control intelligence in relation to your movements while
> your generals write letters giving details. A letter from General van
> Alen to a person not connected with the War Department describes
> your position as intrenched at Chancellorsville. Can't you give his
> sword something to do, so that he will have less time for the pen.[24]

It was basically a problem of security. Hooker went to great lengths to
restrict the leakage of military information by taking special pains to
prevent communication across the river, whether by private citizens or
bored pickets, and to restrict – but gradually – access of visitors to his
camps. The sudden stoppage of all visitors, he wrote, would serve notice
that the army was about to move. He even went so far as to ask the
Postmaster in Washington on one occasion to detain mail from his army
for a period of 24 hours, stating only that he had 'very urgent reasons' for
making this request.[25]

Perhaps the greatest damage caused by the frequent breaches of
security was the impact that it had upon Hooker and his command style. 'I
have communicated to no one what my intentions are,' he confided to the
Union commander at Suffolk the day before he began his operations. 'If
you were here, I could properly and willingly import them to you. So much
is found out by the enemy in my front with regard to movements, that I
have concealed my designs from my own staff, and I dare not intrust them
to the wires, knowing as I do that they are so often tapped.[26]

Throughout the campaign both commanders made extensive use
of cavalry to provide news of enemy activites, and here again the
Confederates enjoyed a decided advantage. Some of the best regiments in
Lee's cavalry originally came from that part of Virginia that now
comprised the theater of operations, and they could always count upon
the enthusiastic support of the local population. Major General J.E.B.
Stuart, the flamboyant Confederate cavalry commander, was still master
of the field and so excelled in reconnaissance that when he was killed a year
later, Lee's first agonizing words were 'He never brought me a piece of

false information'.[27] Although Hooker had recently consolidated his mounted arm into a separate corps, he needed time before the new division and corps commanders could inspire their men, rebuild morale, and learn to succeed in combat. There was a series of small cavalry, but not much in the way of useful intelligence filtered back to army headquarters.

Hooker compounded the problem by sending his new cavalry corps, less one brigade, on a controversial raid against Lee's supply line to Richmond, but the movement, orignally ordered for 12 April, had to be postponed because of rampaging waters and it was not until the 29th that the floods had subsided enough to permit Stoneman's mounted corps to cross the Rappahannock. For the next ten days, during which time the army fought and lost the battle of Chancellorsville, the Union cavalry was out of touch and Hooker's army moved blindfolded into the wilderness.

In one area only did a Union instrument of intelligence enjoy a clear advantage: the observation balloon. Thought had been given to the military possibilities of the balloon as early as the previous century, for a treatise written by an Englishman in the final year of the American Revolution suggested that:

> On the first report of a country being invaded, an *Air Balloon* would save the expenses of messengers, posts, etc., from the coasts to the main army, as at the height it ascends, with the assistance of glasses, the number of the enemy, together with their place of landing, might be communicated with great dispatch. ... A general likewise in the day of battle would derive singular advantage by going up in one of these machines: he would have a bird's eye view of not only everything that was doing in his own, but in the enemy's army.[28]

During the wars of the French Revolution a regular balloon company, the *1ère Compagnie d'Aérostiers* was created to assist in reconnaissance and observation, facilitate signalling between French divisions in the field, and spread revolutionary propaganda leaflets from the air, and for the next few years there was a growing interest in military aeronautics. This soon declined, however, and Napoleon, who relied upon his cavalry for information, showed little interest in the project. Other armies experimented with balloons spasmodically during the first half of the nineteenth century, but not until the Civil War was there any serious effort to use captive balloons for military purposes. By that time 'balloons and aeronauts were no longer rarities: they had become part of American life'.[29]

From the first President Lincoln had demonstrated an interest in the military potential of the captive balloon. Within days of the Union defeat at the first battle of Bull Run, he summoned Professor Thaddeus Lowe, a pioneer aeronaut who had offered his services to the government, to the

White House. Convinced that the recent defeat 'might have been averted if someone in a balloon could have observed the movements of the Confederate forces', Lincoln engaged Lowe as a civilian balloonist at pay equivalent to that of an army colonel. Thanks in large measure to Professor Lowe's efforts, the Aeronautical Corps did useful service throughout the Peninsular campaign, and at the battle of Fredericksburg Hooker's future chief of staff, then a corps commander, made a short ascent to obtain 'a view of the topography, ravines, streams, road, etc., that was of great value in making dispositions and movements of the troops'. Significantly, although there were three balloons in use at Fredericksburg, none of the printed reports reveals that those who had gone aloft had observed the position of the famous stone wall at Marye's Heights.[30]

The Confederates had no balloons at Chancellorsville. Although a Confederate balloon had been reported visible across the Potomac from Washington in 1861 and several months later in the vicinity of Leesburg, Virginia, this was not a source of intelligence available to Confederate commanders. As Confederate General James Longstreet confessed to Professor Lowe after the war: 'At all times we were fully aware that you Federals were using balloons to examine our positions and we watched with envious eyes their beautiful observations as they floated high in the air, well out of range of our guns. ... We were longing for balloons that poverty denied us.'

During the Seven Days' Campaign some Confederates did manage to patch together a balloon made of silk dresses, but because the only gas available was in Richmond, the balloon had to be filled there and then towed either by ship or by rail. On one of its infrequent appearances, when it was attached to a steamer in the James River, the tide went out and both ship and balloon were left stranded high and dry on a bar and subsequently fell into Union hands. 'This capture,' Longstreet later assured Professor Lowe, 'was the meanest trick of the war and one I have never yet forgiven.'[31]

In the Chancellorsville campaign Union balloons frequently were in the air, a thousand feet above the ridge that lines the left bank of the Rappahannock, but any intelligence from this source was limited to what could be seen within six to eight miles and thus would be useful only at the tactical level – unless of course Lee should decide to withdraw from his lines above Fredericksburg to conduct operations elsewhere, in which case the balloons could have provided timely intelligence of the movement.

*   *   *

Except for the balloons, in the Chancellorsville campaign the Confederates enjoyed a distinct advantage in all of the methods of gathering intelligence of enemy strength, capabilities, and intentions.

Lee had accurate information of the strength of the Army of the Potomac on the eve of active operations thanks to the untiring efforts of his cavalry, reports from scouts and messages intercepted by his signal corps, and the accommodating Washington newspapers, although he was inclined to think that the numbers reported were 'much exaggerated'.[32] Hooker, on the other hand, received conflicting reports about the strength and location of Lee's forces. There were persistent rumors of a Confederate build-up to the west, aimed probably at the Shenandoah Valley, and on the eve of battle 'deserters' reported that Hood's and Pickett's divisions, of Longstreet's command, had arrived from the vicinity of Richmond. These reports – all from deserters purporting to be from these two divisions – were so persistent that it cannot have been mere coincidence, and the camp rumor that Lee had been overheard saying that this 'was the only time he should fight equal numbers' reinforces the suspicion that the Confederate commander was a master of deception.[33] Although the Union commander at Suffolk correctly insisted as late as the second day of the battle that Longstreet was in his front, Hooker's information was that Longstreet had already rejoined Lee.[34]

Lee also had a much clearer perception of enemy intentions than did Hooker. As early as 12 March he received information from citizens at Falmouth 'that the enemy will, as soon as roads permit, cross at United States Ford, Falmouth, and some point below, the attempt at Falmouth to be a feint'. Accordingly he ordered the commander at the United States Ford:

> If your position can be strengthened, have all needful work done. Have the road repaired. Learn all that you can about United States Ford. This may be effected by inducing one of the enemy's cavalry pickets to come over to exchange papers or to trade. Let me have timely notice of any movements of the enemy.[35]

Throughout April Lee was kept informed by Stuart of enemy activity along the upper Rappahannock, although it was not clear whether Hooker intended to cross at the upper fords or to send his cavalry to the Shenandoah. As Stuart kept probing, Lee gained the impression that Hooker 'is rather fearful of an attack from us than preparing to attack' – a perception that may well have reinforced some chancy decisions that he felt compelled to make during the battle.[36] By this time Lee had already decided to assume the offensive by 1 May, 'when we may expect General Hooker's army to be weakened by the expiration of the term of service of many of his regiments, and before new recruits can be received' – an assumption that almost certainly was based upon his reading of the Washington papers.[37]

Hooker had a far less acute perception of his opponent's intentions. Obviously he could not establish signal stations deep in enemy territory, as the Confederates could do from the Maryland bank of the upper Potomac, for by the very nature of things, signal stations were more effective to the army on the strategic defensive. Nor could his cavalry systematically penetrate the Confederate cavalry screen or cross the upper Rappahannock except with a considerable force. Scouts were active in rear of the Confederate lines, but often this was a mixed blessing: Lee was well aware that the 'chief source of information to the enemy is through our negroes', who could be 'easily deceived by proper caution', and he therefore pursued a policy of secrecy which, '*aided by rumor*', could mask his intentions by planting misleading reports. Lee's policy was to 'send no dispatches by telegraph relative to ... movements, or they will become known'.[38] Hooker's intelligence was therefore limited to what could be inferred from information obtained from deserters, slaves (or contrabands) and local inhabitants in enemy territory, and even when the intelligence was accurate Hooker often misinterpreted it.

On 11 April, for example, Lee requested that a pontoon train of 350 feet span, with rigging and everything complete, be sent to Orange Court House, obviously in anticipation of his projected operations in Maryland and Pennsylvania. Ten days later Hooker confided to President Lincoln: 'Deserters inform me that the talk in the rebel camp is that when we cross the river it is their intention to fall in our rear and attack our depots at Aquia. The recent arrival of a pontoon train at Hamilton's Crossing lends plausibility to these reports'.[39]

Occasional Confederate reinforcements to the Shenandoah Valley of a regiment or two invariably were enlarged to a division or even a corps by the time the news reached Union headquarters, and when Hooker decided to turn Lee's left and sever his communications with Richmond, he was apprehensive that Lee would fall back once Union forces had crossed the Rappahannock and would retreat over the shortest line to Richmond.[40]

On 14 April, Lee received intelligence that Union cavalry was concentrating on the Upper Rappahannock, where Stuart's cavalry prevented them from establishing a bridgehead on the south bank of the river. A week later small bodies of infantry appeared at Rappahannock Bridge and Kelly's Ford, and two days later some Union infantry crossed the river about 20 miles *south* of Fredericksburg at Port Royal. Lee assumed that these movements were intended to conceal Hooker's designs, 'but, taken in connection with the reports of scouts', they indicated that Hooker's army 'was about to resume active operations'.

On 28 April Union troops crossed the Rappahannock in boats near Fredericksburg, drove Confederate pickets, and proceeded to lay down a pontoon bridge, and the following morning the three corps that Hooker had sent up river started to cross the Rappahannock at Kelly's Ford.[41]

Couriers kept Lee informed of the progress of this massive turning movement. On the 29th Lee learned that enemy cavalry had crossed the Rapidan at Germanna and Ely's Fords, removing any doubt that Hooker's intention was to turn his left 'and probably to get into our rear'.[42] He immediately requested that the remainder of Longstreet's corps be sent to him and alerted his troops in the lines behind Fredricksburg to make preparatory arrangements to move to strengthen his left. The following day Lee was informed that the turning movement comprised the V, XI and XII corps and he ordered the rest of his army, except for one division and a brigade from a second, to march west into the wilderness 'and make arrangements to repulse the enemy'.[41]

The battle began on 1 May, when Hooker advanced along the three roads leading from Chancellorsville toward Fredericksburg, hoping to uncover Banks' Ford, where bridges were to be thrown across the river, thus shortening significantly the line of communication between the two wings of his army. A Confederate division attacked the center column and drove it back, causing Hooker, who had assumed personal command of his forces at Chancellorsville, to withdraw to a defensive position that had been prepared the previous night. This was done, according to the chief of topograhical engineers, Army of the Potomac, because of 'information received since the advance began'.[44]

The information came from Hooker's observation balloons, hovering high above the hills across the river from Fredericksburg and at Banks' Ford. For when Lee decided to move out of his trenches at Fredericksburg to attack Hooker near Chancellorsville, there was ample and timely warning from 'Balloons in the Air' that this was his response. On the 29th there had been reports of Confederate infantry and wagon trains moving to the west. The next day it was noted that 'all of the camps west of the railroad have been struck save one small one', and although the telegraph was not in working order and vision was obscured by an early morning fog, by noon on 1 May Hooker was informed that the largest enemy column was moving on the road toward Chancellorsville, leaving the Confederate strength at Fredericksburg 'considerably diminished'.[45] Shortly before the Confederates attacked he was informed by his chief of staff, at army headquarters across the river from Fredericksburg: 'The enemy will meet you between Chancellorsville and Hamilton's Crossing. He cannot, I judge, from all reports, have detached over 10,000 or 15,000 men from Sedgwick's front since sun cleared fog'.[46]

This timely intelligence, coupled with the planted reports that 'Hood's division arrived yesterday from Richmond', was certainly the reason why Hooker suspended his attack and fell back to defensive lines around Chancellorsville. At the time he made his decision only one division had yet been engaged: two others were within sight of Confederate works guarding Banks' Ford, which he recognized was critical terrain for the success of his operations, and yet Hooker recalled his forces because of news he had just received 'from the other side of the river'.

> Hope the enemy will be emboldened to attack me. I did feel certain of success. If his communications are cut, he must attack me. I have a strong position. All the enemy's cavalry are on my flanks ... which I trust will enable Stoneman to do a land-office business in the interior.[47]

When he suspended his own attack Hooker instructed Sedgwick, who commanded 40,000 men at Fredericksburg, 'to keep a sharp lookout, and attack if you can succeed'. But Sedgwick, who received a steady flow of reports from 'balloons in the air' to the effect that the Confederates had withdrawn many troops from their lines at Fredericksburg to meet Hooker's advance from the west, decided not to attack. Major General John F. Reynolds, who commanded I Corps, cautioned against making an attack and speculated that the Confederates 'have been ... showing weakness, with a view of delaying Hooker, in tempting us to make an attack on their fortified position, and hoping to destroy us and strike for our depot over our bridges'.[48]

In sharp contrast, Lee made the best possible use of his intelligence. Having won the initiative when Hooker fell back to his fortified lines about Chancellorsville, Lee decided to assume the offensive. Acting on reports from his cavalry that Hooker's right flank rested on no natural obstacle and thus was 'in the air', he decided to send Jackson's entire corps to attack the Union right flank and rear. It is possible that Lee and Jackson erred somewhat in their estimation of the exact location of the Union right flank, for in executing the movement Jackson was forced to take a longer route than anticipated to avoid marching across the front of the intrenched XI Corps. Major General Fitzhugh Lee's cavalry brigade, which covered Jackson's marching column, provided the timely intelligence that enabled Jackson's attack to succeed – and Lee to win the most brilliant victory of his career.

Jackson's march did not go unobserved. The balloons at Fredericksburg were too far off to detect the movement through the thick woods, but Jackson's column was observed by Union lookouts in the treetops at Hazel Grove and fired upon by a battery nearby, and about 9.30 a.m. Hooker sent word to the commander of XI Corps, Major General O.O. Howard: 'We have good reason to suppose that the enemy is moving to our right'. Major General Daniel Sickles, commander of III Corps, likewise saw the continuous column of infantry, artillery, trains and ambulances moving across his front in a southerly direction 'toward Orange Court-House, on the Orange and Alexandria Railroad, or Louisa Court-House, on the Virginia Central', but Sickles was uncertain whether this portended a retreat on Gordonsville or an attack upon the Union right flank. Later Howard's scouts and cavalry sent back 'the unvarying report' that 'The enemy is crossing the Plank Road and moving toward Culpeper'.[49] Hooker had assumed all along that once he could maneuver his army across the rivers and astride Lee's line of communications, the Rebels 'may as well pack up their haversacks and make for Richmond'.[50] It seemed logical to assume, therefore, that the long column was probably headed for the Orange and Alexandria Railroad. Hooker and his subordinates were guilty of 'making pictures'.

There is no need to devote more attention to the battle. Jackson's flank attack succeeded brilliantly, although Jackson himself was mortally wounded. The following day, after bitter fighting, the Confederates united to drive Hooker's larger forces into defensive lines north of Chancellorsville, enabling Lee later to send desperately needed reinforcements to the tiny force that fought to delay Sedgwick's advance from Fredericksburg. On 4 May Lee concentrated against Sedgwick, driving him back upon Banks' Ford, and two days later Hooker's army, which still significantly outnumbered that of Lee, withdrew to the northern bank of the Rappahannock.

Jackson's biographer considered Chancellorsville, where 60,000 men defeated 130,000, 'as much the tactical masterpiece of the nineteenth century as was Leuthen of the eighteenth', and most students of the Civil War would agree that it was Lee's most brilliant achievement.[51] And in searching for the reasons why Lee had been able to outmaneuver superior numbers in this week's fighting in the wilderness of Virginia, high on the list would be his superior use of intelligence, both at the operational and the tactical level.

Ironically, while Hooker was hampered in acquiring strategic intelligence, his tactical intelligence was more than adequate. Thanks to his 'balloons in the air', he knew early in the afternoon of 1 May that Lee was moving out from Fredericksburg to attack before there had been any contact on the ground. But instead of utilizing this information, Hooker seemed overwhelmed by it, while Sedgwick convinced himself that this must be a trap. The next day Hooker also had ample warning that a substantial Confederate column was movng toward his flank or rear, and again he did not take appropriate action.

Several weeks after the battle the Balloon Corps was disbanded. In part this was a bureaucratic decision made to resolve a conflict between

Professor Lowe and a captain of engineers who was placed in overall
command of the Balloon Corps: protocol, accountability, and the amount
of pay Lowe received were the issues. And since Hooker's chief of staff
later claimed that he could not recall uses 'of any value' during the battle[52]
it almost appears as if the decision was made to make the balloons the
scapegoat for the battle! The message traffic from the aeronauts published
in the *Official Records*, however, suggests that the problem was not in the
quality of the intelligence, but in the ability of the Union commanders to
make use of it. Had the Union forces in their next battle possessed a
balloon in addition to the signal station on Little Round Top, the course of
the battle, particularly on the second day would have been far different.[53]
Instead the balloons were soon to be sold as government surplus.

NOTES

A version of this essay was first published in the *US Army War College Guide*.

1. John Bigelow, Jr., *The Campaign of Chancellorsville: A Strategic and Tactical Study* (New Haven, 1910), pp.40–49.
2. Major General R.E. Colston, 'Lee's Knowledge of Hooker's Movements', Robert Underwood Johnson and Clarence Clough Buel (eds.), *Battles and Leaders of the Civil War*, 4 vols. (New York, 1888), Vol.III, p.233; Bigelow, *Chancellorsville*, p.xii; *The War of the Rebellion: A Compilation of the Official, 128 vols., Records of the Union and Confederate Armies* (Washington, 1887), XIX, Part 1, pp.801–4.
3. George H. Cassamajor, 'The Federal Secret Service', in Francis Trevelyan Miller (ed.), *The Photographic History of the Civil War* (10 vols., New York, 1911), VIII, pp.269–76.
4. Ibid., p.276.
5. Francis A. Lord, *They Fought for the Union* (New York, 1940), p.133; Bigelow, *Chancellorsville*, p.47).
6. Lord, *They Fought for the Union*, p.133.
7. *Official Records*, XXV, Pt.1, pp.194–5.
8. Ibid., Pt.2, pp.99–100, 630–31.
9. Archie P. McDonald (ed.), *Make me a Map of the Valley: The Civil War Journal of Stonewall Jackson's Topographer* (Dallas, 1973), p.116.
10. *Official Records* XXV, Pt.2, pp.713–15.
11. Robert Debs Heinl, Jr., *Dictionary of Military and Naval Quotations* (Annapolis, 1966), p.160.
12. Casamajor, 'The Federal Secret Service', p.284; John W. Hedley, 'The Confederate Secret Service', *Miller's Photographic History*, VIII, p.286.
13. *Official Records*, XXV, Pt.2, pp.700–1.
14. Ibid., pp.702–3. For other specific reports that clarified Lee's picture of what was happening on the other side of the river, see ibid., pp.598, 642, 646, 691, 724–5.
15. Ibid., pp.101, 114.
16. Bvt. Brig. Gen. Albert J. Myer, *A Manual of Signals for the Use of Signal Officers in the Field* (Washington, 1877).
17. A.W. Greely, 'The Signal Service', *Photographic History of the Civil War*, VIII, p.309.
18. *Official Records*, XXV, Pt.2, pp.738, 752.
19. On 21 May 1863 Hooker's chief of staff forwarded a Richmond newspaper 'of yesterday'. Ibid., p.333.

20. *Official Records*, XXV, Pt.2, pp.239–41, 790.
21. Ibid., pp.258, 269–70, 316.
22. Lord, *They Fought for the Union*, p.135.
23. McDonald, *Make me a Map of the Valley*, p.125.
24. *Official Records*, XXV, Pt.2, p.351.
25. Ibid., pp.153–4, 209, 267, 269.
26. Ibid., pp.257–8.
27. Douglas Southall Freeman, *R.E. Lee: A Biography* (4 vols., New York, 1936), III, p.327. For an account of the role played by Union cavalry throughout the Chancellorsville campaign, see Stephen Z. Starr, *The Union Cavalry in the Civil War, I. From Fort Sumter to Gettysburg, 1861–1863*.
28. Eugene B. Block, *Above the Civil War: the Story of Thaddeus Lowe, Balloonist, Inventor, Railway Builder* (Berkeley, 1966), pp.2–3.
29. F. Stansbury Haydon, *Aeronautics in the Union and Confederate Armies, with a survey of Military Aeronautics prior to 1861* (Baltimore, 1941), Vol.1, pp.1–38, passim.
30. Captain W.Z. Glassford, 'The Balloon in the Civil War', *Journal of the Military Service Institution of the United States*, XVIII (March, 1896), p.265.
31. Longstreet is quoted in Block, *Above the Civil War*, p.96.
32. *Official Records*, XXV, Pt.2, p.752. According to Bigelow, 'throughout the operations ... Lee underestimated the strength of Hooker's army, and Hooker overestimated that of Lee's'. *Campaign of Chancellorsville*, p.158 n.
33. *Official Records*, XXV, Pt.2, pp.198, 322, 327, 332–3.
34. Ibid., p.371.
35. Lee to Stuart, 12 March 1863. Ibid., pp.664, 669.
36. Lee to Stuart, 16 April 1863. Ibid., pp.737.
37. Lee to Davis, 16 April 1863. Ibid., pp.724–5. 'If there are any two-years' men that you consider unreliable, in consequence of the near expiration of their term of service, you will leave them on duty with the division left behind.' S. Williams, Assistant Adjutant-General, to Commanding Officer, Second Corps, 27 April 1863. Ibid., p.267.
38. Ibid., pp.679, 701, 826.
39. Ibid., pp.238, 715.
40. See ibid., pp.114, 253, 728; Bigelow, *Chancellorsville*, p.139.
41. *Official Records*, XXV, Pt.1, p.796; Pt.2, pp.744–45.
42. Lee to Davis, 29 April 1863, ibid., Pt.2, p.756.
43. Ibid., pp.761–62. These 'arrangements' included constructing a defensive line at Zoar Church, about three miles east of Chancellorsville.
44. Ibid., Pt.1, p.199; Pt.2, p.306.
45. Ibid., Pt.2, pp.277–78, 288, 301, 324, 333, 336.,
46. Ibid., p.330. For reports of the arrival of Hood's division, see ibid., p.332–33.
47. Ibid., pp.328, 330, 332–3.
48. Ibid., p.337.
49. Ibid., Pt.1, pp.386, 628.
50. Hooker as quoted in Bigelow, *Chancellorsville*, p.126.
51. G.F.R. Henderson, *Stonewall Jackson and the American Civil War* (2 vols., London, 1906), II, p.470.
52. Glassford, 'Balloon in the Civil War', p.265; Block, *Above the Civil War*, pp.101–102.
53. General E.P. Alexander, *Military Memoirs of a Confederate* (Bloomington, 1962), p.352.

Lee at Gettysburg:
A General Without Intelligence

JAY LUVAAS

With the retreat of the Army of the Potomac across the Rappahannock and the subsequent arrival of Lieutenant General James Longstreet and his two detached divisions from operations around Suffolk, south of the James River, Lee was now free to return to his original plan to invade Pennsylvania. As early as 23 February Jedediah Hotchkiss, Stonewall Jackson's celebrated map-maker and reputedly 'the best topographical engineer' in the army, had been ordered to 'prepare a map of the Valley of Virginia extended to Harrisonburg ... and then on to Philadelphia', and to keep the project 'a profound secret'.[1] Such a move, Lee later reassured the Secretary of War, would offer 'the readiest method of relieving the pressure' on Confederate forces in the west, and he had already begun preparations for his offensive when Major General Joseph Hooker crossed the Rappahannock on his vast turning movement to Chancellors-ville.[2] After the battle, which one authority has described as 'perhaps more nearly a flawless battle ... than any ... ever planned and executed by an American commander',[3] Lee reorganized his army. He expanded his two corps into three, explaining that 30,000 men 'are more than one man can properly handle and keep under his eye in battle ... They are always beyond the range of his vision, and frequently beyond his reach', a consideration now increased by the recent loss of 'Stonewall' Jackson at Chancellorsville.[4] Lee also perfected the battalion system of artillery that had been such a vital factor in his most recent victory.

His most pressing problem, however, was to lay hands on sufficient additional cavalry to organize a second mounted division, which Lee was now convinced he needed. 'If I could get two good divisions of cavalry,' he explained to the President, 'we ought to resist the three of the enemy.' The catalyst in this line of reasoning was the recent raid of Major General George Stoneman's Union Cavalry Corps against Confederate com-munications near Richmond during the Chancellorsville campaign, which had an abrupt effect upon Lee's thinking.

> Stoneman has been running wild over the State, cutting our rail-roads, etc., and even going to within sight of Richmond ... He must be restricted in his operations or we shall be ruined. ... Every

expedition will augment their boldness and increase their means of doing us harm, as they will become better acquainted with the country and more familiar with its roads. Where can we obtain reinforcements of cavalry from?[5]

Lee's cavalry was ultimately strengthened by the addition of two brigades which had been operating in the Shenandoah Valley and western Virginia, but as the next campaign was to demonstrate, this did not enable him to solve the problem.

In many ways the Gettysburg campaign looks like a mirror image of Chancellorsville: this time it was the Confederate cavalry that was absent when the armies met in battle, the Union commander who selected the ground, the Confederate attacks which were ill-timed and disjointed – and it was Lee who was forced to withdraw. The battle itself seems almost like the crowning act of a Greek tragedy, with Lee's supreme confidence in his army replacing the *hubris* in the climax of the drama, for such it is generally viewed to this day.

The battles – Lee's best and his worst – were fought back to back. This study attempts to assess the role of intelligence throughout the Gettysburg campaign, not so much to blame Stuart or to relieve him of the responsibility for what happened, but rather to offer fresh insights into the role of intelligence in Civil War military operations.

Lee's purpose for invading Pennsylvania did not change after Chancellorsville. As early as 16 April he had proposed to President Davis:

> We should assume the aggressive by the 1st of May, when we may expect General Hooker's army to be weakened by the expiration of the term of service of many of his regiments, and before new recruits can be received. If we could be placed in a condition to make a vigorous advance at that time, I think the [Shenandoah] Valley could be swept of [Federals] ... and the army opposite me be thrown north of the Potomac. I believe greater relief would in this way be afforded to the armies in Middle Tennessee and on the Carolina coast than by any other method.[6]

Lee returned to the subject a few days after the battle, claiming that if he could advance beyond the Rappahannock he might draw Union troops away from other threatened points in North Carolina, the Virginia Peninsula, and the Shenandoah Valley. 'It would have been folly,' he later explained to one of his subordinates,

> to have divided my army; the armies of the enemy were too far apart for me to attempt to fall upon them in detail. I considered the problem in every possible phase, and to my mind it resolves itself into the choice of one of two things – either to retire on Richmond and

stand a siege, which must ultimately have ended in surrender, or to invade Pennsylvania. I chose the latter.[7]

Lee later proposed that another Confederate force advance into Western Virginia, that Confederate armies in Tennessee move against weakened Union forces in Kentucky, and that the flamboyant General P.T.G. Beauregard be sent to Culpeper to organize a 'shadow army' that would 'not only effect a diversion most favorable' for his own invading columns, 'but would ... relieve us of any apprehension of an attack upon Richmond during our absence'. Nor did he begin operations of his own until he received 'reliable intelligence' that Union troops at Yorktown and Gloucester Point were moving northward *away* from Richmond – possibly 'to cover some movement of Hooker's to the Lower Rappahannock and across'.[8]

On 3 June Lee began to shift the bulk of his forces from Fredericksburg to the vicinity of Culpeper. Longstreet's corps began its march that day, followed a short time later by that of Ewell. The cavalry under Major General J.E.B. Stuart had been concentrated at Culpeper since the opening stages of the Chancellorsville campaign.[9]

1. The build-up at Culpeper, 3–10 June
2. The advance to the Potomac, 11–15 June
3. The invasion of Pennsylvania, 16–27 June
4. The move to concentrate, 28 June–1 July

Each was governed by what the opposing commanders knew – or did not know – about events 'on the other side of the hill', as the Duke of Wellington once described it, only in this case it was first a river and then a mountain range that helped to conceal the movements of each army from the searching eyes of the other.

* * *

While the infantry of Ewell and Longstreet marched toward Culpeper, Lee remained uncertain about enemy intentions. For in marked contrast to the days before Chancellorsville, it was no longer easy for his spies to penetrate Union lines. Hooker had reorganized his outposts and the Union cavalry had dramatically improved. Indeed, Lee was not even sure that the mass of Hooker's army was near Fredericksburg, for he had been unable to determine 'its exact position or intention'. This uncertainty made Lee fear that Hooker might be planning to embark a force at Aquia, steam down the Potomac and land somewhere up the James, which would force him to call off his offensive and fall back to defend Richmond. He instructed Lieutenant General A.P. Hill, whose corps had remained in the lines at Fredericksburg, to order a signal officer on the Potomac 'to discover what is doing on the Potomac and at Aquia', and to keep him informed about transports passing on the river.[10]

In contrast, Union intelligence knew more of what was happening on the enemy's side of the Rappenhannock than Lee did, for on the eve of the campaign Colonel George Sharpe, a former infantry regimental commander who had been given the job in February of forming an intelligence service, had submitted a detailed estimate of Confederate strength, positions and intentions based on reports from uniformed scouts and undercover agents. It is included here as a good example of intelligence in this stage of the Civil war, and also to help readers set the stage for coming operations. The document came from the Provost-Marshal-General's Office and is dated 27 May 1863.

1. The enemy's line in front of us is much more contracted than during the winter. It extends from Banks' Ford, on a line parallel with the river, to near Moss Neck. Anderson's division is on their left. McLaws' is next, and in rear of Fredericksburg. Early is massed about Hamilton's Crossing, and Trimble's is directly in the rear of Early. Rodes' (D.H. Hill's old division) is farther to the right, and back from the river, and A.P. Hill is the right of their line, resting nearly on Moss Neck. Each of these six divisions have five brigades.

2. Picket's division, of six brigades, has come up from Suffolk, and is at Taylorsville, near Hanover Junction.

3. Hood's division, of four brigades, has also left from the front of Suffolk, and is between Louisa Court-House and Gordonsville.

4. Ten days ago there was in Richmond only the City Battalion, 2,700 strong, commanded by General Elzey.

5. There are three brigades of cavalry 3 miles from Culpeper Court-House, toward Kelly's Ford. They can at present turn out only 4,700 men for duty, but have many dismounted men, and the horses are being constantly and rapidly recruited by the spring growth of grass. These are Fitz. Lee's, William H. Fitzhugh Lee's, and Wade Hampton's brigades.

6. General Jones is still in the Valley, near New Market, with about 1,400 cavalry and twelve pieces of light artillery.

7. Mosby is above Warrenton, with 200 men.

8. The Confederate army is under marching orders, and an order from General Lee was very lately read to the troops, announcing a campaign of long marches and hard fighting, in a part of the country where they would have no railroad transportation.

9. All the deserters say that the idea is very prevalent in the ranks that they are about to move forward upon or above our right flank.

According to Douglas Southall Freeman, this clear and concise report was 'correct in nearly every particular'. Hooker apparently paid little attention to the report, but had Lee known of its existence, such evidence of an improved Union intelligence capability should have given him cause for reflection.[11]

From a variety of sources, it was apparent to Union authorities that Lee was up to something. On 3 June, Brigadier General A. Pleasanton, commanding the Cavalry Corps, forwarded a note to army headquarters from a G.S. Smith, presumably a secret agent, to the effect 'that this movement of General Lee's is not intended to menace Washington, but to try his hand again toward Maryland, or to call off your attention while General Stuart goes there'.[12] From Banks' Ford the Union observation balloon reported the next day that Confederates were moving northward along the Telegraph Road, while on the 5th Brigadier General John Buford, commanding a cavalry division, reported 'reliable' information from a refugee that 'all of the available cavalry of the Confederacy is in Culpeper country'. To the Military Department of Washington it was also apparent that Lee had moved his army from Hooker's front, although where he might be headed was still anybody's guess.[13] Meanwhile a contraband (the term for a slave who had escaped or been bought into Union lines) correctly reported that Lee himself was still at Fredericksburg on the night of 5 June, while A.P. Hill's were positioned in such a way to persuade Major General John Sedgwick, commanding the Union VI Corps, that he could not move 200 yards 'without bringing on a general fight'.[14]

Hooker reacted to these reports on 7 June by ordering his cavalry across the Rappahannock to determine the strength and nature of the Confederate forces at Culpeper. Because it was assumed that Stuart's cavalry was about to start a major raid north of the river, Hooker decided to reinforce his mounted arm with a specially selected force of infantry commanded by Brigadier General Adelbert Ames to help block any advance of enemy cavalry. The infantry, it was specified, must be 'well disciplined and drilled, capable of marching rapidly, and of endurance', to serve as a 'moving point d'appui where the cavalry might rally' and 'which no cavalry force can ... shake'. The cavalry battle at Brandy Station, fought on 9 June, was the largest mounted action of the war. It was also the first time that the Union cavalry had held its own against Jeb Stuart – and it involved the first use of combined arms in the modern sense of the term.[15]

Brandy Station marks the end of the initial phase. Union authorities no longer doubted that Lee was on the move; the only question was where. Pleasanton reported that Stuart's projected raid was intended for Pennsylvania, possibly Pittsburgh, and that it had been learned from a contraband that the Confederates would cross the Rappahannock at Kelly's Ford and march for Aquia Creek if Hooker attempted to attack their rear at Fredericksburg. This particular rumor could well have been planted by Lee to fix Hooker in position for another day or two, for only recently he had commented that 'the chief source of information to the enemy is through our negroes', who are 'easily deceived by proper caution'.[16] In any event, Secretary of War Stanton notified the commander in Pittsburgh that 'this will certainly be the point aimed at by Stuart's raid, which may daily be expected', while General-in-Chief H.W. Halleck sent Brigadier General J.G. Barnard, Chief Engineer of the Washington Defenses, to Pittsburgh to help prepare the defenses and ordered Major General Milroy, commanding a division in Winchester, to fall back to Harper's Ferry 'immediately'. To prepare Pennsylvania to resist the 'invasion', the Department of the Susquehanna was created with headquarters in Chambersburg. Major General Darius Couch, who had commanded II Corps at Chancellorsville, was assigned to command.[17]

* * *

On 10 June Ewell's corps resumed its march, and two days later reached Cedarville, a short distance north of Front Royal, where it was joined by Brigadier General A.G. Jenkins, who had been sent with his cavalry brigade from western Virginia to strengthen Lee's mounted arm in coming operations. Sending Jenkins and an infantry division to dislodge a Union force at Berryville, Ewell moved vigorously upon the Union works at Winchester with the rest of his command. In the second battle of Winchester (13–14 June) the Confederates captured 4,000 prisoners, 28 guns, a considerable quantity of ordnance, commissary and quarter-master's stores, and expelled the Union forces from the Shenandoah Valley at a trifling cost. Longstreet's corps left Culpeper the following day and moved along the eastern slope of the Blue Ridge to occupy Ashby's and Snicker's Gaps, while Hill's corps marched from Fredericksburg to Culpeper, where it arrived on 16 June.

Hooker's initial proposal, once it became apparent that the camps behind Fredericksburg had began to disappear, was to cross the river and 'pitch into Lee's rear', but Lincoln warned bluntly against such a move:

> In case you find Lee coming to the north of the Rappahannock, I would by no means cross to the south of it. If he should leave a rear force at Fredericksburg, tempting you to fall upon it, it would fight in intrenchments and have you at disadvantage, and ... worst you at that point, while his main force would in some way be getting an advantage of you northward. ... I would not take any risk of being entangled upon the river, like an ox jumped half over a fence and liable to be torn by dogs front and rear, without a fair chance to gore

one way or kick the other. If Lee would come to my side of the river I would keep on the same side. ...[18]

On 11 June Hooker ordered his army to be ready to move at short notice, but he was fixed in place by reports from his balloons that the Confederates were daily receiving reinforcements and now enjoyed 'a numerical superiority over me!' On 12 June new Confederate camps were reported at Fredericksburg.[19] The timing of this report, given the fact that no such reinforcements are mentioned by Confederates and had any been available on this date they certainly would have been sent directly to Culpeper, strongly suggests that Hooker was a victim of good deception. The very next day Hill's corps departed for Culpeper!

On 13 June, however, word came from Pleasanton that two boys ('carried off from Fairfax some six weeks ago and ... good Union lads') had left Culpeper the day before and reported that Ewell and Longstreet had passed through, headed for the mountains. Once convinced that the Confederate army was indeed marching toward the Valley, although 'a good many troops and batteries' were still assumed to be at Fredericksburg, and guided no doubt by Lincoln's insistence that 'Lee's army, and not Richmond, is your sure objective point', Hooker decided to transfer operations from the line of the Aquia to the Orange and Alexandria Railroad. That night he ordered his troops to withdraw from their positions on the Rappahannock.[20]

The evidence was overwhelming: Lee was headed for Pennsylvania. 'As matters look now', General Couch reported to Stanton on 15 June, 'all south of the Susquehenna will be swept.'[21]

For Lee's part, all seemed to be going well. He was still concerned about his lack of cavalry, which in his judgement was not 'half as much as I require to keep back the enemy's mounted force in my front', but he enjoyed the initiative, which meant that Hooker's movements would largely be determined by his own. 'I think the enemy had been mystified as to our movements,' he wrote on June 13, 'until the publication of my dispatch to the [War] Department of the cavalry fight on the 9th, and the comments and assertions of some of our Richmond papers. ... Yesterday movements were discovered up the Rappahannock and pickets report they continued all night.'[22]

Obviously Lee still underestimated the flow of intelligence to enemy headquarters, for it was this and not the Press that revealed his movements: Union reports never mentioned the Richmond papers.

Perhaps Lee reacted as he did because of his own reliance upon newspapers for strategic intelligence. Only three days before he had written to President Davis at length regarding 'recent political movements in the United States and the comments of influential newspapers upon

them'. Lee urged the Confederate President to give all the encouragement possible, consistent with the truth, to the rising peace party
of the North. 'As he read the Northern newspapers with care, he was
confirmed in his belief that the projected campaign in Pennsylvania would
strengthen the arguments of the Northern peace party.'[23]

Ominously, Lee wrote to Longstreet on 15 June: 'I have been waiting
for the arrival of Stuart, or of information from him, but as yet have
received none'.[24]

* * *

Rodes' division crossed the Potomac near Williamsport on 15 June and
spent the next three days on the northern bank gathering supplies. On 17
June Lee instructed Ewell to move Rodes' division to Hagerstown 'and
operate in the enemy's country according to the plan proposed. Give
out that your movement is for the purpose of enveloping Harper's
Ferry'. Accordingly, on the 19th Rodes moved his division to Hagerstown,
while Johnson's division crossed to Sharpsburg and Early marched to
Shepherdstown to threaten Harper's Ferry. In these positions Ewell's
divisions waited two days until Lee's other corps had closed up, and on 22
June the march was resumed toward Greencastle, Pennsylvania. Halting
one day at Chambersburg to secure additional supplies, Rodes and
Johnson's divisions pushed on to Carlisle, which they reached on 27 June,
while Early's division crossed South Mountain to Gettysburg and then
proceeded to York to cut the Northern Central Railroad running from
Baltimore to Harrisburg, and to destroy the bridge over the Susquehanna
at Wrightsville. Longstreet and Hill followed Ewell as far as Chambersburg, where their men encamped on the 27th.

Meanwhile the Army of the Potomac was marching fast in pursuit. A
series of indecisive but lively cavalry combats were fought at Aldie,
Middleburg and Upperville (17–21 June), as the Union cavalry endeavored
to penetrate Stuart's protective screen and determine the location of Lee's
infantry. 'Lee is playing his old game of covering the gaps and moving his
forces up the Shenandoah Valley', Pleasanton reported on 20 June.

> Longstreet's corps has not passed through either Middleburg
> or Union. I am holding both. ... Stuart is just in front and has called
> up Hampton's Legion and Fitzhugh Lee from Warrenton. Some
> infantry soldiers with knapsacks on were found on the field
> yesterday. These belong to Garnett's and Pickett's divisions [of
> Longstreet's Corps]. The gaps in the Blue Ridge are guarded, and
> from their signal station they can see every man we can bring against
> them. I judge Longstreet has the covering of the gaps, and is moving
> up his force as the rebel army advances. ... I have been attacking

Stuart to make him keep his people together, so that they cannot
scout and find out anything about our forces. ... We cannot force the
gaps. ... in the presence of a superior force.[25]

For his part Lee was uncertain as to the whereabouts of the Union
forces. 'I have heard nothing of the movements of General Hooker either
from General Stuart or yourself,' he wrote to Longstreet on 17 June.

and therefore can form no opinion of the best move against him. If a
part of our force could have operated east of the mountains, it would
have served more to confuse him, but as you have turned off to the
Valley, and ... all the trains have taken that route, I hope it is for the
best. At any rate, it is too late to change from any information I
have.[26]

During the next two days scouts confirmed that Hooker was moving
toward the Potomac, but whether his objective was Harpers Ferry or
Leesburg was not yet clear. Lee wrote to Ewell on 19 June:

You must therefore be guided in your movements by controlling
circumstances around you ... and carry out the plan you proposed,
so far as in your judgment may seem fit. If your advance causes
Hooker to cross the Potomac ... Longstreet can follow you ... As
soon as I can get definite information as to the movements of
General Hooker ... I will write to you again.[27]

Two days later Lee learned that Hooker had abandoned the line of the
Rappahannock and was falling back toward the Potomac. 'Do you know
where he is and what he is doing?' he inquired of Stuart.

I fear he will steal a march on us and get across the Potomac before we
are aware. If you find that he is moving northward and that two
[cavalry] brigades can guard the Blue Ridge and take care of your
rear, you can move with the other three [brigades] into Maryland
and take position on General Ewell's right, place yourself in
communication with him, guard his flank, keep him informed of the
enemy's movements, and collect all the supplies you can for the
army.

This was the fateful 'order' that led Stuart on his controversial ride around
the entire Union army. The order was submitted through Longstreet, who
suggested that if Stuart could get through by passing around the rear of the
enemy, he would be 'less likely to indicate what our plans are'.[28] Whether
or not Stuart was justified in his interpretation or execution of the order
lies beyond the scope of the study – and sometimes beyond reason.

The following day Lee tried to clarify his intention: after crossing the

Potomac east of the mountains Stuart was to 'move on and feel the right of Ewell's troops collecting information', for as one of the aides privy to Lee's thought at the time has recorded, 'the great object of having his cavalry on our right was to keep us informed of the enemy's movements'. From the moment Stuart struck out on his own nothing was heard from him until he appeared at Gettysburg on the second day of the battle, although he apparently sent at least one dispatch that never reached Lee.[29] True, Lee had other cavalry with the army – one brigade was with Ewell, two brigades continued to guard the passes through the Blue Ridge, and still another was moving along his left flank west of the Cumberland Valley – but two of these brigades were not organic to the Army of Northern Virginia and the others were not commanded by Stuart's favorite subordinates. More to the point, none of these units was in a position to provide the kind of information that Lee needed during Stuart's absence.

On 26 June Lee arrived at Chambersburg. Early's division was within six miles of York and the rest of Ewell's corps had reached Carlisle. Assuming that Hooker had not yet crossed the Potomac, Lee decided to wait until he had some word from Stuart. 'Our army is in good spirits, not overfatigued, and can be concentrated on any one point in 24 hours or less,' he explained to one of his generals.[30]

But by 27 June Hooker had already reached Frederick, with three of his corps encamped at Middletown, one at Knoxville, two at Frederick, and a seventh corps nearby.[31] The next night a scout who had been sent out by Longstreet before the army left Fredericksburg made his way to Longstreet's headquarters with positive information that three Union corps were near Frederick when he had passed through – more accurate information, Longstreet wryly observed, 'than we could have expected if we had been relying upon our cavalry'. The scout was questioned by Lee, who promptly notified Ewell to call off his advance against Harrisburg and march instead 'in the direction of Gettysburg, via Heidlersburg ... *east* of the mountains'.[32]

There is some confusion about the date of this last order to Ewell. The published text, dated 28 July, was reconstructed 'from memory' by one of Lee's former aides years after the war, and because it refers to another communication written the previous evening in which Lee notified Ewell that Hooker was reported to have crossed the Potomac and was then in Frederick County, it could be argued that Lee had received some intelligence of enemy movements *before* the news conveyed by Longstreet's scout. It is more likely, however, that Colonel Marshall's memory was at fault as to the date of the order and that this was in fact written on the 29th, *after* Lee had learned that the Union army had already crossed the Potomac.

In any case, there is contemporary evidence to suggest that Lee had written to Ewell on the 26th to indicate his belief that the coming battle would occur 'near Fredericks City or Gettysburg'. On the 27th he said much the same thing to Major General I.R. Trimble, asking specifically about the terrain around Gettysburg. Trimble recalled that Lee, placing his hand on the map over Gettysburg, had remarked: 'hereabout we shall probably meet the enemy and fight a great batle'. If Trimble's recollections are correct, for at least a week Lee had believed that his march into Pennsylvania had caused the Union forces to be unsure of his location or intentions and therefore 'obliged to follow by forced marches'. Years later Trimble recalled Lee's assessment of the situation:

> They will come up, probably through Frederick; broken down with hunger and hard marching, strung out on a long line and much demoralized, when they come into Pennsylvania. I shall throw an overwhelming force on their advance, crush it, follow up the success, drive one corps back on another, and by successive repulses and surprises before they can concentrate, create a panic and virtually destroy the army.[33]

Obviously Lee had been studying his maps while waiting for news from Stuart, and one glance at the road network on the Hotchkiss map could have told him that Gettysburg, the hub of most roads running through the mountains or leading in the general direction of Baltimore or Washington, would be vital terrain to either army. Indeed, it was for this reason that Major General B.B. McClellan, in his official report of the Maryland Campaign the previous fall, had pointed to the importance of Gettysburg for an army operating in the Cumberland Valley.[34] Despite the lack of news from Stuart, therefore, Lee had pretty much decided where he might expect to meet the enemy, for in this respect strategy, as Jomini had written 25 years earlier, was indeed 'the art of making war upon the map'.[35] This most recent confirmation of enemy movements only indicated the fastest road ('turnpike most of the way') that Ewell could use to get there.

The problem for Union authorities was the reverse: each day brought a greater volume of reports and rumors as army scouts, signal detachments, prisoners or Confederate deserters, civilian refugees, aroused citizens, and newspapers revealed alarming and often conflicting details of Lee's advance. On 17 June the Army of the Potomac was ordered to march to the Potomac via Leesburg and the various corps were instructed to keep in communication with each other: commanders, in the event of an engagement, were told to 'march to the sound of heaviest firing'. 'Try and hunt up somebody from Pennsylvania who knows something, and has a cool enough head to judge what is the actual state of affairs,' Hoker's chief of

staff wrote in obvious frustration. His letter reveals the confusion that
evidently existed at army headquarters.

> Seven or eight thousand men are reported at Williamsport. Couch
> reports his pickets driven in. Enemy reported to have appeared at
> Poolesville, and everywhere else in Maryland, Pennsylvania, and
> Western Virginia. Cavalry enough is reported to have appeared
> to fill up the whole of Pennsylvania and leave no room for the
> inhabitants. Since we were not allowed to cross [at Fredericksburg]
> and whip A.P. Hill, while Longstreet and Ewell were moving off
> through Culpeper ... we have lost the opportunity of doing a thing
> which we knew to a certainty we could accomplish. My impression
> now is that there is not a rebel, excepting scouts, this side of the
> Shenandoah Valley; that Lee is in as much uncertainty as to our
> whereabouts and what we are doing as we are as to his; that his
> movement on the Upper Potomac is a cover for a cavalry raid on the
> north side of the river, and a movement of his troops farther west,
> where he can turn up at some weak spot.
> Our scouts tonight will be in Fredericksburg, Culpeper,
> Warrenton, Salem, and one on the way in from Richmond. Those
> sent up to Western Maryland cannot get there before tomorrow
> night. We cannot go boggling round until we know what we are going
> after.
> Get any news you can that you know is definite and reliable, and
> bring out with you. Will they cashier any of these people who send in
> such stampeding reports?[36]

But to another staff officer at army headquarters the problem was
Hooker himself. 'Halleck is running the Marching and Hooker has the
role of a Subordinate,' the Provost Marshal General recorded in his diary.
Hooker

> acts like a man without a plan and is entirely at a loss what to
> do, or how to match the enemy, or counteract his movements.
> Whatever he does is the result of impulse, now, after having failed so
> signally, at Chancellorsville. ... He has treated our 'Secret Service
> Department' [headed by Colonel Sharpe] which has furnished him
> with the most astonishingly correct information with indifference at
> first, and now with insult. ... We get accurate information, but
> Hooker will not use it and insults all who differ from him in opinion.
> He has declared that the enemy are over 100,000 strong – it is his only
> salvation to make it appear that the enemy's forces are larger than his
> own which is all false and he knows it. He knows that Lee is his master
> and is afraid to meet him in fair battle.[37]

The problem was also too much information – more, in fact, than the system could handle. Indeed, there were too many systems. In addition to Colonel Sharpe's intelligence organization and Pleasanton's cavalry in the Army of the Potomac, the Department of the Susquehenna, which embraced all of Pennsylvania east of the Laurel Hill Mountains, ran its own intelligence operations; so, too, did the Eighth Army Corps or Middle Department, which at one time or another controlled the garrisons at Winchester, Harpers Ferry, and later French's division near Frederick from headquarters in Baltimore. The Department of Washington was actively seeking intelligence of enemy movements in Maryland and Northern Virginia.[38]

But there was no single chain of command or channel of communication; messages were directed to the President, the Secretary of War, the General in Chief, the governors of threatened states, or to each army or military division commander. There was no official distribution list so it is impossible to determine exactly what information any commander had at a given time. Even Brigadier General H. Haupt, in charge of the Military Railway Department, had made 'very extensive arrangements ... to procure information from scouts' and was running what in effect was his own intelligence network.[39]

Because he could not be everywhere at once, Hooker on 25 June announced the formation of a Left Wing comprising the I, III, and XI corps, to be commanded by Major General John F. Reynolds. He ordered Reynold to cross the Potomac at Edwards Ferry and occupy the principal gaps through South Mountain. Almost immediately the picture began to come into clearer focus, if only because Reynolds now received information passed on from XI Corps, which happened to be nearest the Confederates, and from Major General Julius Stahel, commanding the cavalry division assigned to the Department of Washington. Stahel confirmed the next day that there were no Confederates in any of the gaps and no signs that the enemy intended to move east of South Mountain.

The whole rebel army is marching toward Harrisburg. Ewell's whole corps passed through Hagerstown and Smithsburg last Tuesday [23 June]. Sixty-six pieces of artillery, belonging to this corps, passed through Hagerstown on Tuesday, and sixteen pieces belonging to the same corps passed through Smithsburg the same day. Their force is estimated at from 25,000 to 30,000. Both columns were marching in the direction of Greencastle. On Thursday, the 25th instant, [R.H.] Anderson's division, of Hill's corps, passed through Boonsborough about 6 a.m. They were three hours passing through the town. This column crossed at Shepherdstown. Ewell's corps crossed at Williamsport and Shepherdstown.

Stahel also informed Reynolds that he had sent out scouting parties 'of perfectly reliable men' to penetrate Confederate lines and learn their strength and plans. On the basis of this information and reports from the signal station on South Mountain, Reynolds could confirm to Army Headquarters that the entire Confederate army was indeed in Pennsylvania, and that a sizeable force (Early's division) was headed for Gettysburg.[40]

One cannot read the message traffic for the next several days without being impressed by the efficiency of Colonel Sharpe's Secret Service Department and the skill of his agents. After the Confederates had passed through a town Union scouts – many of them familiar with the new Confederate order of battle – would return to question citizens about what they had learned of Confederate strengths, movements, and intentions. One of his most active scouts, a man named John C. Babcock who worked from Frederick, Maryland, sent frequent detailed reports during this crucial phase of the campaign, supplementing messages from the signal station on South Mountain which had an 'extensive and clear view' of enemy movements in the vicinity of Sharpsburg, Boonsborough and Shepherdstown.[41]

On 27 June Hooker was relieved and instructed to turn over command of the Army of the Potomac to Major General George G. Meade. The campaign now entered its final phase.

* * *

In the absence of any intelligence it was impossible for Lee to be sure of his opponent's location and therefore of his intentions, but to protect his own line of communications through the Valley he decided to concentrate the army east of the mountains. On 29 June he ordered Hill's corps to move to Cashtown, with Longstreet to follow the next day. Ewell, as we have seen, had been directed to join the army at Cashtown or Gettysburg, 'as circumstances might require'. The arrival of Union cavalry in Gettysburg was not known to Lee, and the inclement weather caused him to conduct his march through the mountains 'with a view to the comfort of the troops'.

On 30 June Major General Henry Heth, commanding Lieutenant General A.P. Hill's leading division, sent a brigade into Gettysburg to procure supplies. The brigade, however, was unable to accomplish its mission because of the presence of Union troops – how many or what kind they did not know. It was known, however, that Lee had no desire to bring on a general engagement until his army was concentrated, so Brigadier General James J. Pettigrew ordered his men to return to Cashtown.

Hill did not share Pettigrew's concerns. 'The only force at Gettysburg is cavalry', he assured his subordinate, 'probably a detachment of

observation. I am just from General Lee, and the information he has from
his scouts corroborates what I have received from mine ... the enemy are
still at Middleburg and have not yet struck their tents.' Heth then
requested permission to take his entire division the next morning to get
shoes at Gettysburg. Hill agreed, and as Lee rode forward through the
mountains on 1 July, he was startled to hear the sound of distant guns.[42]
Now, probably more than any previous time in the campaign, he needed
Stuart.

Meade, on the other hand, was kept well informed. On 28 June he had
received a detailed report of enemy movements from a scout that could be
confirmed by information from other sources.

> Thomas McCammon, blacksmith, a good man, from Hagerstown,
> left there on horseback at 11 a.m. to-day. Rebel cavalry came first
> a week ago last Monday. General [A.J.] Jenkins having 1,200
> mounted infantry, said to be picked men from Jackson's men, and
> 300 or 400 cavalry of his own. The cavalry went back and forth out of
> Pennsylvania driving horses and cattle, and the first infantry came
> yesterday a week ago – General Ewell's men. He came personally
> last Saturday, and was at the Catholic church Sunday, with General
> Rodes and two other generals. On Monday he left in the direction of
> Greencastle, in the afternoon, Rodes having left the same morning.
> Rebel troops have passed every day, more or less, since; some days
> only three or four regiments or a brigade, and some days, yesterday,
> for instance, all of Longstreet's command passed through excepting
> two brigades. Saw Longstreet yesterday. He and Lee had their
> headquarters at Mr. [James H.] Grove's, just beyond town limits,
> toward Greencastle, last night, and left there this a.m. at 8 o'clock.
> Think A.P. Hill went through last Tuesday. Heard from James D.
> Roman, prominent lawyer and leading Confederate sympathizer,
> who was talking in the clerk's office last night; said that their officers
> reported their whole army 100,000 strong, now in Maryland or
> Pennsylvania, excepting the cavalry. Mr [William] Logan, register
> of wills, and Mr. [William H.] Protzman, very fine men in
> Hagerstown have taken pains to count the rebels, and could not
> make them over 80,000. They counted the artillery; made it two
> hundred and seventy-five guns. Some of the regiments have only 175
> men – two that I saw, 150. Largest regiment that I saw was a
> Maryland regiment, and that was about 700. Don't think their
> regiments would range 400. Great amount of transportation; great
> many wagons captured at Winchester. Horses in good condition.
> Ewell rides in a wagon. Two thousand comprise the mounted
> infantry and cavalry. Saw Wilcox's brigade wagons yesterday or

day before. Saw Kershaw's wagons in town yesterday. Kershaw's brigade is in McLaws' division, Longstreet's corps. Know Hood and Armistead. Have passed through Hood's division and Armisteads brigade. Pickett's division is in Longstreet' corps. The Union men in Hagerstown would count them and meet at night. Officers and men in good condition; say they are going to Philadelphia.[43]

That same day Meade's chief of staff received word that Stuart's cavalry had encamped the previous night between Williamstown and Hagerstown, and on the 29th one of Sharpe's scouts reported that Early's division from Ewell's corps had passed through Gettysburg the day before. Meade ordered scouts to be sent to Gettysburg, Hanover, Greencastle, Chambersburg, and Jefferson to ascertain enemy strengths, positions and movements. Lee's army, he informed Halleck, was in the vicinity of Chambersburg. He would not waste force by useless movements in trying to pursue Stuart's cavalry in his rear, but would submit to the cavalry raid 'in some measure' while concentrating all efforts 'to find and fight the enemy'.[44] On 30 June he alerted his corps commanders from his position between Emmitsburg and Westminster.

> The enemy are advancing, probably in strong force, upon Gettysburg. It is the intention to hold this army pretty nearly in the position it now occupies until the plans of the enemy have been more fully developed. ... Corps commanders will avail themselves of all the time at their disposal to familiarize themselves with the roads communicating with the different corps.

Meanwhile Buford's cavalry was posted at Gettysburg, Mechanicstown and in front of Emmitsburg to warn of any Confederate approach.

'I have pushed out the cavalry in all directions to feel for them,' Meade assured Reynolds, 'and so soon as I can make up any positive opinion as to their position, I will move again. In the meantime, if they advance against me, I must concentrate at that point where they show the strongest force.' The next day 'that point' became Gettysburg, where Reynolds' I corps had been ordered even before 'the positive knowledge of the enemy's withdrawal from Harrisburg and concentration was received', although Buford's reports made it clear that Hill's corps was massed at Cashtown and Ewell had already crossed the mountains from Carlisle.[45]

* * *

The role of intelligence during the battle is easily dealt with. Since Meade had sent Buford and later Reynolds to the spot a day before the fighting, with the mission of advising whether 'the nature of the country' would be suitable for an offensive or defensive position, Union commanders obviously enjoyed a general familiarity with the terrain, and throughout the fighting on the first day Buford's cavalry kept the I and XI corps informed of all Confederate columns approaching from the west and north.[46] Because Meade's army occupied the same ground for the next three days, the terrain offered no unpleasant surprises. The Union signal station on Little Round Top unquestionably played an important part in the battle, but more perhaps for its impact on the Confederates than for any specific information it furnished of enemy movements. Because it located where it could detect any movement over Herr Ridge, Lee insisted on the morning of 2 July that Longstreet's column, which he had ordered to attack the Union left flank, follow a route concealed from the prying eyes of Union signal men, which cost the Confederates precious time and quite possibly the battle.

Lee, on the other hand, was crippled for want of good intelligence. Had Stuart been present in his front on 30 June, Lee would have had a much clearer idea of the nature of the Union force in Gettysburg, and if Stuart been there to 'feel out' the single Union cavalry brigade that blocked Heth's attempt to get to Gettysburg the next day, Hill would have had a clearer picture of what he was up against and there would have been no need for a battle unless determined by Lee. Instead Heth felt compelled to send forward two infantry brigades to determine what force, if any, lay behind the screen of Union dismounted cavalry on McPherson Ridge. Hill then decided to reinforce these units, and by the time Lee arrived on the ground, four of his nine divisions were already engaged in hard combat. Lee therefore found himself in a major battle before his army could be concentrated and no one could tell him precisely how far the rest of the Union army was from Gettysburg or when, and by which routes, it could be expected to arrive. 'Coming unexpectedly upon the whole Federal army,' Lee explained in his after-action report,

> to withdraw through the mountains with our extensive trains would have been difficult and dangerous. At the same time we were unable to await an attack, as the country was unfavorable for collecting supplies in the presence of the enemy, who could restrain our foraging parties by holding the mountain passes with local and other troops. A battle had, therefore, become in a measure unavoidable.[47]

If Lee ever considered Longstreet's proposal on the afternoon of 1 July that the Confederates move south around the Round Tops and secure good ground between the Union position and Washington,[48] without intelligence of enemy movements toward the battlefield it could never have been a serious possibility. Lee's map reveals that the road structure south of the Hagerstown pike probably would not support moving a corps at such a distance and across Marsh Creek, and without Stuart to reconnoiter and determine where Union columns were marching and when they could be expected to arrive, Longstreet's alternative was not an option. Confederate efforts to seize Culp's Hill on the first day also were delayed because of the need to send staff officers to investigate reports of enemy movements beyond Ewell's left flank: here, too, adequate cavalry reconnaissance might have changed somewhat the course of the battle: certainly it would have changed the timing of Ewell's movement against the Union right flank.

The absence of Stuart, however, did not necessarily mean that Lee could not have won the battle. There were many things that went wrong for Lee at Gettysburg: his new corps commanders let opportunities slip, his attacks were disjointed, Longstreet seemed sluggish and Lee may well have been overconfident. For the first time he found himself in a fight where he did not have good knowledge of the battlefield, and the hostile inhabitants of area would not enlighten him. Clearly the absence of intelligence narrowed his options.

One of his most serious errors on the morning of 2 June, however, was his mistaken belief that the Union battle line 'extended upon the high ground along the Emmitsburg road' instead of along Cemetery Ridge, where in fact it remained until Major General Daniel E. Sickles, in violation of orders, moved his III Union corps forward to occupy higher ground at the Peach Orchard. This assumption, which resulted in his giving Longstreet unrealistic orders to attack *up* the Emmitsburg road in the direction of the town of Gettysburg,[49] could probably have been rectified simply by sending forward a regiment or two as skirmishers to reconnoiter. Certainly it cannot be attributed to the absence of Stuart, who reached the area about noon on 2 July.

Clearly it was at the *operational level* that the lack of timely intelligence had its most serious effects. By their very nature offensive operations did not favor use of the signal corps, perched on high peaks where enemy movements could be observed. To fulfill this mission as Lee invaded Pennsylvania it would have been necessary to have occupied ground on South Mountain already held by the enemy, and so this means of acquiring deep intelligence was denied to the Confederates. Nor did a basically hostile population provide much helpful information. This time no one volunteered to conduct a Confederate corps by a concealed route to the Union flank, as had happened at Chancellorsville. Stuart's failure to provide timely information of enemy activities deprived Lee of any opportunity to isolate and defeat Meade in detail, which apparently had been his plan – or at least his hope. Moreover, the lack of timely intelligence of Union strength west of Gettysburg on 1 July sucked the Confederates into a battle before Lee could concentrate his army, which was contrary to his instructions.

This was one of those rare occasions during the Civil War when Lee knew less than his opponent throughout the crucial stage of a campaign, which explains, more than any other single factor, why at Gettysburg he was forced to fight a battle without intelligence.

NOTES

1. Archie P. McDonald (ed.), *Make me a Map of the Valley: The Civil War Journal of Stonewall Jackson's Topgrapher* (Dallas, 1973), p.116.
2. Lee to James A. Seddon, 9 April 1863. Clifford Dowdey (ed.), *The Wartime Papers of R.E. Lee* (Boston, 1961), p.430.
3. Douglas Southall Freeman, *R.E. Lee, a Biography* (4 vols., New York, 1936), III, pp.2–3.
4. Lee to Jefferson Davis, 20 My, 1863, *The War of the Rebellion: A Compilation of the Official Records of the Union and Confederate Armies* (128 vols., Washington, 1880–1901), Ser. I, Vol.XXV, Pt.2, p.810. Hereafter *O.R.*
5. Lee to Jefferson Davis, 7 May 1863, Lee to Gen. Samuel Jones, 9 May 1863, *O.R.*, pp.782–83, 789.
6. *O.R.*, XXV, Pt.2, p.725.
7. *O.R.*, XXV, Pt.2, p.791; Maj. Gen. Henry Heth to Rev. J. Wm Jones, June, 1877, in *Southern Historical Society Papers* (Richmond, 1877), IV, p.154. Hereafter *S.H.S.P.* Lee consistently contended that if his army was ever forced to withstand a siege, 'it will be a mere question of time'. Dowdey (ed.), *Wartime Papers of R.E. Lee*, pp.744, 760.
8. Freeman, *Lee*, III, p.52; Lee to Davis, 23 June, 1863, *O.R.*, XXV, Pt.2, pp.847, 851; XXVII, Pt.3, pp.924–25;
9. *O.R.*, XXVII, Pt.2, p.305.
10. *O.R.*, XXV, Pt.2, p.832; XXVII, Pt.3, p.869; Freeman, *Lee*, III, p.24.
11. Wilbur Sturtevant Nye, *Here Come the Rebels* (Baton Rouge, 1965), pp.29–30.
12. Pleasanton to Brig. Gen. Seth Williams, 3 June, *O.R.*, XXVII, Pt.3, p.32. 'Please show the inclosed note to Maj. Gen. Hooker. He knows who Mr. Smith is.'
13. *O.R.*, XXVII, Pt.3, pp.5, 6, 8, 18.
14. Sedgwick to Maj. Gen. Butterfield, Chief of Staff, Army of the Potomac, 5 June 1863, *O.R.*, XXVII, Pt.3, p.13.
15. *O.R.*, XXVII, Pt.3, pp.15, 28; Pt.2, p.1043.
16. Pleasanton to S. Williams, A.A.G., 10 June; pp.47–8; Pleasanton to Hooker, 10 June, p.49; Lee to Lt. Col. J. Critcher, 26 May, *O.R.*, XXV, Pt.2, p.826.
17. *O.R.*, XXVII, Pt.3, pp.36, 50, 54, 68.
18. Ibid., p.31.
19. *O.R.*, XXVII, Pt.1, p.70; Pt.3, p.36.
20. *O.R.*, XXVII, Pt.1, pp.35–8; Pt.3, pp.84, 104.
21. *O.R.*, XXVII, Pt.1, pp.114–29 *passim.*
22. Lee to Seddon, 14 June, *O.R.*, XXVII, Pt.3, p.886.
23. *O.R.*, XXVII, Pt.3, p.881.
24. Lee to Longstreet, 15 June, *O.R.*, XXVII, Pt.3, p.890.
25. *O.R.*, XXVII, Pt.2, pp.316, 464; Pt.3, p.224.
26. *O.R.*, XXVII, Pt.3, p.900.
27. *O.R.*, XXVII, Pt.3, p.905.
28. Longstreet to Stuart, 22 June, *O.R.*, XXVII, Pt.3, p.915.
29. Major General Sir Frederick Maurice (ed.), *An Aide-de-Camp of Lee, being the Papers of Colonel Charles Marshall* (Boston, 1927), pp.201–211.
30. Freeman, *Lee*, III, p.58.
31. *O.R.*, XXVII, Pt.1, p.59.
32. *O.R.*, XXVII, Pt.3, p.943; Lieut. General James Longstreet, 'Lee's Invasion of Pennsylvania', *Battles and Leaders*, III, p.250; Freeman, *Lee*, III, pp.60–62.

33. Maj. Gen. Isaac R. Trimble, 'The Battle and Campaign of Gettysburg', *S.H.S.P.*, XXVI (1898), pp.119–21.
34. *O.R.*, XXVII, Pt.3, p.943. McClellan reported that it was incumbent upon him 'to move slowly and cautiously' until 'I first obtained reliable information that the enemy's object was to move upon Harper's Ferry and the Cumberland Valley, and not upon Baltimore, Washington, or Gettysburg', *O.R.*, XIX, pp.26–27. The Hotchkiss map is reproduced in *The Atlas to Accompany the Official Records of the Union and Confederate Armies* (Washington, 1891–95), Plate no. CXVI.
35. Baron de Jomini, *Summary of the Art of War*, translated from the French by Major O.F. Winship and Lieut. E.E. McLean (New York, 1854), p.79.
36. Butterfield to General R. Ingalls, 17 June, *O.R.*, XXVII, Pt.3, pp.174–5.
37. David S. Sparks (ed.), *Inside Lincoln's Army. The Diary of Marsena Rudolph Patrick, Provost Marshal General, Army of the Potomac* (New York, 1964), pp.260–61.
38. The abstract from returns of these departments for June 30 reveals the location of garrisons and the various commands. *O.R.*, XXVII, Pt.3, pp.440–48.
39. *O.R.*, XXVII, Pt.1, p.22; Pt.3, p.427.
40. *O.R.*, XXVII, Pt.3, pp.334–5.
41. *O.R.*, XXVII, Pt.3, pp.225–8, 248, 286, 351; Edwin C. Fishel, 'The Mythology of Civil War Intelligence', *Civil War History*, Vol.X, No.4 (December 1964), pp.356–7.
42. James I. Robertson, Jr., *General A.P. Hill: The Story of a Confederate Warrior* (New York, 1987), pp.205–6.
43. *O.R.*, XXVII, Pt.1, p.65.
44. Ibid., p.67.
45. *O.R.XXVII*, Pt.3, pp.419–20.
46. *O.R.*, XXVII, Pt.1, p.702.
47. *O.R.*, XXVII, Pt.2, p.308.
48. Lieut. Gen. James Longstreet, 'Lee's Right Wing at Gettysburg', *Battles and Leaders*, III, p.339.
49. Maj. Gen. Lafayette McLaws, 'Gettysburg', *S.H.S.P.*, VII, pp.67–9.

PART TWO

THE FIRST WORLD WAR

British Intelligence in Mesopotamia 1914–16

RICHARD POPPLEWELL

It is an essential part of the duty of intelligence to size up not only what the enemy should be able to accomplish, but also to foretell what he is likely to attempt to accomplish.[1]

The surrender of General Townsend and 13,000 men at Kut al Amara on 29 April 1916 was the British Army's greatest humiliation in the First World War. In comparison with the 19,000 killed on the first day alone of the Somme the loss of manpower was small, but no other British army surrendered with its colours in the course of the war. Indeed none had done so since the battle of Yorktown in 1781 and none was to do so again until the fall of Singapore in 1942. Such a defeat at the hands of an oriental power like Turkey was difficult for the British to comprehend at the time.

At the beginning of the war the British had every reason to believe that the quality of the Turkish Army was low.[2] Its poor performance throughout the nineteenth century had won Turkey the reputation of the 'sick man of Europe'. This image was reinforced by the serious Turkish reverses at the start of the first Balkan War in 1912, particularly as a result of the sophisticated propaganda campaign which the Turks conducted at that time with the main object of enlisting the support of the Muslim population of India. The pamphlets which they sent to India, such as the harrowing *Come over to Mesopotamia and Join Us*, claimed that Turkish Muslims were being mercilessly slaughtered in the Balkans by their more powerful Christian neighbours.[3] At the same time the Turks played on the sympathies of Western Europeans. The resulting wave of sympathy for the underdog was further stimulated by exaggerated Western press reports of the Bulgarian victories. As a result two pro-Ottoman societies sprang up in London, while the French novelist Pierre Loti wrote his influential Turcophile manifesto, *Turkey in Agony*.

The British government, however, was provided with more reliable assessments of Turkey's military capabilities by the military attaché at Constantinople and Athens, Lieutenant-Colonel Ernest Tyrrell and his assistant, Major Francis Cunliffe-Owen, who served as special military attaché with the Greek Army during the war.[4] Their reports were objective and critical of press accounts of the Balkan War.[5] They appreciated

that political, not military considerations, had shaped the Ottoman
Empire's initial objectives, which imposed overstretched supply lines
on the army. However, they too found much to fault in its organization and performance. The Turk's mobilization was disorganized, and
thoughout the war they suffered from a lack of trained and educated
officers.[6] As a result the initial Turkish offensive ended in the surrender of
an army of 45,000 men in Macedonia at the beginning of December.[7]

The military attachés stressed, however, that the Turkish army fought
vigorously after it had withdrawn to defensive lines.[8] Even so, Tyrrell
regarded the Turkish Army as incapable of attack.[9] Despite the
subsequent military reforms introduced by the Minister of War, Enver
Bey, the Turkish Army had not improved by the outbreak of the First
World War. Cunliffe-Owen, who was by now military attaché, reported in
January 1914 that the Turkish Army was not 'in a condition well-fitted to
take the field'.[10]

Racial prejudice did not distort British appreciations of Turkish
strength. Early twentieth-century British perceptions of oriental races
were complex. If on the one hand the Turks attracted many Western
sympathizers during the Balkan Wars, on the other, the British Foreign
Office regarded their governments as incorrigibly incompetent and
brutal.[11] But there is no evidence that British soldiers felt the same dislike
for the Turks as did British politicians. On the contrary, before the
war British officers generally got on well with their Turkish opposite
numbers.[12] Far from harbouring racial prejudices against the Turks,
British soldiers during the Great War frequently remarked on the fine
physique of Anatolian POWs. The British generals' impression of the
Turkish Army's absolute inferiority was in fact based on objective
assessments of its defective structure of command and supply and upon
the economic weakness of the Ottoman Empire.

The general awareness of Turkish weakness shaped the British
response to the Ottoman Empire's slide into war on Germany's side. On
the outbreak of the war the British Admiralty high-handedly retained two
Turkish dreadnoughts which were being built in England. This led to an
anti-British agitation in Turkey, where the action was widely resented.[13]
However, the Admiralty's decision was subsequently justified by the
actions of the Turkish government which led up to the Anglo-French
declaration of war on 5 November.[14]

Already before the war, there existed a powerful pro-German party
within the Turkish Army. Germany's influence within Turkey had grown
particularly strong after the first Balkan War during which the Turks
received no support from Britain. The strength of the bonds between
Turkey and Germany were made obvious at the end of 1913, when the
Turkish Minister of War, Enver Bey, secured the appointment of the

German General Liman von Sanders as an executive member of the Turkish General Staff.[15] At the start of the First World War Turkey's pro-German sympathies were immediately apparent when it committed a gross breach of neutrality by sheltering two German warships, the *Goeben* and the *Breslau* which had found themselves trapped in the Mediterranean in August 1914. Reports from within the Ottoman Empire from that time onwards confirmed the British government's suspicions of the mounting threat to the British Empire and to Russia.

The British did not have a unified system of intelligence within Turkey. Indeed, the Viceroy, Lord Lytton had criticized the lack of a British secret service at Constantinople as long ago as 1878.[16] In 1914 the Secret Service Bureau (the predecessor of MI6) did not operate inside the Ottoman Empire, which clearly reflected Britain's disregard for Turkey as a power. Intelligence on Turkey was provided by various local agencies on the periphery of the Ottoman Empire which reported on individual regions of it. Thus the military attachés dealt mainly with European Turkey, where the bulk of the Ottoman Army was concentrated; the Intelligence Bureau of the Egyptian War Office covered Sinai and the Levant coast; and the British depended on the Russian General Staff in the Caucasus for information on the Turkish Army Group based at Erzerum. British intelligence activity in the Ottoman Empire was officially divided into two distinct spheres: that controlled by the War Office and that controlled by the Government of India. The latter was responsible for reporting on Persia, Arabia and the area of Mesopotamia downstream of Baghdad. This part of the Ottoman Empire was lightly garrisoned by the Turks. British intelligence there amounted to little more than the reports of the Consuls at Baghdad and Basra, and for Arabia, upon the reports of the Government of India's Foreign and Political Department. The latter were the equivalent of an Indian diplomatic service. As well as in Arabia they represented the British Empire in Persia. The famous explorers Shakespear, Leachman and Gertrude Bell were controlled by the Foreign and Political Department.

The diplomatic service of the Foreign Office was the only unified organization providing information on the whole Ottoman Empire with the exception of Arabia. However, the fragmentation of British intelligence coverage of Turkish affairs was not a disadvantage. It ensured that the various 'professional' intelligence agencies had detailed local knowledge when dealing with the Ottoman Empire which was ethnically and linguistically heterogeneous. It should be noted, also, that the Ottoman Empire was not a soft target for British intelligence. The Turkish authorities were vigilant and the penalties for spying severe.

Turkish mobilization against the British Empire and Russia was barely concealed. From the middle of August until Turkey's entry into the war, reports came in from Sofia, Bucharest and Constantinople itself on a stream of German officers and men entering the country.[17] At the end of September Sir Louis Mallet, the British ambassador at Constantinople, complained to the Turkish government that the presence of 4,000–5,000 German soldiers and sailors had transformed the city into 'an armed German camp'.[18]

At the same time Cunliffe-Owen reported on the Turkish mobilization on all fronts. The Consul at Adrianople, Major (later Lieutenant-Colonel) Rhys Samson, provided reports on the mobilization of the major Turkish army group based there.[19] Samson had been consul since 1907, but his diplomatic status was a cover for his military intelligence operation. He was later, under the codename 'R', to be in charge of the British Secret Service in the Aegean.[20]

Agents of the Intelligence Office (which after the outbreak of war became the Intelligence Department) of the Egyptian War Office followed the movements of the Mosul and Damascus Army Corps,[21] which after their mobilization constantly sent troops south.[22]

Evidence of the Turks' hostile intent also reached London from friendly and Allied governments. The Italians furnished information that Turkish military preparations were not, as Constantinople claimed, purely defensive measures against the Russians,[23] while at the beginning of August the Russian Consul at Erzerum reported that the Turks were hurrying military preparations against the Caucasus and arresting Russian subjects.[24]

Even though the Russians had not strongly reinforced the border, Cunliffe-Owen believed the Turkish government when they assured him that they were not planning an attack on the British Empire, but were afraid of an attack by Russia.[25] Sir Louis Mallet considered that the Turks did not intend war, but were falling in with German designs in order to extract as much as possible from Germany.[26] Their counsel for concilia-tion of the Turks was not heeded by Whitehall or by the Government of India. Already in August 1914 Sir Eyre Crowe of the Foreign Office noted that 'The Turks are, and have been, playing with us'.[27] He was right. The Turkish government had signed a treaty promising to join Germany in the war on 2 August 1914.[28] Through the various sources of information at their disposal within the Ottoman Empire, the British government obtained a clear warning of Turkish intentions. Its resolution to strike the first blow was further strengthened by the many reports that the mobiliza-tion was bringing famine and ruin to the Ottoman Empire and that the Turkish Army would not be able to fight effectively as a result.[29]

Turkey's entry into the war did not frighten the authorities in London and India.[30] Despite the hard-pressed position of the Allied Forces in Europe, the Government of India was primarily concerned about the effect which Turkish belligerence would have upon Indian Muslims and upon the tribes on India's North-West Frontier and in Afghanistan.[31] At the end of September General Barrow, the Military Secretary at the India Office, and Sir Arthur Hirtzel, the Secretary of the Political and Secret Department of the India Office, concluded that war with Turkey was only weeks away but need only be feared if the Turks won over the Arabs to their side, since, as Barrow put it, 'In that case they will proclaim a Jihad and endeavour to raise Afghanistan and the frontier tribes against us'.[32]

Barrow consulted Major Shakespear, the Arabian explorer, who was then in London about the danger of the Arabs joining in a Holy War against the British Empire. Shakespear told Barrow that Ibn Saud would join the British at the first sign they intended to support him. When he did so all Arabia would follow suit. Unlike the British sources of intelligence in the west of the Ottoman Empire, Leachman, Shakespear and Bell were to man anti-Turkish and looked forward to the liberation of the Arabs. Shakespear seconded the opinion of the India Office that inactivity in the Gulf would only lose Arab support.[33] Barrow recorded in his diary:

> I was so impressed that I went over to see Hankey at the Defence Committee Office and enfolded to him a plan to despatch a brigade of the 6th Division from Bombay secretely to the Shatt-al-Arab. This would commit us to supporting the Arabs and be the desired signal.[34]

Admiral Slade, who was the Admiralty's authority on the Persian Gulf, was 'delighted' with the scheme, and its boldness immediately appealed to Lord Kitchener, the Secretary of State for War.[35]

Barrow recommended that an expeditionary force should be sent to the head of the Persian Gulf before the outbreak of war. He advised that: 'So startling and unexpected a sign of our power to strike would at once determine the attitude of the Shaikhs of Mohammerah and Kuwait as well as of Ibn Saud, and the support of the Arabs would utterly destroy all prospect of Turkish success either in Mesopotamia or in Egypt'.[36] The Admiralty and the India Office would have sent troops straight to Abadan on the Persian border with the Ottoman Empire, but for the protests of the Government of India, which did not want its Muslim subjects to feel that the British had aggressive intentions towards their Turkish co-religionists.[37] None the less, on 16 October, two weeks before Turkey's entry into the war, 5,000 men of Expeditionary Force 'D', or 'Dunsterforce' as it was also known, left Bombay for Bahrain, where they stood ready to secure the Abadan oil-fields on the first sign of overt Turkish hostility.

The Indian Army had no pre-war plan for operations in Mesopotamia. In 1912 its General Staff had prepared for the occupation of Basra but had planned for nothing beyond that. This did not deter the India Office and the Admiralty. They were aware that the Turks had only weak forces in Mesopotamia. The Consul-General at Baghdad reported that the estimated 10,000–15,000 Turkish troops in the area were 'mutinous from neglect and ill-treatment', while the Consul at Basra reported that the 1,200 Turkish troops at Basra were 'reserves and mostly without training'.[38] These troops were unlikely to be reinforced once operations opened against the Russians in the Caucasus.

At the root of the assumptions of Shakespear, Barrow and Slade – and it is noteworthy that no voices of dissent to the plan were raised – lay a set of British preconceptions about the behaviour of oriental races. The British assumed that the oppressed groups in the Ottoman Empire had a natural desire to free themselves from the brutality of the Turkish regime at the first opportunity. In fact, the supposedly inefficient rule of the Ottoman Empire maintained the subservience, if not the goodwill, of the Arabs of Mesopotamia for the duration of the war, even after the British had 'liberated' them.

The conduct of the campaign in Mesopotamia was left to the Government of India; since the Expeditionary Force was to be drawn entirely from the Indian Army. While the activities of the Political Department were centred on Persia and Arabia, the Indian Military Department which had to prepare the Expeditionary Force had minimal information on Mesopotamia. The Intelligence Bureau of the Indian Army played no role in intelligence gathering in the Ottoman Empire. Being composed in 1914 of under 20 officers, it was barely sufficient in size to meet the needs of the Indian Army on the North-West Frontier, which was its sole sphere of activity. In this respect, the Intelligence Bureau reflected the limitations of the army as a whole. The poverty of India ensured that the pre-1914 Indian Army was not equipped to fight a European enemy. Its primary role was to ward off border tribes and to protect the Raj against internal unrest. Before the war it was not able to devote resources to securing information on the Ottoman Empire, which did not appear a threat.[39]

Even if the Government of India had foreseen before the war the need to despatch an expeditionary force to the head of the Gulf, it would have proved very difficult to obtain detailed geographical information about Mesopotamia. Even during the war, with the presence of the Indian Army, effective survey work was very difficult because of the hostile attitude of nomadic Arab tribes. Most of Mesopotamia above the port of Basra and below Baghdad was desert. Land communication was very difficult and the main means of travel were the rivers Tigris and Euphrates; at the start of the Mesopotamian campaign the Indian Army's knowledge of local geography did not extend beyond a knowledge of their course. In its ignorance, however, it was equalled by the Turks, who even in spring 1916 lacked the most basic maps of their own province. In October 1914, when 'Dunsterforce' set out from India, all combatants were expecting the war to be over within months. Neither the British nor the Turks could have foretold that the deserts of Mesopotamia would become of strategic importance.

The Turks began hostilities on 29 October when their warships, accompanied by the *Goeben* and the *Breslau*, shelled Russian ports in the Black Sea. On 5 November Britain and France declared war on the Ottoman Empire. On 6 November Indian Expeditionary Force 'D', commanded by General Delamain, landed at Fao, totally surprising the Turkish garrison and sustaining no casualties. Remarkably, since 'D' Force had made little attempt to conceal its departure from India, the Turks had remained completely unaware of its existence.[40] On the other hand, Delamain had a fair knowledge of Turkish strength in Mesopotamia. Before landing he had learned that, as the planners in London had foretold, the majority of the Turkish troops in the East were heading for the Caucasus, and there was only one regular division in Mesopotamia. On 2 November the Government of India informed Force 'D' that its objective was Basra.

Delamain's sources of tactical intelligence were little different from those at the disposal of Sir James Outram, who in 1857 had led a British force against the Persians in the same area. Delamain was greatly helped by the Sheikh of Mohammerah, who provided him with general information of Turkish dispositions. At first Force 'D' was also much dependent on cavalry reconnaissance in ascertaining Turkish strength and dispositions. It was particularly difficult in the desert conditions of Mesopotamia because of the mirage. Edmund Candler, who served with the cavalry from the beginning of the campaign until the fall of Baghdad in March 1917, wrote:

> There is not a cavalry regiment with the force which has not at some time or other mistaken sheep for infantry ... Often in a reconnaissance the enemy are within six hundred yards before the squadron commander can distinguish whether they are mounted or on foot.[41]

The best local sources of information on Turkish strength often proved to be prisoners of war. The limitations of British tactical intelligence were revealed at the battle of Saihan on 17 November, when Delamain attacked a Turkish force which he believed to be 3,100 strong and routed it. The examination of prisoners showed that it had numbered 1,200.[42] Delamain was not able to follow up his victory because he could not be sure of the Turkish Order of Battle. Still, on 20 November 1914 the British occupied Basra without meeting further resistance.

The means of field intelligence at the disposal of the Mesopotamian Expeditionary Force improved over the course of the war, most notably after the arrival of the first aeroplanes in March 1915. However, the basic system of tactical and strategic intelligence used by the General Staff of IEF 'D' for working out Turkish strength and Order of Battle remained fundamentally the same throughout the war.[43]

The Intelligence Section of the General Staff, or I(a) as it was also known, was headed for most of the war by Captain (later Brigadier-General) W.H. Beach. It was divided into two sections, 'strategical' and 'tactical', each of which was run by a General Staff Officer (GSO). Throughout the war, they had only a very small clerical staff at their disposal.[44] There were two sub-sections of I(a): I(b), which was otherwise known as the Secret Service; and I(c), the Topographical Sub-Section.

I(a) was represented at the front line by 'Special Service Officers' (SSOs). This term was peculiar to Mesopotamia, where no Intelligence Corps came into existence. They were very few in number. In 1914 and 1915 there were probably 8 or less of them, while even in 1918 there were only 14.[45] The SSOs kept in touch with officers of the Intelligence Corps in other theatres of the war. Sometimes they were stationed independently in outlying areas. Otherwise they were attached to Corps and Divisions, where Intelligence work was also carried out by 'substantive Intelligence Officers'. The latter were GSOs appointed from within the Corps or Division to perform intelligence duties. The SSOs differed from them in being under the ultimate control of GHQ. They had a generally better knowledge of local geography and languages than the 'substantive Intelligence Officers', and thus undertook the examination of prisoners of war, deserters, and agents.[46] Besides acting as assistants to the Corps and Divisional Intelligence Officers, the SSOs were expected to secure first-hand information and to conduct counter-intelligence at the front.[47]

Interpreters constituted by far the most numerous group in the Intelligence establishment of the Mesopotamian Expeditionary Force. The maximum number was about 500. The majority were not good enough for responsible work. The lack of officer linguists was particularly serious. Few officers could speak Arabic well, and even fewer knew Persian. The almost complete lack of officers at GHQ who spoke fluent Turkish and German was remarkable. Headquarters depended 'for some time' upon a single Turkish-speaking officer who was also the only expert cryptographer, and upon a single German-speaker who was a GSO with normal work to perform besides interpreting.[48]

The tactical section of I(a) dealt with information concerning the Turkish 6th Army which opposed IEF 'D' in Mesopotamia. The strategical section handled information from all other theatres of the war.

Since Mesopotamia was not an important recruiting ground of the

Ottoman Empire, and since only a small part of the Turkish Army was stationed there, the strategical section was largely dependent upon information received from other Allied Intelligence agencies. The four centres in question were: Egypt; the Caucasus; Athens; and Persia. As before the war, the Intelligence Bureau of the Egyptian War Department and the Russian General Staff continued to supply the British War Office with information on Turkish troops movements. For reasons of cipher security they did not communicate direct with the Government of India, let alone with the Mesopotamian Expeditionary Force, and it took about 3–4 days for information to reach the Mesopotamian front from the Caucasus. After the outbreak of war links with the Russian Army in the Caucasus were strengthened by the appointment of Major Marsh as liaison officer on the Russian General Staff. The headquarters of IEF 'D' had much confidence in his work.

The strongest concentrations of the Turkish Army were around Constantinople, and its most important recruiting areas were European Turkey and Western Anatolia. This region, together with Bulgaria, was covered by a motley assortment of homegrown – predominantly Greek – agents, who were run from Athens by Major Samson, the former assistant military attaché at Constantinople. This network, besides reporting on Turkish troop movements, was the most convenient means which the British possessed for gauging the morale of the population in the heartland of the Ottoman Empire.

Intelligence operations in Mesopotamia and in Persia was very closely linked and I(a) covered both areas in its periodical intelligence summaries. The Political Service of the Government of India continued to provide information on Persia. Sir Percy Cox, the former Resident at Bushire, accompanied the Mesopotamian Expeditionary Force to represent the interests of the Indian Political Department and to give advice on the political situation in the Arab world. The service was extended to the conquered provinces of Mesopotamia.

The effective operation of Allied Intelligence at the strategic level against the Ottoman Empire was faced by great difficulties. In the period 1914–15 the British were not able to break Turkish codes with any regularity. Before the war India had set up a small cryptographic department. It was not active on the Mesopotamian Front. There were no obvious points of access to the landlines used by the Turkish 6th Army. The rare pieces of Sigint which proved useful to IEF 'D' were all sent to it by the War Office.

The lack of signals intelligence on the Turkish Army in the early part of the war made human intelligence all the more vital. However, agent networks within the Ottoman Empire were particularly unreliable. Transport was slow and news took time to come through. Often Allied

Intelligence agencies would receive a report from an agent on the movements of Turkish reinforcements and then would hear nothing more from the source for weeks. The force against which the hypothetical reinforcements were heading could only hope that the next news of them would not be their arrival on the opposite side of the battlefield. Moreover, the Turks had a great advantage in possessing internal lines of communications. There were many points of diversion for a force moving in the interior of the Ottoman Empire. For example, a force reported at Mosul might be intended for Mesopotamia, the Caucasus, Persia, or it might be undergoing training at the military school, whose existence at Mosul had been reported by Russian agents.[49] Given these difficulties the interpretation of evidence on Turkish troop movements depended to a considerable extent on probability., Thoughout 1914 and most of 1915 the successful Russian campaign in the Caucasus and, from April to December 1915, the presence of British and French troops at Gallipoli, prevented large transfers of Turkish troops to Mesopotamia.

The greatest problem for British strategic intelligence in the war against the Turks was the small number of troops fighting in Mesopotamia. In 1914–15 there were never more than two Divisions of IEF 'D', or 25,000 men, serving there. If for example, Allied Intelligence in Europe failed to detect the transfer of 10,000 German troops from the Western to the Eastern Front, the result would not be decisive. If, on the other hand, a similar number of Turks had turned up unexpectedly in Mesopotamia, the British Expeditionary Force would have been dangerously outnumbered.

I(a) of the Mesopotamian Expeditionary Force employed a very simple filing system for working out the Turkish Order of Battle. Any reports of value were entered in 'Distribution and Strength Tables', which were simply registers with a separate space ruled off for each Turkish division. Entries were made in the relevant space showing the origin of the information, its date, and a short summary of it. The report was analysed and a detailed record of I(a)'s conclusions was filed, and a short summary of them entered in the 'Distribution and Strength Table'. The report and the analysis were then submitted to the head of I(a), W.H. Beach, who showed them to the Chief of the General Staff and often to the GOC-in-C as well. Though simple the system was felt to be accurate and fast.[50] About once a month the General Staff issued a balance-sheet summarizing the distribution of the Turkish Armies in the five main theatres of war.[51] The most important information was written up in a 'Daily Summary', and issued to Divisional Commanders and Special Service Officers. The 'Daily Summaries' were abbreviated in printed weekly summaries. Estimates of Turkish strength were given in monthly summaries.[52]

Determining the Turkish Order of Battle involved special problems. During the war 'kaleidoscopic' changes took place in the names of Turkish units. Colonel W. Leith-Ross, who served on I(a) from early 1916 until 1920, noted that 'the Turks rarely stopped tinkering with their organization for more than a month together'. Generally this was because shortage of manpower and transport led to a hand-to-mouth existence which enforced improvisation. But there was little method behind the changes. In summer 1916, for example, owing to heavy losses in combat against the Russians, the 5th Army Corps in the Caucasus was renamed the 5th Caucasus Division at a time when a '5th Division' was already serving on that front. The reports submitted by uneducated local agents often omitted the distinctive word 'Caucasus', so that it was impossible to tell which unit was meant. Some changes were even more baffling, and could be explained only by the peculiar character of the Turkish Army. In April 1918 the headquarters of the 21st Division in Assir were renamed the headquarters of the 23rd Army Corps, although the 'Corps' consisted of only 2,400 men. I(a) concluded that the Divisional Commander wanted to draw a Corps Commander's pay.[53]

Leith-Ross claimed that the British system grew to be very efficient.

> Every important strategical movement, every identification of a Turkish unit and every material change in enemy organisation was at once cabled to all concerned either direct or though the War Office. Reports of minor urgency were received by mail.

> It will be readily understood that this close co-operation soon led to almost every unit of the Turkish Army being marked down no matter where it was. Every now and again some regiment or division would disappear from ken; but the disappearance would be only temporary, its movements would be traced before long and its location definitely established on one front or another.[54]

As far as establishing the titular Order of Battle was concerned, Leith-Ross's claims were true, though he did not mention the severe dangers involved when even a single enemy unit was 'lost from ken' when the strength of IEF 'D' was low. Overall, however, British intelligence at the strategic level worked coherently. Early in 1915 Egyptian Intelligence compiled an 'excellent' handbook on the Turkish Army.[55] After less than two years of war with the Turks, the War office was circulating a 'Copy of the Turkish Order of Battle'.[56]

However, the benefits of knowing the Turkish titular Order of Battle so well were considerably reduced by two factors: the very variable strength of Turkish units and the enormous differences in fighting quality between different regiments and divisions. In these respects the Turkish Army was a far harder target for British Intelligence than the German Army. It will be seen that these problems had a decisive effect in the events leading up to the surrender at Kut.

The fighting quality of Turkish units varied enormously. As much as 60 per cent of the forces facing the 'Mesopotamian Expeditionary Force' in the first two years of the campaign might be irregular Arab levies who never stood and fought. More importantly, there was a great difference between the fighting quality of Anatolian Turks and Arab and subject races serving in the regular formations of the Turkish Army.

The numerical strength of units was more difficult to obtain than their locations and titular numbers for the Order of Battle, because in practice the size of Turkish units varied greatly and was generally far removed from theoretical strength. At the beginning of the war a Turkish regular division was supposed to consist of nine battalions totalling about 8,500 infantry. This figure was almost never reached and the modal average soon became about 4,500.[57] The number of desertions from the Turkish Army was huge. It was not uncommon for 50 per cent of a draft to disappear before it arrived on the Mesopotamian front. Indeed, on one occasion a Turkish officer, who had himself deserted, had shortly before been complimented by his Divisional Commander on having arrived from Constantinople with 40 per cent of his draft.[58]

Besides aerial reconnaissance, the main sources for working out the strength of units were deserters, POWs and captured documents. While deserters and prisoners could not be trusted to give the accurate strength of their battalion, reasonably accurate results were obtained by working upwards from the strength of the smallest unit to which a man belonged, whose strength he was sure to know precisely.[59]

The names of commanding officers were often valuable aids to the determination of titular numbers. Since they were often barely numerate, Turkish and Arab soldiers frequently did not know the numbers of the regiments to which they belonged, let alone the numbers of their divisions or army corps, or else they confused these numbers with one another. Agents and travellers, who were equally ill-educated, rarely got hold of a correct titular number at all. I(a) even encountered one man who did not know his own rank: so far as he was concerned he might have been anything from a private to a Field Marshal. On the other hand, even the stupidest man knew the name of his commanding officer.[60]

British intelligence officers often offered prisoners money or drink. They found that 'the Turk in contravention of his religious principles [was] usually a devoted adherent to the bottle'. The reliability and amount of information obtained from POWs depended, as regards the Turks, on the state of affairs at the moment. At the time of the siege and fall of Kut I(a) found it practically impossible to obtain information from Turkish POWs. On the other hand, the heterogeneous character of the Turkish Army worked to the advantage of the British, since Armenians, Arabs, Christians and Jews generally gave what information they had. Turkish refugees from Europe, or Muhajirin, 'were always worth singling out'. They had lost their homes during the Balkan Wars and had been encouraged to return to Turkish territory with the promise of exemption from military service for six years. On the outbreak of war, however, they were ruthlessly conscripted.[61] Deserters were the main source on Turkish reinforcements. Unfortunately for the British, though, the majority found refuge among the Arab tribes or simply returned home.[62]

Occasionally the British captured individual documents of real value, giving Turkish strengths in detail. Helpfully, Turkish and Arab officers were keen diary-keepers. Captured mails frequently proved the means of accurately locating units in other theatres of war.[63] However, the majority of documents which were of any use just showed ration strengths.[64]

I(b), or the Secret Service, came into being from the moment IEF 'D' landed in Mesopotamia. The agents it employed were all local inhabitants. British and Indian troops were never used as agents because their speech and deportment would have given them away instantly.[65] However, though the majority of local inhabitants adopted an attitude of benevolent neutrality towards the British, almost none were willing to render them active assistance for fear that the Turks might one day return.[66] This attitude grew even more pronounced after April 1916 when the Turks inflicted a violent retribution on the inhabitants of Kut al Amara, whom they suspected – wrongly – of having helped the British during the siege.[67] Likewise, numerous attempts were made to induce POWs and deserters to return as spies, but none would run the risk. Men with a taste for espionage joined the Turks, not the British because the punishment on capture by the latter was less severe.[68]

The agents whom the I(b) secured were almost universally unsatisfactory, being poor, ill-educated men, who worked for the sake of money alone. Being completely familiar with the routes over which the British sent them, most would lie up with an Arab tribe and return late with a perfect, fictitious itinerary and a noncommittal story of what they had seen en route based partly on tribal rumour and partly on 'a most intelligent and frequently accurate anticipation of forthcoming events'.[69] In November 1918 the list of agents in Section I(b) of the Mesopotamian Expeditionary Force contained 656 names, of which 608 had a remark such as 'convicted', 'useless', 'dismissed', 'liar', etc. written against them.[70]

Intelligence officers found it difficult to check the veracity of agents before aircraft started to be used on the Mesopotamian front in March 1915. Then the interrogating officer who was familiar with the latest air reports on the locations of Turkish camps could check the claims of his agents. The officers of I(b) also resorted to more devious methods. Often they would leave agents in a room on their own, and then listen in to their conversation through dictaphones. Another device which they found to work very successfully with ignorant people was an electric carpet, upon which the man being interrogated would sit. I(b) wired the carpet to a set of powerful batteries concealed in a cupboard or other suitable places. If the interrogator suspected an agent of lying he would press a button concealed under his desk to deliver him two or three powerful shocks through his legs and pelvis. I(b) found that very few agents continued to lie after that.[71]

The second sub-section of Intelligence on the General Staff of IEF 'D', I(c), or the Topographical Section, comprised only 18 men at the end of 1914.[72] In May 1916 it still numbered only 23, and was greatly under strength for work in a largely unmapped country like Mesopotamia.[73] Furthermore, topographical work in Mesopotamia was beset by unusual difficulties. Because the land was flat, it was impossible for surveyors to make ground surveys of areas in enemy occupation, which could only be done by aerial photography of a quality not reached until the last years of the war.[74] Marauding Arabs made survey work behind British lines difficult. The flatness of Mesopotamia by no means meant that its terrain was predictable. Battlefields along the banks of the Tigris and the Euphrates were chequered by the remains of ancient irrigation systems, which served as impediments to an attacking force. Most seriously, however, ground conditions were difficult because of either a surfeit or a dearth of water. Sudden flooding could change the map of a battlefield overnight.

In the first two years of the war the General Staff's knowledge of the battlefields of Mesopotamia was often as defective as its knowledge of the Turkish strategic routes leading to them. At the end of 1915 the only book which the General Staff had of the crucial strategic route between Mosul and Damascus was the 'Military Report, Arabia, 1904'.[75] By the end of the war I(a) had worked out the details of many routes in Asiatic Turkey and Persia. By this means alone was it possible to forecast whether a body of troops of a given size and known to have started from some place, could or could not be close to the front-line by a given date. On several occasions in Mesopotamia, British offensives were timed before the arrival of reinforcements known to be coming. However, their information on these routes was less precise in 1915 and 1916 and the benefit of these later advantages – which would have been taken for granted by commanders on the Western Front – was absent.[76]

The rapidity of their success in taking Basra surprised the British. However, they realized that this had not sufficiently impressed the Arabs. Far from revolting against the Turks, nomads had started to snipe at the Expeditionary Force. The population of Baghdad, however, was reported to be 'already friendly'. Moreover, the British thought that the Turks were unlikely to offer much opposition to their further advance.[77]

At the end of November, General Barrow, the Military Secretary at the India Office, still hoped that Arab support might materialize. He thought that the British ought to make a demonstration of their strength by taking the town of Qurna, which lay 30 miles up the Tigris from Basra. Like Barrow, Sir Percy Cox, the Indian government's Chief Political Officer with 'Dunsterforce', was a persistent proponent of a continued British advance in order to impress Arab opinion. Cox's opinions on Arab affairs carried great weight. He had a long and extensive knowledge of the Gulf, having held a variety of diplomatic posts in Arabia and Persia between 1893 and 1914, including that of Political Resident for the Gulf from 1909 to 1914.

Convinced that a general Arab revolt was imminent, Barrow and Cox did not consider the consequences of British inactivity once Qurna had fallen. The British were in a dilemma. In an unmapped and unfamiliar land they were numerically weak. British and Indian reinforcements could not readily be spared from the main theatres of war. The Mesopotamian 'side show' had therefore to sustain its own momentum, but this could only be done by gaining Arab support, and in order to obtain this support Force 'D' had to become increasingly overstretched. However, the dangers which this entailed were not fully apparent at the time. At the beginning of December 1914 IEF 'D' attached a force outside Qurna which it believed to number between 1,200 and 1,500, but which subsequently turned out to have been 3,000 strong, and routed it.

However, after the battle of Qurna until March 1915 'Dunsterforce' received repeated warnings of Turkish reinforcements on their way to Mesopotamia from other theatres which counter-balanced pressures for an advance.[78] At the end of December 1914 the Russian General Staff reported that 25,000 Turks were leaving Syria for Mesopotamia. A British representative of the Anglo-Persian oil company claimed to have seen these troops and to have been much impressed with their equipment. At the same time the British embassy at Sofia received information that 10,000 Turks were moving from Constantinople to Baghdad.[79] Various other reports fuelled fears that the Turks and Germans planned to break through to India. At the beginning of 1915 German agents arrived in Persia, which they intended to raise in revolt against British and Russian domination. The British captured the most important agent, Wilhelm Wassmuss who, though he escaped, left papers which revealed an ambitious German scheme to bring down British rule in India.[80]

However, while some Turkish reinforcements were clearly arriving in Mesopotamia in spring 1915, British tactical intelligence on that front failed to detect the presence of the large number of reinforcements which had been reported leaving other theatres. In this period I(a) found it very difficult to estimate the existing Turkish strength in Mesopotamia, because the Turks had set up a screen behind which they were assembling their forces.[81] In the absence of aircraft, the British had difficulties in penetrating it. None the less, at the end of January 1915 the Indian Political Service received information from the Arabs – presumably the Sheikh of Mohammerah's agents – which proved to be a substantially correct statement of the Turkish Order of Battle and battle plans. The Arabs stated, moreover, that the Turks had only 12,000 men in Mesopotamia.[82] By the end of March the Indian General Staff had accepted this local information as definitive, and thought that IEF 'D', which had now been reinforced to a strength of two divisions, should be able to defeat the Turks in detail.

The new commander of 'Dunsterforce', General Sir John Nixon, who arrived at Basra on 9 April 1915, immediately engaged the main Turkish force. At the battle of Shaiba which lasted from 12 to 14 December he inflicted a heavy defeat upon it. But, lacking aircraft, he did not realize that his troops had put the Turks into a disordered flight.

The British victory at Shaiba owed little to the operation of Allied intelligence at a strategic level. While intelligence in other theatres had correctly picked up rumours of Turkish reinforcements, their size and quality had been greatly exaggerated. There were only 7,000 regular Turkish troops at Shaiba.[83] Even the highest estimate by local agents of 16,000 was not as excessive as many reports received the strategic section of I(a).[84] This gave British generals the impression that local, tactical intelligence would be able to provide early warning of the arrival of any substantial Turkish reinforcements.

British tactical intelligence in Mesopotamia was strengthened in May 1915 when the first aeroplanes finally reached IEF 'D'. Mesopotamia was to prove ideally suited to air reconnaissance, because cover from aerial observation there was non-existent. Leith-Ross wrote that:

> It may be laid down as axiomatic that if aerial reconnaissance during operations is thorough and continuous, the enemy cannot make a tactical move of any importance without being observed.[85]

However, the advantage of aircraft was not as great as it was to be by spring 1917, at the time of the successful advance on Baghdad. Pilots took time to grow familiar with the local terrain. This was a particular problem in 1915 when the aeroplanes on the Mesopotamian Front had no photographic equipment and the effectiveness of air reconnaissance depended on the pilot's ability to sketch what he had seen. Moreover, throughout 1915 and for most of 1916 there were very few aircraft with 'Dunsterforce'. Those present were of a cumbersome outdated design and were ill-suited to carrying out observation flights. Difficult climatic conditions ensured that the aircraft were never all operational at the same time.[86] This made it impossible for the intelligence officers of the General Staff to compare a wide selection of observers' reports.

Air reconnaissance performed two roles: it provided information on Turkish strength and dispositions, and it furnished battlefield maps for British forces on the attack. It was possible to estimate the Turks' strength from tent maps of their camps. However, the improvised character of many units of the Turkish Army made this task particularly difficult. Not only were Turkish tents of very diverse shapes and sizes, but also many troops slept rough at night, possessing no tents at all. The possibility of false camps also impeded the working out of Turkish Order of Battle by aerial reconnaissance. These problems were not reduced until later in the War with the provision of photographic equipment of a technical quality much superior to anything available in 1914–15.[87] Despite initial difficulties aircraft reconnaissance gave the British a decisive advantage in their advance after Shaiba.

After his victory Nixon's objectives remained limited to securing the approaches to Basra. He planned first to retake Qurna, which the flooding of the Tigris had forced the British to abandon, and then to block the Euphrates route to Basra by seizing the town of Nasiriya which lay about 70 miles upstream.

The British offensive began spectacularly. The Turkish forces around Qurna were seemingly invulnerable in their positions on the islands around the town which the floods had created. On the morning of 31 May they found the British advancing towards them in small local sailing boats or bellums. Nixon had also managed to get his artillery afloat and the Turkish islands provided an easy target for it. The Turks fled after a brief fight. The next day aircraft reconnaissance established that they had abandoned Qurna and were rushing upstream in every available river-craft. Unlike at Shaiba, this information allowed Nixon to turn the retreat into a rout. His two aeroplanes kept track of the fleeing Turks after gunboats had set out in full pursuit of them. A single British ship, the *Shaitan*, chased the Turks 50 miles up the Tigris to Amara, which was held by 2,000 troops, who fled, leaving the *Shaitan* in control of the town.

On the other hand, the attack on Nasiriya on 5 July suffered an initial setback. Arab reports had put Turkish regular strength at only 2,000. Subsequent examination of prisoners allowed the British Special Service officers present to establish the real strength of the Turkish regulars as about 5,000.[88] As at the second battle of Qurna, aircraft reconnaissance made a vital difference.[89] The water-logged terrain had made field reconnaissance impossible, but after some difficulty a pilot succeeded in sketching the Turkish positions. Again the Turks fled.

Lord Hardinge, the Viceroy, Sir Beauchamp Duff, the Commander-in-Chief of the Indian Army, Austen Chamberlain, the Secretary of State for

India, and General Barrow were all initially opposed to a further British advance in Mesopotamia. But General Nixon argued successfully that he should be allowed to take the town of Kut al Amara, which lay about 90 miles as the crow flies from Amara, the furthest point of his last advance, and about 180 miles from Basra. Nixon's reasons were entirely tactical: the capture of Kut would put both ends of the Shatt al Hai, the channel linking the Tigris and the Euphrates, in British hands; and it would improve the British position in regard to the local tribes on the Tigris line.

As at the battle of Shaiba and Nasiriya, British tactical intelligence provided by I(a) proved a fairly accurate statement of the Turkish OB before the battle.[90] The British had been facing the Turks near Kut since June. Their consistent estimate of Turkish strength at about 8,000 regulars was based on air, cavalry, and infantry reconnaissance,[91] and on agent reports.[92] I(a)'s assessment that Turkish morale was low was also fully borne out both by the course of the battle and by a subsequent examination of prisoners.[93]

Before the battle General Charles Townsend, the British commander in the field, obtained information about the Turkish position, which was stronger than anything the British had so far encountered in the campaign, from aerial observation supported by the naval flotilla and cavalry reconnaissance.[94] This established that an outflanking movement was possible through the dry land between the marshes upon which the Turkish commander had hinged his left flank. The head of the Mesopotamian air flight, Major Reilly provided a map and detailed information of the Turks' position.[95]

Townsend took advantage of the Turks' dispersal on either bank of the unfordable Tigris, and launched his main attack against the heavily fortified end of the Turks' left flank. He first led the Turks into believing that he intended to attack on both sides of the river, and pitched all available tents on the right bank to give the impression that the main British force was there.[96] Early on 27 September the British attacked the Turks' centre; by advancing on an extended front, they made this seem like their main attack. The Turks in the fortifications on the far left of their line were entirely surprised when the British outflanking force carried out the main assault later in the morning.[97] The fortifications fell after a short fight.[98] However, the Turks escaped during the night and set off for an entrenched position 80 miles upstream at Ctesiphon. They had sustained 2,000 casualties and lost 1,200 prisoners and 14 guns.[99]

At this time the British were not only winning battles, they were winning them brilliantly. No other force of the British Empire could match the achievements of Indian Expeditionary Force 'D'. The Turks failed to defend Kut even though they had constructed excellent fortifications.[100] As on previous occasions the British had won decisively at

numerical odds which were less than one to one, even when Arab levies
are not included. At the same time the Turks were failing to hold their own
against the Russian advance in Armenia. Inevitably the impression of
Turkish qualitative weakness was reinforced.

After the battle of Kut the British gained the impression from POWs
that even the Anatolians who formed the backbone of the Turkish Army
were demoralized and hostile to their own government, while local Arabs
in Turkish regular units hoped that the British would win. The British
believed that this change was partly caused by the 'civilized' government
which they had brought to Mesopotamia.[101]

In their weekly intelligence summaries I(a) gave a low assessment
of the Turkish generals, describing Nur-ud-Din, the commander of the
Mesopotamian Army, as an over-confident brute, much disliked by his
troops.[102] His rumoured replacement, Halil Bey, was known only for
having lost badly to the Russians in the Caucasus, and for being Enver
Bey's uncle. The British thought that many Turkish generals owed their
positions to their loyalty to the Young Turks, not to their abilities.

British Intelligence in the Ottoman Empire on the eve of the war
had given the impression that Turkish morale was bad. The reports
of Major Samson's agents still indicated that the population of
Constantinople might revolt if the Allies could only win a decisive victory.
This intelligence had an effect on the decision to hold on to the
Dardanelles for so long. It also influenced events in Mesopotamia.[103]

The extravagant hopes of British planners that the Arabs would rise
against Turkish rule and that the Turkish Army would crumble away,
unsure of its own cause, had not been fulfilled. However, the British
continued to see the main threat from the Turks in Mesopotamia not in
their fighting power, but in the effect which their and the Germans'
propaganda might have upon the Muslims of India, Afghanistan and
Persia.

The intelligence from Persia drawn up by I(a) in its weekly summaries
echoed the impressions of the Indian Political Service that Persia
was drifting into the war on the German side. Wassmuss and his
gang of German agents, backed up by Swedish officers of the Persian
gendarmerie and by the Persian Governor-General of Fars, were stirring
up the local tribes around Bushire and Shiraz.

At the same time the Government of India wanted military success to
impress the Indian population. An attempt at open revolt in the Punjab
had failed thanks to the vigilance of the police. However, 1915 saw
a serious terrorist campaign in Bengal, which came close to causing
the collapse of the provincial administration, and ambitious German
attempts to send arms to Bengal from America and the Far East.

After the battle of Kut the question of whether to continue to Baghdad

was debated in London, India and Mesopotamia. Because of the seriousness of the strategic issue and because IEF 'D' might subsequently have to
draw on reinforcements from England, the decision to advance on
Baghdad needed the approval of both British and Indian governments.
The arguments for and against an advance were complex. This and the
distance between London and India involved a long debate.

Nixon felt that an early advance on Baghdad was desirable. On 25
August, before the fall of Amara, Townshend told Nixon that if he routed
and stampeded the Turks in the coming battle he might follow them into
Baghdad.

By September 1915 the Viceroy, Lord Hardinge, was fully in favour of
Nixon taking Baghdad. This was not a quest for local glory. The
Government of India considered the dangers of doing nothing to
reestablish the British position in Persia, and of putting IEF 'D' at risk,
and found that the former consideration much outweighed the latter. In
this way 'Dunsterforce's' mission remained political. Barrow himself was
now not very keen on Nixon continuing up the Tigris. However, new
political pressures helped to keep IEF 'D' moving onwards. In fact, given
the British low regard for the Turks in the field at this time, the Expeditionary Force's main role – the protection of Persia – was really more
defensive than offensive. In all the discussions on whether or not to
advance on Baghdad the question of IEF 'D' being defeated never
occurred. The worst eventuality, stressed by the War Office, was that the
Expeditionary Force might not be able to hold Baghdad once they had
taken it.

Because of their lack of pre-war information on Mesopotamia the
British were uncertain of the tactical advantages of taking Baghdad.
Nixon and the Government of India argued that its fall would put IEF 'D'
in a strong tactical position. Nixon argued that Baghdad formed the centre
of the 'Turkish lines of advance' and was an important supply centre.[104]
Lord Hardinge hoped that the capture of Baghdad would isolate German
agents in Persia.[105] The General Staff of the War Office, on the other hand,
believed that Baghdad had no natural defences and would be difficult to
supply from Basra, which lay 275 miles away.

The British Cabinet had the greatest hopes of all for the Mesopotamian
Expeditionary Force. They felt that through IEF 'D' Britain could win the
great victory which had eluded its generals in every theatre. The Cabinet
were aware that such a victory had to be won soon, for by 23 October,
when the Cabinet sanctioned the advance on Baghdad, the strategic
situation in the war against the Turks was changing. Bulgarian entry on
Germany's side was imminent and the Austrians and Germans had started
a final attack on Serbia. At Gallipoli the Allies had made no progress and
were menaced by the collapse of Serbia, which would allow Germany to

send munitions direct to the Ottoman Empire. The British Cabinet did not, however, realize that the length of time taken in the debate on whether to advance on Baghdad had itself led to a change in the military situation in Mesopotamia. The Turks had had time to prepare a strong position at Ctesiphon and their morale had recovered. Most importantly, however, they were able to send reinforcements to the Tigris in the nick of time, just as the British began to attack.

Before the battle of Ctesiphon, which was fought on 22 November 1915, Nixon and his General Staff estimated the Turkish regular strength on or very near the battlefield at about 13,000 regulars. In fact there were 20,000 with more on the way. Townsend's force of 9,000 was outnumbered two to one.

Before the battle many warnings of Turkish reinforcements on their way to Mesopotamia had reached Nixon from all theatres of the Turkish war. He and his General Staff were discouraged from heeding these warnings by their experience earlier in the year before the battle of Shaiba, when reports of large Turkish reinforcements from other theatres had turned out to be gross exaggerations and had only encouraged British inactivity in Mesopotamia. The information about Turkish troop movements which reached IEF 'D' from Egypt, the Caucasus, Athens, and from its own secret service, between October and November was again imprecise and confusing but, as will be argued, it by no means amounted to a failure of intelligence at the strategic level.

At the beginning of October the Intelligence Department of the Egyptian War Office informed Nixon that there were 'no signs of anything important going to Mesopotamia'.[106] Two weeks later Egyptian Intelligence reported a general movement of the Turks in the direction of Baghdad.[107] The figures given by the Egyptian Intelligence Department's agents did not, however, seem convincing.[108]

The most persistent reports of Turkish reinforcements moving to the Mesopotamian Front came from Major Marsh, the British liaison officer with the Russian General Staff in the Caucasus.[109] Marsh was basically correct that 7–8,000 Turks were heading for Mesopotamia under Halil Bey. But he was much less accurate about their rate of march south. Most of his reports in November stated that Halil Bey was still at Bitlis.[110] When I(a)'s agents sent in a stream of reports that Halil Bey was at Baghdad they were not believed.[111] Marsh reported that he had left Bitlis only on 17 November, which would not allow his force to arrive at Ctesiphon before Townshend's attack on the 22nd.[112]

Like the reports obtained by Allied Intelligence in Egypt and the Caucasus, those provided by the British Secret Service in the Aegean came entirely from agents. In fact, most of the news of Turkish troops movements to Mesopotamia which Major Samson furnished in the weeks before the battle of Ctesiphon were provided by a single source, designated as 'a very reliable Constantinople agent'. His reports supported the information from the Russian General Staff that Halil Bey was moving south to Baghdad.[113] Most importantly, he gave accurate information that the German Field Marshal von der Goltz, who had reorganized the Turkish Army in 1911, was heading for Mesopotamia to take charge of operations there. However, the 'very reliable agent' was very imprecise about the timing of von der Goltz's departure from Constantinople, which he announced on four separate occasions. Furthermore, he stated incorrectly that von der Goltz was taking a large number of troops with him to Baghdad.[114]

The agent network run locally by Sub-Section (b) of the General Staff also came up with information about Turkish reinforcements. But these reports were more contradictory and more imprecise than those from other theatres.[115] It is easy to see why Nixon had no faith in either his own agents or those run by Allied intelligence in the Caucasus, the Aegean and Egypt. As I(b) was aware, native agents in the Ottoman Empire were very unreliable. However, Nixon's disregard of strategic intelligence reports in November 1915 shows that he regarded Secret Service activity against Turks as fundamentally useless. He and his general staff made no allowances for a system of human intelligence which, if incapable of providing accurate information on the numbers of Turkish reinforcements, proved none the less capable of giving timely warning of major Turkish movements. The War Office and the General Staff in India had much greater confidence in the work of British Intelligence on the Ottoman Empire at a strategic level and were more anxious about the situation in Mesopotamia than Nixon. In fact, the sheer volume of reports of Turkish reinforcements to Mesopotamia in November 1915 was the nearest that the strategic system could come to giving Nixon a definitive warning.

In the first three months of 1915 the strategic situation in the war with the Ottoman Empire had made large reinforcements to Mesopotamia unlikely. By November 1915 every probable strategic circumstance pointed to the accuracy of the many reports of Turkish movements to the Tigris. The entry of Bulgaria into the war eased the Turkish position in Europe. The Egyptian Intelligence Department thought that this made all reports of a move on the Mesopotamian Front inherently probable. The Turks, they felt, were very unlikely to yield Baghdad without a fight.[116] The General Staff at the War Office were aware that the Turks realized that the British had their hands full everywhere. This meant that they could confidently and easily spare up to 60,000 reinforcements for Mesopotamia from other fronts.[117]

Nixon's disregard for agent intelligence which reached him in November

1915 was founded on a confidence that local, tactical intelligence would provide him with a month's warning of the arrival of any sizeable force in Mesopotamia. General Barrow wrote that since Townshend was halfway to Baghdad he might have been expected to get reliable information.[118] I(a) estimated that the Turks had been reinforced by October 1915, bringing their strength up from 10,000 to 13,000 regulars. They did not thereafter detect any large reinforcements. Prisoners of war had always been a reliable source of information in the past. In October and November 1915 they gave little indication of a further increase in the strength of the 6th Army.[119] Moreover, POW information suggested that the new units were not good fighting material. In fact the 45th Division, which had arrived in Mesopotamia in September, was mainly composed of Anatolian Turks and was a considerably better unit than the 35th and 38th Divisions which the British had easily defeated in the past.[120]

Aircraft reconnaissance likewise did not indicate the arrival of fresh Turkish troops in Mesopotamia in November. From early October Major Reilly and his squadron carried out observation flights over Baghdad. These continued without locating any new Turkish formations until 13 November, when an aircraft was lost near Baghdad, leaving only six aircraft at the front. Nixon gave orders that no more long-distance reconnaissances were to be undertaken. Thus at a time when reliable information about the arrival of Turkish reinforcements was essential, he was obliged to restrict aircraft to local flights. However, on 21 November Townshend sent Major Reilly on flight over Baghdad. Four miles east of Ctesiphon he observed a change in Turkish dispositions, which indicated that large reinforcements had arrived. However, the Turks shot him down as he returned. While full intelligence that Turkish reinforcements were on their way came from many sources, Reilly alone would have shown how close these reinforcements were. By this time, though, Townshend was so close to the enemy that a withdrawal without fighting might not have been possible.[121]

Despite the failure of their reconnaissances I(a) had managed to work out the Turkish titular order of battle at Ctesiphon with considerable accuracy. They did not foretell how close one of the two Turkish divisions which had arrived in Mesopotamia since the battle of Kut was to the battlefield but they were aware of its presence. However, they estimated the strength of the new units – the 45th and 51st divisions – at an average strength.[122] In fact, as W.H. Beach, the Head of I(a) later realized, 'the strengths of the newly arrived formations were much in excess of those of their predecessors' and, abnormally for the Turkish Army, were close to their theoretical sizes.[123]

The Commander-in-Chief of the Indian Army, Sir Beauchamp Duff, was not confident that the British would win at Ctesiphon. He wrote to

Lord Hardinge on 19 November: 'We have now no idea of what the actual strength of the Turks may be and it seems clear that Nixon himself does not know'.[124]

However, Nixon was not concerned with estimates of Turkish numbers alone when he attacked the Turkish positon at Ctesiphon. It is remarkable how little the British generals on the spot were bothered by all the threats of Turkish reinforcements. On the contrary, on the night of 21 November Townshend and his men were very optimistic about the battle the next day. This optimism was based entirely on their low estimate of the fighting quality of Turkish units. Indeed, had the reinforcements whose presence Nixon so readily disregarded been of the same quality as the enemy troops the British had encountered so far, then Nixon would have made the right decision. On previous occasions intelligence estimates of Turkish strength had proved too low and the British had little difficulty in beating the Turks. Even at Ctesiphon they won, albeit only a Pyrrhic victory. But the deciding factor there was not just the quantity of Turkish troops unaccounted for but also their quality. The 51st Division which had arrived at Baghdad from the Caucasus some days before the battle, and whose presence at the front line the British Intelligence had not expected, was a crack Anatolian unit greatly superior to anything which had faced IEF 'D' so far. The 45th Division which the British had estimated as poor fighting material also proved to be a formidable adversary. Thus at the battle of Kut the irregular makeshift character of the Turkish Army worked greatly to the disadvantage of the British.

The British also suffered a certain amount of bad luck at the battle of Ctesiphon. At the start of the battle a British aircraft observed the 51st Division moving up to the front line, but was shot down.[125] This was the last chance Townshend had of correctly establishing Turkish strength before battle was joined. He was left with only two aircraft which were fully occupied in guarding against Turkish outflanking movements. However, the battle of Ctesiphon began like the previous actions of IEF 'D'. Early on the morning of 22 November Indian infantry expelled the Turks from the most fortified part of their line. However, the Turkish Army did not dissolve into a rabble, for the 45th and 51st Divisions moved into the line and checked all further advance. On the afternoon of the next day the Turks took the initiative and the 45th Division charged the British repeatedly in an attempt to regain the positions the Turks had lost the day before. In a ferocious fight it lost half its men. Never before in the Mesopotamian Campaign had Turkish units ever made a serious attempt to regain positions they had lost. They did not succeed and during the night the Turks withdrew, convinced that they had faced 20,000 not 9,000 troops. However, the British had lost half their force in the battle and could not continue their attack. On 25 November Townshend decided to retire back down the Tigris to Kut.

The British did not by any means consider that they had suffered a decisive setback at Ctesiphon. The General Staff noted on 24 November that:

> The enemy is in no condition to assume the offensive after the severe handling he has had, neither are we, until fresh troops arrive ... It was hard luck we could not complete our victory by pushing through to Baghdad, but losses and the superior forces of the enemy simply made further operations impossible for the time being.[126]

The disparity in strength between the two armies only became certain when the Turks attacked the British on 1 December.[127] The attack was beaten off and the British arrived at Kut without further opposition.

Kut provided a very strong defensive position. It was situated in a loop between the Tigris and the Shatt al Hai, and commanded both waterways. Unfortunately it proved as easy for a small Turkish force to contain the British there as it did for the British to repel Turkish attacks.

Contrary to his later claims, Townshend was not forced to stop at Kut by the exhaustion of his men. Some British units retreated downstream to safety before the Turkish investment began.[128] Despite the crisis at Gallipoli, it was difficult for the British to appreciate that the Turkish Army they were fighting after Ctesiphon was qualitatively different from that which had confronted them before. Nixon was reluctant to give up any of his gains over the past year. By holding Kut he hoped to check a Turkish advance down the Tigris until two divisions which were on their way from France arrived. Thus while Nixon's decision to fight at Ctesiphon was partly based on inadequate intelligence on Turkish numbers, the decision to hold Kut was founded on an inadequate assessment of the quality of the Turkish Army.

Nixon's decision to defend Kut was greatly reinforced by the need to check German intrigue in Persia. The British felt restricted in their strategic options. On 30 November Lord Hardinge telegraphed to Sir Austen Chamberlain, the Secretary of State for India:

> To regard the capture of Baghdad as impossible would be to give up our best means of countering the German intrigues in Persia and Afghanistan against India and should therefore be dismissed from our calculations. Our success hitherto in Mesopotamia has been the main factor which has kept Persia, Afghanistan and India itself quiet...[129]

The decision to hold Kut did not seem nearly so dangerous in December 1915 as it did by the end of January 1916. Most assumed that the British relief forces, whose departure from France had been hastened, would easily be able to break through Turkish defences, which had stopped no British force in Mesopotamia until now. The lack of success of Imperial forces at Gallipoli was not an obvious warning that the Anatolian soldier might prove formidable in defence, for the most obvious reason for his success there was the enormous natural advantages which the cliffs of the peninsular coastline afforded him. Sir Beauchamp Duff, the Commander-in-Chief of the Indian Army, was in a minority at this date in thinking that the relief of Kut would be difficult.[130] For if Townshend's forces were included, the British in Mesopotamia might be expected almost to equal the strength of Turkish regulars in Mesopotamia in the new year. Barrow noted that the Turks would have 'probably less than 30,000 men, against our 24,000, a proportion of about 2 to 3. I think the history of all our fighting in Mesopotamia shows that we are quite equal to tackling the Turks in those proportions'.[131]

The new commander of the British forces in the field, General Aylmer was faced by strong pressures to attack as soon as possible.[132] At the beginning of January 1916 Townshend reported that his food supplies would last only until the end of the first week of February, while throughout the first two months of 1916 the British were in constant fear of the arrival in Mesopotamia of more of the possible 60,000 Turkish troops which were thought to have been released for action in any theatre by the change in the strategic situation. These fears were fuelled by the unexpectedly rapid build-up of Turkish forces throughout Mesopotamia to a total of 30,000 men by mid-December 1915.[133]

However, if the Turkish forces besieging and downstream from Kut were of better quality than those whom the British had defeated in the past, the new divisions arriving from France were not the élite force that Townshend's troops had become. Their departure from Europe had been more hurried than planned and their equipment was inadequate. Above all they lacked sufficient aircraft. In the crucial period from January to February 1916 the Turks, supplied with a few German Fokker fighters, had air superiority. The soldiers themselves were not used to the harsh climate of Mesopotamia, while their training had prepared them for the border wars of the North-West Frontier and for the trenches of Flanders, but not for the mirage and the floods of Mesopotamia. The relief forces' lack of familiarity with local conditions was matched by its commanders' ignorance of the terrain along the Tigris downstream from Kut. Though the British had fought over this area before, they had no accurate knowledge of its topography, which had been inadequately mapped. Moreover, sharp changes in climate had caused great alterations in the terrain.

The Turks skilfully chose their position to block the British advance on

Kut. On the right bank of the Tigris, upon which the town was situated, they constructed a series of trench lines between the river and some impenetrable marshes to the north. On the left bank the Turkish flank was hinged on the desert, which was likewise a severe barrier to any out-flanking movement.

The character of the campaign to relieve Kut was very different from the mobile operations which Nixon and Townshend had conducted in 1915. The scope for tactical skill on Aylmer's part was limited. On 6–9 and 13–14 January the relief force was decimated in a series of frontal assaults upon Turkish forces who would not yield. By the beginning of March 1916 the British realized that the Turkish force on the Tigris had not been reinforced to the extent expected, nor was it likely to receive many new additions for some time, since the strategic situation had turned into the Allies' favour.[134] However, by this time the British had already frittered away their strength. The uncertainty in the strategic situation after the battle of Ctesiphon was not the fault of British intelligence but the product of the Turks' basic ability to move troops from one theatre to another relatively quickly thanks to their possession of the internal lines of communication. Only a mastery of Turkish codes could have given the British the precise warnings of Turkish movements which they needed at this time.[135]

The recriminations which followed the fall of Kut on 29 April 1916 reflected the inability of the British to believe that the Turks could have beaten them in the field 'in a fair fight'. It is too easy to blame the dramatic end of the first part of the Mesopotamian Campaign upon equally spectacular faults of the British commanders and upon the incompetence of their intelligence officers. The decisions which Nixon took at the time were all reasonable up to the fatal decision to hold Kut. Nixon after all had won continually until then, even at Ctesiphon. The confidence of British commanders might be accounted a critical failure to interpret intelligence. But throughout 1914 and 1915 the British and Russians had trounced the Turks on the Egyptian, Caucasian and Mesopotamian Fronts and only the immense natural fortifications at Gallipoli seemed to allow them to hold their own there. There was no reason why the Allies should esteem the Turkish soldier. The impressions gained at the beginning of the First World War overshadowed the important conclusions which the officers of British military intelligence had made about the character of the Turkish Army during the first Balkan War. Indeed, what happened to Townshend is similar to what happened to the Bulgarians after the seemingly decisive defeats which they inflicted on the Turks in Macedonia in 1912. In both cases the Turks retired to a strongly fortified position nearer their supply centre. They then seemed to undergo a mercurial change of character and resisted tenaciously.

Ironically it was precisely the weaknesses of the Turkish Army which handicapped British intelligence so severely in the early part of the war. Turkish units varied considerably in fighting quality. There was a very great difference between units like the 51st Division, which was made up of Anatolian Turks, and the Arab regular units which the British had initially opposed. Just as important in the intelligence failure before Ctesiphon was the diversity in the sizes of Turkish units. The possession of a Turkish titular Order of Battle was of much less advantage to the British than the possession of a German OB. The Turkish Army was a more difficult target for British Intelligence than the German Army whose regular organization and generally high motivation made it a much more formidable opponent on the field. In fact the disaster at Kut was to a large extent the product of the makeshift character of the Turkish Army.

The Mesopotamian Expeditionary Force suffered from its own improvised organization. Tactical intelligence was made difficult by a lack of intelligence personnel and by a shortage of aircraft. But above all the main problem facing the British in Mesopotamia was the size of the Expeditionary Force. This meant that the sudden arrival of one élite Turkish division before the battle of Ctesiphon turned a spectacularly successful 'sideshow' into a strategic disaster.

NOTES

I would like to thank Dr John Ferris of the University of Calgary for suggesting this topic to me and for locating most of the source material. I would also like to thank him and Dr Christopher Andrew of Corpus Christi College, Cambridge, for very valuable advice.

1. National Army Museum (hereafter NAM), Leith-Ross Papers, 8312–69–10, 'The Strategic Side of I(a)', p.21.
2. The subject of British appreciations of the quality of the Turkish Army before the First World War has been discussed by David French in 'The Origins of the Dardanelles Campaign Reconsidered' in *History*, 1983. In this respect, French's excellent article is misleading. He argues that British disdain for the Turks before the Gallipoli landings was based on press accounts of the performance of theTurks in the Balkan Wars. These he claims, led to 'the destruction of the Turks' military reputation', and that 'more accurate reports ... reached London too late to prevent this'. He does not, however, explain why the War Office was more convinced by journalists than by its own military attachés. Indeed, he does not discuss British Military Intelligence in the Ottoman Empire. Moreover, it did not take the Balkan wars to destroy Turkey's military reputation. The reputation of the Turkish Army within European military circles had been low since at least the Crimean War and had not improved after the Russian War of 1877–78, though admittedly accounts of Russian successes were exaggerated.
3. This pamphlet was proscribed by the Home Department of the Government of India. India Office Library and Records (hereafter IOLR), Home Department (Political) Proceedings, B Series, June 1912, nos.1–6, IOR.POS.9831.
4. For Cunliffe-Owen's previous career as a British intelligence agent at New York engaged in watching Irish and Indian subversives see Richard Popplewell, 'The

Surveillance of Indian 'Seditionists' in North America, 1905–1915', in Christopher Andrew and Jeremy Noakes (eds.), *Intelligence and International Relations 1900–1945* (Exeter, 1987).

5. Military Attaché's report, dated Constantinople, 26 October 1912, Public Record Office (hereafter PRO) FO195/2436 (5608).

6. Tyrrell wrote of the initial offensive that 'in spite of the graft of modern ideas, the Turk tends to revert to his original ideals. The formation of irregular hordes is in his blood, and the half of the volunteers and Mustahfiz Corps which are now springing up like mushrooms are simply our old friends the bashi bazouks under a new name'. Report by Lt.Col. Tyrrell, dated Constantinople, 23 October 1912, PRO FO195/2436 (5604).

7. For details of the end of the Turkish Army in Macedonia, see PRO FO195/2436(6528). French is wrong in his implication that the Turks escaped virtually unscathed after their trouncing at the hands of the Bulgarians in the battles of Kirk Kulisse and Lulé Bulgas.

8. At the beginning of December Tyrrell reported that 'the army is very different in a material and moral sense, from what it was three weeks ago'.

9. Report by Military Attaché, dated 2 December 1912, PRO FO195/2438(6621).

10. Report by Cunliffe-Owen, dated Constantinople, 12 January 1914, PRO FO195/2457(60). The Turkish Army had, moreover, been weakened in the Balkan Wars by the loss of a large number of guns.

11. Thus on 10 January 1917 the British and French advocated 'the turning out of Europe of the Ottoman Empire as decidedly foreign to western civilization' in reply to President Wilson's peace proposals.

12. For example, some of the British officers in the Mesopotamian Expeditionary Force had had affectionate memories of the septuagenarian Circassian General, Mohammed Daghistani, who commanded Turkish operations in Arabistan until his death in 1915.

13. In 'Intelligence and its Interpretation: Mesopotamia 1914–1916', in Andrew and Noakes (eds.), op.cit., Peter Morris argues that numerous British actions between August and November 1914 *might* have been construed as by the Turks as provocation. Many within British governing circles later regarded the retention of the two warships as a mistake. Sir Beauchamp Duff, the C-in-C. of the Indian Army and Sir Louis Mallet, the Ambassador at Constantinople, argued that it was unwise of the British government to station two warships inside Turkish waters. However, they were concerned that this action might seem like provocation of the Turks to Indian Muslims, not that it might push Turkey into the German camp, for it was there already. Morris completely disregards the hostile movements of the Turkish Army directed towards Egypt and the Caucasus, and, unjustifiably, dismisses reports German military assistance to Turkey as 'unfounded'. The sheltering of the *Goeben* and the *Breslau* was a gross breach of neutrality which it was not possible for the British government to overlook. Morris fails to appreciate that the Young Turk triumvirate had already on 2 August 1914 signed a treaty pledging their support to Germany in the coming war. An account of the negotiations leading up to the formation of the alliance is given in Djemal Pasha, *Memories of a Turkish Statesman* (London, 1922), Ch.3, pp.107–17.

14. Russia had already declared war on Turkey on 2 November.

15. The British Military Attaché noted that Liman von Sanders would 'doubtless be in a position to scrutinize intelligence and political information relating to other countries and to advocate strategical plans ...'. Report by Cunliffe-Owen, dated 12 January 1914, PRO FO195/2457 (60).

16. Letter from Lytton to Staplehurst, 27 April 1878, Lytton Papers, IOLR MSS.EUR.E. 218/25A.

17. Telegram from Bax-Ironside, Sofia, to FO, 25 August 1914, PRO FO371/2138 (43125). Telegram from Mallet, Constantinople, to FO, 28 August 1914, PRO FO371/2138 (44220). The military attaché reported that at least 600 German officers and men had arrived in Constantinople in August 1914. Telegram from Mallet to FO, 5 September 1914, PRO FO371/2138 (46758). Telegram from Mallet to FO, 21

September 1914, PRO FO371/2138 (45385). Telegram from Mallet to FO, 19 September 1914, PRO FO371/2138 (512064). Telegram from Mallet to FO, 23 September 1914, PRO FO371/2138 (52354). Telegram from Bax-Ironside, Sofia, to FO, 28 August 1914, PRO FO371/2139 (44159/44217).

18. Telegram from Mallet to FO, PRO FO371/2138 (51418).
19. See the many reports by Samson in PRO FO195/2457 (215): 'Military information subsequent to 4 August 1914'.
20. By beginning of 1918 Samson was head of the Political Branch of MI1(c), the Secret Service.
21. Various reports by Egyptian agents are contained in PRO WO157/687, Intelligence Summaries: Egypt, September 1914.
22. The Foreign Office summarized Turkish moves hostile to Egypt in a statement which they issued on 1 November 1914. This is contained in a telegram from Grey to Mallet, dated 24 October 1914, PRO FO371/2139 (62834).
23. Telegram from Sir R. Rodd, Rome, dated 19 August 1914, PRO FO371/2138 (41038). The Italians informed the British on 30 August that the Caucases was the main Turkish objective. PRO FO371/2138 (45057).
24. Telegram from Sir G. Buchanan, St. Petersburg, to FO, 20 August 1914, PRO FO371/2138 (41532). Telegram from Sir G. Buchanan, St. Petersburg, to FO, 21 August 1914, PRO FO371/2138 (41748).
25. Telegram from Mallet, Constantinople, dated 23 August 1914, PRO FO371/2138 (42379).
26. Telegram from Mallet to FO, 27 September 1914, PRO FO371/2138 (53560).
27. Minute by Sir Eyre Crowe, dated 16 August 1914, PRO FO371/2138 (38623).
28. For example, telegram from Constantinople to FO, 16 August 1914, PRO FO371/2138 (39808); telegram from Mallet to FO, 18 August 1914, PRO FO371/2138 (40642); telegram from Mallet to FO, 20 August 1914, PRO FO371/2138; telegram from Mallet, PRO FO371/2138 (49871). When the Russian military authorities wanted to close the Bosporus Mallet and the Russian Ambassador at Constantinople successfully resisted them, being 'opposed to such a policy which is playing into the hands of Germany', PRO FO371/2138 (46082). At the end of September 1914 Mallet still argued that it was 'unlikely that Turks seriously contemplate engaging in a war in 3 distinct localities'. PRO FO371/2138 (53560).
29. As early as 15 August 1914 the Military Attaché reported that: 'the activity displayed by the military party led by Enver Pasha and inspired by his German advisers has been a blunder which has produced the most unfortunate economic results and which may eventually prove to be a disaster the consequences of which it is impossible to foresee'. Telegram from H. Beaumont, Constantinople, to FO, 15 August 1914, PRO FO371/2138 (46995). At the end of the month Cunliffe-Owen claimed that 'the country is entirely ruined' by the mobilization, Telegram from Mallet, Constantinople, dated 23 August 1914, op.cit. Telegram from Mallet, 2 September 1914, PRO FO371/2138 (45688).
30. The Russians regarded the Turkish military threat with similar equanimity. See, for example, telegram from Mallet to Grey, dated 27 August 1914, PRO FO371/2138 (43850).
31. Sir Beauchamp Duff, the Commander-in-Chief of the Indian Army, wrote that 'since from the material point of view Turkey can give Germany no useful help, German influence must be wholly directed to turning the spiritual influence of the Caliphate to the best advantage; in other words to starting a great Pan-Islamic movement and if possible a 'Jehad'. Letter from Beauchamp Duff to Hardinge, 6 October 1914, Hardinge Papers, Vol.88, part A, p.284a.
32. Memorandum entitled 'The Role of India in a Turkish War', Barrow Papers, IOLR MSS.EUR.E.420/12.
33. Minute by Sir E. Crowe entitled 'The Arabs and Turkey', 26 September 1914, PRO FO371/2139 (53671).
34. Barrow, diary entry, 25 September 1914. IOLR Barrow Papers, MSS.EUR.E.420/36.
35. Letter from Barrow to Lord Crewe, 25 September 1915. IOLR Barrow Papers

MSS.EUR.E.420/12.

36. Memorandum entitled 'The Role of India in a Turkish War', Barrow Papers, IOLR MSS.EUR.E.420/12.
37. Letter from Beauchamp Duff to Hardinge, 6 October 1914, op.cit.
38. Telegram from Mallet to FO, dated 26 August 1914, PRO FO371/2136 (43529). Telegram from Mallet to FO, dated 31 August 1914, PRO FO371/2138 (45058).
39. The Government of India's Department of Criminal Intelligence, which provided information on the activities of native threats to British rule was similarly run on a low budget. Despite the existence of a strong revolutionary movement in North America and in the Far East, the Department of Criminal Intelligence had no details of shipping routes in the Pacific in 1914. See Richard Popplewell, 'British Intelligence in the Far East, 1914–1918' (*Intelligence and National Security*, forthcoming).
40. A.T. Wilson, *Loyalties – Mesopotamia 1914–1917* (Oxford, 1930), p.8.
41. Edmund Candler, *The Long Road to Baghdad,* Vol.I, Ch.9, p.111 (London, 1919).
42. War Diary of the General Staff, Force 'D', November 1914, PRO WO95/4965. The General Staff of IEF 'D' only landed on 16 November 1914.
43. Leith-Ross said that the system of collating information used by the British in Mesopotamia 'stood the test of 4 years of war'. 'The Strategical Side of I(a)', p.8.
44. NAM Leith-Ross Papers, 8312–69–10. 'The Strategical Side of I(a)', pp.1, 9.
45. NAM Leith-Ross Papers, 'Character and qualifications of intelligence personnel'.
46. NAM Leith-Ross Papers, 'The Tactical Side of I(a)', p.18.
47. Ibid, p.19.
48. 'The Character and qualifications of intelligence personnel', op.cit., p.2.
49. Telegrams from the Chief of the General Staff to the GOC, IEF 'D', 11 November 1915.
50. 'The Strategical Side of I(a)', pp.4, 8.
51. Ie Europe, Anatolia, the area from Cilicia to Aden, Mesopotamia and the Caucasus.
52. By the end of 1915 the bi-weekly summaries were printed. 'The Strategical Side of I(a)', p.10; 'The Tactical Side of I(a)', pp.16, 23.
53. 'The Strategical Side of I(a)', p.7.
54. 'The Strategical Side of I(a)', p.4.
55. *Official History*, Appendix XXX.
56. 'Copy of the Turkish Order of Battle, 30 August 1916, forwarded by the Director of Military Intelligence, War Office', IOLR L/MIL/5/734.
57. 'The Strategical Side of I(a)', p.14.
58. 'The Strategical Side of I(a)', p.17.
59. 'The Strategical Side of I(a)', p.14 Leith-Ross claimed that the average of 6 or so statements would give an accurate figure.
60. 'The Strategical Side of I(a)', p.18.
61. 'Secret Service or Intelligence, Sub-Section (B), GHQ', pp.9–10.
62. 'The Strategical Side of I(a)', p.17.
63. 'Secret Service or Intelligence, Sub-Section (B), GHQ', p.11
64. 'The Strategical Side of I(a)', p.14.
65. 'Character and qualifications of intelligence personnel', p.5.
66. In Leith-Ross's opinion no particular race among the inhabitants of Mesopotamia was better than any other. He made the folowing conclusions. Jews and Christians were the best educated, but with very few exceptions they lacked the requisite courage for agent work. Kurds were plucky but extremely grasping and not too bright. Arabs were more intelligent than Kurds but inveterate liars, prone to exaggerate and sometimes timid. Persians were more nimble witted than Arabs, but even worse liars. 'Character and qualifications of intelligence personnel', p.7.
67. 'Secret Service or Intelligence, Sub-Section (B), GHQ', p.1.
68. 'Character and qualifications of intelligence personnel', p.5.
69. 'Secret Service or Intelligence, Sub-Section (B), GHQ', pp.2–3.
70. 'Character and qualifications of intelligence personnel', p.7.
71. 'Secret Service or Intelligence, Sub-Section (B), GHQ', p.6.
72. NAM Leith-Ross Papers, 'Report on surveys, Mesopotamia Expeditionary Force',

p.5.
73. NAM Leith-Ross Papers, 'Note on the method of working the Topographical Sub-Section I(c) of intelligence in Mesopotamian Expeditionary Force', p.1.
74. 'Report on surveys, Mesopotamian Expeditionary Force', p.1.
75. Daily Intelligence Summary, 1 September 1915, PRO WO157/779.
76. All the evidence for Turkish travelling times which Leith-Ross cites, comes from 1917.
77. Telegram from Viceroy to Secretary of State, in 'Précis of Correspondence Regarding the Mesopotamian Expedition; Its Genesis and Development' (prepared in the Military Department of the India Office), Barrow Papers, IOLR MSS.EUR.E.420/12.
78. On the basis of agent reports the Egyptian Intelligence Bureau reported on 23 December that the Turkish 4th Army Corps, numbering 36,000 men, or 7 times the size of 'Dunsterforce', was moving from Syria to either the Red Sea or Basra. The latter seemed quite likely because the force was equipped with boats. Subsequent information, however, showed that the 4th Army Corps was not heading for Basra. Nevertheless, indefinite information of large Turkish reinforcements on their way to Baghdad continued to arrive from Egypt and other sources.
79. Telegram from Sir G. Buchanan, Petrograd, to Sir E. Grey, 28 December 1914. Telegram from War Office to the Chief of the General Staff, India, 29 December 1914. The findings of Soane, the employee of the Anglo-Persian Oil Company who was repatriated to England via Aleppo, were repeated in a telegram from Secretary of State to Viceroy, dated 10 March 1915. 'Précis of Correspondence Regarding the Mesopotamian Expedition: Its Genesis and Development', Barrow Papers, IOLR MSS.EUR.E.420/12.
80. In the early part of the war the British consistently over-estimated German organizational ability, regarding the Germans' ambitious plans to raise India and Afghanistan at face value. The Germans intended at this time to create a revolt in India by shipping vast quantities of arms to revolutionary groups in India. By 1916 the British realized that they could check these conspiracies with only a small secret service operation. See Popplewell, 'British Intelligence in the Far East', op.cit.
81. Telegram from Viceroy to Secretary of State dated 3 March 1915, in 'Précis of Correspondence Regarding the Mesopotamian Expedition: Its Genesis and Development', Barrow Papers, IOLR MSS.EUR.E.420/12.
82. Report received through the Political Resident, Persian Gulf (Bushire), from Vice-Consul, Ahwaz, transmitted in telegram from the Senior Naval Officer, Persian Gulf, to the Admiralty, 22 January 1915. 'Précis of Correspondence Regarding the Mesopotamian Expedition: Its Genesis and Development'. IOLR Barrow Papers MSS. EUR.E.420/12.
    Bushire was the centre of the Political Department's intelligence-gathering in Persia. The Political Resident there was also Consul-General, and thus served both the Government of India and the Foreign Office.
83. Official History, Vol.II, pp.217–18. General Moberly had access to a translation of a postwar account of the Mesopotamian Campaign by Staff Bimbashi (Major) Muhammed Amin of the former Turkish 6th Army.
84. Report by Lieutenant R.O. Harvey, 10 April 1915, forwarding information received from Ali Ghalib Effendi, a former officer of the Turkish Police. PRO WO157/776.
85. NAM Leith-Ross Papers, 'The Tactical Side of I(a)', p.12.
86. Only one of the first batch of two Maurice Farman biplanes was operational a month after their arrival in Mesopotamia. Maurice Farmans were particularly prone to overheating in Mesopotamia. Weekly Summary of Intelligence, 23 June 1915, PRO WO157/776.
87. NAM Leith-Ross Papers, 'The Tactical Side of I(a)', pp.3–7; 'Report on advanced air-photo compilation section, Mesopotamian Expeditionary Force.
88. Daily Intelligence Summary, 10 July 1915, PRO WO157/777. Weekly Summary of Intelligence, 7 July 1915, PRO WO157/777. The actual strength of the Turks, according to the Official History, Vol.II, p.297, was 4,200 regular troops.
89. Summary of Intelligence, 23 July 1915, PRO WO157/777.

90. Weekly Summary of Intelligence, 2 October 1915, PRO WO157/780. The Turks had 38 guns, not the estimated 23.
91. Weekly Summary of Intelligence, 23 June 1915, PRO WO157/776. Daily Intelligence Summaries, 16 and 19 September 1915, PRO WO157/779.
92. Telegram from GOC, Amara, to Genstaff, Intelligence, Basra, 21 June 1915, PRO WO157/776.
93. Weekly Summary of Intelligence, 23 June 1915, PRO WO157/776. Daily Intelligence Summary, 29 September 1915, PRO WO157/779.
94. In the pre-battle reconnaissance of the Turkish position the General Staff placed great reliance on air reconnaissance. See, generally, War Diary of the General Staff, IEF 'D', September 1915, PRO WO95/4965.
95. Major General Sir C.V.F. Townshend, *My Campaign in Mesopotamia,* General Staff, War Diary, 17 September 1915, PRO WO95/4965.
96. Although some Indian trans-frontier troops deserted to the Turks the night before the battle and informed Nur-ud-Din that Townshend intended to make his main attack against the Turkish left, Nur-ud-Din took their story as a ruse.
97. The operation map prepared by air reonnaissance gave a fair indication of the relative position of the different topographical features. However, the wide variations of its compass bearings with those made personally by the Royal Engineer leading Delamain's column made it inadvisable to include any compass bearing in the orders issued to the column. At that time the Air Force in Mesopotamia had not got a really reliable compass for aeroplane work. *Official History,* Vol.I, p.321.
98. Daily Summary of Intelligence, 2 October 1915, PRO WO157/780.
99. Daily Summary of Intelligence, 2 October 1915, PRO WO157/780.
100. Telegram from Nixon to Chief of the General Staff, India, 29 September, 'Telegrams relating to Sir John Nixon's advance on Baghdad', Barrow Papers, IOLR MSS.EUR. E.420/12.
101. Weekly Intelligence Summary, 4 October 1915, Intelligence Summaries, Egypt, October 1915, PRO WO157/696.
102. Weekly Summary of Intelligence, 2 October 1915, PRO WO157/780.
103. A large number of reports from Samson's agents are contained in 'Intelligence Reports from Athens', PRO WO158/922.
104. Telegram from Nixon to the Chief of the General Staff, India, in 'Précis of Correspondence Regarding the Mesopotamian Expedition: Its Genesis and Development'. Details of the topography around Baghdad were drawn up by I(a) in Summary of Intelligence, 22 October 1915, PRO WO157/780.
    The difficulties which the Turks had in supplying their units in the Baghdad area after the city's fall in March 1917 justified Nixon's argument.
105. Private telegram from Viceroy to Secretary of State, ibid.
106. Weekly Summary of Intelligence, 16 October 1915, Intelligence Summaries: Egypt, PRO WO157/780.
107. Intelligence Summary, 2 November 1915, Dardanelles General Headquarters Intelligence Summaries, PRO WO157/652.
108. For example, an agent reported that 16,000 men had left for Baghdad. Intelligence Summaries, Egypt, October 1916, PRO WO157/696. On 14 November the Intelligence Department reported that 15,000 men had left Syria for Baghdad.
109. His reports at this time took only a day to reach Mesopotamia. See, generally, Daily Summaries of Intelligence for November 1915 in PRO WO157/781.
110. Daily Intelligence Summary, 8 November 1915, PRO WO157/781.
111. Daily Intelligence Summary, 14 November, PRO WO157/781.
112. Daily Intelligence Summary, 17 November 1915, PRO WO157/781.
113. Intelligence Summary, 16 November, Dardanelles, General Headquarters: Intelligence Summaries, PRO WO157/652.
114. Intelligence Summaries, 9, 10, 16, 19, 26, 28 November, Dardanelles Headquarters, Intelligence Summaries, PRO WO157/652.
115. Local agents first reported heavy reinforcements at Baghdad at the end of October: Daily Intelligence Summary, 3 November 1915. However, a week later this infor-

mation was contradicted by an agent at Mosul: Daily Intelligence Summary, 4 November 1915. Agents greatly exaggerated the numbers of Turkish troops at Baghdad. The General Staff received reports that there were 20,000 Turks there on 23 October: Daily Intelligence Summary, 11 November 1915. By 19 November agents reported the presence of 50,000 Turks there: Daily Intelligence Summary, 19 November 1915. PRO WO157/781.

116. Intelligence Summary, 27 October–2 November 1915, Intelligence Summaries: Egypt, October 1915, PRO WO157/696.
117. Telegram from Secretary of State to Viceroy, 21 October 1915, 'Précis of Correspondence Regarding the Mesopotamian Expedition: Its Genesis and Development'. Barrow Papers, IOLR MSS.EUR.E.420/12.
118. Note by Barrow in 'Précis of Correspondence Regarding the Mesopotamian Expedition: Its Genesis and Development', Barrow Papers IOLR MSS.EUR.E.420/12.
119. See generally, Mesopotamia General Headquarters, Intelligence Summaries, for October and November 1915, PRO WO157/780–781, and the War Diary of the General Staff, PRO WO95/4965.
120. POW information contradicted accurate reports that the new troops were likely to stand and fight, as did the 45th Division's precipitate withdrawal as the British advance guard arrived near Ctesiphon early in October 1915. The General Staff remarked: 'It's always the same story; the moment we show any signs of force the enemy disappears!', War Diary of the General Staff, 12 and 28 October 1915, PRO WO95/4965.
121. Sir Beauchamp Duff thought that Nixon had now to attack the Turks. Letter from Beauchamp Duff to Hardinge, 19 November 1915, Cambridge University Library (hereafter CUL) Hardinge Papers, Vol.90, part A, p.389.
122. I(a) estimated that there were about three and a half divisions present – the correct figure was three and two-thirds, and that they numbered about 4,000 infantry each.
123. *Official History*, Vol.II, Appendix XXX, op.cit.
124. Letter from Beauchamp Duff to Hardinge, 19 November 1915, op.cit.
125. Account of Muhammed Amin, in *Official History*, Vol.II, p.82.
126. General Staff, War Diary, 24 November 1915, PRO WO96/4965.
127. General Staff, War Diary, 1 December 1915, PRO WO95/4965.
128. General Moberly wrote that, 'General Delamain's opinion as to the physical condition of the men of his own brigade on their arrival at Kut makes it clear that the exhaustion of the men was not a contributory factor to the occupation of Kut', *Official History*, Vol.II, p.160.
129. Hardinge to Chamberlain, 30 November 1915, CUL Hardinge Papers, Vol.90.
130. Sir Beauchamp Duff wrote to Lord Hardinge on 15 December 1915: 'It is unfortunately beginning to look as if we may have very great difficulty relieving Townshend, while the more I hear of his actual position at Kut, the less I like it'. CUL Hardinge Papers, Vol.90, part A, p.441.
131. 'Appreciation of the Situation in Mesopotamia by the Military Secretary, India Office', dated 24 January 1916, Barrow Papers, IOLR MSS,EUR.E.420/12.
132. General Aylmer took over command of the British forces in the field on 12 December 1915. Nixon remained Commander-in-Chief until his resignation because of ill health and replacement by the former Chief of the General Staff, India, Sir Percy Lake, on 19 January 1916.
133. 'Memorandum by His Excellency the Commander-in-Chief, dated the 16th December 1915', CUL Hardinge Papers, Vol.90, part A, p.442.
134. In Caucasus the Russians had resumed their advance, while Russian detachments had entered Northern Persia, as a successful deterrent to Persian support for Germany. In Egypt the British position was secure.
135. The decisive advantages which possession of Turkish ciphers gave the British in 1917 has been discussed in John Ferris's definitive article on 'The British Army and Signals Intelligence in the Field During the First World War', *Intelligence and National Security*, Vol.3, No.4 (October 1988).

Institutionalized Deception and Perception Reinforcment: Allenby's Campaigns in Palestine

YIGAL SHEFFY

The British Campaign in Egypt and Palestine during the Great War (1916–18) was distinguished by several features which greatly differed from those of the warfare in the main theater of war, the Western Front. Mobile warfare, extensive use of cavalry and mounted formations, operational-logistic struggle against severe desert conditions and a constantly changing battle-ground were some of the characteristics marking the Egyptian Expeditionary Force (EEF) – the official title of the British and Commonwealth formations in this campaign.

The Campaign's unique nature has given rise to the probability that an additional weapon-system – deception – was extensively exploited. Two major deception operations were implemented in the course of the Palestine Campaign. The first was executed before the Third Battle of Gaza, on the southern border of Palestine, in October 1917. This battle resulted in the EEF advancing into Palestine. The second was carried out a year later (September 1918) during the Battle of Megiddo, which crushed Turkish disposition in Palestine and Syria and consequently, decided the war's fate in this theater.

The deception operations initiated by the British in Palestine are considered the forerunners of modern deception and their imprint was to be found in succeeding major deceptions during the Second World War. However, the existing literature has so far discussed only some isolated sensational episodes of these operations, while overlooking the EEF's novel concept of deception as an integral ingredient of operational plans and battle-procedure. Likewise, it has not weighed up the part played by the deception in causing the enemy's overall surprise and its effect on the Turks' reactions. This study will endeavour to clarify these issues.

THE THIRD BATTLE OF GAZA

The Turkish Army's attack on the Suez Canal at the beginning of 1915 stimulated the British decision to advance into the Sinai Peninsula in order to protect this vital waterway. The successful advance took place in 1916 and by March 1917 both armies were deployed on the Egypt–Palestine border along a line stretching from Gaza on the Mediterranean shore eastward to the desert town of Beersheba. In the same month, General Archibald Murray, then Commander of the EEF, launched his first offensive on Gaza, and following its failure, the Turkish retreat was stopped. In April, the Second Battle of Gaza began but this also failed, despite the use of tanks, close naval gun support, gas shells and flame-throwers.

The Turkish setbacks during the war and the desire to restore its honor and credibility brought the Turkish Supreme Command and its German advisers to the conclusion that it was imperative to carry out an impressive militry operation. Within this framework, the renewed conquest of Baghdad – Operation 'Yilderim' (Lightning) – was planned. However, delays in assembling the force and the fear that a Britisah offensive in Palestine would foil the plan compelled the Turks, at the end of summer 1917, to divert forces from the north towards the Palestine front.

In June, the British government decided that it would not stop at mopping-up the Sinai Peninsula, but would take all of Palestine, since it sought to end the stalemate on the Western front as well as provide a means for diverting the Turkish forces assembling for Yilderim in Northern Syria. By the end of June, General Allenby was appointed Commander of the Egyptian Expeditionary Force.

The British Plan of Operation

During the British planning stages, the Turkish Army was deployed in southern Palestine together with the 8th Army HQ under the command of the German General Kress von Kressenstein, who had three corps HQs and eight divisions at his disposal. Of these, a three-division corps was deployed in the Gaza area, a similar corps in the Tel Sheria-el Hareira area and a two-division corps, one of them a cavalry division, in Beersheba (see Map 1). The reinforcing of the sector was carried out in parallel with British planning and preparations. The overall strength of the force in the front line was estimated at about 33,000 infantry, 1,400 cavalry and about 300 artillery pieces.

The Egyptian Expeditionary Force was organized in three corps, also consisting of eight divisions (two more divisions having arrived during September–October). The major part of the British force was deployed in the Deir el Belah-Rafah area, while units from two cavalry divisions were deployed in the southern part of the northern sector, between Gamali and Abasan el Kebir. The fighting force of the Expeditionary corps numbered some 60,000 infantry, 12,000 cavalry and about 450 artillery pieces.[1]

In July 1917, General Allenby approved the main outlines of the offensive plan. Unlike previous occasions, the British planned to surprise the enemy by diverting their main effort towards the left flank of the enemy disposition in Beersheba. Their aim was to push toward the main Turkish disposition while 'bending' it back towards Gaza; a secondary effort was to attack Gaza frontally.

The following is a summary of the phases, the forces and their assignments:

> Phase 1: the taking of Beersheba from the south by the Mounted Desert Corps (two divisions) and the XXth Corps (four divisions).
> Phase 2: the taking of the frontline in the Gaza sector from the South-West by the XXIst Corps (three divisions).
> Phase 3: the attack of the Turkish left flank on the Tel el Sheria-Tel el Hariera line from Beersheba and forcing it back towards Gaza by the XXth Corps and the Mounted Desert Corps (seven divisions in all). The Mounted Desert Corps would outflank the Turkish disposition and advance north of the XXth Corps to capture water sources and secure the flank. This phase was to begin 24–48 hours after the launching of Phase 2. 'Z'-Day was set for 31 October 1917.[2]

The British were to transfer six divisions (two of them mounted) to the sector of the main effort. To surprise the enemy there, they planned to conceal the assembling of the force before the offensive began, while diverting the enemy's attention to Gaza. To this end, a large-scale deception operation was initiated. The allocation of sizeable forces to the secondary effort in Gaza was to enable Allenby to operate in an alternative direction, should the main effort fail.

The British Intellignce Picture

On the even of the operation, the Expeditionary Force had at its disposal an intelligence network which gradually improved as 'Z'-Day drew nearer.

A number of factors contributed to this:

- The stability of the line of following the second Gaza offensive did not necessitate many changes in the enemy disposition.
- Most of the Turkish divisions were deployed along the front line. This proximity facilitated collection.
- An efficient collection system based on several main agencies:

> 1. *Sigint*. From October 1916 British intelligence had effective access to most of the codes and ciphers used by the German and Turkish headquarters and formations in Palestine. They read much of the enemy radio traffic in the theater and their interception, processing and deciphering capability went as far as penetrating

MAP 1

THE ADVANCE THROUGH PHILISTIA: SITUATION AT 6 P.M. ON 29 OCTOBER 1917

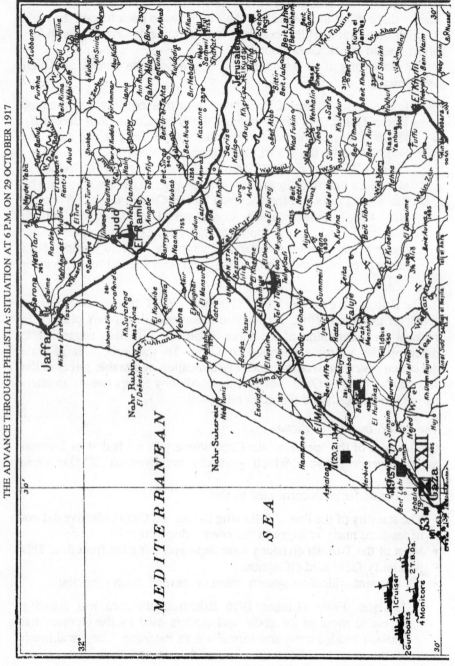

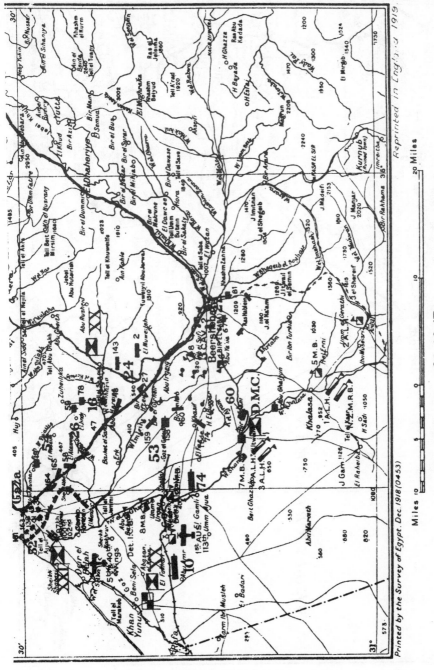

Situation at 6 p.m. on 29-10-17 as known at G.H.Q.E.E.F.

Printed by the Survey of Egypt. Dec. 1918 (0-4-53)

Reprinted in England 1919.

MAP 2

THE ADVANCE THROUGH PHILISTIA: SITUATION AT 6 P.M. ON 31 OCTOBER 1917

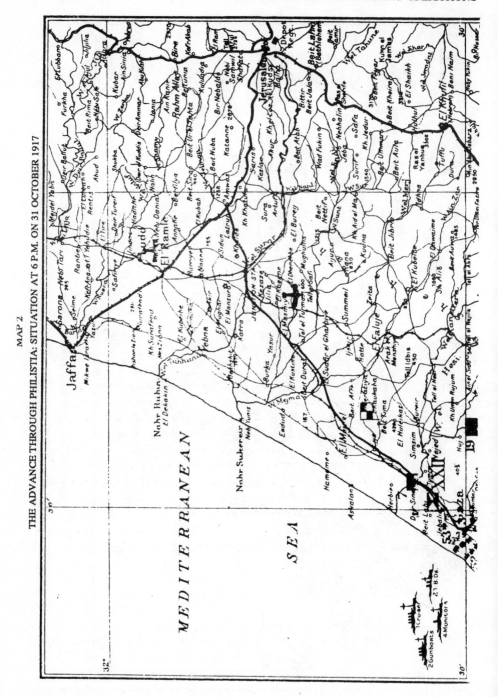

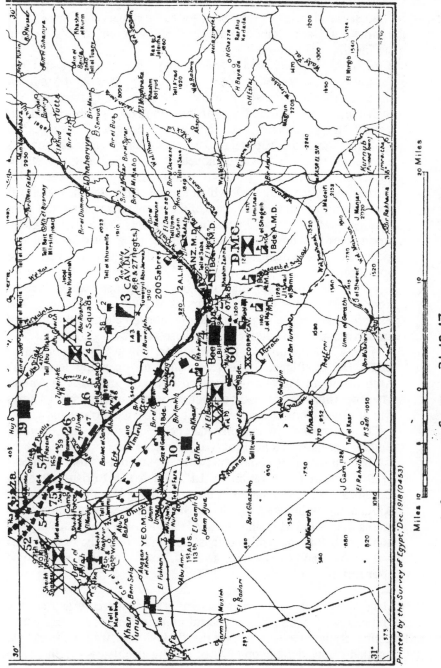

Situation at 6 p.m. on 31-10-17 as known at G.H.Q.E.F.F

Printed by the Survey of Egypt; Dec.1918 (0453)

communications between Turkish Army Group HQ and its subordinate armies. The British acquired a remarkable amount of
information from Sigint and it played an important role in forming
the intelligence picture.[3]
2. *Airborne reconnaissance, observation and photography.* The
capability to carry out sorties grew as the number of aircraft
allocated for the purpose increased and their quality improved. To
each corps was allocated a squadron or flight, which carried out
tactical reconnaissance. A long-range dedicated photography
squadron was at the disposal of the Expeditionary Force HQ, as was
a balloons unit, which was deployed in the front and was used for
observation purposes. In-depth observation patrols were also
carried out by naval aircraft, which took off from British vessels off
the Palestine coast. In 1917 some of the reconnaissance aircraft were
already fitted with radio communication sets, so that they could
report their findings in real time. The carrying-out of sorties was
made easier, as British superiority in the air was achieved before the
operation.[4]
3. *POWs.* A sizeable quantity of intelligence was obtained
from interrogation and debriefing of POWs and deserters. The
Expeditionary Force's intelligence officer even claimed that most of
the information was derived from these sources.[5]
4. *Agents.* The Intelligence Bureau in Port Said in Egypt (a branch of
EEF GHQ Intelligence) was responsible for operating Jewish and
Arab agents in Palestine, Syria and Lebanon and in Asia Minor.
Their opertion was carried out indirectly by means of special ships
which sailed along the eastern coast of the Mediterranean.

There are some indications that field formations also operated
Beduin agents for tactical local assignments.

The following espionage network was formed from members
of the Jewish organization 'NILI', which the British called 'A
Organization'. It was based in an agricultural experiment center in
Atlit, a few kilometers south of Haifa. Its members volunteered
their services in 1915, while most of their activity took place in 1917
until just before the British offensive. At that time, the organization
was exposed and its members arrested. Some died or were executed
after torture.

NILI comprised about 40 members in its idealistic core and several
dozen more Jewish sympathizers and informants dispersed in key points
in Palestine, Syria, and even among the Turkish military. The organization supplied a considerable quantity of intelligence that was reliable, up
to date, and of considerable use. It included topographic intelligence and

visual intelligence about the ground and aerial activity, deployment and Orbat (order of battle) of the enemy. More important, it assembled information and documents about enemy intentions, its expected reserves, its strength and further intimate information from within the army's ranks which were gleaned from Turkish and German military personnel. It succeeded in obtaining ciphers or code lists, which served high-grade communications linking Damascus to Turkey and Germany. The information was assembled in Atlit and given to couriers who landed from a mother ship and boarded it again the next day. This ship would thereupon sail directly to Cyprus and the highlights of the information would be transmitted from the intelligence station on the island to Egypt. Thus much time was saved.[6]

Arab agents operated mainly in the coastal areas of Lebanon and Syria as loners and concentrated mainly on visual intelligence.

The intelligence picture which the British forces drew up was not uniformly accurate. The Expeditionary Force had an accurate picture of the enemy's strategic intentions and the identification of the enemy formations deployed on the line.[7] On the other hand, the picture was deficient in overestimating of the combat strength of the formations and in the exaggeration of the amount of reserves and reinforcements the enemy could muster against the Expeditionary Force.[8]

As the date for launching the offensive drew nearer, these over-estimations were gradually corrected, and the British forces had a reasonably good picture of the Turkish–German intelligence capability and of its intelligence estimate.

Various indications lead one to conclude that the decision to adopt a plan of deception had already been taken at an early stage of the operational planning and was accepted as an inseparable part of it. Lieutenant-General Philip Chetwode, then commander of the Eastern Front and originator of the operational concept, had written in the first draft submitted to the new OC in C on 21 June:

> We must give the enemy every reason to believe until the last moment that we will contemplate renewing our efforts against his right. Subsidiary operations against portions of his Gaza front will, I think, be unnecessary.[9]

A month later, Allenby stated that his policy was to encourage the belief that the attack would come against Gaza and that some measures to strengthen this belief had already been implemented.[10] In mid-August, six weeks before 'Z'-Day, he ordered the commanders of his recently-created Corps to carry out deception activity 'as will cause the enemy to be apprehensive of a serious atack against the right and right centre'.[11]

The intelligence estimate at the disposal of the deception planners[12] –

among them the very resourceful and active GSO2 (intelligence) of the
Expeditionary Force, Major Meinertzhagen – emphasized that:

- The Turks were aware of the British intentions to attack. For this
  reason and owing to the impressive British order-of-battle, it would not
  be possible to conceal the preparations for the offensive.
- The proven capability of the Turkish Intelligence (especially in
  the field of air observation) would not permit the concealment of the
  concentration of the force against the Turkish left flank.[13]
- The enemy intelligence estimate determined that the British attack
  would be launched from the direction of Gaza, which was the
  dangerous direction: 'It is there [Gaza] that the Turks at present expect
  us to attack and I hope to keep their attention so fixed'.[14] General
  Allenby's officers believed that prevailing circumstances might help to
  convince the enemy that Gaza would be again the main target. Among
  them were the precedent of the two previous attacks, the concentrating
  of British forces in the northern-western sector (in front of Gaza)
  and the tactical and logistical advantages of approaching from this
  direction, as opposed to the difficulties in the other flank. Moreover, a
  westerly attack would facilitate close naval fire support and enable
  auxiliary sea-landing. The Turks actually expected an enemy landing
  north of Gaza, a fact well-known to British intelligence.
- In order to avoid visual detection of the deception in the initial
  movement phase, enemy aircraft must be kept at a distance by
  augmenting the air defence disposition.

The deception had two objectives:

> 1. *Strategic:* to pin down the four or five Turkish divisions deployed
> in the Aleppo area (for Operation Yilderim) and thereby prevent
> the reinforcement of the disposition in Palestine.
> 2. *Operational:* to pin down the deployed enemy forces and reserves
> in the Gaza sector, both before 'Z'-Day, as well as during the first
> two phases, thereby assisting the forces attacking Beersheba (phase
> one) and the main defense position (phase two). Consequently, the
> deception was to continue to fulfill its function throughout the initial
> phases of the offensive.

The British intended to coax the Turkish intelligence into formulating
the following intelligence picture:

> *At the strategic level:* The British offensive planned in the Middle
> East front would take place in northern Syria by seaborne forces
> landed apparently in Alexandretta Bay. It is not known whether the
> landing was to be presented as the main effort, or just as a secondary
> one.

At the operational level: The main British effort in the south would be carried out in the Gaza sector, by a frontal ground attack and a flanking sea-landing. A feint attack would be launched in Beersheba, the goal of which is to attract the enemy reserves in that direction, both before 'Z-Day as well as after the onset of the main effort against Gaza. 'Z'-Day would not occur before 4 November 1917 and would probably be around mid-November. ('Z'-Day was actually 31 October 1917.) The viewing of the attack on Gaza as a secondary effort rather than as just a diversion (to which only token forces are allocated) directly served the deception story and its intention.

The British aimed at achieving a misleading type of deception, in order to channel the enemy into a definite – wrong – conclusion. But the above assessment established that the actual preparations 'may cause the Turks to expect an attack on their left'.[15] They hoped, therefore, that in such a case, the Gaza-orientated preparations would at least cause the enemy to fall into an ambiguity-increasing deception which 'will still leave him in doubt as to which is the feint and which is the real attack'.[16]

Implementation of the Strategic Deception

The project of a naval landing – genuine or notional – on the Syrian coast and the Gulf of Alexandretta (Iskanderun) made many periodical appearances upon the Mediterranean military scene during the Great War. An actual landing was first considered in December 1914 as a diversion to disrupt Turkish communications with Syria.[17] As early as July 1916 the British War Committee, while advising the Commander in Chief, Egypt, to prepare for an advance to El Arish in Sinai, recommended that 'The Admiralty and General Staff should develop naval and military measures designed to make the enemy expect a landing at Alexandretta or Smyrna'.[18] Apparently this recommendation was adopted by the authorities in Cairo and was implemented in the second half of the year. Consequently, Naval Intelligence office in Port Said carried out an amateurish deception attempt to convince the Turks that they would soon face a landing in Alexandretta via Cyprus. Its objective was to draw forces from the Sinai and Mesopotamia Fronts by dissemination of rumors and signposting throughout Cyprus, which hinted at an expected massing of forces.[19] An alternative operational plan to flank the Turkish line through the east bank of the Jordan River recommended in August, 'a demonstration based on Cyprus and Egypt to force the enemy to maintain his coast-defense troops in position'.[20]

There is no concrete evidence on when Allenby decided to create this notional threat. In mid-September, answering the CIGS' questions

MAP 3

THE GAZA OFFENSIVE: SCHEMATIC OPERATIONAL PLAN

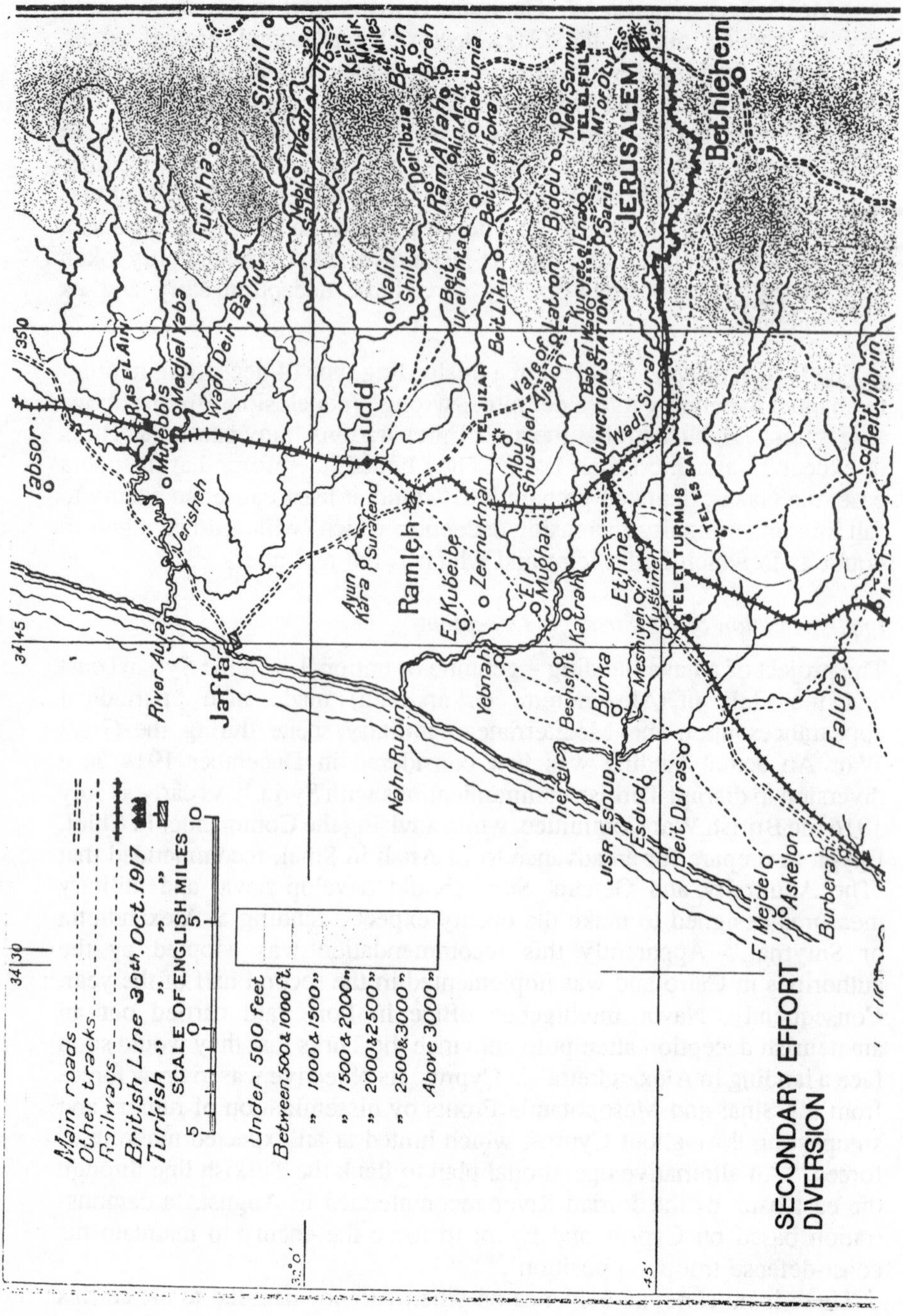

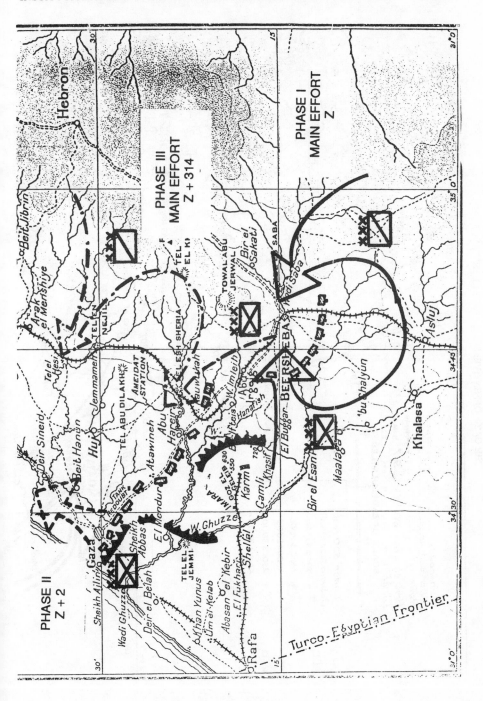

MAP 4

THE GAZA OFFENSIVE: SCHEMATIC DECEPTION PLAN

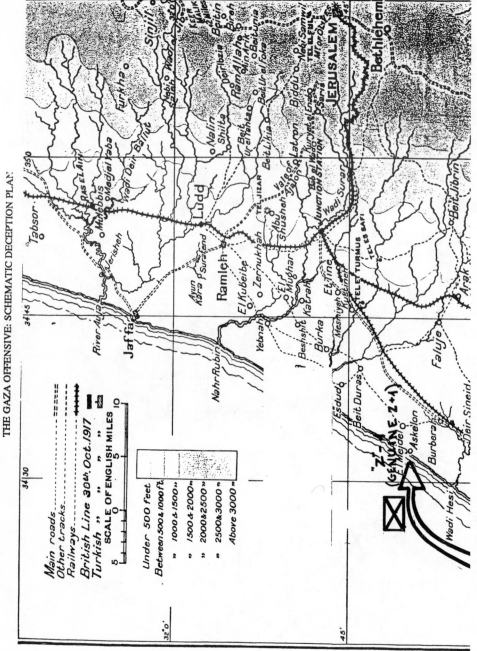

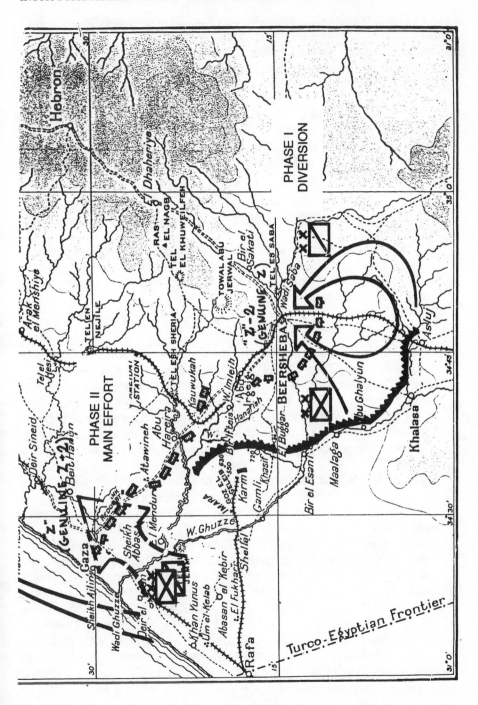

concerning possible assistance of the French Navy, he concluded: 'I think
they would do most good by threatening the Northern Coast of Syria. In
connection with French naval operations, manifestations of activity in
Cyprus might be useful – real and stimulated'.[21] Yet the Commander in
Chief did not mention in his answer any existing plan to create such a
deceptive picture.

The actual deception plan to create a picture of a landing threat on the
Syrian coast was approved by Allenby's HQ on 6 October ('Z'-Day –25).
The channels that were to mislead the Turks into concentrating on Cyprus
were based upon visual and wireless deception and rumor-spreading.
Their activity included:

• Marking sites for new camps and beginning to construct them.
• Intensifying the movement and activity of the small garrison stationed
  in Cyprus.
• Radio communications activity, which included deceptive messages.
• Apparent interest of dealers in purchasing merchandise and provisions
  on a large scale for troops in the island as well as for overseas forces
  following a landing operation.
• Overt preparations on piers and ports for loading of equipment,
  soldiers and horses.

Word of the activity obviously reached the Turks. According to Turkish
sources (quoted in the official British history), on 17 October, 11 days
after the deception began, a special air reconnaissance sortie was dispatched over the island. Its findings indicated that no unusual activity
or preparations were taking place in Cyprus. At any rate, there is
no evidence to indicate that a change in the Turkish intelligence estimate or military activity had taken place as a result of the deception
attempt.

The official British history attributes the failure to lack of sufficient time
to create a convincing visual picture between the beginning of the
operation and the enemy sortie. It seems that the failure was more deeply
rooted. In 1917 the German GHQ apparently estimated that there was a
possibility of a sea-landing of the Entente forces in Alexandretta Bay,
since this would be advantageous to the attackers and would hasten the
end of the war. The Turkish Command, on the other hand, did not attach
much importance to this possibility.[22] This might be for several reasons:
rejection of this course of action as very unlikely, or dismissal of its value
and chances of success, even if carried out (as a lesson learned from the
Dardanelles campaign). It is even possible that the Turks were prisoners
of their own desire to implement Operation Yilderim and tended to
dismiss any indications that might hamper their plans. Even after the
danger to the Western flank of the Army Group become more acute, its

Turkish and German commanders estimated that the danger from the south (from the Gaza area) was far more threatening and real.[23]

Consequently, the British had taken it upon themselves to change the enemy's estimate of the situation. But to succeed in this, far greater resources and efforts were required. The short timetable was just another contributory factor. The attempt to change the enemy's basic perception was the prime cause of the failure.[24]

Operational Deception

In order to put the deceptive message across to the Turkish command, the British adopted a variety of means. The main channels for leaking the deception story were:

1. *Wireless Channel*:[25] From 'Z'-Day, a number of false messages were transmitted daily on the regular radio communications network. These were transmitted within the framework of 'innocent' conversations of officers and radio operators, as well as official traffic and ciphered telegrams, which were read by the Turks, since the key for reading them *en clair* had been deliberately leaked by the British. One of these messages informed its readers that preparations were being made for a large-scale patrol reconnaissance in force towards Beersheba, although it is not the main offensive. The message was given credence by real patrol activity. Patrol reports indicated that the Beersheba area could not be crossed by cavalry formations. Other messages stated that General Allenby would be absent from the area between 29 October and 4 November. The meaning of this was clear: no offensive was to be anticipated between these dates.

2. *The 'Loss of Documents–Haversack Ruse'*: On 'Z'-Day–48, the British tried to abandon in the field a haversack with documents bearing deceptive material, in the hope that the Turks would find it. The purpose of doing this at such an early stage was probably to give the Turks enough time to digest the information, draw conclusions and act upon them, as well as to enlarge the collection capability with which the contents of the documents would endow them. Two attempts to abandon the haversack during contact with the Turkish line failed. Consequently, on 'Z'-Day–20, Major Meinertzhagen, who originally conceived the idea, assumed personal responsibility for 'losing' the material. The attempt was successful; to this day, it is considered a classic ruse example and was copied on several occasions during the Second World War.

The haversack contained the following documents:

- Subjects for discussion in GHQ from which it could be concluded that the main offensive would be launched against Gaza and would be accompanied by landing from the sea, while the preparations in Beersheba were just a feint.

- A staff officer's notebook, which included, among others, details about difficulties of transport and water supply for a large force in the Beersheba area, and notes about the British inability to cope with these problems.
- An order to study details of a model of a section of fortifications in the Gaza area. The timetable for studying the model ended in mid-November.
- Several private letters of officers, expressing the frustration of the officers in the Beersheba sector due to the postponement of the attack and the feeling that the direction chosen – Gaza – was a mistake.
- Personal documents, letters and money to add authenticity.

To facilitate the absorption of the documents by the Turks, a number of steps were taken:

- The number of people in the know was limited to a minimum.[26] As soon as the loss of the haversack became known to officers who were not privy to the secret, several genuine steps were innocently taken, as would be necessary in such a situation, such as sending patrols to locate the documents and reporting the incident by radio to higher HQs and to Units in the field.
- The loss of the haversack and the steps to retrieve it were reported in the daily order of one of the formations. A patrol on a mission near enemy lines intentionally left some sandwiches in the field wrapped up in this daily order.

3. *Psychological Warfare.* Unrelated to the deception, a secret operation was conducted with the aim of encouraging Turkish soldiers in Gaza to smoke opium cigarettes. In the preparatory phase beginning in August, regular cigarettes (a rare commodity much in demand) were dropped over the town. The cigarettes were wrapped in propaganda leaflets. The leaflets, while being originally a camouflage to accustom the Turks to collect the cigarettes, helped to support the deception story by strengthening the Turks' feeling that Gaza was the focus of British interest.[27] Additionally, rumors were spread about preparations being made in the Dir el Belah sector for a landing via the sea.

4. *Visual Channel.* This includes the preparations for the offensive on Gaza, which provided a realistic deception picture. The emphasis given to the field security effort came to full expression in this plane.

By September the Royal Navy had already been integrated into preparations for the deception. Its intended duties are quite enlightening and indicative of the British concept that the deception should be maintained even beyond 'Z'-hour:

A) Possible feints prior to the commencement of operations, designed to induce the enemy to think we contemplate a landing on the coast at some point north of Gaza, e.g. ordering and collecting of small crafts, unobtrusive taking of soundings off the coast etc.
B) Possible feint of landing during operations, e.g. appearance of small crafts off Deir el Belach, a show of embarking troops and departure of the vessels just before nightfall.
C) Bombardment of targets north of Gaza.[28]

The following steps were taken in the preparatory phase until 'Z'-Day−10:

- All the forces allocated for the offensive on the right flank were left in their original locations, wset of the front.
- A naval force was assembled, as suggested, in the Dir el Belah area to simulate preparation for landing.
- Royal Navy auxiliary vessels sailed along the coast displaying water depth measuring.
- From August, once every two weeks, a mounted patrol was sent to the Beersheba line to accustom the enemy to activity that would almost certainly increase as the date of the attack drew nearer.

In the deployment phase from 'Z'-Day forces were gradually transferred to assembly and forming up areas in the British right flank. The movement began with limited forces, gradually increasing as it approached the line and went southward. Most of the movement took place on the night of 28−29 October, during which time the deployment was completed.

The successful movement of over six divisions, consisting of 45,000 infantry, 11,000 mounted troops and about 200 artillery pieces, is considered an outstanding military feat, both from the point of view of its planning and its maintenance-operations aspects. The following points are worthy of special emphasis:

- The movement was carried out in 'hops', where each night new formations took up positions vacated by those who had 'hopped' a stage further south or east.
- Troop movement and railway and water-pipe extensions eastward were carried out only at night. During the day, the soldiers stayed put in wadis, maintaining strict concealment and camouflage discipline. Each morning, the newly constructed sections of the railway and water pipelines were camouflaged.

- In the abandoned camps in the Rafah–Dir el Belah area staged routine was continued by a small number of soldiers, while strictly maintaining night illumination.
- Massive reinforcing of air units and air defense was carried out. According to the British sources, only one Turkish reconnaissance aircraft succeeded in carrying out a photography sortie over the moving units, and, before returning to base, was shot down and its pilots were captured.

It appears that the emphasis was on concealing the extent of the movement, rather than its existence.

Concealment was the order of the day. The importance that the commanders attached to it is clearly reflected in a letter written by Major General P. Chetwode, Commander of the XXIst Corps, to his division commanders:

> While it is impossible to conceal the movements of so large a force entirely, we may be able to deceive the enemy as to the strength which we intend to put against him. I would ask you to give your personal attention to every device by which enemy airmen may be deceived, such as have your present bivouac areas looking as much occupied as possible by leaving tents standing and digging holes wherever you have blanket shelters, not pitching Brigade Field Ambulances or showing their flags, and allowing no new ground to be used whatever. I would ask that the troops of the 60th, 74th and 53rd divisions when east of the Wadi should be kept concealed as much as possible in wadis, gardens, near buildings, etc., and that the strictest aeroplane discipline is enforced, all ranks lying flat when the whistle is blown, and remaining so until the 'carry-on' is sounded. It is particularly important that no motor lights, either Ford or ambulance, should be shown east of the Wadi after Z day, and then as little as possible.[29]

The activity in the Gaza Sector was designed to draw attention to the area even after the onset of the attack on Beersheba:

- From 'Z'-Day–15 forces from the XXIst Corps were moved forward along the line in the Gaza area.
- From the eve of 'Z'-Day–6, an artillery bombardment was begun in the area and was gradually intensified until 'Z'-day +2 (the 'Z'-Day of the XXIst Corps). On 'Z'-Day–2 Royal Navy ships joined the bombardment effort (at a time when movement of forces southward was to reach its peak).
- On the eve of 'Z'-Day +(31 October–1 November), a ground raid was carried out in the area.

- 'Z'-Day +1: Preparations for immediate sea-landing were simulated. Hundreds of workers from the Egyptian Labor Corps marched towards the Dir el Belah beach in military formation and boarded ships. Under cover of darkness, the workers disembarked, although the illuminated boat movement between the ships and the shore continued. At midnight the flotilla set sail for the open sea. Some of the ships were intended to reach Wadi Hassa estuary the next morning. This activity was not concealed from the local inhabitants.
- 'Z'-Day +2: Onset of the XXIst Corps' offensive

The Turkish Reaction to the Deception

Knowledge of how in fact the deception was received by the Turks is sparse, as almost no official Turkish or German documents from that period have been published or even released, apart from those that have appeared in British publications.

The basic intelligence estimate, formulated by the German commander of the Eighth Army, von Kressenstein, at the beginning of August, determined that the British forces were planning to launch an offensive between the beginning and middle of November. He estimated that, by that date, the British forces would be massively reinforced and would achieve complete superiority over his own forces. Therefore he concluded that the offensive would be started along the whole front, that the main effort would be directed against the Gaza sector and that a strong flanking attack against the eastern sector (i.e. Beersheba) would be launched by the enemy cavalry formations.[30] Their estimate of the British Orbat at the time was correct and they anticipated its reinforcement. Proof of the centrality of Gaza in the estimate could be found in the fact that in September von Kressenstein rejected his commander's recommendation to deploy the reserve division (19th), in Beersheba and, instead, placed it in the center of the front.[31] During September–October, this preconception was strengthened and the attack on Beersheba was believed to be a secondary effort.

Most of the historians (including writers of the official history), as well as the Commonwealth commanders and intelligence officers who had taken an active part in the events, regarded the deception (especially the haversack ruse and the early bombardment of Gaza) as the main reason for this assessment, e.g.:

- Immediately after the abandoning of the documents, the British noted that the fortification work in the Turkish left flank had been reduced and was significantly increased in the right flank.
- Orders and documents captured during the campaign indicated that the documents found were analysed and even brought to the Army

MAP 2

TURKISH ESTIMATE OF THE EEF'S ORDER OF BATTLE BEFORE THE THIRD GAZA OFFENSIVE

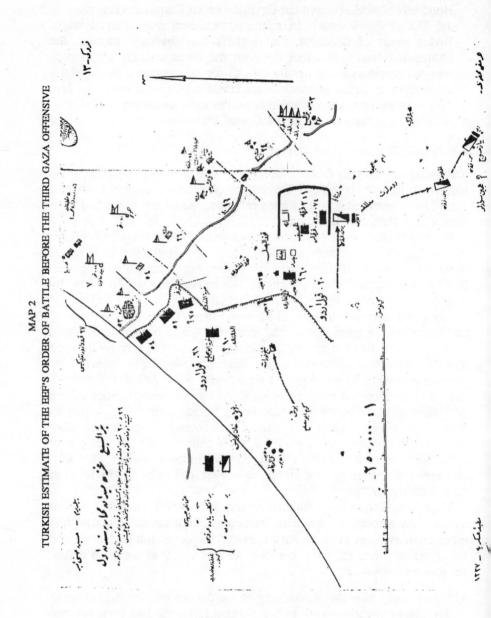

Commander.[32] The latter did not rule out the possibility that the documents were fakes, but according to these sources apparently tended to accept their authenticity in the end. His refusal to send reinforcements to Beersheba after the attack began, despite requests of the local commander to do so, and his underestimation of the size of the British attacking force, are evidence of this belief.[33]

- A series of Turkish situation assessments on 28 and 29 October at the Corps, Army and Army Group levels, talked of an expected diversionary attack in the direction of Beersheba by a force of two divisions, and a main effort in the direction of Gaza by a force of six divisions.[34]

This, however, is only one side of the coin. Further examination of the facts raises several questions:

1. *Identifying the deception*: Von Kressenstein claimed that, at first, he evaluated the 'lost' documents as authentic, but was finally convinced that this was a British deception attempt because preparations for immediate action were observed in the field – contrary to the contents of the documents, which indicated the postponement of the offensive.

Von Kressenstein further claimed that the reconnaissance activity opposite Beersheba was viewed as an indication that one should expect the worst (i.e. that the British were planning to attack this flank, contrary, of course to the intention of the deception).[35]

2. *Location of the movements*: The Turks almost accurately estimated the location of the changes in the British deployment from 25 October (i.e. two days after they began), and kept constant track of them, mainly by air and ground reconnaissance.[36] On 'Z'-Day−3 they discovered that the camps in the north were really deserted (!) and on 'Z'-Day−2 they had an astoundingly accurate picture of the British forces deployment. They even mistakenly identified the intended deployment of the mobile formations three days before it actually happened, when on 25 October, they located 4–5 cavalry and camel brigades in the Khalasa–Asluj area.[37] Von Kressenstein himself later explained that, even when various signs in the field indicated that Beersheba was the threatened sector, he continued to stress his western flank – Gaza – since he estimated that a penetration of this sector would be more dangerous to his forces than a breakthrough from Beersheba.[38] Furthermore, the spotting of the activity and the cavalry concentrations on the eastern flank corresponded with the German-Turkish basic intelligence assessment, which predicted a strong, if secondary, attack there. Yet, even this does not explain why the German commander had adhered to his former estimate that the main effort of six divisions would be directed against Gaza, particularly when he had an accurate enemy Orbat picture, unless, despite his retrospective

denials, the 'documents' and other deception steps strengthened the preconception that the British wished to portray.

3. *The step in the field*: the two reserve divisions, upon arrival, were deployed in the rear of the central front (24th Division in Jemana and 19th Division in Araq el Menshiya). The closer 'Z'-Day became, the more reinforcements were sent to Beersheba and to the central sector and not to the right flank of the Turkish disposition (Gaza):

* The 24th Division was sent towards Kauwuka, while one of its brigades reinforced Beersheba on 28 October.
* When the fighting began, the 19th Division was transferred to Huj, near Gaza (near the present-day town of Sderoth). But on 'Z'-Day +1, before the onset of offensive on Gaza, it was moved towards Tel el Sheria in the center. It was used in battle, however, with considerable hesitation, because of the consideration that it would be better utilized later on the flank (Gaza).[39]
* The 7th Division (the reserves of the 21st Corps), which was deployed in Dir Sineid so as to prevent landings from the sea, was advanced southwards on 'Z'-Day – indicating that the notional landings were not 'swallowed' by the Turkish Command.[40]

To sum up the reception picture: despite the fact that the Turks located the British concentrations in the southern sector, they adhered to their belief that the main offensive would be launched from the direction of Gaza. Their actions in the field, however, fulfilled only part of British expectations: in spite of the fact that Beersheba sector was barely reinforced, the reserves were not deployed in the Gaza area either.

At that point the British Intelligence picture on the eve of the operation (28–29 October) had several inaccuracies and was over-optimistic about the success of the deception. According to the intelligence picture, only two reserve divisions (19 and 7) were transferred to the northern sector and deployed near the coast.

THE MEGIDDO CAMPAIGN

After its victory in the Gaza campaign, the Egyptian Expeditionary Force advanced northward, along the coastal plain ('Philistia' as it was officially called), and paved its way through the Judean Hills. On 11 January 1918 it captured Jerusalem.

Allenby's forces crossed the El Auja (Yarkon) River and established a defensive line. This began east of Jerusalem, passed through the Judean Hills, north of Ramallah, bore west towards the lowland ('Sharon') and continued north-west along the coastal plain, to terminate in the Mediterranean Sea near the location of the present town of Herzeliya.

TABLE 1

THE MEGGIDO CAMPAIGN – BASIC TIMETABLE FOR THE DECEPTION MOVES

Date	Days Before 'Z'-Day	Western Sector	Central Sector	Jordan Valley	Transjordan
August 1 Beginning of month	45	*DISSEMINATION OF OPERATION ORDER*		Reinforced with 2 infantry bns.	Beginning of movement from Aqaba eastwards
8	41	Beginning of open departure of 4th Cav. Div.		Beginning of return of 4th Div.	
15	34			Beginning of concealed departure of 5th Div.	
18	31	Beginning of concealed arrival of 5th Cav. Div.		Beginning of concealed return of 'Anzac' Div.	
23	26			Beginning of concealed departure of Australian Div. Assigning partial responsibility to Chaytor Force HQ	
26	23	Beginning of concealed arrival of Australian Div.			
30	21				Beginning of Arab movement towards Azrak
31	20		Beginning of departure of 75th Div. from the line to the rear staging area		
September 5	14			Beginning of concealed departure of 4th Div. Assigning full responsibility to Chaytor Force HQ	
10–11	8–9		Transfer of Arty. Bde. westwards		
11	8	Completion of 5th Div. assembly			
12	7				Completion of concentration at Azrak
13	6		Beginning of departure of 60th Div. from line and movement westwards New and extended deployment of XXth Corps. Continued transfer of Arty. units to western sector		Beginning of Arab movement to Amman and to the north

TABLE 1 (contd.)

Date	Days Before 'Z'-Day	Western Sector	Central Sector	Jordan Valley	Transjordan
September					
15	4	Completion of 5th Div. concentration			
16	3	Arrival of 'Mounted Desert Corps' HQ		Departure of 'Mounted Desert Corps' HQ	
17	2	Completion of concentration of all the forces in staging and assembly areas			Beginning of diversion activity in Deraa area
Night of 18–19	1	Movement to forming up lines	Beginning of operational activities of XXth Corps		
19		Beginning of Operation			

The Jordan Valley and East Bank of the Jordan (hereafter Transjordan) remained under Turkish control. There, south of the Dead Sea, the Arab forces of Feisal were already operating. (See Maps 7 and 8.)

Winter conditions, with transport and supply difficulties, caused the cessation of the fighting and stabilization of the line. Thus, the objectives of the Campaign were effectively realized: i.e., the foiling of Operation Yilderim and the accentuation of the initiative and activity of the Entente, as against the drawn-out stalemate in the Western Front.

In February 1918 the Supreme War Council of the Entente in Versailles decided on the war plan for the first half of the year. This included the continuation of the defense in France and, simultaneously, the execution of a large-scale offensive in Palestine, with the objective of routing the Turks and causing their withdrawal from the war. In the wake of this decision, Allenby began to plan his next phase.

Allenby planned to execute his plan gradually. First, he wanted to protect his eastern flank by gaining control of the Jordan Valley and destroying the Hejaz railway – the artery connecting Arabia to Syria (and from there to Palestine and the remaining parts of the Ottoman Empire) – thereby aiding the Arab revolt. At the same time he wished to advance towards the Tul Karem line in Samaria. Following this, at the end of the rainy season, he planned to launch the main offensive which he calculated would bring him, by the end of July 1918, to the Tiberias–Nazareth–Haifa line. In the wake of a request by the CIGS to continue the offensive beyond this line, he extended his plan: to advance along the coastal plain up to the Tripoli area, thereby outflanking the entire Turkish disposition and threatening Damascus through the Tripoli–Hama gap. It appears that the general idea to transfer the main offensive to the Western flank of the front had already taken shape in the British general's mind in the first months of 1918, while the actual plan was formulated only during the course of the year. The climax of the plan was the large-scale successful offensive against the Turkish disposition in September, known as the 'Megiddo Campaign'.[42]

The Confronting Forces

The situation of the Entente Forces in France, where Germany had launched its major offensive, in February 1918 forced Allenby to relinquish considerable trained forces, which were dispatched to the front in the west and, in their stead, absorb fresh and less trained forces. When the reorganization was completed in August, the Expeditionary Force consisted of three Corps HQs, seven infantry divisions, four mounted/cavalry divisions and several additional independent infantry elements. The force was deployed in the following order, from west to east:

- XXIst Corps (four infantry divisions) in the Coastal Plain and the Sharon;
- XXth Corps (three infantry divisions) in the Samaria Hills;
- Desert Mounted Corps (four cavalry/mounted divisions) – three in the Jordan Valley and one in the Coastal Plain rear.

In all, the strength of the fighting force numbered about 57,000 infantry, 12,000 cavalry and 540 artillery pieces.[43]

In March, General Liman von Sanders, the hero of the defense of Gallipoli, was put in command of Turkish Army Group F ('Yilderim' Force), which was responsible for the defense of Palestine. At his disposal were 12 infantry divisions, a cavalry division, two German infantry brigades and an independent cavalry brigade. There are no accurate data regarding their numerical strength. The figures range between 20,000–32,000 infantry, 3,000–4,000 cavalry and 400–500 artillery pieces.[44]

The Turkish force deployed west of the Jordan River in two armies, and at the beginning of April another Army HQ was established in the Jordan Valley and in Transjordan:

- The 8th Army (five infantry divisions, a German infantry brigade) in the west flank of the front, the Coastal Plain and the Sharon.
- The 7th Army (six infantry divisions) in Samaria, the mountain ridge area and the Jordan Valley foothills.
- The 4th Army, which was established later in the east flank of the front,

had at its disposal three infantry divisions and all the cavalry formations of this front.

The Situation in the Field

Following its forced reorganization, the Expeditionary Force had to postpone its offensive and make do with active defense.

Between February and August, limited operations took place in Palestine, most of them initiated by the Expeditionary Force and almost all in the east sector of the front, i.e., the eastern part of the Samaria and Judean Hills, the Jordan Valley and Transjordan. This eastern activity had an important role in designing the future reactions of Turkish Army Group F to the deception efforts and operational activities of the Expeditionary Force. These operations were:

· 1. The capturing of Jericho, in the month of February and improving the British line in Samaria and the foothills of the Jordan Valley in the beginning of March. The operation was intended primarily to protect the east flank of the disposition and improve positions. Four divisions, two of which were mounted, participated in it.
2. The first raid into Transjordan at the end of March, of two-divisional strength, directed towards Amman and As-Salt. Its stated objective was to assist the Arabs under the command of Sherif Hussein in Hejaz and in Transjordan by hitting at the main Turkish communications routes, pinning down their forces and diverting their attention. The raid did not achieve most of it territorial objectives and two weeks later the force withdrew back to the west.
3. The second raid into Transjordan at the beginning of May was initiated in order to capture the town of As-Salt. Its immediate objective was to cut off the strong Turkish force between the town and the Jordan River which appeared to threaten the British flank. The raid was also intended to assist the advance of Faisal's forces. Its strategic objectives, if such existed, are considered later. The raiding force, which numbered almost four divisions, mostly cavalry or mounted, failed in achieving its stated objectives and after fierce fighting returned to its bases.
4. Limited Turkish and British attacks were conducted between April and September. Most of them were initiated by the British, in the area between East Samaria and the Jordan Valley, and were intended to train the new troops. In the western sector one British three-division strong attack failed (the Berukin offensive in April). The mutual raids did not bring about any real territorial gains.

A Turkish intention to launch an offensive against the Arab forces in Transjordan was thwarted after a British divertive attack in the Aqaba area.[45]

5. Arab activity in Transjordan. 'The Northern Arab Army' under the command of the Emir Feisal and T.E. Lawrence operated between Aqaba and the Dead Sea. Its 'strategic' objective was to gain control of the area between the Hejaz railway in the east and the Dead Sea in the west and cut off the railway, thereby assisting the Egyptian Expeditionary Force. The sector was active during the entire period, with the Arabs operating against the railway and against the local Turkish garrisons and trying to capture small towns, while the Turks carried out counter-attacks and pre-emptive attacks.

The Operational Plan

Allenby's plan underwent much rethinking and several changes, although its main theme, which concerns us, did not undergo any essential change. The following, therefore, is the final plan of operation as published in 'Operation Order No.68' on 18 September 1918.

The objective of the operation was: 'Inflicting a decisive defeat on the enemy and driving him from the line Nablus–Samaria–Tul Karem–Caesareia'.[46] This was to be achieved by breaking through the Turkish disposition and swiftly securing the Beisan (Beit Shean) and Afule areas which were considered as vital junctions, thereby cutting off the 7th and 8th Armies.

Using the mirror image of the Gaza Campaign (where the right flank of the line had been penetrated), Allenby now planned to concentrate the main effort in breaching the left flank of the enemy in the coastal plain, to move a mounted force quickly through this gap northwards, along the coastal plain and to outflank the enemy disposition by bearing eastwards deep into its rear. In its right-eastern flank, he intended to hold defense initially and then to advance northwards.

Phases, forces and assignments:

- Phase A: Breaching the Turkish disposition in the coastal plain and the Sharon by the five infantry division-strong XXIst Corps and simultaneously attacking along the front in the middle of Samaria by the two division-strong XXth Corps.
- Phase B: Outflanking the enemy disposition from the west via the Sharon and the Jezreel Valley, capturing the Beisan–Afule area and preventing the retreat of the Turkish Armies. This was to be achieved by three mounted/cavalry divisions of the Desert Mounted Corps which would pass through the gap made by the XXIst Corps.
- In the Jordan Valley a task force commanded by General Chaytor (the

Chaytor Force) would be established whose main role was to secure the
weak British right flank and appear to threaten the Turkish disposition
in the area. The force would be composed of a cavalry division and
several infantry units.
• The roles assigned to the 'Arab Army' were to harass, to confuse and to
act as a diversion along the Hejaz railway line and in the Deraa sector.
• 'Z' Day and 'H' Hour were set for 19 September 1918 at 0430 hours.

Allenby planned to surprise the Turks as he did in the Third Battle of
Gaza: concealing the main effort and hiding the force concentration
and the preparations in the western sector while diverting the enemy's
attention to his eastern flank. The self-imposed assignment was by no
means easy, since in order to carry out the plan, two cavalry divisions, two
infantry divisions and a very considerable number of artillery battalions
and batteries were to move from the Jordan Valley and the Samaria Hills
to the coastal plain. At the same time the XXth Corps was to redeploy in its
sector in order to fill with sparse forces the gap created by the transfer of
the forces westward. As in Gaza, here, too, the British general and his
staff resolved to deceive the enemy.

The British Intelligence Picture

During 1918 the capability of British intelligence in Palestine progressively improved. The collection assets developed and the intelligence picture
became more accurate.
Sigint: Initiated actions were carried out to destroy the enemy's line
communications infrastructure, in order to force it to use wireless
communications more extensively.[47]
Aerial Reconnaissance and Photography: Several aspects of the aerial
collection assets were considerably improved: the number of aircraft was
increased, advanced equipment was introduced, including cameras,
stereoscopic interpretation equipment and production gear, and
improved techniques were implemented. These techniques encompassed
the fields of: photography, area and point coverage, interpretation and
quick distribution of the final product (reports, photographs and sketch
maps). It seems that aerial photography gradually replaced the visual
observation sorties.[48]
POWs and Deserters: During the British operational activity a large
number of prisoners were taken from the majority of army units in varying
intervals and provided abundant information. (About 1700 POWs were
taken within three and a half months.) No less fruitful were the deserters,
the number and variety of whom were indeed very impressive.[49] The
updating of the intelligence picture from Humint sources was, therefore,
current and regular.

Captured Documents: Their vital importance in the past taught the British to treat these sources with reverence. Units on raids were instructed to collect documents from HQs and other similar locations. We have no details of the overall value of the many documents collected, but at least some of them contributed directly to the deception planning (see below).

The intelligence picture, as regards enemy organization, Orbat and deployment, was accurate and up-to-date. A comparison between the actual changes which took place and the British Orbat maps of that period indicate that most of the changes were observed swiftly, in fact within a few days. (For example, the movement of the Turkish 3rd Cavalry Division and the 2nd Cavalry Brigade which took place on 24 March, were marked in the British intelligence map of the same date.)[50]

Naturally, British intelligence made mistakes and had its shortcomings. To this day criticism is expressed of British underestimations of the Turkish numerical strength. However, these errors had no significant bearing on the campaign's moves or on the deception plan.

The British analysed fairly accurately the Turkish intelligence assessment as regards the intentions of the Egyptian Expeditionary Force. The capability of the Turkish collection system was also quite well known to them. These advantages assisted the deception planners to adapt their story to suit the Turkish assessment, to carry out deception activity that would be picked up by its collection agencies and to keep track of the effect of the deception on their enemy's moves.

Thus, for example, in order to deceive the enemy, British troops were made to march on a route which was exposed to Turkish ground observation.[51] The nature of the activities and the reports which Alllenby sent give the impression that he tried to adapt his deceptive messages to Turkish intelligence concepts as he understood them.

Basic British Hypotheses and the Intelligence Estimate for Deception

The operational activity in the east flank of the front drew the attention of the Turks to the Jordan valley and Transjordan. The Egyptian Expeditionary Force was aware of the Turkish-German way of thinking. Documents captured during the raids indicated that the enemy interpreted the limited British activity as an intention to break through to the north and north east through the Jordan Valley or Transjordan. The British received further reinforcement of this view from the massing of forces and building of the new Turkish HQs in the east flank.

Allenby himself pointed to the realization of his basic assumption: 'The enemy was thought to be anticipating an attack in these directions (Madeba or Amman) and every possible step was taken to strengthen his suspicions'.[52]

Additional basic assumptions had to be taken into account in planning the deception:

- The need for concealment was the first condition for the success of the deception and the achievement of surprise.
- The hilly terrain on the mountain ridge area and the dense coverage of citrus plantations and groves in the Sharon and coastal plain were likely to ensure concealment of the preparations from ground or aerial observation.
- The elements likely to reveal the preparations were aerial reconnaissance and photography sorties. Therefore, it was vital to achieve maximum air superiority and prevent enemy forces from approaching.
- The front line was not continuous and enabled enemy agents to infiltrate. This phenomenon necessitated meticulous camouflage of the troop concentrations from ground observation. On the other hand, it facilitated erroneous identifications of field agents to be exploited for deception purposes.

It appears that Allenby believed that the environmental conditions and the operational activity level would make it possible to conceal the preparations for the offensive entirely. Unlike in the Battle of Gaza, where the British had understood from the beginning that they could only divert the enemy's attention to the wrong direction, in Megiddo they tried to hide the very existence of the future offensive. The conditions prevailing in the field appear to justify this belief, since the Turks were basically aware many months before of the British intention to launch a large-scale offensive and this awareness might have dulled their senses. During those months, the Turks received reports about enemy intentions, but these 'intentions' either did not materialize at all or consisted of only limited local attacks.[53] They thereby grew accustomed to early warning indications which did not yield the expected results. The planners of the operation could therefore assume that, even should the preparations for the operation become partially exposed, the enemy would none the less reach the same conclusions as before.

The Objective of the Deception

When did Allenby decide to use the operational activity in the east flank as a ruse to distract enemy attention? The answer to this question will enable us to conclude whether or not Allenby set for himself a long-range continuous deceptive objective as a preliminary phase for a tactical short-range deception to take place on the eve of the operation.

The authors of the official history of the war, as well as commanders and historians, have determined that, in addition to the different immediate objectives of each of the eastern operations, they all had a long-range objective in common: to divert attention towards the East, to pin down enemy forces and even draw additional units to this arena.[54] Allenby himself did not leave behind a diary or memoirs, thus making it hard for us to comprehend his perception of the future, at each and every phase. In his Report on 18 September he wrote, that among the reasons for the eastern activity was the possibility that: 'the enemy might transfer a portion of his reserves from the west to the east of the Jordan, thereby weakening his power to make or meet any attack on the main front'.[55]

It should be remembered, however, that this report was written on the eve of the offensive. By that time, the aim of the deception was clear, and it is difficult to say whether or not the above quotation reflects wisdom after the event.

What can be ascertained is that the turn towards the east, at the beginning of 1918, had real operational-political reasons which might be attributed to the way in which Allenby perceived the possibilities for continuing his advance and to the fact that he attached political strategic importance to the Arab Revolt at the time. Allenby assessed that there was a possibility of continuing his advance northwards via Transjordan. There is evidence pointing to the fact that the operation against As-Salt in March, which the CiC later called a 'raid', was aimed at permanently holding the territory to be taken at the first phase of the advance.[56]

Allenby believed that the Arab Revolt would also contribute to the war effort of the Expeditionary Force. Consequently the reports that he sent to the War Office clearly indicate that one of his prime objectives in the eastern activity between February and April was to assist the 'North Arab Army' by reducing the Turkish pressure on it.[57]

As the year went on, the long-term results of his eastern policy and, in parallel, his operational plan for the main offensive from the western flank became clear to Allenby. He therefore adopted a 'deceptive' concept which maintained that continuing to pursue the activity in the east would divert enemy attention from the sector designated for the main effort. Despite the difficulty in dating this concept, and contrary to the generally accepted notion that puts it as early as the beginning of the year, it appears more likely that his deception concept was formulated in May, when the failure of the activity at As-Salt almost certainly contributed to this.[58]

As far as the objectives of the deception leading up to the Megiddo Campaign are concerned, we find that, unlike the Battle of Gaza, it had no strategic or operational objectives. Rather, it had long-term continuous objectives, to be achieved during the entire deception period, as well as immediate ones to be accomplished only a short while, relatively speaking, before 'Z'-Day.

The long-term range objective was to draw enemy forces to the eastern sector of the front and pin them down there for a lengthy period. These activities aimed at applying this objective began in May (some four months before 'Z'-Day).

The immediate short-range objective was to cause the Turkish-German forces to stay put in their positions along the entire front line generating two seemingly-conflicting results: the British main effort's sector would not be reinforced by the enemy before 'Z'-Day and the Turkish forces deployed there would remain in their positions, not withdrawing before the onset of the attack. A reinforced enemy might complicate British efforts but premature withdrawal would cause the EEF to attack a depleted disposition and hence fail to achieve the destruction of major enemy units.[59]

THE DECEPTION STORY

The British deception planners expected the Turks to form the following intelligence picture during the entire deception period:

- The Deraa area in southern Syria was the main objective of the Expeditionary Force, since it represented a vital communication junction. Thus, if the Turks lost this junction, they would be cut off from their rear area and be compelled to withdraw their forces from all of Palestine and Transjordan, or risk being annihilated.
- To achieve this objective Allenby designated the Jordan Valley and Transjordan as the sectors of his main effort.
- The raids against Amman and As-Salt and the British and Arab activity initiated in the east flank were carried out within the framework of preparatory activity before the offensive.
- In the existing environmental conditions (terrain, distances, enemy, availability of forces) the British would use mounted forces in the main effort. Their presence in the Jordan Valley, therefore, indicated the direction of the main effort as well.

Towards the execution of the deception, several new themes were added:

- No change had occurred in the original plan to attack the eastern flank, which is why the mobile formations were deployed in this sector. However, their deployment was routine and peaceful, since the attack date was not in the immediate future.
- The force in the Jordan Valley was of a strength such as would enable it to carry out a full-scale attack and threaten the Turkish disposition when the time came. With the onset of the offensive, this point was to have convinced the Turks that there was still a dangerous potential in the east flank, despite the threat developing in the west.

Unlike the Battle of Gaza, where the deceptive force also served as a secondary effort, the main operational role of Chaytor Force in the Jordan Valley was to secure the flank, while its deceptional role was to create an atmosphere of calm. Even in the very last few days before 'Z'-Day, when it recived the additional diversionary role, there was no intention to create a picture of an impending main thrust eastwards, rather the impression of an additional potential threat. It would appear that this is why the forces allocated to it were relatively few.

Implementing the Deception: the Early Stage

The deception's planners concentrated, in the first phase, on methods of diversion and feints, and in the second phase on concealment and cover. Then, just before 'Z'-Day, they redoubled their efforts to divert attention eastwards once more.

Allenby's first operational plan was formulated, as mentioned above, in May, so that the planners had four months at their disposal. The General Staff of the Expeditionary Force began to plan the deception operation between May and June. When Lawrence met Allenby and his officers in mid-July, he had already been briefed on the deception's main themes, which were intended to conceal the forces in the eastern sector. The methods presented to him corresponded to the visual means applied in the field several months later.

At the same time, Allenby instructed Lawrence to prepare for the taking of Deraa not long before the onset of the main offensive. This was a means of deception aimed at diverting Turkish attention from the western flank.[60] Thus, in fact, the CiC determined that all the future Arab activities in Transjordan would from now on be dedicated to reinforcing the deceptive element.

However, apart from the Arab aspect, no additional exclusive steps at the first stage were taken for the purpose of a long-term deception. If Allenby had initiated a directed long-term deception effort, one would expect that he would have passed on additional deceptive messages, such as rumors, forged documents left in the field during raids, communications deception, etc. None of these means, which worked well in the Battle of Gaza, was employed here.[61]

Scholars and historians such as Cyril Fulls (author of the official history) and Field Marshal A.F. Wavell believed that the stationing of the mounted troops in the Jordan Valley was the result of a long-intended deception effort. In contrast, the Australian official history, which analysed the activities of the mounted troops in greater detail, reached the reasoned conclusion that their deployment to the Jordan line derived only from operational and logistic considerations.[62]

Although the deception plan had been formulated several months before the offensive, it was implemented in a limited manner at that time. Only later was it carried out to the full.

Implementing The Deception: The Main Phase[63]

In order to put into effect the later phases, in which emphasis was placed on concealment and cover, the Expeditionary Force had to prepare itself for deceptive activity against four focal points of possible exposure:

> Mass movement from sector to sector.
> The deployment of forces in the western sector.
> Thinning out of the disposition in the Jordan Valley.
> Field security leaks which could reveal the date or direction of the attack (from rumors, revealing of plans, etc.).

During August–September 1918 all the forces to participate in the main effort were to assemble gradually in the coastal plain, while the rest of the sector would be thinned out.

The deception was based mainly on visual means, understandable considering that its main objective was concealment.

Concealment of the movement westwards. The divisions and the artillery units were moved at night only. The movement procedure was planned in such a way that towards dawn, a force that had not yet reached its destination would stop in citrus groves or woods and remain hidden there until nightfall. Only then would it begin to move again. The concealment steps adopted during these stopovers were intended mainly against air reconnaissance sorties as well as against ground surveillance on the part of the enemy agents.

The concealment was considered an element which affected pace and pattern of movement and came at the expense of speed. Thus, for example, the movement of the 60th Division, which in fact covered a distance of just 54 miles, took six whole nights, and the transfer of the XXth Corps artillery to the XXIst Corps took seven nights. The long timetable allocated to movement enabled adherence to the rules of concealment.[64]

Concealment of the concentrations in the western sector. The problem of the concentration of thousands of troops and horses as well as hundreds of guns was solved in two ways: accustomization and concealment.

The type of vegetation cover dictated the nature of the deception. In the line's rear sector, south of the Yarkon River, the area chosen for the concentration of the cavalry formations, the citrus groves and woody areas allowed full concealment, while north of this sector, where the infantry units were to deploy, the terrain was more exposed and called for accustomization techniques designed to show, for about two months, that a much larger force was constantly deployed in the area than actually was there.

The following were the accustomization techniques:

- *Open Camps.* From the month of July, for accustoming purposes, battalion-size camps were built with double the capacity necessary for the forces in the field at the time. The forces then present in the area manned the camps in a dispersed manner – one battalion for every two camps. When the reinforcing forces arrived, the longstanding battalion was assembled in one camp, while the fresh battalion entered the other. Thus the force was doubled without requiring additional tents or unusual concentrations and continued its camp routine as before.

- *Closed Camps.* These served the concealment objective. They were set up inside groves south of the Yarkon River for calvary and were designed to hide their very existence from air observation and from enemy agents. Therefore, all daytime activity and movement were forbidden. Providing water for the horses, essential in these formations, was preplanned and used the internal irrigation system inside the groves at predetermined times, when a special aerial effort was made to ensure 'clean skies' over the deployment area.

- *Artillery Positions.* These were dug during the month of August. Each position was camouflaged and inspected from the air in order to spot faults in the camouflage. The positions themselves were manned just before 'Z'-Day.

- *Bridging.* The operational plan necessitated the bridging of the Yarkon River at a number of additional points in British-held territory so as to alleviate the passage of forces. The erections of the bridges was to take place during the last few days before 'Z'-Day. In order to accustom the enemy to the presence of the bridges the deception planners made use of bridging training centers set up in July or in the beginning of August near the Yarkon River. In these centers, under the watchful eye of the enemy, bridges were repeatedly assembled and dismantled. There are differences of opinion as to whether these centers were set up especially for the purpose of deception or whether they just served the purpose of the deception post factum.[65] One thing is clear: the bridges were used for purposes of accustomization, and just before 'Z'-Day they were reassembled and remained in place ready for use.

Concealment of the thinning out activity in the Jordan Valley and Samaria. In accordance with the deception objective of creating the impression that in the Jordan Valley it was 'business as usual', even after the forces had left, the thinning-out was concealed by the following means:

- Presenting a picture that the forces had not left at all.

- Revealing the reinforcement of the Jordan Valley as a counterweight against the possibility that the movement westwards would be exposed. This theme also helped the secondary later deception objective, according to which an offensive threat was developing in the Jordan Valley against the Turks in the sector.

To this end the following techniques were adopted:

- Leaving the vacated camps, while presenting them as active and even growing. This was done by leaving there soldiers unfit for combat who would display a regular camp routine during the day and at night, including lights and smoke.[66]
- Setting up new camps with a skeletal staff, which would be 'reinforced' during the day. (See below.)
- Dummy horses. This dramatic means was later to become the symbol of the deception operation in the Megiddo Campaign. The British built 15,000 (!) dummy horses (with wooden frameworks and military blankets) and placed them in the vacated cavalry camps in the Jordan Valley. The dummies were mainly designed to deceive air reconnaissance and air photography sorties. But an oblique ground photo seen by the author indicated that they could also deceive local enemy Beduin or Arab agents, if they were to carry out brief ground observation from a distance.
- Faking activity, by raising dust clouds by means of wooden sledges and branches dragged along by mules between Jericho, the Dead Sea and Jordan River. The nature of the terrain allowed for the raising of extremely large dust clouds by single movements. The deception-planners hoped that, in addition to deceiving the enemy, the clouds would hinder Turkish observation.
- The 'reinforcement' of the Jordan Valley. The reinforcement was simulated by two infantry battalions which marched every day in daylight hours along the Jerusalem–Jericho road eastward to Jericho, where they entered the 'new' camps mentioned above. At nightfall, they were returned in trucks westwards and the next day set off, once again, on a march, simulating additional forces. Their route was purposely exposed to enemy eyes. The deception-planners took pains to make every movement eastwards appear as a reinforcement. Even the routine supply vehicles were organized in convoys to make them more conspicuous.
- Communications Deception. Only one case is known and it was brief: when the Mounted Corps HQ left its position at Tlaat ed Dum and moved westward to the coastal plane on 'Z'-Day −2, it left behind some HQ facilities, including its wireless station, which continued to function as normal.[67]

Diversion of attention eastwards. For the purpose of implementing this objective, additional steps over and above the visual deception were undertaken. These consisted primarily of rumor-spreading during the period before the offensive and of distracting operational activity carried out close to the launching of the main offensive and in its initial phases.

Rumors were spread about the anticipated concentration of forces in Jerusalem and conspicuous overt preparations were made for the 'transfer' of the Expeditionary Force GHQ to the city in the near future. A hotel in the city was vacated and signs were affixed to the doors of its rooms indicating branches of the GHQ. Telephone landlines were drawn nearby and billets were marked out.

From mid-August, Lawrence of Arabia's men, who were almost certainly unwitting agents, carried out a series of actions likely to be interpreted as preparations for an offensive on Amman. Within this framework, messengers were sent to Arab tribes in the Amman area to buy considerable quantities of fodder for British forces, who, they were told, would arrive on the scene within about two weeks. Local agents in Amman were asked to enter negotiations for the purchase of all the sheep in the vicinity. Two large airstrips were marked and local Arab workers were hired to guard them. Arab staff officers in the 4th Turkish Army, who were among Lawrence's agents, were warned not to remain in Amman.

These actions by Lawrence are worthy of special reference. Unlike the other sources, Lawrence claims that the diverting of attention to Amman had not been initiated by the Expeditionary Force GHQ, but that he himself initiated it for purposes of *local* deception, to distract attention from his main objective, Deraa: a sort of deception within a deception. He claims that he thought that this activity would also contribute to the general deception effort, and indeed it seems that it did correspond to Allenby's overall aims. However, in principle this is to be considered an example of a local uncoordinated deception initiative presenting a story different from that presented by the overall deception picture.[68]

The Arab forces in Transjordan were employed first and foremost as part of the deception concept. Lawrence's testimony as regards the instructions he received orally from Allenby illustrate this more than anything else: 'Three men and a boy with pistols in front of Deraa on September the sixteenth would be better than thousands a week before or a week later'.[69]

If we allow ourselves to deviate for a minute from the factual description, this instruction reveals Allenby's deep insight into the deception concept. He feared that a too-successful deception operation early in the game might even trigger off the enemy's withdrawal from the

TABLE 2

THE BRITISH DEPLOYMENT IN THE TURKISH–GERMAN VIEW

Formation East to West	Correctness of Location			Deceptive Interrelations		
	General	Internal deployment & structure	Subordination	Correlation to British intention	Effect of deception effort	
XXI Corps						
HQ	–			1	x	
60th Div.	–	–	–	1	(–)	
7th Div.	+	–	+	1	x	
75th Div.	–/+	–/+	+	2	(–)	
3rd Div.	+	–	+	1	x	
54th Div.	–	–	+	3	(–)	Apparently identified as 6th Div. not in sector at all
French Force	–	–	+	3	(–)	On the line, identified as Italian
XX Corps						The change in sector width and thinning out was not spotted
HQ	+			?	?	
10th Div.	+	–	+	1	x	
53rd Div.	–	–	–	1	(–)	
Mounted Corps						
HQ	–			1	x	
5th Div.	+	+	–	2	(–)	
4th Div.	–	–	+	1	x	
Australian Div.	–	–	+	1	x	
Chaytor Force						Its setting up was not spotted
HQ	–			1	x	
Anzak Div.	+	+(?)	–	1	x	
Infantry Forces	+	+	–	1	x	

+   Similar/identical
–   Different
1   Corresponds to deception intention
2   Contradicts deception intention
3   Of no effect
x   Deriving from deception effort
(–) Not deriving from deception effort

line it held in the Sharon area. Thus the deception's success would turn into a two-edged sword and the British might strike at an empty line.

All the activities in Transjordan fro May onwards should, therefore, be viewed as deceptive. The 'North Arab Army' was to assemble in the Azrak area about a week before the offensive was launched and begin

operating against the Hejaz railway and around the town of Deraa as from
'Z'-Day–3. These activities were put into effect within the timetable
determined in the planning, while on the same day Deraa was bombed by
the Royal Air Force for the first time.

Chaytor Force was the second operational dimension in the plan. The
operation order, after specifying its operational roles (responsibility for
defense of the line in its sector, advance northwards) defined its deceptive
role:

> Will take such measures as he finds possible from Z-day inclusive to
> make the enemy believe that attacks both east and west of the Jordan
> are imminent, and so preventing the enemy from concentrating
> troops to attack the right flank of the XXth Corps.[70]

The order giving the force a limited deceptive role, to be in force from 'Z'-
Day only, contradicts Allenby's later report that this force was also
intended to conceal the departure of the mounted troops from the area,[71]
that is to say, before the onset of the offensive.

The advance of the XXth Corps on the east flank was scheduled to begin
on the eve of 'Z'-Day, several hours before the forces in the coastal plain
started their advance. The intention, apparently, was to fool the enemy as
to the real offensive sector.

Deception in the timing. Because of the emphasis placed on the concealment aspect, little effort was made to deceive the enemy about the date of
the offensive. Possibly this was because such activity in itself could expose
the very existence of the impending operation, thereby endangering the
deception objective. The only activity undertaken, the first roots of which
were evident in the Battle of Gaza, was the public declaration by the
commander of the Expeditionary Force that on 19 December ('Z'-Day) a
horse-racing event would be held in Jaffa. One cannot rule out the
possibility that, in addition to the attempt to mislead the enemy, this was
also a field security measure directed at the troops themselves.

Field security and prevention measures. Written operation orders were
disseminated only to corps and division commanders, while orders at
divisional level and below, including those given to staff officers in the
divisions, were given orally, two or three days before execution. Strict
limitations were set out as regards the nature of the operational information to be given in each order.[72] Approval of the plans was also
carried out orally.

At the same time, rumors were spread within the various units about the
possibility that they would be transferred to the eastern sector before an
initiatied attack. The intention was that the resentment of the troops
would not only aid the security, but would also reach the ears of enemy
agents.

Superiority in the air. As mentioned above, this was the key to the success of the deception, concealment and prevention. In the eight weeks which preceded 'Z'-Day, three-quarters of all enemy aircraft were shot down, thereby preventing extensive reconnaissance sorties. On 'Z'-Day, for example, there were only five serviceable aircraft at its disposal. British sources claimed that the the aerial effort was successful to such an extent that during the period when the forces were assembling, only four enemy aircraft succeeded in crossing the line (apparently referring to the western sector only), compared with some 100 penetrations made in June. Allenby himself defined the control of the skies as the main factor for achieving secrecy.[73] Even German and Turkish sources admitted that they had encountered great difficulties in obtaining intelligence by aerial assets.[74] Yet, contrary to the above-mentioned claims, the Germans still succeeded in covering key areas along the front line and the rear areas near it, as is evident from the aerial coverage map (see Map 6).[75] What the interpreters managed to glean from this coverage is, however, unclear.

The Enemy Reaction to the Deception

The importance and centrality with which the Turkish leadership and the Army Group Commander, Liman von Sanders, viewed Transjordan were the result of considerations totally unconnected to the deception. In the Turks' view, Transjordan served as a vital link joining the center of the Ottoman Empire to the centers of Islam and the holy cities in Hejaz. The religious-symbolic-propaganda importance of their southern flank for the integrity of the Empire was, in their eyes, greater than that of Palestine.[76]

Von Sanders' defensive approach had already been formulated a short time after he arrived on the scene. He apparently saw Transjordan as the key terrain for defense of the entire area, through which the attacker could reach vital ground in Deraa with relative ease. On the other hand, Transjordan and the Jordan Valley could also serve as main axes of retreat for his forces, should the Palestine front collapse. So steadfast was his belief that he even regarded the British taking of the As-Salt area as a step designed to block the retreat routes of the armies in Western Jordan.

The east flank, therefore, appeared to the defenders more important and more *dangerous* at the very beginning of the establishment of the new front line, without any connection to the intensive British activity later on. Even before the first raid on Amman, von Sanders had already begun to reinforce the sector at the expense of other sectors, primarily with his mobile-mounted formations (3rd Cavalry Division and 2nd Cavalry Brigade). As mentioned earlier, the British raid on Amman in March was effected out of operational (not deceptive) considerations. This strengthened his belief in the 'eastern policy' of his enemy and in the possibility that in the near future the attempts to break through the Jordan

Valley would be renewed. Therefore, he reorganized the entire defense disposition in the area, transferred the 4th Army HQ for Damascus to Transjordan, transferred additional forces there and organized all the units within a framework of two new divisions and Corps HQ.[77]

Between May and August, as already stated, deceptive intentions were also added to the British and Arab activities in the eastern sector. These activities, together with the deployment of the mounted formations in the Jordan Valley, confused the basic concept of the commanders of F Army Group as regards the direction of the British effort in the future.

Apart from the reinforcements and changes mentioned above, the Turks responded in the field to the operational deceptive activity of their adversaries by the following steps:

- Out of all the limited reinforcements which reached the sector during the summer (eight Turkish infantry battalions, three German infantry battalions and about 10,000 soldiers to fill in manpower shortage), about half the Turkish troops and the entire German contingent were transferred to the 4th Army sector in the east
- On the eve of the operation, the only reserve division of the front, the 24th Infantry Division, went down to the vicinity of the front line and was placed under the command of 4th Army.
- The outstanding German force stationed in the western sector of the 8th Army near the coast including three augmented infantry battalions, was transferred eastwards to the 7th Army sector border. To compensate for this, a few Turkish units were transferred westwards. The quality of the latter, however, was inferior to that of the German troops who were all directed eastwards.

The launching of the Arab diversion activity in Transjordan on 'Z'-Day-3 compelled the Turks to send part of their limited reserves to the Deraa area. The sending of the reserves, which numbered only 300 men, would not have changed the trend of the battle, even if the small force had been directed towards the real main effort, but it does provide indication of the Turkish perception.

The offensive launched on 19 September surprised the Turks and quickly brought about the collapse of their defenses. What interests us is the reaction of the 4th Army, which from 'Z'-Day stood in front of Chaytor Force totally inactive, while in the west the battle was raging. For the first three days of the battle, the Army did not take any initiative, offensive or otherwise, and only on the fourth day did it begin to withdraw northwards. Was it because of the strength of the imaginary force that it had to contend with? There is no authoritative answer, especially since Chaytor himself reduced his overt activities in these three days.

MAP 6

CAPTURED GERMAN MAP OF BRITISH FRONT LINE AND REAR COVERED
BY GERMAN AERIAL PHOTO SORTIES BEFORE THE MEGIDDO CAMPAIGN

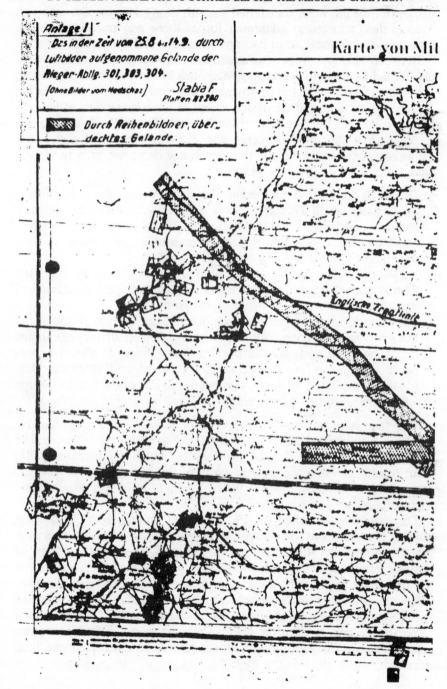

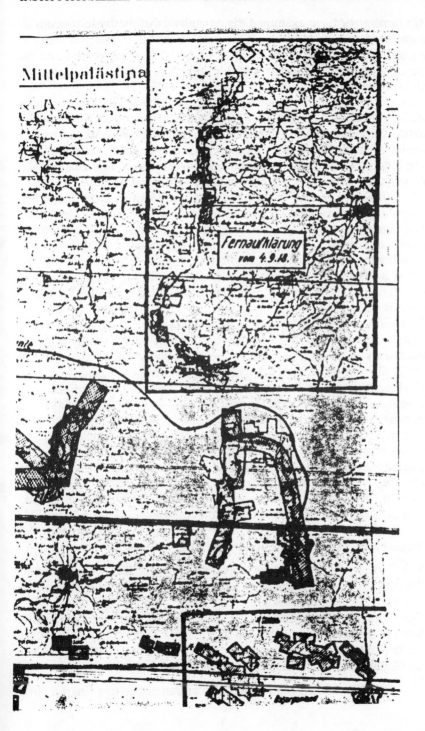

Up to now we have examined the formulation of the basic concept on the one hand and the reactions in the field on the other. We now move to the intermediary aspect – the building of the intelligence picture and the concrete situation assessment. Did the Turks indeed ignore the danger to their west flank?

As early as April, von Sanders estimated that the British were liable to launch an offensive, perhaps on a large scale, on the coastal plain and the Sharon. The estimate as regards the date of the offensive and its westerly direction strengthened as the month of August approached. In the middle of the month von Sanders wrote to the Minister of War in Constantinople: 'We probably may expect a great attack in the coast section'.[78]

The possibility cannot be ruled out that the German general reached this evaluation after receiving information from the Arab leader Sherif Feisal during contacts between the latter and the Turks concerning his shift of loyalty from the British and 'Arab Army' to their enemy. According to von Sanders, Feisal told the Turks in the middle of August that the British were planning a major offensive in the coastal area. The information was rejected by the Turks, who suspected that it was a deception attempt.[79]

In the first week of August, an irregularity was discerned in British activity routine, with long periods of uncanny quiet suddenly being disrupted by concentrated artillery fire towards targets deep inside the Turkish disposition. After 14 September, the firing increased, while the Turks located intensive British patrol activity at least in the eastern sector. The actual extent of the irregularity of this activity aside, it stimulated the Turks, at the front line at least, to sense that a British attack was imminent.[80] On 17 September the Turkish 8th Army Commander, Cevet Pasha, informed the Yilderim Army Group Commander that in the near future the enemy was about to launch an attack all along the front, while its main thrust would be directed towards the western sector.[81]

Reports of German air reconnaissance sorties on the eve of the campaign and a German enemy disposition map dated 17 September ('Z'-Day –2) which were captured by the British (see Map 7), show how the deception and concealment efforts were received.

• The Turks spotted most of the main changes which had occurred within the ranks of the Expeditionary Force upon departure of the forces to France and its reorganization.
• The enemy Order-of-Battle picture of the theater was basically correct.
• Most of the cardinal errors were the result of Turkish failure to locate the deployment changes on the eve of the operation, all of which were accompanied by deception efforts. The Turks believed that:

   There were two main force concentrations: in the Sharon (five divisions), and in the east (four divisions). The majority of the mobile-mounted force (three divisions) were still deployed in the Jordan Valley. The valley itself had been reinforced with infantry forces, according to one source, amounting to a full division.[82] The Mounted Corps HQ, for example, was still situated in its old location in the east.

The XXth Corps was still deployed in its original pattern, while the 60th Infantry Division (which had actually relocated to the coastal plain) was still in its old location in the center of the front.

On the other hand, despite the deception effort, the Turks succeeded in locating the concentration of the 5th Cavalry Division and that the 75th Infantry Division had withdrawn from the front line to the rear.[83]

The last explicit warning reached the Turks on 'Z'-Day −2 when an Indian sergeant deserted from the Western sector and informed them about the imminent attack and its direction. As a result, some staff officers of the Army Group recommended a withdrawal from the front line to a rear position, thus taking just the step that the British were afraid of. However, von Sanders apparently ignored all the warnings and rejected the information, not believing its authenticity, and possibly seeing it as a reiteration of previous unconfirmed reports and rumors.[84]

The mistaken assessment of Army Group F, therefore, had two origins: the basic concept on the one hand and intelligence errors on the other.

The most convincing proof is von Sanders' explanation of why he rejected Feisal's warning. Based on past experience, he estimated that he could contain an offensive in the western sector: '... But the situation of the Army Group would become critical if we were beaten on the Jordan or east of the Jordan. Retreat would be impossible'.[85] This concept of the threat was derived from environmental conditions and basic concepts rather than from a concrete specific threat of the enemy and its intentions.

The Turks also erred in the intelligence aspect. The erroneous intelligence estimate revolved around two axes: the first, 'innocent' collection errors, which did not have their origins in British deception efforts, and the second, the failure to locate changes and the misinterpretation of enemy actions (the Arab operations in the Deraa area for example). The latter were a direct result of a successful deception and concealment operation.

As far as the Turkish intelligence collection effort is concerned it was naturally focused on the eastern sector. Its routine early warning findings which were sometimes mistaken, solely because of Turkish 'honest' errors, helped to substantiate the 'Eastern' view. In this fashion, limited operations which had been carried out in the eastern flank for entirely operational reasons were estimated several times as large-scale offensive

MAP 7
BRITISH DISPOSITIONS AS SHOWN BY ENEMY INTELLIGENCE SERVICE

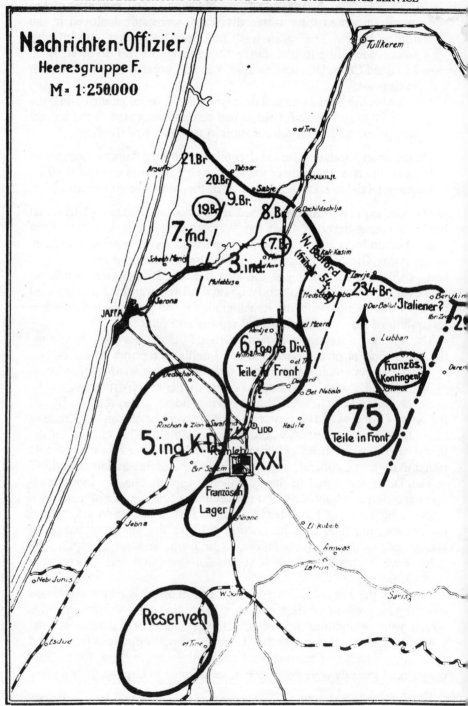

Nachrichten-Offizier
Heeresgruppe F.
M = 1:250.000

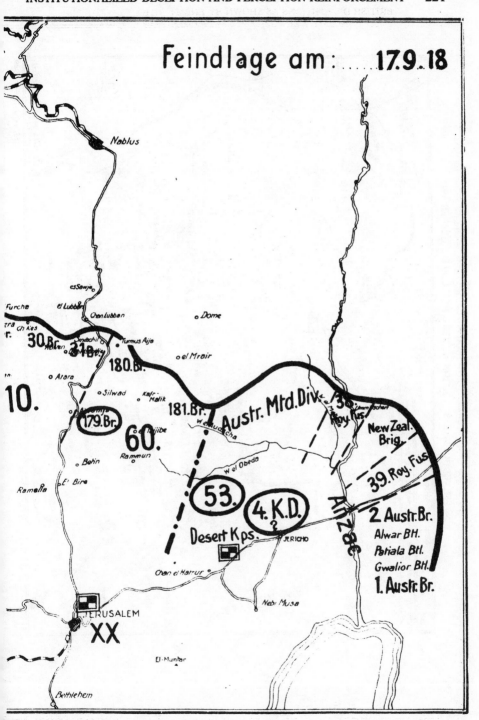

Feindlage am: 17.9.18

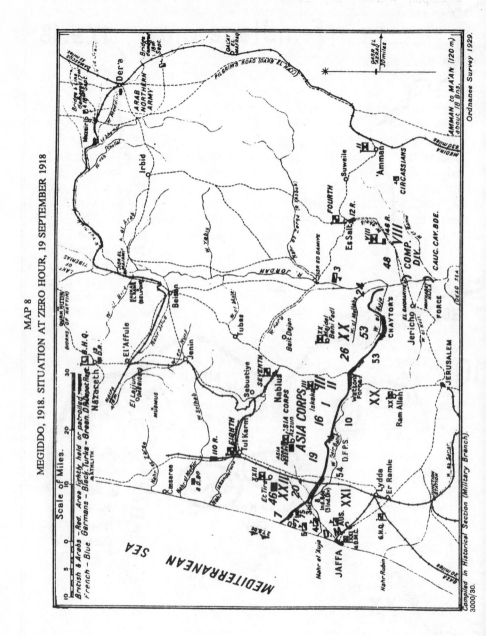

MAP 8

MEGIDDO, 1918. SITUATION AT ZERO HOUR, 19 SEPTEMBER 1918

attempts, without any British intention of creating such a false impression.

In addition, the Turks grew accustomed to a large volume of traffic between the Jordan Valley and the coastal plain, which contributed to the intelligence errors.

In July two cavalry divisions left the Jordan Valley for rest and recuperation. They moved overtly without any special concealment, and the Turks noticed the movement, which was not part of the deception plan. When the divisions returned in August, this time according to the deception requirement, the Turks noticed this movement too. The enemy, therefore, grew accustomed to seeing large-scale movements within short spaces of time in both directions. With no apparent reason to identify them as irregular and, on the basis of its experience during July–August, the enemy was not persuaded by these movements in the long term, to change significantly its picture of British deployment.

It is understandable that, in the short time at their disposal, the Turks did not manage to spot the changes in location and the movements which took place in the very last few days before 'Z'-Day (i.e., the movement of the 60th Infantry Division, which began four days before the Enemy Disposition Map was drawn (Map 7), and the transferring of the Mounted Corps just one day before this). What is much harder to accept as a natural collection error is the failure to locate the movement of the two mounted divisions along the entire front – a movement which had begun several weeks earlier. Failures such as this could more feasibly be attributed to the success of the deception plan.

TABLE 3
BRITISH DISPOSITION (DIVISIONS), 17 SEPTEMBER 1918

	WESTERN SECTOR	CENTRAL SECTOR	EASTERN SECTOR	TOTAL
GENUINE	F- 7 (3-CAV) T-7 R-	F-3 T-3 R-	F-1(+)(CAV) T-1(+) R-	F- 11 T-11 R-
ENEMY ESTIMATE	F-2/3 T-5 R-3/2(1-CAV)	F-2 T-2 R-	F-2(+)(CAV) T-4(+) R-2 (1-CAV)	F-6/7 T-11 R-5/4

F = Front line   R = Rear area   T = Total

The deception, therefore, had a double impact. First in the realm of the intentions assessment and the Turkish rejection of the information which indicated an offensive in the west flank of the front, the deception played an important, if not exclusive, role. Several factors linked together:

- Basic misperceptions accompanied by an erroneous, innocent and directed intelligence estimate (deployment of forces, the 'presence' of the mobile strike force in the Jordan Valley, the failure to locate the preparations for an imminent operation).
- Arab operational activity in Transjordan, which, in its final stages, was primarily the result of deception considerations. This illustrated, in the basic Turkish view, that the threat was becoming more real.
- The fear that the information received was 'planted' or unreliable.

Secondly, in the realm of practical responses in the field, most of the basic Turkish dispositional changes in the eastern flank including the arrival of a considerable portion of the reinforcements, occurred even before the deception operation began. Apparently, the main reason for the *reinforcement* was the basic concept and the belief that the eastern flank was highly vulnerable.

The deception activity in the summer, however, including the Arab activity in Transjordan, contributed mainly to the *pinning down* of the forces to this area, including the mobile and élite forces.[86]

The main deception objectives were attained, both because they corresponded to the Turks' basic concept and because they were re-inforced and rendered more effective by other deception activities.

In the long-range plan, the enemy's attention was diverted to the east and during the year it reinforced its forces in the area at the expense of other sectors.

In the immediate short-range plan, the reinforcement of the western sector was prevented and the forces in the front line remained in their place, not withdrawing on the eve of the offensive.

The eastern sector was not reinforced very strongly immediately before the offensive, and this proves that von Sanders had not expected a large-scale offensive of any kind until the attack was actually launched – another point to the credit of the deception planners.

The enemy's surprise gave rise to the fact that 35,000 infantry and 9,000 cavalry, supported by about 380 cannons, charged in the main sector on 'Z'-Day, opposed by only 8,000 defenders and 130 cannons.

CONCLUSIONS

The same Commander-in-Chief who had led the Egyptian Expeditionary Force in the Battle of Gaza also headed the Megiddo Campaign. In both cases he was personally involved in the planning of the deception effort and its execution. It is no wonder, therefore, that there are common themes in both campaigns.

The conceptual difference between them stems from the different intelligence estimates before the execution of the deceptions, estimates which were fundamental vital elements for the continuation of the planning and execution, without which there could have been only a random chance of success.

Before the Battle of Gaza, it was decided that it would not be possible to conceal the preparations for the offensive itself. Before the Megiddo Campaign, on the other hand, the deception planners thought that they could *conceal* its very existence. From this basic difference derive the differences in objectives, in deception stories and in techniques and means.

In the first campaign the deception attempted to convince the enemy that the inevitable offensive would be launched in a flank different from that planned and at a later date. The dominant method was *diversion* in the direction of Beersheba and it was implemented by a variety of methods and means. In the second campaign, the deception was intended, first and foremost, to *conceal* the very existence of preparations. This may, perhaps, explain the over-emphasis placed on the visual means used at the expense of others.

The success of the deception gave rise to the fact that, in Gaza, the Turks were surprised by the timing of the offensive and even more so by the direction in which it came, while in the Megiddo campaign its very launching came as a surprise to them. What then was the weight of the surprise among the elements leading to the British victory and what was the part of the deception in achieving this surprise?

The surprise was an important element in achieving the victory, since without it, it is very doubtful whether it could have been achieved with such relative speed and ease. Surprise disrupted the thinking of the enemy commanders and made it difficult for them to adapt to the new, un-anticipated situation. The unexpected timing of the offensive in Gaza meant, among other things, that on 'Z'-Day the fourth reinforcement division was still on its way from Northern Syria, and gave rise to a situation where all the command chain in Syria and in Palestine was caught in the midst of a reorganization process as well as physical change of location, [87] a process which upset the Turks' ability to function properly in the campaign.

In the Megiddo campaign the surprise element was even stronger since the rejection of the information about the forthcoming offensive caused the Turks to leave their forces in place in the front line. Upon the break in the defenses in the Sharon, the surprise was one of the factors which made it difficult for von Sanders to perceive the extent of the penetration and understand its nature.

None the less, in the two battles other factors played no less an important role in the British victory:

- The overall superiority, qualitatively and quantitatively, of the British forces over their adversaries along the entire front in infantry, cavalry and artillery. Towards the Megiddo campaign, the poor standard of the Turkish Army and its soldiers deteriorated even more in all aspects: morale, command and control and even logistics. In the Gaza campaign, the differences in strength made it possible to turn the effort in the Turkish right flank into a secondary flank for all sakes and purposes, as against just a diversion effort. In Megiddo this principle was not needed, because the differences in strength limited, at the outset, the Turks' ability to react, irrespective of the surprise element.
- Power struggles in the Turkish-German leadership in the Middle East also contributed to slowing down the reinforcement during the Gaza and Megiddo campaigns and to the last-minute problems in command and control during the Gaza battle.[88]

A comparative examination of the characteristics of the forces, the quality of the command and the war principles of both armies clearly shows that, almost without exception, all were weighted in favor of the British.[89] This total superiority was *the* vital factor in achieving victory. The surprise, coupled with other war principles, represented a decisive factor 'only' in its nature and method of achievement.

In our estimation, the Turks' basic perception of the situation was the crucial factor in achieving the surprise. In October 1917, the Turkish Command refused to believe that the enemy would refrain from attacking via an area that would endow it with clear advantages. In September 1918, it had apprehensions about its east flank, which seemed dangerously vulnerable. The preconceptions which the Turks formed even before the deception efforts of their adversaries began, combined with a wider conceptual outlook, were what brought about the acceptance of the early warning indications, true or false, which strengthened their conceptions as regards 'Gaza/Transjordan first'. Therefore, they rejected most of the information which did not suit these concepts and failed to carry out any activities in the field, even though the information was not totally rejected. Only thus can one explain the willingness to ignore the information about the abandoning of the camps and the location of new concentrations in 1917 and the information about the offensive a year later.

It is the goal of every deception planner to attain points of persuasion which correspond to the basic concepts of his victim. The reason why

Allenby's deception succeeded was that, both intentionally and incidentally, it reinforced the 'concept'. Both campaigns proved that the more precisely the deception initiator evaluates the basic perceptions of his enemy and the better he manages to adapt his deception effort to these perceptions, the easier it will be to coax the enemy into accepting the message, thereby enabling it to be channelled into the desired direction. When the British tried their hand at strategic deception which contradicted the basic Turkish conception, they failed. The lesson one learns from this has become a universal axiom, which has since been proved again and again in tactical and strategic deception operations. It finds expression in the report of the Israeli Agranat Commission on investigating the reasons for the surprise in the Yom Kippur War of 1973: 'In the days which preceded the Yom Kippur War, the Israelis had at their disposal an abundance of early warning indications. The Intelligence Corps did not assess correctly the warning in this information because of its doctrinal adherence to a conception and its willingness to find a pretext for the enemy deployment ...'.[90]

Naturally, this conclusion points to the importance of a solid preliminary basic intelligence for the success of the deception. It involves two aspects: first, familiarity with the enemy's outlook, concepts, beliefs and thinking (over and above the current intelligence as regards its strength, deployment and moves); the second is the enemy's evaluation of the deception initiator and his operational intentions. In Allenby's campaigns we also saw that the British had reliable information about the Turks' estimate of them.

Both campaigns had a unique deception aspect: their novelty. The main principle of the deception lay in General Allenby's ability to view its role and its method of planning and implementation in an original and different light.

'Deception which for ordinary Generals were just witty hors d'oeuvres before battle, had become for Allenby a main point of strategy.'[91] Thus wrote T.E. Lawrence about the Commander of the Expeditionary Force. It summarizes Allenby's basic original concept which raised deception almost to the level of a war principle.

His predecessors, when tackling the subject, regarded it as a kind of personal sporting match of intellect between them and the enemy commander, an extra which one could do with or without. Allenby, on the other hand, regarded the planning of the deception and its implementation as an integral and institutionalized part of the staff work in the combat procedure phase as well as during the conduct of operations. The deception story and its implementation method were decided on the basis of an orderly situation assessment in the same way as the operational plan was determined, and not on the basis of the arbitrary desire of the deception initiator. It is possible that Allenby, who had served under General Roberts in the Boer War, was impressed by the deceptive techniques used to lift the siege from the town of Kimberley.[92] However, it was Allenby who transformed the deception idea into an institutionalized concept. This institutionalization was expressed in the planning at GHQ level and its assimilation at all echelons. The subject of concealment, for example, was clear demonstration of this fact as it was emphasized in the operation orders, at every level, from the Expeditionary Force GHQ level, through the Corps HQs down to the orders of the divisional HQs.[93] This was not a one-man show, but a process backed by an entire organization.

The deception achieved its objective with the aid of a series of factors, some of which were not even derived from a planned deceptive effort, while others, comprising a variety of methods and complementary means, were the results of the originality of Allenby's approach:

• A long time before the Battle of Gaza and before the Megiddo Campaign, large-scale operational activity had taken place in the flanks, which were later to become the deceptive flank. The first two offensives on Gaza and the raids into Transjordan were executed out of operational-strategic considerations, with no relation to a deceptive idea of any kind. However, they did contribute considerably to shaping the enemy's perception, and to accustom it to seeing Beersheba and Jordan as flanks constantly under threat. The deception plan exploited this situation and even strengthened it.

• The long time that elapsed between the moment it was decided to carry out the operation and 'Z'-Day itself helped to facilitate the conveying of the desired message to the enemy, to accustom the enemy to it and to dull the enemy's wits. The main potential deficiency, which, luckily for the British, did not materialize, was that the danger of leaking and exposure increased as time elapsed. The tremendous prevention effort put into guarding the secrecy reduced the danger and thereby pointed to the strong connection between deception on the one hand and prevention and counter-intelligence on the other.

• In both deception operations one can discern originality and novelty. Use was made of modern technology, from the deceptive use of radio communication systems to the intentional exploitation of enemy air photographic sorties to give a false impression. As a complementary means, the British took pains to destroy important communications junctions, thereby disrupting the communications, command and control systems on 'Z'-Day.

• Allenby's conception of deception gave rise to almost complete co-ordination between the genuine operations and the deceptive activity.

In order to achieve deceptive aims, real activity and troops were used on a significant scale.

The main fault which arose in the Battle of Gaza lay in the Turkish exposure of the troop movements. In different circumstances, this exposure could have endangered the entire deception effort. In the Megiddo Campaign, the main error appears to be that too great an emphasis was placed on visual deception while other means and techniques were relatively neglected.

Is it possible that this negligence derived from the fact that the highly imaginative Meinertzhagen left the arena upon the completion of the Gaza Campaign? If this proves true, then we have before us clear illustration of the need for a combination of thorough staff work and of creative thinking and vivid imagination, which few are blessed with. This combination would provide the optimal solution.

One cannot fail to mention the effect these successful deception campaigns had on the future. Several prominent military commanders, Field Marshal A.F. Wavell being the most conspicuous among them, continued Allenby's pioneering work during the Second World War. At first Wavell served as the liaison officer of the Imperial General Staff in Allenby's GHQ and was fully involved in the planning and activities – both operational and deceptive – of the Expeditionary Force. Before the Megiddo Campaign, he was appointed Chief of Staff to the XXth Corps.

The deception operations left a deep impression on him, both with respect to their value as a weapon and with respect to the need, as he saw it, to infuse institutionalized procedure to carry it out. As Commander of the British Forces in the Middle East between 1939 and 1941, he carried out deception activities directed against the Italians in East Africa and on the Egyptian–Libyan border. Some of the characteristics of his concept have a familiar ring about them: the establishment of a dedicated deception organization in his GHQ under the direct command of the Supreme Commander; precise planning and preparation of long-term deceptions; relying on intelligence estimates when defining objectives and constructing deception stories; the use of a variety of visual deception means and communications and leak channels; the 'loss' of documents, rumor-spreading and psychological warfare; siumultaneous use of dummy, notional and real forces, and carrying out the deception in co-ordination with field security and prevention efforts.[94] Deception efforts which succeeded in the operations of the Egyptian Expeditionary Force were again adopted by the British during the Second World War: deception as regards the day set for D-Day, the planting of documents, the absence of the commander from the scene of activity and the concealment of the real rate of advance. All came into expression in deception plans which preceded or accompanied operations like Alam Halfa, El Alamein in North Africa as well as in the invasions of Sicily, at Anzio and in Normandy.[95]

Although the deceptive operations of the Egyptian Expeditionary Force in Palestine were not the sole contributor to the major surprise inflicted upon the enemy, they undoubtedly were the main factor that caused this surprise to affect the enemy in such a decisive way. Allenby's greatness was that his *modus operandi* for deceiving the Turks intensified all other causes and crucially reinforced his enemy's grave misconceptions. Apart from his other achievements, Field Marshal Sir Edmund Allenby will always be remembered for the original and novel dimensions of the concept of deception that he introduced so successfully into the modern battlefield.

NOTES

I am indebted to Professor Michael Handel, who first suggested that I adapt and develop a short Hebrew article about the deception operation in the Third Battle of Gaza into its present English form, and who has been a source of constant encouragement. I also wish to thank the Wolfson Foundation for supporting the English as a Foreign Language Writing Project for Israeli Graduate Students, which provided encouragement in the preparation of this study.

Air Ministry and War Office documents referred to (AIR and WO respectively) have been cited from British Public Record Office's files currently in the possession of Israel State Archive.

1. The details of the strength of the two sides differ in various sources. The data in the article were based on Cyril Falls, *Military Operations Egypt and Palestine*, Vol.I (London, 1930), p.35 (hereafter: Official History). See also A.F. Wavell, *The Palestine Campaigns* (London, 1931), pp.112–15.
2. 'Force Order No.54 by General Allenby' dated 22 October 1917 in Official History, pp.676–80.
3. I am greatly indebted to Dr John Ferris, Department of History, University of Calgary, Canada, for his enlightening comments regarding Sigint collection in the campaign. According to Liddell Hart, T.E. Lawrence told him that each morning Allenby received a log of Turkish telegrams intercepted and deciphered during the previous day. See B. Liddell Hart, *T.E. Lawrence* (London, 1964; originally 1934), p.312. As regards the interception capability, see R. Meinertzhagen, *Army Diary* (London, 1962), p.225. Patrick Beesly, *Room 40* (London, 1982), p.180.
4. For details of air force order of battle see Wavell, *Palestine Campaign*, p.141. The subject of naval air sorties is described in L.B. Weldon, *Hard Lying* (London, 1925). For the importance of this source see note 6. As regards the quality of intelligence collected, see Peter Mead, *The Eye in the Air* (London, 1983), p.180. General Allenby, for his part, estimated that six air reconnaissance squadrons would be needed for the coming operation. See Allenby to Imperial General Staff, 9 October 1917. WO 106/718/268.
5. Meinertzhagen, *Army Diary*, p.224.
6. The best published information about the operation is to be found in two sources: *Hard Lying* by Captain Weldon, the military intelligence representative on board the intelligence ship *Managem*, which liaised between Egypt and Palestine (see note 4);

Livneh Eliezer, *Nili, A Chapter in Political Daring* (Hebrew), (Tel Aviv, 1971) contains original messages sent by 'Nili' and appreciation of British commanders and intelligence experts about the intelligence contribution of that organization.

7. Allenby's appreciation submitted to the CIGS. 12 July 1917. WO 106/721/30; A series of intelligence assessments in, 'General Staff (Oper.) Appreciations of the situation in Palestine. 1 July 1917–3 January 1918'. WO 158/661.
8. A situation assessment compiled by EEF. GHQ in July stated: 'Before long all [Turkish] divisions in Palestine will have been brought approximately up to full strength as regards the fighting strength'. WO 158/611/55. For the official estimate on probable enemy reinforcements, see Allenby to General Robertson, the CIGS and to the War Office, 9 October 1917. WO 106/718/268.
9. 'Notes on the Palestinian Operation'. 21 June 1917. WO 158/611/69.
10. Allenby to Robertson, 26 July 1917. WO 106/718/193.
11. 'Notes by Lt. Col. Wavell regarding Plan of Operation on the Palestine Front'. WO 106/718/123.
12. There are many sources dealing with the details of the deception. The most important and noteworthy ones are in my opinion: Wavell, *Palestine Campaign*, pp.106–9; Official History, pp.73–90; Meinertzhagen, *Army Diary*, pp.222–3; 282–5; George Aston, *Secret Service* (London, 1930), pp.186–98.
13. In his after-battle report, Brigadier, General G.P. Dawnay, the B.G.G.S. of the Expeditionary Force, stated that, before the Gaza offensive, the enemy 'has full knowledge that our offensive was imminent. His estimates of our strength were by no means far at fault'. 13 December 1917. WO 106/718/78.
14. Allenby to Robertson, 21 August 1917. WO 106/718/169. According to a previous letter, dated as early as July, the British commander was confident that the Turkish main concern was their Western sector. WO 106/718/193.
15. WO 106/718/169.
16. 'Notes by Lt. Col. Wavell'. WO 106/718/. I owe the conceptual distinction between the two variants of the deception to Donald Daniel and Katherine Herbig who defined it clearly in their article 'Prepositions in Military Deception', in *Strategic Military Deception* (New York, 1982) by the same authors.
17. Official History, p.20.
18. Ibid, p.231.
19. Weldon, *Hard Lying*, pp.140-41.
20. 'A plan submitted by Major Galet', 30 August 1917. WO 106/721/59.
21. Allenby to Robertson, 16 September 1917. WO 106/718/98.
22. Marshal von Hindenberg, *Out of My Life* (London, 1920), p.295.
23. Details of the different perceptions of the two sides and the mutual relations between them are explained in the excellent book by Jehuda Wallach, *An Anatomy of Military Assistance* (Hebrew), (Tel Aviv, 1981), pp.200–6. Von Kressenstein, when describing in his memoirs the Turkish-German situation assessment leading up to the 'Yilderim' Operation, does not mention the landing threat at all. See Kress von Kressenstein, *Mit den Turken zum Suezkanal* (Berlin, 1938), pp.264–5.
24. The inadequate allocation of resources and efforts is distinctly demonstrated by the fact that although naval forces naturally play a crucial role in the planning and implementation of every seaborne landing, whether real or notional, no such role had been assigned to the Royal Navy concerning the Cypriot deception scheme. It seems that London was unaware of, or did not relate any importance to, this plan. Otherwise, it would be hard to explain the British reaction to a French suggestion at the beginning of October, three weeks before 'Z'-Day, that the Entente would initiate a genuine landing of several divisions from Cyprus on the Syrian Coast, co-ordinated with the main offensive. The General Staff and the Admiralty, while studying the suggestions seriously, did not consider the implications of the planned deception for such an operational initiative and did not look into the possibility that such a move might endanger the French plan, once adopted, by shifting the enemy attention to the northern sector. Foch to Robertson, 5 October 1917. WO 106/718/87; Exchange of memorandums between the D.M.O. and the First Sea Lord, 10–15 October. WO 106/718/88; WO 106/718/94.

25. According to a Turkish source, the British had already tried to carry out a communications deception in the second Gaza Campaign in April 1917. On 14 April a Turkish monitoring station in the front intercepted an enciphered telegram which contained part of the plan expected to be implemented three days later, according to which Gaza was to come under frontal attack and on the same night another division would simultaneously landed in Ashkelon and would attack Gaza from its rear.
     I tend to be skeptical about the authenticity of the event, since, first, it does not seem likely that the British would reveal an exact offensive date; secondly, at the time, they did not know exactly which of their codes and ciphers were being read by the enemy, and thirdly, the event is not mentioned in any other source. See Djemal Pasha, *Memories of a Turkish Statesman* (New York, 1973) (originally 1922), pp.179–80.
26. Meinertzhagen claims that only five men were fully in the know as regards the event: Allenby, his military secretary, the C.O.S. of the Expeditionary Force and his assistant, and, of course, Meinertzhagen himself (*Army Diary*, p.222). This is a very small number on any scale.
27. From Meinertzhagen's testimony, which is the source of the story (*Army Diary*, pp.224–9), it transpires that Allenby, as supreme commander, officially forbade the introduction of drugs, but apparently turned a blind eye when his intelligence officer continued its implementation of his own accord.
28. Notes for D.M.O. and C.I.G.S. WO 106/725/128.
29. Dudley Ward, *The 74th Division* (London, 1923), p.80. Several days later, on 30 September, General Chetwode again stressed the importance of field security measures.
30. The author is grateful to the Turkish Commission of Military History for providing the information based upon the Archives of the Military History and Strategic Studies. (hereafter ATASE Archives). Here: ATASE Archives No.4/7302, Kls.3221, Dos.H-76, F.1–1, 1–2.
31. For details of the Turkish-German perception following the operational and deceptive activity directed against them, see Official History, pp.43, 61; Meinertzhagen, *Army Diary*, p.284.
32. The orders of the Commander of XXth Corps and Commander of 8th Army of 11 October, mentioning the importance of the documents captured in the haversack as an example of the need for field security, are quoted verbatim in: Meinertzhagen, *Army Diary*, p.285.
33. Official History, p.61.
34. A captured document summarized in *A Brief Record of the Advance of the Egyptian Expeditionary Force* (London, 1919), page facing plate 4 (hereafter *Brief Record*). The *Record* itself is an important source, since it contains part of the reports that Allenby sent to the Minister of War and original British situation maps of the Expeditionary Force HQ which show the British deployment and intelligence estimate of Turkish dispositions.
35. Kressenstein, pp.268–9.
36. A.F. Wavell, *Allenby, Soldier and Statesman* (London, 1946), p.17.
37. ATASE Archives, op.cit.
38. Kressenstein, pp.269; 274–5.
39. For the movements, see Wavell, *Palestine Campaign*, p.131; Official History, p.24.
40. It also appears that the idea of the seaborne landing itself did not bother the Turkish-German Command, since it believed that it could handle such a threat successfully. In relation to this, see the report that the German liaison officer (Major Von Papen) sent from 8th Army HQ to the Yilderim HQ, *Brief Record*, ibid.
41. See British Situation Maps dated 28, 29, 30 October. *Brief Record*, plates 3, 4, 5.
42. At the beginning of 1918 Allenby was in favor of a moderate and careful approach as regards the advance in Palestine and preferred the more gradual and slower attack. His territorial objectives were also limited. London, on the other hand, out of global considerations, pressed him to capture larger areas at a faster pace. Official History, pp.298–9; Wavell, *Allenby*, p.200.
43. Wavell, *Palestine Campaign*, p.196; Official History, p.674.

44. The official report Allenby sent to the Minister of War, dated 31 October, gives the following figures for the beginning of September: the combined strength of the 4th, 7th and 8th Turkish Armies consisted of 23,000 rifles, 3,000 sabers and 340 guns. The total strength of the fighting elements facing the E.E.F. including the reserves and the forces dispersed east of the Jordan River was estimated at 32,000, 4,000 and 400 respectively. Turkish documents maintained that the total strength of the three armies comprised 40,600 men including 20,000 rifles, 4,000 swords and 500 guns. (We do not know if these figures include reserves and forces stationed in Southern Transjordan.) General Liman von Sanders claimed its actual strength was far less, while in the opinion of the Australian Official History these figures were in fact an underestimation. See *Record*, p.25; ATASE Archives, No.4/10832 Kls.3718 Dos.28, F.1—124; Liman von Sanders, *Five Years in Turkey* (US Naval Institute, 1927), p.270; H.S. Gaullett, *The Australian Imperial Force in Sinai and Palestine* (Sydney, 1936), p.681.
45. For details of operational activity during the period February–August 1918, see *Brief Record*, plates 32–8; Official History, pp.302–92, 429–38.
46. For the development of the plan, see Wavell, *Allenby*, pp.224–5.
47. According to Lawrence, his men used to cut Turkish telegraph landlines: Liddell Hart, *T.E. Lawrence*, p.312.
48. Technical and Photographic Reports by H.Q. Palestine Brigade, RAF during 1918. AIR 2/98.
49. Between 1 June and 19 September the British took 1,680 prisoners, 69 of whom were officers. In the month of August some seven deserters reached British lines daily from all units in the sector. *Brief Record*, p.23; Official History, p.453.
50. The comparison is between von Sanders, *Liman*, p.210, and *Brief Record*, plate, p.196.
51. The taking into consideration of the Turkish observation appears in R.M.P. Preston, *The Desert Mounted Corps* (London, 1921), p.196.
52. *Brief Record*, p.27.
53. In April von Sanders had already assessed that the British were planning a large-scale offensive in the near future: von Sanders, *Liman*, p.215.
54. See, for example B. Gardner, *Allenby* (London, 1965), p.172.
55. *Brief Record*, p.18.
56. According to Liddell Hart, Allenby, in a private letter that he sent before the raid on As-Salt, instructed General Chauvel, Commander of the Mounted Corps, that the moment that he gained control of the Amman-As-Salt area, he should prepare to move north towards Deraa (Liddell Hart, *T.E. Lawrence*, p.299) Lawrence also indicated that in his meetings with Allenby at the beginning of the year he received the impression that the Commander in Chief was considering the possibility of moving northwards through his eastern flank and that he planned to stay in As-Salt permanently after capturing it. See T.E. Lawrence, *Seven Pillars of Wisdom* (New York, 1935), pp.503–4.
57. On the value of Transjordan and the Arab Desert, the author of the Official History writes: 'It was ... fortunate in that the British Commander in Chief thoroughly understood its [the Arab movement] value to himself and therefore gave it all the support in his power' (p.406).
58. Wavell, *Palestine Campaign* (p.180) claimed that the strategy of the eastern activity as a diversion prevailed as early as February, when the activity against Jericho began. Liddell Hart (*T.E. Lawrence*, p.299) also hints at this, although, it seems that he described a local diversion within the framework of the activities in Transjordan. The Official History, on the other hand, begins to mention (p.565) the deception motive only in connection with the raid on As-Salt. Lawrence (*Seven Pillars*, p.526) claims that Allenby told him about this concept in May for the first time.
59. The British fears are illustrated in the words of Brigadier General Bartholomew, assistant to the Chief of Staff of the Expeditionary Force: the withdrawal of the Turkish forces 'would save their army and leave the British like a fish flapping on dry land' (Gaullet, *Australian Imperial Force*, p.678).
60. Lawrence provides enlightening details of the staff procedure concerning the operation

234   INTELLIGENCE AND MILITARY OPERATIONS

and deception plans which he encountered in the Expeditionary Force GHQ in the months May–July. See Lawrence, pp.256; 538–9.

61. Simple repetition of the 'haversack ruse' of October 1917 could in fact have been exposed and this is what may have been at the basis of the British apprehension. However, it should be recalled that during the raids, which characterized 1918, many documents fell into enemy hands, almost as routine. The Turkish commanders even adopted the contents of some of them as the base for his intelligence estimates. See von Sanders, *Liman*, p.217.

62. Falls claims that the transfer of the Australian Mounted Division to the Jordan Valley in the summer months was part of the deception plan. Wavell, *Palestine Campaign*, (p.164) even extends this claim to include the entire Mounted Corps. Gaullett, (*Australian Imperial Force*, p.679), on the other hand, points to other considerations as being decisive, such as nature of the terrain, the need for mobility, water sources at the line, etc. See Cyril Falls, *Armageddon 1918* (London, 1964), p.55.

63. Details of the deception: Wavell, *Palestine Campaign*, p.201; Official History, pp.461–3; Preston, pp.189, 197; W.T. Massey, *Allenby's Final Triumph* (London, 1920), p.99.

64. For details of the transfer of the artillery units westwards and the concealment measures taken, see P.H. Dalbiac, *History of the 60th Division* (London, 1927), p.225; Dudley Ward, *History of the 53rd Division* (Cardiff, 1927), p.227.

65. Massey (*Allenby's Final Triumph*, p.102) writes that the training centers were set up especially for the purpose of the deception, while Falls represents the other approach. In my estimate, Massey's reports should be viewed with caution, since his descriptions, as the military correspondent of the London press in the Expeditionary Force, tend towards exaggerated sensationalization.

66. The technique of leaving lights on its vacated camps as a deceptive means had, since the Gaza Campaign, become an almost routine operation in the Expeditionary Force. The Australian Mounted Division also acted thus when it left the camps on its way to the raid on As-Salt at the end of April. See Official History, p.368.

67. The Turks carried out communications deception in the sector at an earlier stage in order to mislead the British as regards the strength of their forces in the Jordan crossing areas and present them as stronger than they really were. Their mobile stations in the rear and in the flanks transmitted enciphered messages about approaching reinforcements. They adopted this means several times, apparently, on the assumption that the British would be able to pick up the transmissions, locate the transmitters and decipher their contents. See von Sanders, *Liman*, p.28.

68. Apart from Lawrence, all other sources present the deceptive activity directed against Amman as if it was just an integral part of the overall deception plan. The details of the deception appear in Lawrence, *Seven Pillars*, p.231–5; 332.

69. Ibid., p.539.

70. Official History, p.715.

71. *Brief Record*, loc. cit.

72. A good example of the restrictions is to be found in Operation Order No.42 of the XXth Corps dated 13 September 1918: '... Only such portions [of the Corps's operation order] will be communicated verbally to brigade commanders as is essential for the performance of their tasks. Brigade and regimental orders will define only their own objectives and those of units in immediate touch with them and will give no indication of the general Corps plan' (Official History, p.720).

73. *Brief Record*, loc. cit.

74. Von Sanders, *Liman*, pp.272; 275. Generalmajor Hans Guhr, who was commander of the Turkish 1st Division in the Western sector, did not see a single German aircraft over his front during this period. See Hans Guhr, *Als Turkischer Divisionkommander* (Berlin, 1973), p.236. According to German documents captured by the RAF after the battle, the photographs taken during June 1918 amounted to 674; during 2–17 August to 325 and in the last three weeks preceding the offensive declined to 230. See AIR 2/98/ 57. The Turkish Commission of Military History came to the conclusion that the partial knowledge of the redeployment of the British formations before 'Z'-Day derived from

ground observation and reconnaissance activity and from agents' reports rather than from aerial assets (letter to the author, 26 October 1987).
75. AIR 2/98/57.
76. For the political-religious significance of Hejaz and its holy cities to the Ottoman Empire as a general concept, and especially for the implementation of political war aims, see G. Lenczowski, The Middle East in World Affairs (New York, 1968), pp.44–6; Ahmed Emin, Turkey in the World War (New Haven, 1930), pp.174–87.
77. Von Sanders' basic situation estimate determined that the coming battle phases for Palestine would revolve around a Turkish defense and British initiated offensives. On his considerations, see von Sanders, Liman, pp.205, 215, 221, 263.
78. Ibid., p.260. See also a captured letter of a German officer in which he writes on 18 September ('Z'-Day −1!) that he expects a great offensive in the coming days. Official History, p.341.
79. Von Sanders, Liman, p.262. Circumstantial testimony substantiates the authenticity of the story, despite the amazement revolving around it. Lawrence, who knew the details of the British plan long before the date mentioned, was in touch with Feisal and may have described the plain to him in outline. For verification of Feisal's contacts with the Turks, see Liddell Hart, T.E. Lawrence, p.317.
80. Guhr, pp.238–9.
81. ATASE Archives, No.1/1399, Kls.3787, Dos.H-37, F.11.
82. Letter of the Turkish Commission of Military History.
83. On 15 September ('Z'-Day–4), while most of the mounted troops were already deployed in the Western sector, a German air reconnaissance patrol did not succeed in locating them and estimated 'some regrouping of cavalry units in progress behind the enemy left flank. Otherwise, nothing unusual to report'. On 17 September ('Z'-Day–2) another air reconnaissance report determined that there was no reduction in the level of cavalry force in the Jordan Valley and there was even evidence that 23 squadrons had been added: Gaullett, Australian Imperial Force, p.687; Preston, Desert Mounted Corps, p.198.
84. The Official History (p.468) relies in this account on the memoirs of the Commander of the Turkish XXth Corps which were published after the war. Von Sanders himself (p.274) expresses doubt about the account of the event without giving any explanation. None the less, one cannot ignore the fact that the German Commander was known to be a tactician whose doctrine maintained mainly static defense as against a mobile one, for example.
85. Von Sanders, Liman, p.21.
86. In this respect, I tend to differ from the approach of those who see the reinforcement mainly as the result of intentional British deceptive activity (see for example: Wavell, Palestine Campaign, p.188).
87. The 'Yilderim' HQ was split. Part of it began to take up position in Jerusalem on Z-Day, and another part, including the Supreme Commander himself, remained pinned down in Allepo. The Seventh Army HQ, which reached Hebron, several days before Z-Day, was to assume command of the IIIrd Corps in Beersheba and of two divisions of the XXth Corps on the same day. See Official History, p.42.
88. For details of the power struggle, see Wallach, especially pp.192–5, and Chapter 7 'Yilderim'; Ulrich Trumpener, Germany and the Ottoman Empire 1914–1918 (New Jersey, 1968), pp.188–90.
89. Comprehensive and comparative details can be found in US Department of Commerce, A Survey of 'Quick Wins' in Modern War (Washington, 1975). For additional information on the subject (including details of deceptive measures) see A. Kearsey, Summary of the Strategy and Tactics of the Egypt and Palestine Campaign, revised 2nd edition (Aldershot, n.d.; original edition, 1919), Ch.II, 'Principles of War', pp.63–8.
90. The Agranat Commission Report (Hebrew)(Tel Aviv, 1975). For main conclusions, see Chapter II, p.19. With regard to tactical deception operations, see Yigal Sheffy, Deception in the Western Desert in World War II (Hebrew), (Tel Aviv, 1988).
91. Lawrence, p.537.
92. For the effects of General Roberts's campaigns on Allenby, see Wavell, Allenby,

236 INTELLIGENCE AND MILITARY OPERATIONS

p.168; John Connell, *Wavell, Scholar and Soldier* (London, 1966), p.125.

93. See, by way of example, Operation Order No.40 of the 53rd Division dated 15
    September, in addition to the orders of the Expeditionary Force and the order of the
    XXth Corps mentioned above, 53rd Division, pp.269–70.

94. For details of the deception campaigns of Wavell and other British commanders in
    North Africa, see Sheffy, op. cit.
95. For an enlightening summary on the subject, see Michael Handel, 'Introduction:
    Strategic and Operational Deception in Historical Perspective' to *Strategic and
    Operational Deception in the Second World War* (London, 1987), pp.1–91.

PART THREE

THE SECOND WORLD WAR

Flawed Perception And Its Effect Upon Operational Thinking: The Case of the Japanese Army, 1937–41

ALVIN D. COOX

Strategically we should despise all our enemies, but tactically we should take them all seriously. This also means that we must despise the enemy with respect to the whole, but that we must take him seriously with respect to each and every concrete question ... in dealing with concrete problems and particular enemies we shall be committing the error of adventurism unless we take them seriously.

Mao Tse-Tung, November 1957

INTRODUCTION; THE LOW ESTATE OF JAPANESE INTELLIGENCE

Although the practice was by no means unique among armies of the world, the component of the Army General Staff (AGS) held in the highest esteem, by far, in the old Imperial Japanese Army (IJA) was the First (Operations) Bureau. Theoretically, all staff bureaus were supposed to possess identical authority in the military decision-making process; the Army Chief of Staff rendering his judgements with the assistance of the deputy if necessary. In fact, priority was given to operations thinking, an emphasis that was definitely excessive. In General Sugiyama Hajime's day, for example (during the crucial period between 1940 and 1944), the AGS Chief was said to be practically a robot, with the real power held in the First Bureau.[1]

Army General Staff Colonel Hayashi Saburo has commented that the Operations Bureau, 'with its own dictum concerning the 'secrecy of supreme command', adopted ultra-secret policies and acted like a law unto itself, with utter self-satisfaction. It was common knowledge among staff officers serving at the Tokyo level when the Pacific War broke out, remarks Hayashi, that 'the driving force behind the commencement of hostilities stemmed from the First Bureau advocates'.[2]

Influenced greatly by the old Prussian-German tradition the IJA always 'headed straight for the sound of enemy guns'. Mission, in other words, must take precedence over intelligence estimates. It became the habit for Japanese field officers to reach relatively quick combat decisions rather than to ponder matters over extended periods. By and large, there was a tendency in the Japanese armed forces to treat intelligence lightly or not at all.[3]

Psychological considerations certainly played a large part in shaping the IJA outlook. Deliberate negative concepts were often deemed to be unmilitary, whereas positive or aggressive attitudes were highly regarded and typically triumphed, particularly after the eruption of the China conflict in 1937. By extension, intelligence officers who adopted a broad and sometimes pessimistic view, could be equated with anathematized passivity. High-spirited and 'glamorous' combat officers disliked the 'plodders' and 'worriers' who seemed to infest intelligence (and logistics) organizations. When a certain general officer told one graduating War College class that staff officers would be better off relying on field glasses than sabers, he was almost cut down on the stage by a furious fellow-general famous army-wide for his skill in the martial arts.[4]

Historically speaking, Japanese intelligence had functioned in the shadows until the First World War. Intelligence work was undramatic and methodical, slow but sure. After the First World War, emphasis began to center on large-scale activity, on corps instead of regiments. The former reliance on detailed analysis of enemy strength began to erode, and was supplanted by what some regarded as risky and dangerous 'leaps in the dark'.[5]

Nevertheless, considering the fundamental outlook, inaccurate or unsound intelligence work – even when detected – served only to reinforce the extreme attitude of operations types which can be summed up in the statement that, 'whatever an intelligence staff officer might know, an operations staff officer would *most assuredly* know!' The intelligence section was typically excluded from operations staff deliberations.[6] A classic example of underestimating intelligence usefulness was the step taken by Southern Army Headquarters in 1942, without approval from the High Command in Tokyo, combining the Intelligence Section staff with Operations Section after the successful first-phase campaigns of the Pacific War. The Southern Army simply assumed that the intelligence staff had lost any *raison d'être* by that time. This degradation of intelligence functions in the midst of a full-scale war to the death is underscored by the fact that the Intelligence Section of the Southern Army was not reactivated until February 1944.[7]

"Despite structural and historical factors, one central reason helps to explain the chronic low estate of IJA intelligence: the army's tendency to despise the fighting qualities of all foes, actual or hypothetical – whether Chinese, Russian, British or American. Feelings of contempt were generally accompanied by ignorance of, lack of interest in, or under-estimation of, enemy potential. The Japanese Army could not or would

not comprehend or estimate realistically the scale of modern Great
Power foes, who operated more rationally, more systematically and more
massively than the Japanese.

Some say that the failures in IJA perception stemmed from viewing
matters exclusively through insular Japanese eyes. The 'common sense
Japanese', one IJA officer lamented, simply could not fathom the 'super-
natural' scale of Soviet or American thinking. 'Being delicate island folk,
the Japanese tend to worry about small and trivial matters, taking it for
granted that the enemy will too. But he never did!'[8].

PERCEPTION OF CHINA

The unflattering IJA evaluation of the Chinese military underwent no
appreciable improvement after 1894–95, when Chinese forces were
severely trounced. A Japanese observer's remarks made in 1932 are
typical:[9]

> It would appear a gross exaggeration to say that Chinese soldiers
> are bandits in official uniforms and that bandits are disbanded
> soldiers but this is one of the incredible truths about China.
> Soldiers to all appearances, [Chinese troops] in fact are a uni-
> formed rabble. ... They are untrained, cowardly, unpatriotic,
> treacherous, mercenary, and everything else a soldier should not
> be. ...

After the so-called China Incident broke out in 1937, the Japanese High
Command's attitudes toward China continued to be characterized by
optimism and disdain. An IJA section chief in Tokyo, for example,
reacted to the news of the very dangerous armed clash at the Marco Polo
Bridge at Peking in July by telephoning his superior to say that 'something
interesting' had just occurred. Later a staff officer visited the general's
office and berated the central headquarters for opposing the dispatch of
troops to China. 'You simply do not know what the Chinese are like,'
jeered the section chief. 'That is why you are voicing such negative
opinions in anticipation of serious trouble. But, I assure you, the incident
will be settled if Japanese vessels loaded with troops merely heave to, off
the Chinese coast.' As usual, IJA intelligence experts were excluded from
the decision-making process.[10]

The AGS did not contemplate committing more than eleven divisions
to fight China, or an absolute maximum of 15 divisions if the divisions from
reserve were drawn upon. Yet, by the end of 1937, the Japanese had
already had to send 16 divisions and 700,000 men, approximately the
number of soldiers in the entire standing army to date. By the end of 1939,
IJA forces in China numbered 23 divisions, 28 brigades (the equivalent of

242	INTELLIGENCE AND MILITARY OPERATIONS

another 14 divisions), and an air division. The number of Japanese troops in China had risen to 850,000.[11]

This level of commitment was maintained until around 1943, when transfers to other theatres began, under Allied military pressure. Still, at the end of the war in 1945, the Japanese Expeditionary Army in China was the largest of the armies stationed overseas: 1,050,000 officers and men (19 per cent of the entire Japanese Army); 26 infantry divisions (15 per cent of the total); plus one tank division (25 per cent) and one air division (7 per cent). In addition, 64,000 Japanese Navy (IJN) personnel were on duty in China.[12]

The size of the Japanese military involvement in China hardly tallies with the notion, held widely in Japanese government circles, the general public and the army, that China 'did not count'. According to one IJA colonel, his single infantry regiment, 3,500 men strong, engaged three Chinese so-called divisions under a general officer, during the Suchow offensive in 1938, and 'made mincemeat out of them'.[13]

Although the casualty statistics bear out the Japanese colonel, one has to admit that part of the Japanese Army's confidence, and hence grandiose designs for defeating China, derived from a gross under-valuation of the capabilities of the Chinese Army and guerrillas. The Japanese High Command long nurtured the idea that Nationalist China could be brought to bay only if foreign aid routes could be severed and the capital seized (first, Nanking; then Hankow; finally, the unattainable Chungking). In the end, the Chinese paid an enormous price for their contribution to the Allied victory over Japan, but Chinese forces were definitely in on the kill. It was Chinese troops who recaptured Lashio and Mandalay, and Liuchow, Kweilin and Taichow; who drove within 56 miles of Nanking; and who were about to mount a great assault against Kwangchowan, north of Indo-China – all before the Pacific War ended in August 1945.

PERCEPTIONS OF THE WEST WITH PARTICULAR REFERENCE TO THE USA

The Japanese Navy did not underrate the British and the Americans. The Japanese Army, however, had an entirely different set of enemies: the Chinese, whom they had been fighting and beating in the 1930s, and the Russians, who were always regarded as the main foe they directed strategic planning against, but who were rarely encountered in combat before 1941. Contrary to the general impression in the West, the Japanese Army was not very interested in, let alone impressed by, such Western armies as the British, Dutch, or French – gin-and-tonic warriors best at chasing Hottentots and Moroccans in the Riff. The US Army, only two years before Pearl Harbor, ranked twentieth by size in the world, smaller than those of Sweden, Switzerland, Portugal and Greece. It had a reputation for recklnessness on the attack and helplessness on the defense. 'The amateurishness of [all the world's] armies – except the Germany Army,' wrote a British observer, 'never ceased to astound the Japanese.'[14]

To have admitted to inferiority was unthinkable to the Japanese military, which had, or professed to have, a veritable 'scoring system' to indicate the level of contempt felt for all enemies. This measure was expressed, subjectively of course, by the number of foreign soldiers that one Japanese warrior could thrash in battle. During the Second World War, when the Japanese forces began to suffer defeats, they typically rationalized the reversals by reference to superior Allied material. The most that a Japanese soldier might admit was that an enemy fought well enough to be compared favorably with the Japanese.

The Japanese Army was convinced that Great Britain was senile and 'over the hill', for it had often appeased Japan during the confict in China and had been humiliated at Dunkirk. By 1940–41 it was considered inevitable that German submarine and air attacks, coupled with troop landings on the British Isles themselves, would bring down the British. United States assistance to Britain was largely ignored as a factor of significance in the short run, which seemed all that mattered. It goes without saying that the Japanese Army was mesmerized by Germany's brilliant operations against Poland, France, Belgium and Holland. Simply put, the Japanese were sure they knew who would win the war in the West, and they wanted both to be on the winning side and to share the spoils in the East.

The Japanese High Command's *Weltanschauung* was remarkable for the tendency to overestimate Germany and downgrade other countries. Colonel Matsutani, later head of AGS war guidance, has said that from the standpoint of IJA operational planning, 'It is embarrassing to have to admit that there was almost no consideration of Britain and the United States'.[15] Only after the Third Reich collapsed in the spring of 1945, and the Allied counter-offensive neared the Japanese homeland, did the IJA get around to devoting serious thought to and planning against the Anglo-American powers.

Emphasis in Military Education

The foreign languages that Japanese Army officers studied or did not study played a very important part in their acquaintance with, interest in, and friendship toward other countries and armies. Language tracks depended on the type of school that had been attended by prospective officers before they entered the military academy. Those who came in from the military preparatory schools were exposed to German, French or

Russian for three years. Traditionally, only those who had attended high school ever studied English as a 'special subject' for three years. Chinese language was another 'special subject' open to high school products, but an entering cadet might have studied no Chinese before attending the military academy.[16]

The effects of the language tracks upon subsequent IJA careers is seen in the fact that most officers sent abroad as attachés or students were products of the military prep schools, not high schools. These officers were selected on the basis of class standing at the time of graduation from the Military Academy. This meant that, in practice, most of the foreign postings were to locations regarded as 'prizes' by the Army: Germany, France or Russia. In turn, it was the officers who returned from those choice posts who were assigned to the most important job slots in Tokyo. For the very few officers who had studied in America or Britain, career advancement prospects were proportionately slim.

Skipping North America

It was this system that contributed to the meager comprehension of the United States and England in the Japanee Army. The ignorance of senior officers was especially pronounced. Even officers returning from Europe usually went home via the Trans-Siberian Railway or the Indian Ocean. Of 134 full generals in the Japanese Army from its inception in the 1870s until its demise in 1945, only three ever served in the United States. Even in the more cosmopolitan navy, only about seven of 77 full admirals were stationed in America.[18]

When Tojo Hideki was ordered back from Europe in late 1921, he briefly observed the proceedings of the Washington Conference; but since he was unfamiliar with the English language and anxious to get back to Tokyo, he soon took a train for San Francisco, where he would board a ship home. Probably his brief experience in the United States exerted a permanent influence on Tojo. It has been suggested that he 'viewed the Americans of the roaring twenties as undisciplined, unmilitary, and unconcerned with anything except pursuit of the jazzy life'.[19]

Some Who Tackled America

The attitude of Tojo was the reverse of Sugita Ichiji's who, as a captain and major, was stationed in the United States between 1936 and 1938, and in Britain in 1938 and 1939. Sugita argued that even one tour of America might have been very instructive to IJA officers. 'When you landed in San Francisco,' Sugita reminisces, 'you could see enormous numbers of motor vehicles jamming the streets – no match for Japan. One could have discerned America's national strength from the automobiles alone.' But, adds Sugita, it was the general feeling in IJA circles that the United States was a country whose soldiers would flee at the first taste of combat.[20]

In 1939, when Sugita visited IJA attachés in all the major capitals of Europe and asked to see copies of the cable traffic to Tokyo, he was dismayed to note that no messages from Germany, Italy, Poland, Romania or Turkey alluded to American matters. Only the post in London (and to a lesser degree, that in Paris) had anything to say about the United States. If the military attachés in Europe were paying little or no attention to America, it was inevitable that the staffs in the War Ministry and the AGS were similarly ignoring that country. Sugita tried to remind his superiors and his colleagues that the American mobilization capability was high – that the United States had sent approximately one million troops to Europe in 1917–18.

Sugita did not feel that he made a dent in IJA thinking. The leaders did begin to expect war with the United States, but the danger appeared to be preponderantly naval. Even if the US Army ever undertook offensive operations, the level would be minuscule. Sugita deplored the High Command's disinterest. He thought that when Lieutenant-General Yamashita Tomoyuki led an important mission to Germany in 1940. Yamashita should at least have been asked to inspect the United States on the way. Instead the AGS sent Sugita, a mere major, to visit America at the end of 1940.[21]

Yet Sugita was essentially ignored by the Germanophile AGS, even after he reported the secrets of Hawaii. There, after arrival in early January 1941, he was shown the defenses by a US Army staff officer, an old friend who had been his company commander when he was attached to an American infantry regiment in New York State in 1937. (Ironically, the ill-fated General Walter Short, now commanding the Hawaiian Department, had been Sugita's division commander in New York. Sugita would have liked to pay a courtesy call on Short in Hawaii, but the general was away at the time.)

Sugita was astounded by the extent of the US military build-up in Hawaii, which was entirely unknown to the Japanese. As soon as he could, Sugita rushed the startling information to Tokyo. At the time, he was sure that his reports were at least being read by top-ranking officers on the General Staff. After the war he learned that his messages were pigeon-holed by somebody and therefore did not go up the reporting channels. Apparently that 'somebody' and his colleagues were unimpressed by Sugita's information. The Americans could never have revealed as much to Sugita as he claimed; even if they did, it was merely a bluff.[22]

The experience and attitudes of Kan Haruji (a graduate of a high school before entering the Military Academy) are similarly instructive. During the First World War, when he was a junior officer, he was considered for technical schooling in the United States, but he preferred to study in France or Japan, since 'military technology was not very advanced in America at that time'. Kan was accordingly sent to the engineering college at Tokyo Imperial University, 'the best in the world in those days'. Later, between 1927 and 1929 as a captain and major, Kan served in England and France. Contrary to the reticence of many other returning attachés or students, Kan wanted to return via the United States, especially since he had recently been reading General Sato Kojiro's book, *If Japan and America Fight*. Tokyo turned Kan down and ordered him to come back via Siberia. Kan (an eventual lieutenant-general) comments: 'Looking back at that time, if only the Army had let me see America I might have been of some help later. Though we had been looking down on US technology, I think that it had progressed considerably by then. The IJA brass must still have been taking America lightly.'[23]

Hara Tomio, another eventual lieutenant-general, had graduated from military prep school, the Military Academy, and the engineering college at Tokyo Imperial University. In 1935 he was sent to a German technical school to study automotive technology, but what he learned there was 'the American system'. Consequently, when his tour in Germany was up the following year, he asked to be allowed to return via the United States in order to perfect his knowledge. The War Ministry replied that he might travel back through America, but that additional travel expenses would not be authorized. If he could manage within the allowance set aside for travel across Siberia, that was his decision. Hara scrimped and saved, and somehow squeezed out enough money to finance a low-budget trip of about a month in America.

Assisted by Army Attaché Washizu, who made reciprocal arrangements with the American side, Hara became the first IJA officer to inspect the Aberdeen Proving Ground and a US Army tank school. Though Hara was not particularly impressed by what he saw, he at least was able to update IJA intelligence on American armor; 'it was useful to observe the US tanks at first hand'. Colonel Washizu thought that Hara was exaggerating when he reported what he had seen, but Hara was *persona grata* with the Americans and took the whole IJA staff in Washington with him to inspect a US Army experimental mechanized infantry regiment stationed at Camp Eustis. Hara even had to decline the unusually gracious American offer to stage a march-past for his benefit (something too grandiose for a mere major, he protested).

Hara later explained his success: 'IJA officers who went to the United States were too timid, so they ended up never seeing an American tank. I achieved my objective because I was ignorant of American customs and was very pushy.' As for his military observations, Hara found that the US peacetime army was truly small, their ordnance poor, their technology primitive, and studies small-scale. 'They were so far behind,' recalled Hara, 'that even I was respected by them.' All in all, his self-directed trip to America had been very useful, Hara concluded.[24]

Lieutenant-Generals Hara and Kan remained within the career path of technicians. Washizu rose to the rank of lieutenant-general, but this expert on the United States went into retirement the very month of Pearl Harbor at the age of 56. Sugita, an eventual colonel, found his English language skills of ironic use when serving on General Yamashita's 25th Army staff at the time General Percival surrendered Singapore.

THE EXPERIENCES OF SATO KENRYO

One question that emerges from the preceding account of the very rare, but first-hand IJA inspections of a foreign army is whether familiarity breeds contempt (as the saying goes) or fosters more profound perception. The experiences of Sato Kenryo shed particular light on the matter. Assigned to the United States between 1930 and 1932, Sato was one of the very few IJA officers with service in America to reach high levels of responsibility in Tokyo. He became a War College instructor in 1935, Military Affairs Section desk chief in 1936, IGHQ Press Bureau chief in 1938, Military Affairs section chief in 1941, Military Affairs Bureau chief in 1942, and lieutenant-general commanding an infantry division in 1945.

Sugita describes Sato's outlook on the United States, when Sato was Military Affairs Section chief, as follows: 'I know [all about] America, so you don't have to come around [and fill me in]'.[25] What had Sato really learned during his stay in the United States? English had been one of his favorite subjects in high school days, but he lost interest in the language after he entered the army and graduated from the Military Academy in 1917. He was delighted to go to America in 1930, escaping from unsatisfying duty in the War Ministry and from the burdens of managing family finances on a captain's pay. With high hopes and cheerful dreams about unknown America, he sailed across the Pacific on a new cruise ship. He intended to improve his English and master conversation in particular, but he soon found American English pronunciation to be formidable and again lost interest in the language. Homesick for Japan, he spent too much time with the many Japanese living in Washington, and of course his English did not improve. Colonel Washizu sent him to Boston, where orders then sent him to San Antonio for attachment to the 12th Field Artillery Regiment for six months. After seriously banging up a knee in an automobile accident while driving back to Washington from Boston, Sato then drove 2,700 miles, alone, to his assignment in Texas. Sato learned about America mostly from his experience in the San Antonio area.

First, a local Japanese provided the following advice: 'Japanese males are smaller than Americans and have the habit of bowing too often. This would convey the impression that Japanese are subservient; so when you shake hands with superior officers, don't avert your eyes. Look up, right into their eyes.'

Sato was given a room in Bachelor Officers' Quarters (BOQ), where everybody was very kind to him. What troubled him most was the fact that the girlfriends of American officers visited the BOQ at night and made noise. How very greatly did US military discipline differ from that of the Japanese Army! But the American officers carried out their duties quite satisfactorily in the daytime, so apparently they could separate dallying with women at night from behaving properly by day.

Since his knee was still bothering him, Sato was excused from riding, until some US officers asked him whether Japanese horses were smaller than American horses. Suspecting that the Americans were implying that he was afraid of their large horses, Sato decided to ride a mount into the ground, whether or not his knee survived the ordeal. Miraculously, his knee pain disappeared; apparently he had untwisted a wrenched muscle by riding so hard.

It was the era of Prohibition, but the American officers unabashedly served Sato moonshine corn liquor cut with ginger ale and lemon. Once he was shown barrels of the booze in the basement of the house of a US Army Air Corps captain.

Sato participated in a series of two-week maneuvers. As opposed to IJA practice, the US Army never commandeered civilian homes. It was Sato's understanding that the quartering of troops was prohibited by the Constitution, which in turn was based upon adverse experience learned from wartime experience in Europe; namely, that when government forces camped for extended periods in the houses of anti-establishment people the soldiers ended up being hassled by the inhabitants.

Whereas in Japan, troops might not camp in the field for more than three nights at a time, out of concern for the health of the men, the Americans camped for the full two weeks under the stars. Sato expected that this would be very hard on his health, but when he awoke each morning on his cot in his tent, he felt fine. The air in Texas was quite dry and there was nothing like Japan's night dew to soak the grass.

To Sato's surprise, the US Army took off each Sunday, even during the maneuvers. Officers' kin drove out to the campsites with picnic lunches and enjoyed family outings. It was unthinkable for Japanese officers to have family visits during maneuvers. His company commander invited Sato to the family picnics, but none of the other single officers, noncoms, or soldiers could receive visitors. 'Apparently there were no hard feelings,' noted Sato. 'It must be due to a difference in customs.'

At the bivouac, the American flag was hoisted each morning and lowered each evening. Whenever Sato heard the bugle play, he emerged from his tent and saluted the flag, but a lieutenant told him that there was no need to do this if he was inside the tent when the flag ceremony began. Sato had thought that anybody not engaged in official duties must honor the flag, whether inside a tent or lying down; instead it looked as if people outside a tent would hustle inside whenever the flag ceremony was at hand to avoid the trouble of saluting. Saluting the flag must have originated from the fact that the United States, a federal republic, needed to unify the country in time of war; but in peacetime the necessity for unity of the nation decreased, and the salute to the flag became a mere formality. At hotels and other public places, many national flags were posted in parallel. The American people seemed to like their own flag, but only in an ornamental capacity.

Sato felt that, apart from differences in ethnic characteristics, the basic distinction between Japanese and American officers and men stemmed from the differing mobilization base: obligatory in Japan, voluntary in the United States. Japanese soldiers were subjected to rules of absolute obedience, which greatly curtailed their individual freedom. Under the volunteer system, however, it seemed that American officers were not particularly concerned with the personal lives and welfare of their troops, on duty or off. The feeling of camaraderie between officers and soldiers was weak – nothing like the bonds in the Japanese Army.

With respect to military discipline, the Americans punished transgressions strictly by the book; otherwise, free-spirited volunteers could not be kept in line. In the Japanese Army, on the other hand, company commanders and other officers were often affectionate toward their men and might overlook violations of the letter and skip punishments.

The practices observed by Sato reflected 'subtle differences' between the two armies, in peacetime and wartime application. One could not, however, assess the superiority or inferiority of fighting strength merely on the basis of the mobilization systems in use. Both a draft army and a volunteer army, after all, must aspire to the same end: successful operations. In Japan, the military was strong and dragged along the nation. In the United States, the military was not influential, and national economic power and industrial technology dragged along the military.

How the American public reacted to the Manchurian Incident of 1931 and the Shanghai Incident of 1932 interested Sato greatly. He concluded that Americans 'love a hero'. In Manchuria, the actions of the Kwantung Army were so swift and bold, some Americans actually cheered on the Japanese Army, though it was really operating against the interest of the United States. When the Japanese forces did not overcome Chinese resistance at Shanghai with equal ease, the American people seemed disappointed and drew the conclusion that Japanese troops performed nicely against bandits, but could not do too well against regular. It was then that the Chinese became the heroes, and the image of Japan and the Japanese Army deteriorated in America. Part of Japan's good press was derived from the fact that Manchuria was *terra incognita*, whereas Shanghai was a cosmopolitan city in the limelight of China. Once the Japanese were able to crush the resistance at Shanghai and then pull out, the Americans began applauding the Japanese again.

From the events of 1931–32, as seen from the United States, Sato drew a number of impressions that stayed with him thereafter: that Stimson was a bully who later teamed up with Roosevelt and Hull to provoke hostilities against Japan; that the China Lobby, funded by the Chinese government, manipulated all-important public opinion in the United States – something that Ambassador Debuchi flatly refused to do in behalf of Japan; and that the American press was excessively pro-Chinese in its sympathies.

These, then, are the perceptions of an IJA officer who was chief of the very important Military Affairs Section of the War Ministry as a major general, on the eve of Pearl Harbor, and who 'knew all about America'. Can we say that his experience in the United States had served his army and his country in good stead? Sato himself had the following to say about the six months he spent with the American field artillery regiment in Texas: 'I could not find a thing worth learning, be it ordnance, equipment, training and education, or unity between officers and men. With respect to training, in particular, I felt like teaching *them* a thing or two'.[26] Sato, indeed, seems like the prototype of Colonel Hayashi's critique of the High Command *c*. 1941:[27]

> The [Japanese] military had a strong tendency to disbelieve – and to treat as astronomical – official United States Government data indicating the rate of production of American industry. In addition, they made light of America's spiritual fiber. The majority believed that the United States would find it difficult to instill a martial spirit throughout the nation as a whole. After all, isolationism was rampant there, and most of the advocates were influential figures.

Matsuoka's Parable

The perceptions of one last Japanese 'expert' on the United States warrant mention: those of the University of Oregon-trained foreign minister in 1941, Matsuoka Yosuke. Asked by a newsman, 'What are the American people like?' Matsuoka replied:[28]

> Let us say there is only one path running through a field. It is so narrow that one person can hardly pass at a time. You are walking along the path in one direction; and an American from the other.

You and the American run into each other, face to face, in the middle of the field. You will not yield; neither will he. After you stare at each other for a while, the American blows his cool and strikes you in the face. If you bow and yield to him out of instinctive reaction, that will be the end of you, for the American will conclude that is the best way to deal with you. He will punch you again, every time he meets you. But if you refuse to yield and you hit right back, he will be astonished and take a second look at you. He will think: 'Hey, he's O.K. after all!' This will provide the opportunity for you and the American to become very good friends.

CONCLUSIONS

We have seen that Japanese military perceptions of foreign armies and countries before the Second World War were a mixture of untruths, half-truths, and sound insight. Painting over one's own faults was imperative; accentuating enemy debilities was constructive. To offset the foe's material strength in weapons, manpower and mechanization, it was necessary to consider the intangibles of leadership, soldierly quality and national character.

In the previously mentioned book *If Japan and America Fight*, Lieutenant General Sato Kojiro, 'the Japanese Bernhardi', wrote that, 'in point of discipline and skill in the art of war, the Americans are the worst of all the nationalities. Moreover, the method of command adopted by the American officers is infantile compared with that of the Japanese Army'. Ethnic strife would cripple the polyglot United States domestically in time of war. Blacks were a particularly subversive force, supplemented by the Japanophile Mexicans and naturalized Germans and Austrians. The American armed forces were ill-disciplined, permeated by drunkards and brawlers, and prone to desert or resign. In the First World War, the US Army participated for only half a year, during the period of Allied victory; it engaged in no serious fighting, yet lost one out of every 12 men. There was no reason to think that America's martial capabilities had improved since then. In Sato's view:[29]

> The American resembles the Yedokko [a citizen of Yedo, now Tokyo]. The Yedokko is known to make a show of authority with his characteristic caustic remarks, giving the devil to his adversary. But if the adversary should face him with pluck, the Yedokko will prove to be unexpectedly coward at heart.

Updating Sato's critique, a leading Japanese daily newspaper, *Asahi Shimbun*, appraised America's military posture in far less insulting terms, only five weeks before Pearl Harbor.[30] There was a shortage of commanders in the US Army, wrote the *Asahi*'s military commentator. Battalion commanders were usually majors, but they were old majors, the age of 45 being comparatively young for them. IJA battalion commanders were more than ten years younger, on average. Since ages and ranks did not coincide in the US Army, a shortage of commanders had resulted. At least ten years were required to train mid-range officers; one wondered whether the supply of officers would suffice even if the United States mobilized a huge army.

Men of draft age (21 to 35) numbered 16 million in all of the United States, but the target of America's five-year plan was only 25 per cent of that number, so there was still considerable leeway to conscript more manpower. The United States lacked experience in fighting for its life, because the nation had been exposed to liberalism, the American role in the First World War was far from impressive, and the US Army had lacked hypothetical foes. 'Young America' was weak; there were many reports of conscripts hugging their girlfriends in public and weeping as they entered service.

Since the United States was a rich country, the *Asahi* continued, it was a common characteristic for Americans to feel that there was no need to struggle and to risk one's life. This attitude could be deemed a weakness of the democratic system. Seriousness of purpose might not grip America until an enemy landed on its shores and presented a credible threat to life and limb. Still another weakness of a democracy was labor's demand for high wages, with workers and the nation teaming up to clamor for freedom and struggling to evade governmental pressure.

In order to demonstrate the alleged excellence of improved army ordnance, the US government was announcing new weapons, and running photographs under banner headlines. It was doubtful, however, that the new tanks and anti-aircraft guns were more than official propaganda, and that they possessed the capabilities claimed for them. Still, America's production technology was advanced, as shown by the world-famous 'automobile culture'. The US government was utilizing excellent technocrats in the military munitions industry, demanding tough working hours from labor and driving hard to expand production. Given these facts and the country's vast material potential, it would not take long for the United States to achieve its dream of creating a newly equipped army. In addition to civilian factories, the United States had established governmental munitions plants, whose productive capabilities would have moved into high gear between mid–1941 and the spring of 1942. This, in turn, would facilitate the build-up of mechanized American forces. The United States was hampered by one factor, however: in parallel with the development of its own armed forces,

FLAWED PERCEPTION AND OPERATIONAL THINKING

253

America was obliged to serve as an arsenal for all the anti-Axis nations – Britain, the Soviet Union, and China.

Somehow, the cool comments of the *Asahi Shimbun*'s military critic and of *rara avis* intelligence officers such as Sugita Ichiji serve to remind us that Japan was not entirely devoid of good sense and introspection on the eve of Pearl Harbor. Unfortunately, the flawed perceptions and the ignorance of hotheads, Germanophiles and hysterics colored what should have been hard-headed thinking and crisis management. IJA plans of that era were consequently sketchy, broad, opportunistic and undistracted by detail. To cite but one instance of sheer ignorance: Colonel Takayama Shinobu recently revealed that both the Japanese Army and Navy General Staffs had no idea about the function of the US Marine Corps, as late as 1941. It was thought that the Marines were merely like IJN landing parties (*Rikusentai*) such as those employed at Shanghai in 1932. Takayama told Colonel Hattori Takushiro, the head of the all-important AGS Operations Section, that US Marines were stronger than any force in the US Army or Navy, and that one day the Marines might prove fatal to Japan. 'But Hattori's outlook was no better than that of his colleagues at the time,' Takayama laments, 'and he, too, regarded the US Marines as no different from our own *Rikusentai*.'[31]

Sun Tzu once said that 'what is called "foreknowledge" cannot be elicited from spirits, nor from gods, nor by analogy with past events, nor from calculation. It must be obtained from men who know the enemy situation'.[32] But, as it has been suggested, a peculiar national trait of the Japanese is that they are not particularly interested in intelligence. The IJA thus fought, typically, without sufficient information.[33] The price was ultimate catastrophe for a major army and a major people.

NOTES

This paper was presented at the US Army War College Conference on 'Intelligence and Military Operations', Carlisle Barracks, Pennsylvania 22–25 April 1986. Copyright US Army War College Foundation. The views expressed in this article are those of the author and do not reflect the official policy or position of the Department of Defense or the US Government.

1. Interviews with Imaoka Yutaka, Hayashi Saburo, Nishihara Yukio.
2. Saburo Hayashi in collaboration with Alvin D. Coox, *Kogun: The Japanese Army in the Pacific War* (Quantico VA, 1959), p.27. First published by Iwanami Shoten as *Tailheiyo Senso Rikusen Gaishi* (Tokyo, 1951).
3. Interviews with Hayashi, Nishihara, Imaoka.
4. Interview with Imaoka.
5. Interview with Nishihara.
6. Interview with Katakura Tadashi; Takayama Shinobu, *Kaiko*, Jan. 1979, p.8.
7. Hayashi, *Kogun*, p.45.
8. Interviews with Inada Masazumi, Sato Kotoku.

9. Akimoto Shunkichi, *The Manchuria Scene* (Tokyo, 1933), pp.292–5.
10. Kawabe Torashiro, *Ichigaya-dai kara Ichigaya-dai e: Saigo no Sanho Jicho no Kaisoroku* (Tokyo, 1962), pp.137–8; Tateno Nobuyuki, *Showa Gunbatsu; Gekido-hen* (Tokyo, 1963), p.251; Katokawa Kotaro, *Kaiko*, Jan. 1979, p.8.
11. Hata Ikuuhiko *et al.*, *Taiheiyo Senso e no Michi* (Tokyo, 1963) 4 (part 2): 24,41,63; Hata Ikuhiko, *Nitchu Senso Shi* (Tokyo, 1961), p.249.
12. Hayashi, *Kogun*, pp.149–50, p.182.
13. Interview with privileged IJA source. Also see Albert C. Wedemeyer, *Wedemeyer Reports!* (New York, 1958), pp.325–6.
14. Arthur Swinson, *Four Samurai: A Quartet of Japanese Army Commanders in the Second World War* (London, 1968), p.25.
15. Matsutani Makoto, *Kaiko*, Jan. 1979, p.9.
16. Hasegawa Kiyoshi, ibid., pp.9–10; Hayashi, *Kogun*, pp.23, p.199.
17. Interviews with Hayashi and Takahashi Tsuruo; Hayashi, *Kogun*, p.23; Katokawa, *Kaiko*, Jan. 1979, p.9; Hasegawea, ibid.; Sugita, ibid.
18. Sugita, *Kaiko*, Dec. 1978, pp.8–9.
19. Alvin D. Coox, *Tojo* (New York, 1975), p.19.
20. Sugita, *Kaiko*, Dec. 1978, p.10; Takahashi Toshiro, ibid.
21. Sugita, *Kaiko*, Dec. 1978, p.8; ibid., Jan. 1979, p.8; and *Kaiko*, March 1978, p.7.
22. Interview with Sugita; and Sugita, *Kaiko*, Jan. 1979, p.9.
23. Kan Haruji, *Kaiko*, Aug. 1980, p.21.
24. Hara Tomio, *Kaiko*, June 1981, pp.6–7.
25. Sugita, *Kaiko*, Jan. 1979, p.8.
26. Sato Kenryo, *Sato Kenryo no Shogen* (Tokyo, 1976), pp.51–66.
27. Hayashi, *Kogun*, p.23.
28. Matsuoka Den'ichiro, *Oyaji Matsuoka*, cited in Matsuoka Yosuke Denki Kanko-kai, *Matsuoka Yosuke; Sono Hito to Shogai* (Tokyo, 1974), p.45.
29. Kojiro Sato, *If Japan and America Fight* (Tokyo, 1921), pp.16, pp.82–3, pp.87–93, pp.96–102.
30. *Asahi Shimbun*, 30 Oct. 1941, p.5.
31. Takayama, *Kaiko*, March 1978, p.8.
32. Sun Tzu, *The Art of War*, transl. Samuel B. Griffith (Oxford, 1963), p.145.
33. See Alvin D. Coox, 'Recourse to Arms: The Sino–Japanese Conflict, 1937–1945', in Alvin D. Coox and Hilary Conroy (eds.), *China and Japan: Search for Balance Since World War I* (Santa Barbara, CA, 1978), p.311.

The British Army, Signals and Security in the Desert Campaign, 1940–42

JOHN FERRIS

Speed, flexibility, reliability and security are the characteristics required of any signal system. Without these it cannot provide the means whereby immediate and accurate information is supplied to commanders and timely and effective execution of operational and administrative plans can follow. These characteristics are of especial importance under desert conditions where distances are great and dispersion considerable, where there are constant and rapid changes in the situation and where units and formations move frequently from one command to another.[1]

The following examples of the misuse of routine may serve as a guide to [the] proper use (of radio-telephones):

a.   In June 1942 an Italian Second Lieutenant in a radio intercept company was awarded the German Gold Cross for 'Saving the 15th Panzer Division in the Western Desert near Bir Hachem'. The 15th Panzer Division was cut off from its supply trains and was almost out of fuel and ammunition. The Italian intercepted a conversation *in the clear* between two British commanders concerning their *intended actions* in disposing of the unfortunate German division. This information enabled the German commander to collect and fuel a few of his tanks and break through the encircling British forces to reach his supply trains, and so to extricate his whole division.

b.   During the British stand on the Alamein line, a British regimental commander whose position was near the south flank sent a desperate call, *in the clear*, saying, in effect: 'I am out of fuel, out of ammunition. Will someone please do something'. Fortunately, in this case the Germans did not.

c.   Two British brigade commanders were talking on the air. One asked: 'Can you do anything about closing the 3000 yard gap between your left and my right flank?'

The second replied 'No, I can't. Can you?'

'No, I can't either.'

Twelve hours later the Germans did something about it.

d.   A British Armoured Division on the Tunisian Front intercepted a message *in the clear* from a German air support party calling for a dive bomber attack on a British position at a stated time, and stating that the target area would be indicated by ringing it with artillery smoke. The British commander ordered his artillery to register on a nearby German strongpoint. When the Stukas arrived on schedule the British artillery ringed this point with smoke. The subsequent Stuka attack was thorough and effective.[2]

Only a traitor used radio, only a fool did not; this dilemma haunted all commanders of the Second World War. In order to control the operations of millions of men scattered over as many square miles, states had to rely upon the least trusted medium of communication on earth. Although radio was a uniquely supple and speedy form of signalling, it was also extraordinarily vulnerable to interception. The use of this device simultaneously increased both the ability of a state to co-ordinate its forces and the chance that an enemy would discover its intentions. Without radio there was no certainty of command. With it there was no guarantee of secrecy. The rise of radio led to a new system of relationships (which might be called 'C³IS') between command, control, communications, signals intelligence and signals security. Indeed, it sparked a revolution in the art of war. The connection between information, command and communication lay at the heart of this revolution.[3]

Intelligence shapes a commander's understanding of how his forces can best be used to further his aims while communication systems carry the messages which lead both to knowledge and to action. If it can maintain adequate communications or deny the enemy access to accurate intelligence, conversely, an army should be more likely to defeat its opponent. Ideally, it should be able to establish the technically maximum standard both of signals and of security at one and the same time. The more dangerous the enemy's source of intelligence, the greater the standard of defence needed against it. All this seems simple; all becomes complex when that threat is the most deadly of them all – signals intelligence. For any improvement in an army's standard of communication will tend to weaken that of its signals security; any tightening of security will tend to strangle signals. Indeed, improvements in signals or security alike may actually hinder an army's ability to achieve victory. These paradoxes stem from the dialectical nature of C³IS.

The flow of communications is the lifeblood of command. One would expect orders and information to move most efficiently through an army when the latter has a simple and flexible command structure. One would also expect this level of efficiency to fall as that structure becomes more complex and hierarchical, and especially as more levels of command are interposed between a field commander and his fighting units. Too many generals spoil the battle. Of course, any headquarters will have a limited span of command: it can control only so many sub-units and assimilate only so much information at any one time. Thus, a field commander will need intermediate levels of command both to amplify his power over his fighting units and to filter out the information rising from below. In principle, however, these intermediate levels should be as few as possible and they should serve primarily as relay stations for the transfer of orders and information. The more intermediate levels of command, the greater the likelihood that the transfer of messages will be slowed and their meaning misunderstood. The more independent and powerful these levels become, the more likely they will be to pursue their own aims and thus confuse the process of command. Nothing, then, could seem less efficient than a C^3 system with many intermediate levels of command, each having a small span of command, all joined by rigid hierarchical bonds. The ideal C^3 system would have the maximum possible span and the fewest possible levels of command.

An army could exert its power to the full through such a fine-tuned system – if every part always functioned with high efficiency and without interruption. Armies, however, must sometimes enter a realm of friction where only the crude survive. Under the stress of war, some or all command links will disappear, the transmission of orders and information will be unexpectedly delayed, action and knowledge alike will be hampered. To survive these conditions, the sub-units of an army must co-operate without co-ordination from above, while headquarters must act even when enveloped in the fog of war. This is most likely to occur when an army has many intermediate levels of command, each an independent centre of power with a small span of command, all connected by rigid hierarchical bonds which can maintain control over large segments of an army even when under the gravest stress known to man. Such robust C^3 systems will be far less efficient than fine-tuned ones; even this greatly diminished quality of command can be maintained only when signals systems operate at their maximum level of performance.

The purpose of military signals is to transfer up and down a chain of command that volume of information and instructions at that velocity which an army needs to achieve a given task. The volume and velocity which can be provided depends upon the efficiency of a signals service. What is needed will vary with the aim and with the army at hand. The more urgent and unpredictable the problem, the greater the call for speed; the larger and structurally more complicated the army, the greater the need for size. Modern military organizations require fast-working and dense signals links with subordinates, superiors, with that host of other units which fight beside them or which meet their logistical needs.

These communication structures must necessarily be complex; they are correspondingly vulnerable to dislocation.

In crude terms, the efficiency of a communication system may be measured in terms of its volume (the maximum quantity of groups of traffic which can be transmitted between all its stations at any one time) and of its velocity (the mean, the minimum and the maximum times required for any station in the system to receive messages of a given length from any other). A military communication system will be most efficient when all its traffic can be sent at the highest possible rate of speed and through an uninterrupted set of links. The friction of war, however, will degrade this level of efficiency. For example, whether for technical reasons or because of enemy action, individual stations or links in a network may cease to function. This will happen without warning and its effect will vary with the length of time and the level of command involved. At worst, this problem can entirely block irreplaceable channels of communication during critical periods. While less spectacular, another form of friction is no less deadly.

Security against traffic analysis, codebreaking and cryptanalysis will degrade the functioning of any communication system. The use of the most simple and rapid modes of signalling such as radio transmission in plain language will be curtailed; the adoption of time-consuming matters like code and cipher will become essential. One lapse from a complex and continually changing set of procedures, and security will slide towards the pit. Only well-trained and constantly monitored personnel can avoid such slips and only at a price. Every security system offers a compromise between the need for secrecy and the usability of signals. For example, speed of transmission is crucial in communications; secure systems are slow. Thus, in 1944 operators using Morse code by key could transmit about 300 plain language groups of traffic in 10 minutes. When they used high-grade British systems such as the Typex cipher machine or one-time pad (OTP), the encipherment and the transmission of this traffic required a period six to 14 times greater.[4] Such friction will occur whenever any signals security system is used. The more communication an army needs in order to function, the greater the effect of this problem. The aggregate effect of these delays in the velocity and the reduction in the volume of traffic may be a signals failure. In any case, when guarded by the full panoply of security precautions, any communication network will function at a small fraction of its full theoretical efficiency. Thus, effective procedures for signals security will cripple again the already diminished level of efficiency of any C^3 system. In no other case does the mere pursuit of defence against a hostile source of intelligence so harm the work of any army; security against the enemy's sound-ranging service, for example, will not reduce the scale of one's artillery fire by two thirds. A signals intelligence service need not read a single message in order to hamstring its enemy.

In using means of communication which an enemy can intercept, the more technically perfect signals become, the less so security must be, and vice versa. For example, a robust C^3 system will have dense layers of main and fallback communication links between units and headquarters. Effective signals security procedures, however, will be correspondingly more difficult to enforce upon this increased number of operators; the enemy's codebreakers and traffic analysts will simultaneously receive an increased quantity of traffic to attack. Conversely, reductions in the number of links will make a communication system more secure but more fragile. Only a signals system which is never used is certain to be secure; any form of signals security is certain to cripple communications. Of course, one can sometimes establish secure means to transmit traffic by plain language; or reduce the volume of communications which is necessary during operations by training an army to act automatically in certain circumstances without first requesting and receiving orders; or devise techniques to transfer some types of information and orders quickly and flexibly throughout an army. These means can reduce the scale of the problem; they cannot eliminate it. The imperatives of communication and of security are in conflict; the stakes at risk are the quality of one's command and the secrecy of one's strategy.

There is no simple escape from this dilemma. Signals security, of course, is not an absolute virtue, an unbreakable but unworkable crypto-graphic system is worse than none at all. Communication is the primary purpose of signals, security a secondary consideration. Despite this relative ranking, however, in absolute terms each of these matters is a vital concern: to ignore signals security is to risk fatal consequences. One cannot escape the need to choose between evils: one can merely select the least of them. Thus, 'the old struggle between "security" and "signals"'[5] must end in a complex compromise. Their requirements must be balanced at the highest possible level of marginal efficiency, where no further gains can be made in either direction save by suffering greater losses in the other. It is difficult enough to create a technically effective system for either C^3 or signals security; one must, however, strive to achieve both at the same time.

It is never easy to balance these imperatives. During 1940–42 it was even harder than usual for the British Army to draw the 'most effective compromise between theoretical security and operational requirements',[6] because it was poorly prepared for either the use or the security of radio. Indeed, Britain discovered that virtually no such compromise was possible at all. The combination of small numbers of radio operators, and those inexperienced, of large volumes of traffic, of emergency conditions and of poorly designed cryptographic systems created this danger: any use of security procedures might cause a breakdown of communication, any use of radio one of security. During these years the British Army was notorious for lax signals security and for constant signals failures. From late 1942 until 1945, however, it possessed the most powerful, flexible and secure system of military communication on earth. An examination of the process by which the British Army entered and escaped its predicament will contribute to the study of the desert campaign, of the signals intelligence struggle of the Second World War, and of the general relationship between command, control, communication, intelligence and security.

The purpose of military communications is to support the operations of armed forces; the shape of signals reflects an army's approach to war. Between 1919 and 1939 the British Army suffered from financial stringency, from Whitehall's refusal to let it prepare for major wars, from its own misunderstanding of the nature of modern ones.[7] Similarly, the Royal Corps of Signals was starved of funds, denied the opportunity to train with higher formations and to prepare for mobile operations. If the army was Britain's Cinderella service, signals was its Cinderella corps.

In 1939 Britain had 1,400 regular signals personnel, augmented by another 38,500 less well trained men. This total strength was to increase fourfold to 154,661 men by 1945. During this period the signals strength of the Indian Army (including seconded British personnel) increased tenfold, from 6,411 to 71,395 men.[8] This expansion was particularly marked regarding radio personnel, and with predictable consequences. Genius was not required to handle signals equipment: as the Chief Signals Officer (CSO) of the Eighth Army noted in 1945, 'Gurkhas, who are notoriously thick in the head, make good signallers'.[9] Proper training, however, was essential: another authority stated in 1943 that 'signals personnel are either good or useless. There is no half-way. To be good, they must have long periods of combined training, and they must specialize in the particular job for which they are to be employed'.[10] Years of training would be required to make these British personnel 'good'. Moreover, the British Army would have to recentre its entire signals system while within earshot of the sound of the guns.

For the army entered the Second World War with its communication system of the first. This elaborate structure of telegraph and telephone lines had a symbiotic relationship with a stable front. Neither could exist without the other. This system could do anything but move; during mobile operations it could not carry a large or rapid flow of instructions and information between a commander and the commanded. Radio was a tertiary component within this system. It was used far less than technically possible and was handled with neither security nor effect. Confronted with the choice between the risk of interception and the inconvenience of code, signals personnel tried to avoid the use of radio, but when this proved impossible usually sent their messages in clear.[11] Most of these characteristics resurfaced in British signals during 1939–41.

Of course, all forms of communication are complementary and no single one can handle all tasks. Even in the desert, landlines were an essential signals service: by 1942 the Signals Officer in Chief (SO in C), Middle East, noted that 'the pendulum has now swung' and the value of these systems was underestimated.[12] They were less vulnerable to interception than radio and hence a more secure medium of transmission. Since landline links could carry plain language traffic, they reduced to a degree out of all proportion to their number the problems caused by signals security. Where available, cable was more than worth its weight in radio sets. In mobile operations, however, landlines were not enough: radio-telephone (R/T) and wireless-telegraphy (W/T) were necessary to maintain tactical and operational control.

In September 1939, unfortunately, these systems were not available to the British Army. Corps and army headquarters had, respectively, two or three and six to nine radio sets. One set each for forward and for rear and lateral communication linked British divisions to brigades and the latter to infantry battalions or armoured regiments. Battalions had no forward radio links at all, although armoured car squadrons, artillery batteries and every tank were equipped with a radio set. R/T and W/T did not even provide a full fallback network for the British Army. Their tactical use was limited to purely armoured operations or to artillery support. Individual command links did not even possess a dedicated communication circuit: a corps might have to command three divisions or a division three brigades through one set. This would be a certain cause of apoplexy of command. The artillery circuits were the only element of redundancy in the system; throughout 1940–42 these links all too often provided the only means for communication within infantry brigades during emergencies. No allowance was made to carry administrative messages. Radio was treated as an auxiliary service which would handle a small load of traffic. Should this system suddenly become a principal means of communication, it would not carry enough operational traffic to maintain a high standard of control: the standard volume of administrative messages would bury it alive. The throat of command might be cut if accident or enemy action wrecked even one radio set.

Not only would these failings soon become obvious, but they had been predicted. During the interwar years radical thinkers had argued that armies would move more quickly and more flexibly in the future than in the trenches, and hence would require new modes of communication; so too had chiefs of the imperial general staff. In 1922–23 Lord Cavan wanted

the army to abandon landlines entirely and trust in wireless.[13] In 1929 Lord
Milne insisted that instead of being 'tied up in a network of line communications tending to paralyse rather than invigorate its functions', the army
needed 'mobility and elasticity in [its] means of communication'. Only R/
T and W/T offered this possibility. They should, therefore, become the
principal means of communication in front of corps headquarters. While
this view remained official policy until 1939, as with so many of Milne's
proposals haste was made too slowly.[14]

Financial restrictions and institutional inertia alike hampered the
adoption of radio. In any case, the army did not prepare signals fit for
mobile war because it did not believe that one would occur. Most army
officers held that any new continental war would be akin to the last; hence
a variant of their old signals system would meet the army's needs.
Operations would unfold at a stately pace. Command could be exercised
in a sure rather than swift fashion, with plenty of time to receive information, to assess options and to issue orders. Shielded from enemy action by
a stable front, a landline network would carry with the requisite rapidity
an enormous volume of instructions and information. In the Great War
such procedures had allowed hastily improvised headquarters to turn the
largest, most complex, most unwieldy, human organizations ever known
into the most perfect meatgrinding machines ever seen. Surely this could
be done again.

By 1939 the army's use of radio had advanced little since 1918; its
procedures for security had actually regressed. By 1917–18 the army's
system for signals security matched that of any belligerent.[15] Between
1919 and 1932 the War Office preached the necessity of this matter to its
officers. It emphasized the extreme vulnerability of radio traffic in
the field, particularly between the headquarters of divisions and their
brigades. It provided hints on the best means to minimize such risks; it
planned to establish signals security sections to monitor such dangers in
war.[16] The genius of the army's signals security between 1919 and 1939,
unfortunately, did not lie in an infinite capacity for detail. Although
British forces in Egypt noted during 1936 that 'great importance has
always been attached in strict wireless discipline',[17] the War Office was
strikingly lax in these areas.

For example, the basic elements of signals security were systems of code
names for units and places and call signs for communication stations. Until
October 1941, however, each army radio station received an individual
call sign. Thus, through patience and direction finding, an enemy could
follow the movements of each station and often identify the units to which
they were attached. Then, through inference and scrutiny of the patterns
and the levels of inter-communication, an enemy could determine
Britain's order of battle in any theatre and forecast British intentions with

striking accuracy. Although these individual call signs changed every day, British forces did not simultaneously change their patterns of inter-communication. Thus, an enemy could quickly identify some of these new call signs, connect these to their sets or nets (communication stations which serviced given command links) and finally reconstruct the entire system. If British procedures for signals security were too primitive for safety's sake, British personnel were also too untrained to use them. Thus, in 1939 GHQ France warned that 'unless something were done to simplify communications while at the same time ensuring a reasonable degree of security, the whole mechanism of command and administration was in danger of breaking down' – all because the personnel of the BEF could not use a system of unit and geographical code names![18] In the British Army the phrase 'signals security' was essentially a synonym for 'wireless silence'; this offered little security once silence ceased.

Between the wars, superenciphered codebooks were the main high-grade cryptographic system used by the British Army.[19] Such systems, however, were extremely slow (in 1937, for example, two hours were needed to encipher, transmit and decipher a message of 110 groups on the RAF's superenciphered codebooks)[20] and were cryptographically vulnerable when used to transmit large quantities of radio traffic. Nor, contrary to the implication in *British Intelligence in the Second World War*, did the use of Typex cipher machines overcome this problem. Although these devices were issued down to the divisional headquarters of the British Expeditionary Force (BEF), they were not often used by the latter during May–June 1940. Until early 1942 these machines were in agonizingly short supply in the Middle East. Although they were issued to corps heaaduqarters during the Crusader offensive of November 1941, their value was initially limited. Until special vans were devised to shield these devices 'from sand and rain ... Typex machines were more often out of order than in order – now [spring 1942] very much the reverse is the case'. Even during the Gazala operation of May–June 1942, Typex carried only rear headquarters, and essentially administrative, traffic.[21] Until early 1943 British divisions and corps had no simultaneously secure and flexible high-grade system to carry their operational messages.

In any case, formally powerful systems are not the only ingredient in cryptography. As the head of RAF signals security noted in 1944, 'the mistakes of cypher operators form almost the principal weakness of cypher systems in general. Left to themselves, it is extraordinary what mistakes even trained operators can make'.[22] During the first years of the war, the British Army was desperately short of trained operators. In the Abyssinian campaign of 1941 and the Burma one of 1942, it overcame this problem only by conscripting almost every English woman in Khartoum, Nairobi and Rangoon.[23] In January 1941 the radio operators of even so critical a centre of command as GHQ Middle East constantly made errors so elementary as to respond in plain language to messages sent in the signals service code.[24] The army's cipher personnel had to master their trade as they practised it; this crippled signals and security alike in the interim. These problems were even greater at lower levels of cryptography and command.

During the Great War the army had found it hard to construct proper low and medium-grade systems for front line traffic; by 1918 all these codes and ciphers had been either extremely clumsy to use or entirely lacking in security. The army retained this tradition throughout the interwar years. Though signals personnel recognized the need to develop 'improved ciphering arrangements' for traffic in the field, the War Office did not do so. The army's low and medium-grade systems offered little security and gravely hampered communication. As in 1918, this would tempt operators and officers alike to square the circle by sending all their traffic in clear. In any case, during May–June 1940 many British units seem to have had no low or medium-grade systems at all. Staff officers planning the evacuation of British forces in Narvik over the Norwegian civil telephone system were forced to rely on the use of 'parables' for security: the withdrawal orders for one British infantry battalion in Belgium were 'given over the telephone by means of a code which involved discussion on the film *The Invisible Man*'. The orders issued to one British armoured regiment attached to the First Armoured Division on the Somme front arrived 'on a grubby bit of paper, one paragraph of which read: "Frequencies and code names as for last brigade exercise in Wimborne." Luckily somebody had a copy of the code'.[25] By 1939 the British Army was prepared neither for the safe nor the effective use of radio in the field. As the War Office admitted in 1946,

> From the examination of captured documents and interrogation of German intercept personnel, it has been established that valuable information at all levels was acquired through the insecure use of wireless.
>
> At the beginning of the war very scant attention was given to signal security and it was only by painstaking effort and by perseverence that this aspect of training was given the attention it deserved as a operational necessity.
>
> Signal security reached a high level only during the latter years of the war ... .[26]

During the initial years of this conflict, Britain and its army alike paid dearly for these failures of signals and those lapses in security.

This British system provided an ideal target for blitzkrieg, that style of warfare into which the *Wehrmacht* stumbled during 1939–41. The latter forced its foes to fight for high stakes and at a fast pace. Unexpectedly rapid decisions had to be made by armies with confused command structures over fragile communication networks. Poland, France, Britain, Russia, all learned in succession that ineffective command and communication systems were a combat divider. The Germans struck straight at the heart of these systems; the centre could not hold, neither could the front.

In 1940, for example, information and orders percolated through the many levels of an extraordinarily rigid and convoluted Anglo-French command. The actions of formations could not be co-ordinated until a complete sequence of communications had been completed up from units through every single intermediate headquarters to the high command and back down again. If any link broke, every action would be paralysed. Moreover, during days when critical decisions had to be made, these armies had first to determine who should make them. No action could be taken against the Germans until several higher headquarters with over-lapping responsibility had been consulted. This process was often completed only after the possibility of successful action had already been forestalled, or never at all.[27] This failure stemmed in part from the unusual weakness of the Allies' signals network.

The French higher commands relied for communication upon notoriously poor civil telephone systems; the highest of them possessed fewer telephone sets than did a British battalion. One British officer attached to the French First Army during 1940 later described his experiences with this system in these words:

> You could get through to no one, you could beg, you could beseech, you could implore, you could curse but nothing melted the cast-iron obduracy of the operators. It was if some telephonic sadist was gloating over [one's] agonies .... The French members of the staff were made of sterner stuff and never seemed to tire of shouting into the microphone, *'Priorité, Priorité' d' opérations, Priorité de première urgence'*, but I don't think that they achieved much.

Another British witness wrote of General Billotte, commander of the Northern Group of Armies of 800,000 men: 'After the second day of the battle (of France) his sole communication was one civilian telephone. He had no telegraphic communication between his H.Q. and Armies at all. The result was that he completely lost touch with his Armies and was never in the picture at all'.[28] Billotte soon died by accident; the French command by its own hand.

The British Army, too, inflicted wounds upon itself. When its forces failed to find a stable front, its signal system had to perform in a role for which it had not rehearsed, movement. It was simultaneously exposed to enemy action. The ability of this system to carry orders and information declined, which crippled command precisely when it most needed power. Although the army sought to solve this problem by increasing its use of radio, this at first could not carry all the requisite traffic. Neither could undertrained and overstrained operators maintain an adequate level of wireless security. These problems increased the chances that an enemy could damage the British Army, which in turn would exacerbate the initial difficulties with signals and security, *ad infinitum*. Once within this vicious circle, the British Army found it hard to escape.

By 1939 the German Army, like its British counterpart, had developed a signals service fit for the war which it expected to fight. The *Wehrmacht*, however, placed a greater emphasis on the use of radio because it expected that future operations would be immediate, mobile and decisive. The communication system which it devised to meet these circumstances proved all too suitable for those of blitzkrieg. Although German wireless equipment was technically superior and its higher formations possessed more radio sets than did those of the British Army, the real difference between these forces was not in material but in understanding. The *Wehrmacht* was more willing to rely on radio, had a better idea of its value and limitations and had drawn a far more efficient balance between the needs for signals and for security.

Thus, it utilized a system (which the British later called the 'link sign' or the 'single call' procedure) by which call signs were assigned not to radio sets but to radio nets: on a given day each member of any net used the same call sign. Only skilled operators could handle this system, but the latter could cripple the ability of hostile traffic analysts to identify nets and sets and to observe changes in their composition and interaction. Moreover, through the Enigma cipher machine, German formations down to divisional headquarters were able to transmit large volumes of operational traffic with great speed and security. This device should not be judged a failure just because it was ultimately solved: until summer 1942 it was the most flexible and secure means to transmit operational traffic possessed by any army on earth. With a car, a radio set and an Enigma machine, a German general could roam at will throughout his command and yet be in constant and secret touch with all his superiors and subordinates – if he so wished. Erwin Rommel, of course, held that even by this means no commander could simultaneously appreciate the shape of a mechanized battle and communicate with his rear. He preferred to maintain physical contact with some of his leading troops at the cost of abandoning signals touch with all of his headquarters for days at a time.[29] This was simply a poor approach to command. As a better Panzer leader, Heinz Guderian, showed, the German approach to signals allowed any general to lead from the front while staying in constant communication with his rear. Without this system, blitzkrieg could never have come into being.

Not only had the German Army raised the standard level of its security; it had also learned when that level should be reduced. In particular, it understood the proper role of plain language. It used this for tactical traffic and for operational emergencies, when the need for speed outweighed the risk of interception, when the enemy could not use the information thus compromised before one had acted upon it. Conversely, without the lubrication provided by the constant use of plain language, Britain's entire C^3 system would grind to a halt. During 1939–41 the German Army often suffered from breakdowns of communication and of security, yet still it possessed the finest signals service of any army on earth. Only if the British Army entirely abandoned security could it match the ease of use of German signals; it could match the latter's security only if it did not use radio at all.

In signals as in all areas of the British Army, the bill for 18 years of neglect fell due in May 1940. Throughout 1939–40 the BEF was desperately short of signals and especially radio equipment and personnel. GHQ, for example, received its signals staff only by stripping them from the divisions sent as labour to the Somme. Even in May 1940 it could establish its radio service solely by borrowing two wireless sets from its corps. These shortages crippled GHQ's ability to meet its functions; those regarding cipher personnel almost negated it. Thus, by 19 May 1940, with the débâcle in full swing, the War Office pressed GHQ to send by radio 'live cipher messages' regarding operations. This order had to be cancelled after precisely two such messages had been sent 'owing to the congestion in Cipher Offices' at GHQ. When during the next two days GHQ had to rely on hand speed wireless for communication with London, 'the cipher office got inundated and delays on cipher messages became very serious'.[30]

The BEF faced not simply difficulties with communication but also with security, for reasons which would continually recur until 1942. With so few trained personnel and so many signals problems, security was an even more secondary concern than usual. The army also lacked either interest or expertise in these issues. The BEF, for example, had precisely one fulltime signals security section in April 1940 while the first one was apparently not established in the Middle East until autumn 1940.[31] All this reduced the sophistication of the signals security precautions which the army could follow. The BEF was reluctant to adopt so elementary a precaution as to change its radio call signs and frequencies regularly. Moreover, in December 1939 it discovered that its own call sign procedure was far less secure than the German 'link sign' one. The BEF, however, declined to use the latter;[32] when adopted by the Eighth Army in October

1941, this same system inflicted immediate and irreparable blows upon German signals intelligence. Finally, as would continue for two years, until it ceased to be the only accepted practice for signals security, an almost religious devotion to wireless silence before battles began made it impossible to detect and to correct signals and security problems before they became operational ones.

When the British Army entered Belgium, its communication system had to move for the first time since 1919. Not until 17–19 May, however, when the BEF began to retreat under continual pressure, did serious signals problems emerge. In the midst of a constantly shifting operational situation, the BEF's signals staff had to improvise a service based on all available channels of communication and with unprecedented reliance on radio. GHQ, meanwhile, seemed bent on increasing the BEF's problems in this sphere. General Gort's penchant for fragmenting his own command structure hampered communication, as did a characteristic lack of liaison between signals and operational staffs. Thus, the head of GHQ signals discovered only 'by chance' on 19 May that the BEF planned to launch a corps level assault on the next day near Arras. 'When G. Staff were remonstrated with for not informing Signals, they pleaded that they thought Signals had no resources so that it was not worth worrying them about it'.[33]

Amid this chaos, the Royal Corps of Signals achieved a remarkable feat. Up to the moment that the BEF escaped at Dunkirk, it generally received the volume and velocity of communication between brigades, divisions and corps, which it needed for operational purposes. This reflects both the ability of the signals corps and the fact that the BEF was spared the worst of the German onslaught. None the less, these weeks revealed flaws in the army's approach to communication and to security. The signals system of the Great War was shown to be unfit for mobile war. Continually throughout May communication within and between British units simply vanished when under any kind of serious pressure. Within the British formations which suffered the heaviest German blows, such as the rearguard of the BEF or the divisions of the Somme Front, communication within and between brigades was constantly broken, often for periods of up to twelve hours at a time.[34] Moreover, one can safely assume that the entire British system for the security of tactical traffic collapsed. Ironically, this probably did not matter in that campaign; tactical signals intelligence was small beer compared with the successful rupturing of the Allied front. In other circumstances, however, its value might rise considerably. These experiences showed that the British Army had many lessons to learn regarding signals and security. These flaws in its procedures would not be addressed for another year, however, in part because defeat by Germans was followed by victory over Italians.

During the two and a half years following the evacuation from Dunkirk, the lands around the eastern part of the Mediterranean Sea and in the Middle East became the centre for the operations of the British Army. Its campaigns in Abyssinia, Crete, Egypt, Greece and Libya were all dogged by grave shortages of signals equipment and personnel. In August 1940 the army had exactly six (soon augmented by another eight) wireless stations for all its intercommand communication within the Middle East.[35] in January 1941 General Wavell, the British Army's Commander in the theatre, reported that his operations in the western desert, Greece and Abyssinia were 'all in danger of coming to a halt, not from want of fighting troops, but for want of transport, signals, workshops and such …. Commanders in all three theatres are seriously hampered by lack of signals personnel'. His Signals Officer in Chief (SO in C) more irritably noted that 'we have not got signals growing on gooseberry bushes'.[36] Imperial assistance alone let Britain meet these needs. More Australian, New Zealand and Southern Rhodesian than British radio personnel may well have served in the desert; India and especially South Africa provided virtually all the signals for the Abyssinian campaign.

Until mid-1941 radio communication between Middle East command and its subordinate headquarters even in operational areas was poor, though this was assisted by cable. In January 1941 Cairo could not establish a single dedicated radio link with Khartoum, a centre for the large-scale offensive in Abyssinia. Such links were maintained with Athens only through help from the RAF. Even in summer 1941 communication between Cairo and Baghdad was in a 'parlous state'.[37] Throughout the theatre critical signals functions could be met only by robbing those marginally less vital. In May 1941 the newly formed headquarters on Crete found its signals staff only by stripping them from its units, increasing the latter's communication troubles. Three months later the headquarters at Baghdad reversed the process, by surrendering most of its own radio personnel so to bolster its divisions' communications. That in turn created the 'danger of breakdown of Signal Communications at this H.Q.'.[38] The British Army's campaigns in the Mediterranean and the Middle East rested upon a flimsy foundation of communication.

In late 1940 and early 1941, British imperial armies smashed far larger Italian ones in Abyssinia and the western desert. Radio was the primary means of communication for forces advancing over such vast and primitive areas. With signals as with all things, these offensives were run upon a shoestring. The demand for wireless equipment and personnel had swelled, the supply to units and formations had not. For example, in September 1940 exactly 16 wireless sets were available in the Sudan for all field operations.[39] The success of these campaigns was astonishing; so, too, was the fact that signals met the army's needs in those circumstances.[40] These achievements increased the army's faith in the value of R/T and W/T. The Seventh Armoured Division, for example, emphasized that these facilities alone allowed rapid inter-communication within mechanized formations, 'in the handling of which information is of such importance and speed so often vital'.[41] Unfortunately, these successes blinded Britain to the flaws in its system of signals and security.

During these operations, the headquarters of infantry battalions and armoured regiments had only one radio set for rear or lateral communication with other units or brigades. Brigade and divisional headquarters had only two or three for forward, rear and lateral signals, while administrative links were extremely limited. The Fourth Indian Division, for example, had precisely one (and that unreliable) set to handle all its administrative traffic during the Sidi Barrani offensive.[42] This fragile web of intercommunication could easily be torn assunder. Not only was tactical communication as vulnerable as ever, but the loss of one radio set could suddenly eliminate control over a regiment; the loss of three, command by a division. Throughout these campaigns accident or atmospherics frequently disrupted signals while whenever the Italians fought with determination, most notably at Keren in Abyssinia, communication within brigades unravelled for several hours. Here, as in the battle of France, the army's communication system could scarcely withstand any operational stress at all. It was precisely during long and intense battles against an aggressive foe that Britain would most need communication; it was precisely these conditions which its signals system was least suited to survive. Moreover, given the small carrying capacity of this network and the untrained nature of its personnel, the army's needs for signals security had to be subordinated to those for communication to an extraordinary degree.

Thus, the Abyssinian campaign was a case-study in signals insecurity and not just on the Italian side. Small numbers of radio operators, many of whom 'only received their cipher training as operations proceeded', transmitted almost all British operational traffic, and mostly in low-grade codes. Italian traffic analysis certainly maintained a clear picture of the British signals system (and hence of its order of battle in Abyssinia) despite changes in frequencies and call signs.[43] Whether the Italians broke British operational codes during the campaign is unclear: it would not have been difficult. Yet even these elementary security precautions seriously impeded communications. One report noted that 'the delay on coding and decoding under the present system reacts against efficiency and even if there is the risk of ciphers being broken, it is surely better to employ some such machine as the "Syko" [an RAF device intended to provide 24 hours' security for messages] rather than owing to the present delay, tempt commanders and staffs to send messages in clear, because there is no time to employ cipher'.[44]

Temptation was not resisted in the desert. Before the Sidi Barrani offensive began, wireless silence was almost total; during its course, the use of plain language was almost universal. Influenced by the scale of this success and the limits to its radio facilities, the army concluded that signals security and mechanized operations were mutually exclusive. A staff study of the desert operations of December 1940–February 1941 argued that

> Modern mechanised warfare demands quick movement, quick thinking and quick decisions; and the more open and unrestrained the country the greater the demand for all three. There simply is not time to put a decision into writing or the opportunity to put it into effect may be lost; and it is the *effect* of the decision that matters, not the writing of it. Consequently, we have to seek another means of conveying decisions and, fortunately, such means are available in the form of R/T.

In mechanized operations, the use of cipher was counter-productive. Despite the army's emphasis on verbal orders,

> cases did occur of written orders being transmitted in cypher. Not only did this cause delay but it was frequently found that the material transmitted was out of date before deciphering had been completed ... the conditions of warfare of this sort are such that, in fact, the use of cypher is seldom justified. The question which staff officers and others should ask themselves before making use of a method which has so many drawbacks in fast moving warfare is: 'Will the information (or the Order or Instruction) which I want to transmit really be of any use to the enemy by the time he has intercepted it, translated it and taken action on it?' In the majority of cases the answer will probably be 'No'.[45]

Because of over-confidence in its own abilities and of a misunderstanding of the need for signals security because of the strained communication situation in the Middle East, during the spring of 1941 the British Army scarcely modified its system for signals and security. Indeed, this remained almost identical to that of September 1939. This fragile system, however, had worked only because of the strategic passivity and the tactical ineptitude of the Italian Army. It might have been tailor-made to suit Erwin Rommel.

The Afrika Korps was not composed of supermen, while the reputation of Rommel's generalship outshines its reality. His flaws as a commander were legion. His tendency to lead from the front while breaking contact with the rear sometimes allowed him to react to situations before his enemy knew that they existed. More often it left Rommel leading battalions while colonels commanded the Afrika Korps. Rommel more-over was ever-ready to take hasty decisions based upon incomplete and misinterpreted fragments of information. This behaviour was particularly shaped by his most formative moment as a soldier. Whenever he scented confusion in the enemy command he no longer saw the desert but Caporetto. For Rommel, nothing was easier than to imagine an enemy on the verge of collapse, nothing more natural than to gamble everything he had for the highest of stakes. This daring led him to remarkable successes against inferior enemies; this recklessness led him to ruin against able ones.

Rommel, none the less, was a good tactician, an excellent trainer of troops, an inspiring leader of men, a formidable enemy. He moved rapidly and sought to exploit every opening which fortune offered him. He was also lucky in his army and his enemy. The Afrika Korps was tough, aggressive, amply supplied with first-rate officers, better suited to armoured operations in the desert than the British and perfectly formed to exploit the latter's system of signals, security and command. It could force the British to fight long, intense and mobile battles, during which British forces would increasingly need to communicate and be decreasingly able to do so. The German signals system was somewhat better placed to withstand such strain. Even if it did not, however, the German command structure was better prepared than that of its enemy for life in the fog of war. The superior German battle drill, flexibility of command, initiative and tactics were well suited to conditions of broken-backed warfare. British officers, conversely, would seek authorization before action, they would debate options, they would question commands, and they would do so via R/T and in the clear.

Not only would the Germans smash the fragile signals of the British Army – they would also feed upon its flimsy security. The German Army emphasized the acquisition of signals intelligence at a tactical level; in the desert the British Army specialized in offering it. Under Rommel's command was the Third Radio Intercept Company, led by Captain Alfred Seebohm. While one can scarcely blame Germans for boasting of their successes in intelligence – they have had so few of them – this company does not appear to have been notably better than its Italian or British counterparts.[46] Initially, however, it had extraordinarily easy hunting. This company was particularly trained in traffic analysis, in the inter-ception of plain language messages and the breaking of low-grade codes. Until autumn 1941, owing to the poor British call sign systems and R/T procedure, the company easily traced the British Army's strength and movements and monitored the latter's condition and intentions. For Rommel this material was equivalent in value to Ultra. Whatever his other flaws, Rommel thrived on intelligence which was both 'hard' and 'hot'. Before the war, he had emphasized that an army must be 'untiringly active in determining [through physical reconnaissance] precise information regarding the enemy and the terrain', and stressed the need to 'report observations rapidly, for delay lessens the value of any information'. During the war he stated that 'reconnaissance reports must reach the commander in the shortest possible time; he must take his decisions immediately and put them into effect as fast as he can. Speed of reaction decides the battle'.[47] Given information which stated unambiguously what an enemy intended or was able to do and in time to act, Rommel could strike like a snake. Seebohm and the British in conjunction gave him precisely this.

A lack of trained signals and cipher personnel, of sound procedures for security, and of radio facilities alike placed the British Army in tragic circumstances by spring 1941. It had no effective and secure means of signalling in the field. It could barely meet the minimal operational demands for communication, let alone balance this need against that for security. Given the British Army's lack of radio circuits and its clumsy low-grade ciphers, its only possible means to maintain a high volume and velocity of communication in the field was by plain language over R/T – which would inform Rommel of British intentions as fast as these were formulated. As matters stood, the British Army would find it extremely difficult to enforce a stricter level of signals security. Should it succeed in doing so, however, the result would be to slow and to confuse its reactions. Nothing could be more fatal against Rommel's style of operations; nothing would play further into his style of intelligence than poor signals security. Rommel did not need the genius of Napoleon to win in the desert during the first half of 1941. He merely needed the British Army as his enemy.

Between April and June 1941 the flaws in British signals and security became as plain as their language. The campaigns in Libya and Greece, in Crete and Libya again, were marked by extraordinary failures of communication which sparked ones of command. During the Greek campaign, so the commander of British land forces in that theatre later wrote, 'generally speaking it was the exception to be in communication with any H.Q. except by liaison officer, a process which involved at least 24 hour round trips'.[48] Cyrenaica Command, the headquarters for British forces in Libya during April, quickly and entirely lost its ability to communicate with and thus to control its subordinates. The main formation defending that region, the Second Armoured Division, frequently could contact neither its subordinates nor its superiors for up to

24 hours at a time.[49] Communication on Crete was even worse.[50] Throughout these campaigns, signals failures frequently left units and formations such as the Fourth New Zealand Brigade standing on the brink of annihilation.[51] Meanwhile, lack of cipher staff multiplied the handicaps on command. On 24 May General Freyberg's headquarters on Crete had precisely one trained cipher officer; not surprisingly, when this body moved during the crisis of the battle, it asked GHQ Middle East to keep 'cipher traffic minimum during next 24 hours'.[52] In Libya only the occasional presence of landlines saved the cipher staffs of the Second Armoured Division 'from complete breakdown'. In the absence of landlines, 'delays in priority messages of 8 hours or more were not uncommon and the use of clear, with all possible security precautions, was authorised more than once in order to relieve the Cipher Staffs'.[53]

Luck and leadership allowed the Commonwealth commanders to maintain the necessary level of control during the retreat from Greece. Here, moreover, Imperial forces followed a simple plan and, blessed by geography, were generally able to make their enemy fight according to the British timetable of phased withdrawals. Conversely, the Germans stamped their confusing and fast-moving style of warfare upon the battles of Libya and Crete. The collapse of communications during these operations brought down Britain's entire command structure, leaving each individual unit to fight alone, leading the British Army to defeat in detail. In itself, this factor was the difference between triumph and disaster during the battle of Crete. When all signals links disintegrated, Freyberg's headquarters entirely lost its touch with operations and its ability to affect the battle. Nor were energetic actions taken to overcome this wasting malady. Meanwhile, in the absence of constant co-ordination from above, far too many British and Dominion units failed to co-operate with each other or to take any positive action at all, save to retreat.

The German Army faced a far harsher environment: its command and communications systems were far more fit to survive. The circumstances of these operations broke the British Army's system of command and of signals security alike.

During these campaigns every previous problem in the sphere of security emerged and some new ones as well. No means had been arranged to change call signs, code words and radio frequencies in battle. So they were not: no regimental commander was 'willing to risk failure of communications during operations in order to gain in signal security', by adopting, for example, new callsigns which his squadrons might not have received.[54] Brigade and divisional headquarters had neither medium-grade facilities nor special systems for use in dangerous areas where physical compromise was possible. Consequently, in Greece and Crete they had only one secure system, the army's universal high-grade code books. The army thus had this choice: either to use these systems in battle, risking their capture and the compromise of much of its traffic throughout the world, or to destroy both them and the possibility of secure communications for any operational traffic.

During the Greek campaign most units 'destroyed their books in ample time (but) in certain instances the books were destroyed before they need have been'. For several days some units could communicate with GHQ Greece only by plain language or through a slow and insecure transposition cipher.[55] Conversely, one RAF officer held his books in hand through all the perils of evacuation, 'under the mistaken impression that he was making a praiseworthy effort'.[56] Nor was this the only example of amateurish preparations for cipher security. On 24 April, some three days before the covering forces withdrew from Greece, the cipher and signals branches of the battle headquarters ashore (the Second New Zealand Division) were permanently separated, which 'meant, of course, that all cipher messages reaching the headquarters remained indecipherable'.[57] On Crete such failures proved costly. At Maleme airstrip the Germans captured much of the RAF's high grade superencipherment system while Freyberg could communicate with his brigades, which had destroyed their high-grade systems, only in plain language. Indeed, by 28 May he could contact GHQ Middle East solely through one 'badly working R.A.F. set and only code SYKO which is easily broken'.[58] These cryptographic failings placed at risk all British operational traffic carried by radio during the campaigns in Crete, Greece and Libya. British signals security hinged not on its skill but rather on the limits to that of its enemy.

Until these campaigns such failures had slowed signals within divisions, shattered command within brigades, caused tactical setbacks. Now communications within divisions could vanish for a day, commands lose their ability to control, campaigns be lost.[59] Of course, German signals were no better in Libya and far worse on Crete. The British Army, however, needed what one Chief Signals Officer (CSO) called 'one hundred per cent efficiency'[60] in communication in order to function; the German Army did not. Britain's failures in signals security had no less serious results. The Middle East commands concluded that during the Greek campaign, 'a failure to appreciate the finer aspects of signals and cipher security ... was responsible for the enemy being aware of the dispositions of our forces and the movements of our aircraft'.[51] What was inconvenient in Greece became fatal in Libya. Failures in signals security gave the Afrika Korps an accurate picture of British dispositions before the Battleaxe offensive of June, nine hours' warning of its start, information on British intentions, perceptions and concerns during its course. The German counterstroke was based on an almost letter-perfect knowledge of the distribution of the British Army, which revealed a deadly gap between the latter's forces; its development was blessed by accurate indications of the confusion at higher levels of command, the heavy losses and the shortages of ammunition and supplies which haunted the foe.[62] Rommel need not have asked for anything more.

However bitter these failures, they at least forced the British Army to recognize its desperate position regarding signals and security. The poverty of its approach to cryptography was obvious as was the fact that 'the British Army is painfully behind the German Army' in signals.[63] As the CSO of the Fourth Indian Division noted after Battleaxe, 'In mobile operations of this nature where distances are considerable, the problem of intercommunication will require the most careful thought and on the signal plan may depend success or failure'.[64] The British Army began this process in June 1941; it had much to think about. It would learn these lessons with remarkable speed but not fully profit from this technical education because of its failures in greater spheres.

Large amounts of equipment and trained personnel were needed to overcome these problems in signals and security, things which were in short supply for the British Army in the Middle East during 1941–42. In November 1941 it was apparently 6,000 men short of its needs. By April 1942 its continual requests to redress these problems sparked this rebuke from London: 'Your demands for signals drafts greatly exceed our ability to supply'.[65] The army had also to train new personnel and to establish an entirely new structure for signals, based primarily on radio. Naturally, this could not be done to perfection; unfortunately, the insistence on strict wireless silence before operations began masked these failings. The CSO of Advanced Eighth Army headquarters wrote during the Crusader offensive of November 1941 that many problems were obvious once silence was lifted 'but it took, to me, an agonisingly long time before they could be put right'. Many signallers had never handled their equipment in the field before the operations began: others were unable even to find nets or to maintain frequencies. The Eighth Army noted after Crusader that 'all sides of Signals had to learn a lot and run themselves in during the campaign itself ... this was done quickly but during the first days of the campaign when as in any campaign good communications are of vital significance, Signals was learning its job'.[66].

The Eighth Army suffered through this learning period. During Crusader even so crucial a formation as the Seventh Armoured Division met its internal needs for communication only by cannnibalizing all signals personnel from units which had been fortuitously (in this sense, if in no other) withdrawn for refitting. It warned that unless these problems were overcome in the future, 'there will be a grave risk of a complete breakdown in communications'. The total collapse of important and irreplaceable links, and delays in the transmission of important messages for periods between half to the whole of a day, were not uncommon. When exactly four wireless sets were knocked out on 22 November, command in and control over the Fourth Armoured Brigade, the Eighth Army's only reserve armoured formation, equivaleñ in numerical strength to a Panzer Division, vanished for 24 hours during the crisis of the battle because no fallback signals system existed. Radio could not be issued to all replacement tanks – indeed, barely to all those of troop commanders. Infantry units and formations had exactly the same unsatisfactory signals establishment as in 1939, while administrative links were badly overstrained.

These signals shortages, combined with failures of organization, made it difficult for higher commands to keep track of the reality of Crusader, to co-ordinate their actions and to control their units. As would continue until August 1942, the continual and sudden reorganization of commands during battle magnified every problem of signals, forcing formations to function within an entirely new system of intercommunication, often with overlapping frequencies and different sorts of radio equipment. This created 'very dangerous results' which crippled the value of the change of command. Formations, moreover, did not draw the optimum balance between 'the wish to get forward for operational control and the necessity to avoid outstripping administrative control'. (After the Gazala battle of May–June 1942, the CSO of 13th Corps argued that an advanced headquarters should be placed within W/T reach of its headquarters and R/T reach of those of its subordinate commands.) The paucity of circuits made communication a bottleneck for command at all levels. Corps, for example, were expected to control two divisions (which might be fighting complex battles separated by 100 miles) over exactly the same links. As would continue until the 'J' service was formed in summer 1942, the tactical information contained in the signals of British units and lower formations took far too long to pass up the British chain of command, and was often never passed down at all. The Second New Zealand Division, for example, later reported that 'information was always scanty about formations on our flanks except when we were able to make contact with them ourselves'. Thanks to Seebohm, Rommel was often better informed of such British communications than his opposite numbers.

The combination of these failings led to the confusion which marked all levels of British command during Crusader. One South African armoured officer summarized the experience of many Commonwealth units thus: 'We were to get used to the daily "swans" into nothingness after nothingness, pursuing mirages of enemy conjured up by imagination and fear, mixed-up communications, mistranslated codes and nerve-racked commanders'. The disintegration of communication links during the first week of the struggle left the armoured formations scattered throughout the southern part of the battlefield to fight in isolation from their fellows. Meanwhile, the Commonwealth infantry formations in the north learned of even the most critical of events to their south only by establishing communications themselves with other formations and by intercepting the traffic of forward British units. The headquarters of the Eighth Army and of its two corps alike failed to meet their central tasks of circulating information to or of coordinating the activities of their formations. Indeed, their own knowledge of events on the front was all too often 24–36 hours out of date. The tempo of delay in communication contributed to a remarkable cycle of exultation and despair on the part of senior British officers.[67]

These problems were serious, yet their scale should not be exaggerated. Even by Crusader the army had more units in the field with more W/T and R/T links than ever before; even during Crusader its communications never collapsed so badly as they had done so universally in the spring of 1941. Crusader, indeed, was a technical success for British signals. If this system was more fragile than desirable, it proved less so than the German one. Even on 22 November, four days after the battle began, Rommel wrote: 'Our signals networks could hardly be worse. This is war the way the ancient Teutons used to fight it. I don't even know at this moment whether the Afrika Korps is on the attack or not'.[68] From the moment that the Afrika Korps' headquarters, its signals and its cryptographic equipment were captured on 23 November, combined with the confusion which Rommel's dash to the wire imposed upon his own no less than his enemy's command structure, British communications were simultaneously more secure and more effective than those of the Germans. The new headquarters of the Afrika Korps had only two radio sets, while as General Auchinleck, the British Commander in Chief in the Middle East noted by 30 November, 'Enemy has been sending all operations orders in clear for last two days, which is significant of haste and disorganisation'.[69] Meanwhile, British signals carried that volume of traffic at that velocity which a steady command needed in order to salvage a gravely threatened position.

The system tested under such stress in Crusader was modified in detail over the next six months. It was not for want of a radio set that Gazala would be lost. Again, especially during the first week of the struggle, British signals worked more effectively than those of the Afrika Korps, handicapped, as ever, by Rommel's own love for fragmenting his command structure. Dedicated R/T and W/T circuits linked all connections of command between formations and down to armoured car, tank and artillery regiments and infantry battalions. Every armoured car and tank, each artillery battery and most infantry companies had a radio set for rear and lateral communications. The system as a whole was shielded by dense layers of redundancy. For the first time each infantry division had a forward R/T link with its brigade headquarters while a forward W/T net supplemented the old R/T one between armoured divisions and their brigades. These and other channels provided flexible and immediate means of communications during operations and robust and effective fallback systems during emergencies. Thus, when on 27–28 May the headquarters signals of the Seventh Armoured Division had to flee from the enemy, were overrun and then forced to flee again for half a day, divisional communications were not seriously disrupted for more than two hours – a far cry from the situation with the Fourth Armoured Brigade eight months before. The same was true when the joint tactical headquarters of the Seventh Armoured Division and the Fifth Indian Division were overrun on 5 June. Although control over sub-units broke down for the better part of a day in both of these instances, the communication system needed to establish command remained in being. Unfortunately, the ability to use the latter did not.

During Gazala the British had another advantage over Crusader: instead of carrying their signals with them into battle, until the last stages of the operation they fought from a prepared position with an established landline network. This carried a vast quantity of clear yet secure traffic for higher formations and solved much of the problem surrounding administrative messages. One headquarters officer even claimed that communications in Gazala were 'almost faultless, there being few occasions when Army HQ was out of telephonic communication with either Corps'. Landlines also carried much inter-formation traffic even during mobile operations. Within armoured divisions temporary cables were laid each night between brigade and divisional headquarters, allowing a much freer and more secure discussion of such essential matters as 'tank states' (unit strengths) and the question of 'tomorrow's plans'. Until the Eighth Army itself was smashed at the Knightsbridge battle, communication at and above the brigade level was not often impaired for more than a few hours at a time. Even during the débâcle of the following month, signals never fell near to their nadir of Crusader. After Gazala, commands and CSOs wanted detailed improvements in their communication system, yet they conceded that it had worked through the shock of a devastating defeat.[70]

British signals in the desert are usually mentioned only in the context of failure, of an inability to maintain communication at this, that or the other vital moment. As one account noted regarding Crusader, 'There were comparatively few radio sets, and at all levels down from Army H.Q. they could be relied upon to fail, or for traffic to become indecipherable when most needed'.[71] One must not, however, confuse the failure of a medium with that of its message, of a signals service with that of command. Slow and faulty communications are part of war, one which armies are designed

to overcome. Such situations may result not from technical failures by a
signals service but from the nature of a campaign. In the desert small
numbers of men fought in confusion over vast areas. There was no stable
front – indeed, headquarters and signals units rather often experienced
the sharp end of war. To an equal extent for British and Germans alike,
headquarters were overrun, signals facilities smashed, the flow of
information and of orders dammed. British signals matched the quality of
their German counterparts in these circumstances; British commanders
did not.

Rommel preferred to fight battles of manoeuvre; he made the British
do so. He believed that such circumstances would cripple the regular
transmission of messages; his tendency to operate out of radio contact
with his headquarters made this a self-fulfilling prophecy. Whatever the
flaws to his system of command, however, it was at least suited in part to
this problem. Moreover, when out of communication with Rommel his
subordinates acted with speed and with effect. Indeed, in November 1941,
at Sidi Rezeg, General Cruwell commanded the Afrika Korps as he saw fit
rather than wait an hour for an order from Rommel, already received, to
be decoded. Subsequently, in violation of orders from Rommel but in
accordance with realities in the field, a colonel at rear headquarters
ordered the abandonment of the Afrika Korps' dash to the wire. The
Germans lost battles but no minutes. British commanders were less
willing to act until they had received enough information to form a clear
picture of events, a picture which with Rommel ran like quicksilver. The
British military machine needed a far steadier flow of orders and a greater
amount of time in order to work than did the Germans. It could not win in
the desert with the best signals it could receive; the failure was not of
communication but of command. Moreover, because the Eighth Army
needed a higher standard of signals in order to function than the Afrika
Korps, it would suffer to a greater extent from the imposition of effective
signals security.

The months between Battleaxe and Crusader witnessed the most
radical improvements in the signals and cipher security of the British
Army during the Second World War. By October 1941 a common inter-
service programme for these matters was instituted down to unit level in
the Middle East. More signals security officers were provided and their
status was enhanced. These personnel received more professional
training, including practical courses in cryptanalysis without which they
'would be of little use and would not know what faults to look for'.[72]
The transmissions of British operators were continually monitored, a
necessary precaution given their lack of experience. All this was essential
if the army were seriously to improve its practice of signals security.

Firm steps were also taken against the perils of traffic analysis.

Although 'many heads were shaken' in doubt that operators could use so complex a system, on 16 October 1941 the Eighth Army adopted the link sign procedure for call signs. These heads were shaken in vain, for this was one of the army's greatest achievements in signals security of the entire Second World War. As Seebohm's company noted after Crusader, the institution of this system

> *eliminates practically all the basis of former wireless intelligence work* ... the difficulties of wireless intelligence in the ensuing period caused a decline in results and later further measures were taken to increase the security, notably the reduction of traffic sent in clear ... *The new procedure* made possible no important identifications of the units taking part after the commencement of the battle on the first days of the attack. Mention must also be made of the smart passing of wireless traffic as well as of the excellent wireless discipline within the 7 Armd. Div. This allowed little scope for the Interception Service ... Neither the time of the attack nor the strength of the forces employed at the commencement were known. The reasons for this were the wireless silence, the measures taken to preserve wireless security, and *the new wireless procedure* adopted.[73]

From Crusader onward, all German observers praised the 'excellent wireless security' of the Eighth Army before battles began. The link sign procedure, of course, was not perfect. By April–May 1942, assisted by various operators' errors and the capture of sections of the link sign book, Seebohm's company penetrated part of the system and thus reconstructed elements of the British order of battle.[74] This, however, required great effort and for limited success. At one stroke Seebohm, and through him Rommel, lost the ability to monitor British dispositions or intentions before operations began. The only source on these matters remaining were the solutions of the encoded radio traffic of the American army's representative in Cairo, Colonel Fellers, in whose 'little fellers' Rommel placed great faith.[75] These were, however, no replacement for traffic analysis: simply because a great technical achievement is required to produce a source of intelligence does not necessarily make it a more valuable one. Rommel began every battle which he fought between October 1941 and August 1942 with strikingly inaccurate assessments of British strength and intentions – for example, the scale and the timing of the Crusader offensive caught the Afrika Korps entirely by surprise, while it also underestimated by one third the number of British tanks on the front before the Gazala operation. The paradoxical nature of intelligence and of its denial alike are revealed by the comment about this failure by Rommel's chief of intelligence, F.W. von Mellenthin: 'Perhaps, fortunately, we underestimated the British strength, for had we know the full facts even Rommel might have baulked at an attack on such a superior enemy'.[76] For the British Army, perhaps, less security in signals might have produced less damage in battle.

Compared with its triumph in this sphere, the British Army proved far less able to improve the defence of its traffic once operations began. In the summer of 1941, it flirted with the idea of using high-grade systems for inter–formation traffic in the field. Thus, in the Syrian campaign OTP was to be used for 'all repeat all' operational messages between divisions, corps and force headquarters. OTP, however, was far too clumsy, slow and labour-intensive to carry much, let alone all, operational traffic. In 1942–43 it would be used only to render absolutely secure certain categories of information warranting such treatment, in which the transmission of tank states ranked alongside Ultra. Moreover, although Typex was issued to corps headquarters during Crusader and Gazala, it carried primarily administrative traffic. Not until the Tunisian campaign was this device with its combination of high security and volume available to help British operational traffic.[77] Denied the use of high-grade systems for such messages, the British Army turned to devising effective low- and medium-grade ones. Unfortunately, it failed to do so and through this chink in its cryptographic armour Britain was to suffer wounds from Rommel.

Low- and medium-grade systems are, for any army, the most difficult to create: they must be used by a host of often poorly trained operators or officers and they must carry an extraordinary volume of traffic which refers to matters of which the enemy knows. It is hard to make such systems usable, harder still to make them secure, hardest of all to achieve both ends at once. The Germans found as many troubles in this sphere as the British. Throughout 1941–42 the British Army experimented with many field ciphers and R/T codes in order to meet these needs. None of them proved very suitable – indeed, even those used in 1945 had flaws. The combination of the weaknesses of these earlier systems and the conditions of the desert war proved almost fatal to the Eighth Army.

In technical terms, these systems offered little security. Given the absence of the records of Seebohm's codebreaking *Staffel*, any conclusions regarding the Germans' exploitation of this opportunity must be provisional. None the less, in July 1942 the Germans found 'little difficulty' in solving the 'Sheetex' R/T code, which was then in common use; indeed, during 1943–45 they often read its successors, the 'Codex' and 'Slidex' systems. Further, the field ciphers used by the Eighth Army were rather vulnerable to solution. They were widely distributed and, like their German counterparts, were often captured when headquarters were overrun. One report after Gazala noted that the 'very frequent compromisation of ciphers and keys seriously interrupted cipher work'; another, that circumstances 'when the Army MEBC (Middle East

Brigade Cipher) keys have been compromised (is) a common state of affairs'.[78] Altogether, in 1941–42 the Germans probably had some access to British R/T codes and field ciphers, and thus to all operational communications from corps headquarters down. They scarcely need to have bothered, however; they could have had all this simply by tuning their radio sets to British frequencies.

The real flaw of these systems was not their insecurity but their clumsiness. During operations the use of cipher caused a 'bottleneck' in communication, particularly because trained cipher operators were as ever in short supply. Thus, by 2 December 1941 the advanced head-quarters of Eighth Army noted, 'Cipher office swamped. 3 day delay on D messages. Outstanding cipher messages'; scarcely surprising, since it had only one trained cipher officer. After Crusader the CSO of Seventh Armoured division, referring to the value of R/T codes, stated that

> ... the lack of use of Cipher was amply justified as the consequent speed up in communications was enormous. In the latter stages of the operations, the Division was placed under Command of a Corps which used Cipher very extensively and the consequent delay in traffic was very apparent.[79]

Throughout Crusader and Gazala the Eighth Army used far more R/T and W/T than ever before. This was handled by imperfectly trained personnel and by senior officers who had little experience with the medium, who treated it like a line telephone system, and for whom even this unprecedented volume and velocity of signals was not enough. Moreover, during these operations the need for quick communication was as overwhelming as Rommel. The combination of slow and clumsy systems, of emergency and of untrained personnel led, as ever, to the use of plain language. Of course, so one German intelligence officer noted, these messages were usually 'masterpieces of understatement ... [which] seldom [revealed] the real state of affairs in all its seriousness'. Still, aware as it was of British habits of expression, the Afrika Korps naturally placed weight on statements such as this from the Fourth Armoured Brigade to the Seventh Armoured Division on 29 November 1941: 'I am without ammunition and in urgent need of it'. The British, moreover, tried to minimize the risks through the use of guarded language, for example, by substituting officers' nicknames for those of formations, or sending operational orders in veiled allusions. One can, however, call the 22nd Armoured Brigade, one of the best and strongest British tank formations, 'Scotty' only so many times before the meaning becomes obvious; then so too becomes the significance of the fact that on 25 November 1941 the commanders of neither the 13th nor the 30th Corps 'know where Scotty is – nobody knows!'[80] There was often poetry in guarded language – 'the fox is killed in the open' after Beda Fomm; 'come on the Greys, get out your whips' during the crisis at Alem el Halfa. There was little security.

Indeed, in the heat of operations even veiled speech evaporated. Thus, on 1 December 1941 while planning the breakout of his surrounded forces, the commander of the Second New Zealand Division, General Freyberg,

> ... called up Headquarters 30 Corps by RT and spoke to General Norrie about his intentions. Sergeant Smith stood by the set while the General spoke and listened in horrified silence while he described his plan in the plainest of plain language, quite umblemished by the merest pretence of RT procedure or security precautions. Smith bounded over to OC A section: 'Did you hear what he said? Did you hear?' he yelled and, without waiting for answer, 'Tiny [General Freyberg] said that we are going to break out at dusk-four miles east, nine miles south-east over the escarpment and then flat out for the wire! *And all in clear!*' The last words were almost a shriek. Throwing out his arm in the direction of the sinister black shapes squatting on the distant skyline to the north, he turned and peered earnestly into the face of Lieutenant-Colonel Agar, who had come up to see the fun. 'And what does he think those bastards out there are going to do about it, sir?' As he sauntered off dejectedly, fragments of his mournful soliloquy floated back to his hearers. '... nine miles to Point 192 ... east to wire ... nine miles to Hell, more like ...'[81]

All this was inevitable in the circumstances; so was the result. Throughout Crusader and Gazala, the more intense and confused the battle, the more routinely did British regimental, brigade, divisional and even corps and army commanders communicate in clear. As one cynic wrote, 'there were codes to be fumbled with and compromised so that resort had to be made to veiled language ... the more senior the officer on the wireless, the more likely he was to break the code' [sic].[82] Seebohm was a passive partner to these discussions, Rommel a recipient, the Eighth Army a victim. Interception of plain language transmissions was the simplest form of signals intelligence during the Second World War and Ultra the most sophisticated. Rommel, however, gained as much from the former during operations as any Allied land commander ever did from the latter.

Through this means, from within about five days of the start of Crusader until its end, Seebohm's company reconstructed most of the British order of battle. It maintained as accurate a picture of British strength and dispositions as did the latter's command, and provided advance warning of many of the enemy's intended actions. Such information helped the Afrika Korps to aim its blows and to assess their effect, if to a rather lesser extent than during Battleaxe. Fortunately, the Germans threw away this advantage and the battle alike. Rommel, who 'used to get this hunch that I knew where the enemy would give way',[83] interpreted fragments of intercepted traffic to indicate that that the enemy would give way all over. He turned from annihilation in the desert before him to pursue the mirage of Caporetto on the horizon. Thus, he suffered a stinging defeat. In January 1942, however, Seebohm's company contributed to Rommel's revenge. Units of the main British force on the new front, the Second Armoured Brigade, broadcast their tank states in clear. This revelation of the weakness of the enemy sparked Rommel's second offensive into Libya; the debate which the commander of the Eighth Army and his subordinates carried out in plain language over R/T regarding their reactions guided his steps towards victory.

Unfortunately, since the records for Seebohm's organization during Gazala have not survived, any judgement regarding the value of its work during that battle must be regarded as unusually provisional. However, remaining evidence indicates that during the first two weeks of Gazala, Seebohm's company provided far less useful material than it had done during Crusader. Even the problem with the use of plain language, the gravest flaw remaining in British signals security, had declined in scale. Still, this source gave the Afrika Korps some unnecessary advantages, most notably by showing how best one of the two German armoured divisions could be saved from deadly peril after the first day of the battle. In any case, by 11 June 1942 – the eve of the decisive engagement in Gazala – through the interception of plain language messages, Seebohm's company reconstructed the Eighth Army's strength and dispositions. It also provided a useful if not entirely accurate picture of British intentions, which spurred Rommel on to one of his greatest triumphs. After the Knightsbridge battle of 12 June, signals security procedures seem to have been increasingly forgotten and senior British commanders driven to use R/T in the most desperate of circumstances. For the next week, Seebohm's organization briefly matched the scale of success which it had known during Crusader. It revealed the collapse of British command and the tempo of the rout of the Eighth Army, providing background knowledge which no doubt helped Rommel to score his stunning victory at Tobruk. However, the triumph of Seebohm's organization was fleeting: in late June and early July 1942 at Mersa Matruh and El Alamein, the Afrika Korps experienced intelligence failures which were remarkable even by its own chequered standard.[84]

This decline in the success of German signals intelligence against the British Army was to continue throughout the high summer of 1942 and down to the end of the war. Indeed, as an authoritative post-war study of the signals intelligence of the German Army during the Second World

War concluded, the British Army's radio communications would become 'the most effective and secure of all those with which German communication intelligence had to contend'. It is usually argued that the capture of Seebohm's company in July 1942 provided such proof of the flaws in British signals security that the latter immediately and radically tightened its procedure.[85] This, however, is inaccurate. The British Army more fundamentally improved its techniques of signals security in autumn 1941 than in autumn 1942, when, in essence, it simply strengthened the details of its system. Indeed, the reasons for this change do not even stem directly from technical improvements in signals security.

Throughout the British Army's success in Crusader, its humiliation during Gazala and its triumph at El Alamein, its system of signals and security did not fundamentally change. Indeed, by Crusader Britain had evolved a basic approach to such matters which it retained until 1945. The value of this system was initially constrained, however, because signals and security are the servants and not the masters of the field. Until July 1942 Rommel made the British fight the war he wanted, and at his pace. He could create confused conditions of warfare which broke the British command. Given their superior training and tactics, even when out of communication German units fought with effect; even Rommel in the course of his desert excursions had sometimes to appear at a decisive place before the British knew that it existed. British units, meanwhile, came on and went back in the same old way. British commanders, losing faith in their men and themselves, desperately striving to reassert their grip on events, looking for the means to form a picture of the battle, reached for the radio telephone like drowning men. This medium amplified the context of command but at a price: it increased the power of poor no less than of sound decision-making. In the case of the British command this medium magnified all their worst characteristics: indecision, lack of discipline, the debating of orders, 'belly-aching'.

Yet after July 1942 this same system of signals and security met British needs, not because the former changed but because its circumstances did. The British Army ceased to make war as the Germans wished. Instead, it made the Afrika Korps stand and fight like Englishmen. General Montgomery mastered the British Army which then beat the German one. He forced Rommel to fight surely rather than swiftly, a style of war at which the British matched the Germans and Montgomery surpassed Rommel. Montgomery quite deliberately slowed the pace of battle; he forced Rommel to fight at a speed which suited the less flexible British system of command and its less well trained forces. It was precisely to deny Rommel the opportunity of ever again stamping his mark upon events, of regaining the initiative, that Montgomery adopted the cautious approach for which he has so often been criticized. The new commander of the

Eighth Army, moreover, reached back for old memories. He adopted a modified version of the style of war by which British and Dominion armies had smashed the Germans in the summer and autumn of 1918. It would do so again. British units would come on in a new way while the level of confusion on the field would decline. This eased the psychological strain on British commanders, who needed to use R/T less often and with less desperation, and hence did so with greater security. In the British case, security was sapped by failure in the field and bolstered by success. From this basis the British Army would shortly forge the most powerful and flexible C³IS system of the Second World War.

NOTES

I am indebted to Michael Handel, Elizabeth Herbert, Richard Popplewell, Tim Travers and to the participants at the Third United States Army War College Conference on Intelligence and Military Operations in May 1988 for comments upon an earlier draft of this paper. I am grateful to Jill and Michael Handel for hospitality and to Yael, Benjamin and Ethan for entertainment. All the primary sources cited in this paper are held at the Public Record Office, Kew, and appear by the permission of the Controller of Her Majesty's Stationery Office.

1. WO 169/1016, memorandum by Middle East GHQ, 13 March 1942.
2. AIR 23/5526, training memorandum by Allied Force Headquarters, 17 March 1943.
3. The following comments have been influenced by Shelford Bidwell and Dominick Graham, *Fire Power, British Army Weapons and Theories of War, 1904–1945* (Boston, 1985) pp.248–50; Martin van Crevald; *Command in War* (Cambridge, 1985), pp.1–16 and Gordon Welchman, *The Hut Six Story, Breaking The Enigma Codes* (New York, 1982).
4. WO 204/8792, Colonel Bailey to 'G', 7 April 1944; WO 203/5157, memorandum by S.O. in C., South East Asia command, 25 March 1945.
5. WO 169/1016, memorandum by CSO, 13th Corps, undated but early 1942 according to internal evidence.
6. AIR 23/6180, memorandum by RAF headquarters, Middle East, 1 Oct. 1941.
7. For accounts of this issue see Brian Bond, *British Military Policy between the Two World Wars*, (London, 1980) and John Ferris, *The Evolution of British Strategic Policy, 1919–1926* (London and New York, 1989).
8. WO 244/98, memorandum by Signals Staff, Army Headquarters, Delhi (undated but late 1943–early 1944 according to internal evidence), *passim*; War Office, *Study on Signal Communications during the Second World War*, (1950, copy in Whitehall Library, Old War Office, no author cited), pp.13,17,90. cf. R.F.H. Nalder, *The Royal Corps of Signals, A History of its Antecedents and Developments (circa 1800–1955)*, (London, 1958), pp.223–64.
9. WO 170/4205, memorandum by CSO, Eighth Army, 21 Feb. 1945.
10. WO 204/6595, memorandum by Bedell Smith, 19 Feb., 1943.
11. R.E. Priestly, *The Signal Service in the European War of 1914 to 1918 (France)* (Chatham, 1921); John Ferris, 'The British Army and Signals Intelligence in the Field During the First World War', *Intelligence and National Security*, Vol.3, No.4 (October 1988).
12. WO 201/126, SO in C, Middle East to Director of Military Training, 20 April 1942.
13. WO 279/54, report on army staff exercise, 10–11.22, undated; WO 279/55, report on army staff exercise, 4.23, undated.
14. WO 32/3057, memorandum by Milne, 14 Nov. 1929, *passim*.

15. Ferris, 'The British Army'.
16. WO 33/1073, 'Secret Supplement to Signal Training', 1925; 'Secret Supplement to the Manual of Military Intelligence in the Field', 1923 and 1931 (copies in Whitehall Library, Old War Office); WO 33/249, 'Memorandum on the Security of Wireless Signals in the Field', 11 May 1931.
17. WO 191/60, memorandum by Fifth Division, 12 June 1936.
18. WO 197/11, memorandum 'Points which have arisen', undated but Oct. 1939 by internal evidence, no author cited. A slightly different problem arose for Commonwealth forces in Egypt during autumn 1940, when

> ... Security became a fetish and censorship was rigid. Code-names were allotted to units and to those holding the principal appointments in them. Telephone conversations thereafter were marked by hilarity or exasperation, according to the mood of the caller and the urgency of his call. To stand by and hear the Adjutant, irascible and red-faced, say 'Pansy of Lulu speaking,' was too much for the orderly-room staff, and though the business was serious it took some time to train all ranks in correct telephone security procedure.

[D.W. Sinclair, *19 Battalion and Armoured Regiment, Official History of New Zealand in the Second World War, 1939–45* (Wellington, 1954), pp.13.]
19. John Ferris, 'The British "Enigma": Britain, Signals Security and Cipher Machines, 1906–1946', *Defense Analysis*, Vol.3, No.2 (May 1987).
20. AVIA 8/356, memorandum A.359, no author cited and undated, but *c.* autumn 1938 according to internal evidence. (I am indebted to Tony Gorst for this reference.)
21. F.H. Hinsley *et al, British Intelligence in the Second World War, Its Influence on Strategy and Operations*, Vol.II (London, 1981). pp.640–41; Ferris, 'The British "Enigma"'; WO 169/1016, memorandum by CSO Eighth Army, 23 Oct. 1941, *passim*.
22. AIR 20/1531, 'Security of R.A.F. Signal Communications', no author cited and undated, but *c.* December 1944 according to internal evidence.
23. John Ferris, 'Whitehall's Black Chamber: British Cryptology and the Government Code and Cypher School, 1919–1929', *Intelligence and National Security*, Vol.2, No.1 (January 1987); Nalder, *Royal Corps of Signals*, pp.303–4, 330; Compton Mackenzie, *Eastern Epic, Volume One, September 1939–March 1943, Defence* (London, 1951), p.518.
24. WO 201/95, RAF headquarters Greece to SO in C, Middle East, 18 Jan. 1941.
25. WO 32/3057, Senior Signals Officers Conference, 12 June 1930; Joan Bright (ed.), *The Ninth Queen's Royal Lancers, 1936–1945, The Story of an Armoured Regiment in Battle* (Aldershot, 1951), p.4; David Scott Daniell, *History of the East Surrey Regiment, Volume IV, 1920–1952* (London, 1957), p.80; *Great Britain, Cabinet Office, Cabinet History Series, Principal War Telegrams and Memoranda, 1940–1943, Miscellaneous* (Nendeln, 1976), 'Hist (C)1', Memorandum by Auchinleck, 19 June 1940, p.51.
26. WO 165/76, War Office Signals Liaison Letter, Nov. 1946.
27. Michael Glover, *The Fight for the Channel Ports, Calais to Brest 1940: A Study in Confusion* (London, 1985), pp.31–3, *passim;* Brian Bond, *France and Belgium 1939–1940* (London: Davis-Poynter, 1975), pp.34–5, 81, 96, 103–4; Walter Lord, *The Miracle of Dunkirk* (London, 1982), p.15; Gregory Blaxland, *Destination Dunkirk, The Story of Gort's Army* (London, 1973); Bernard Montgomery, *Memoirs* (London, 1958), pp.55–8, *passim*.
28. WO 178/8, memorandum by Knox, 17 May 1942; Miles Reid, *Last on the List* (London, 1974), pp.26–7.
29. B.H. Liddell Hart (ed.), *The Rommel Papers* (London, 1953), pp.13, 122, 167, *passim;* Bidwell and Graham, *Fire-Power*, pp.219–20.
30. WO 197/11, memorandum 'Discussions in London', undated, no author cited; WO 197/92, 'Historical Record of SO in C [*sic*] B.E.F. during the Battle of France', undated; WO 165/76, Directorate of Signals War Diary, entry 19 May 1940.
31. WO 167/19, BEF, Special Wireless Section C War Diary, Oct. 1939; WO 167/7, General Staff Intelligence Weekly Progress Reports, 21 and 28 April 1940; WO 169/420, No.3 Headquarters Signals Company War Diary, 8 Nov. 1940.
32. WO 167/17, memorandum by GSO3 Wireless 29 Dec. 1939.

33. WO 197/92, op.cit., J.R. Colville, *Man of Valour, the Life of Field-Marshal the Viscount Gort* (London, 1973), p.190.
34. For material on problems regarding communication within British units and formations during the French campaign, see A.C. Bell, *History of the Manchester Regiment, First and Second Battalions, 1922–1948* (Altrincham, 1954), pp.342–64; W.R. Beddington, *A History of the Queen's Bays (The 2nd Dragoon Guards) 1929–1945* (Winchester, 1954), pp.13–14, 19–22; Blaxland, *Dunkirk*, pp.87, *passim;* Guy Courage, *The History of 15/19 Royal Hussars, 1939–1945* (Aldershot, 1949), pp.26–34; D. Dawnay et al., *The 10th Royal Hussars in the Second World War, 1939–1945* (Aldershot, 1948), pp.13–16; Roger Evans (ed.), *The Story of the 5th Royal Inniskilling Dragoon Guards* (Aldershot, 1951), pp.263–74; Glover, *Channel Ports*, pp.55–61, *passim;* Basil Karslake, *1940, The Last Act; The Story of the British Forces in France After Dunkirk* (London, 1979), pp.68–9, *passim;* Lord, *Miracle*, pp.65; David Rissik, *The D.L.I. at War, The Story of the Durham Light Infantry, 1939–1945* (London, 1954), pp.40–42; Hugh Williamson, *The Fourth Division, 1939 to 1945* (London, 1951), pp.18, 22.
35. WO 169/420, SO in C, Middle East to GHQ Middle East, 1 Aug. 1940.
36. Great Britain, Cabinet Office, *Cabinet History Series Principal War Telegrams and Memoranda, 1940–1943, Middle East I* (Nendeln, 1976), 'Hist (B) 1 Final', p.39, C. in C., Middle East to War Office, 27 Jan. 1941; WO 201/61, SO in C. Middle East to CSO, Crete, 14 May 1941.
37. WO 201/76, C.S.O. RAF Headquarters, Middle East to Air Officer Commanding in Chief, 4 Nov. 1940, *passim;* WO 169/1092, memorandum by CSO, Iraq, Oct. 1941; WO 169/2677, CSO Sudan Force War Diary, entry 26 Jan. 1941.
38. WO 169/1092, G.O.C. Iraq to Army Headquarters, Delhi, 13 Aug. 1941; D.M. Davin, *Crete, Official History of New Zealand in the Second World War, 1939–45* (Wellington, 1953), p.47.
39. WO 169/2677 CSO Sudan War Diary; 1 Sept. 1940.
40. WO 201/294, report by Cunningham on Abyssinian operations, November 1940 –April 1941, undated; J.F. MacDonald; *The War History of Southern Rhodesia, Volume One,* (Salisbury, 1947), pp.63, 81; Neil Orpen, *The East African and Abyssinian Campaigns, South African Forces, World War Two, Volume One* (Cape Town, 1968), p.66, *passim;* P.C. Bharucha, *The North African Campaign, 1940-1943, Official History of the Indian Armed Forces in the Second World War* (Calcutta, 1956), p.95, *passim;* Anthony Brett James, *Ball of Fire, The Fifth Indian Division in the Second World War* (Aldershot, 1951), pp.36–121; G.M.O. Davy, *The Seventh and Three Enemies* (Cambridge, 1952), p.37; William Moore, *The Durham Light Infantry* (London, 1975), p.45; Dudley Clarke, *The Eleventh at War* (London, 1952), p.137, *passim.* Bisheshwar Prasad, *The East African Campaign, 1940–41, Official History of the Indian Armed Forces in the Second World War* (Agra, 1963), pp.54–6, *passim;* cf. notes 41, 42 below.
41. WO 201/352 'Operations of the Seventh Armoured Division in December 1940'.
42. WO 201/353, memorandum by Fourth Indian Division on the operations of November-December 1940, undated.
43. WO 169/3196, memorandum by Callan 5.12.41; WO 201/294, op. cit. F.H. Hinsley et al., *British Intelligence in the Second World War, Its Influence on Strategy and Operations,* Vol.I (London, 1979), pp.380–81.
44. WO 201/352, 'Lessons affecting Particular Arms and Services from Operations in Eritrea', Prasad, *Campaign*, p.79.
45. WO 201/352, 'Report on Lessons of the Operations in the Western Desert, December 1940', copy No.25.
46. Hans-Otto Behrendt, *Rommel's Intelligence in the Desert Campaign, 1941–1943* (London, 1985), *passim,* and also Albert Praun, *German Radio Intelligence* (paper prepared for Historical Division. Headquarters European Command, United States Army, undated but post-1945), pp.51–6, 117–20, offer useful accounts of the work of Seebohm's company. Neither source, however, is sufficiently critical regarding these issues: Behrendt pp.156–58, for example, entirely omits the crucial fact that the Afrika Korps badly misunderstood British dispositions before the battle of Gazala.

47. Liddell Hart, *Rommel Papers*, p.200; Erwin Rommel, *Attacks* (Vienna, VA, 1979), pp.7, 263; Behrendt, *Rommel's Intelligence*, p.80 recognizes that it 'was (Rommel's) intuition, his instinct about his opponents' likely behaviour that was the decisive factor', but fails to address critically the question of the quality of Rommel's use of intelligence. J.A.I. Agar-Hamilton and L.C.F. Turner, *Crisis in the Desert, May–July 1942, Union War Histories* (London, 1952), p.17; David Hunt, *A Don at War*, (London, 1966), pp.72–3, 113; and David Irving, *The Trail of the Fox*, (New York, 1977), pp.122–6, show clearly how poor that quality could be.
48. WO 201/53, memorandum by General Wilson, undated but 1941.
49. WO 169/1016, memorandum by CSO, Second Armoured Division, 2 Nov. 1941; Nalder, *Royal Corps of Signals*, pp.299.
50. WO 201/99, memorandum by Inter-Services Committee on the Crete campaign, June 1941.
51. C.A. Borman, *Divisonal Signals, Official History of New Zealand in the Second World War, 1939–45* (Wellington, 1954), pp.118–19; Howard Kippenberger, *Infantry Brigadier* (London, 1949), pp.40–41.
52. WO 201/101, Crete headquarters to GHQ, Middle East, 24 May 1941, Creteforce Signal Instruction No.4, 12 May 1941; WO 201/53, op. cit.
53. WO 169/1016, op. cit.
54. Ibid.
55. WO 201/54, memorandum C.C. (42) 26, 12 March 1942.
56. AIR 23/6180, op. cit.
57. Borman, *Divisional Signals*, pp.116.
58. WO 201/99, op. cit.; WO 201/101, Crete headquarters to GHQ Middle East, 25 April 1941, 28 May 1941.
59. David Belcham, *All in the Day's March*, (London, 1978), pp.75–9; Barucha, *Campaign*, pp.176, 179; Borman, *Divisional Signals*, pp.98–165; Davin, *Crete*, pp.411–12, passim; Kippenberger, *Infantry Brigadier*, p.41, passim; Gavin Long, *Greece, Crete and Syria, Australia in the War of 1939–1945* (Canberra, 1986), p.37, passim; G.H. Mills and R.F. Nixon, *The Annals of the King's Royal Rifle Corps, Volume VI, 1921–1943*, (London, 1971), pp.151–3; Peter Singleton Gates, *General Lord Freyberg, VC* (London, 1963), p.159, passim; Tony Sampson, *Operation Mercury, The Battle of Crete, 1941* (Hong Kong, 1981), pp.241–2, passim.
60. WO 169/1016, memorandum by CSO, Fourth Indian Division, 30 Oct. 1941.
61. WO 201/54, op. cit.
62. Behrendt, *Rommel's Intelligence*, pp.99–100; Liddell Hart, *Rommel Papers*, pp.145; F.W. von Mellenthin, *Panzer Battles*, (Norman, 1955), p.94; R.H.W.S. Hastings, *The Rifle Brigade in the Second World War, 1939–1945* (Aldershot, 1950), p.73.
63. WO 201/99, op. cit.
64. WO 169/1016, op. cit.
65. *Great Britain, Cabinet Office, Middle East I*, 'Hist (B) 9 Final', War Office to C in C, Middle East, 18 April 1942; Bharuccha, *Campaign*, p.206; John Connell, *Auchinleck, A Critical Biography* (London, 1959), p.310.
66. WO 169/1015, CSO Advanced Eighth Army headquarters to SO in C, Middle East 22 Nov. 1941, memorandum by CSO, Eighth Army, 3 March 1942, passim.
67. Ibid.; WO 201/538, memorandum by GHQ, Middle East, 25 March 1942; J.A.I, Agar-Hamilton and L.C.F. Turner, *The Sidi Rezeg Battles 1941, Union War Histories* (London, 1957), pp.220–21, passim; Belcham, *March*, pp.99–102; Bharucha, *Campaign*, p.225, passim; Borman, *Divisional Signals*, pp.180–210; Clarke, Eleventh, p.207; Connell, *Auchinleck*, pp.348–98; Robert Crisp, *Brazen Chariots, An Account of Tank Warfare in the Western Desert, November–December 1941* (London, 1959), p.32; Davy, *The Seventh and Three Enemies*, p.134, passim; David Erskine (ed.), *The Scots Guards, 1919–1955* (London, 1956), p.87; Geoffrey Evans, *The Desert and the Jungle* (London, 1959), pp.91–3; Kippenberger, *Brigadier*, pp.132–5; Ronald Lewin, *Rommel as Military Commander* (London, 1968), p.65, passim; Barton Maughan, *Tobruk and El Alamein, Australia in the War of 1939–1945* (Canberra; 1966), pp.456–61, passim; G.L. Vernay, *The Desert Rats, The Story of the Seventh Armoured*

Division, 1938 to 1945 (London, 1954), p.76; A.D. Woozley (ed.), *History of the King's Dragoon Guards, 1938–1945* (Glasgow, n.d.), pp.130, 142.

68. Irving, *Trail*, p.129.
69. Connell, *Auchinleck*, p.385.
70. WO 169/1016, memorandum by H.N. Crawford, *passim;* WO 201/538, memorandum, 'Notes on the Employment of L.O.s', 12 August 1942; Agar-Hamilton and Turner, *Crisis in the Desert*, pp.66, *passim;* Brett James, *Ball of Fire*, pp.195–9, 220; Neil Orpen, *War in the Desert, South African Forces World War Two, Volume Three* (Cape Town, 1971), pp.229, 250; I.S.O. Playfair *et al., The Mediterranean and Middle East, Volume III (September 1941 to September 1942), British Fortunes reach their Lowest Ebb, History of the Second World War, United Kingdom Military Series* (London, 1960), pp.270–73; Vernay, *Desert Rats*, pp.106–7.
71. Mills and Nixon, *Annals*, p.182.
72. WO 169/1092, memorandum by Venham, 10 Dec. 1941; AIR 23/722 contains the standing orders for cipher and signals security for the RAF in the Middle East during 1941–42.
73. WO 169/1016, memorandum by CSO, First Armoured Division, 13 July 1942; WO 204/3896, Allied Forces Headquarters to formations, 2 Feb. 1943.
74. Von Mellenthin, *Panzer Battles*, p.94; Behrendt, *Rommel's Intelligence*, p.180, *passim.*
75. Irving, *Trail*, p.152.
76. Von Mellenthin, *Panzer Battles*, p.94.
77. WO 201/73, GHQ Middle East to Palestine Command, 5 June 1941; WO 169/1016, memorandum by CSO, Eighth Army, *passim*; AIR 23/6008, memorandum by Leonard Williams, 25 Nov. 1942.
78. WO 169/1016, memorandum by CSO, 10th Indian Division, 9 July 1942, *passim;* WO 201/538, memorandum by GHQ Middle East, 5 Dec. 1941.
79. WO 169/1015, Advanced Eighth Army Headquarters Signals war diary, entry 2 Dec. 1941; WO 169/1016, memorandum by CSO, Seventh Armoured Division.
80. Behrendt, *Rommel's Intelligence*, pp.105, 109, 115.
81. Borman, *Divisional Signals*, p.202.
82. Hastings, *Rifle Brigade*, p.4.
83. Behrendt, *Rommel's Intelligence*, p.80.
84. Irving, *Trail*, p.154; Playfair *et al., Mediterranean and Middle East, Volume III*, p.139–40; Hunt, *Don*, p.95; Lewin, *Rommel*, p.105; von Mellenthin, *Panzer Battles*, p.97; Liddell Hart, *Rommel Papers*, pp.156, 169, 240; Behrendt, *Rommel's Intelligence*, pp.105–27, *passim.*
85. Behrendt, *Rommel's Intelligence*, pp.168–9; Praun, *Radio Intelligence*, op. cit.; Ronald Lewin, *The Life and Death of the Afrika Korps, A Biography* (London, 1977), pp.35–6; Irving, *Trail*, p.195.

Convoy PQ 17:
A Study of Intelligence and
Decision-Making

PATRICK BEESLY

The destruction of PQ 17 was by no means the worst convoy disaster suffered by the British in the Second World War, but it has the unenviable distinction of being the only convoy to be abandoned by its escort in the face of predictable and devastating attack by the enemy. How did it come about that 34 merchantmen were left defenceless against the onslaught of Dönitz's U-boats and Goering's bombers despite the Royal Navy's centuries-old tradition of sacrificing its own ships and men to ensure the 'safe and timely arrival' of vessels entrusted to its care? The reason was that the convoy was ordered to scatter. The effect of an order to scatter is for its constitutent ships to abandon their close and disciplined formation and to proceed on separate, predetermined and diverging courses to their individual destinations. It was a recognized tactic for a convoy attacked by superior surface forces on the broad oceans and had been successfully used in 1940 by convoy HX 84 in the North Atlantic when, thanks to the sacrifice of its sole escort, the Armed Merchant Cruiser *Jervis Bay*, the great majority of the convoy had been enabled to escape from the 11-inch guns of the pocket battleship *Admiral Scheer*. But PQ 17 was not sailing on the vast expanse on the North Atlantic: it was on its way to North Russia, penned in to the north by the Arctic ice and to the south by the hostile Norwegian coast. It was under constant observation and attack by U-boats and aircraft. Evasion was impossible: disaster was inevitable unless the convoy and escort stuck together and somehow fought their way through to Murmansk. In the event only eleven merchant ships and two rescue ships, out of the total of 34 British, Dutch, American and Russian merchant ships and three rescue ships finally struggled into North Russian ports. No ship of the escort was sunk. Apart from a few aircraft the Germans also suffered no losses. It was a humiliating defeat for the Royal Navy, bitterly resented by its officers and men, and a shattering blow to the morale of all Allied merchant seamen. The decision to order the convoy to scatter, which deprived its escort of any possibility of protecting it, was taken by none other than the First Sea Lord of the Admiralty, the professional head of the Royal Navy, Admiral Sir Dudley Pound. It was taken, so far as can be seen, against the advice of almost all his staff and against the wishes of Sir John Tovey, Commander in Chief of the Home Fleet, of Rear-Admiral Hamilton, commanding the cruiser covering force and of Commander J.E. Broome, commander of the close escort. Pound believed, in the light of the intelligence available to him, that unless the convoy scattered, every ship in it, and all its escorts, would be sunk not so much by air and U-boat attack as by the over-powering strength of a German surface ship task force centred on the battleship *Tirpitz*.

The intention of this study is to examine the information available to Pound, to set out the advice given to him and to consider whether, as his supporters claim, he had no alternative but to act as he did, or whether, as his critics believe, different instructions would have at least mitigated the Allied losses in men, ships and morale. Despite the great changes that have taken place in the last 45 years in the techniques of gathering, analysing and disseminating intelligence, not to mention in maritime strategy and tactics, I believe that some of the problems which confronted Dudley Pound in June 1942 still have relevance today and that there may even be lessons to be learned by modern intelligence and operations staff officers.

THE BACKGROUND SITUATION IN JUNE 1942

When Hitler treacherously attacked his non-belligerent but subservient ally, Stalin, in the summer of 1941, Winston Churchill, despite his longstanding aversion to Bolshevism, immediately promised Russia all the help that Britain could give. Germany by then occupied the whole western coast of Europe from the North Cape to the Spanish frontier: the battle for control of the Mediterranean was raging and the Dardanelles were closed: access to Russia was available at only three points: via the Pacific to Vladivostock; via Persia (Iran) to Caucasia; and via the Barents Sea to Murmansk and Archangel. The first was far too remote both from Britain and the war zone. The second involved the long haul round the Cape of Good Hope and across neutral if not hostile Persia, where communications were primitive. That left only North Russia to which supplies of all sorts of war material (there was no possibility of sending a British army) could be transported. But, on the face of it, the use of this route was strategically and tactically quite unsound. The climatic conditions were appalling – ferocious gales, ice, fog, almost perpetual darkness for six months of winter succeeded by perpetual daylight during the summer. Throughout the 10–14 day voyage convoys (whose speed of advance was theoretically 10 knots, but more often seven knots or even less) were within easy reach of German reconnaissance planes and liable, for three-quarters of their voyage, to repeated attacks by U-boats and bombers based in North Norway. Evasion was virtually impossible: as in the Mediterranean, it would be a question of fighting each convoy right through to its destination. But the imperative necessity of preventing Russia being knocked out of the war compelled the Admiralty to attempt the seemingly impossible. Before long, therefore, a steady and regular flow of convoys bearing tanks, aircraft, guns and every possible sort of munition (desperately needed by the hard-pressed British for their own use) were sailing for Murmansk.

At first the Germans seemed unaware of the volume and value of the supplies that were reaching the Russians, but by February 1942 the Germans had collected a balanced force of U-boats, aircraft and surface ships in North Norway, partly as a result of Hitler's fears, stimulated by British commando raids, that a full-scale invasion was intended, but also to attack the convoys and Russian shipping in the Arctic area. By the end of May they had two pocket battleships, *Scheer* and *Lutzow*, two heavy cruisers, *Hipper* and *Prinz Eugen*, above all, the *Tirpitz*, with supporting destroyers, based on Trondheim and Narvik. There were also twelve U-boats and a powerful force of long-distance reconnaissance, bomber and torpedo aircraft. All this constituted a most serious threat.

What could the Western Allies do to counter-balance this formidable array? The short answer is not enough! Both the British and US Navies were, at this time, stretched to the limit. In May 1942 the British were struggling desperately to reinforce Malta, to secure Madagascar and retain some measure of control in the Bay of Bengal, where the Japanese had reached the frontiers of India. At the same time German U-boats were enjoying their second 'Happy Time' in the Atlantic, off the eastern seaboard of the United States and in the Caribbean, while in the Pacific the Battle of the Coral Sea was being fought: that of Midway was still to be won. The Russians were being driven still further back and suffering enormous losses on their land front: their Northern Fleet was small, primarily a coastal defence force, and unable if not actually unwilling to assist in the protection of the convoys whose arrival in Murmansk Stalin so stridently demanded. The British Home Fleet, based on Scapa Flow and responsible for the protection of the North Russian convoys and also for preventing any breakout by German surface forces into the Atlantic, could rarely muster more than two modern battleships and one modern aircraft carrier. Experience gained in sinking *Tirpitz*'s sister ship *Bismarck* twelve months earlier had convinced the Admiralty that two ships were needed to deal with the *Tirpitz*, which unlike the British *King George V* class, had been secretly designed and built in excess of the limitations laid down by the Washington treaties. British aircraft carriers, although in some respects the best in the world, were, thanks to the inter-war wrangle with the Royal Air Force over the control of the Fleet Air

Arm, not yet equipped with modern aircraft capable of standing up to attack by the Luftwaffe's latest shore-based planes, a lesson which the Royal Navy had learned to its cost during the Norwegian campaign of 1940,. Small escort carriers were only just beginning to come into service and were not yet available to reinforce the big fleet carriers. Nor had the British nearly as many cruisers as they needed, particularly as, once again, the Germans had ignored the tonnage limitations for this class of warship. Both the strategic and tactical situations were bleak, to put it mildly, but unless supplies continued to reach Russia there seemed a very real danger that Russia would be knocked out of the war or that, at the very least, Stalin would make another compromise peace with Hitler.

THE INTELLIGENCE SCENE

The British did, however, hold one possible trump card – their Intelligence was now far superior to that possessed by the Germans. Bletchley Park had broken the Luftwaffe's Enigma cipher early in 1940 and the German Navy's Enigma at the end of May 1941. It is true that the introduction of fourth Enigma wheel by the German Navy in February 1942 had deprived BP of the ability to penetrate radio traffic to and from U-boats in the Atlantic, but fortunately U-boats and surface ships in the North Sea and Arctic continued to use the old three-wheel system so that any *radio* messages and relevant to operations against the Allied convoys to North Russia could still be read. It must, however, be remembered that, invaluable though this was, decrypting of enemy radio messages had (and must always have) definite limitations. In the first place only messages sent, and successfully intercepted by radio, could be decrypted. Messages sent by landline, or orders given in writing in advance of planned operations, could not be subjected to this form of eavesdropping. Secondly, despite BP's expertise, the process of decryption was liable to delays. The settings for the naval 'Homewaters' Enigma were changed daily at noon so that the cipher had, in effect, to be broken afresh every 24 hours. As it happened, for technical reasons, the problem of breaking the second 24 hours period of changes in settings was easier than that presented by the first, so that the delays in decryption generally occurred every 48 hours, to be followed by 48 hours of increasingly current reading until the next major change took place. It was a matter of pure chance whether the gaps in this vital flow of information took place at a critical moment during operations at sea or not, and in the case of PQ 17 this was to prove a factor of the greatest importance.

The British had one further and unusual source of first-class information – Swedish cryptanalysis. Sweden had preserved its neutrality only by making concesssions to the Germans, and a section of Swedish opinion and the Swedish government was, as in the First World War, inclined to be pro-German. Other Swedes, including most fortunately the deputy head of the Intelligence Service, felt that their duty lay with their Norwegian cousins and the allies. The Norwegian military attaché and the British naval attaché, Captain Denham, benefited from a considerable supply of information from Swedish Intelligence, all the more vital because it included, on occasions, the results of Swedish decryption of German messages sent by landline via Stockholm to the German commands in Norway. Other valuable information came from the Norwegian resistance movement although, in the first half of 1942, it had not yet been possible to establish agents or to provide them with means of rapid and regular communication in one or two vital areas.

It should also be noted that, even with sophisticated naval radio transmitters, radio reception in the Arctic was notoriously difficult: There was no guarantee that the British would be able to intercept every German signal made, and even the Germans themselves experienced difficulties in receiving their own signals. This also meant that direction-finding was unreliable, while radio fingerprinting and other such techniques for identifying the source of radio transmissions were at this time of more interest to experimental scientists than to practising intelligence officers. Finally, it must be pointed out that the British did not have reconnaissance aircraft with sufficient range or in sufficient numbers to guarantee regular coverage of German bases in North Norway, and even if they had, the appalling weather conditions sometimes made reconnaissance impossible. Russian co-operation in basing RAF aircraft in North Russia was grudging and incompetent, which in no way helped the obvious solution to this particular problem.

So, to sum up, although the British had a great advantage in the Intelligence field, it was not an advantage which could be counted on to produce results in all circumstances. It might, or might not, prove a broken reed: operational plans could not be made on the basis that it would be infallible.

We turn now to the organization which the British had created to deal with the analysis and dissemination of maritime intelligence. It must be remembered that the British Admiralty, unlike the British War Office or Air Ministry – or indeed the US Navy Department – was an operational authority, with powers to take charge of operations at sea over the head of commanders-in-chief concerned (a power which some thought was exercised too often). Be that as it may, it followed, rightly so in my opinion, that all intelligence bearing on the war at sea, and particularly operational intelligence, was funnelled into the Admiralty's Naval Intelligence Division (NID) for analysis, consideration by the naval staff and dissemination to authorities outside the Admiralty and to commanders-in-chief at sea. The section of NID responsible for analysis and promulgation of operational intelligence was the Operational Intelligence Centre (OIC), which was itself divided into a number of sub-sections of which the most important, in the present context, were those dealing with the surface ships of the German Navy, the submarine tracking room, the direction-finding team and the air section. OIC's sources of information included direction-finding, air reconnaissance, agents and diplomatic reports, reports from British and Allied warships and merchant ships, and, most valuable of all, decrypted messages received from BP, translated into English but otherwise exactly as received. By early 1942 the co-operation between BP and OIC was extremely close: telephone and telex messages, on direct and secret lines, flowed constantly to and from, and although, in the ultimate, responsibility for the appreciation of enemy movements and intentions rested with OIC, much reliance was placed on the views of BP's naval section and on its extensive card index system and its knowledge of the significance of the nature and volume of German radio traffic – traffic analysis. The Royal Navy had been well ahead of the other two services in establishing a system for the secure dissemination of information derived from cryptanalysis by means of signals with the special security classification Ultra, transmitted in one-time pad ciphers.[1] For administrative and security reasons one-time Ultra pads were issued only to Flag Officers (and only to those of such exalted rank with a need to know). Officers of lesser rank, even captains in command of escort groups, were not indoctrinated and did not receive the detailed information contained in Ultra signals, although it was sometimes possible to convey to them some guidance in bowdlerized form. The Director of Naval Intelligence, the brilliant John Godfrey, had further refined the system by a simple system of grading intelligence signals: A to E for reliability of source and 1 to 5 for NID's estimate of the validity of the source's information. Thus Ultra was A.1, while a grading of B.3 indicated a good source passing information of which the validity seemed uncertain, while E.2 indicated an unknown or unreliable source passing information which nevertheless was assessed as accurate. In addition, Godfrey directed that factual information conveyed in an NID signal must be clearly differentiated from any conclusions derived from it by the word Comment, thus giving the recipient not only the benefit of the NID point of view but the chance to draw his own and possibly different conclusions based on local information available to him but not to NID. While in port, the C-inC Home Fleet was in direct touch with OIC by telex and scrambler telephone and was kept completely up-to-date with the latest information including the cryptanalysis position at BP. In retrospect it is hard to think of a better system, given the technology of the time but, as already remarked, there could be no advance guarantee that the flow of

intelligence would be either completely comprehensive or without interruption at critical moments.

THE PERSONALITIES INVOLVED

Although Winston Churchill, when First Lord (political head) of the
Admiralty, had interfered constantly with quite minor administrative,
operational and even tactical matters, when he became Prime Minister
and Minister of Defence in May 1940, he did confine himself, so far as the
navy was concerned, more to broad strategic issues, and I have no firm
evidence that, apart from insisting that PQ 17 must be sailed, he otherwise
greatly influenced the course of events.

His successor as First Lord was the Labour politician A. V. Alexander.
A capable man, he played a much more conventional role and did not
attempt to dictate to the Naval Staff. For some reason which I have never
understood he was not fully indoctrinated into Special Intelligence, saw
no decrypts and only very occasionally visited the OIC and then under
what I must call 'strict surveillance'. He played, so far as I know, no part in
the operational or intelligence decisions affecting PQ 17. The First Sea
Lord, the professional head of the Navy and Chief of the Naval Staff, was
Admiral of the Fleet Sir Dudley Pound. In 1942 he was 65 years old and
had borne an immense burden of responsibility since he assumed office in
mid-1919. Was he too old and was he still physically fit for this most
demanding post? He had for many years suffered from painful osteo-
arthritis and found difficulty in sleeping at night. There are plenty of
reports that he frequently appeared to be dozing during meetings of the
Chief of Staff, but his supporters claim that it was merely a mannerism that
he closed his eyes and that he was fully alert at all times. He died,
apparently of a tumour on the brain in October 1943, and some believe
that the disease may have affected him even two years before this, so that
'his memory, judgement and mental alertness, but not his powers of
decision were waning'. This too is most vigorously denied by some who
were in close contact with him. It is something that can never be proved
one way or the other. Pound certainly was an officer of the old school: he
had commanded a battleship at Jutland and gave the appearance of being
stern, reserved and taciturn to all except those who knew him well. He had
great moral courage, although he has been criticized for not opposing
some of Churchill's more harebrained plans sufficiently resolutely. He
never seems to have realized the strength of his own position. Churchill,
after causing Fisher's resignation in 1915, would not have wished to force
another First Sea Lord to take the same step in the Second World War.
Although a most experienced staff officer, Pound does not strike me as
one who really understood the intelligence world: he very rarely visited

OIC and can have formed no valid opinions about the capabilities of its staff. I believe this was another important factor in the PQ 17 affair.

The Commander-in-Chief of the Home Fleet was Admiral Sir John Tovey, aged 57. An able and courageous officer, he had been responsible for the destruction of the *Bismarck*, and both directly and through his chief of staff kept in close touch with OIC whose ability he recognized and whose dificulties he understood. He resented but could not effectively oppose Pound's tendency to indulge in 'back seat driving' from the distant Admiralty. It should be noted that, although 'Y parties' to deal with low-grade Luftwaffe codes were embarked on occasions in flagships, Tovey, like all other flag officers, was dependent for high-grade cryptanalysis on such information as the Admiralty saw fit to send him once he was at sea. This was almost certainly inevitable in the state of the art at that time, and, so far as OIC was concerned, great efforts were made to supply him with every scrap of information immediately it became available from BP or elsewhere.

The admiral commanding the 1st Cruiser Squadron (CS1), which provided the distant escort for PQ 17, was Rear-Admiral L.H.K. Hamilton. He was a popular if in some ways slightly old-fashioned officer who was not afraid to voice his opinions when he considered, as he often did, that Churchill, the Admiralty or the Royal Air Force were letting the navy down. Naturally he felt himself bound to carry out orders from his superiors even if he disagreed with them. As a flag officer, he was a recipient of OIC's Ultra signals.

The commander of the considerable close escort of the convoy was Commander J.E. Broome, another experienced and forthright officer who had not much love for shore-bound staff officers who attempted, from their 'armchairs' in the comfort of the Admiralty, to dictate to those who had to bear the ultimate responsibility at sea. In accordance with established practice he was not Ultra-indoctrinated, a fact which did not help when he had to decide how to dispose his escort forces when the convoy was ordered to scatter.

So far as the Intelligence Division was concerned only three officers need to be considered because the Director, the extremely able Rear-Admiral Godfrey, was absent from the Admiralty on tour during the critical days: in any case it was his firm policy to delegate control and presentation of operational intelligence to his subordinate in charge of the OIC, the Deputy Director (DDIC), 'Jock' Clayton. Clayton, aged 54, had retired shortly before the war with the rank of rear-admiral. He had been recalled in August 1939 to take charge of the OIC in the rank of captain. Like Broome, he would much have preferred to be at sea, but he was a most intelligent man and a good intelligence officer, lacking only that degree of ruthlessness which might otherwise have taken him to the top of his profession. As with Hamilton, a lifetime in the Royal Navy had taught him to obey orders from senior officers without arguing the toss once those orders had been issued.

Clayton had two brilliant subordinates. The one most directly concerned with the decisions taken to scatter PQ 17 was Paymaster-Commander N.E. Denning, the officer in charge of the section responsible for information about all German surface ships. He was a born intelligence officer and had in fact formed the OIC in 1938 and been largely responsible for its development ever since. He probably knew more about the German Navy than any other British naval officer. He was at this time aged 38, but, by the time he finally retired after holding the posts first of Director of Naval Intelligence and then that of Deputy Chief of Defence Staff (Intelligence), he had reached the rank of vice-admiral and had been knighted. In 1942, however, he still had to contend with the rather patronizing and slightly snobbish attitude of many officers of the Executive branch towards their non-executive brethren in the Supply and Secretariat branch of the Royal Navy. 'Ned', as he was universally known in the navy, worked very closely with BP, particularly with the young Harry Hinsley, then deputy head of BP's naval section, later Vice-Chancellor of Cambridge University and author of the official history of *British Intelligence in the Second World War*.

Ned's colleague in charge of the Submarine Tracking Room was a peacetime lawyer, Rodger Winn, a temporary commander in the Special Branch of the RNVR and quite as brilliant an intelligence officer as Denning. He, too, subsequently rose to the top of his profession – a Lord of Appeal and also a knight. Crippled by polio in his youth, he might have made a legal fortune during the war but preferred to serve his country for the modest pay offered by the Admiralty. This did, however, give him, a civilian in uniform, a freedom to speak his mind not enjoyed by his regular service colleagues. It is interesting to speculate whether, with this independence and his remarkable forensic talents, he would have been more successful, had he been in Denning's shoes, in putting over the intelligence appreciation to Pound.

PRELIMINARIES

The earlier PQ convoys had been escorted only by destroyers and light craft, but, with the gradual build-up of heavier German forces in North Norway, two or more cruisers had to be added to the escort and then, with the arrival of *Tirpitz*, it became necessary for the Home Fleet to put to sea to provide more distant cover – distant cover because the increased threat from the Luftwaffe meant that the Home Fleet had somehow to cruise in an area from which it could intercept the German Task Force if it put to sea, yet without approaching the Norwegian coast so closely as to render itself liable to the full weight of attack by shore-based aircraft, unless there was a real hope of destroying the *Tirpitz*.

At the beginning of March PQ 12 sailed from Iceland, was soon located by German reconnaissance planes and threatened by the departure of the *Tirpitz* from Trondheim, facts immediately detected by British intelligence. It is unnecessary to follow here the various moves and counter-moves which ensured. Suffice it to say that in the next six days the Germans failed by the narrowest of margins to find the convoy, while the Home Fleet would not have been in a position to attack the *Tirpitz* with aircraft from the fleet carrier *Victorious* had not the Admiralty, on the basis of OIC's more correct appreciation of the situation, intervened to redirect Tovey. Unfortunately, the attack failed and *Tirpitz* was able to escape unharmed back to Trondheim. His almost successful intervention must have reinforced Pound's conviction that 'Father knows best'. Nevertheless both Pound and Tovey considered that, with summer approaching and the formidable strength of the German opposition, operations to run convoys to Russia were quite unsound and should be abandoned for the time being. Churchill was inclined to agree with this view but his protests were sharply rejected by both Stalin and Roosevelt, so, fearful of the reaction of his two allies, Winston somewhat reluctantly gave the order for the convoys to continue: even if only half the ships got through he felt the results would be worthwhile. They did, with the torpedoing and loss of two of the Royal Navy's valuable heavy cruisers. As a result, the cruiser covering force was in future forbidden to accompany the convoy all the way through to Murmansk.

On 18 June Captain Denham sent a most important signal from Stockholm to the DNI in London:

FOLLOWING IS GERMAN PLAN OF ATTACK ON NEXT ARCTIC CONVOY. IT IS HOPED TO OBTAIN EARLY RECONNAISSANCE REPORT WHEN EASTBOUND CONVOY REACHES VICINITY OF JAN MAYEN. BOMBING ATTACKS FROM AIRCRAFT BASED IN N. NORWAY WILL THEN COMMENCE. NAVAL MOVEMENTS MAY TAKE PLACE FROM THIS MOMENT AS FOLLOWS:

1. POCKET BATTLESHIPS WITH SIX DESTROYERS WILL PROCEED TO ALTENFJORD ANCHORAGE...

2. *TIRPITZ* WITH *HIPPER*, TWO DESTROYERS AND THREE TORPEDO BOATS [SMALL DESTROYERS] WILL PROCEED TO NARVIK AREA ...

NAVAL FORCES MAY BE EXPECTED TO OPERATE FROM THESE ANCHORAGES ONCE THE CONVOY HAS REACHED THE MERIDIAN OF 5 DEGREES EAST. THE INTENTION FOR THE TWO GROUPS OF SURFACE FORCES IS TO MAKE A RENDEZVOUS ON THE BEAR

ISLAND MERIDIAN AND TO MAKE A SIMULTANEOUS ATTACK ON CONVOY SUPPORTED BY U-BOATS AND AIR UNITS ...

Two further parts of Denham's signal went on to set out German fuel oil shortages and the dispositions of the Luftwaffe divisions which were to attack the convoy. The information, obtained from the Swedes, which Denham graded A.3, was an accurate summary of Admiral Raeder's intentions as signalled to his fleet commander and the Admiral Commanding in North Norway. It was a remarkable coup for Denham but unfortunately, as so often with information derived from cryptanalysis, it was incomplete: it did not and could not include most secret written or verbal instructions given by Hitler. The Führer, alarmed by *Tirpitz*'s narrow escape during PQ 12 from suffering *Bismarck*'s fate, had refused Raeder permission to commit his prestige-laden battleship to the possible dangers of an attack on PQ 17 unless and until the Home Fleet had been located and the risks from its carrier-borne aircraft eliminated.

Pound must have felt that an attack by the German task force was inevitable and it may have been that it was after receipt of this alarming information that he telephoned Tovey in Scapa Flow. Unfortunately, no record of the exact nature and date of this call can be traced. It does, however, appear that Tovey, possibly briefed by Denning, was very doubtful whether the Germans would risk *Tirpitz*. Pound, on the other hand, stated that in certain circumstances it might be necessary for the Admiralty to order the convoy to scatter, to which Tovey is said to have replied that such an order would be 'sheer bloody murder'. Pound does not appear to have been influenced by Tovey's views, because when PQ 17 did sail its order did contain provisions for scattering if so ordered. They also contained provisions for the convoy to reverse course should this appear desirable.

One must ask at this juncture, whether, if Pound was so pessimistic about the chances of less than half the convoy getting through, he should not have made a further attempt to persuade his political masters to agree at least to postponement until the darker days of autumn. But nothing is certain in war and perhaps Pound was hoping that luck would be on the British side and that all would be well on the day. If so, he certainly was not prepared to trust in the goddess of fortune when the moment of crisis finally arose.

OPERATION KNIGHT'S MOVE

The German code word for the proposed attack was *Rösselsprung*, Knight's Move. *Tirpitz* and the heavy cruiser *Hipper* were at Trondheim ready to move north to the Narvik area once the convoy had been detected at sea. The two pocket battleships, *Scheer* and *Lützow*, were at Narvik and would also move north, in their case to the anchorage of Altenfjord, close to the North Cape. Eleven destroyers and three torpedo boats would accompany the heavy ships. Twenty U-boats were based on Trondheim, Narvik and Kirknes. The Luftwaffe had assembled 103 Junkers 88 bombers, 15 Heinkel torpedo bombers, 30 Junkers 87 dive bombers and 74 reconnaissance aircraft.

When PQ 17 finally sailed from Iceland on 27 June, it consisted of 34 British, American and Russian merchant ships, with three rescue ships and was carrying 157,000 tons of war supplies. The close escort, under Broome, consisted of six destroyers, four corvettes, three minesweepers, four trawlers, two anti-aircraft ships and two submarines. Because the Home Fleet was much depleted due to other commitments it had been temporarily reinforced by an American Task Force. Hamilton's cruiser force consisted of four heavy cruisers, *London, Norfolk,* and the USN's *Tuscaloosa* and *Wichita*, and three destroyers. Tovey, giving the distant cover with the Home Fleet, had under command his flagship *Duke of York*, the rather more powerful USN *Washington* (in theory a match for *Tirpitz*), the modern fleet carrier *Victorious*, with about 40 aircraft embarked the heavy cruisers *Nigeria* and *Cumberland* and 14 destroyers. This was a formidable force except for the vital lack of sufficient air power. In addition eight British, one Free French and four Russian submarines were stationed off the North Cap and special air patrols arranged. Tovey's intentions were to route the convoy as far north as possible, not to take the Home Fleet much east of Bear Island and for Hamilton not to proceed east of Jan Mayen unless it was clear that there was no threat from *Tirpitz*.

Tovey was fully supplied with all the intelligence available to OIC, including, at his special request, the exact state of play at Bletchley Park: throughout the operation he was therefore kept informed not only of all relevant decrypts as they reached OIC but also when BP expected to break the next 24 hours' traffic, when this actually occurred and when each period's reading had been completed. For example, at 0510 on 30 June (double British Summer Time, two hours ahead of GMT) he was told:

INFORMATION FOR 29TH JUNE NOW AVAILABLE, ANTICIPATE 30TH JUNE ABOUT MIDDAY

or at 1819 on 3 July:

ALL IMPORTANT INFORMATION HAS NOW BEEN STUDIED. INFORMATION FROM 1200/3 IS NOT EXPECTED BEFORE 2359/4

and so on. Nor was it only positive information that was sent to Tovey and Hamilton, as is shown by an Ultra signal sent late on 30 June, stating that 'from negative information' it was probable that *Scheer* and *Lützow* were still at Narvik. The two flag officers had therefore good reason to be confident that they would receive every scrap of information as soon as it became available in the Admiralty and that they would also be kept aware of OIC's current appreciation both from positive and negative indications of German moves or lack of them: but they had also been warned that there could be no guarantee that even Special Intelligence would necessarily reveal every German move.

For the first few days both PQ 17 and the returning westbound convoy, PQ 13, had uneventful voyages. There was a good deal of fog about and it was not until 1432 on 1 July that the Luftwaffe's first sighting report PQ 17 was received in the Admiralty, coinciding with an Ultra signal to Tovey that settings for the 24-hour period ending 1200 on that day had been broken. This was the second of the 48-hour cycle already mentioned and late on 2 July OIC had to signal that:

INFORMATION FROM 1200/1 TO 1200/3 NOT YET AVAILABLE. EXPECTED TIME UNCERTAIN BUT PROBABLY BY 0800/3

In fact, the settings were broken by 0515 on the 3rd, but in the meantime, on the afternoon of 2 July, Luftwaffe Enigma had already disclosed that an air attack on the convoy would be made that evening, which by then was roughly between Jan Mayen and Bear Island, as was also the westbound PQ 13, in which the Germans were not in fact interested. At 2349/2 OIC gave the C-in-C its appreciation that there were

NO DIRECT INDICATIONS OF MOVEMENTS OF ENEMY MAIN UNITS

but added that the Luftwaffe had placed its coastal fighters on the alert and had been trying to locate the convoy's heavy covering forces.

It should be pointed out that all signals whether from OIC, the Operations or Trade Divisions were transmitted 'From Admiralty'. The receipient could therefore only deduce from the nature of the contents which department had originated it. All had the same authority whether initiated by the First Sea Lord or a junior watchkeeper on Denning's staff.

PQ 17 was now approaching the most critical period of its voyage and a very great deal depended on whether the combination of BP and OIC could provide those at sea with up-to-date and accurate assessments of the Germans' intentions and actual moves. At 0810/3 OIC signalled Tovey as follows:

1. SHADOWING AIRCRAFT WERE STILL IN CONTACT WITH PQ 17 AT 0200/3. GERMANS STATED WEATHER CONDITION MADE IT DOUBTFUL WHETHER IT WOULD BE POSSIBLE TO CONTINUE SHADOWING. 2. AT 2104/2 BRITISH BATTLEFLEET HAD NOT BEEN LOCATED SINCE 2100/1. UNVERIFIED REPORT HAD BEEN RECEIVED OF A SKUA

[CARRIER-BORNE AIRCRAFT] 60 MILES WEST OF TRONDHEIM AT 1600/2 WHICH LED GERMANS TO SUGGEST THAT CARRIER WAS POSSIBLY OFF TRONDHEIM.

3. AT 0300/3 AIR OFFICER COMMANDING LOFOTENS REPORTED THAT CLOSE AIR ESCORT FOR OPERATION CONCERT WOULD PROBABLY NOT BE POSSIBLE ON ACCOUNT OF WEATHER.

4. LUFTWAFFE INTENTIONS FOR 3 JULY WERE (A) RENEWED RECONNAISSANCE FOR CONVOY AND (B) OPERATION KNIGHT'S MOVE.

5. U-BOATS WERE IN CONTACT WITH PQ DURING 2 JULY. COMMENT; OPERATIONS CONCERT AND KNIGHT'S MOVE ARE PROBABLY CONCERNED WITH ENEMY MAIN UNITS.

Between 0950/3 and 1422/3 four more Ultra signals were sent to Tovey which indicated that *Scheer* and *Lützow* were on the move and that *Lützow* had been 'detached', that *Tirpitz* was also at sea at 2303/3, that U-boats had been given the estimated position of the convoy and told to search along that latitude but if they made no contact a Bear Island patrol line was intended. At 1745/3 a further long Ultra signal was sent to Tovey and Hamilton which concluded with the following comment:

IT APPEARS CERTAIN *SCHEER* HAS MOVED NORTHWARDS FROM NARVIK, PROBABLY ACCOMPANIED BY DESTROYERS. MOVEMENT OF *LÜTZOW* IS UNCERTAIN BUT SHE WAS INDEPENDENT OF *SCHEER*.[2] *TIRPITZ* and *HIPPER* MAY HAVE LEFT TRONDHEIM AREA SINCE 0001/3.

This signal was followed quickly by one stating that:

ALL IMPORTANT INFORMATION HAS NOW BEEN STUDIED

and, ominously:

INFORMATION FROM 1200/3 IS NOT EXPECTED BEFORE 2359/4.

which meant that no reliable intelligence, except possibly from Luftwaffe codes or RAF reconnaissance, temporarily based in North Russia, could be counted on just when accurate information about the progress of Knight's Move was vital. RAF reconnaissance failed, but BP, despite the crisis in the fighting in the Western Desert, had just obtained authority to concentrate its limited stock of 'bombes', for breaking the various types of Enigma, on the defence of PQ 17. Despite all BP's efforts, it was not until 1934/4 that OIC was able to signal Tovey and Hamilton that

NOON 3RD TO NOON 5TH NOW AVAILABLE.

It is not difficult to imagine the rising tension in the Admiralty. According

CONVOYS PQ 17 AND QP 13, 3–6 JULY 1942

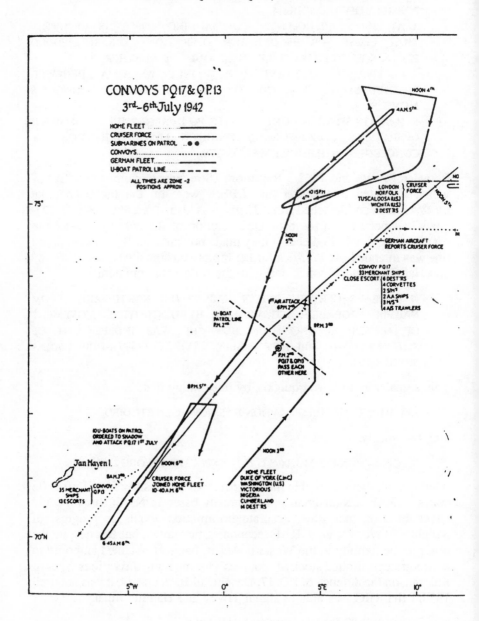

Source: S.W. Roskill, *The War at Sea,* Vol. II (London: HMSO, 1957)

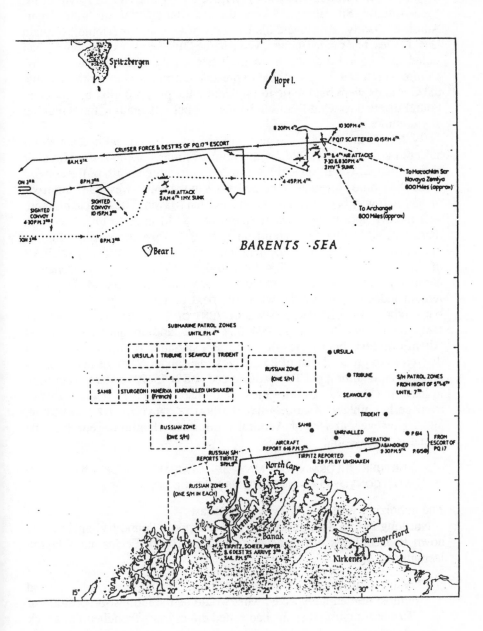

to Ned Denning, who slept in the Admiralty and was therefore either on duty or on call throughout the operation, the Vice-Chief of Naval Staff, Vice-Admiral Sir Henry Moore, the Assistant Chief of Staff, Rear-Admiral 'Daddy' Brind, and his Director of Operations (Home), Captain 'Jas' Eccles, had made frequent visits to the OIC ever since the convoy had sailed, but Pound did not do so until late on the night of the 3rd. The picture which Denning was able to present to him certainly suggested that the Germans were beginning to implement the plan reported by Denham. Pound listened to what Denning had to say but left again without making any comment.

By 2300/3 the convoy was just north of Bear Island and had not so far suffered any casualties, although within 400 miles of the Luftwaffe's air base at Banak. Hamilton and his cruisers were a little north of the convoy while the Home Fleet was some 250 miles to the south-westward, approximately half way between Bear Island and Jan Mayen. The critical moment was rapidly approaching when Hamilton would have to turn back, but there was little that OIC could do until BP broke the settings for the period from 1200/3, for an accident had interrupted air patrols by the RAF of the North Cape. At 0250/4 OIC told the C-in-C that a sequence of German naval transmissions made at hourly intervals since 1407/3 might remain indecipherable even when the next period's traffic was broken, but might 'INDICATE THE COMMENCEMENT OF A SPECIAL OPERATION BY MAIN UNITS' and then at 1145/4 that *Scheer* and an oiler had reached Altenfjord. Possibly as a result, Admiralty signalled Hamilton giving him discretion to proceed east of 25 degrees east (about 60 miles ahead of his position at the time), but Tovey disagreed and at 1512/4 ordered Hamilton to leave the Barents Sea once the convoy had reached 25 degrees east or even earlier unless 'ASSURED BY ADMIRALTY THAT *TIRPITZ* CANNOT BE MET'. However, at 1858/4 Admiralty informed Hamilton, repeating the signal to Tovey, that

> FURTHER INFORMATION MAY BE AVAILABLE SHORTLY. REMAIN WITH CONVOY PENDING FURTHER INSTRUCTIONS.

The agonizing wait in OIC was over at last.

Not long before this, during the late afternoon, Pound had again come down to Denning's office, accompanied by Brind, Eccles and Clayton Denning recounts:

> ... he sat down on a stool in front of the main plotting table ... and almost immediately asked what would be the farthest-on position of *Tirpitz* assuming that she had sailed direct from Trondheim to attack the convoy ... Brind estimated that she could be within striking distance [at that very time]. I interjected that it was unlikely she

would have taken a direct course ... I also considered that she would put into Narvik or Tromso to refuel her escorting destroyers .. Pound gazed at the plot but said very little ... Pound then left, but Eccles and Clayton remained and shortly afterwards Harry Hinsley ... phoned on the direct scrambler line to alert me that the awaited break was imminent ... Eccles [immediately] drafted the signal to Hamilton [quoted in the preceding paragraph]. Both Eccles and Clayton then went out, I presume to discuss the proposed signal with Pound ...

As was customary, Bletchley gave priority to decrypting the latest urgent intercepts and these began arriving in the teleprinter room just before 1900. [One of the first was a signal timed 0040/4 indicating that the aircraft shadowing PQ 17 had sighted a battleship, one heavy cruiser, two light cruisers and three destroyers on an easterly course.] Clearly, the formation was the cruiser covering force under Hamilton. Misidentification in ship recognition by the Luftwaffe was not unusual. The question was: what credence would the German naval Staff place on this report? This teleprint was followed within a few minutes by the following:

FROM C-IN-C FLEET (IN *TIRPITZ*). TO ADMIRAL COMMANDING CRUISERS. IMMEDIATE. ARRIVING ALTA 0900. YOU ARE TO ALLOT ANCHORAGE TO *TIRPITZ* OUTER VAGFJORD. NEWLY ARRIVED DESTROYERS AND TORPEDO BOATS TO COMPLETE WITH FUEL AT ONCE.

I was in the process of drafting an Ultra to the C-in-C and CS 1 based on the information in these two latest decrypts when Clayton and Eccles returned accompanied by Pound ... I was immediately asked what I proposed to say. I gave the gist of the two intercepts and a proposed comment that all the indications pointed to *Tirpitz* and accompanying ships being still in harbour at Alta. Pound apparently considered the comment premature and my proposed Ultra was whittled down to the bald facts.

The Ultra signal, despatched with little delay at 1918/4, read as follows:

C-IN-C *TIRPITZ* ARRIVED ALTENFJORD 0900/4. DESTROYERS AND TORPEDO BOATS ORDERED TO COMPLETE WITH FUEL AT ONCE. *SCHEER* WAS ALREADY PRESENT AT ALTENFJORD. AT 1622/3 TWO U-BOATS WERE INFORMED THEIR MAIN TASK WAS TO SHADOW CONVOY.

This was fine so far as it went, but contrary to practice up to this moment, it did not contain, as Denning had wished it to do, the Admiralty's appreciation of what all this portended. One must ask why Pound did not delay a few minutes longer to ask Denning why he believed *Tirpitz* was still at anchor, to accept or refuse Denning's arguments, and then to give Tovey and Hamilton his own views of the position. But no, the signal had to go at once. Then, and only then, did Pound start to cross-examine Denning.

> Pound resumed his seat on the stool at the head of the table and enquired how long it would take the destroyers to top up with fuel. I had already mentally calculated this as about three hours. Then he asked me what was likely to be the speed of *Tirpitz*. I replied probably 25 or 26 knots provided the weather was favourable for the destroyers, but two or three knots less if the pocket battleships were in company. Taking up the dividers, Pound remarked that if *Tirpitz* had sailed from Alta that morning, she could be up with convoy about midnight.

If Denning is correct, this was a miscalculation since even at 26 knots the earliest possible time would have been 0230 the following morning. A small point but perhaps indicative that Pound was already thinking seriously of scattering the convoy. Or was he just worn out? Denning's assistant recalls 'a very tired looking Dudley Pound sitting gazing at a small-scale chart of the Barents Sea area, calculating with a pair of dividers where *Tirpitz* could be at that time'.

To return to Denning's narrative:

> He then asked me why I thought *Tirpitz* had not yet left Alta. I expounded what had happened during the sortie against PQ 12. I pointed out that up to noon that day no decrypt had been received ordering U-boats to keep clear of the convoy and even now radio direction finding of U-boat transmissions showed that they were still in contact. Despite intensive air reconnaissance the Luftwaffe had not yet relocated Tovey's force. They had indeed located the cruiser covering force early that morning but the formation was reported including a battleship, and the Luftwaffe had now reported sighting an aircraft in its vicinity. Therefore the German Naval Staff could not ignore the possibility that this might be a major force supporting an aircraft carrier. I continued that although Bletchley had not yet broken the Enigma from noon that day, nevertheless the nature of radio transmission intercepted during the afternoon revealed none of the characteristics normally associated with surface ships being at sea. Moreover there had been no sighting report from our own or Russian submarines patrolling off the North Cape ... Clayton interjected occasionally supporting my reasoning and Brind and Eccles

intervened with questions and comments, but Pound spoke very little and played idly with the dividers, apparently sunk in thought. After a time he got up to proceed to the U-boat Tracking Room, but before leaving he turned to me and asked 'Can you assure me that *Tirpitz* is still in Altenfjord? My reply was to the effect that although I was confident she was, I could not give absolute assurance but fully expected to receive confirmation in the fairly near future when Bletchley had unbuttoned the new traffic.

One can hazard a guess that when Pound arrived in the Submarine Tracking Room it was some time after 1930. The news had arrived from BP that the traffic from 1200/4 to 1200/5 had been cracked, which meant that virtually current reading of the enemy's signals would soon be possible. The U-boat situation disclosed by Winn was not good, but no precise record of what was said now survives, nor can we be sure how long Pound remained with Winn. He did not return to see if Denning had any fresh information, but went up to his own office and called an urgent meeting to consider what action should be taken. This haste was most unfortunate. We must return to Denning's account.

At about 2000/4 the current decrypted traffic began to be passed on the teleprinter, and almost the first was the following signal, German time of origin 1327/4:

FROM U-457. TO ADMIRAL COMMANDING NORTHERN WATERS. HEAVY ENEMY FORCES IN SIGHT IN 1542.

That position was about 80 miles north east of Bear Island. To the German Naval Staff this would possibly have been seen as confirming the presence of a battleship in CS 1's formation reported by the aircraft at 0040 that morning. However, if so, they would have been perplexed by the following:

FROM FLIEGERFUHRER LOFOTENS. TO ALL. MOST IMMEDIATE. SHADOWER REPORTS AT 1422 ENEMY FORCES REPORTED CONSIST OF 3 HEAVY NORTH AMERICAN CRUISERS, ONE HEAVY BRITISH CRUISER, THREE DESTROYERS, COURSE EAST, SLOW SPEED

However, Admiral Northern Waters had already assumed a major force was present for the following intercept, German time of origin 1458/4, was then received:

FROM ADMIRAL COMMANDING NORTHERN WATERS, TO EISTEUFEL. [The U-boat Group pursuing the convoy.] BOHMAN TO CONTINUE TO SHADOW CONVOY. BRANDENBURG TO

CONTINUE TO SHADOW BATTLESHIP FORMATION. U-BOATS
ARE TO ATTACK ON BRANDENBURGS REPORTS.

In accordance with routine, these messages would have been passed
immediately by my duty watchkeeping officer to the U-boat
Tracking Room [with another copy coming immediately to
Denning]. Clayton and I presume Pound was still there. The
following decrypt was received [at 2031/4] German time of origin
1130/4 [i.e. earlier than the one just quoted]:

FROM ADMIRAL COMMANDING NORTHERN WATERS TO
EISTEUFEL.
NO OWN FORCES IN OPERATIONAL AREA. POSITION OF HEAVY
ENEMY GROUP NOT KNOWN TO PRESENT BUT IS MAIN TARGET
FOR U-BOATS WHEN ENCOUNTERED. BOATS IN CONTACT WITH
CONVOY ARE TO KEEP AT IT. NO AIRCRAFT IN CONTACT WITH
CONVOY AT THE MOMENT. RECCE IS BEING OPERATED.

Clearly *Tirpitz* had NOT sailed that morning and I hastened to find
Clayton, only to bump into him in the corridor outside my room. He
was on his way to attend an urgent meeting called by Pound and I was
only able to hand him the teleprinter message and exchange a quick
word with him. I returned to my room and, as was my wont, tried to
sum up the situation as it appeared in the eyes of the German Naval
Staff from such information as was available to them and in the
sequence in which they received it. I cannot recall my exact thought
process but it must have been something on the following lines:-

The convoy and escort are approximately 120 miles north east of
Bear Island. They are being shadowed by U-boats and air attacks
have been made on them. A surface force has been located some 30
miles north of the convoy and is being shadowed by a U-boat. Its
exact composition is now known but may include a battleship, and
could possibly be a major force supporting a carrier. At present it is
the main target for attack by U-boats. The heavy group with an
aircraft carrier reported by reconnaissance on 1st July had not been
located despite intensive air reconnaissance. It is possible therefore
that there may be two major forces supporting the passage of the
convoy. Therefore, unless and until the position and composition of
these forces is estabished, it would be taking an unjustifiable risk to
commit our only worthwhile surface force to attack the convoy at
present. Thus for the time being we will continue to attack and harass
the convoy by U-boats and aircraft.

Based on this thinking I started to draft an Ultra to C-in-C Home
Fleet and CS 1. After giving the basic information in the decrypts, I
added a comment to the effect that it was considered the *Tirpitz* and

accompanying ships were still in Altenfjord at 1200/4. Indications pointed strongly to them not having *yet* sailed. It was unlikely that they would sail until the Germans had located and established the location and strength of the forces in support of the convoy. Normally I would have despatched the Ultra without formal consultation with higher authority but in view of what had happened I felt obliged to wait until Clayton returned from Pound's meeting.

Denning's position was a difficult one. He had already had a rather less strong comment struck from the earlier Ultra by the First Sea Lord himself: Ned's reaction was inevitable. But OIC's whole tradition was to dispatch information to those at sea quickly and to leave any operational decision which needed to be taken to a separate signal sent by Operations or Trade Divisions or by the man on the spot. What would have been the effect if Ned had turned a Nelsonian blind eye and sent his signal? For him personally it would almost certainly have been disastrous, but Tovey and Hamilton might well have acted very differently from the way they soon did had they received, as they previously had done, this clear appreciation of OIC's, an appreciation which was, incidentally, firmly supported by Hinsley at BP. When OIC signalled Tovey at 1930/4 that the Enigma had at last been broken, he was some 375 miles away from PQ 17, steering south-west at economical speed. He at once reversed course to the north-east. Had he then increased to maximum speed and ordered the convoy also to reverse course, their combined speeds would have been at least 30 knots. By 0230/5, when Pound anticipated the *Tirpitz* would fall upon PQ 17, aircraft from *Victorious* would have been in a position to attack the German ship. That, after all, was what the Home Fleet was supposed to do. Unfortunately, the decision was immediately taken out of Tovey's hands. Tovey was, as usual, maintaining strict wireless silence: might he not deliberately have disclosed his position so as to warn *Tirpitz* off? Hamilton was just ahead and to the north east of the convoy. At 1809/4 he had signalled Tovey and the Admiralty that he intended to withdraw to the westward about 2200/4 once his destroyers had refuelled. He might have considered that Denning's comments would have given him the discretion to remain a little longer, despite the threat from the U-boats and his very small anti-U-boat destroyer screen. Such speculation is not altogether idle, because without it one cannot decide whether Pound had any alternative but to order the convoy to scatter.

We left Denning with his drafted Ultra in his hand waiting for Clayton's return. 'Then,' he tells us, 'Commander Rodger Winn ... came into my room to discuss an Ultra he was drafting concerning U-boat activities ... I showed Rodger my proposed Ultra and I was perturbed by his remarks, as he said he understood from the discussions which had just taken place in his room that *Tirpitz* was *already at sea* and that there was some talk of dispersing the convoy.'

It is of course, quite impossible to establish whether Pound or the other senior staff officers who had accompanied him to the Tracking Room did believe that there was positive evidence the *Tirpitz* had already sailed from Altenfjord. But Winn was an exceptionally astute man, a peacetime lawyer accustomed to judging the reactions of judges and juries. It seems to me highly probable that some if not all of those present had either misunderstood Denning's views or that they had already gained the impression that Pound had rejected them. Nor is there any precise record of what went on when the meeting assembled in the First Lord's room. This cannot have been before 2045 and it did not last more than three-quarters of an hour. Those present included, as well as Pound and Clayton, Brind, Eccles, Moore (Vice-Chief of Naval Staff) and Rear-Admiral E.L.S King (Assistant Chief of Staff – Trade): there may have been others. According to the only published reconstruction of the meeting Pound had already decided that, because of the U-boat threat, Hamilton's cruisers must get clear of the area quickly. Pound could never rid himself of the habits of a junior staff officer: like Oliver, the Chief of the War Staff in the First World War, he often drafted even quite unimportant signals himself. He did so on this occasion and the results were unfortunate. Within a few minutes of the opening of the meeting of the following signal, with time of origin 2111/4, had gone out to Hamilton, repeated to Tovey:

CRUISER FORCE WITHDRAW TO WESTWARD AT HIGH SPEED

It was given, unnecessarily, the highest priority, Most Immediate. Typically of Pound, brought up in the tradition of 'theirs not to reason why', it contained no explanation for the movement ordered even by reference to those U-boat warning signals already sent out by the Tracking Room. It was fatally liable to misinterpretation and, taken together with two further signals, misinterpreted it was by all its recipients.

The First Sea Lord is then said to have inquired of all those present what should be done with the convoy to avoid its destruction by the German surface force within the next few hours: he stated that in his opinion it should be dispersed. According to this account they all, with one exception, were against immediate dispersal. The exception was Moore, who pointed out that if the convoy was to be dispersed, this must be done very quickly owing to the limited sea room available. What Moore did not say was that, even if the manoeuvre was carried out immediately, no individual ship could, within the four or so hours thought to be available, be more than a maximum to twelve miles from one another. This was little better than remaining in convoy as a defence against a surface force but, as

Tovey had already said, sheer bloody murder from the point of view of U-boats and aircraft. Nobody seems to have called for a large-scale chart and plotted the cruising formation of the convoy and the effects of Moore's proposal. It was all too hurried. We do not know what Clayton said, if anything: whether he produced the decrypt, already nine hours old, which Denning had thrust at him as he hurried to the meeting, telling U-boats that there were no German surface ships in the area. Pound, as usual, listened to such debate as did take place with his eyes closed. Eccles thought he had fallen asleep, but Pound finally reached for a signal pad and wrote out the following signal addressed to C-in-C Home Fleet and Cs 1 and the Escorts of PQ 17:

> IMMEDIATE. OWING TO THREAT FROM SURFACE SHIPS CONVOY IS TO DISPERSE AND TO PROCEED TO RUSSIAN PORTS.

But an order to disperse means that the individual ships should leave their ordained formation in the convoy and proceed direct and at their own chosen speed direct to their destinations. Many, depending on their speed, would remain bunched together. This was not what Pound wanted: he intended them to 'scatter' so that each ship would proceed on pre-determined and diverging course, not necessarily on the most direct route. Moore pointed this out and quickly drafted an amendment. This was dispatched thirteen minutes later (2136/4) but with priority 'Most Immediate' in the hopes that it would reach the recipients at the same time as the previous instruction. It read:

> MY 2123/4. CONVOY IS TO SCATTER.

Whether Pound was right to come to a decision so quickly, without waiting for further information, and whether, even if his haste was justified, he could or could not have devised a different or better plan, is a matter of opinion. What is undeniable is that the three signals, sent in such quick succession, were just about as badly drafted as any in recent British naval history. The recipients had been provided ever since the convoy sailed with a frequent, full, if occasionally spasmodic, flow of information and appreciation about German movements and intentions. They had been aware from the outset that there was a threat from *Tirpitz*. Tovey and Hamilton, though not Broome, were aware of BP's difficulties in breaking the traffic for the 48 hours starting noon on 3 July. Then within the space of an hour and a half, they were told first that information might shortly be available, secondly that the cruisers were to withdraw at high speed, thirdly that the convoy was to disperse because of the threat from surface forces and, finally, with even higher priority, that the convoy was to scatter. They may have wondered why these signals were not accompanied by any factual Special Intelligence in an Ultra signal, but there was only one conclusion to be drawn – *Tirpitz* was at sea and her masts might appear over the horizon literally at any moment. Hamilton and his four cruisers and his meagre escort of three destroyers turned back to the west, determined to do or die in an attempt to keep the enemy away from the ships of the convoy. Broome, who at first could not believe the order he had received, finally came to the conclusion that there was very little he could do to protect the rapidly scattering merchantmen. He decided, and regretted his decision to his dying day, that he must take his destroyers, but not the rest of the escort craft, at maximum speed to reinforce Hamilton. He has been criticized by some but I believe his decision was a very courageous one: there was indeed little that he could do for his former charges. In the event 23 merchant ships and one rescue ship were sunk, not by *Tirpitz* but by the U-boats and aircraft against, which as independent ships, they had no effective defence.

It is easy with hindsight to suggest alternative instructions Pound might have given. I do, however, feel that nothing could have had worse results than the orders he did issue and that these instructions were issued without sufficient consideration and with unnecessary speed. Why was the convoy not ordered to reverse course and Tovey ordered to close the gap as quickly as possible? Why, if the cruisers could not be sacrificed, was the convoy not kept together to let Broome do what he could? He claims he could have hidden it in a nearby fog bank, and we know, again with hindsight, that, thanks to inhibiting orders from Hitler, German admirals were reluctant to risk their ships in the way that the British and Ameican officers were normally expected to do. Unfortunately, on this occasion, the British also had an 'All Highest' ashore, who thought he knew better than the men on the spot, although it must be pointed out that Pound took full responsibility because he felt it was unfair to leave the decision to so junior an officer as Broome.

Pound's fatal order to scatter is really the end of this story but, for the record, I must give Denning the last word.

I suppose that it would have been about 2130/4 that Clayton returned from his meeting and I learned that because of the U-boat threat, the cruiser covering force was being ordered to withdraw to the west-ward at high speed and that because of the possible threat of attack by surface forces on the convoy, Pound had decided to disperse it. Clayton was clearly perturbed and I showed him the Ultra I had prepared. After studying it, he expressed his full agreement. I therefore suggested that he might like to consider taking it up to Pound. After some hesitation he agreed. He was not away very long and said to me on his return 'Father says he's made his decision and is not going to change it now.' Eccles had come back with Clayton and I

seem to recall that we were joined by Brind ... I overheard Clayton
discussing my proposed Ultra with Eccles and presently they went
out together. Sometime later Clayton phoned me and asked if there
was any later information. There was nothing I could give him. I
presume I must then have gone to lie down on my camp bed in an
adjoining office for the next thing I remember was being awakened
by my watchkeeping officer who showed me a copy of the Ultra
message which he had been given by Clayton to send. It read:

1. IT IS NOT REPEAT NOT KNOWN IF GERMAN HEAVY FORCES
HAVE SAILED FROM ALTENFJORD, BUT THEY ARE UNLIKELY TO
HAVE DONE SO BEFORE 1200/4. 2. IT APPEARS THAT GERMANS
MAY BE IN SOME CONFUSION WHETHER A BATTLESHIP IS IN
COMPANY WITH CS 1. 3. GERMANS DO NOT REPEAT NOT APPEAR
TO BE AWARE OF THE POSITION OF C-IN-C HOME FLEET.

It was precisely the signal that Ned Denning had wished to send five
hours earlier. I do not know whether Clayton sent the signal on his own
authority, or that of Eccles or Brind, or whether Pound had finally agreed.
But it was now far too late: the die was cast, and the fate of the convoy
settled. Further decrypts during the early hours of 5 July disclosed that the
Germans were aware that Hamilton was proceeding at high speed away
from the convoy, and then that the Luftwaffe had finally located the Home
Fleet some 260 miles north west of Bear Island, steering south-west and
therefore in no position to give any assistance to PQ 17, by now some 500
miles to the eastward and scattered. *Tirpitz* was in no danger and Hitler's
restrictive precautions no longer applied. At 1052/5 the German task
force was ordered to put to sea. It did so and all the signs of this happening
were revealed to the British exactly as Denning had predicted. The sortie
was, of course, now unnecessary. Why risk *Tirpitz*? She and the rest of the
task force were recalled in the afternoon.

POSTSCRIPT: A PURELY PERSONAL VIEW

It is easy for all of us now, more than 40 years on, to sift slowly through the
relevant records, neatly arranged in proper chronological order, and ask
ourselves, with the additional benefit of hindsight, why clues were missed,
why appreciations were faulty, why incorrect decisions were taken. Those
who have never experienced it should not, however, forget the 'fog of war'
factor, the atmosphere of urgency, the pressures, the strain, day after day,
week after week, year after year, to try to solve the problems and complete
the jigsaw puzzle – or rather puzzles, because, in a world war, no single
problem can be considered in isolation: there are dozens of them, each
calling for swift and most of them for immediate action. The more senior

the individual concerned, the more likely it is that he will have to switch his
attention at any time during the day – or night – from one end of the world
to the other, from the land to the sea or to the air, from the tactical
situation to the long-term implications, from the possible reactions of the
enemy to the behaviour of allies. Nothing is simple, nothing is certain, but
everything is important. War is a young man's job and, in fact, requires
almost as much if not as much, physical fitness and mental alertness – you
cannot have one without the other – from those in headquarters as from
those in the firing line.

Pound was 65, suffering from painful osteo-arthritis and possibly also
from an incipient brain tumour. I believe that Churchill should have
replaced him at least by the end of 1941, just as he had done the 62-year-old
but more active Callaghan, Commander-in-Chief of the Grand Fleet on 2
August 1914. Of course one's views on age are relative – Winston was 40 in
1914 but 68 in 1942! One must also remember the quite impossible hours of
work imposed on Pound by the Prime Minister. But, despite his many
great qualities, Pound was, I am sure, past his peak by the time of PQ 17.
The trouble is that old men seldom recognize that it is time for them to give
way to younger men, and their subordinates, out of a mistaken sense of
loyalty, urge them to stay on even if they do.

Quite apart from age and health, and despite his great experience as a
staff officer, Pound did not, in my opinion, understand the intelligence
scene. Although the OIC was only a few minutes' walk from his own office
he very rarely visited it. He appreciated neither the strengths nor the
weaknesses of Special Intelligence: he required 'Yes' or 'No' answers to
his questions ('Can you assure me that *Tirpitz* is still in Altenfjord?') –
something which even the very best intelligence officers can seldom give.
In all intelligence problems there must always be some element of
uncertainty, always a last piece of the jigsaw puzzle which can only be
filled in by guesswork. It may be inspired intuition, but it should always be
based on a thorough background knowledge of the enemy and his way of
thinking. After three years of war it ought to have been obvious that
Denning, one of the most brilliant intelligence officers of either world
war, had this gift, but Pound could not bring himself to rely on so junior an
officer's opinion. Events proved Denning right and Pound wrong. Senior
officers, who have to take the final responsibility, must not only fully
understand the sources, methods and extent of their intelligence
organization, but also personally know their intelligence officers
sufficiently well to assess their capabilities and to rely on their assessments
or, if they are not satisfied, replace them.

It might be suggested that the First Sea Lord's responsibilities were so
great and far-ranging that he could not afford the time to make frequent
visits to the OIC. If one accepts this view – which I do not – he should have

delegated responsibility for control of current operations to his Vice-Chief of Naval Staff: but Pound was a centralizer, almost as incapable of delegation as Oliver was in the First World War. He could not rid himself of the habits of a junior staff officer, even to the extent of drafting signals in his own hand and to concerning himself with trivial details. This did not help him when it came to taking major decisions.

Denning reproached himself subsequently for not having put over his case more forcefully but, in the circumstances and given Pound's formidable and withdrawn personality, it is hard to see what more a paymaster-commander could have done to persuade an Admiral of the Fleet and First Sea Lord to change his mind, because I believe that Pound had virtually determined to scatter the convoy before it ever sailed and that his visits to the OIC were merely to confirm that there was no incontrovertible evidence available which would compel him to make a different decision. The evidence was not, and could not be, cast iron and some will no doubt agree with Sir Harry Hinsley, who, despite his complete support for Denning at the time, now feels that Pound had no alternative but to act as he did. Hinsley does not, however, examine whether there were any alternative courses of action open to Pound. I have indicated that I believe that some alternatives did exist, but only a high-level war game would prove whether they would have mitigated or even have prevented the disaster which, in fact, resulted from Pound's decisions.

With hindsight we can see that Hitler would never have permitted Raeder to send *Tirpitz* to sea had the Home Fleet and the 1st Cruiser Squadron not been withdrawn so that they could not even threaten the German Task Force on its return to Altenfjord or Narvik after its sortie. The considerable number of British, French and Russian submarines stationed off the North Cape might also have inflicted serious losses on the German surface ships. Surely, in any case, it was with these very possibilities in mind that all the British forces were deployed in the way in which they were: what was the point of these dispositions if the threat from *Tirpitz* was considered unanswerable? Here was a chance to destroy *Tirpitz*, which, like the *Goeben* in the First World War, exercised a quite disproportionate influence upon British maritime strategy.

I get the impression that both Pound and Raeder were bluffing. Both of them were 'big ship' men and neither of them was, *au fond*, prepared to risk their battleships. If so, Pound's nerve certainly cracked before Raeder had to make a decision, and for this, I believe, the very excellence of British Intelligence was partly responsible.

British Intelligence had certainly done a superb job, but, not for the first or the last time, it was unable to provide that last and vital clue to the intentions of the enemy – a glimpse into the mind of the All Highest on the other side. I do not think that sufficient attention had been given to the impact on Pound of Denham's signal from Stockholm. A Napoleon, a Nelson or a Wellington, having listened to his contemporary Denning, would probably have taken a less cautious and pessimistic view. I come back again to the questions: what was the Home Fleet's purpose? If Tovey's capital ships could not be risked, why had Pound, however reluctantly, acquiesced in Churchill's fatal decision to send *Prince of Wales* and *Repulse* to Singapore? No doubt their fate had also influenced Pound's thinking?

When PQ 18, the next convoy, sailed for North Russia in September 1942 it was not escorted by the Home Fleet but by a 'fighting' escort of sixteen Home Fleet destroyers and, equally important, one of the first escort carriers. Tovey remained, sensibly, at Scapa Flow to direct operations from there. The convoy fought its way through with the loss of thirteen of its original total of 40 ships but inflicted significant losses on German U-boats and aircraft. Hitler refused all requests to allow his precious surface ships to make a sortie. One must agree with the subsequent judgement of the German Naval Staff that the smaller success achieved on this occasion was 'due to the fact that the convoys [PQ 18 and QP 14] maintained their close formation in the face of heavy and persistent attacks'. On 31 December 1942 an attack on convoy JW 51B by a German pocket battleship and heavy cruiser was driven off by the bold tactics of Captain Sherbrooke's destroyers and Admiral Burnett's inferior couple of cruisers. Exactly a year later the *Scharnhorst* was sunk by Sir Bruce Fraser in the *Duke of York* in the final attempt by the Germans to use their surface ships offensively – a classic example of how centralized intelligence should be used without in any way taking away initiative from the man on the spot.

These three cases show that the British learned the lesson of PQ 17 and, indeed, despite the apparent odds against them, of the 813 ships which set out on the perilous voyage from Britain to North Russia between August 1941 and May 1945, 720 arrived safely at their destinations. All this we know with hindsight. Pound was faced with a political *Diktat* to which he could find no effective military solution. A greater admiral might have done so, but PQ 17 was only an isolated defeat which was soon redeemed. 'War is hell,' said General Sherman, and supreme commanders are compelled to take ruthless decisions. Perhaps one should not judge Dudley Pound too harshly.

NOTES

This paper was presented at the US Army War College Conference on 'Intelligence and Military Operations', Carlisle Barracks, Pennsylvania 22–25 April 1986. Copyright US Army College Foundation. The views expressed in this article are those of the author and do not reflect the official policy or position of the Department of Defense of the US Government.

1. Information derived from decrypts is now erroneously if conveniently, referred to as Ultra. The description used by the Royal Navy and to a lesser extent by the other Services in the Second World War was Special Intelligence. Ultra was merely a security classification and followed a practice introduced by the Admiralty in 1917 to deal with decrypts from its famous Room 40. The Director of Naval Intelligence had reintroduced this system in 1939 in anticipation that BP would sooner or later crack German ciphers. On 13 May 1940 he signalled the C-in-C Home Fleet that the previous security classification, Hydro, was to be replaced by a new one, Ultra, the first use of this now famous word that I have been able to trace. References here to Ultra mean signals containing information derived from decrypts to be despatched in one-time pad to authorised recipients.
2. *Lützow* had in fact hit an uncharted rock and was unfit to take part in the operation. This, however, was not known to the British until later, who therefore had to continue to reckon with her participation in one form or another.

SHORT BIBLIOGRAPHY

The destruction of Convoy PQ 17 bids fair to generate as much controversy and produce as many accounts of it as did the Battle of Jutland. A high proportion of books so far published deal with the experience of those who were involved at sea. There was much heroism and some cowardice, but, naturally (as with Jutland) little reference to the Intelligence factors which were, in my opinion, decisive. This study may seem rather cold-blooded. That is an Intelligence officer's lot. Curiously, although I was Winn's deputy in the Submarine Tracking Room at the time, I do not have any clear personal recollections of Pound's fateful visit to the OIC on the evening of 4 July. I can only conclude that I went off duty before he visited the Tracking Room.

I have not referred to German plans and action except in so far as they were known or deduced by the British at the time.

I cannot claim that I have done any fresh original research since the publication of the story of the OIC, *Very Special Intelligence*, in 1977, but quite a lot of published or easily accessible information is now available, of which I recommend the following:

British Intelligence in the Second World War, by F.H. Hinsley *et al.*, Vol.II (London: H.M.S.O., 1981). Excellent and authoritative short accounts of both PQ 12 and PQ 17, including, in Appendix II, a list of the Ultra signals sent to the Home Fleet between 30 June and 8 July. I am not sure whether all the purely U-boat signals sent by the Submarine Tracking Room (as opposed to the Ultras sent by Denning) are included. Hinsley's judgement is that, even if Pound had delayed ordering the convoy to scatter until there was more positive evidence the *Tirpitz* was about to sail (i.e. at 1517/5), he would then have had to do so. I am not sure that I agree. The alternatives are not examined.

The War at Sea, Vol.II by S.W. Roskill (London: H.M.S.O., 1957). Roskill saw, but was then not permitted to refer explicitly to, at least some Ultras. His account is, therefore, necessarily muted so far as Intelligence is concerned, but is otherwise all that one would expect from this great naval historian.

The Destruction of Convoy PQ 17 by David Irving (London: Cassell, 1968; revised ed. William Kimber, 1980). First published by Cassell & Co. in 1968, this book resulted in a successful and very expensive libel action brought by Broome against the author and publishers. It was, moreover, written without any access to or precise knowledge of Special Intelligence. A second edition, published by William Kimber in 1980, has been revised to take account of these failings. Like all Irving's books, it is the result of the most painstaking research and claims to be the result of interviews with many participants now dead. I have relied on it for the account of Pound's staff meeting on the evening of 4 July, the only published account of which I am aware. It rings true to me, but I am bound to issue the caveat that, in acknowledging help from many individuals, including myself, Irving names one or two who I know were either unwilling or unable to give him information. Nevertheless, this is a most valuable source.

Convoy is to Scatter by Jack Broome (London, 1972). A personal account by the commander of the close escort. It includes many signals made during the course of the operation, although not any Ultras. It is very anti-Pound, but brings out clearly the reactions of those at the 'sharp end'.

Room 39 by Donald McLachlan (London, 1968), McLachlan served in NID (although not in OIC) and was subsequently Deputy Editor of the *Daily Telegraph* and Editor of the *Sunday Telegraph*. He was able to talk to many of the participants, particularly those in the Intelligence Division and was given access to some records then secret, but was forbidden to make any reference to Special Intelligence. He therefore had the difficult task of writing *Hamlet* without once referring to the principal character. Not to be relied on implicitly for detail, but excellent for atmosphere.

PQ 17 Vice-Admiral Sir Norman Denning. Typescript, 1979, Churchill College Archives, Cambridge. Copy in my possession. My old friend and boss in OIC from 1940 until the end of 1941 was always most reluctant to record his wartime experience. However, about 1978, I persuaded him to attempt to set out his recollections of his innvolvement in PQ 17. He produced a number of drafts which he sent to me for comment, but sadly died suddenly, in 1979, just as he had completed what I believe would have been the penultimate version. The quotations in this paper are from that draft which, with the permission of his brother, Lord Denning, and with the help of Stephen Roskill, I passed to Hinsley, who made good use of them in his official history. Old men's memories are notoriously fallible, but Ned was a great intelligence officer and well aware of this danger. I believe that his account forms an accurate record of the events which had taken place 36 years previously.

I am grateful to Lord Denning for permission to quote from his brother's account and to Her Majesty's Stationery Office for permission to reproduce the map from S. W. Roskill's *War at Sea*.

Ultra Intelligence and General Douglas MacArthur's Leap to Hollandia, January–April 1944

EDWARD J. DREA

During the past decade, historians and former signals intelligence practitioners have focused much attention on the role of Ultra intelligence in operations during the Second World War. The European and Mediterranean theaters have received extensive treatment as have naval operations in the Atlantic – particularly the U-Boat War – and the Pacific. Historians, however, have offered little critical analysis of Ultra's influence on the campaigns of General Douglas MacArthur, especially the major role it played in MacArthur's operations along the northern New Guinea coastline in early 1944.

As the United States government continues to open formerly classified compendia of Second World War intelligence documents to the historical community, a critical examination of Ultra in the Pacific land campaigns is long overdue. This is all the more important because without a proper understanding of Ultra and its role in MacArthur's leap to Hollandia on 22 April 1944 one loses perspective on the contributions of signals intelligence to the operational level of warfare.

Before discussing those contributions, a brief description of military developments in the southwest Pacific to 1944 will set the operational context in which to evaluate Ultra's importance to MacArthur's campaigns. Japan's war with Great Britain and the United States opened in December 1941 with a series of Japanese triumphs culminating in the capitulation of the great British base at Singapore on 15 February 1942. With the American Pacific fleet settled in the sand of Pearl Harbor, the British naval deterrent sunk, and the American and Filipino defenders of the Philippines bottled up on Bataan, the Rising Sun extended throughout the Pacific. In early February 1942, as a link in their long-range defensive chain, the Japanese occupied New Britain with its strategic anchorage at Rabaul and the next month seized Lae and Salamaua, Northeast New Guinea and moved into the Solomon Island chain in order to protet the southern approaches to Rabaul. The first stage of Japanese operations ended an unparallelled success (See Map 1).

The second stage, though, proved disastrous. In May 1942 the Battle of the Coral Sea spelled the end of Japanese ambitions to seize Port Moresby, Papua New Guinea, by sea and the following month the naval battle of Midway blunted Japanese offensive naval power. Nevertheless, the Japanese moved ahead with plans to attack Port Moresby overland, and in July 1942 landed troops on the north coast in the Buna-Gona region.

In the meantime, General Douglas MacArthur had escaped from the Philippines and arrived to a hero's welcome in Australia where, on 18 April 1942, he established the Southwest Pacific Area Theater (SWPA). MacArthur was slow to react to the Japanese land threat to Port Moresby, and only after a protracted campaign of attrition, in which the Australians carried most of the burden, did the Allies eject the Japanese from Buna in January 1943. During these operations, however, the Japanese had developed air bases and supply depots along the northern New Guinea coast, built Rabaul into a major naval base, and still fought the Allies for control of Guadalcanal in the Solomons.

In March 1943, following the Japanese withdrawal from Guadalcanal, Imperial General Headquarters ordered Japanese forces in the Rabaul–New Guinea–Solomon area to hold their positions at all costs as Japan entered the third stage of its Pacific war. The next several months witnessed the intensification of the Allied effort to isolate Rabaul by land, sea, and air against the tenacious Japanese defenders.

American landings on New Georgia and New Britain as well as Australian–American efforts on New Guinea in 1943 did produce hard-won gains but with significant Allied casualties and at a seemingly slow pace. Put differently, after grinding battles of attrition on the ground, in the air and at sea, it had taken the Allies 16 months to recapture about one third of New Guinea from the Japanese. One factor in MacArthur's hitherto deliberate tempo of operations was SWPA's uncertainty about the exact Japanese dispositions and plans because, throughout this early period, Imperial Japanese Army codes, unlike their counterparts in the Imperial Navy, remained generally impenetrable to Allied decryption efforts.

My contention in this analysis is that signal intelligence played a paramount role in MacArthur's decision to advance his operational timetable and to implement extended leapfrog maneuvers deep into the enemy's rear areas. Signal intelligence provided MacArthur with an accurate knowledge of Japanese dispositions and defensive strategies, and allowed him to craft his operational plans to take greatest advantage of Japanese weakness. He did this throughout all phases of his Hollandia operation by cutting the Japanese convoy routes, by destroying Japanese air power, and finally by enveloping Japanese ground forces. This Ultra dimension affords the opportunity both to reassess MacArthur's

MAP 1
JAPANESE-CONTROLLED AREA, MARCH 1944

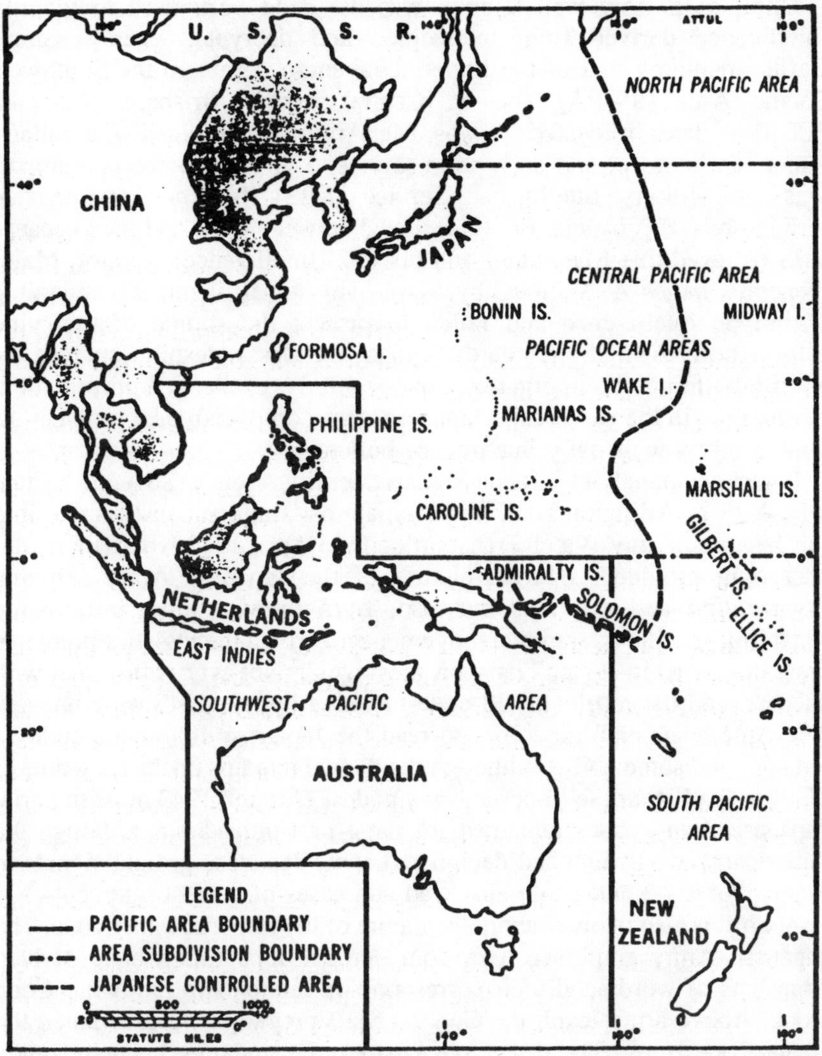

Source: E. Drea, 'Defending the Driniumor: Covering Force Operations in New Guinea, 1944', Leavenworth Paper No. 9 (US Army Command and General Staff College, 1984).

campaigns in the southwest Pacific and to glean fresh insights into
the relationship between the conduct of large unit operations and
intelligence.

Ultra, as is now well known, was the code-word used to identify
intelligence derived from intercepted and decrypted enemy signals
traffic, including that of the Imperial Japanese Army. In the Southwest
Pacific Area (SWPA) Theater, Central Bureau Brisbane, Australia
(CBB) – later relocated – was MacArthur's combined Australian–
American intercept and decryption service. The Washington counterpart
was the Military Intelligence Service (MIS) then headquartered at
Arlington Hall, Virginia. Friction existed between CBB and MIS because
MIS believed that MacArthur and his G-2 (Intelligence) director, Major
General Charles A. Willoughby, were over-casual, if not lax, regarding
Ultra-type intelligence and failed to protect the source of this vital
information to MIS standards. None the less, despite charges of
empire-building, both organizations regularly exchanged information,
particularly in the case of the Japanese Army cryptanalytical problem, as
evidenced by their daily intelligence bulletins.[1]

In fact personnel of CCB and Signals Security Agency (SSA) co-located
with MIS at Arlington Hall, Virginia, almost simultaneously broke into
the Japanese Army Water Transport code in April 1943 which thereafter
'not only provided a broad picture of the Japanese Army shipping
organization and activities but also, from time to time, information
regarding specific operational movements of which the logistics problems
were discussed in Water Transport messages'.[2] Not every effort met with
success, and the results of US code-breaking by late 1943 were uneven.
The Americans had the ability to read the Japanese diplomatic codes –
(Magic) and some ability, although the degree remains unclear, by the US
Navy to read Japanese Imperial Navy codes. Through 1943 most Imperial
Japanese Army codes remained for large part unreadable, although the
Americans and British had deciphered some Japanese ground signals in
September 1943 and could also read addresses of current intercepts.[3]

A word is also in order about the nature of the Imperial Army code. The
Japanese Army employed a random number substitution code derived
from lists of words and their corresponding numbers in the Army Code
Book. Above army level, the General Staff prepared and distributed the
Army Code Book. The respective Japanese headquarters' echelons then
enciphered this number from the code book by adding corresponding
numbers taken from a random numerical register, what SSA called the
key book.

Regimental and lower echelons as well as air ground signals used
a three-digit system while higher echelons had a four-digit one. There
were 'common' and 'special' higher echelon codes, the former divided

between division and army level and the latter for use by air force, communications, shipping, military police, and other specialized units. A special calculator table offered another form of cipher wherein numerical substitution, i.e., 0 = 3, altered the basic encoding before the addition of the random register numeral. There were about 250 variations of the 'common' code alone in 1941 and nearly 400 by 1945. Code books were valid for one year; random numerical registers for one to three months; and special calculator tables for 5–30 days. Tokyo signalled field commands in which code book and key register or conversion table were in effect or passed rules of encipherment. A signal officer at Eighteenth Japanese Army in New Guinea enciphered a message by selecting from the Army Code Book the appropriate four-digit numeral corresponding to the word he wanted to transmit and then adding to that basic numeral another four-digit number from a register of random numbers. To complicate attempts to penetrate the cipher, this addition did not include carrying of tens, so $3219 + 6982 = 9001$. He then used a substitution table to encipher 9001 as 4758, thereby completing a double encipherment.[4]

Then, in late January 1944, the capture of the main Japanese Army codes and ciphers 'brought a sudden embarrassment of riches to Arlington Hall, and early in February the Japanese section began to be deluged with a daily flow of thousands of readable Japanese Army messages'.[5] The exact provenance of this seizure of the Japanese Army codes remains unclear. According to one account, US troops landing on the northern New Guinea coast in January 1944 discovered a 'trunkful of Japanese Army codebooks, buried in the sand along the beach'. More recent versions credit the seizure of the code books from a sinking Japanese submarine off New Guinea in early 1944. In any event, a compromised code book clearly provided the major crib the Allies needed to break into the Imperial Army codes.[6]

Allied codebreakers made available thousands of readable Japanese signals. Since 'there were never enough' competent Japanese translators,[7] I determined to assemble available significant Japanese Army signals for the period and to compare the original Japanese language messages with the resulting English language translations that appeared in the Ultra classified Special Intelligence Bulletin (SIB) issued by SWPA in order to evaluate the accuracy of the translated information. Substandard translations naturally would have diminished the overall value of the intelligence. Suffice it to say that the translated decryptions are of the highest quality and accurately state the contents of the decrypted Japanese signal.

With that background, I contend that from late January until 22 April 1944 – the date of the Hollandia landing – General MacArthur based his operations along the north New Guinea coast on his Ultra-derived knowledge of the Japanese dispositions and intentions. With the veil shrouding the dispositions of Eighteenth Army units in New Guinea pulled away, MacArthur and his staff were privy not only to enemy order of battle information but also to the very intentions of Lieutenant General Adachi Hatazo, commander of that army. Exact casual relationships in MacArthur's command decision-making process may never be clear because security considerations prohibited transcripts of discussions based on signal intelligence sources. None the less, based on circumstantial evidence and limited direct documentation, it seems apparent that signal intelligence derived knowledge of his opponent significantly influenced MacArthur's strategic and operational planning.

The 15 January SIB reported Eighteenth Army's estimate of the situation following the 2 January 1944 Allied landing at Saidor and detailed Japanese counter-measures that included future dispositions of Japanese 20th and 41st Infantry divisions. Of special interest to SWPA planners was the importance Eighteenth Army placed on the defense of the Madang and Hansa Bay area, the critical terrain for General Adachi.[8]

Eighth Area Army, headquartered at Rabaul, New Britain, which controlled Eighteenth Army until March 1944, also unknowingly provided a treasure trove of signal intelligence for SWPA. A 19 January 1944 Eighth Area Army message to Operations Division, General Staff, Tokyo revealed in great length and exactitude Japanese plans to defend the Madang–Hansa Bay area and urged Imperial General Headquarters (IGHQ) in Tokyo to hurry reinforcements to those locations for the purpose of strengthening defenses against an anticipated Allied attack.[9] (See Map 2).

MacArthur's decision to seize the Admiralty Islands on 29 February 1944, one month ahead of his originally scheduled invasion date, was, in part, based on his knowledge that Japanese air and sea arms were withdrawing from the area and there was little to fear from them. The Admiralty operation, in turn, allowed him to accelerate his drive up the New Guinea coast and provided him with airbases in the Admiralties from which to support his operations along that coast. The acquisition of those forward bases and Ultra revelations probably led MacArthur to cancel his proposed Hansa Bay landings in favor of a direct jump to Hollandia.[10]

In fact, MacArthur's Reno series of operations plans originally called for an invasion of the Hansa Bay area. G-2 intelligence reports for February, based in the main on Ultra, revealed that the Japanese were reinforcing that very area in anticipation of future Allied landings there. Willoughby, based on the unfolding intelligence picture, favored a leap to Hollandia as did Brigadier General Bonner Fellers, Planning Section Chief, G-3. Fellers' superior, Major General Stephen J. Chamberlin,

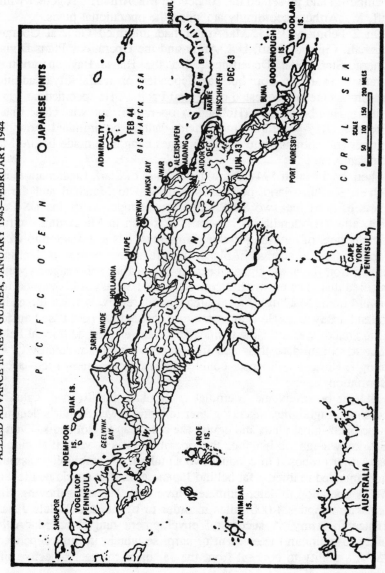

MAP 2

ALLIED ADVANCE IN NEW GUINEA, JANUARY 1943–FEBRUARY 1944

○ JAPANESE UNITS

Source: As for Map 1.

however, termed it a 'wild scheme'. Nevertheless, Fellers circumvented Chamberlin and presented the concept to MacArthur.[11] Together with his staff, MacArthur accordingly amended the operational plans.

On 2 February 1944, MacArthur had informed General George C. Marshall, Chief of Staff, U.S. Army and the Operations Plans Division, General Staff, War Department, that the Hansa Bay operation was tentatively set for 26 April but was 'dependent on availability of additional amphibious means requested of Central Pacific'. He specified no date for a future Humboldt Bay (Hollandia) operation, but was clear that the 'Geelvink Bay-Vogelkop movement cannot be initiated prior to 1 October and entrance into the Philippines cannot be made before March next year'.[12]

Then, on 5 March 1944, through his Chief of Staff, Lieutenant-General Richard K. Sutherland, he proposed instead to Marshall and the Joint Chiefs of Staff that two SWPA divisions, supported by the US Pacific Fleet, attack Hollandia on 15 April, as a step in MacArthur's ultimate strategic goal of returning to the Philippines. His justification to General Marshall for the change in plans, in part, seems based on intelligence derived from Japanese signals because MacArthur's message to Marshall specified that 'The enemy has concentrated the mass of his ground forces forward in the Madang–Wewak area leaving relatively weak forces in the Hollandia Bay area. He is attempting to concentrate land based air forces in the area of western New Guinea and is developing additional fields in order to consolidate this area into a bulwark of air defense'.[13] Only through Ultra intelligence could MacArthur possess such accurate information.

The daily, mundane, cumulative signals intelligence data, with occasional highlights, taken together influenced MacArthur's decision to revise his original plans and devise the bold leap to Hollandia. Even with such knowledge of his foe, the operation was a very high-risk one. MacArthur proposed to conduct two simultaneous amphibious assaults – later amended to three – far behind Japanese lines. It would be the largest SWPA operation to date, ultimately involving 217 ships moving 80,000 men with supplies 1,000 miles in order to bypass and isolate Japanese Eighteenth Army. A successful envelopment hinged on MacArthur's ability to maintain the element of surprise which, in turn, depended on SWPA's ability to conceal from the Japanese the real objective of the Allies.

The manner in which MacArthur and his staff tailored their operations to accomplish the strategy and the role of Ultra in such planning encompassed sea, air and land phases of combat. I will address each phase separately, although it must be borne in mind that naval, air and ground campaigns proceeded simultaneously, competing for limited resources in

MacArthur's orchestration of joint and combined operations. Let us begin with the naval operations.

Yet another Eighth Area Army message, this one of 1 February and issued by SWPA on 5 February, detailed naval convoy traffic and resupply schedules from Palau, Caroline Islands to Rabaul, New Britain and Wewak, New Guinea. This signal, from Eighth Area Army Chief of Staff to Eighteenth Army, provided a list of supplies, cargo, personnel reinforcements, convoy size, escort force, and, most significant, arrival time for five convoys scheduled for Wewak from early February to early March.[14] According to an official post-war assessment of Ultra in the Pacific, 'The messages were issued in sufficient time for our action'.[15]

That flat statement concealed the fate of at least twelve Japanese freighters sunk en route to resupply Wewak between 29 February and 24 March 1944 by Allied air or naval action.[16] Eighth Area Army's message sealed the fates of the respective convoys and illustrates the critical role of Ultra intelligence in anti-convoy operations.

On 14/15 February Wewak Convoy Number 19, four ships plus escorts arrived and unloaded at, and departed from, Wewak as scheduled without incident, probably because inclement weather prevented Allied interception. Two weeks later, however, the next convoy in this series suffered serious losses. Despite three naval escorts and 30 to 80 fighter aircraft providing air cover, the four ships of Wewak Convoy Number 20 fell prey to the US submarine *Gato* that torpedoed and sank the transport *Daigen maru* Number 3 on 26 February with the loss of 404 reinforcements of the 66th Infantry Regiment, 51st Division. The Eighth Area Army signal relaying this disaster did note that the regimental colors were safe.[17]

The remaining three transports arrived safely at Wewak on 29 February and departed at 0100 on 1 March for Hollandia. After discharging aviation fuel and personnel reinforcements at Hollandia the convoy headed back to Palau, but may have lost a second transport to air action during its return voyage.[18]

On 29 February Hollandia Convoy Number Six carrying the Sixth South Seas Detachment left Palau for Hollandia as previously announced. Alerted by Ultra, the US submarine *Peto* attacked the convoy and sank the 4,368 ton passenger cargo ship *Kayo maru*, resulting in the deaths of 45 Japanese soldiers including the detachment commander Colonel Matsuo Yutaro.[19] The remaining 240 troops of the convoy reached Hollandia on 4 March, a fact noted by SWPA in its 14 March SIB. Ironically the same bulletin commented that part of the Sixth South Seas Detachment had reached Hollandia earlier on 20 February and the ill-fated Colonel Matsuo had probably assumed command of the garrison at that time.[20]

On the night of 15 March, SWPA night air patrols, again forewarned

from Ultra sources, attacked a barge convoy moving from Hollandia to
Wewak and sank two 1,000-ton vessels and drove another one aground.[21]
The worst disaster, however, befell Wewak Convoy Number 21 on the
night of 18–19 March. Based on an intercept of 9 March providing revised
convoy schedules, SSA had alerted MIS which, in turn, by 17 March, had
notified SWPA and the US Navy of the schedule of the impending four-
ship convoy. Two B-24s of the 63rd Squadron, 43rd Bombardment
Group, equipped with a new radar bombsight, first discovered the convoy
at 0230, 60 miles northwest of Hollandia. They attacked and sank
one transport, probably the *Yakumo maru*. The remaining three ships,
including two Submarine Chasers (Auxiliary) serving as escort vessels,
stood by rescuing survivors.

This fixed their location the following morning when US heavy
bombers and at least 80 fighter bombers attacked the remainder of the
convoy and sank all the ships. Japanese intercepts available by 28 March
acknowledged the loss of four ships whose 'crews and all aboard were
lost'.[22] Among other losses when these freighters were sunk was a 100-man
air surveillance unit together with its radar equipment that the Japanese
intended to use to cover the south and south eastern approaches to the
major Japanese base of Hollandia. Their presence was sorely missed just
two weeks later when massive Allied air raids against Hollandia destroyed
Japanese air power in eastern New Guinea. More important, though,
IGHQ ordered the suspension of large ship convoys to Wewak on 24
March when it signalled Eighth Area Army, 'In view of the present
successively occurring losses of Wewak convoys we regret to say that it has
been decided to stop for a short time the transportation by large type ships
from Palau to Wewak'.[23]

The rash of sinkings, though, did not lead the Japanese to suspect that
the Americans had compromised Japanese codes. US Fifth Air Force
conducted routine night patrols over Hollandia and Wewak that
accustomed the Japanese to the presence of American aircraft. Furthermore, reconnaissance aircraft appeared conspicuously in the sectors
where signal intelligence had alerted the Allies to the probable presence
of Japanese convoys. The resulting aerial attacks led the Japanese to
conclude that the reconnaissance plane had called for the air strikes.[24] As
for submarine attacks, at this stage of the war, only about one in four
Japanese merchantmen reported sighting an enemy submarine. Statistic-
ally, at least, the Japanese could attribute the sinkings by submarine
attack to ill fortune.

The Japanese also believed that Allied scouting patrols sent by sub-
marine reported on convoy arrivals and departures.[25] Indeed the Allied
Intelligence Bureau constantly had small teams of agents active behind
Japanese lines and their presence probably fueled Japanese estimates of

their effectiveness. In any case, the net result of such prohibitive losses left Tokyo no alternative but to cancel the convoy runs to Wewak, although this deprived Eighteenth Army of its major source of resupply. The foreknowledge of Japanese convoy schedules that Ultra provided had allowed the Allies to intercept and sink Japanese transports thereby isolating Eighteenth Army from resupply by sea.

Ultra played an equally important role in the struggle for air superiority over the north New Guinea coast. On 30 September 1943, IGHQ had ordered the strengthening of defenses in Western New Guinea, the Marianas and Carolines in preparation for forthcoming Allied offensives. In particular, desperately needed aircraft and pilot replacements were to augment a series of 35 new airfields planned for Western New Guinea. Japanese doctrine called for three echelons of airfields, a main airfield, an advanced field, and a rear field for dispersal in case of attack, thus the large number of required new airfields. The over-ambitious projection of 35 airdromes in New Guinea proved impossible to achieve because of a combination of lack of heavy construction equipment, shipping losses, and Allied air raids. Thus the Japanese had to concentrate their airpower at Hollandia. The evolution of the Hollandia base illustrates in microcosm the problems the Japanese faced as they tried to rebuild their air strength in New Guinea.[26]

In April 1943 IGHQ transferred Hollandia from Southern Army (Singapore, Malaya) to Eighth Area Army (Rabaul) as a rear area base. From June to November the Japanese built two airstrips at Hollandia and constructed a road from the bay to the airfields. The Japanese also completed work on a third runway in January 1944, but the following month they suspended construction of two additional strips due to lack of material and equipment. Nevertheless, Hollandia served not only as a base for Headquarters Fourth Air Army, but also had developed into the major resupply base for Eighteenth Army operations in eastern New Guinea.[27]

In spite of the battles of attrition in eastern New Guinea in 1943, delays in the airfield construction program, and shortfalls in aircraft production, IGHQ remained determined to replace the losses in first line air units, and, lacking alternatives, ordered the transfer of existing combat air units to concentrate on the Hollandia area. On 9 February SWPA's Special Intelligence Bulletin noted these Japanese air reinforcements staging from Halmahera to Hollandia. Three days later SWPA announced that the Japanese had scheduled five new air regiments for Hollandia including 81 bombers and 80 fighters to add to the existing 151 bombers and 205 fighters in New Guinea. By 16 February 1944, MIS picked up the intelligence and reported that the realignment of Japanese Army Air Forces in New Guinea was under way as the 8th Air Brigade (33rd, 77th and 60th Air regiments) was scheduled to arrive Hollandia on 15 February. MIS also expected two more fighter regiments from the Philippines to be subordinated to 8th Air Brigade. The mission of these units was to support the defense of Hansa Bay from the Hollandia bases.[28]

By 18 February, the Allies knew that approximately 150 Japanese aircraft had augmented the fewer than 100 airplanes of Fourth Air Army. In particular they learned that 8th Air Brigade was headquartered at Hollandia and two of its regiments, the 33rd and 75th, had a total of 56 operational aircraft. On 23 February SWPA reported that the five air regiments originally identified in signals intercepts as reinforcements eleven days earlier had now arrived at Hollandia via Wakde and Halmahera.[29] Furthermore, on 28 February, responding to an inquiry of 23 February, General Willoughby signalled the War Department that 'recent ultra evidence of Japanese aircraft' in New Guinea identified at least 101 aircraft at Hollandia (33rd, 77th and 75th Air regiments) as well as 34th and 61st Air regiments with another 74 aircraft.[30] On 29 February 1944 SWPA reported that aerial photo reconnaissance of 26 February has confirmed the presence of the Japanese aircraft at Hollandia.[31]

Despite Allied reconnaissance flights, however, the Japanese believed themselves secure at Hollandia because of its distance from Allied fighter bases. Hollandia lay within range of Allied heavy bombers, but beyond the range of the Allied fighters that had to escort the bombers to Hollandia, for the Japanese correctly judged an unescorted heavy bomber attack as suicidal. For their part, the Japanese planned to overcome distance by staging from forward bases like Tadji (Aitape) or Wewak thereby both employing their fighters, but, at the same time, preserving the bulk of their precious aircraft well out of range of land-based Allied fighters. Unknown to the Japanese, however, SWPA had already identified Hollandia as a lucrative target because 'The forced canalization of ... air reserves from the west through Hollandia would probably result in a reckless and undispersed concentration of air strength taxing to the utmost the facilities of the four known Hollandia–Wakde airdromes'. On 22 March SWPA called attention to another 22 Japanese aircraft reinforcing Hollandia and remarked on 'the preeminence of Hollandia in the sphere of enemy air operations for New Guinea'.[32]

Another reason for the Japanese false sense of security was that to date MacArthur had not had carrier aircraft available to support his amphibious operations, so the Japanese failed to consider the possibility of carrier-based airstrikes against their rear bases. Consequently, they believed that, as in the past, MacArthur would have to seize forward air bases somewhere between Madang and Aitape in preparation for a later invasion of Hollandia. MacArthur acknowledged the apparent validity of the Japanese estimate of the situation as he explained that, without carrier support, the limit of air protection for land operations 'was the possible radius of operation of our fighter planes ... from the actual location of our ground air bases. This required the seizing or construction of such new bases at each forward movement'.[33]

The Japanese were also confident that they could detect any Allied bombers early enough to intercept the unescorted formations before they could seriously damage the rear bases. Detection, though, depended on a reliable early warning system and accurate intelligence estimates of Allied capabilities. The Japanese were deficient in both areas. Although the Japanese had signal intercept stations at Wewak and Hansa respectively as well as coastwatchers scattered along the north shore, they had no central air intelligence unit at Hollandia to analyse or synthesize the assembled data from field units.[34] The radar early warning unit had, of course, gone to the bottom with Wewak Convoy Number 21.

Nevertheless, the very presence of such large numbers of Japanese land-based aircraft within striking distance of his carriers was a source of much concern to Admiral Chester W. Nimitz, Commander in Chief, Central Pacific Area, who had agreed to provide carrier air support for MacArthur's multiple amphibious landings at Hollandia and Aitape. At a conference on 25 March in Brisbane, Australia, MacArthur's air chieftain, Lieutenant General George Kenney, Commander, Allied Air Forces, SWPA and Fifth Air Force, promised Nimitz 'to have them rubbed out by 5 April'. As Kenney knew the location, disposition, and operational strength of Japanese Fourth Air Army, this was not an idle boast.[35]

In February Kenney had received new P-38s modified with wing tanks to extend their range, and he also converted P-38s already in the theater to equip them with wing tanks. To deceive the Japanese at Hollandia into believing they were safely beyond his fighters' range, he ordered these modified aircraft to fly no missions beyond existing ranges, thereby giving the Japanese no indication of their improved range.[36] He also secretly staged his heavy aircraft in forward bases undetected by the Japanese. In sum, his Ultra-based knowledge of the major concentration of enemy air strength allowed Kenney to plan his operation secure in the knowledge that the lucrative, and unsuspecting, Japanese air bases awaited him.

By late March Kenney knew that, by basing the bulk of their air strength in illusory safety at Hollandia, the Japanese probably had about 180 fighters and 130 bombers available in the New Guinea theater to combat Allied offensives. On the day of the first major Allied air strike against Hollandia, 30 March, SWPA reported that Fourth Air Army had 113 aircraft 'ready for action', including 47 fighters.[37]

That day, again using a photo reconnaissance aircraft both to confirm the presence of the Japanese air units at Hollandia and to mask his source

of intelligence, Kenney attacked the Japanese base at Hollandia with 60
B-24s escorted by 80 P-38s with the extended range with tanks. He
continued the attacks on 31 March and, following a stand-down for
weather, again on 3 April when 63 B-24s plus 171 B-25s and A-20s,
escorted by 76 long-range P-38s, demolished what was left of Japanese air
strength at Hollandia.

The initial flight profiles along the north coast intentionally concealed
the exact American target. At 0845 on 30 March, Hollandia scrambled 40
fighters to intercept a large formation of enemy aircraft reported by
Wewak. Ten minutes later Aitape signalled Hollandia that the enemy
aircraft had turned southeast, i.e., toward Allied bases, after making an
attack. Hollandia then recalled its aircraft for refuelling, but the
American warplanes swung back westward. Thus Kenney's main force
surprised the Japanese as Allied aircraft formations appeared 'like clouds'
over the mountains approaching Hollandia's airdromes from the
south and southeast, the area the Japanese early warning system left
uncovered.[38]

Kenney's raids destroyed most of the 131 operational Japanese aircraft
at Hollandia on the ground and smashed forever any Japanese ambitions
to regain aerial superiority in New Guinea skies. Once again Ultra
intelligence had allowed an Allied commander the flexibility, born of
awareness of his opponent's order of battle, to tailor his operational plans
to deliver the most damaging attack at the time the enemy was most
vulnerable. By early April then MacArthur's forces had isolated Japanese
Eighteenth Army by sea and by air. The ground envelopment awaited
completion as the culmination of the Hollandia operation.

Ultra provided MacArthur and his SWPA staff with a comprehensive
portrait of Japanese Eighteenth Army deployments from mid-January
1944 through the Hollandia landings and beyond. Eighteenth Army radio
message traffic proved so lucrative a source of information not only about
Japanese plans for New Guinea but also for other theaters that in June
1944 General Marshall sent the following somewhat contradictory
request to General MacArthur:

> So long as 18th Jap Army remains physically isolated and in radio
> communication with other Jap units it will continue to afford US
> valuable source of cryptoanalytic assistance. To the extent that it will
> not interfere with your present operations, it is highly desirable that
> this situation be preserved and fully exploited. Will advise when this
> advantage to us ceases.[39]

The following examples of Ultra intelligence available to MacArthur
highlight the significant intercepts and demonstrate the value Marshall
attached to their preservation. They represent only a handful of

the hundreds of other decrypted Japanese signals that taken together provided a running commentary on the evolution of Japanese preparations for the defense of New Guinea.

On 4 February SWPA reported a 19 January radio from Eighth Area Army to Tokyo detailing its counter-measures against Allied offensives and recommendations for strenghthening defenses in the Admiralties, Madang-Hansa, Wewak, and Hollandia sectors. The same day an Eighteenth Army message confirmed for SWPA the 'enemy intention to cling to Madang. It also tends to fix his defensive position'. Subsequent intercepts available during February related that the Japanese 41st Division experienced great difficulty in moving into position because of the enemy air raids and heavy rain (6 February); that the 20th and 41st divisions were each to receive 2,000 replacements and, in February, the 51st Division 4,500 replacements (12 February); that the projected reorganized strength of the 51st Division was about 10,000 men and the 20th Division around 15,000 (19 February); and that the mission of the 51st Division probably was the defense of Wewak (21 February). On 22 February, based on further analysis, SWPA was able to subdivide the strengths of the 51st and 20th divisions according to those engaged with the enemy, those available at Wewak, and those *en route* from Japan. Eavesdropping electronically on Japanese signals also provided SWPA with the strength of reinforcements arriving for Wewak and Hollandia in late February and Japanese troop requisitions for March.[40]

IGHQ reacted to MacArthur's seizure of the Admiralties in early March 1944 by placing Eighteenth Army under operational control of Second Area Army, headquartered at Davao, Mindanao, Philippine Islands. Intercepts alerted the Allies to this shift and to the subordination of Fourth Air Army to Davao as well.[41] The evolution of Eighteenth Army planning as General Adachi adjusted to his isolation from Rabaul caused by the loss of the Admiralties and his new command relationships passed into SWPA's hands via signals intercepts. Regimental and division level deployments such as the realignment of the 78th Infantry Regiment from defense forward of Madang to its parent 20th Division at Hansa Bay also appeared in intercepted traffic. SWPA learned of Eighteenth Army Headquarters move to Wewak and relocation of its forward combat command posts to Hansa Bay from where 'surprise operations will be directed'.[42]

By 20 March SWPA knew that 41st Division had been diverted to Madang in order to prepare to counter-attack and destroy an Allied landing 'at any time or place'. The composition of the 5,000 man unit also appeared in signal traffic as did its mission, to hold the Madang area as an 'independent fortress' thereby preventing its use by the Allies as long as possible. Aside from the valuable intelligence, analysis of the continual shifting of Eighteenth Army units indicated to SWPA that it 'will be in a transitory, unprepared state during March and probably most of April'.[43] Furthermore, SWPA also knew that Eighteenth Army was short of weapons and equipment because of intercepted messages of 9 March requesting two-thirds of the normal weapons' allotment for a division in order to re-equip the divisions under Adachi's command.

On 24 March SWPA's SIB reviewed its knowledge to date of the missions of Second Area Army, Eighteenth Army and Fourth Air Army. Eighteenth Army had to hold Wewak in strength yet redeploy its forces westward toward Hollandia in order to secure its hold on Wewak. The Fourth Air Army had to destroy enemy forces attempting to land west of Madang, support convoy escort and reconnaissance missions requested by Eighteenth Army, and deploy, as necessary, part of its strength to defend the Carolines.[44]

On 28 March Ultra revealed that Fourth Air Army's mission was to co-operate with the Area Army in crushing a landing by enemy task forces in the area west of Madang, support convoy escort and reconnaissance missions requested by Eighteenth Army, and deploy, as necessary, part of its strength to defend the Carolines.[44]

On 28 March Ultra revealed that Fourth Air Army's mission was to co-operate with the Area Army in crushing a landing by enemy task forces in the area west of Madang, thus reconfirming Japanese intentions to defend the Hansa Bay sector.[45] The following day an Estimate of the Allied Situation by General Anami Korechika, Commander-in-Chief, Second Area Army, dated 25 March, became available. Anami's lengthy commentary, an unprecedented look into the enemy commander's thinking, displayed, according to SWPA:[46]

> No serious contemplation of an Allied offensive against Hollandia, though a possibility is suggested. Attack against Carolines presumed. Our occupation of Madang and Hansa Bay are accepted as foregone conclusion. Allied advance expected after June. Conclusion: On D-day of the Hollandia operation, the bulk of 18th Army will probably be in Wewak. Transfer of a division back to Hollandia ... is still possible prior to D-day.

Two days later, as SWPA analysts continued to assess Anami's estimate, they reported that Eighteenth Army laid particular stress on immediate counter-attacks in case of a landing in Hansa Bay, before the Allies could consolidate their beachhead.[47] The 1 April MIS echoed this assessment and reported that it had alerted Allied intercept stations to watch carefully message traffic of the Japanese 36th Infantry Division at Sarmi, about 150 miles west of Hollandia, for any indications that the 36th might move to reinforce Hollandia. The lack of significant signals traffic from Hollandia, however, MIS viewed as a strong indicator in itself that the Japanese planned no such move at present.[48]

As the 22 April date of the Allied landings at Hollandia and Aitape drew near, SWPA, too, ordered special emphasis and attention to developments there. On 1 April SWPA reported the presence of 8647 general troops and 7650 air troops (2250 of whom were air duty personnel) at Hollandia. Despite the impressive numbers, the units, as SWPA commented, were overwhelmingly service elements, base defense, construction, and air service types. Perhaps, SWPA judged, the Japanese had one combat maneuver battalion available to defend Hollandia. Moreover, in a hand-written note appended to this SIB, Willoughby informed Colonels Walter Buck, Chief, Operations G-2, SWPA and Paul Cooper, Chief, Theater Intelligence, SWPA, that 'In view of the pressing situation in Hollandia, it is essential to hammer away at the tactical enemy capabilities in that area, in the Special Intell as well as, guardely [sic], in the daily'.[49] Not coincidentally Willoughby's 'suggested' comment appeared verbatim in the next day's SIB.

SWPA G-2 could also validate the claims of US pilots by reporting a Japanese message on 4 April that stated that the airfields at Hollandia were unserviceable because of Allied air raids, doubtless a source of comfort to Admiral Nimitz. There were, however, indications that Japanese concern over a landing in Dutch New Guinea might accelerate their westward withdrawal and reports that Eighteenth Army Headquarters was moving to Hollandia by submarine, although a considerable portion of the Army would remain at Wewak.[50]

Then without warning on 8 April all Japanese Army high-level cryptological systems that the Allies had been reading were changed and MIS acknowledged that 'at the present time no messages in such system are being read currently'.[51] Nevertheless, traffic analysis filled this void temporarily until the codebreakers could again reconstruct readable segments of the Japanese Army code. MIS reported on 21 April that 'Despite this [Japanese] recognition of the importance of Hollandia and a speculation by the Chief of Staff Southwestern Area Force that US communications might indicate a landing there, Japanese Army traffic has thus far failed to disclose any of three divisions of 18th Army have established a division or regimental headquarters west of Wewak'. Traffic patterns also indicated that Second Area Army's only strategic reserve, the 36th Infantry Division, still remained immobile 150 miles west of Hollandia at Sarmi.[52]

That the three Eighteenth Army divisions remained fixed defending Hansa Bay was not accidental. In particular a decrypted Japanese message, transmitted 28–29 February and available to SWPA shortly thereafter, offered SWPA planners an unparalleled insight into the

thinking of their Japanese adversaries. The message formed the core of a
staff appreciation of Japanese defensive planning for New Guinea and
subsequently appeared in a SWPA, G-2 (Intelligence) Memorandum to
the Assistant Chief of Staff, G–3 (Operations) SWPA. According to the
intercepted signal, which became the basis for the subsequent Allied
deception plan, the Japanese anticipated that the Allies' next major
amphibious operations would occur on the north New Guinea coast
between Madang and Awar. General Adachi planned to counter such a
landing by attacking its beachhead from the east with his 41st Infantry
Division and from the west with his 20th Infantry Division thereby
'ambushing' any Allied invaders (See Map 3).[53]

On 7 March MacArthur approved this deception plan to accompany the
Hollandia operation. Feeding on Ultra revelations of what General
Adachi and his staff were predisposed to believe anyway, SWPA staged
air raids and bombed targets in the Hansa-Madang area to reinforce
Japanese preconceptions of imminent future Allied landings there. The
Allies conducted conspicuous reconnaissance flight to map and photo-
graph the Hansa Bay terrain. Motor torpedo boats were very active off
Hansa Bay to mislead the enemy. Air units dropped dummy parachutists
near Hansa and scattered leaflets agitating Korean and Taiwanese conscripts to desert their Japanese masters. Submarines left empty rafts
ashore suggesting reconnaissance patrols had landed to scout the beaches
for possible landing area. US Navy destroyers conducted deceptive feints
and shelled the Hansa Bay area on 10 April.[54] So successful was this
operational level deception campaign that in a 17 April signal to Marshall
detailing the Hollandia operation MacArthur confidently stated, 'Our
feints in the Wewak–Hansa Bay front have held the mass of the enemy's
forces forward making possible the envelopment of his entire 18th Army
with an estimated strength of 60,000'.[55]

That same day, the Japanese naval communications center at Rabaul,
based on radio intercepts of Allied air and naval special high speed
message traffic, issued a warning about the imminent probability of Allied
landing operations along the New Guinea coast. Eighth Area Army
rebroadcast this warning to all units. Despite Japanese naval aircraft
sightings on 18 April of the Allied naval task force near the Admiralties
and on 19 April an Eighth Area Army reconnaissance plane sighting of the
transport convoy about 200 miles due north of Wewak, the Japanese
were unable to forecast accurately where the enemy might land.[56] Eighth
Area Army, for example, on the 20th, signalled all units that Allied
landings were most likely at Wewak or the Ninigo Islands north of New
Guinea. Consequently the heavy airstrike by US Navy carrier-based
aircraft against Hollandia from the morning of 21 April failed to alert the
Japanese defenders to the approaching invasion fleet.

MAP 3
ANTICIPATED AND ACTUAL ALLIED LANDINGS, APRIL 1944

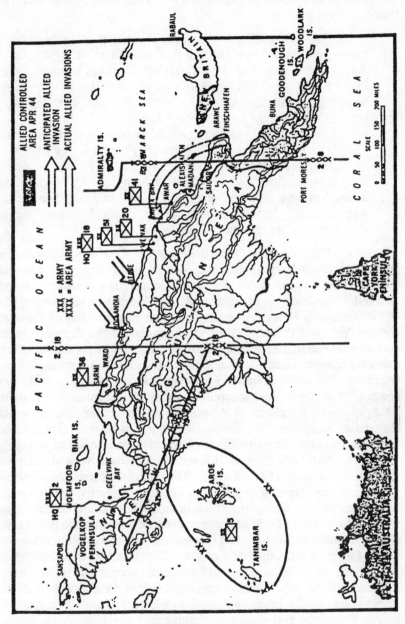

Source: As for Map 1.

Indeed the deception operation did mislead the Japanese. The day before the Allied landings Eighteenth Army signalled Davao and Rabaul that:[57]

> Judging from enemy trends, there is a 90 per cent probability that the enemy plans a new landing on the north coast line in the latter part of April. Based on the military situation, we estimate the most likely places are Madang, Hansa, or Karkar Islands. According to the general situation a landing in the Wewak sector is next in probability. In light of the recent bombings of Hansa, of reconnaissance and naval bombardment of Wewak, and the dropping of pamphlets by the enemy stating that they would land on Wewak on 24 April, it is necessary to be vigilant for it. While it cannot be said there is no possibility of a Hollandia landing, enemy submarines and destroyers have not reconnoitered the area in force. The air attack was simply a destructive measure. It is not felt these are clear indications of an imminent landing.

Another US deception contributed greatly to this Japanese misperception of Allied intentions. The three Allied convoys sailed on roundabout routes some 200 miles longer than a direct voyage to Hollandia required. Rear Admiral Daniel Barbey, Commander of the VII Amphibious Force, Seventh Fleet, and in command of the assault convoy, believed the northward route convinced the Japanese that the convoy was heading toward Truk in the Carolines or possibly might turn eastward toward Rabaul. Regardless, the Japanese spent 20 April searching the area behind the convoy and never again made visual contact.[58] The final Allied deception came on the morning of the landings, 22 April, when hundreds of Australian and American aircraft attacked Hollandia, Aitape and Wakde-Sarmi in such force that respective local Japanese forces believed their sector was the main invasion target.[59]

Thus MacArthur's leap to Hollandia and Aitape with simultaneous, multi-division landings on 22 April 1944 caught the Japanese defenders of Eighteenth Army totally unprepared, in effect facing the wrong direction in order to defend Hansa Bay.[60] Ultra alone was not, of course, responsible for his success. Intelligence, no matter how accurate, is only valuable if a commander armed with that information acts to exploit his knowledge of the forces on the other side of the hill. It is a tribute to MacArthur's generalship that he could rapidly revise operational plans to take advantage of the windfall Ultra presented to him. Lesser or more cautious commanders might have vacillated and let the chance slip from their hands. The corps and divisions commanders involved in the operation fully realized that failure would 'discredit MacArthur's entire bypassing strategy'.[61] But MacArthur's boldness and resolution capitalized on the intelligence gleaned from intercepts of Japanese radio signals and he used the information to amend his operational plans accordingly.

Finally, the historical campaign I have just described affords a classic illustration of the current US Army emphasis on the operational level of warfare.[62] MacArthur used Ultra intelligence to 'see deep' into the enemy's rear areas. He adapted the intelligence to seal off his battlefield by the air and sea interdiction of Japanese lines of communications. He attacked the so-called 'soft-skinned targets', transports and barges that provided the sinews of war to Eighteenth Army.

His strategic objective was the return to the Philippines and his operational objectives from the Admiralties through Sansapor were all integrated and designed to contribute to that strategic end by eliminating the Japanese forces in New Guinea and thus opening the way for his triumphal return to the Philippines. The sequencing of events best employed the means available to MacArthur to achieve the greatest gains in the least time with the minimum casualties.

He achieved this end by judicious employment of his air and sea forces for interdiction, reconnaissance, counter-air, and air superiority missions. SWPA's deception plan encouraged enemy convictions while it diverted Japanese attention from MacArthur's synchronization of three simultaneous amphibious landings far to the rear of Eighteenth Army's main forces. Operational maneuver decisively influenced the New Guinea campaign because American forces concentrated in a manner that forced General Adachi's units to fight at times and places of MacArthur's choosing. The Ultra edge allowed MacArthur to select the battlegrounds and, with this advantage, the destruction of Eighteenth Army became really a matter of time. Perhaps the seeds of Inchon may be found in the New Guinea operations of early 1944. In any case, these overlooked campaigns merit fresh study as the US Army grapples with the question of operational maneuver and the conduct of large unit operations.

APPENDIX
CHRONOLOGY OF THE WAR IN THE SOUTHWEST PACIFIC THEATER,
DECEMBER 1941–APRIL 1944

1941

7 December	Japanese attack Pearl Harbor, Hawaii
8 December	Japanese invade Malaya
10 December	Japanese invade Philippines

1942

15 February	Singapore surrendered to Japanese
9 April	American surrender of Bataan
18 April	General Headquarters of Southwest Pacific Area (GHQ, SWPA) established
6 May	Japanese capture Hollandia, Dutch New Guinea
7–8 May	Battle of Coral Sea
3–6 June	Battle of Midway
23 July to 23 January 1943	Papuan Campaign
7 August to 21 February 1943	Guadalcanal Campaign

1943

16 February	Sixth Army established in SWPA
11 May	US 7th Infantry Division invades Attu
30 June	New Georgia landings (US 43rd, 37th, and 25th Infantry divisions engaged)
21 August	US and Canadian forces occupy Kiska
4 September	9th Australian Division lands at Lae area
16 September	Lae captured
22 September	Australians land at Finschhafen
2 October	Finschhafen captured
1 November	Bougainville landing
20 November	Gilbert Islands (Tarawa) landings
15 December	Arawe, New Britain landings by 112th Cavalry Regiment

1944

2 January	Saidor, New Guinea landings by 126th Regimental Combat Team
1 February	US invades Marshall Islands
29 February	Invasion of Admiralty Islands (1st Cavalry Division)
30 March	Hollandia bombed and Japanese air power destroyed
22 April	Hollandia and Aitape landings

NOTES

Abbreviations

MMBA	MacArthur Memorial Bureau of Archives, Norfolk, Virginia.
NARS	National Archives and Records Center, Washington, DC.
NIDS	National Institute for Defense Studies, Military History Archives, Tokyo, Japan.
USAMHI	United States Army Military History Institute, Carlisle Barracks, PA.

The following SRH series documents used in the essay are in 'Index of NSA/CSS Cryptologic Documents offered to and accepted by The National Archives of the United States', Record Group 457, National Archives, Washington, DC:

SRH-044	'War Department Regulations Governing the Dissemination and Security Communications Intelligence,' 1943–45.
SRH-059	'Selected Examples of Commendations and Related Correspondence Highlighting the Achievements of U.S. Signal Intelligence during World War II', 10 January 1946.
SRH-107	'Problems of the SSO System World War II', August 1952.
SRH-140	'History of the "Language Liaison Group", Military Intelligence Service, War Department', 22 September 1945.
SRH-169	'Centralized Control of U.S. Army Signal Intelligence Activities'.
SRH-203	'General Headquarters, Southwest Pacific Area, Military Intelligence Section, General Staff, 'Special Intelligence Bulletins', Part 2, No.210–329 (1 December 1943–31 March 1944) and Part 3, No.330–390 (April 1944–31 May 1944).
SRH-266	'Japanese Signal Intelligence Service', Third Edition (SSA,1 November 1944)
SRH-349	'The Achievements of the Signal Security Agency in World War II'.
MSJAS	US War Department, Office of the Assistant Chief of Staff, G-2, Special Branch, Military Intelligence Division, 'Magic Summary Japanese Army Supplement', SRS 01–30, Supplement, 10 February 1944–31 March 1944 and SRS 31, Supplement, April–May 1944.

This paper was first presented at the US Army War College Conference on 'Intelligence and Military Operations' Carlisle Barracks, Pennsylvania, 22–25 May 1986. Copyright US Army War College Foundation. The views expressed in this article are those of the author and do not reflect the official policy or position of the Department of Defense or the US Government.

1. On 10 July 1945, Major General Clayton A. Bissel, Assistant Chief of Staff, G-2, in a memorandum to General George C. Marshall, Chief of Staff, US Army observed, 'Akin [Major General S.B. Akin, SWPA's chief signal officer] has built a signal intelligence empire in Central Bureau which in my opinion, judged by results in others areas and by other agencies, is not very efficient'. SRH-169, p.76. See the criticisms of Central Bureau and MacArthur's G-2 by MIS Special Officers stationed in SWPA which appear in SRH-127, pp.23, 29–34, and 181. SRH-349, 12 and 26. Central Bureau followed MacArthur's Southwest Pacific advance moving from its original base at Melbourne to Brisbane (September 1942) to Hollandia (late summer 1944) to Leyte (October 1944) to San Miguel (May 1945) and to Tokyo (September 1945) where it was deactivated (November 1945).
2. SRH-349, 26. SSA evolved from the Signals Intelligence Service (SIS) of the 1930s which transformed into the Signal Intelligence Division then the Signal Intelligence Branch, the Signal Security Branch, the Signal Security Service, and, on 1 July 1943, the Signals Security Agency (SSA). Ibid., p.9.
3. Ibid., p.27. On the Japanese codes and ciphers see Kamaga Kazuo, 'Nihon Rikugun

ango wa 'antai' datta', (The Japanese Army Codes Were Secure) *Rekishi to jinbutsu,*
(September 1984), 270–82 and Kamaga Kazuo, Fujiwara Kuniki and Yoshimura
Akira, 'Zadanka: Nihon Rikugun ango wa naze yaburarenakatta ka', (Discussion:
Why Couldn't the Japanese Army codes be broken?) *Rekishi to Jimbutsu* (December,
1985), pp.150–65. Both Kamaga and Fujiwara served as signals intelligence officers in
the Imperial Japanese Army during the Second World War.

4. Kamaga, op. cit., pp.278–9, and Kamaga, *et al.*, op. cit., pp.155–6.
5. SRH-140, p.5. Kamaga argues persuasively that Eighth Area Army's poor signals
   security procedures facilitated the Allies ability to penetrate Japanese Army codes and
   ciphers. Kamaga, p.275. As each Japanese area army and army enciphered their own
   message traffic, one weak link could compromise radio signals received from all other
   headquarters' echelons on that particular radio net. This seems to have been the case
   with Eighth Area Army, Eighteenth Army, and Fourth Air Army.
6. The buried codebooks version is from Clay Blair, *Silent Victory: The U.S. Submarine
   War Against Japan* (Philadelphia, 1975), p.606. The capture from a disabled Japanese
   submarine appears in SRH-349, pp.28–9.
7. The information on the paucity of Japanese translators comes from SRH-349, p.12,
   SRH-140 explains that MIS overcame this problem by employing a small group of
   scanners, able to read some Japanese, to read all messages searching for specific words
   or units and to select the most worthy of full translation. After translation Lieutenant
   Colonel Edwin O. Reischauer, later US ambassador to Japan and distinguished
   Harvard University Professor, and Paul V. Gerhard, the most experienced Arlington
   Hall translator assigned to the Japanese military problem, checked the results before
   dissemination to the field. Presumably SWPA used a similar system to establish
   priorities for full translations.
8. SRH-203, SIB, 15 January 1944.
9. Ibid., 4 February. The original Japanese signal appears as 'Oka ho sanden dai 283 go',
   (Eighth Area Army Chief of Staff Message No.284) 20 January 1944, in *Nanto Taiheiyo
   homen [dai 8 homengun, dai 17 gun, dai 18 gun, dai 4 kokugun] kankei denpo tsuzuri*
   (Southeast Pacific Front [8th Area Army, 17th Army, 18th Army, 4th Air Army]
   Related Miscellaneous Signals) Showa 19 nen 1 gatsu (January 1944), p.131, in NDIS.
   Hereafter cited as NT with date. The Japanese Army operated on Tokyo time and this
   accounts for the discrepancies in dates throughout the essay.
10. On MacArthur's decision to leap to Hollandia see D. Clayton James, *The Years
    of MacArthur, Vol.2. 1941–1945* (Boston, 1975), pp.331–5; US Army, Far East
    Command, General Staff, Military Intelligence Section, *A Brief History of the G-2
    Section, GHO SWPA and Affiliated Units* (Tokyo, 1948), p.18: Robert Ross Smith,
    The Approach to the Philippines. US Army in World War II (Washington, DC, 1953),
    pp.6–9: Edward J. Drea, 'Defending the Driniumor: Covering Force Operations in
    New Guinea, 1944', *Leavenworth Paper* No.9 (Fort Leavenworth, KS, 1984), pp.9–
    14; and Walter Krueger, *From Down Under to Nippon: The Story of the Sixth Army in
    World War II* (Washington, DC, 1953), pp.45–52. Krueger was, of course, the
    lieutenant-general commanding Sixth Army.
11. *Brief History*, p.25: Smith, pp.4–7: James, pp.444–5. The Reno series were SWPA's
    plans for operations in the Bismarck Archipelago, along the northern coast of New
    Guinea and thence to Mindanao, Philippine Islands. For his efforts, Chamberlin
    relieved Fellers who subsequently became MacArthur's military secretary.
12. OPD (Operations Division, General Staff), Top Secret Message File, (1–29 February
    1944) SWPA to WAR [Department], 02 February 1944 in Registry Group 165, A 48–
    12, Box 5, NARS. The Operations Division was the main war planning agency and
    central command post to assist Marshall in his strategic direction of the military forces
    in the various theaters of war.
13. Ibid. (1–15 March 1944) CG, Rear Echelon, SWPA to WAR, 5 March 1944. A slightly
    abbreviated version of this message may be found in Supreme Commander for the
    Allied Powers, *The Reports of General MacArthur: The Campaigns of MacArthur in
    the Pacific,* Vol.1 (Washington, DC, 1968), p.142.
14. SRH-203, SIB, 6 February 1944. 'Oka ho san ni dai 276 go' (Eighth Area Army Chief of

Staff Signal No.276) 2 February 1944, NT (February 1944), pp.17–19 in NDIS.
15. SRH-059, p.26.
16. MSJAS, 31 March 1944.
17. 'Oka ho san ni den dai 459 go', 28 February 1944, Ji Showa 19 nen 1 gatsu itaru Showa 19 nen 12 gatsu Dai 8 home gun hatsuden tsuzuri (yon kan) [Miscellaneous Eighth Area Army Signals: January–December 1944] Vol.4, 1340 in NDIS identifies the *Daigen maru* Number 3 as the torpedoed vessel. Theodore Roscoe, *United States Submarine Operations in World War II* (Annapolis, 1949), 318 identifies the *Gato* as the US submarine.
18. The fate of the second transport, allegedly sunk by air action, is not clear. MSJAS, 13 March 1944 reported the loss of two transports on 29 February, one to air and one to submarine. SWPA's Fifth Air Force, however, recorded no successful convoy attacks that day. See Kit C. Carter and Robert Mueller (comp.), *The Army Air Forces in World War II: Combat Chronology 1941–1945* (Montogomery, AL and Washington, DC, 1973), pp.281–2. A series of five Fourth Air Army messages, all transmitted on 1 March 1944, relate that four aircraft from 68th Fighter Squadron, flying air escort over Wewak for the convoy, sighted two P-38s, engaged them, and shot one down allowing Wewak Convoy 20 to enter port without incident. Bad weather then prevented further Allied attacks. See especially 'Yon ko gun san den dai 2528 go' (Fourth Air Army Chief of Staff Message Number 2528), 1 March 1944, NT, March 1944, 5 in NDIS.
19. Boeicho, Boei kenshujo, senshishitsu (Japan, Defence Agency, National Defense College, Military History Section) (ed.), *Senshi soosho*. Vol.75, *Daihon'ei rikugunbu* (8) *Showa 19 nen 7 gatsu made* (Official War History, Vol.75, Imperial General Headquarters (part 8) To July 1944)(Tokyo, 1974), 214. The National Defense College is today's National Institute for Defense Studies.
20. SRH-203, SIB, 14 March 1944. Roscoe, 544. The USS *Peto* recorded the sinking as 4 March. The Japanese reported that the submarine attack began at 2330 on 3 March. In any case the 5,500 ton *Kayo maru* exploded with such violence that the *Peto* first reported destroying an ammunition ship.
21. MSJAS 13 March 1944 alerted appropriate theater commanders to the impending barge convoy schedule. MSJAS 15 March 1944 stated it based the results on a SWPA 15 March 1944 communiqué. *Combat Chronology*, 294 reports a Fifth Air Force attack on a Japanese convoy off Hollandia on that date.
22. MSJAS 28 March 1944, stated that Japanese intercepts now available confirm sinking of four ships, including two escorts, although operational reports claimed five ships sunk. See also George C. Kenney, *General Kenney Reports: A Personnel History of the Pacific War* (New York: Duell, Sloan & Pearce, 1949), pp.374–5: *Daihon'ei rikugunbu* (8), 218: and 'Yon ko gun sanden dai 2841 go', 25 March 1944, p.136.
23. MSJAS, 31 March 1944: NT (March 1944), p.263: *Daihon'ei rikugunbu*, p.234.
24. SRH-349, p.22, states SWPA regulations prescribed such tactics. Evidence of the Japanese growing conditioned to the presence of American aircraft on night patrol over Hollandia or Wewak may be found in 'Mogo sanden dai 771 go' (Eighteenth Army [Rear] Staff Message Number 771), 22 February 1944 in NT (February), p.137. The message relates the nightly raids by B-24s and B-25s.
25. *Campaigns MacArthur*, p.116, note 26.
26. SCAP, *Reports of General MacArthur: Japanese Operations in the Southwest Pacific Area*, Vol.II Part 1 (Washington, DC, 1966), pp.258–60: Kimata Jiro, *Rikugun koku senshi* (Combat History of the Army Air Force) (Tokyo, 1982), pp.88–9.
27. Boeicho, Boei kenshujo, senshishitsu, ed., *Senshi soosho*, vol.22, *Seibu Nyugineya homen rikugun koku sakusen* (Army Air Force Operations on the Western New Guinea Front) (Tokyo: Asagumo shinbunsha, 1969), p.255: Kimata, 96. IGHQ established Eighteenth Army at Rabaul in November 1942 with the mission to take control of operations in New Guinea. Army Heaquarters moved to New Guinea in April 1943. Southern Army moved from Singapore to Manila in May 1944.
28. SRH-203, SIB, 9 February 1944; 12 February 1944; MSJAS, 16 February 1944; and *Seibu Nyugineya*, pp.205–8; *Daihon'ei rikugunbu*, pp.21–2 has the IGHQ order. The Allies may have also intercepted a 9 February signal from Chief of Staff, Second Area

Army to Chief of Staff, Eighth Area Army which amplified the aircraft arrivals and mission. See 'Ki sandan dai 543 go', 9 February 1944, Ji Showa 18 nen 12 gatsu itaru Showa 19 nen shichi gatsu Dai ni homengun hatsuden tsuzuri (Miscellany of Second Area Army Messages from December 1943 to July 1944), 4–8, in NDIS. Of interest, and indicative of friction between Eighth Area Army and IGHQ, was the fact that these air squadrons came under direct command of Second Area Army, not, as would have been in accordance with existing command and control arrangements, Eighth Area Army. *Daihon'ei*, p.22.

29. SRH-203, SIB 23 February 1944.
30. Rear Echelon, GHQ, SWPA to WAR, 28 February 1944, OPD, Top Secret Message File, NARS.
31. SRH-203, SIB 29 February 1944.
32. Ibid., 8 February 1944; 6 March 1944; 22 March 1944.
33. *Reports MacArthur, Japanese Operations*, p.263. MacArthur's views may be found in Letter, General Douglas MacArthur to Major General A.C. Smith, Chief, Military History, Department of the Army, 5 March 1953, RG 10, 'Personal Correspondence, March 1953', MMBA.
34. *Seibu Nyugineya*, p.256 and Kimata, p.97. In order to strengthen western New Guinea defenses, IGHQ had transferred elements of the Fourth Air Army Intelligence Regiment to Biak and attached others to Eighth Air Intelligence Regiment in early March 1944. 'Nihon Rikukaigun no joho kiko to sono katsudo' (The Intelligence Structure of the Japanese Army and Navy and its Activities) *Kenkyu shiryo* 84 SRO-2H (Research document SRO-2H), mimeo., 180–5 in NDIS.
35. Kenney, p.377.
36. Ibid., pp.373–4.
37. SRH-203, SIB 30 March 1944, US Fifth Air Force operational reports estimated that 40 Japanese fighters intercepted the U.S. bombers and that American pilots claimed to have shot down ten with seven other probable kills. Kenney, p.380. A 29 February Fourth Air Army signal reported 133 operational aircraft, although errors in encoding make the 113 figure more reliable. See 'Yon kogun sanden dai 3018 go', in NDIS.
38. Kenney, pp.379–81; 84 SRO-2II, pp.184–5; *Seibu Nyugineya*, pp.263–6; and SRII-266, p.20. Eighteenth Army had a signal intercept detachment at Wewak and the 20th Division one at Hansa.
39. 'For MacArthur From Marshall', 11 June 1944, Chief of Staff Record Files, CINC US Army Forces, Pacific, RG-4, Box 14, MMBA.
40. SRH-203, SIB 4, 6, 19, 21, and 22 February 1944 and MSJAS, 12 February 1944. Cf the 4 and 12 February intercepts with Japanese messages 'Oka ho sanden 284 go', 10 January 1944 and 'Oka ho sanden 850 go', in NT (January), pp.113–15 and 131 in NDIS. Eighth Army staff message 850 was subtitled 'Sakusen renraku no ken' (Matters Related to Operations).
41. SRH-203, SIB 13 March 1944 and MSJAS 16 March 1944.
42. SRH-203, SIB 15 March 1944.
43. Ibid., 20 March 1944.
44. Ibid., 24 March 1944. SWPA was listening in to the ongoing differences between Eighth Area Army and IGHQ over defensive priorities in New Guinea. Eighth Area Army emphasized Eighteenth Army's critical role in the defense of Madang as primary. IGHQ, admitting that Madang was important, was more concerned about future Allied operations and therefore wanted to strengthen western New Guinea. Thus as Second Area Army urged Eighteenth Army to withdraw westward as quickly as possible. Eight Area Army promoted Eighteenth Army as the defender of Madang. See *Daihon'ei*, pp.212–13.
45. SRH-203, SIB 28 March 1944.
46. Ibid., 29 March 1944. 'Hi san ni den dai 262/263 go', 26 March 1944, Nanpogun (reika butai) kankei denpo tsuzuri (Miscellany of Signals related to Southern Army [and subordinate units]), pp.32–4 in NDIS. Anami's lengthy signal appears in full in the 29 March SIB.
47. SRH-203, SIB 31 March 1944.

48. MSJAS, 1 April 1944.
49. SRH-203, SIB 1, and 2 April 1944. Willoughby's handwritten note is appended to the 1 April SIB.
50. Ibid., 7 April 1944.
51. MSJAS, 8 April 1944. SWPA's SIB for 29 March 1944 announced that it was believed that the Japanese changed their code on 26 March after the loss of Wewak Convoy No.21. SRH-349, p.29, is ambiguous, stating, 'After some early compromises in 1944 the Japanese signals systems were read from time to time'.
52. MSJAS, 21 April 1944₁. This bulletin refers to a 'Southwestern Area Force' which may be the Southwest Area Fleet. The 9th Fleet, the main Japanese naval headquarters in New Guinea, passed from Southeast Area Fleet Headquarters, Rabaul to Southwest Area Fleet in March 1944. Southwest Area Fleet controlled all naval units in the Netherlands East Indies and was directly subordinate to the Combined Fleet. Smith, p.95.
53. Brief History, pp.25–8, Plate No.9 and accompanying text.
54. Ibid. Campaigns MacArthur, pp.144–45.
55. CG, Rear Echelon, SWPA, Brisbane, Australia to WD, 'MacArthur Eyes Alone Marshall', 17 April 1944, OPD Message File, NARS.
56. Japanese Operations, p.266.
57. My translation of 'Mo sanden dai 489 go', (Eighteenth Army Staff Message No.489), 22 April 1944 in Ji Showa 19 nen 3 gatsu itaru Showa 19 nen 12 gatsu Dai juhachi gun hatsuden tsuzuri (fu 20D/51D) kan go (Miscellany of Eighteenth Army Signals (appendix 20 and 51 divisions) from March 1944 to December 1944, Vol.5) in NDIS. A different version of this message may be found in Brief History, p.28.
58. Daniel E. Barbery, MacArthur's Amphibious Navy: Seventh Amphibious Force Operations, 1943–45 (Annapolis, 1969), p.167.
59. Japanese Operations, p.266.
60. For land operations after 22 April 1944 see Smith, op. cit., for the entire New Guinea operation and Drea, op. cit., for the Aitape operation.
61. See, for example, the comments of Lieutenant General Robert L. Eichelberger, Commander Reckless (Hollandia) Task Force which was I Corps reinforced, who wrote on 23 April 1944: 'Our route was such that our arrival was a complete surprise ... While we are not out of the woods, we are a long way on the road to victory. Had expected more Japs and a bitter fight. What a lucky break!', and, the following day, 'A week ago if I could have anticipated conditions as good as they are today I would have been very happy ...'. in Jay Luvaas (ed.), Dear Miss Em: General Eichelberger's War in the Pacific, 1942–1945 (Westport, CT, 1972), p.107. Vice-Admiral Barbey wrote that, 'I was ready to give twenty years of my life if the convoy could get in close enough to open fire before being discovered, fired upon, and perhaps blown out of the water'. Barbey, p.170. General Krueger recalled, 'Again success depended very largely on strategic and tactical surprise, on outguessing the enemy'. Krueger, p.59. Major General Charles P. Hall, Commander, XI Corps Commander, claimed 'General MacArthur had had much difficulty in convincing the JCS of the feasibility of bypassing Hansa Bay and Wewak'. Had the operation failed, Hall believed, '[T]he JCS would have immediately put a brake on General MacArthur's movements. The entire theory of by passing would then have to be discarded and MacArthur would have been somewhat discredited'. Major General William H. Gill, Commander, 32nd Infantry Division, in turn, felt himself under enormous pressure from army and corps' level to 'wrap up the campaign' so that MacArthur could continue operations in western New Guinea. Gill Papers, USAMHI.
62. The emphasis is expounded in Headquarters, Department of the Army, Field Manual 100–5, Operations (Washington, DC: 20 August 1982).

German Air Intelligence in the Second World War

HORST BOOG

Much has been written about the intelligence services of the main powers involved in the Second World War. Professor Hinsley's three-volume work on *British Intelligence in the Second World War*[1] reveals how important a source the Luftwaffe radio traffic was for the British. This prompts the question: how much did the Luftwaffe know about Britain, the Royal Air Force and the other main opponents? As far as Luftwaffe radio intelligence is concerned, this can hardly be ascertained in view of the fact that at the end of the war, the Luftwaffe itself destroyed about 97 per cent of its records, among them apparently all intercepts. This is particularly regrettable since about 70 to 80 per cent of all intelligence information was provided by radio intelligence. Only through the post-war study by Gottschling[2] do we know about some tactical successes of Luftwaffe radio intelligence (*Funkaufklärung*). No details are known as to when and how far enemy codes were broken and what was learnt from these intercepts. Before the Luftwaffe intelligence service, about which hardly anything has as yet been published, is described, it is necessary to survey the German intelligence community,[3] of which Luftwaffe intelligence was just a part.

More than a dozen such services were controlled by government agencies, by the Nazi Party, and by the armed forces. State-run services included:

- the Postal Ministry;
- the Ministry of Economics with its Foreign Economy and Statistical Departments collaborating with the War Economy and Armament Staff of the Supreme Command of the Armed Forces;
- the Foreign Office with its Political, Commercial, and Press Branches, a code-breaking establishment, a spy branch, and a radio-monitoring service;
- the Ministry of Propaganda with its Press Agency DNB also using the radio-monitoring service;
- Hermann Goering's *Forschungsamt* (Research Office)[4] linked to the Prussian state and engaging in wire-tapping and intercepting diplomatic, commercial and press material;
- the Ministry of the Interior with the Secret State Police (Gestapo).

The Nazi Party ran the so-called SD (*Sicherheitsdienst* or Security Service). This was connected with the Gestapo, as SS Chief Heinrich Himmler was also Minister of the Interior, and was headed by the same people who were in charge of the Gestapo; Reinhard Heydrich, Ernst Kaltenbrunner and Walter Schellenberg. Other party intelligence services were

– the Foreign Organization (*Auslandsorganisation* – AO) of the NSDAP under Ernst-Wilhelm Bohle;
– the office of the Reich Press Chief Otto Dietrich.

The armed forces had at least four intelligence services:

– the Army High Command with the 3rd and 12th Departments of the General Staff, which were concerned with Foreign Armies West and East. The chief of the latter was the famous General Reinhard Gehlen. In addition, there were the Army Communications Chief with his Signal Intelligence Branch and the Army Postal Service.
– the Supreme Command of the Armed Forces under Wilhelm Keitel with its War Economy Staff and Foreign Economy Branch as well as with Admiral Wilhelm Canaris' Foreign Information and Counter-Intelligence Office (Amt *Ausland/Abwehr*), the three divisions of which engaged in espionage (I), sabotage (II), and counter-espionage (IIII). Canaris also had at his disposal a Foreign Information Division and a Press Evaluation Group. There was also the Armed Forces Communications Chief with his Cipher Branch.
– the Navy, with the 3rd or Foreign Navies Department and the 2nd Department of the Admiral Staff. The latter was called B-Dienst (observation service). This Signal Intelligence Department gained particular importance in submarine warfare in the Atlantic.
– the Air Force with the 5th Department in its High Command General Staff. There was, in addition, a General of Reconnaissance, a main Aerial Photography Branch, and the Air Signal Communications Chief Wolfgang Martini with the Cipher Office.

At lower levels, the intelligence agencies in the troop staffs and their officers were usually designated 'Ic' (G2/A2 or S2 today). Requests by the military intelligence staffs for agent information had to be directed to Canaris' office, which tried to fulfil them. Military attachés were not allowed to participate in espionage. The military intelligence agencies also received information from POW interrogations, radio intelligence, published sources, patrols and air reconnaissance.

The amazing thing about this maze of intelligence services was that they were rather uncoordinated, each working for itself. There was duplication of effort and much rivalry between them. No committee or clearing

agency existed to sift results and co-ordinate activities until the last year of
the war, when Hitler ordered the SS to take over military intelligence.
The individual channels of intelligence information ended with Hitler,
to whom each intelligence chief reported directly or through his
commander-in-chief or minister, often also with the intention of gaining
advantages over others. Only in the person of Hitler did the individual
streams of information meet. But he could not possibly digest everything
and form a proper picture of the situation, nor was he informed regularly,
not did he always want information.

So much for the overall picture of the German intelligence services.[5] Let
us now turn to air intelligence in particular.

Intelligence in the German Air Force did not enjoy high prestige.[6]
The best general staff offices or troop officers were usually assigned
elsewhere. The long-time Chief of the Intelligence Department of the
Air Force General Staff, Colonel Josef (called 'Beppo') Schmid, had
no particular knowledge of foreign languages. For years he ran the
Intelligence Department in addition to working as Hermann Goering's
Ministerial Officer.[7] He had a reputation for embellishing his reports to
please Goering and to strengthen the morale of the flying personnel
fighting against the English, especially during the Battle of Britain and in
1941.[8]

Intelligence officers in troop staffs as well as in the General Staff
were subordinated to the operations officers or department.[9] It was the
operations officer who prepared the situation assessment, because the
basis for all evaluations of the situation were the Luftwaffe's own
operational intentions, objectives or missions.[10] The Army Manual H.
Dv 89 g of 1941, the regulations of which were also adhered to by the
Luftwaffe, went even further and stated that it was the commander
who prepared the situation estimate together with his chief of staff or
operations officer and not his intelligence officer, who was only heard
before – if at all.[11] Thus the Chief of the Intelligence Department of the Air
Force General Staff was subordinated to the Chief of the Air Operations
staff, who was sometimes also the Chief of the Operations Department or
Ia in personal union. At other times he was identical with the Chief of the
General Staff. In the staff of air fleets the Ic (or A2) was part of the
Operations Branch headed by the Ia (A3).

Intelligence officers and branches were regarded as 'maids of all
work'.[12] Their responsibility included troop welfare, propaganda and
censorship.

The attachés were not given much guidance by the Intelligence
Department of the General Staff, as we know from complaints by the air
attaché in Turkey and others.[13] (In the navy, however, it was different.)
When General Friedrich von Boetticher returned from the USA in the

spring of 1942, Hitler did not ask him for his views on America.[14] Hilmer von Bülow, air attaché in Italy, was reprimanded by Hitler for his negative reports on the Italian Air Force, which Hitler did not want to hear as he did not consider it Bülow's business.[15] Colonel Heinrich Aschenbrenner, the air attaché in Moscow, was instructed (in circumstances described below) by the Chief of the General Staff, General Hans Jeschonnek, to abstain from collecting intelligence.[17] This attitude increased, when failure became common in the later years of the war, and climaxed in a radical distrust of intelligence after it was discovered that this service had been infiltrated by members of the Communist spy ring, the *Rote Kapelle*.[18]

Air intelligence was not organized suitably and centrally, although centralization had already been demanded after the Polish campaign as a result of experiences there. No basic manual was available for intelligence work; drafts for such a manual were written only late in the war.[19] There were about eight intelligence collection agencies: the Foreign Countries and Counter-intelligence Office of the Armed Forces Supreme Command, the Air Force Signal Intelligence Service, the Long-distance Reconnaissance Group of the Commander-in-Chief of the Air Force, the War Booty Staff of the Air Technical Office, the Air Force Interrogation and Evaluation Centres West (*Oberursel*) and East, Goering's above-mentioned Research Office in part, the air attachés, and the press group.[20] Only the latter two were directly subordinated to the Intelligence Chief of the Air Force General Staff. With the others there was only a loose co-operation. Signal Intelligence with the important cipher service of the Commander-in-Chief of the Air Force was a sort of private domain of the Chief of Air Signals Communications, the aforementioned General Martini.[21]

The evaluation of information took place in the 5th, the intelligence, and the 8th Departments, the Air Historical Department, the Foreign Air Armament Department of the Director-General of Air Armament, the troop command staffs, and the office of a Professor Steinmann which was camouflaged as the Construction Office.[22] Information on radar was evaluated by ten different agencies.[23] Thus there was no central evaluation, but much rivalry and friction especially between the most important agencies, the 5th Department of the General Staff, the Foreign Air Armament Branch, and the Chief of Signal Communication.[24] Instead of immediately forwarding technical information to the 5th Department – supposedly the central intelligence agency – the Foreign Air Armament Department first prepared the information meticulously in the engineers' way, which could take several weeks.[25] Information was quite frequently withheld from others because knowledge meant more power.

Personnel in the East and West Groups of the Intelligence Branch was increased only after events, for instance, after the Battle of Britain, for

which better intelligence would have been helpful, and after the setback
before Moscow, where air reconnaissance had not been thorough enough
to discover the intensity of Soviet troop movements from Siberia.[26]

The Intelligence Department was in many instances not informed early
enough for timely collection of intelligence on certain countries because
there was no general war plan. Intelligence on Norway had to be collected
within a few weeks and on the basis of travel guides. Intelligence work on
France was quite inadequate, and it was only the quick success of
the fighting troops that saved the Intelligence Branch from exposure.
The Balkans, Crete and the Mediterranean were other examples of
intelligence collection at short or at no notice.[27]

As already pointed out, it was not until the last year of the war that
attempts were made to intensify and centralize air intelligence work.

The quality of intelligence work must be measued by its results. They
can be summarized as gross underestimation of the three main opponents
in the crucial first three years of the war.[28] After that the intelligence
picture became more realistic, but could no longer alter the course of the
war. The die was cast.

TABLE 1

MILITARY AIRCRAFT PRODUCTION FIGURES OF THE MAIN AIR POWERS FROM
1919 TO THE END OF THE SECOND WORLD WAR

Year	Japan	Germany	Britain	USA	Soviet Union*
1939	4467	8295	7940	2141	10382
1940	4768	10826	15049	6019	10565
1941	5088	11776	20094	19433	15735
1942	8861	15556	23622	47836	25436
1943	16693	25527	26263	85898	34900
1944	28180	39807	246461	96318	40300
1945	8263	7541	12070	47714	20900
Total	76320	119328	137499	305359 **	158218

  * In 1938 the Soviet Union built 5469 front line aircraft.
** The total US production including civil aircraft from 1939 to 1945 was 324,750 aircraft.
    (*Source*: Holley, pp.548 ff.; Craven and Cate, Vol.6, p.350; Postan, pp.484 f; Lusar,
    pp.168 ff.; and Soviet Air Forces, p.400; Von Hardesty, p.252).

The destruction of most of the Luftwaffe's records makes it impossible
in most cases to trace the path of individual intelligence information from
its source to the final intelligence estimates in order to evaluate the
influence of those estimates on operational and strategic decisions
or to find out where errors and mistakes slipped in and who committed
them. The underestimation must be taken as a fact. Consequently, the
Luftwaffe suffered heavy losses over England and, because Germany did

not have air superiority, Britain was never occupied but served later on as a springboard for the bomber offensive against the Third Reich and for the invasion. In the case of Russia, the German bomber force suffered greatly from attrition in close air support, thus draining Germany's air potential. The neglect of the industrial capacity of the USA decided the war.[29]

BRITAIN

Studie Blau ('Blue Study')[30] was the first attempt at central collection and evaluation of the available information on Britain. It was completed in the first half of 1939 under the direction of the Chief of Intelligence of the Luftwaffe General Staff and in co-operation with civilian experts on foreign trade, with scientists, with representatives of industry, economy, technology, with attachés and with political as well as military experts. The study covered the entire military, social, economic and political scene of Great Britain. This undertaking was not continued during the war, however, owing to lack of personnel and because of other priorities. It would have been of great benefit to Lutwaffe intelligence if projects like this had been generally pursued and with respect to other countries as well.

Before the war the intelligence assessment about the air armament position of the potential enemies was at first objective and carefully weighed.[31] According to a report in the spring of 1938[32] the readiness for war of the major air forces in Europe was still considered to be relatively low. From the summer of 1939, however, a significant increase in air power was predicted for Britain and France, but not for the Soviet Union. The Luftwaffe Operations Staff Intelligence Department considered in the summer of 1938 that the Luftwaffe was not yet capable on its own of winning the battle against the British arms industry.[33] In the report of 2 May 1939 on the air situation in Europe,[34] one month after the British guarantee of 31 March 1939 to stand by Poland, Schmid, however, considered it '*quite possible*' that in spite of the pact and promises the war arising in Eastern Europe could be localized, because the West's forces were hardly capable of operations as an instrument of foreign policy owing to internal politics. It is not clear in what way and with what justification he came to this important political conclusion. The existing air capacity of the Western armed forces, including their overseas sources of assistance, was described as 'inadequate to catch up with the major advance in the expansion of the air forces achieved by Germany during the next 1–2 years'.[35] In fact, only a year later the British were producing 50 per cent more aircraft than Germany. An increase in the number programmed until then appeared 'at first out of the question'; at best 'keeping up the present strength' was considered to be realistic, because it was doubtful whether an increase in aircraft numbers and anti-aircraft defence 'could be obtained in addition to the existing armaments programme *in terms of production* and personnel, even with the inclusion of the reserves of the personnel in the Empire'. Only in the 'technical *development*' of fighter aircraft and heavy anti-aircraft guns was the 'strength of the German *units* matched'; in bombers and other air force equipment the Western Powers were in fact inferior to Germany.[36]

Therefore, taking into consideration the usual lengthy development time, it was patently believed that the Western Powers were some two to three years behind in fighters and heavy anti-aircraft guns, and even further behind in bombers and other air force equipment. This statement was to be disproved a year later at Dunkirk by the Spitfire,[37] and by Galland's request to Goering that his fighter squadrons be equipped with Spitfires,[38] and also in the autumn of 1939 and summer of 1940 by other reports about the building of British four-engine bombers.[39] The opinion that American aid to Britain could not become effective until after a certain period following the start of the war[40] was correct. On the other hand, the statement that the air defence of Great Britain would only suffice 'at the expense of the complete exposure of the rest of the country for the complete protection of the air defence region of Greater London' was exaggerated and optimistic. Moreover, the existing air defences of Britain and France were 'too weak' to protect adequately the sensitive points of both countries. Hardly credibly, it goes on that on account of the inferiority in the air at that time, and of the geographically conditioned disadvantage in the air, which increased with the increasing ranges and speeds, Britain was '*very vulnerable from the air*', especially in the east because the defender of the insular position had to face 'more difficult problems' than the attacker. This was written at a time when German bombers in the event of war had to make a detour round Holland and Belgium in order to reach England. It added, however, that only powerful German attacking forces could militarily and decisively exploit British vulnerability in the air. German air defence was considered so strong 'that any combined attack by the British and French air striking forces had only a small chance of reaching its targets'. The final opinion ran:

> The *German Luftwaffe* is at present superior to any single European air force, and this applies not only to the numbers and quality of the equipment and *armament of the troops*, but also to the *organization, training*, and especially the *tactical* and command side of the preparation for war in the air.

This was thought to apply also 'to 1939', even if the British and French Air Force 'emerge simultaneously as enemies'. Because neither Poland nor Russia could mount an effective air offensive against Germany one would not 'have, for the time being, to reckon on an equally strong threat from east and west'. Schmid, however, appeared to doubt whether the rapid advance in German air armament could be maintained in the following years. The last part of the final verdict was to the point. The report was a mixture of truth and falsehood, which certainly made it difficult to recognize the underestimate of enemy strength it contained.

The German chances were assessed much too favourably in the 94-page study, which corresponded to observations of the attitude in the Reich Air Ministry made with great uneasiness by the German air attaché in Washington, General von Boetticher, before the war.[41] Such reports also appear to have succeeded in impressing Goering. It was certainly not only from euphoria of victory and deliberate exaggeration made for scaring-off purposes that he proclaimed on 9 September 1939 in his long drawn-out 'peace speech' to the armaments workers in the Rheinmetall-Borsig works in Berlin that the British could not deny 'that our superiority in the air, not only in defence but especially our offensive capability is overwhelming'.[42] In May 1939, on the other hand, during an exercise carried out by Luftflotte 2 in the presence of the Luftwaffe CGS, the State Secretary Milch, and the Chiefs of Staffs of Air Fleets 1 and 3 to assess the prospects of German victory in a possible air war against Britain, a generally quite different picture had emerged, particularly in respect of German armament, training, tactics and organization described by the 5th Department as superior. The operational range of the He 111 was too short, the equipment was inadequate for successful attacks on British warships, there were too few military aircraft for such an extensive field of operations, and the blind flying training of the crews was inadequate. A war decision in the air within a short time in 1939 could not be expected. Concerning air defence there was an inherent weakness caused by the organizational splitting of responsibility in the coastal area between the Luftwaffe and the navy.[43] These sobering conclusions reached by General Felmy, the Commander of Luftflotte 2, were the basis of the exhaustive appraisal made by the Luftwaffe General Staff of the 'operational objectives of the Luftwaffe in the event of a war against Britain in 1939' dated 22 May 1939.[44] It was also pointed out that an air war against British imports could not be successful because the western and southern ports lay beyond the range of the Air Fleet 2 concerned, and furthermore that terror attacks on London as the stronghold of the enemy air defence would hardly have a catastrophic effect or contribute significantly to a war decision. They would only strengthen the British will to resist. Attacks on a British expeditionary force would have little effect because more distant French ports could be used for shipping traffic. The war against the British Royal Air Force would only lead to great German losses caused by British fighters and divert the effort against vital targets in Britain. Success of some sort could be expected only from attacks by very small units on the widely dispersed British air armaments industry in weakly defended areas.

On 16 May 1939 Generalleutnant Geisler, who had just been appointed to Air Fleet 2 as General for Special Duties and who was previously Commander of the Naval Air Arm, was instructed to investigate the still unanswered question of an air war beyond the sea, and to specify the requirements of this in terms of command, organization and training. In matters that concerned his sphere of activity he could, after notifying the Commander of Air Fleet 2, communicate directly with the Chief of the Luftwaffe General Staff. Geisler came to essentially more unsatisfactory conclusions than Felmy in his investigation of 7 August 1939 into the preparedness for, and conduct of, an attack across and on the sea and along the coast.[45] Starting from operational objectives, which, after gaining control in the air, aimed at crippling the British war economy, cutting off British maritime trade, severely damaging the Royal Navy, causing grave delays to and destruction of British military transports to the mainland, and which included the threat of invasion, he came to the following conclusion: taking into account the German forces available in the summer of 1940, the technical and tactical performances of the He 111 and Ju 88, the training of the units, navigation, and replacements, 'an air war against Britain *in 1940* can only result in *partial*, though *important, success,* which *could not have an effect, and threaten* the British conduct of the war, before the *second year of the war*'. This would, however, only be possible 'with the most rigorous concentration of all forces, and provided their operations could be sustained *for a longer period* leading to the breakdown of the enemy defence and gradual expansion of the German squadrons'. Further investigations into the chances of success in an air war against Britain in 1942 revealed 'that by no means could there be a decisive turning point in the war, not even by the mass deployment of all the Geschwaders' (for which there would not be sufficient operational airfields anyway) and 'that a noticeable or effective paralysis of the British Air Force' at the very start of the war could not be expected. Apart from that it would, because of the generally unfavourable weather conditions, not be possible to detail as many squadrons for simultaneous attack as would bring about a noticeable weakening of the enemy in the first days of the war'. The British Air Force would split itself up and thus be even harder to engage.[46] Hitler himself maintained at his conference with the commander-in-chief of the services of the *Wehrmacht* on 23 May 1939 that it was a foregone conclusion that the Luftwaffe would be able to subdue Britain; and in fact an OKW Directive of 17 January 1940 states that no all-out air war against Britain would be possible without adequate operational bases and equipment.[47] Such sobering assessments of the situation appear to have had some effect on Goering in that they induced him in August 1939 to make whatever effort he could for peace, and, at the start of the war against Poland, made him violently castigate the Foreign Minister von Ribbentrop as being solely responsible for the war, and exclaim after the expiration of the British ultimatum on 3 September 1939: 'If we lose this war then God have mercy on us.'[48] (But, as pointed out above, Goering had outwardly assumed an optimistsic attitude already six days later after the first successes in Poland.)

These situation appraisals did not basically differ from the first memorandum about Britain[49] dated 22 September 1938 by General Felmy, in which he had concluded that because of the inadequate range of German bombers a successful air war against Great Britain would only be possible after the occupation of Holland and Belgium, and that the state of aircrew training for war across the sea was still unsatisfactory. The final judgement read: 'A war of extinction against Britain seems to be excluded, given the means at present available'. At the time Goering had commented on this matter in his own handwriting: 'I have not called for a report which considers existing chances of success and points out our weaknesses – I know all this better than anybody else – but I want to know, rather, how you think we could exert maximum effort with the planned means and what you need as a prerequisite for this'. Jeschonnek added that judgements like these discredit the Luftwaffe and were a smack in the eye for Goering, who had believed that the sky over London would darken when he ordered the whole of the Luftwaffe to attack Britain. Jeschonnek himself was of the opinion as early as 1938 that the Luftwaffe alone could defeat Britain within a few months without any support from the navy.[50] Goering was certainly not so happy about the results of the investigations carried out by Luftflotte 2 and the Operations Department of the Luftwaffe General Staff as he was while reading the study made by his Director of Intelligence, which was quite different. On Hitler's orders the troublesome fault-finding Felmy was relieved of his post at the first opportunity in connection with the Mechelen incident.[51]

The Director of the 5th Department nevertheless retained his optimistic view of a successful outcome for Germany of a war against Britain. He was of course not alone in this opinion. The Quartermaster General, 6th Department, in a report of 15 May 1939 about the armaments situation of the Western Powers had indeed likewise reckoned on German air superiority and implied that it would diminish after 1940. Even more optimistic, but leading to the same conclusion, was an opinion expressed by the Director-General of Air Armament, Department of General Planning, on 13 May 1939 about military aircraft production.[52] In the autumn of 1939[53] after the German victory in Poland, Schmid judged

the British entry into the war as a political success for Germany, because
Great Britain, as regards armaments, had entered the war too early and
was now faced with the alternatives of fighting or losing prestige. Since
Britain acted on the assumption of a long war and could catch up in
armament by 1940, he considered it to be 'decisive ..., to begin with the
real war against Great Britain', Germany's most dangerous enemy, 'as
soon and as vigorously as possible in any circumstances still during the
current year'. 'In respect of the better all-weather flying training of our
units purely tactical prospects of success are seen for us even if the British
Air Force – which is not to be expected – strikes back as often and with
equally strong forces'. In the Studie Blau issued at the end of June 1939
by the 5th Department with the co-operation of Udet, Milch and
Jeschonnek, and judged by Goering and Milch to present a true picture,[54]
Schmid had expressed himself even more cautiously, pointing to the
possibility of the British catching up in armaments, and had described the
period of time which the Luftwaffe would need to reach its goal against
Britain as indeterminable. Schmid wrote after the war that the study had
not indicated that the British leadership's capacity for improvisation and
the toughness of the British might possibly prevent a capitulation as a
result of aerial attacks alone and might necessitate an invasion of the
island. Also, the Studie Blau did not mention that the prerequisite for this,
the defeat of the British fleet, would be impossible to achieve by the weak
German naval forces and that therefore Luftwaffe forces must be
available in sufficient strength. He maintained, however, that he did
mention these matters when briefing Goering, Milch, Jeschonnek and
Felmy on 26 July 1939 at List on Sylt.[55] In this connection he expressed the
opinion that 'a prudent Luftwaffe leadership', on consideration of Studie
Blau and Germany's own striking power, would not even have started the
Battle of Britain. He thereby concealed the fact that, in the autumn of
1939, he had turned away from his cautious prognoses, abandoned his
more moderate judgements under the influence of the euphoria of victory
soon spreading ever wider and had urged the attack, saying that the
inherent risk was low. This view corresponded exactly to the deliberations
to the top leaders of the Wehrmacht, particularly of Hitler, who, conscious
of the technical superiority of Luftwaffe armament communicated to him,
but also for economic reasons and in view of the probable loss of
Germany's lead in armaments already foreseeable in 1939, believed that
there was a once and for all chance to win, which he would have to take.[56]

In January 1940[57] Schmid estimated the combined British and French
Air Forces to be 'definitely inferior to the German Luftwaffe in terms of
numbers and equipment (for a foreseeable future)'. Even if the USA,
without entering the war, put the weight of its aircraft industry at the
disposal of the Western Powers and if the sea lanes were protected, no

decisive improvement in the strength of air armaments compared with Germany could then 'immediately' be expected during the course of the war in 1940. Schmid further doubted that the British fighters 'in view of the better dogfight performance and defensive armament of the Me 110' would have any chance against this German twin-engine fighter. This statement was made on the basis of the success of the German single and twin-engine fighters in the air battle over the German Bight on 18 December 1939 and in similar fashion supported by Messerschmitt in February 1940.[58] Within six months it was carried to the point of absurdity. In the air battles over England the German twin-engine fighter proved distinctly inferior to the RAF fighters with their better curve performance and higher speed, could only protect itself by forming defensive circles with others or needed single-engine fighter cover, and finally had to be withdrawn. All this, and the fact that they had been built at the expense of the single-engine fighter force.[59] Schmid also asserted, incomprehensibly, that the air armament position of the Western Allies would be 'all the more adversely affected the sooner heavy losses occurred – even on both sides'. He forgot that the bases for personnel training of the Luftwaffe were restricted, while the British could train their air crews in Canada. The successful Norwegian campaign and the rapid collapse of France, which confirmed the intelligence appraisal of this country, strengthened the belief of the Luftwaffe Ic in his own capability[60] as well as the optimism of the Luftwaffe leadership concerning the chances of success against Britain and made Goering (although he was at times sceptical)[61] and particularly the younger people like the CGS Jeschonnek[62] and the Director of the 5th Department 'rather presumptuous in the assessment of the European Great Powers as enemies', as Propaganda Minister Josef Gœbbels wrote in his diary[63] as a summary of a later conversation with this Director. They believed at first that the RAF could be knocked out of the sky in two to four weeks,[64] felt to be its superior, and calculated at the end of July 1940 that a decisive success in the air war against Britain could be achieved still in the same year.[65] This feeling of optimism also rubbed off on Hitler at first, because in mid-September he still believed in the possiblity of decisive results of the air attacks against Britain, given four to five days of good weather.[66]

Intelligence reports must have been the basis of these much too optimistic expectations. Thus Colonel Schmid again emphasized in a comparison of the military fighting power of the Luftwaffe and the Royal Air Force on 16 July 1940,[67] even if not without qualification in respect of the Me 110, the superiority of the German fighters, particularly of the Me 109F. In the belief that there was a distinct possibility of success he urged that the real air onslaught on Britain should begin at once. This was in spite of the fact that the Me 109F could not yet play any part because it was not going to be put into operational service until January 1941. Even then, as a teleprinter message of complaint from Field Marshal Kesselring to Udet's letter to Messerschmitt of 4 April 1941[68] proves, this aircraft had plenty of faults and teething troubles. The British bombers were considered inferior because of insufficient armour-plating and bomb-aiming equipment, without any thought being given to corresponding weaknesses in the German bombers. The British ground defences were considered inadequate. The replacement of crews, in fact the greatest bottleneck in British Fighter Command, was reckoned to be adequate. Because of lack of knowledge of the true industrial capacity it was assumed that with the intensification of the air war against Britain there would be a decline in aircraft production and in the front-line strength of the Royal Air Force. It turned out to be exactly the opposite. The top command was thought to be inflexible, the middle command to be too old and its commanders unable to fly, which applied still more to the German Luftwaffe. In contrast to the Royal Air Force the German Luftwaffe was considered able to mount decisive day attacks on the island because of insufficient air defence there. Schmid overlooked the high repair capacity of the British, and estimated the monthly production of fighters to be only 180–200, whereas Britain had in fact already produced 496 fighters in July 1940 alone. The radar-controlled British defence system was not mentioned at all, although the Luftwaffe had known since 1938 at the latest that the British were experimenting with radar; but even in 1940 it did not yet seriously occupy itself with the study of how to overcome this system. There were no engineers in the 5th Department who had paid adequate attention to the British radar system, to which the British had turned in 1939/1940 to reinforce the defences in time for the expected German air attack.[69] In addition the Germans considered their defence system to be superior. Hence, in a letter of 7 August 1940 circulated to the Air Fleets and Air Corps,[70] Schmid came to the conclusion that radar control of the British fighters tied them to their own bases and prevented short-term assembly of fighters at crucial sectors and that this system must collapse under massive attacks. The Luftwaffe was to find that it had been fundamentally misled when it started its daily attacks.

A comprehensive air armament comparison between Great Britain and Germany[71] for the period of 1 July 1940 to 31 December 1941, which was produced from data available till 10 August 1940 by the DGAA at the suggestion of, and in conjunction with, the Luftwaffe Operations Staff Intelligence Department, likewise showed symptoms of victory euphoria, of a non-factual ideological attitude, and especially a considerable absence of the technical knowledge and clear-headed judgement essential for an appraisal of the enemy situation. While in the British economic and armaments system an over-strong conservative attitude allegedly hampered research and development, it said, there was on the other side the 'globally unrivalled success of German air armament against the British system'. Authoritarian Germany was supposed to be better equipped to provide for the future. In Britain an 'individualistic' attitude solely directed towards economic profit made it impossible to regard armaments 'as a whole' and a 'liberalistic' way of thought prevented Britain from overtaking the German armaments lead with public assistance.[72] This description of the British armaments economy seems to have applied, within certain limits, rather to the German *Blitzkrieg* economy. The irrational belief in the superiority of the German air armament industry, which was supposedly 'uniformly directed from above', and of the authoritarian system became here the basis of the assessment of the British. Hitler, too, used almost the same phrases a little later while describing to Mussolini the American air armaments industry.[73] The question whether the Ic transmitted 'embellished' reports upwards, because that was what they liked to read, cannot be answered definitely. More obviously it seems that he had believed such things himself because of his political conviction.

In particular, it was further maintained that the German 'outstandingly superior' Me 110 twin-engine type destroyer and the Me 109 fighter were superior to the British fighters on account of their better offensive armament with the new Pmk high-explosive phosphorus ammunition with steel core and their DB 601N high-altitude engines driven by 100-octane petrol.[74] In this respect the negative experience with the new British Spitfire fighters over Dunkirk, though mitigated by poor weather and unfavourable deployment of the German fighters at the limit of their range, had not really entered consciousness. The diary of the Director of the Operations Department in the Luftwaffe General Staff expressed only satisfaction about the heavy material losses suffered by the British at Dunkirk, but it contained nothing about the failure of the Luftwaffe to gain air superiority and about the superior quality of the Spitfire.[75] Hitler and Goering, too, did not take the Dunkirk experience seriously.[76] In addition it seems that the compilers of the comparative armaments analysis had not been aware of the fact that even in September 1940, at the height of the Battle of Britain, by no means all of the single and twin-engine German fighters had been equipped with the new high-altitude engines. In 1941 only 480 Me 110 twin-engine fighters, which in any case were inadequate for employment against Britain, and only 80 Me 109s in operational units were fitted with the new highly efficient engines.[78] The compilers also appear not to have considered the fact that at the start of the war only a maximum of 3000 tons per month, i.e. only 10 per cent of the aircraft petrol production and 2 per cent of the mobilization demand for high-performance air engine fuel could be prdouced. At the end of 1943 still only a quarter of the aircraft engine fuel production consisted of high-performance fuel.[79] After the war it was in fact maintained on the British side that: 'it was the British Spitfire plane, built around the Rolls-Royce engine and its 100-octane fuel, which won the Battle of Britain by the narrowest of margins – a margin which depended on the fuel'.[80]

In the bomber performance appraisal emphasis was placed on the superiority of the German bombers with their very high bomb load and cruising speed. The He 177 was mentioned,[81] though in fact it was not in service at all, and was never to live up to the expectations placed on it. It was unhesitatingly emphasized that in an air war against Britain, which had already begun and the intensive phase of which was to start within a few days, the greater German repair capacity was a decisive element in German superiority. This neglected the fact that damaged but still reparable German aircraft would in reality hardly ever come down within the territory held by the Germans, but would more likely be shot down over England and the Channel from where they could not be salvaged.[82] The British fighters were not recognized as having much chance of success against German daylight bombers over England because of their having 'only' eight wing-mounted machine guns with a very limited amount of ammunition, although these fighters had proved a danger to the German bombers at Dunkirk. The bombers were nevertheless believed to have a good chance over England despite their inadequate defensive armament.[83] Especially emphasized were the better bomb-aiming equipment and the method of bombing – the dive-bombing practised by the German bombers.[84] There was no consideration of the fact that the point target aiming (diving) method depended on the ability of the pilot and had been mastered by only a small number of pilots, not that the plane was temporarily exposed to great danger from anti-aircraft defence when it pulled out of the dive. The existing mechanical Goerz bombsight for bomb release from level flight was unsatisfactory. The optical Lotfe 7 C-sight was only in the process of being introduced, and like the B.Z.G.2 bombsight, was hardly used. Not until the end of 1941 was training gradually changed over to the Lotfe 7D sight which, for the first time, permitted accurate level flight bombing. Some crews, however, still declined to use this and other equipment as being too complicated for them. Methodical training in bomb aiming, which was considered to be a minor problem compared with finding the target, had, therefore, not been started until the establishment of the Luftwaffe Air Bombing School at the beginning of the war, when there was less and less time available for the training.[85] Already in October 1940 the German bombers had to be withdrawn from day attacks and transferred to night attacks because the losses were too severe.[86] The Stuka also soon had to be withdrawn from employment against England because of its vulnerability to British fighters.[87] There was no mention that the Me 109 was conceived as an interceptor and not as an escort fighter, and that because of its short range it would be at a disadvantage in terms of endurance compared with the British fighters operating close to their own bases. The battle of fighter against fighter, or fighter against twin-engine fighter or dive-bomber was inadequately analysed or not at all, and regarding the dive-bombing method only the advantages were praised, whereas the disadvantages were not discussed.

Finally the probable total production of military aircraft in Britain including new construction and repairs for the period of 1 July 1940–31 December 1941 was given as 9,630 planes, compared with 4,900 in America and 19,730 aircraft in Germany.[88] Only the German actual production agreed surprisingly accurately with these figures. Germany produced 19,519 aircraft, including 5,007 repaired ones during the period considered. That was, however, 1300 fewer than had been calculated in advance for the much-praised German aircraft repair industry.[89] The British built at least 28,000 during the same period, the Americans at least 22,000 military aircraft – approximately 300 and 450 per cent respectively more than expected.[90] The Technical Officer's estimate of 1 July 1941 for the 1941 American aircraft production was 17,000 (1,700 too low); for 1942 it was 28,200 (19,636 too low) and for 1943 it was 31,000 (54,898 too low).[91]

Errors and inaccuracies in intelligence work cannot be avoided because of the complicated and mostly very incomplete source situation. Wrong estimates by factors of three or four are, however, very serious. The Western Allies made a wrong estimate of German aircraft production from 1941 to 1944; they, on the contrary, overestimated this production for the critical years until 1942/43 by 100 per cent, fighter production by 50 per cent. But from 1943/44, in overestimating the effects of their bombing attacks, they began to underestimate German fighter production by three fifths, and aircraft production as a whole by one third of the numbers actually produced,[92] which thanks to Allied air superiority and the impending shortage of aviation fuel in the Luftwaffe, did not have any adverse consequences. The French in 1938/39 likewise believed the Luftwaffe to be stronger than it was. The underestimation of British and American aircraft production by German air intelligence lasted until 1943 and then gave way to an overestimate.[93]

The Luftwaffe enemy situation reports as a whole were very much concerned with purely military matters, which are important for the start of a confrontation or for a short war, that is with operational strengths and the particular tactical and technical features of the aircraft, but hardly at all with in-depth armament and with the industrial potential of the enemy. Wishful thinking was dressed up in flowery ideological language and was obviously intended to cover up the lack of necessary in-depth analysis. This method of assessment remained on the surface and corresponded to Germany's armament in width which was directed to large numbers of effective operational squadrons and to production instead of investment. It also matched the General Staff training, which was to produce the necessary number of staff officers during shorter and shorter periods, so that the acquisition of knowledge and understanding of the economy as the basis of armament production had to be abandoned. As regards Great Britain there was a deep reliance on the *Studie Blau*, which formed the basis of the planning of the bomber offensive,[94] but which had the disadvantage that it was mainly based on source material for 1937. According to this, British production of aluminium was only one sixth of that of Germany. Only limited import of aluminium into Britain was believed to be possible.[95] The possibility of a rapid expansion of British air armaments and of American supplies to Britain was not generally recognized because of an out-of-date basis of calculation, as Schmid stated after the war.[96] The Chief of the General Staff, Jeschonnek, had great faith in this armament comparison, as his optimistic statements during the attack on Britain indicate.[97]

The inadequacy of Luftwaffe intelligence about the enemy, to some extent excused by lack of experience in the matter of strategic bomber warfare, also revealed itself in the choice of targets, on which, as Douhet had already recognized, the greatest difficulty in a strategic air war rests. It is the correct choice here that reveals the ability of the commander of a strategic air force.[98] The ultimate blame for unsystematic target selection lay of course with the top leadership of the armed forces, which for a long time could not make up its mind whether and when to go for a landing operation or whether an independent strategic air war was to be conducted.[99] Certainly Goering and his CGS Jeschonnek bore the responsibility for the frequent changes of targets and the lack of sustained attacks on certain targets (as for example the British fighter airfields during the Battle of Britain), and also to a large measure for the resultant lack of success of the Luftwaffe's effort.[100] Already on 19 June 1939 Goering, in agreement with Jeschonnek, expanded the targets from the group of air industrial targets, which, according to the opinion of the 1st Department of his General Staff, offered the only prospect of success in England, to 'all places'. This shift, however, did not take place until the matter had been referred back to the Director of the 5th Department.[101] In fact the conduct of a strategic air war more than that of a co-operative one must be based on top echelon intelligence assessments, because it is only there that all the information about targets in the enemy's hinterland can be evaluated comprehensively, which is necessary for the employment of a strategic air force. That the air war against Britain had to be 'conducted primarily by the chief of intelligence' was just as obvious to the pertinent intelligence expert[102] as it was perhaps unusual in the eyes of Goering and Jeschonnek. In any case the part played by the Luftwaffe Operations Staff Intelligence Department in the inadequate German conduct of the air battle over England was, on account of the peculiarity of this type of air war, considerable even if it can no longer be substantiated in detail because of the lack of sufficient documents. There was indeed an England Committee obviously including General der Flieger Wenninger, the former air attaché in London, representatives of the Foreign Office, science and politics, which was listened to and helped the 5th Department in the selection of targets,[103] but otherwise seems to have played only a minor role. Economists and engineers do not appear to have been appointed to this committee. Thus the choice of targets that would have most effectively paralysed the British power to resist was, it seems, mostly the concern of the 5th Department. Nevertheless the final decision generally seems to have rested with Goering and Jeschonnek, who were not particularly knowledgeable about strategic air warfare. In contrast, the British and Americans engaged a very much greater number of civilian scientific, technical and economic experts as well as high-ranking politicians in determining the targets to be attacked in Germany. They set definite priorities and plans for the targets, for example the 'Oil Plan', the Western Air Plans already conceived before the war, and the 'Casablanca Directive' of January 1943. This caused Speer to remark at the armaments conference on 1 December 1944: 'One must be quite clear about the fact that those people who plan the enemy bomber attacks on our economy have an understanding of German economic life; their planning is shrewd in contrast to that of our own bomber attacks.'[104] Insight into the unavoidable need to involve civilian experts in the determination of strategic targets does not appear to have taken place in the Luftwaffe High Command until a new start on strategic air warfare was made in the summer of 1943, when Jeschonnek replied thus to the proposal made by Luftflotte 6 for the setting up of a special staff to conduct the strategic air war:

> This staff will, however, only have to concern itself with carrying out attacks against the targets assigned to it by the C-in-C of the Luftwaffe. Work with archival documents in order to make the right choice of the various targets and to find out whether they are worth of being attacked etc. cannot be part of its terms of reference. This target information can only be ascertained by an office that is in close contact with those sections whose task it is to study and appraise the enemy war industry; it must have access to all sources of research and intelligence. This task must therefore continue [!] to remain with

the C-in-C of the Luftwaffe, who in this context works in close collaboration with the corresponding agencies of the German war economy.[105]

Hence there was confusion about the choice of targets, not only on the part of Goering and Jeschonnek, but especially of the Intelligence Department. The Director of Operations of the Luftwaffe General Staff had already in 1936 pointed out this shortcoming and its very great significance in a bombing war[106] in his paper on the Basic Principles of the Strategic (*'operativ'*) Conduct of the Air War. It was obvious that the knowledge and experience of the military about the functioning of technical-industrial systems and thus about their relative vulnerability were inadequate. So there was now a preference for the choice of a large number of targets for simultaneous attack as a precaution, lest one important target be left out, rather than concentrating on the most important targets, as was clearly laid down in the Air War Manual L. Dv. 16. Thus no systematic method of paralysing a particular section of industry was arrived at; much more were inflated hopes placed on a psychological paralysis of the population. To help the present-day reader to understand this it should be simply stated that the concept of a civilian population easily panicked by repeated bombing attacks had been an integral part of the air warfare philosophy of the air powers since the First World War. This applied particularly to Britain, where the press, leading politicians and military leaders gave repeated expression to this philosophy, especially in the 1920s and 1930s, and where the government was much influenced by this anxiety and was – of course not only for this reason – driven to the policy of appeasement. Against a background of the Bolshevik October Revolution there developed from this belief the fear of a possible uprising of the population as a result of bombing. Those who pointed out the opposite view that the will to resist of the civilian population might harden as the result of the bombing could find no public support for their opinion in Britain at that time.[107]

The proposals for targets, as discussed on the German side during the air war against England in the summer and autumn of 1940, included the bombing of residential areas of London in order that the approach roads to the planned invasion area would be choked by fleeing people, and panic and mass hysteria would break out. This was wanted particularly by Jeschonnek,[108] and by Goering.[109] Others wanted London's working-class districts to be bombed, in the obvious hope also put forward by the England Committee[110] and by Hitler[111] that the poorer working class would thus be incited against the rich ruling class and bring about a revolution that would make Britain ready to talk about peace. There were also deliberations about the bombing of London's public utility and traffic system, the newspaper district[112] and alternatively the armament centres in the Midlands, where 'the war can indeed be won'. The England Committee which was more oriented ideologically and sociologically thereby wanted to hit the 'invested capital' supporting the British government, 'that class of solid conservative, stubborn Englishness proper at home, ... the mental and spiritual basis of Great Britain's will to resist and to see it through'.[113] Group III of the 5th Department, which was responsible for Britain, was more in favour of the destruction of the aircraft industry, which was to be paralysed 'indirectly by attacks on individual places of concentration of the sub-contractors' works.'[114] There were very different opinions about industrial targets. Items discussed were the destruction of power stations and the electricity supply grid, steel works, food manufacturing factories, fighter aircraft factories, centres of aluminium and magnesium extraction from raw materials, window glass factories, aircraft engine works, and port installations.[115] There was a vacillation between 31 and 51 of the most varied targets selected for destruction, to each of which by Jeschonnek's order of 2 September 1940[116] only a few specially picked crews were to be assigned, also with a view to splitting the British defences.[117] In mid-October 1940 Goering even ordered 'frequent changes of targets ... in order to achieve the necessary effect on the population of London and to confront the enemy's defences with a new situation'.[118] But everywhere there was a lack of fundamental analysis of the overall strategic effects of the destruction of the many individual groups of targets, so that *Gruppe* III of the 5th Department had begun some appropriate preparatory work in order to be prepared for 'new situations with which it was confronted (by the top Luftwaffe command) sometimes quite incidentally'.[119] Co-ordination of efforts between the 5th Department and the analysts of enemy armament with DGAA in respect of targets in the British aircraft industry to be selected for destruction obviously did not start until the beginning of November 1940, not without the technical expert responsible to Udet being surprised by the short notice of the order.[120] All this goes to show that the personnel on whom strategic air warfare was especially dependent were ill-prepared and badly instructed about target analysis concerning industrial targets of strategic interest and appraisal of effects of bombing, which demanded more than mere military knowledge.

The choice of targets was made more difficult by the lack, until 10 November 1940,[121] of 'really objective reports and a comprehensive appraisal' of the effects of the German air attacks on Great Britain, and there were no other useful agents' reports, statements made by prisoners of war, or reports from attachés, and until 1944 no official British aircraft production numbers were known. From 1941/1942 on there was also no more German aerial photographic reconnaissance of the British aircraft industry.[122] The price now had to be paid for the inadequate peacetime reconnaissance of Britain, although the strategic photographic reconnaissance unit, the *'Hansa-Luftbild-Abteilung B'*, under Colonel Theodor Rowehl had been carrying out espionage missions over Britain since 1938. In this situation there suddenly appeared, for the first time in June 1940, reports from an agent with the cover name of 'Ostro'[123] about British armament, which to a great extent formed the basis of the situation appraisal of Britain made by the Luftwaffe Operations Staff Intelligence Department.[124] 'Ostro' was controlled by the Foreign Information/Counter-intelligence Office of the Supreme Command of the Armed Forces – Luftwaffe Intelligence was forbidden to engage in active spying.[125] The 'Ostro' source was considered reliable, well-informed and faultless. 'Ostro's' evaluation of the British aircraft industry were highly esteemed.[126] In ignorance of the true facts, 'Ostro' reports were interpreted much too favourably for the German side although people in the 5th Department did not want to believe them at first, not because their reports of British aircraft production capacity appeared to them to be too low but because they were too high when compared with information from captured documents and serial reconnaissance reports. In a 5th Department's instruction about the Royal Air Force of 1 September 1938[127] the basis had been a monthly production of 230 aircraft at the start of 1938, which at that time was about 80 more than the actual production; at the end of the year, however, it was reduced by a third. In July 1939 the Planning Department of the DGAA assumed a production of 200 aircraft for September 1938,[128] when it had already reached 326 aircraft, and 230 military aircraft for May 1939 when 702 were actually built. Still in December 1940 it was believed that the production numbers reported by 'Ostro' for July, August, and September were far above the numbers actually manufactured,[129] although these were up to 100 per cent higher. Even at the end of July 1941 Luftwaffe Intelligence estimated the current British and Canadian aircraft production including supplies from USA at only approximately 700 aircraft per month.[130] No one knew that the numbers 'Ostro' reported of British production were much too low.[131] A comparison in Luftwaffe Intelligence records[132] of 'Ostro' numbers with the true British aircraft production numbers[133] clearly shows how the Luftwaffe Operations Staff was misled (see Table 2).

The 5th Department's estimates for 1940 exactly stuck to the 'Ostro' figures. Based on these a memorandum was prepared for the CGS with a forecast of British annual aircraft production in 1941 of only 7,200, compared with an actual figure of 20,094 aircraft.[134]

Certainly the agents' and attachés' reports concerning the effect of the German attacks on Britain were very ambiguous and different from each other in that they mentioned the serious effects, which Jeschonnek in

TABLE 2
BRITISH AIRCRAFT PRODUCTION FIGURES

	according to 'Ostro'	actual figures
July 1940	1100	1665
Aug. 1940	811	1601
Sept. 1940	803	1341
Oct. 1940	650	1419
March 1941	711	1730
May 1941	742	1708
July 1941	839	1668
Aug. 1941	915	1793
Nov. 1941	1220	1806
Aug. 1942	1700	1827

particular willingly believed, as well as the less decisive results of bombing.[135] It was thus difficult for anyone in the Luftwaffe leadership to form an accurate picture. Briefing notes of the England Group of the Intelligence Department dated 28 September 1940 state that if the 'Ostro' report, according to which it had been necessary to extend all British armaments order delivery dates by 50 per cent, was 'only approximately true, then that means a battle won'. There was a 'firm conviction that by *intensification and widening of the indirect effects* on the British military aircraft industry ..., *in combination with planned attacks on the targets already ordered*, the British aircraft industry will be paralysed within a very short time, and that the effects *will decide the outcome of the war*'. The technical experts assigned to the study of Britain expressed their opinion on 25 October 1940 thus: 'If the situation in the British industry is only approximately the same as "Ostro" portrays it, then there must soon come a complete standstill'.[136] A drop in the British aircraft industry in November 1940 was described 'as being of decisive importance for the conduct of the war'.[137] In the summer of 1940 in the military-tactical plane, the operational readiness of British fighters were crucially underestimated by Goering and his Intelligence Chief, although the radio listening service reported higher and truer numbers.[138] According to Schmid's calculations based on 'Ostro', the British Fighter Command should have been virtually eliminated by the beginning of September. In fact, however, its numerical strength increased, although there was a temporary shortage of pilots. The period for defeating the Royal Air Force was put at two to four weeks or less, which, like the estimate of a few weeks to overpower the British armaments industry from the air, was much too low.[139] At the end of September 1940 the DGAA was still proposing the immediate establishment of a department for the administrative control and stock-taking of the British aviation industry and its research and development results in the event of the occupation of

Britain.[140] In October 1940 the Director of the Operations Department in the Luftwaffe General Staff, Generalmajor Hoffmann von Waldau, had to admit that the Luftwaffe leaders had underestimated British Fighter Command by 100 per cent.[141]

Very serious, too, was the above-mentioned underestimate of British and American aircraft production during the summer of 1940 in what was the first proper appraisal of the US armaments by the Luftwaffe Operations Staff Intelligence Department.[142] In the summer of 1942 Goering still regarded it as impossible that Britain was building not only more bombers but also more fighters than Germany,[143] and in October 1943 he believed that the British could not deploy as many fighters against the attacking German bombers as Germany could against the British massed formations.[144] The Director of Technical Intelligence with the DGAA, in August 1942, considered the figure of 265 four-engine bombers produced in Britain per month as improbable.[145]

It was only from June 1944 onwards and after lasting doubts about the accuracy of the agent's reports as well as after the British government (Cripps, Beaverbrook) had first published production numbers, that the Luftwaffe Operations Staff Intelligence Department became aware of the fact that it had for years been deceived by false agents' reports.[146] Since mid-1942 'Ostro' had been joined by 'Hector' and 'Josephine', who allegedly occupied high positions in Britain, but were probably the product of the imagination of a German intelligence agent in Stockholm, who obtained his information through liaison with secretaries in the Swedish Defence Ministry handling the reports from the Swedish Air Force and naval attachés in London, and who, in fact, was receiving large sums of money from German Counter-intelligence to pay the (phantom) agents allegedly 'managed' by him. The Foreign Air Forces West Section of the Luftwaffe Operations Staff Intelligence Department had to admit: 'Because of the false reports of agents our own assessment of the enemy particularly in 1940/1942 and to a lesser extent also in 1944 came to wrong conclusions about the strength of the Royal Air Force'.[147] The 8th (Military Science) Department of the Luftwaffe General Staff gave its opinion in a study in August 1944: 'Our intelligence service must be blamed for not having recognized in time the extent of foreign armaments and the General Staff for not having seen the consequences of such armament production to initiate timely counter-measures in the meantime and make them available [!] in sufficient quantity'.[118] The prevailing general assessment of Britain was characterized by the Foreign Air Forces West Section on 24 September 1944 as follows: 'The British aircraft numbers ... have, on the basis of our present knowledge, probably been assessed too low in 1940/1941 and too high at the beginning of 1944. They have, however, in the period of time concerned provided the basis for all our own appraisals'.[149]

The Luftwaffe intelligence assessment of Great Britain can be characterized as follows:

- Political deliberations based in ideological bias were not allowed to enter into intelligence assessments. British society, for example, was described as being individualistic, liberalistic, and solely out for profit, and thus incapable of a united effort. This capability, however, was ascribed to the authoritarian German society (*Volksgemeinschaft*), and to German industry. German society could take more punishment than British society which, it was said, would revolt against its government.[150] The British, in fact, united at once in a common war effort, whereas the German system was rather chaotic and intent on preventing the German population from realizing that there was a war on.

- As far as the front-line strength, equipment, training, organization, and matters of a tactical and operational nature were concerned, the intelligence assessments – with exceptions of the kind just mentioned – usually proved right, though sometimes only with the help of information from signal intelligence. The assessments of the overall war and armament potentials were generally incorrect, at least in the first years of the war. Thus British aircraft production figures were substantially underestimated, which, in 1940, was also a result of euphoria over the successes in Poland, Norway and France. In the Battle of Britain, it was to the disadvantage of the Luftwaffe that Goering believed the British had to scratch together their last fighters for the defence of London and thus he started his air offensive against London early in September, not heeding the warnings of his signal intelligence. Actually Britain had produced many more fighters than Germany. It was different with the Allies. They overestimated German aircraft production in the early war years because they wrongly assumed full economic mobilization in Germany, and they gave it too little credit in 1943–44 because they exaggerated the effects of their own bombing offensive.

- German air intelligence was deceived by the double agent 'Ostro', who (after the breaking-off of the strategic air offensive against Britain, when there was hardly any German air reconnaissance over the island) was the only source of information. When later in 1944 the deception was discovered in the German Air Force General Staff Intelligence Department, it was too late, because air superiority could no longer be taken away from the Allied air forces, which dictated the course of the war in the air.

THE SOVIET UNION

Germany's second major enemy in the Second World War, the Soviet Union, was at first also generally underrated by the most important Luftwaffe leaders, although one must make distinctions here between Goering, Milch, the Chief of the General Staff, and the Luftwaffe Operations Staff Intelligence Department. The Luftwaffe, however, was not alone in arriving at a false picture of the Russian situation, as Hillgruber, Moritz and Reinhardt[151] have fully demonstrated in respect of the army, navy and OKW. The British General Staff, too, and the Americans underestimated Russia in the early 1940s.[152] The order for intensified reconnaissance of the Soviet Union was given only after, with Hitler's Directive No. 21 'Barbarossa', the political and strategic decision to attack this country had been taken.[153] This is typical evidence of a leadership and command doctrine that stressed offensive operations more than the supporting activities like logistics, training and intelligence, a leadership based too much on operational objectives rather than on logistics in the widest sense. On 10 January 1941 Colonel Schmid, chief of the Intelligence Department of the Luftwaffe General Staff, was directed to prepare the target data for targets as far east as the general line Archangelsk–Leningrad–Ilmen Lake–Dnepr and to reconnoitre the Soviet Air Force.[154] This order was received in the department with surprise, since the air offensive against Britain had not yet come to an end.

The German Air Force already had done routine reconnaissance towards the east, but the results were still negligible.[155] The means and possibilities of obtaining intelligence information about the Soviet Union were very limited because of the rigid maintenance of secrecy, the strict measures of control and isolation there, and the Russian mistrust of foreigners. Agent activities were almost impossible. Attempts to infiltrate higher political and military staffs by spies had remained unsuccessful. The controlled Soviet press and professional literature contained only general information which permitted no exact conclusions about the strength, organization and operational readiness of the Soviet Air Force. Only the radio listening service was able to provide some valuable though fragmentary information about it, which, however, did not suffice for a complete picture. Even the long-distance reconnaissance flights conducted on orders from the Supreme Command of the Armed Forces (OKW) since 1934 at high altitudes by the special reconnaissance squadron under Theodor Rowehl,[156] also called '*Fliegerstaffel z.b.V.*' and, by 1937, '*Hansa-Luftbild-Abteilung B,*' could not entirely cover the huge area. Though providing some information on the ability of the Soviets to build modern aeroplanes and to fly in formation during air parades, the German military attaché in Moscow, General Kostring, did not succeed in getting deeper insight into the Soviet Air Force and armament production potential.[157] For the rest the knowledge about the Air Force of the Red Army was widely determined by the impressions German officers and engineers gained in the period of the secret German–Soviet military collaboration until the early 1930s. At that time the Soviet Air Force and air armament industry were just being built up and still in a state of learning. The Stalin purges had later left the impression that the Soviet Union was military power without a head.[158]

The Condor Legion had great respect for the new Soviet fighter I 16 in the Spanish Civil War, but the performance of Soviet air units employed there was altogether unconvincing. Operational leadership was clumsy and insufficiently trained from a general staff point of view. Many a shortcoming, however, could be balanced to a certain degree by dexterity and improvisation. The employment of the Red air units was characterized by lack of concentration of power and of mobility in attack and defence so that their losses were high. The flying crews were brave and aggressive over their own, timid over enemy territory. There were only a few able pilots. The flight training of the units was insufficient, especially with the fighters. Soviet bombers played only an insignificant role in Spain owing to lack of relevant training. Their main mode of employment was close air support. Some progress was observed with the anti-aircraft artillery, especially with the light and medium guns. There were considerable shortcomings in radio communication, which was no separate branch of service, badly organized and too inflexible for mobile operations.[159]

In view of the scarce information on the Soviet Union the Luftwaffe, too, attributed special value to reports of immigrants and German resettlers from this country, all the more so since their depreciatory tendency matched very well with the prevailing traditional feeling of German cultural superiority over the east European peoples and with the National Socialist conviction of the 'racial' superiority of the Germans over the Slavs, a belief with which NS propaganda had attempted to indoctrinate the armed forces and which played its part in preventing a realistic assessment of the Soviet Union and its air force.[160] So the otherwise sober and factual Chief of the Operations Department of the Luftwaffe General Staff, Generalmajor Hoffman von Waldau, called the Soviet state a 'state with a maximum centralization of executive power and of below average intelligence'.[161]

The scarce and biased pre-war knowledge of the Luftwaffe General Staff about the Soviet Air Force is reflected in the Considerations of the 5th Department of the Air Situation in Europe of 2 May 1939.[162] In the report an ever-increasing desultoriness in the control of Soviet armament economy and administration as well as a lack of tight and unified top command of the armed forces was observed. Reports estimating the Soviet Air Force's strength at 10,000 to 12,000 aircraft were expressly rejected. Their strength was assumed to be 6,000 planes, 5,000 of them being first-line aircraft and only 3,300 being deployed in Europe. The Soviet air striking force and its ground organization and logistics as well as the anti-aircraft artillery were rated as insufficient, the armament industry as highly vulnerable to air attack because of its dependence on the traffic communication system, which had always been considered to be a critical bottleneck of the Russian armament economy.[163] The striking power of the Soviet Union was considered to be low and forceful Soviet air operations against Germany were regarded as improbable. The air armaments industry was at best thought to be capable of covering the normal needs and the usual wear and tear. The prospective employment of the Soviet flying units was expected to be mainly in co-operation with the ground forces. The idea of independent strategic bombing to be carried out by the heavy bomber corps did not seem to be pursued any further. That the temporary weakness of the Soviet Air Force would some day be overcome was not denied, but this was assumed to be possible at an 'Asiatic' pace only and with organizational deficiencies. In contrast it was considered 'probable by all means' that the Soviet Union 'will collapse when exposed to strong outside pressure.'

As soon as the German–Soviet agreements of August/September 1939 had been signed, Hitler issued an order forbidding on principle any espionage against the Soviet Union, although intelligence on the Soviet Air Force was completely unsatisfactory, the meeting with the Soviets in Eastern Poland in September 1939 having produced no essentially new information.[164] Hitler was glad to have a free hand in the east in order to fight the west unhampered and did not want to irritate his new partner unnecessarily. Obviously this prohibition did not include the routine evaluation of information otherwise collected by the General Staff, but it caused Admiral Canaris, chief of the Foreign Information and Counter-intelligence Office of the Supreme Command of the Armed Forces, to cease intelligence operations against the now neighbouring country and seems to have led to a restriction or even temporary cessation of the strategic reconnaissance flights of Rowehl's unit over the USSR.[165] Intelligence work on the Soviet Union in the Intelligence Department of the Luftwaffe General Staff was, moreover, seriously reduced by the redistribution of personnel from the East Group ordinarily responsible for Russian affairs to the West Group and by the fact that information on that country stayed out to a considerable degree.[166]

Typical of this situation were Jeschonnek's words to the newly appointed German air attaché, Colonel Heinrich Aschenbrenner, when briefing him before his departure for Moscow: 'Establish the best relations to the Soviet Union, but do not worry about collecting intelligence'.[167]

During the summer of 1940 relations between Germany and the Soviet Union became increasingly strained and deteriorated gradually. The Soviet Union took advantage of Germany's engagement in the western campaign to expand towards the west, and also gained importance in Hitler's calculations for the defeat of Britain. So the acquisition of intelligence about the east was newly activated by the Luftwaffe. In response to a request from the army Hitler, in an order of early October, personally requested Rowehl, now commander of the Long-Distance Reconnaissance Group of the C-in-C Luftwaffe, to fly reconnaissance missions with the proper forces as far as 300 km deep into Soviet territory and especially to cover all airfields. The order was to be carried out until 15 May 1941. Afterwards all Soviet airfields in this prospective operational zone had to be checked again by aerial reconnaissance within a week.[168] It was more or less only tactical and not also strategic reconnaissance in the proper sense, because it was to serve the operations of the ground forces in the first place. For this reason, and because of the lack of far-reaching aircraft the region of, and behind, the Ural Mountains was not explored by aerials reconnaissance, although knowledge of this part of the Soviet Union with its already huge industries could have been enlightening for the Luftwaffe High Command.

In the meantime the Luftwaffe General Staff's optimistic assessment of the spring of 1939 had apparently been confirmed by the performance of the Soviet Army and Air Force in the Russo-Finnish Winter War of 1939/40, which was rated low. Although it was conjectured that the Soviets might have been bluffing, the weaknesses shown by the Red Army in the fight against Finland entered most of the German intelligence assessments of Soviet Russia, not only those of the Luftwaffe General Staff Intelligence Department.[169] Obviously the facts that, for some time, only the forces of the Leningrad Military District were engaged against Finland and that the Red Army had beaten a Japanese army in Mongolia the preceding summer were overlooked. At the end of November 1940[170] the Luftwaffe's Intelligence Chief, Colonel Schmid, rated the Soviet flying troops again as limited in strength and not up-to-date, the anti-aircraft artillery as 'extremely mediocre', and judged the growth of the Soviet air forces in the European part of Russia as a 'preliminary deployment towards west', the completion of which would take 'a long time as was usual under the conditions obtaining in Russia'.

The systematic photo-reconnaissance of the Soviet Union, which was not fully under way before the winter of 1940/41, was seriously prevented for some time by the weather. Reconnaissance missions were generally flown at altitudes of 9000 m by aircraft of the types He 111, Do 214, Ju 88 B and Ju 86 P equipped for high-altitude flying with pressure cabins and specially prepared engines. In pursuance of the policy of 'appeasement' which Stalin, at that time, exercised toward Hitler, the Soviet Union abstained from energetic protests against these reconnaissance flights. Soviet fighters were even forbidden to shoot at German reconnaissance planes. German crews repeatedly reported such 'peaceful' encounters in the air, which were surprising to them. After the war Soviet historiography blamed the 'traitor Beria', who at that time, commanded the border troops responsible for the protection of Soviet air space, for having 'practically' opened Soviet air space to German aerial espionage by forbidding the fighters to shoot.[171]

From the end of 1940 onwards the Counter-espionage Department of the OKW and the air attachés in Moscow, Ankara, Tokio, Stockholm, Helsinki, Washington and in the Balkan states were also ordered to gather intelligence about the east within the possibilities open to them. The Rowehl group dropped agents by parachute. The radio listening grid was tightened. A group of former Tsarist officers helped in evaluating intercepts and deciphering Soviet secret codes. It was first of all the radio listening service that produced valuable results, which were mostly used as the basis for the disposition of photo-reconnaissance missions. In view of the short notice allowing only unsatisfactory preparations, the activities of the OKW Counter-intelligence Department were not very successful. The attachés could gain hardly any insight into the Soviet Air Force and air armament production.[172]

The information gathered by the air attaché in Moscow was, in a way, an exception to this. He was able to get hold of the 'Atlas of the Red Commander' containing many details about Russian railways and industrial plants, and of a telephone directory from which conclusions could be drawn about the size of the industries in the Ural region. Otherwise it was but a superficial and quite restricted local source of information.[173]

In February 1941 it was stated in the Basic Orientation Manual about the Soviet Union:[174]

> The leadership [of the Soviet Air Force] is rigid and relentless. It lacks any *instruction* in modern operational experience. It is inclined, like all Russian command, to rigidly patterned precedure, and is not competent to conduct a successful war against an enemy armed with modern weapons .– A *methodical* employment and concentration of forces of the Russian flying units cannot be ascertained ... The *ground organization* is ... *out of date* ... Thus the *operational readiness* of the units is seriously affected ... the

organization of supply is at a low level ... The striking power of the Soviet Air Force is *essentially* less than that of the German Air Force. Considering the size of the area concerned the *numerical strength* of the front line units is *insufficient*. With regard to *operational* employment it is doubtful in terms of training and leadership that there is a basis for close *co-operation with the army*. As a result of the clumsiness of the leadership and the difficult communications one *cannot* count on *concentrated* employment *of forces* in correspondence with changing situations. In consideration of the defects of the ground organization and in the supply system and in view of the low technical ability of the Russian people the operational readiness must be regarded as *inadequate*. The operational strength of the front line units will therefore be *considerably* lower (at the most 50 per cent) than the nominal strength. It will *quickly* continue to shrink in a war against a highly armed enemy using modern weapons. The *operational capability* of all the flying units will be in doubt in a relatively short time as soon as the airfields and supply establishments will be attacked by air and in view of the poor supply situation and the dependence of the airfields on seasonal weather conditions .2.. The Russian anti-aircraft artillery is *badly* equipped ... and gives only *insufficient protection* to the Russian armed forces if the size of the country is considered. Even in *peacetime* conditions the Soviet Union is *not able* to meet the needs of the armaments industries and, at the same time, ensure a sufficient supply of food, clothing etc. to the population. ... In many fields the quality of the goods produced is still unsatisfactory. Reject production is very high ... . In all industries ... there is a *severe shortage of skilled workers* and of a sufficient number of trained *managers* ... . During a prolonged war the aircraft industry will not be able to prevent a *rapid collapse* of the front line forces ... The concentration of the metal and armaments industry still lies in the European area of the USSR west of the Urals ... . Interruptions [of the east-west and north-south railway network intersections] ... must have an *extremely adverse* effect on the transport and supply system ... . Compared with this breakdown of the goods traffic concerning all economic tasks in the event of war the other expected deficiencies fade into the background.

It was, however, at the same time also stated in the manual: 'In spite of the existence of a series of bottlenecks in the war economy ... *no branch of the economy* can, on account of the great spatial extent of the armaments industry and its concentration into well protected areas, be paralysed to such an extent that the overall supply of the USSR could be *decisively neutralized'*.

The Stalin purges were believed to have decapitated the industrial management. There was still supposed to be a lack of sufficiently trained engineers and skilled labour. For these reasons substantial improvements of the production process or technological innovations were not expected. The very favourable judgement of the French aviation industrialists Louis Breguet and Henry Potez, who had visited Russia in 1936, on the great achievements and the progress in production methods of the Soviet aviation industry apparently did not receive proper attention. Centres of Soviet aviation industry were considered to be located in the regions around Moscow and Leningrad as well as in central Russia, the Ukraine and the Ural region.[175] But, as just noted, the centre proper of Soviet armaments industry and economy was still considered to be located west of the Ural mountains, especially in the Ukraine and the Donbas–Donets Basin, and it was not believed at all possible to shift, by the early 1940s, 40 to 50 per cent of the total industrial production to the Ural–Kutsnetsk region. Information about the industrial network in the Asiatic part of Russia and in the Far East was scanty.

The fuel situation was, despite large oil deposits, especially in the Caucasus and the Ural Mountains, regarded as unsatisfactory because of increasing consumption, great losses during transport and the wear and tear of refineries. Aviation fuel was supposed to be in especially short supply. Already in peacetime the air and ground forces would be supplied only when allocations to the economy and the population were cut at the same time.

The railways handled about 90 per cent of the entire transport of goods and personnel. Despite this it could not yet be built up adequately. The building up of the inland waterway system, which handled 8 per cent of the freight traffic, still needed much time for completion. The road network was supposed to be still incomplete, too thin and in bad condition; at any rate, should the necessity arise, it could not essentially relieve the railraod system. Motorization was also unsatisfactory. So it was only to the railroad system that any importance in case of war was attributed. Civil aviation was considered important for the Soviet Union because of its intended conversion for military use in case of war, but the technical condition of access roads and aircraft was rated primitive and, therefore, the military utility of civil aviation deficient.

These opinions were undoubtedly pertinent in so far as they concerned the low military striking power of the Soviet Air Force, particularly in the first phase of the German attack,[176] but they generally underestimated the Soviets in many respects.[177]

Already the faulty assessment of Soviet aircraft strength was very serious. The total strength of the Soviet Air Force at the start of 1941 was assumed to be 10,500 aircraft, including about 5,000 modern aircraft; 7,500 planes were supposed to be deployed in European and 3,000 in Asiatic Russia. In the European part of the Soviet Union there were reckoned to be only 2,980 fighters, 2,100 bombers, 620 reconnaissance and 1,800 transport aircraft.[178] further estimates in the spring of 1941 gave an operational readiness of the opposing Soviet air striking force of 1,490 fighters and 1,360 bombers and long-distance reconnaissance planes, hence about 50 per cent of the existing total strength.[179] The army exercise 'Otto', carried out by Army Group A without Luftwaffe officers in St. Germain on 5 February 1941, proceeded on an assumption of only 4,000 Soviet aircraft in Europe, of which about two thirds were fighters and one third bombers, and only 50-60 per cent were assumed to be ready for operations. Ground organization, technical skills, striking power, and training of the Soviet Air Force were likewise rated low.[180] In the situation reports of the Luftwaffe Intelligence Department of May 1941 the tactical strength of the Soviet Air Force in Europe was estimated to be at least 7,000 and in Asia 2,000, aircraft. It was calculated that there were in the European sector 2,000 fighters, of which only 300 were up to date types, 800 short-range reconnaissance planes, 1,800 mostly obsolescent bombers, 700 ground attack aircraft and the same number of seaplanes, besides about 10,000 training aircraft. There was no essential change in the overall assessment of the Soviet Union.[181] Radio signals intelligence at the beginning of June indeed reported a total of 13,000 to 14,000 aircraft in Western Russia, yet in spite of that the Luftwaffe staff proceeded on the basis of a very much smaller number. They even put it, on 22 June 1941, at a total of about 5,800 Soviet front-line aircraft, only 1,300 bombers and 1,500 fighters being completely ready for operations, and they considered the combat value of the Soviet Air Force to be low in spite of its numerical superiority several times over.[182] Not until 19 July 1941 did the estimates of the Luftwaffe approach realistic numbers. They now started from a Soviet total aircraft strength in the European sector of 8,700 aircraft, including 4,000 fighters, 2,900 bombers and 1,800 reconnaissance and other front-line aircraft at the beginning of the war, to which were to be added about 7,500 training aircraft. According to Soviet sources, however, the Soviets had, at the start of the eastern campaign, about 18,000 front-line aircraft, 50 per cent of which (approximately 5,300 fighters, 2,800 bombers, 450 reconnaissance and 400 ground attack aircraft) were deployed in the west.[183] If one rejects the much higher 1943 German estimates of 28,000 aircraft in June 1941,[184] the German estimates of the total Soviet Air Force front-line strength before the campaign were too low by about half, of the air squadrons deployed in the European sector by about 30 per cent; of fighters by more than half and of bombers by about one third. All this was a fatal underestimate, because the actual strength of the Luftwaffe squadrons deployed on the eastern front, including the transport and army co-operation squadron, as well as the communications aircraft amounted to only a little more than one third of the front-line strength of the Soviet air striking force there.[185] With an actual strength of all Luftwaffe front-line squadrons of 5,599 aircraft and an operational readiness of 68 to 59 per cent, or approximately 3,859 aircraft on June 1941, there were in the east approximately 3,100 aircraft, 2,400 of them ready for operations,[186] not including the Finnish and Romanian squadrons, courier, transport, and communications aircraft as well as single- and twin-engine fighter training and replacement groups.

Even more serious was the underestimate of the Soviet aircraft production and production capacity so important for a prolonged war. The former, which in 1939, with an output of 10,382 aircraft, was about 2,000 aircraft higher than the German, was still reckoned in February 1941 to be only 600 aircraft per month;[187] in July 1942 still only 450 to 500 per month.[188] The Luftwaffe General Staff Intelligence Department in May 1941 calculated a whole year's production capacity of the Soviet aircraft industry at only 3,500 to 4,000 front-line aircraft.[189] Actually it had no accurate knowledge of the Soviet aircraft production and for a while simply subtracted the Soviet losses from the assumed Russian strength at the start of the war,[190] so that the picture of the enemy situation at first appeared increasingly advantageous to Germany.

In fact the Soviet Union not only kept in step with German aircraft production in 1941 in spite of the loss of extensive industrial areas, but it even exceeded it by 3,000 aircraft, and in 1942 by about 10,000 aircraft thanks to its great armaments effort in the unoccupied areas and to the relocation of the aircraft and other industries to the Ural region and to Siberia. The underestimation of the strength situation soon became evident in fact,[191] but by then the campaign which was to wear down the Luftwaffe was already under way. The Director of the Operations Department of the Luftwaffe General Staff noted on 3 July 1941: 'The military power of the Soviet Union is quite considerably stronger than could be learned from the pre-war investigations on 22 June. We had considered many strength data to be propagandistic exaggerations. The quality of the material is better than expected ... the great numbers will not at the moment be destroyed.' The Director of Air Defence Administration (*Luftwehr*) on 19 December 1941 was also aware of the very great underestimate of the military, economic and political strength of Russia. Goebbels later confided in his diary:

Concerning the Russian campaign the Luftwaffe experts, as Colonel Schmidt [!] openly admits, have had far-reaching illusions. It was believed that the Soviet Union would have been defeated by the autumn of 1941, and the whole weight of the Luftwaffe could be thrown against Britain ... The experts themselves do not know what Russia is actually building. But in spite of that it would be best for us to rate the numbers and quality of the aircraft relatively high.[192]

Goering too complained at the end of 1943 before the assembled Gauleiters:

And then came the Russian campaign! Yes, gentlemen, at that time I also indulged myself in the hope that we would not need to call off the campaign against England. At the start it was said: these Geschwaders were only to go to the east for the first four days in order to impress the Russians and to reinforce the effort. But what went east did not return, it remained in the east.[193]

In 1942, in a mood of disappointment, he reproached the German aircraft manufacturers that they had 'only very small cramped premises ... very small workshops for the mechanics ... compared with the huge factories of the Soviet aircraft industry',[194] and Hitler publicly announced on 3 October 1942: 'We had no presentiment of how gigantic had been the preparations of this enemy against Germany and Europe'.[195]

The optimistic assessment of Soviet Russia by the Intelligence Department influenced the top Luftwaffe leaders, although they did not all agree to the campaign plan. Rather some doubts were raised against it. Goering did not basically reject a German attack on the Soviet union, but only for that time since he did not consider the Soviet menace to be so serious. Besides, Britain was, for him, the main enemy, and he feared an excessive demand on the Luftwaffe in a war on several fronts and in view of the wide expanse of Russia. He foresaw dangers of the operations resulting from a possible breakdown in supplies. With this in mind he tried in the autumn and winter of 1940/41 to divert Hitler to the Mediterranean, particularly to Suez and Gibraltar, where Britain in his opinion would be seriously vulnerable, and he believed it to be a mistake to break off the air offensive against Britain. However, he also believed that Soviet armaments would not be adequate before 1942/43, nor even before 1944.[196] In addition to that Hitler appears to have dispelled Goering's doubts by hinting that within six weeks he would be able to resume the air war against Britain, and several hundred thousand soldiers from the Army units would become available as a work-force for air aramaments,[197] an optimistic view which Goering attempted to impart to Milch.[198] Shortly before the start of the campaign Goering who, in contrast to Hitler, had his doubts because of the very small amount of information about the Soviet Union, and who, since the middle of 1940, had made repeated warnings about the strength of the Soviet Air Force,[199] was optimistic about its outcome,[200] saw it to be essentially a supply problem[201] and believed that the Communist regime would collapse after 14 days at the most, and that within four to six weeks at the most the River Volga or the Urals would be reached.[202]

Milch too was at first opposed to the campaign on account of the danger of war on several fronts and of the probable entry of the USA into the war, and asked Goering to dissuade Hitler from this venture.[203] In contrast to Hitler, Goering and Jeschonnek he had actually fought in the east during the First World War. His doubts about the duration of the campaign made him, according to his own post-war statements, prudently supply the Luftwaffe with winter clothing in the face of opposition from the army.[204] But they were soon dispelled by the huge initial success, and gave way to a very optimistic attitude. This of course appears to have been overshadowed from time to time by moments of anxiety: for example in the spring of 1942 when he, together with Speer and Generaloberst Fromm, was said to have adopted the opinion that the war in the east had to be won by October 1942 with the existing forces, otherwise it would be lost. A little later, on his fiftieth birthday, he received a gift of 250,000 Reichsmarks from Hitler. His anxiety now appeared to have been silenced.[205] Irving, in his biography of Milch, which the Field Marshal had checked before publication, does not mention the latter's warning. Consequently, therefore, this attitude appears not to have been typical of his assessment of the sitaution in the east at that time. There is in fact ample evidence of this. In front of a group of assembled manufacturers he said on 18 September 1941: 'In the past we have perhaps underestimated the Russian. Today he is weak'.[206] Hitler, too,[207] the Chief of the Army General Staff,[208] and the Chief of the *Wehrmacht* Operations Staff[209] soon considered the war in the east as won. On 15 October 1941 Milch described the bomb and ammunition demands of the Luftwaffe Quartermaster General as 'to some extent much too high when based on the war situation, according to which the great campaign against Russia will come to an end in the foreseeable future'.[210] On 7 August 1942, two months after he, together with Goering, had demanded that the Germans must work as if the war were to last 30 years,[211] he stated that as far as the east was concerned the war 'will be over next year',[212] and exactly 14 days later he expressed the opinion at a DGAA-conference that the 'Russian war will be over at the end of September 1942'.[213] At the end of October 1942 he had become more cautious and hoped that the war against Russia would 'be finished in 1943, perhaps even by the middle of that year', and regarded the year 1944 as no longer being mainly determined by events in the war against Russia.[214] In the summer of 1943 Milch appeared still to be convinced that, as he put it, Russia would not survive the coming 'winter with troops capable of fighting; that is out of the question! She has nothing to eat and no longer any means of transport. Russia is in it up to the neck! Production will not rise any further, but will fall, slowly now, but more rapidly towards autumn. On that point we have very accurate particulars and up to date reports'.[215] Five weeks later he again stated that Russia would be ground into the dust if the Germans could manage to stay in possession of the Donets Basin and the Ukraine over the winter.[216] Not all these statements can be regarded as a conscious glossing over the situation – as Milch leads one to believe in his memoirs[217] – in order to stimulate his colleagues and to 'restore to them confidence and belief in our victory, hope, and hence pride in their duty and joy in their work'. The memoirs prove, rather, that he obtained no dependable and relevant information about the Soviet armaments from his Department for Foreign Armaments, that he was taken in by the underestimation of the Soviet Union, and that, indeed, his undeniable initial resistance to the eastern campaign cannot have been as strong as he let it be described after the war.[218]

The Chief of the Luftwaffe General Staff, Jeschonnek, concerning whose reaction to the prospects of a war with the Soviet Union hardly any sources are in existence, appears to have put forward no greater objections and to have been 'positively committed' to this new task.[219] He said to his Intelligence Chief Colonel Schmid, in this context: 'At last a neat and tidy war'.[220] This attitude of the Chief of the General Staff of the Luftwaffe was not quite so frivolous and superficial as it seems. Jeschonnek was aware of the failure of the air offensive against Britain, which, although still going on when he made this remark, had proved that the Luftwaffe was not capable of conducting an independent strategic air war against the vitals of an enemy country. The campaign in the east, however, was to be conducted by the Luftwaffe in co-operation with the army. This was the type of war in which the Luftwaffe had always been successful in Spain, Poland and France, and Hitler, in his Directive No. 21, had expressly stressed the co-operative mission of the Luftwaffe in Russia and had forbidden any strategic employment of it until the campaign had reached its goals. Against this background Jeschonnek's remarks must be measured. There were strong views against the planned campaign held by Generaloberst Löhr and his chief of staff, General-major Kortn. They both had made a realistic appraisal of the insurmount-able difficulties of a Russian campaign, and wanted to follow up the success of the Balkan campaign with a strategic move into the eastern Mediterranean aimed at cutting off the lines of communication of the British Empire. They were supported by the Director of the Operations Department, Generalmajor Hoffmann von Waldau, a man of above average talents, far-sighted and clear-headed, who in contrast to Jeschonnek, thought not only primarily in military, but also in political and economic terms.[221] Full of misgivings, he said a few weeks before this war while crossing the Grosser Stern Square with its Victory Column in Berlin: 'I wonder whether this place will come to be called "Red Army Square"'.[222] The Quartermaster General of the Luftwaffe, General Hans-Goerg von Seidel, expressed his opposition to the eastern campaign to Jeschonnek and Field Marshal Kesselring, because he was convinced that the Luftwaffe was not strong enough to wage war on two fronts.[223] Generally the ideas of the Luftwaffe leaders, which do not seem to have been sustained and brought forth vigorously enough, had no effect on Hitler's resolve concerning the war in the east.[224]

In spite of his optimism in public Goering also appears to have had apprehensions about the strength of the Red Air Force. Through his air attaché in Moscow in March 1941, he sought the permission of the Soviet government for German experts to inspect the armaments and research establishments of the Soviet aviation industry.[225] Besides the air attaché and the Luftwaffe engineers Tschersich and Schwencke, who were responsible to the DGAA for planning and foreign armaments, representatives of the firms Daimler-Benz, Heinkel, Askania, Mauser, and other companies took part in an extensive tour of inspection from 7 to 16 April 1941. They were shown aviation research institutes and aircraft and aircraft engine factories in Moscow, Rybinsk and Perm. During the farewell ceremony, the famous Russian aircraft designer Artem Mikojan, a brother of the People's Commissar for Economy, warned the Germans unambiguously: 'We have shown you everything we have and can do; whoever attacks us will be smashed'. The team of experts were 'extremely impressed' by the size of the establishments and the quality of the production. Their report reflected this opinion. They were, however, not believed. Goering rejected them as exaggerators and reprimanded the authors of the report as victims of Soviet bluff. The report[226] of the two Luftwaffe engineers, according to whom just one of the aero-engine factories inspected had been found to be six times larger than the main German engine works, roused Goering's wrath. He is said to have forbidden them to speak about it, called them grumblers, and threatened them with the concentration camp. The reports had a depressing effect on Hitler.[227] He reacted to them with the words: 'Well, look how far these people [the Russians] have advanced. We must start at once'.[228]

Intelligence assessment of the military efficiency of the Soviet Air Force proved generally correct in the first months of the campaign.[225] This applied to organization, training, weapons, equipment, signal communications – which were considered deficient – and leadership. It was true that Soviet pilots were badly trained and lacked initiative and that leaders were unable to command larger units. When a leader was shot down the rest lost their heads or continued to fly in formation without altering direction until the last of them had been shot down. This changed, of course, later in the war. Furthermore, it was rightly judged in May 1941 that the Red Air Force was in the process of re-equipment with new aircraft, which weakened it temporarily. But there was no knowledge that in the year and a half before the outbreak of war, the Soviets had already produced 2,739 aircraft of most modern types: 399 1, 1309 MiG 3 and 322 LaGG 3 fighters, 460 two-engine Pe 2 bombers and 249 IL 2 ground attack aircraft, which were among the best of their kind ever built in the world.[230]

German air intelligence strangely underestimated the value of para-military training of youths in Soviet Russia (although the Hitler Youth vigorously pursued a similar programme) and the ability of the Soviets for improvisation, which compensated for many shortcomings in their ground organization and lines of supply and communications. The capability of the Soviet soldier to camouflage and defend himself against low-level air attacks with all possible means, including infantry arms, was not sufficiently recognized.

Underestimation of the Soviet air armament production potential, of Soviet morale, and of the role of the civilian consumption sector within the entire war economy, was, as in the case of Great Britain, crucial. The production potential for 1941 was believed to be one-third of the actual production. The strength of the Red front-line air force was more than 50 per cent higher than German intelligence assumed, but was believed to be counterbalanced by the German superiority in training and equipment. There was no worst-case calculus if the optimistic assessment should turnout to be wrong. In reality, morale was not so bad that the Soviet state collapsed; consumer goods could be reduced much more than in Western societies because of the primitive life and inhuman pressure to which the Soviet population was accustomed.

Underestimated also was the ability to shift whole industries from the western parts of Russia to regions east of the Ural mountains and the size of industries already existing in Siberia. The failure to appreciate Soviet potential became obvious when the war in the east could not be successfully concluded before Christmas 1941.[231]

THE UNITED STATES

If German underestimation of Brtain's and the Soviet Union's air strengths was chiefly attributable to the conclusions drawn from air intelligence work, this applied only to a lesser extent to the assessment of the United States of America, because there were numerous published reports about the air armaments of the country in the press, and there were the reports of the Washington air attaché, General von Boetticher. These contained occasional warnings of the impending danger to Germany in the event of an American entry into the war on the side of Britain and about the unusually rapid growth of America's air and land forces, which Boetticher predicted would be ready for war in 1942. Of course these reports had little impact because they were generally diluted with a confusing amount of presumptuous National Socialist ideology, irrelevant subjective statements of German superiority and embellishing interpretations of the bulk of the information, and, moreover, the air attaché wrongly assumed that the Americans would engage themselves primarily with Japan in the Pacific.[232]

It is in any case unbelievable that the Director of Development in the Technical Office could still say in 1942 that he had known nothing about the development of American four-engine bombers, and had been taken unawares by the news about them.[233] In the Luftwaffe experimental establishment at Tarnewitz even before the war research was conducted on the possibilities of shooting down such large bombers, experiments which were, however, stopped by Udet as unnecessary.[234] The USA continued to be underestimated, as shown by the above mentioned air armaments comparison of August 1940 and as indicated by the air armaments comparison between Germany and Italy on the one hand, and Great Britain and the USA on the other, dated 30 August 1941.[235] The Anglo-American superiority given for 1943 was said to amount at the most only to 48 per cent in fighters and 63 per cent in bombers in Europe and only to 50 per cent as regards aluminium. This was just another very great underestimation of American air armament potential. It compares strangely with the German 'Elch' aircraft production programme, which was originally meant to quadruple the size of the Luftwaffe, but was soon reduced by 50 per cent because of a shortage of aluminium.[236] In fact Britain and American together in 1943 built 34,715 fighters and 37,083 bombers compared with only 11,198 fighters and 8,295 bombers and other attack aircraft on the German side.[237] This corresponded to a threefold Anglo-American superiority in fighters, and more than four-and-a-half-times as many bombers. Moreover, in the armament comparison the four-engine bombers, 14,100 of which were built in Britain and America in 1943, had actually been calculated two for one so that the underestimation was even more serious. Certainly the underestimation was mitigated by the statement that the 'economic knowledge about *aluminium production* and about the *industrial expansion* possible on both sides clearly shows that the new supply programme B [Elch] in combination with the Italian production *cannot prevent the enemy superiority becoming ever stronger* from the spring of 1942' on.[238] But still in June 1941 the Director of the 5th Department optimistically believed that the 'USA will not be capable of active participation in the air war in the foreseeable future'.[239] Compared with the lead which we ... had at first,' as the head of this department added after the war,[240] 'no one could imagine ... that the Western Allies could manage to produce armaments to that extent'. One did not believe what one already knew, even though the official aircraft production numbers of the Americans were first published as late as the autumn of 1944.[241]

American industrial superiority was, however, recognizable early enough, and therefore the underestimation of the USA is an example of wilful suppression of a disagreeable truth and of the fact that the intelligence information, even if faulty, did not have its implications taken seriously enough by the top Luftwaffe leaders and Hitler, which in the critical phase before the German declaration of war against the USA was decisive. Hitler had, at the end of July 1940, clearly understood Roosevelt's intention of supporting Great Britain, and had a presentiment of what the enmity of the USA would mean for him. For that reason he wanted to deter America from declaring war on Germany by a quick victory over the Soviet Union.[242] Even though, in 1941/42, he was concerned in playing down to himself and his entourage the danger which the enmity of the USA signified – which worked so fatally well in the case of Goering – he appears not yet to have taken seriously the contents of a memorandum from the aircraft manufacturer Fritz Siebel, dated 7 October 1940, about American air armament.[243] The breathtaking and not at all fanciful tempo of American rearmament was pointed out, as was the fact that the Americans would appear not with hundreds but with thousands of heavy bombers. The memorandum, warning of the vast American air armament and demanding at least equal air armament for Germany, was submitted to Hitler in the autumn of 1940 by Udet and Goering, who were deeply affected by it. Between the lines it contained proof that Germany could not win a war with the USA, because it would be a war of factories, and in this respect Germany was by far inferior. Hitler immediately discovered the only error of calculation in it, an interchange of kilograms and pounds, and laid the memorandum aside with the remark that the Americans had insufficient light alloys, which was indicated by a report about the collection of old aluminium saucepans and other aluminium equipment of American households.[244] Thereupon the memorandum was gone over once more by Siebel and Dr Justus Koch, considerably enlarged and brought right up to date.[245] In October 1941 it was again presented to Udet, Goering, Jeschonnek, and Hoffmann von Waldau. The Reich Minister of Weapons and Munitions, Dr Todt, took it along to Hitler in order to explain its significance and point out the critical importance of the Luftwaffe and of air armament in the war. Hitler slapped Udet, who was also present, on the shoulder and said that it could indeed be possible that the gentlemen were right, but he already had victory in the bag.[246] According to another version of the meeting he is said to have instructed Goering to dismiss Udet on account of his weakened nerves.[247] He also gave the order to keep quiet about this memorandum.[248] It is difficult to judge how far Hitler himself believed in his conscious belittling of the obvious threat of American war potential. It seems, however, that it did not weigh heavily on his mind because his land-oriented thinking was permeated with anti-American ideology. At Christmas 1940 he reprimanded Generalmajor Osterkamp because of his warnings about the expected strength of American air armament, and defended the opinion that it was not the air force that was decisive, as the Battle of Britain had shown, but the number of divisions, of which America could not create enough.[249] On the eve of the eastern campaign at the Führer's headquarters Hitler tried again to play down America's strength: 'America is a private capitalist country, and the transition to an entirely state-controlled economy must lead to friction, which would prevent the highest efficiency'. The high numbers of the output of the United States armaments industry he described as 'pure humbug'. As soon as the Soviet Union was defeated, which he thought would take four months at the most,[250] there would no longer be any shortage of raw materials and labour for Germany, and its armaments would be equal to any potential alliances in the world.[251] As to the reports from the German military and air attaché in Washington, General von Boetticher, concerning the American production of four-engine bombers, Hitler, who regularly read them carefully, 'exploded' about them[252] in the autumn of 1941, the more so since Goering and General Thomas, the Director of the War Economy and Armaments Office, considered them to be authentic. He again brought in ideological arguments, as a basis for his disagreement.[253] Still in the summer of 1942 he described a report checked by Boetticher on American air armaments as 'nonsense' and 'pessimism', although the number contained therein were already kept 35 per cent below the actual figures in order to make Hitler read the report and thus get at least a vague idea of the strength of America.[254] He did not ask the attaché on his return from America about the military situation there, but delivered a monologue on the weakness of American armaments in which he strongly believed.[255] Even in 1943 Hitler refused to have a threefold increase in the strength of the Reich's air defences and remarked that the figures supplied to him concerning America were too high.[256]

Goering soon accepted Hitler's misplaced confidence, in spite of scruples at first, about the incompetence of the Americans, as he had also earlier concurred with Hitler's opinions, which he more or less echoed, as Ansel[257] has written. The two finally confirmed each other in their depreciatory attitude, as when, for instance, Hitler said Goering had reassured him that the American Flying Fortresses were of miserable quality.[258] When in December 1941, shortly before the start of the war with the USA, an officer of the 5th Department spoke to Goering about the state of American air armament and forecast a production of over 100,000 aircraft in 1944, Goering retorted angrily that the Americans could only make refrigerators.[259] Reports that contradicted this biased judgement he also described in 1942 as 'dangerous to the common weal' and 'rubbish'. Whoever could write like that should have his head examined.[260] Hitler and Goering did not want to believe that America could become so powerful.[261] In October 1942 the latter said to Milch that 'all these American airplanes were not worth very much and would make no trouble at all for Germany' and that, 'in spite of their four engines etc., we can calmly face the future'.[262] When Milch on 4 January 1943 put before him the true figures about the Allies' aircraft production, amounting to several times that of Germany, Goering accused Milch of being a defeatist and shouted that the Americans, too, could only cook with water.[263] Even in the autumn of 1943 Goering explained to his State Secretary, upon the latter's futile attempts to let his experts on enemy armament brief the Reichmarshal, that the Führer had told him that the high production numbers were enemy propaganda, purely misleading, and had taken in the 'defeatists' in the Air Ministry.[264] Again in May 1944, long after he had realized that Britain and America had not only outstripped Germany in air armaments as regards quantity, but also in terms of quality,[265] he still had no inclination to believe the enemy production numbers, which Colonel Engineer Schwencke passed on to him.[266] One can, with Ansel, indeed only describe this as an 'ostrich approach to US air potential'.[267]

In contrast, Jeschonnek's attitude to the armaments reports from America, appears to have been less thoughtless, even if it was over-shadowed by his loyalty to Hitler and his obedience to Goering. He had obviously given credit to the importance of the attaché reports from General von Boetticher about American air potential. When Boetticher went to see him after his recall from America, and after a visit to Hitler at the end of May 1942, Jeschonnek's first question was about Hitler's reaction to Boetticher's reports from America, and whether Hitler had made any comments about the Luftwaffe and the defence of Germany by fighter aircraft. Hitler had not mentioned these matters. Jeschonnek complained bitterly: 'This is typical ... Exactly the same experience that I have had for months, even years. Did he say anything at all about the plans for the improvement of our over-committed Luftwaffe?' When this question was again answered in the negative, Jeschonnek is said to have sat down on a bench and to have uttered in a tearful voice:

Boetticher, we are lost. For years I have, on the basis of your reports, forwarded demands to Goering and Hitler, but for years my requests for the expansion of the Luftwaffe have not been answered. We no longer have the air defence I requested and which is needed for our German soil. Conflicting demands have been made by Hitler. We now no longer have any time ... to provide ourselves with the weapons to fight the dreadful threat which you have predicted and reported to us. Then we will be covered from the air with an enemy screen which will paralyse our power to resist. They will be able to play with us![268]

The CGS seems in fact – though late – to have taken the trouble to draw conclusions from the danger threatening in the west from American air power, and not to have suppressed it like Hitler and Goering, but was obviously restricted in his endeavours by the high losses in the east and the armaments priority for the army. Especially on account of his special, inner attachment to his Führer, which is so unusual for a General Staff Chief, and knowing his personal situation, which hampered him from carrying out what he knew to be correct, Jeschonnek seems to have been affected much more deeply by his clear knowledge of the mighty superiority of American air power, and to have been subject to greater mental conflict than Milch, whose assessment of American air potential still shared signs of a certain amount of powerful self-deception.

To the Industry Council Milch declared on 18 September 1941 that the Americans would build 16,000 aircraft in 1942.[269] In fact they built 47,836 warplanes in that year. In July 1942 Milch spoke of wanting to reach the numbers stated by Roosevelt for the American air power.[270] In spite of his belief that Germany, in comparison with the Allies, could 'never arm too much', and in spite of his previous statement, according to which the Anglo-Americans in 1942 had built over five times more fighters and four times more bombers than the Reich, he stressed in a DGAA conference[271] in January 1943 that Germany 'could equal this in terms of single- and twin-engine fighters by 1944 (in terms of numbers)', and 'if one considers the quality ... then it is a fact that parity already exists in 1943', because the Americans also needed material to fight the Japanese. 'In 1943, we could therefore,' as he concluded, 'fight the enemy with our single-engine and twin-engine fighters with complete prospects of real success. For 1944 we would, with almost the same numbers, be able to achieve a considerable superiority over the double front of Britain and America'. The bomber ratio, in Milch's view, was to be 'looked at in a different light ..., because in fact the enemy was not at all in the position to deploy this weapon in the small space available to him; he cannot do that, he does not have so many airfields very close to Germany as to be able to operate and accommodate them all'. He also pretended not to know 'what, by all means, the enemy wants to do with this great number of warplanes'. In October 1943[272] Milch still informed Goering and Speer of his 'hope to intersect in approximately November 1944 the production graph of the Americans as regards front-line aircraft ... The enemy intends to level out here and no longer to climb higher, although he could do that'. Milch made these statements although he knew that it 'would become not easier, but harder for the enemy is able to step up air armaments production on a very different scale from what we can do'[273] and although he (of course vigorously denied after the war)[274] had exclaimed several times in a conference of the Reich Minister, Secretaries of State, and Gauleiters with Goebbels on 2 August 1943 after the heavy air attack on Hamburg: 'We have lost the war! Definitely lost!'.[275] Milch's optimistic ideas quoted in respect of German and enemy air armaments show that the otherwise sober-minded, energetic Milch, like German air intelligence, succumbed to self-deception in the evaluation of American industrial capacity, which he nevertheless otherwise recommended should be imitated and not underrated. After the war he appeared intent on hushing up this error.[276]

It must be pointed out generally that it is difficult to determine in each case whether Hitler and Goering simply did not believe the high figures on enemy potential eventually presented to them or did not want to believe them despite better insight.

THE LUFTWAFFE RADIO INTELLIGENCE SERVICE

Having taken a general view on air intelligence, we must now take a closer look at the Luftwaffe radio intelligence service, from which 70 to 80 per cent[277] of useful information about the enemy stemmed. Unfortunately the end product, the intelligence report, does not show how the individual pieces of information it contained were gained. Moreover, the records of the radio intelligence service of the Luftwaffe including the deciphered intercepts are no longer available. Therefore the following examples of successful radio intelligence activities cannot be substantiated by any original records as it is the case with Ultra.[278] They are based on the memories of specialists engaged in it as collected by Colonel of the Signal Corps Kurt Gottschling in his post-war study on Luftwaffe radio intelligence.[279]

The signal or radio intelligence service of the Luftwaffe comprised radio-listening, radio deception, radio-camouflaging and radio-jamming, referred to under the collective term *Funkhorchdienst* (radio-listening service) until well into the war, towards the end of which it was called *Funkaufklärung* (radio intelligence). It was surrounded with very much secrecy, maintained by the members of this service even after the war. The Luftwaffe radio intelligence service co-operated closely with the Armed Forces Signal Service (*Wehrmachtnachrichtenführung*) and with respective services of the army, navy and other organizations. Radio intelligence activities were carried out by special air signal companies organized in independent battalions and air signal regiments. In general only one air signal battalion was allocated to an air fleet, and an air corps was furnished with one company only. These units were subordinated to the intelligence officer (Ic) of the pertinent staff only tactically. Their central control and direction rested with the Cipher Office of the Commander-in-Chief of the Luftwaffe. This office consisted of sections A (collection and evaluation of enemy material), B (evaluation West), C (evaluation Southwest and Southeast), D (evaluation East) and E (deciphering East and West). The Cipher Office was the nucleus of the 3rd (Radio Intelligence) Department of the Chief of the Luftwaffe Signal Communications Service, renamed *Generalnachrichtenführer* (General Officer Commanding Air Signals) in 1944. This 3rd Department handled all radio intelligence, jamming and wire-tapping activities and, in addition to the two independent sections for general operational and personnel matters, consisted of groups II (radio-listening service, III (radar observation and jamming service) and IV (code control and development).[280] So, as already pointed out, radio intelligence was the domain of the General Officer Commanding the Air Signal Service who was directly subordinated to the Chief of the General Staff of the Luftwaffe but not to the Intelligence Branch of the Luftwaffe Operations Staff. In matters concerning radio intelligence this Branch was – like other officers of the Air Ministry – only authorized to submit directives to, and to ask for services of, the 3rd Department and/or its Cipher Officer. Such orders were also placed there by the air fleets and air corps. Otherwise the radio intelligence units continually had to carry out tactical and political-strategic radio reconnaissance or, depending on the situation, radio deception, camouflaging (*Verschleierung*) and jamming as well as radar and telephone observation tasks. The radio intelligence regiments and independent battalions furnished intelligence directly to the intelligence and operations officers or chiefs of staff of the requesting air fleet and air corps or to the air force units immediately concerned. Intelligence of strategic importance or intercepts that could not be deciphered were forwarded to the Cipher Office of the Commander-in-Chief of the Luftwaffe for final decoding, evaluation and dissemination.[281]

Towards the end of the war all radio intelligence units were subordinated administratively to the Higher Commander of Radio Intelligence (*Höherer Kommandeur der Funkaufklärung*). In 1944 the Office of the Chief of Radio Intelligence within the Reich (*Funkaufklärungsführer Reich*) was established for the central tactical control of all radio intelligence units engaged in the air defence of Germany.[282]

The following successes of the Luftwaffe radio intelligence service have been reconstructed from memory by former air signal officers after the war[283] and may therefore contain some errors in details.

During the 'Phoney War' it was learnt in 1939 on the basis of a long experience in peace time and through listening to the radio traffic of British air units and to private dialogues between British signal personnel that Great Britain, at that time, was not planning any offensive operations in the West. This knowledge was highly important for Hitler's strategy.[284]

In publication about the so-called Air Battle over Heligoland Bight (*Luftschlacht über der Deutschen Bucht*) on 18 December 1939, the first major victory of the German fighter arm over the British bomber force in the Second World War that cost the latter at least twelve out of 24 Wellingtons against only four German fighter losses and forced RAF Bomber Command to discontinue daylight raids and change over to night attacks, it is usually to the experimental 'Freya' radar sets of the German Navy and Air Force on the islands of Wangerooge, Borkum and Heligoland that the main credit for the timely location of the enemy planes and alerting of the fighters is given. Apart from the fact that this 'success' forced Germany to establish a very expensive night fighter defence system, it was actually the Luftwaffe radio-listening service of the listening and direction-finding station at Pewsum near Emden run by the 10th company of the IIIrd battalion of 2 Signal Regiment that tracked the British bomber squadrons first and kept Fighter Wing Schumacher (No. 1) informed about their route. The 'Freya' radar sets had a range of only about 120 to 130 km. The radio-listening station, however, located the bombers already while tuning their radio sets shortly before take-off from the vicinity of the Wash at a distance of about 540 km and tracked their flight across the Dogger Bank and farther east.[285] The radio-listening service was quite familiar with the call signs and specialities of individual British flying units because of a long experience dating back to peacetime. The success of the Air Battle over Heligoland Bight caused the radio-listening service in subsequent years to engage gradually more and more in tactical activities instead of sticking to its original strategic[286] objectives: intercepting information of strategic importance. Another reason for this shift of interest seems to have been that the yield in these strategic activities was quite negligible. So the continuous defensive patrol flights across Heligoland Bight could be reduced substantially, since the air situation could be reconnoitred sufficiently by radio listening. However, the information gained through radar was still necessary to supplement and confirm the results of the radio listening service.

The co-operation between the flying units and the radio listening service of the Luftwaffe first exercised over Heligoland Bight was intensified in the air war against Britain in the summer of 1940. In particular it was the radio-listening and direction-finding station

Wissant[287] that was quite successful. The station was closely connected
with the airfields on the Channel coast and continuously reported the
bomber, reconnaissance, and fighter units taking off from British bases.
Because of its complete detection of the radio telephone traffic of the
British fighter units over south-east England it could make out the entire
employment of British fighters including their ground radio stations, their
zones of operation, the units, their state of readiness. Reports with
charts were continually forwarded to the Luftwaffe Operations Staff/
Intelligence through the C-in-C of 2 Air Fleet, Field Marshal Kesselring.
British fighter strength diminished at first and reached a low point around
20 July 1940. The commanding officer of the IIIrd battalion of 2 Air Signal
Regiment reported this to 2 Air Fleet at the right time for immediate
successful attacks. Although he received an award for this, nothing
happened, because the German preparations for an invasion of Britain
had not yet advanced sufficiently. Later on British fighter strength
increased continually despite great losses, which was duly reported by
the radio-listening service. The Chief of Intelligence of the Luftwaffe
Operations Staff was, however, more inclined to trust the calculations of
his own department, which were based on false figures and on the
underestimation of British capacity for aircraft production. Contrary to
the actual figures he predicted a complete breakdown of British fighter
defences by early September. This also provoked, as it turned out later,
Hitler's and Goering's precipitate and faulty decision to turn from attacking British fighter bases to raiding London and certain industrial targets.
Successful radio intelligence work did not, in this case, also lead to
operational success; on the contrary it could not prevent the Luftwaffe
from failing strategically over England.

The radio-listening service at the Channel front distinguished itself
further in locating British convoys, in uncovering the identification friend
or foe key of the enemy fighters and bombers, and in alerting the German
fighters in time to intercept approaching enemy aircraft, as well as in
continually informing them about the enemy air situation. Until 30
August 1940 German fighters on the Channel coast shot down 63 enemy
planes solely on the basis of intelligence from Wissant. The radio-listening
service also discovered deceptive ground-air signal traffic executed by
British ground stations solely for the purpose of trying to simulate larger
fighter missions.[288]

As already mentioned the Reich air defence experienced the growth of
a new defensive: tactical-dynamic radio intelligence developing itself
from a radio-listening system which was originally conceived to be of a
strategic and static nature.[289] This development was supported by Colonel
Schumacher of 1 Fighter Wing (*Jagdesgeschwader* 1) and Generals
Kammhumber and Schmid as air officers commanding XII and I (Night-

Fighter) Air Corps. It climaxed when, in 1944, most of the radio-listening and jamming units engaged in Reich air defence were subordinated to the Air Officer Commanding Radio Intelligence in the Reich, who also ran the Central Operational Headquarters of the Radio Listening Service in Treuenbrietzen.[290] This headquarters could give tactical orders to all radio-listening units of the Reich air defence and to their reporting centres. It also housed the operational headquarters of the chief of the radio-jamming service. Altogether this set-up was a vital supplement of the aircraft reporting and radar locating service. Had there not already existed a tactical and strategic radio listening service of the Reich air defence at the time when the German radar sets of the air warning service were paralysed by British 'Window' counter-measures during the attack on Hamburg at the end of July 1943 and later, an effective fighter defence would no longer have been possible from then on. The reporting centres 1 to 5 installed between the Central Operational Headquarters of the Radio Listening Service and the radio-listening units, especially reporting centre 1, were engaged with

- the direction of systematic reconnaissance and surveillance of the enemy installations for command, radio transmission, radio telegraphy, navigation and flight safety;
- the continuous collection of reports and intelligence on enemy activities, intentions of employment and preparations on the bases and within the entire territory of the enemy (e.g. an up-to-date air situation estimate about England);
- reporting daily at 1600 hours whether there would be an air attack during the coming night;
- reporting daily at 1800 hours whether there would be a daylight attack on the following day;
- locating the take-off, gathering and departure of enemy air units;
- information on changes of enemy mission planning and on the frequent premature breaking off of missions;
- working out methods independent of each other as well as of radar about continuous tracking of the routes taken by Allied bomber formations e.g. over England, in the approach and over the target area as on the return flight until touch-down;
- informing and directing pertinent radar stations towards the expected area of attack;
- orientation about air warning and visual observation service;
- the preparation of a combat report a few hours after an air raid including details on engaged enemy units, their strength, bases, landing areas, diversions, casualties, damage reports, futile recalls etc.

- the very difficult differentiation between main, harassing, mock and decpetion attacks important for ordering the fighters to the right place in time and for precautionary alerting other defence units and special early warning of possible areas of attack. This was one of the most significant achievements of the radio intelligence service.[291]

This description reveals that a radar defence system by itself would have been utterly insufficient for home air defence, because it could not furnish any advance information about the planning and preparation of bombing raids twelve hours or more before the event. It is not possible to express in numbers the benefits which Reich air defence gained from radio intelligence, but it can safely be said that the Allied bomber losses would have been smaller, the damage in Germany larger without the Radio Intelligence Service. This may be demonstrated by the following examples.

The first is the British bombing raid on Nuremberg in the night of 30 March 1944.[292] This was the raid generally recognized as the one with the highest casualty rate ever inflicted on Bomber Command during the Second World War. In fact the British lost 165 out of 795 bombers including 106 total losses; 545 air crew were killed and 159 taken prisoner. The Germans lost 19 fighter pilots and 110 civilians. There is an unproved tale that the plan for this attack had been betrayed to the Germans. It is much more probable that the event was a success of the radio-listening service. By 4.30 p.m. on 30 March Headquarters Air Fleet Reich had already been informed by the Chief of Luftwaffe Signal Communications that a heavy bombing attack was expected for the coming night. The radio-listening service had obtained this intelligence information through technical observation of RAF radio traffic. Already an hour later the radio-listening service reported the approximate strength of the attacking forces, which amounted to between 700 and 800 bombers, and also the fact that the target was located in southern Germany. It is possible that this intelligence was concluded from the observation of the intensity of preparations, of the bases where the units were stationed and from special characteristics of British test reports as well as from the development of the weather. German fighter units were ready for take-off in good time. The majority of the bombers came across the Belgian coast, while a smaller unit flew towards Heligoland Bight probably in order to simulate an attack on Hamburg or Berlin and to split up German air defence. Air Fleet Reich, however, knew what the main attacking force was, because the aircraft flying north were, as the radio-listening service found out, not equipped with H2S radar sets necessary for major area attacks. The fighters were, therefore, massed along the prospective route of the main bomber force. Diversionary attacks of Mosquito bombers on Cologne,

Aix-la-Chapelle and Kassel were recognized as such. The jamming by British jamming stations of the radio telephone traffic between German ground control stations and fighters was countered effectively by switching over to new frequencies. The cloudless cold night and the clearly visible trails of the bombers made it easy for the fighters to keep in touch with the bomber stream and to find their targets. All this together led to the catastrophe marking the end of the Douhetian 'bomber dream' cherished by the Commander-in-Chief Bomber Command and rendered his protest against the contemplated tactical employment of Bomber Command for Overlord worthless.

Another example of the efficiency of radio intelligence was the American air raid on Ploesti on 1 August 1943.[293] East of Benghasi in North Africa the Americans had erected a model of the oil-mining and refining district of Ploesti, Romania, in order to familiarize the bomber crews of the 9th US Air Force with the area and train them for their first major operation. The radio-listening service discovered and observed these training activities for several weeks. The Germans knew, therefore, that an extraordinary air attack was to be expected. On 28 July training activities were suddenly discontinued and a conspicuous radio silence followed. When, therefore, at 7 a.m. on 1 August the ground station started its characteristically one-sided radio activities, and as there was much more tuning than was customary for flights to Sicily, Italy and Greece, the Germans were certain that this was the day of the expected major attack. The route of the 177 B-24 'Liberator' bombers was initially tracked on the basis of the Allied aircraft reporting grid. It stretched to Italy and then turned across the Adriatic Sea to Ochrido Lake and from their northeast to Ploesti. The information obtained from the radio-listening service enabled a timely alert of all defensive forces in the southeast, the laying of a smoke-screen over the oil-mining and processing area, and the reinforcement of fighter forces. The bomber units could be split up. The return flight developed into a catastrophe, as shown by the many SOS-calls which were frequently transmitted in disregard of regulations. Only 92 bombers returned to base; others had to make emergency landings in Turkey, Cyprus, Sicily and Malta, and 54 bombers and 532 air crew were lost. Romanian oil which was extremely important for German warfare, especially in Soviet Russia, was thus spared new air raids until eight months later, 5 April 1944.

Towards the end of the war Allied bombers could be tracked by locating their panorama radars.[294] The equipment of the so-called weather-Lightnings with Meddo-radar sets enabled the radio-listening service to predict for instance the selected bombing targets of the 15th US Army Air Force a day in advance. These reconnaissance plans operated their Meddo sets at higher pulse rates over the planned target areas – probably for photographic purposes. This could be heard in the earphones of the Korfu-direction finding set, which was a special centimetre-wave receiver. This set responded perfectly to the British 9-cm and the American 3-cm panoramic radars. Since the reconnaissance planes could be tracked continuously, the target photographed could easily be made out by the simple means of time comparison.

From radio intelligence in air defence we now turn to its employment in the co-operation of the Luftwaffe with army and navy.

The operational orders of the Commander-in-Chief of the Yugoslav Air Force could be intercepted and deciphered so rapidly that there was time enough for German counter-measures. This helped greatly in bringing the campaign to a quick end.[295]

The role of Luftwaffe radio intelligence in determining the actual strength of the Red Air Force in June 1941 has already been mentioned. In the war against Soviet Russia radio intelligence proved to be the Luftwaffe's most important and most reliable source of information.[296]

During the early stages of the eastern campaign it was possible to ascertain the rout and dissolution of the Soviet front on the basis of the discontinuation of Soviet radio traffic, while its subsequent gradual increase indicated the stabilization of the front and the consolidation of the Red Air Force. The detection of the location, strength and types of aircraft of newly established Soviet flying units as well as of air depots permitted a continuous supplementation of the estimate of the enemy situation. Combat aircraft could be detected especially by means of surveillance of the radio traffic between Soviet pilots. The positions of such aircraft were immediately reported to the German fighter ground control stations, which deployed friendly fighters accordingly. Through this type of co-operation with radio-listening service alone German fighter units shot down 600 Soviet planes until April 1943.[297]

Again, during the early stages of the eastern campaign, in the operational area of Army Group Centre on the Eastern front, the XXIVth mechanized Army Corps with 400 to 500 tanks was located in a forest by a Soviet reconnaissance plane. The pilot did not radio his message at once but returned to base and reported his findings orally. The Soviet radio station at Bobruisk broadcast the news in clear language and with high energy to all flying units in the area and gave the exact location of the massed tanks. The radio-listening service of the IIIrd Battalion of the 2nd Air Signals Regiment picked up the message and forwarded it immediately to the German fighter units in the vicinity (*Jagdgeschwader* 51 and 27). They were able to intercept the Soviet bombers already on their approach or even at their bases. The Soviets lost 180 aircraft. A similar situation occurred in the north where another tank corps got stuck near Schaulen for lack of fuel. It was saved by the radio-listening service and furnished with fuel by airlift so that it could proceed toward Riga, while the attacking Soviet bomber units were decimated.[298]

In the autumn of 1941 the radio-listening service of 1 Air Fleet discovered the transport of Siberian troops to Tichvin which was effected within fourteen days. Hitler, however, did not want to believe this. The Soviet attack on the German assembly positions, therefore, was unexpected. Its success prevented Finns and Germans from meeting east of Lake Ladoga and thus completing the encirclement of Leningrad. Its consequences were the fierce fights on the Volchov River and the encirclement of a German Army corps near Demjansk.[299]

German radio intelligence was generally in a position to detect changes in the Soviet Air Force ground organization and the concentration of Soviet flying forces in time. Around Stalingrad the movements of the ground organization for the establishment of five Soviet air armies was reported very early and it was pointed out by air intelligence that owing to this massed concentration of forces heavy air activity of the Soviets had to be expected. These reports were, however, treated with scepticism.[300]

In February 1943 a Soviet ground force under General Popov assembled near Isjum to attack south toward the See of Azov and cut off German forces along the River Mius. German army and air force radio intelligence units were able to observe Soviet operations continuously and track their movements so that this offensive could be thwarted by timely German counter-measures. An intercepted radio message of one of the army corps under Popov's command was very enlightening: 'By all means,' it read, 'we have to revise our keys and superencipherment of co-ordinates, because all our operations ordered by radio messages are being thwarted by instant counter-measures of the enemy. We are betraying ourselves.'[301]

From Konstanza in Romania the German air listening service could observe the south-eastern part of the eastern front, especially the Soviet Black Sea Air Force consisting of five air regiments. Radio traffic was carried out by radio telegraph and radio telephone and on frequencies which were changed daily, with certain frequencies continually repeating themselves. Call sign structures and encipherment did not distinguish themselves from those ordinarily used by other Soviet flying units. Reconnaissance aircraft were recognized in time by detection of tuning traffic. They operated between the Crimea and Konstanza. Their position could be detected by cross-bearing as soon as they transmitted their reconnaissance reports. In this way, located German convoys could be protected by German fighters. So it was possible to destroy large numbers of Soviet planes approaching German convoys during the evacuation of the Crimean peninsula in 1944. The fact that Soviet reconnaissance planes operated mainly in the area of the Black Sea coast and did not fly further south than the 44th degree of latitude allowed German convoys to travel between Sevastopol and Konstanza for a month without being harassed by Soviet aircraft.[302]

Luftwaffe radio intelligence units also kept close surveillance on British supply traffic in the Mediterranean and through Africa. From Sicily and Crete the deployment of British fighters, bombers, torpedo and observation aircraft in Malta and the approach of supply planes, as well as the passing through of transport vessels and couriers, were observed steadily. From Athens and Kavalla air signal units observed Turkey, the Near and Middle East, North Africa and the supply routes across central Africa from the Gold Coast via Khartoum to Egypt. The activities of the Royal Air Force in the Near East, the newly supplied aircraft types and the state of airfields could be discerned. The employment of weather observation aircraft could be spared by deciphering British weather reports.[303]

The sinking of the Italian battleship *Roma* and the damaging of the *Italia* by means of gliding bombs was made possible through the Luftwaffe signal service which located the Italian naval force while it left the port of La Spezia and reported its course to Luftwaffe bomber units.

There are also some examples of the engagement of Luftwaffe signal communications units in radio deception and jamming. Jamming operations were conducted steadily in home air defence, although mostly only as reactions to enemy measures. They were directed against the entire Allied radar service, against radio telephone traffic of enemy day- and night-fighters and against radio navigation of enemy air forces and ground control of bombers using blind bombing methods. Radio deception measures were usually co-ördinated with the other services, particularly if they were to convince the enemy of certain simulated strategic operations.

The breakthrough of German battleships through the English Channel in February 1942[304] was the first larger radio screening and jamming operation carried out by the Luftwaffe and the navy together in the Second World War. The accompanying German fighter and destroyer aircraft flew at low altitude in order to evade radar detection by the British and kept silence until the beginning of the air battle after the ships had passed the narrowest stretch of the Channel. The frequencies, positions and ranges of British radar stations along the Channel coast had been detected by radio observation, the danger zone regarding the detectability of the German aircraft had been fixed and jamming stations against British radar had been developed well in advance. The Germans abstained from any jamming measures before the event. Only when the battleships were passing the critical section of the Channel did all jamming stations become active at once. Their activities were also directed against airborne radar of British reconnaissance aircraft. German bombers equipped with radar simulated the approach of strong striking forces, against which the British dispatched fighter forces which were thereby diverted from the ships. The British kept being confused even after they had unmistakably located the German men-of-war and after the latter could no longer be deceived away. The success of this breakthrough operation, however, depended not only on these German jamming and deception measures, but to a much larger degree on bad weather and good chance. The radar instruments of two British observation planes failed to operate at the right moment so that the ships were discovered too late. This large-scale radio-jamming and deception operation had only an ephemeral success, because the British developed such a great variety of radar apparatuses with different frequencies that Germany, short of both specialized labour and appropriate electronic material, was not in a position to produce the necessary numbers and types of radar sets to meet this challenge and jam all the frequencies.

In the spring of 1942 the Germsn succeeded in safely shipping about 20 tanks to Tripoli which Rommel needed for a new offensive. That the convoy arrived there safely must be attributed to the radio intelligence service of the IIIrd battalion of Air Signal Regiment No. 2. By jamming it had to prevent or impair the transmission of the radio messages of enemy reconnaissance aircraft about the course of the convoy. Moreover, radio deception had to be carried through by way of infiltrating British radio traffic without arousing the suspicion of the British and Italians. The radio intelligence service transmitted faked position reports of the convoy. Thereupon the British strike forces were deployed the following night in an area located approximately two meridians east of the actual route. There the bombers searched in vain for the convoy, and when they repeated requests for its position, the jamming station, re-entering the radio traffic, answered in a dilatory manner so that the aircraft, running out of fuel, either had to return or make forced landings before reaching the coast. The convoy reached its port of destination without being attacked and without any losses. The British now resorted to measures rendering further German jamming operations of little use.[305]

A few days before the campaign in the west was started in May 1940, the Luftwaffe, following a similar operation of the army, tried by means of a large-scale radio deception operation to screen the actual centre of concentration of its bomber and close-air support units which lay with 2 Air Fleet and its Air Corps IV, VIII and I. By intensified simulation of radio and flight traffic with the IInd and Vth Air Corps of 3 Air Fleet and by radio-simulated transfer of 7 (Parachute) Air Division to the Stuttgart area, attempts were made to divert the enemy from the actual centre of attack. Similar radio deception took place before the surprise attack on the Soviet Union in 1941,[306] when the withdrawal of the flying units deployed against England was to be hidden, and in the summer of 1942, when the offensive in the south-east toward Stalingrad and the Caucasus was to be screened by making the Soviets believe that the German air strike forces were transferred to Luftwaffe Command East in the middle of the eastern front.

The time and area of the invasion in June 1944 were discerned by Luftwaffe radio intelligence.[307] In the evening of 5 June there were many indications of imminent larger enemy operations. Enemy broadcasting stations transmitted orders for sabotage to partisan groups in France at about 9 p.m. to be carried out within 24 or 48 hours. At 10 p.m. weather observation planes of the heavy US bomber units transmitted weather reports. Weather observation for the tactical American air force began around 11 p.m. The transfer of British close air support forces to the south was recognized by this time. The assembly of heavy US bomber units north of London was observed at 2.30 a.m. on 6 June. Nevertheless, the invasion came as a surprise. The blame for this rests with higher headquarters, not with the radio intelligence service.

Summing up, it can be said that the highly secret Luftwaffe Radio Intelligence Service was very effective not only with regard to the relatively large amount of enemy information it produced but also because this information, owing to its nature, was reliable and true. Of course, as in other countries' intelligence services, the information had to be used in combination with intelligence gained through other channels and from other sources. Originally set up for strategic reconnaissance of higher command echelons it soon changed into a predominantly tactical means of reconnaissance, thus replacing many squadrons of observation aircraft.[308] Consequently its successes seem to have been mostly of a tactical and not of a strategic nature. No outstanding achievements in the field of grand strategy have been related. In fact Luftwaffe radio intelligence was primarily engaged in the observation of enemy air forces while the observation of the radio traffic of state and civilian agencies had to be ordered now and then by the Commander-in-Chief of the Luftwaffe via the Chief of Luftwaffe Signal Communications and his Cipher Office from the *Forschungsamt* or other agencies.[309] The latter tasks, however, increased during the war. To give a general idea of the success of Luftwaffe radio intelligence: out of 125,000 American five-letter groups about 25,000 could be decoded. It must have been similar with English radio traffic. In the Mediterranean theatre of war about 5,000 radio intelligence specialists were engaged on the part of the Luftwaffe. Luftwaffe radio intelligence is supposed to have employed a total of about 10,000 specialists,[310] but it seems there were many more engaged in this activity. So the opinion voiced when the British Ultra secret was uncovered about ten years ago that the history of the Second World War would have to be rewritten cannot be maintained, because the Germans also had a capable, though not in the least as efficient, radio intelligence service.

CONCLUSIONS AND EXPLANATIONS

In sum, German air intelligence was characterized by the following main traits:

- as far as radio intelligence is concerned it was predominantly of a tactical nature;
- it was usually correct in its assessment of enemy frontline strength, training, organization and equipment, i.e. in the field of tactics and operations; it failed in its estimates of a grand strategic nature, economy, production capacities, and morale;
- underestimations of enemy war potential took place during the first years of the war and, therefore, were decisive for its outcome; correct assessments in later years can be disregarded as having had no effect on the course of the war.
- ideological bias and euphoria about the success of the first war years blinded German air intelligence, subjected Luftwaffe leaders, particularly Goering, to rapidly changing moods, and prevented a sober and true intelligence picture of the enemy;[311]
- there was a conspicuous lack of worst-case calculation;
- as in other countries, true intelligence information was not always believed by responsible leaders.

The following explanations might offer some answers concerning the reasons for some of the main characteristics of German air intelligence:

1. General staff officers in charge of the major posts within air intelligence were trained more in the military fields of tactics and operations and not so much in fields pertaining to grand strategy, namely economics, science, technology, industrial production methods, mentality of other peoples, because

> a) There was a strong tradition of short-war thought in Germany. Experience in our history of the preceding 150 years had shown that a long war could not be sustained due to the lack of resources and that, therefore, all possible force should be applied right at the beginning of a war in order to win it. In a short war that had to be decided by the forces available at the beginning. The potential that might be developed later on was not considered relevant.
> b) Fighting qualities in the field and tactics and operations were, in a society shaped by military tradition, of a higher value than good

performance in assignments in rear areas, in infrastructural sectors, and at the desk of the intelligence officer, who, therefore, was *de facto* subordinated to the operations officer.

c) There was even a traditional disdain for intelligence work in Germany,[312] which was regarded as close to spying and therefore dirty. That good intelligence was essential for a realistic ends-means calculation especially in a long war, and that intelligence work was mainly a collecting and collating activity based on scholarly method, for example of the historian, was not seen clearly enough.

2. The shortcomings in officer training were not compensated for by a better organization and linkage between all agencies necessary for conducting a modern war of attrition so as to include also civilian specialists and agencies that were knowledgeable in the various economic, scientific, technical and political fields. Military intelligence, and air intelligence in particular, were considered until too late in the war to be mere military business. Consequently, there were no joint organizations and committees that guaranteed a steady flow of all pertinent information, as for example in England.[313] Instead, Hitler's Basic Order No. 1 for the Safeguarding of Military Secrecy forbade anyone to know more or any earlier than he needed for the execution of his task. There was no war plan reaching further than the Blitz against Poland. Because Hitler himself made his intentions known only partly and only at short notice, there were no long-range perspectives for intelligence work, which, in the decisive first years of the war, was repeatedly directed to new countries and subjects on an *ad hoc* basis. Intelligence developed a long-range activity of its own only when it was too late to have any effect on the war.

3. In German air doctrine the principle of the offensive was paramount. It was conditioned by Germany's unfavourable geo-strategic position, which, in the eyes of German military planners, demanded that a war should be carried into enemy country from its outset in order to protect Germany and obtain a glacis, from which to establish an early warning air defence system. An attacker usually wants to impose his will upon the defender by sheer force, and to be strong enough for this purpose is more important than obtaining information about the defender, though this does not mean that the attacker does not need any information at all about the defender. Only when Germany was thrown upon the defensive did the air force intensify its intelligence work, because defenders, being usually weaker than their attackers, must make up for their weakness by good intelligence about the enemy in order to take appropriate measures.[341]

The underestimation of foreign air power, war potential, and morale and the overestimation of German air strength by German air intelligence before the war and in its early years contributed substantially to corroborate Hitler's false view that he could successfully wage a succession of victorious campaigns against individual opponents unpunished and build up a racially determined continental empire unhampered.

APPENDIX
SECOND WORLD WAR GERMAN AND ANGLO-AMERICAN GENERAL OFFICER GRADES COMPARED

German	British	US
Generalmajor	Air Commodore	Brigadier General
Generalleutnant	Air Vice-Marshal	Major General
General der Flieger		
General der Flakartillerie	Air Marshal	Lieutenant General
General der Luftnachrichtentruppe		
Generaloberst	Air Chief Marshal	General
Generalfeldmarschall	Marshal of the RAF/ Field Marshal	General of the Army
Reichsmarschall (Marshal of the State)	No equivalent	

NOTES

Abbreviations and special terms used

Abt	*Abteilung* – department
Abw	*Abwehr* – Counter-intelligence Department of the Foreign Information and Counter-intelligence Office of the OKW
Abw I Luft	Luftwaffe Group in the Counter-intelligence Department
a.D.	*ausser Dienst* – retired
Amt Ausland/Abwehr	Foreign Information and Counter-intelligence Office of the OKW
Ang	*Angelegenheit* – issue, letter, directive concerning the same matter
BA-MA	*Bundesarchiv-Militärarchiv in Freiburg* – Military Archive Department of the Bundesarchiv in Koblenz
Befh	*Befehlshaber* – higher commander, corps and higher level
Befh NW	*Befehlshaber Nordwest* higher commander of the northwestern air region
B No.	Registration number
CGS	Chief of the General Staff (of the Luftwaffe here)
Chef	Chief
ChefdGenSt	*Chef des Generalstabes* – Chief of the General Staff
ChefdLfl 2	*Chef der Luftflotte* 2 – Commander (not Chief of Staff) of Air Fleet 2
ChefdSt	*Chef des Stabes* – Chief of Staff (troop staffs)
Chefs	*Chefsache* = matter concerning department or staff chiefs only, higher degree of secrecy
DGAA	Director-General of Air Armament (or *Generalluftzeugmeister* – GL)

FrLwW	*Fremde Luftwaffen West* – Foreign Air Forces West Section of the 5th (Intelligence) Department of the Luftwaffe General Staff
FüAbt	*Führungsabteilung* – 1st (Operations) Department of the Luftwaffe General Staff (also used for Operations departments of air fleets)
FüSt	*Führungsstab* – Operations Staff of the Luftwaffe General Staff
g	*geheim* – secret
G.B.	Great Britain
GenQu	*Generalquartiermeister* – Quartermaster General
Gen zbV	*General zur besonderen Verwendung* – general for special duty
gk	*geheime Kommandosache* = secret operations matter (degree of secrecy higher than just secret)
GL	*Generalluftzeugmeister* – DGAA
gRs	*geheime Reichssache* – secret State matter
Ia	1st (Operations) Department of the Operations Staff of the Luftwaffe General Staff or 1st Department of the Luftwaffe General Staff (also used for operations officer sections in other staffs), corresponds roughly to A 3
Ic	5th (Intelligence) Department of the Operations Staff of the Luftwaffe General Staff or 5th Department of the Luftwaffe General Staff (also used for intelligence officer sections in other staffs), corresponds roughly to A 2
Ic/III	Group West of the Intelligence Dept.
I L/T	Group Luftwaffe in the Foreign Informations Department of the Foreign Information and Counter-intelligence Office of the OKW
Kafü	*Jagdfliegerführer* – fighter leader (brigade level)
KM	*Kriegsmarine* – Navy
Lfl (Kdo)	*Luftflotte* – Air Fleet (Staff)
LwFüSt	*Luftwaffenführungsstab* = Operations Staff of the Luftwaffe General Staff
LwFüSt Ic	5th (Intelligence) Department of the Luftwaffe General Staff
Luftflotte	Air Fleet
MD	Milch Documents
MGFA	*Militärgeschichtliches Forschungsamt Freiburg* – Office of Military History in Freiburg
MilAmt	Central Military Foreign Information and Counter-intelligence Office
NS	National Socialist (Nazi)
ObdL	*Oberbefehlshaber der Luftwaffe* – C-in-C Luftwaffe
OKL	*Oberkommando der Luftwaffe* – Luftwaffe High Command
OKM	*Oberkommando der Kriegsmarine* – Navy High Command
OKW	*Oberkommando der Wehrmacht* – Supreme Command of the Armed Forces
o.S.	*ohne Signatur* = without designation
PRO	Public Record Office
RdLuObdL	*Reichsminister der Luftfahrt und Oberbefehlshaber der Luftwaffe* – Reich Minister for Aviation and C-in-C Luftwaffe
RH	Designation for army records
RL	Designation for Luftwaffe records
RLM	*Reichsluftfahrtministserium* – Air Ministry
RM	Designation for Navy records
Rob(inson)	Cover name, Advanced Headquarters of the Luftwaffe General Staff

RSHA   *Reichssicherheitshauptamt* – Reich Security Main Office of
                     the SS
SKl   *Seekriegsleitung* – Naval Operations Staff
1.Skl   1st (Operations) Department of the Naval Operations Staff
StdLuGenInspLw   State Secretary of Aviation and Inspector General of the
                     Luftwaffe

This paper was originally presented at the US Army War College Conference on 'Intelligence and Military Operations', Carlisle Barracks, Pennsylvania, 22–25 April 1986. Copyright US Army War College Foundation. The views expressed in this article are those of the author and do not reflect the official policy or position of the Department of Defense or the US Government.

1. F.H. Hinsley, with E.E. Thomas, C.F.G. Ransom and R.C. Knight, *British Intelligence in the Second World War: Its Influence on Strategy and Operations*, Vol.II (London, 1981), pp.283–7.
2. Kurt Gottschling, *Die Funkorchaufklärung der Luftwaffe, Militärgeschichtliches Forschungsamt* (MGFA) Lw 36/1 and 2.
3. See David Kahn, *Hitler's Spies: German Military Intelligence in World War II* (London, 1978), p.44.
4. Ulrich Knittel, *Reichsluftfahrtministerium-Forschungsamt. Geschichte and Arbeitsweise eines Nachrichtendienstes*, in BA-MA o.S. 250; David Irving (ed.), *Breach of Security: The German Secret Intelligence File on Events leading to the Second World War* (London, 1978).
5. Kahn, *Hitler's Spies*, pp.42–63.
6. Horst Boog, *Die deutsche Luftwaffenführung 1935–1945. Führungsprobleme – Spitzengliederung – Generalstabsausbildung* [Command and Leadership of the German Air Force] Vol.21 of *Beitrage zur Militar – und Kriegsgeschichte*, ed. by *Militärgeschichtliches Forschungsamt* (Stuttgart, 1982), pp.76–82.
7. About Schmid see Herbert-Joachim Rieckhoff, *Trumpf oder Bluff? 12 Jahre deutsche Luftwaffe* (Geneva, 1945), p.149.
8. Oral Statement by Brigadegeneral (ret.) Richard Heuser of 8 May 1975, MGFA.
9. *Handbuch für den Generalstabsdienst im Kriege* (Army Manual g 92), (Berlin, 1939), p.19, No.60.
10. *Heeresdienstvorschrift* (Army Manual) 300, 'Truppenführung' [Command of Troops], p.10, No.36; p.19, No.60.
11. *Heeresdienstvorschrift* (Army Manual) g 89, Entwurf der Vorschrift 'Feindnachrichtendienst' [Provisional Intelligence Service Manual] (Berlin, 1941), pp.11 ff., No.16.
12. See Kahn, *Hitler's Spies*, pp. 382, 403; and *Richtlinien für die Fuhrung und Bearbeitung der Feindlage bei den Kommandobehorden und in der Truppe*, 19 August 1944, in Bundesarchiv-Militärarchiv (BA-MA), Freiburg, E-2027, p.3.
13. Colonel (ret.) E. Morell, *Erinnerungen und Erfahrungen aus der Tätigkeit als Gruppenleiter in der 3. Abteilung des Generalstabes der Luftwaffe bzw. im Luftwaffenfuhrungsstab Ic., und als Luftattache in der Turkei 1940–1943*, 7 April 1956, in BA-MA Lw 135.
14. Friedrich von Boetticher, General der Infanterie (ret.), *Soldat am Rande der Politik, Erinnerungen*, Written on the basis of his diaries by Major Dr. Kehrig, 1960 (private manuscript), p.210.
15. Hilmer Freiherr von Bülow, Generalleutnant a.D., *Die Abteilung 'Fremde Luftmächte' im Reichswehr- und Reichsluftfahrtministerium 1927–1937* (post-war study), pp.3 ff., in BA-MA Lw p.135.
16. Andreas L. Nielsen, Generalleutnant (ret.), *Die Nachrichten beschaffung und – auswertung für die deutsche Luftwaffenfuhrung*, p.140 f., study kept by MGFA, lw 17.
17. Statement of Lt. Colonel (GS) Walter Kienitz during interview by Professor Richard Suchenwirth on 3 April 1956, in BA-MA Lw 135. Josef Schmid, (called Beppo), Generalleutnant (ret.), *Die 5. Abteilung des Generalstabes der Luftwaffe (Ic) 1*.

January 1938–1941. October 1942. Memoirs written 1945, in BA-MA Lw 101/11, pp.51 ff.
18. Ibid., p.52.
19. *Merkblatt für den Dienst des Ic-Offiziers in der Truppe. (A.III.c), Luftwaffenführungsstab Ic Fremde Luftwaffen Ost* No. 4256/44 g., February 1944, in BA-MA 4406/250 (copy); *Richtlinien für die Führung und Bearbeitung der Feindlage bei den Kommandobehörden und in der truppe* (19 August 1944), in BA-MA E-2027.
20. Cf. Nielsen, op. cit., pp.104 ff.
21. Ibid., pp.18 ff., 21 ff.
22. Ibid., pp.2 ff., 104 ff.
23. *Aktennotiz* gk of 8 March 1945, signed Zetzsche, in BA-MA RL 2/547. This memorandum was written by an air intelligence officer while the war was still going on, and is a fundamental criticism of the German air intelligence system.
24. Vortragsnotiz (briefing note) Luftwaffenführungsstab Ic, Fremde Luftwaffen West No.30897/44 g (A) of 25 October 1944, in BA-MA RL 2/647.
25. Luftwaffenführungsstab Ic, Fremde Luftwaffen West No.55017/44 g of September 1944, Ibid.
26. Letter Major von Dewitz to Lt. Colonel von Lindeiner, Robinson Ic, of 10 October 1940, in BA-MA RL 2/671. Cf. Boog, *Luftwaffenführung*, p.110.
27. Nielsen, op. cit., pp.59, 118.
28. Boog, *Luftwaffenführung*, pp.90–123.
29. The German aircraft losses at the eastern front were heavy especially in the first year of the campaign, but they were not so decisive as Olaf Groehler, 'Starke, Verteilung und Verluste der deutschen Luftwaffe im Zweiten Weltkrieg', in *Zeitschrift für Militärgeschichte*, No.3/1978, pp.316–336, puts it, because for the duration of the war in the east they amounted on average to only one third of Germany's total losses in aircraft, two thirds therefore being attributable to action of the Western Allies. Cf. the December 1944 statistic of the 6th Department of the Luftwaffe General Staff, BA-MARL 2III/734. Even the economic expert Dr Rolf Wagenfuehr of the Institute of Economic Cycle Research in Berlin estimated at the beginning of 1940 that the British and US air armaments potential was very low. He was wrong (Wagenfuehr, *Mehr Flugzeuge – aber wie?* (Berlin, 1940), pp.11, 33, 41, 50).
30. See notes 54 and 94 below.
31. Compare Hilmer Freiherr von Bülow, 'Luftrüstungen des Auslandes', *Jahrbuch der deutschen Luftwaffe* 1937, pp.73–87, and Harro Schulz-Boysen, 'Wehrchronik (Luftwaffe) 1938', in *Jahrbuch der deutschen Luftwaffe* 1939, pp.34–43.
32. Annex I to RdLuObdl GenSt 5. Abt. No.360/38 gk, in BA-MA RL 2/534, p.43.
33. Karl Klee, *Das Unternehmen 'Seelöwe'*, Vol.4a (Göttingen, 1958), p.40.
34. Annex to RdLuObdL, ChefdGenSt No.700/39 gk (5. Abt. I) of 2 May 1939, in BA-MA RL 2/535. See Karl Gundelach, 'Gedanken über die Führung eines Luftkrieges gegen England bei der Luftflotte 2 in den Jahren 1938/1939', in *Wehrwissenschaftliche Rundschau*, 1960, No.1, p.41.
35. Annex to RdLuObdL, ChefGenSt No.700/39 gk (5. Abt. I) of 2 May 1939, in BA-MA RL 2/535, p.43/
36. Ibid., p.44.
37. A Me 109 could not equal in altitude and speed a Spitfire flying at an altitude of 13,000 m. See also Hans-Adolf Jacobsen, *Dunkirchen* (Neckargemund, 1958), p.199 f.
38. Adolf Galland, *Die Ersten und die Letzten* (Darmstadt, 1953), p.97.
39. Abw Abt. I No.20112/39 I L/T of 29 August 1939 to 5. AbtGenSt Luft (Agent report of 26 August about an almost completed four-engine bomber of the Short factory in Rochester), sgd.: Grosskopf; GenSt5. Abty (VIB) of 2 August 1940 to LwFüStIc/III re: New aircraft types G.B. (4-engine bombers Short Stirling and Handley Page Halifax) Ic draft on new types of aircraft G.B. of August 1940, and Ic/III briefing notes of 15 November 1940 on Short-Stirling, all contained in BA-MA RL 2/447.
40. Annex to RdLuObdL. ChefdGenSt. No.700/39 gk (5. Abt. I) of 2 May 1939, in BA-MA RL 2/535, pp.45 ff., 48, 27, 92 ff.

41. Boetticher, op. cit., p.190 ff.
42. Archiv der Gegenwart 1939, 4220.
43. Lflkdo FüAbt No.7093/39 gk Chefs of 13 May 1939, in BA-MA RL 7/42. See also Karl-Heinz Völker, *Die deutsche Luftwaffe 1933–1939* (Stuttgart, 1967), p.161; Karl-Heinz Völker, *Dokumente und Dokumentarfotos zur Geschichte der deutschen Luftwaffe* (Stuttgart, 1968), pp.460 ff., and Gundelach, op. cit. [Considerations concerning the conduct of an air war against England], pp.42 ff.
44. GenSt 1. Abt (Chef) No.5094/39 gk Chefs of 22 May 1939, MGFA, Greffrath Collection. See also Klee, op. cit., pp.41 ff.; Gundelack, op. cit. pp.41 ff.; *Völker Luftwaffe*, 162, and Irving, *Die Tragödie der deutschen Luftwaffe. Aus den Akten und Erinnerungen von Feldmarschall Milch* (Frankfurt/Main, Berlin, 1970), pp.123 ff.
45. Annex I to Gen zbV Lflkdo 2 ChefdSt B No.100/39 gK Chefs Nur durch Offizier (to be handled by officer only), of 7 August 1939, 3, in BA-MA RL 7/29. See also Gundelach, op. cit., p.44, and Völker, *Luftwaffe*, p.161.
46. Gen zbV Lflkdo 2 ChefdGenSt B No.100/39 gK, Chefs, Nur durch Offizier, of 12 August 1939, and same, II. Ang of 14 August 1939, in BA-MA RL 7/29. As to the weakness of the Luftwaffe in the summer of 1939 see also Karl Koller, *Der Letzte Monat* (Mannheim, 1949), pp.19 ff., and Völker, *Luftwaffe*, pp.184–94.
47. Rudolf Bogatsch, 'Polititsche und militärische Probleme nach dem Frankrichfeldzug', in *Aus Politik und Zeitgeschichte* 1962/15, pp.157, 159. Hans-Adolf Jacobsen, *1939–1945. Der Zweite Weltkrieg in Chronik und Dokumenten* (Darmstadt, 1959), pp.95 ff.
48. Klee, op. cit., p.44, note 124.
49. Völker *Luftwaffe*, pp.159 ff.; and Gundelach, op. cit., pp.35 ff.; Irving, *Tragödie*, pp.116 ff.
50. Walter Ansel, *Hitler confronts England* (Durham, NC: Duke University Press, 1960), pp.111, 191. Rieckhoff, op. cit., p.17.
51. Erroneous landing of two Luftwaffe officers of Felmy's Air Fleet No.2 near the Belgian town of Mecheln on 10 January 1940. The officers had the plans for the western campaign on board.
52. GenQu GenSt 6. Abt. of 15 May 1939, re: Luftrüstungslage der Westmächte [Air Armaments Situation of the Western Powers], 1 April 1939 to November 1940, and GenSt 5. Abt No.750/39 gk (I) of 12 May 1939, both contained in BA-MA RL 2 III/606. Cf. Edward Homze, *Arming the Luftwaffe. The Reich Air Ministry and the German Aircraft Industry, 1919–1939* (Lincoln and London, 1976), pp.244 ff.
53. LwFüSt Ic No.7300/39 gk (I) of 22 November 1939: *Beurteilung der Kriegführung gegen Grossbritannien vom Standpunkt der Luftwaffe* [Assessment of the Air War against Great Britain from the Point of View of the Luftwaffe], in BA-MA RL 2/342.
54. Milch Diaries (MGFA), entry of 26 July 1939: 'List [town on the Island of Sylt]. Report by Schmidt [!] on England. Very good'. See Klee, op. cit., Vol.4a, p.42. Blue Study no longer exists. Only Vol.II is available: *Anlagen der Auswertung der Sonderstudie Grossbritannien* (Annex to the Evaluation of the Special Study on Great Britain). RdLuObdl LwFüSt Ic No.7080/39 gk (I) of 25 October 1939, in BA-MA RL 2/402.
55. Josef Schmid, Generalleutnant a.D., *Die 5. Abteilung des Generalstabes der Luftwaffe (Ic)*, 1 January 1938–1 October 1942, 1945 in BA-MA Lw 101/11, 11, 31: Nielsen, op. cit., pp.62 ff.
56. Gerhard Förster, *Totaler Krieg und Blitzkrieg, Die Theorie des totalen Krieges und des Blitzkrieges in der Militärdoktrin des faschistischen Deutschlands am Vorabend des Zweiten Weltkrieges* [Total War and Blitz Campaign. The Theory of Total War and Blitz Campaigns in the Military Doctrine of Fascist Germany on the Eve of the Second World War], (Berlin (East), 1967), pp.106 ff.; see also Homze, op. cit., pp.244 ff., 248.
57. ObdL FüSt Ic No.7600/40 gk (I) of 12 January 1940: *Beurteilung der Luftrüstungslage der Westmächte nach dem Stand vom 1.1.1940* [Assessment of the Air Armaments Situation of the Western Powers from 1 January 1940], in BA-MA RL 2/342.
58. Cajus Bekker (pseud.), *Angriffshohe 4000* [Luftwaffe War Diaries], (Hamburg, 1964), p.87; Armand van Ishoven, *Messerschmitt, Der Konstrukteur und sein Flug-*

zeuge [The Designer and his Aircraft] (Vienna and Berlin, 1976), p.214.
59. Galland, op. cit., pp.79, 103; Kesselring, *Soldat bis zum letzten Tage* (Bonn, 1953),
    p.102; Irving, *Tragödie*, pp.161 ff.; Theo Osterkamp, and Franz Bachér, *Tragödie
    der Luftwaffe? Kritische Begegnung mit dem gleichnamigen Werk von Irving/Milch*
    (Neckargemünd, 1971), p.128; Georg W. Feuchter, *Der Luftkrieg. Vom Fesselballon
    zum Raumfahrzeug*, Frankfurt/Bonn, 1964) 3rd ed., p.138; ChefdLfl 2 u Befn NW Ia
    4434/40 g of 4 October 1940 to Obdl, LwFüSt, sgd. Kesselring, Field Marshal, with
    Appendix 1, Jafü 1: *Gedanken zum Einsatz von Zerstören* [Considerations regarding
    the employment of twin-engine fighters] of 15 September 1940, and Appendix 2, Jafü
    2 Abt Ia No.1682/40 g: *Stellungnahme des Jafü 2 zu 'Gedanken zum Einsatz von
    Zerstörern' des Jafü 1* [Opinion of Fighter Leader 2 about Fighter Leader 1: Con-
    siderations regarding the employment of twin-engine fighters], all in BA-MA 8A-771.
60. Derek Wood and Derek Dempster, *The Narrow Margin. The Battle of Britain and the
    Rise of Air Power 1930–1940* (London, 1961), p.105; Kesselring, op. cit., pp.89 ff.
61. Irving, *Tragödie* p.164; Christian Freiherr von Hammerstein, *Mein Leben* [My life]
    (privately printed without date and place), Institut für Zeitgeschichte I (Institute
    of Contemporary History) Munich, ED 84, 131 F.; Richard Suchenwirth, *Hans
    Jeschonnek, Ein Versuch über Wesen, Wirken and Schicksal des vierten General-
    stabschefs der deutschen Luftwaffe*, MGFA Lw 21/5, 72; Bekker, op. cit., p.176.
62. Also in the summer of 1940 Jeschonnek stood for an all-out attack on Britain with the
    entire Luftwaffe. Obviously he saw chances of success as he had done in the case of
    Dunkirk. Cf. Ansel, op. cit., pp.75, 85, 118, 164 ff.
63. Josef Goebbels, *Kriegstagebuch* [War Diary], September 1942 IfZ ED 83/2), 29
    September 1942, Goebbels was of the opinion that the leaders of the Luftwaffe were,
    at the beginning of the Battle of Britain, convinced they would be able to soften up the
    island by air attacks alone so that it would be inclined to sue for peace. Schmid himself
    admitted in his post-war study about the 5th Department, op. cit., pp.37 ff., that he
    had underrated the British.
64. Franz Halder, *Kriegstagebuch. Tägliche Aufzeichnungen des Chefs des Generalstabes
    des Heeres 1939–1942*, 3 vols. (Stuttgart, 1962, 1963 and 1964). Vol.2, p.18, (entry of
    11 July 1940); Ronald Wheatley, *Operation Sea-Lion. German Plans for the Invasion
    of England 1939–1942* (Oxford, 1958), p.59; Rieckhoff, op. cit., pp.107 ff.
65. Halder, op. cit., Vol.2, pp.41 ff. (29 July 1940); Wheatley, op. cit., p.59.
66. Halder, op. cit., Vol.2, pp.99 ff. (14 Sept. 1940).
67. LwFüSt Ic *Beurteilung der Schlagkraft der britischen Luftwaffe im Vergleich zur
    deutschen Luftwaffe* [Assessment of the Striking Power of the Royal Air Force in
    Comparison with that of the German Air Force] as of 16 July 1940, in BA-MA E-2221;
    see also Wood/Dempster, op. cit., pp.106 ff.
68. Ishoven, op. cit., pp.229 ff.
69. Barry D. Powers, *Strategy without Slide-Rule. British Air Strategy 1914–1939*,
    (London, 1976), p.208. As to the German neglect of the British radar system see also
    Basil Collier, *The Defence of the United Kingdom* (London, 1957), p.162.
70. Wood/Dempster, pp.113, 274. See also the report on experiences of Torsten Christ to
    the Chief of the Operations Department of the Luftwaffe General Staff of the
    beginning of May 1940, BA-MA RL 2/210. Cf. Len Deighton, *Fighter. The True Story
    of the Battle of Britain* (London, 1977), pp.196, 204.
71. *Generalluftzeugmeister* (DGAA), GL No.740/40 gk of 10 August 1940, in BA-MA
    RL 2/356.
72. Ibid., pp.52 ff., 60 ff.
73. Andreas Hillgrüber (ed.), *Staatsmänner und Diplomaten bei Hitler. Vertrauliche
    Aufzeichnungen über die Unterredungen mit Vertretern des Auslandes* [Statesmen
    and Diplomats with Hitler. Confidential minutes of his Conferences with Foreign
    Representatives], Vol.1: 1939–1941 (Frankfurt 1967), p.284. Wood/Dempster, op.
    cit., pp.103, 116, seem to see the reasons for the failure of German air intelligence
    against Britain more in Schmid's desire to please Goering, in the lack of contact of the
    Intelligence Department with the front line units, and in the lack of information.
74. *Generalluftzeugmeister* (DGAA) GL No.740/40 gk, 10 August 1940, pp.11 ff., 16 ff.,

25 ff., 28 ff., 33 in BA-MA RL 2/356.
75. Otto Hoffmann von Waldau, General der Flieger, *Private Kriegstagebücher* [War Diaries], Vols. I and III, March 1939 to 8 August 1942, in BA-MA RL 200/17, 25 May and 9 June 1940 (14, 20 f.), and Appendix 3; Adolf Galland, 'Defeat of the Luftwaffe', in Eugene M. Emme, *The Impact of Air Power, National Security and World Politics* (Princeton, Toronto, London and New York, 1959), p.251; Feuchter, op. cit., pp.125 ff.
76. Oral statement by Generalmajor a.D. Eckard Christian of 24 June 1972, item 48.
77. Walter Grabmann, Generalmajor a.D., *Geschichte der deutschen Luftverteidigung 1933–1945* [History of German Reich Air Defence 1933–1945], MGFA Lw 11, 11; and conferences between the 1st Department of the *Generalluftzeugmeister* (DGAA) (GL 1 and the 6th Department of the *Generalquartiermeister* [Quartermaster General] of 24, 31 May, 12, 19, 26 July, 9, 30 August, 14, 27 September, 19, 26 October, 6, 21 November, and 6 December 1940 as well as of 22 January 1941, in BA-MA, MD, Vol.44, pp.7307, 7301/1, 7285, 7289, 7278 ff., 7274, 7625, 7259, 7252, 7239, 7232, 7228, 7220, 7211 and 7192 ff.
78. GL 1/GenSt 6. Abt. conference of 22 Jan 1941, in BA-MA MD Vol.44, pp.7192 ff. It was planned to re-equip 1230 aircraft until 1 April 1941. How far this was achieved is not known. At any rate the re-equipment could have had no effect on the Battle of Britain.
79. Wolfgang Birkenfeld, *Der systhetische Treibstoff 1933–1945. Ein Beitrag zur national-sozialistischen Wirtschafts- und Rüstungspolitik* (Göttingen, Berlin and Frankfurt, 1964), pp.172 ff.
80. Frank A. Howard, *Buna Rubber. The Birth of an Industry*, quoted from Birkenfeld, op. cit., p.172.
81. GL No.740/40 gk of 10 August 1940, p.25, and Appendix 3, in BA-MA RL 2/356.
82. Ibid, pp.14, 19.
83. Ibid., pp.27 ff.; Cf. Feuchter, op. cit., p.138.
84. GL No.740/40 gk of 10 August 1940, pp.19, 26, in BA-MA RL 2/356.
85. Herbert Krauss, Generalmajor a.D. *Die Ausbildung im Bombenwurf und im Bombenzünderwesen bei den Kampfverbänden (ohne Ju 87 Verb.)* [Bombing and bomb fuse training of the bomber units (except Ju 87 dive bomber units], study of 1 November 1945, MGFA Greffrath Collection, A/67, microfilm roll 141. RAF Bomber Command was, at the beginning of the war, also faced with the surprising fact that it had not developed an accurate bomb-aiming method. Cf. Sir Charles Webster, and Noble Frankland, *The Strategic Air Offensive against Germany 1939–1945*, Vols.1–4 (London, 1961), Vol.1, pp.107–26.
86. Feuchter, op. cit., p.144; Irving, *Tragödie*, p.169.
87. Osterkamp/Bachér, op. cit., pp.123 ff; Galland, *Die Ersten und die Letzten*, p.79; Bekker, op. cit., p.205.
88. Appendix 2b to *Generalluftzeugmeister* GL No.740/40 gk of 10 August 1940, in BA-MA RL 2/356.
89. Combat aircraft production (including repair) from 1 September 1939 to 31 March 1945 (without sea planes and gliders) in BA-MA Lw 112/6.
90. The same underestimation of British aircraft production is evident from the intelligence documents contained in file BA-MA RL 2/447.
91. In LwFüSt Ic. FrLwW(B3), draft of 28 January 1945, in BA-MA RL 2/449.
92. David Mac Isaac (ed.), *United States Strategic Bombing Survey (USSBS)* 10 vols., (New York and London, 1976), Vol.2, *Aircraft Division Industry Report*, p.74.

COMPARISON OF ALLIED INTELLIGENCE ESTIMATES OF GERMAN
AIRCRAFT PRODUCTION WITH ACTUAL PRODUCTION
(Average monthly figures for six month intervals)

	Single-Engine Fighters		Total Aircraft Production	
	Estimates	Actual	Estimates	Actual
1st half 1941	325	244	1575	880
2nd half 1941	360	232	1725	870
1st half 1942	410	323	1820	1115
2nd half	435	434	1880	1241
1st half	595	753	2030	1985
2nd half 1943	645	851	2115	2172
1st half 1944	655	1581	1870	2811

93. Compare with material in BA-MA RL 2/447, 2/449; BA-MA MD Vol.53, pp.1262 ff.;
    BA-MA E-2699; BA-MA Lw 103/32.
94. Wood/Dempster, op. cit., p.103.
95. RdLuObdL LwFüSt Ic/No. 7080/39 gk (I) of 25 October 1939: *Auswertung der
    Sonderstudie Grossbritannien, Fruhjahr 1939* [Evaluation of special Study on Great
    Britain, spring 1939], Vol.II, Annex, in BA-MA RL 2/402, See especially Annex 18.
96. Schmid in Niesen, op. cit., pp.126, 130.
97. So he once told Goering that he believed the air victory over Britain would take only
    six weeks (Suchenwirth, *Jeschonnek* p.72), and in the autumn of 1940 he mentioned to
    Generalmajor Osterkamp 'that the British are already completely demoralized and
    that the next bomb could make the barrel overflow'. Theo Osterkamp, *Dursch Höhen
    und Tiefen jagt ein Herz* (Heidelberg, 1952), p.269.
98. USSBS, Vol.1, IX.
99. Wood/Dempster, op. cit., p.114.
100. On the blunders of Goering and the Luftwaffe General Staff in the conduct of the
    Battle of Britain see especially Alan L. Gropman, 'The Battle of Britain and the
    Principles of War', in *Aerospace Historian*, Vol.18, No.3 (1971) pp.128–44, and op.
    cit., p.60.
101. Supplement of 22 June 1939 to GenSt. 1 Abt. (Chef) No.5049/39 gk of 22 May 1939:
    *Operative Zielsetzung für die Luftwaffe im Falle eines Krieges gegen England im Jahre
    1939* [Strategic aims of the Luftwaffe in case of war with Britain in 1939], copy of copy,
    Greffrath, Karlsbad, 14 June 1944, MGFA Greffrath Collection C IV/1.
102. Letter Major von Dewitz, Ic/III Kurfürst, to Lt. Col. von Lindeiner, Robinson Ic, of 4
    November 1940, in BA-MA RL 2/671.
103. This committee was also known as Ic/Pol as shown in the documents of file BA-MA
    RL 2/671.
104. Albert Speer, *Erinnerungen* [Memoirs] (Berlin, 1969), p.362. Compare *USSBS*,
    Vol.2; Aircraft Division Industry Report, pp.45–8. More or less directly engaged in
    target selection for the British Bomber Command were the Prime Minister, the Chiefs
    of Staff of the three services, the Defence Committee of the Cabinet, the Joint
    Intelligence Committee, the Joint Planning Committee and the Joint Planning Staff
    respectively, the Prime Minister's Statistical Section, the Operational Research
    Section of Bomber Command, and especially the Ministry of Economic Warfare.
    Targets were selected in accordance with British grand strategy. Already before the
    war an Industrial Intelligence committee was set up. See Webster/Frankland, op. cit.,
    Vol.1, pp.87, 92 ff., 103, 141 ff., 146 ff., 155 ff., 230 ff., 260–70, 281, 289 ff., 299, 301,
    312, 346 ff., 458, 492. The US Army Air Forces had, among others, an Air Plan
    Division. See Wesley Frank Craven and James Lee Cate (eds.), *The Army Air Forces
    in World War II*, 7 vols., (Chicago, 1950–1958), Vol.1, pp.146 ff.
106. Published in Völker, *Dokumente*, pp.454 ff.
107. See Powers, op. cit., pp.21 ff., 56 ff., 59 ff., 108, 122 ff., 127 ff., 156, 195 ff., 202, 204 ff.

108. Ansel, op. cit., pp.297 ff.; Irving, *Tragödie* pp.160, 164; David Irving, *Hitler und seine Feldherren* [Hitler and his Generals] (Frankfurt/Berlin/Vienna, 1975), p.163; Wheatley, op. cit. pp.85 ff.; Halder, op. cit., Vol.2, pp.99 ff.; P.E. Schramm, in collaboration with Hans-Adolf Jacobsen, Andreas Hillgruber and Walther Hubatsch (eds.), *Kriegstagebuch des Oberkommandos der Wehrmacht (Wehrmacht führungsstab) 1940–1945* [War Diary of the Supreme Command of the German Armed Forces (Armed Forces Operations Staff)], 4 vols. (Frankfurt, 1961–1965) (cited as *OKW War Diary*), Vol.1, p.27.
109. Ansel, op. cit., p.296.
110. Represented here in particular by Dr Hesse, but without full support of Ic/II (compare notice von Dewitz of 10 September 1940 in BA-MA RL 2/671, 185 ff.). See also notice 'Wiederholung der im Englandausschuss am 20.9.1940 gemachten Ausführungen' and Ic/III briefing notes of 25 September 1940, notes of 10 October 1940 and letter of 17 October 1940, according to which IIc/III speculated about revolutionary uprising, worth considering only if the air war in its present form and intensity were to last another half year, and demands for this purpose particularly the bombing of the London public utility and supply installations. BA-MA RL 2/671.
111. Bernhard von Lossberg, *Im Wehrmachtführungsstab. Berich eines Generalstabsoffiziers* (Hamburg, 1950) 2nd ed., p.89, and Speer, op. cit., pp.296 ff. (Hitler's vandalism/destructive intoxication).
112. England Committee on 20 September 1940, in BA-MA RL 2/671.
113. Ibid., LwFüSt Ic/Pol. briefing note of 21 October 1940, and letter von Dewitz to von Lindeiner of 25 October 1940.
114. Ibid., Letter von Dewitz to von Lindeiner, Robinson Ic, of 10 October 1940.
115. Materials ibid., see especially letter von Dewitz to von Lindeiner of 2 November 1940.
116. ObdL FüSt Ia No.5937/40 gk, in BA-MA 8A 771.
117. Ic/III of 6 October 1940; Ic/III to Lt. Col. von Lindeiner, Rob, of 21 September 1940, in BA-MA RL 2/671.
118. ObdL FüSt Ia No.7682/40 gk (op 1) of 19 October 1940, in: BA-MA OKM GE 967, 338.
119. Letter von Dewitz to von Lindeiner, Rob Ic, of 24 October 1940, in BA-MA RL 2/671.
120. Ibid., Letter von Dewitz to von Lindeiner, Rob Ic, of 6 and 9 November 1940, and Ic/III briefing note of 6 October 1940.
121. Ibid., Letter Major von Dewitz to Lt. Col. von Lindeiner of 10 September 1940.
122. According to report LwFüSt Ic/III A of 14 January 1942 on the British air armaments industry, situation end of 1941, in BA-MA RL 2/447, there had been no control of the British aircraft factories by aerial photography for the past year to eighteen months. According to LwFüSt Ic FrLw W W No.6927/44 gk (B2) of 14 December 1944, briefing note (BA-MA RL 2/547), and to statement by General Karl Koller, Chief of the Luftwaffe General Staff, of 16 July 1945 (BA-MA RL 2/v.3401), there had been no photographic reconnaissance of England since the middle of 1941.
123. Cover name. According to Anthony Cave Brown, *Die unsichtbare Front. Entschieden Geheimdienste den Zweiten Weltkrieg?* (Munich, 1976) [Original title: *Bodyguard of Lies* (New York, 1975)], p.464, this was Paul Fidrmuc, who represented an American pharmaceutical firm in Lisbon and worked as a double-agent for the Germans as well as for the British. He was probably engaged in a deception (double-cross) game of the British Intelligence Service, as his systematic underestimation of British aircraft production figures in the decisive years of the war from 1940 to 1943 seems to indicate. Suspicion was already voiced in 1944 by Count von Posadowsky-Wehner, a specialist at that time in the Intelligence Department of the Luftwaffe Operations Staff, Foreign Air Forces West Section (Appendix to LwFüSt Ic FrLwW No. 5567/44 gkk (C2) of 14 June 1944, in BA-MA RL 2/649). According to David Kahn, *Hitler's Spies*, p.356, 'Ostro' was not identical with Fidrmuc. After the war Fidrmuc was a foreign correspondent of *Der Spiegel* magazine in Spain.
124. LwFüSt Ic FrLwW No.18149/44 g (C2) of 14 June 1944 to Abw I Luft c/o Lt. Col. von Dewitz concerning 'Ostro' reports on aircraft production in Great Britain, in BA-MA RL 2/547; Amt Ausll/ Abw No.2882/40 Abw I Luft/E of 17 June 1940 (BA-MA RL 2/

447) concerning Great Britain, its supply, air force, industry, communication, technology and new developments in the British aircraft industry, according to which the British armaments industry was not in a position to make up for the material losses suffered in Flanders within the next three years; 1 Amt Aus 1/Abw No.3275/40 Abw I Luft/E of 16 July 1940 to LwFüSt Ic, re Great Britain, 1. Effect of German air raids, 2. RAF, in: BA-MA RL 2/447; LwFüSt Ic FrLwW No.31073/44 g (Bz, Appendix 1, of 27 October 1944, in BA-MA RL 2/547.

125. Interview with Colonel (ret.) Rudolf Wodarg, ex-chief of Luftwaffe Intelligence (5th Department), 18 April 1972.
126. Amt Ausl/Abwe No.2882/40 Abw I Luft/E of 17 June 1940 and No.3725/40 Abw I Luft/E of 16 July 1940 to LwFüSt Ic, in BA-MA RL 2/447.
127. BA-MA RL 2/368.
128. RLM GL 1 No.2160/39 g of 1 July 1939, in BA-MA 3-1638, and M.M. Postan, *British War Production* (London, 1957), p.484.
129. *Generalluftzeugmeister* GL 1 of 7 December 1940 to LwFüSt Ic in BA-MA RL 2/447.
130. LwFüSt Ia (KM) to OKM/1. Skl, and briefing notes Ic/IIII A. Both of 31 July 1941, in BA-MA OKM GE 958, pp.53 ff.
131. Ic/III briefing notes of 6 October 1940, in BA-MA RL 2/671.
132. BA-MA RL 2/447, BA-MA RL 2/547, BA-MA RL 2/671.
133. Postan, op. cit., pp.484 ff.
134. Ic/III A of 17 February 1941, in BA-MA RL 2/671.
135. Compare *OKW War Diary*, Vol.1, p.123, with p.125 (entries of 23 and 24 October 1940), also Halder, op. cit., Vol.2, p.125 (4 October 1940) with p.286 (20 February 1941).
136. Ic/III briefing note of 28 September 1940 and letter von Dewitz to von Lindeiner of 25 October 1940, in BA-MA RL 2/671.
137. LwFüSt Ic/III of 21 December 1940: British Aircraft Industry (3rd issue) as of the end of December, in BA-MA RL 2/447.
138. *OKW War Diary*, Vol.1, p.86 (23 September 1940); BA-MA RL 2/671, pp.182 ff.; LwFüSt Ia of 16 September 1940, in BA-MA8A-2486; MGFA, Milch Diaries, 32172 (16 September 1940); Osterkamp, op. cit., pp.325 ff. 369, 386; Feuchter, op. cit., p.140; Theo Weber, *Die Luftschlacht um England*, (Wiesbaden, 1956), pp.89 ff., 117, 126, 142; Irving, *Tragödie*, pp.164 ff., 168; Wood/Dempster, op. cit., pp.115 ff.; Wheatley, op. cit., p.59; Olaf Groehler, *Geschichte des Luftkrieges 1910–1970* [History of War in the Air] (Berlin (East), 1975) pp.166, 271; Deighton, op. cit., pp.225 ff.; Kahn, *Hitler's Spies*, pp.384 ff.; Klaus Maier, 'Die Luftschlacht um England' [Battle of Britain], in *Das Deutsche Reich und der Zweite Weltkrief*, Vol.2, ed. by MGFA, (Stuttgart, 1979), pp.287, 390 ff.
139. Bogatsch, op. cit., pp.161 ff.; Klee, op. cit., Vol.46, pp.335, 353 ff.; Halder, op. cit., Vol.2, pp.18 (11 July 1940) and 98 ff. (14 September 1940).
140. *Generalluftzeugmeister* GL No.909/40 gk ChefdSt, of 28 September 1940, re *Industrieerfassung in England* [Registration of Industries in Britain], in BA-MA 4378–388. See also BA MA, MD, Vol.65, 7243.
141. Halder, op. cit., Vol.2, p.128 (October 1940).
142. Nielsen, op. cit., p.183.
143. *Reichsmarschall* Conference of 29 June 1942 in the Reichsjägerhof, conference notes No.109/42 gk, in BA-MA MD Vol.62, 5241. According to Postan, op. cit., p.485, Britain, in June 1942, turned out 528 bombers of all types and 814 fighters, whereas Germany, on the basis of the statistics of the 6th Department of the Luftwaffe General Staff of 28 June 1945 (BA-MA Lw 103/84), produced in this month only 405 bombers and dive bombers and 352 single- and twin-engine fighters, night-fighters and destroyers.
144. *Reichsmarschall* Conference of 9 October 1943 on the Obersalzberg, Conference-notes No.109/453 gk in BA-MA MD Vol.63, 6312. According to Postan, op. cit., p.485, Britain produced 925 fighters in October 1943, Germany (in accordance with above statistics of the 6th Department) only 853 fighters of all kinds, and destroyers.
145. *Generalluftzeugmeister* conference of 20 August 1942, in BA-MA MD Vol.15, 1965.

Actually Britain built, again according to Postan, op. cit., p.485, 182 four-engine bombers in August 1942, in October 1942 249 and in January 1943 282.

146. LwFüSt Ic FrLwW No. 18149/44 g (C 2) of 14 June 1944 to Abw I Luft E in BA-MA RL 2/547; LwFüSt FrLwW No. 19784/44 g of 1 July 1944 to RSHA MilAmt I Luft stating that the 'Ostro' report submitted by MilAmt on 28 June 1944 was absolutely false, in BA-MA RL 2/649; Appendix to LwFüSt Ic FrLwW No. 5567/44 gk (C 2) of 22 September 1944, re: Ostro, Josephine and Hector as part of an enemy deception (double-cross) scheme. The author of this analysis, Count von Posadowsky-Wehner of the Foreign Air Forces West Section of the 5th Department, distinguished between four developmental phases of this scheme. From the middle of 1940 to the middle of 1941, 'Ostro' was the only 'well-functioning' espionage organization in Great Britain. During this period, 'Ostro' reported far too low British aircraft production figures and exaggerated the effects of German air raids against England, in order to cause the Luftwaffe to shift the mass of its attacks from the British aircraft industry to other targets. Until the middle of 1942 'Ostro' continued to report figures on British aircraft production, which were too low, and at the same time concealed the start of the production of four-engine and high altitude (Mosquito) bombers. The Foreign Air Forces West Section, therefore, had already been criticizing these reports since early 1942. From the middle of 1942 to the end of 1943 and with the stopping of the German advance in the east and the foreseeable invasion in the west, the danger of an increase of POW-information arose. Therefore the new organizations 'Hector and Josephine' were established around the middle of 1942/early 1943 with the purpose of rehabilitating 'Ostro' by, in the beginning, reporting approximately the same figures. New developments were, however, not reported. Since the end of 1943 the reports started to diverge from each other perhaps to prevent 'Hector' and 'Josephine' being unmasked as both controlled by the enemy. As to 'Hector' and 'Josephine' see, besides Brown, op. cit., pp. 444 ff., especially Kahn, Hitler's Spies, pp. 306–12, 315, 335, 366, 386. According to him these 'organizations' were just cover names which Dr Karl-Heinz Krämer, counter-intelligence agent and trade attaché with the German embassy in Stockholm, gave his various sources. Each name stood for several sources, some of them involuntary. 'Josephine' stood for the reports allegedly obtained from two Swedish attachés in London through female secretaries in the Swedish Defence Ministry, with whom Krämer entertained good relations. The information gained this way was mixed with information gathered from newspapers and magazines and forwarded as agent reports. On 'Ostro' see also John C. Masterman, The Double-Cross System in the War of 1939 to 1945 (New Haven and London, 1972), pp. 4, 151, 180.

147. LwFüSt Ic FrLwW No. 6927/44 (B 2) of 14 December 1944, in BA-MA RL 2/547.

148. 8. Abt.: Die Kampfführung der eigenen und der anglo-amerikanischen Luftwaffe [Methods of operation of the German and Anglo-American air forces], Study of 22 August 1944 (copy), in BA-MA Lw 106/10.

149. OKL FüSt Ic FrLwW No. 28343/44 g (C 2/C 3) of 23 September 1944 to OKL ChefGenSt 8. Abt., re Britische and amerikanische Flugzeugbestande [British and American Strength in Aircraft]; LwFüSt Ic FrLwW No. 17316/44 g (c 2), briefing notes of 7 June 1944, in BA-MA RL 2/447. Compare with Nielsen, op. cit., p. 131.

150. Generalluftzeugmeister, GL No. 740/40 gk of 10 August 1940 55 ff., 60 f., in BA-MA RL 2/356.

151. Hillgruber, Hitlers Strategie, pp. 221, 229. Klaus Reinhardt, Die Wende vor Moskau. Das Scheitern der Strategie Hitlers im Winter 1941/42 [Turning Point Moscow. The Failure of Hitler's Strategy in the Winter of 1941/42] (Stuttgart, 1972), pp. 8–26; compare also Otto Wien, Ein Leben und viermal Deutschland. Erinnerungen aus 70 Lebensjahren 1906–1976 (Düsseldorf, 1978), pp. 288 ff. (on Jodl and Halder).

152. Hans-Joachim Lorbeer, Westmächte gegen die Sowjetunion 1939–1941 (Freiburg, 1975), pp. 36 ff., 99 ff. (Session of the British War Cabinet of 7 February 1940, excerpts from PRO Cab 65/5, 172), pp. 102–111 (Military Implication of Hostilities with Russia in 1940, excerpts from PRO Cab 66/6), pp. 100–105: Weak Points in the USSR System, item 6; Soviet Military Potential, items 7, 8; General Conditions Governing

Attack on Russian Oil Supplies in the Caucasus, items 40–53). As for the USA it must suffice to mention its fears about the possibility of a sudden breakdown of the USSR after the German onslaught in summer 1941. According to Haywood S. Hansell, Jr., *The Air-Plan that Defeated Hitler* (Atlanta, 1972), pp.92, 97, US intelligence predicted the collapse of the Red Army for the spring of 1942 at the latest.

153. Compare Kahn, *Hitler's Spies*, p.445.
154. Nielsen, op. cit., pp.148 ff.
155. Kahn, *Hitler's Spies* pp.451 ff.; Nielsen, op. cit., pp.137, 139 ff.; Walter Schwabedissen, Generalleutnant a.D., *Die russische Luftwaffe mit den Augen deutscher Kommandeure gesehen,* in MGFA Lw 22, pp.112 ff.; Hermann Plocher, Generalleutnant a.D., *Der Feldzug im Osten 1941–1945. Der Einsatz der deutschen Luftwaffe an der Ostfront.* MGFA Lw 4/1–26, Vol.4/5 pp.738 ff.; Heinz Höhne, *Der Krieg im Dunkeln. Macht und Einfluss des deutschen und russischen Geheimdienstes* [War in the Dark. Power and Influence of the German and Russian Intelligence Service], (Munich, 1985), p.352.
156. Theodor Rowehl, *Chronik der Aufklärungsgruppe des Obdl,* 4, BA-MA Lw 108/16; Kahn, *Hitler's Spies,* pp.449 ff; Karl-Heinz Eyermann, *Luftspionage* [Air Espionage], 2 vols., (Berlin, 1963), Vol.2, pp.131 ff.
157. Kahn, *Hitler's Spies,* pp.454 ff.
158. Schwabedissen, op. cit., p.6., Reinhardt, op. cit., p.20.
159. Erhard Mortiz, 'Zur Fehleinschätzung des sowjetischen Kriegspotentials durch die faschistische Wehrmacht in den Jahren 1933–1941' [Concerning the undestimation of the Soviet armed forces by the Fascist Forces in the years 1933–1941] in *Auf antisowjetischem Kriegskurs* (Berlin, 1970), pp.176 ff.; Schwabedissen, op. cit., pp.74 ff.
160. BA-MA RL 3/63, pp.7397 ff.; Kahn, *Hitler's Spies,* pp.445 ff.; Reinhard, op. cit., p.19.
161. Hoffmann von Waldau, op. cit., p.54 (3 July 1941, item 4).
162. Annex to RdLuObdL, ChefdGenSt Nr. 700/339 gk (5. Abt. I): 'Die Luftlage in Europa, Stand: Frühjahr 1939' [Air Situation in Europe in spring 1939], pp.59–66, 77 ff., 92 in BA-MA RL 2 II/446.
163. Lt. Col. Macht, 'Engpässe der russischen Wehrwirtschaft' [Bottlenecks in the Soviet armaments economy], in *Die Luftwaffe* 3, No. 1 (1938), pp.53–76.
164. Kahn, *Hitler's Spies* p.453; Heinz Höhne, *Canaris. Patriot im Zwielicht* (Munich, 1976), pp.430 ff.; see also Höhne, *Der Krieg im Dunkeln,* pp.322 ff.; Schwabedissen, op. cit., p.13.
165. Eyermann, op. cit., Vol.2, p.139, attributes the more than 500 violations of Soviet air space by German reconnaissance planes to the year 1939 and the first half of 1941. M.N. Kozevnikiv, *Kommandovanie i stab VVS Sovetskoj Armii v Velikoj Otecestvennoj Vojne 1941–1945 gg.* [Command and Staff of the Air Forces of the Soviet Army in the Great Patriotic War 1941–1945] (Moscow, 1978) p.28, mentions 324 such violations for the first half of 1941. The *Geschichte des Grossen Vaterländischen Krieges der Sowjetunion* [History of the Great Patriotic War of the Soviet Union], ed. by the Institut für Marxismus-Leninismus beim Zentral-Komitee der Kommunistichen Partie der Sowjetunion (Berlin (East), 1964) 6 vols., knows of only 152 violations: Vol.1, p.562.
166. Nielsen, op. cit., p.142; Boog, *Die deutsche Luftwaffenführung 1935–1945,* p.110.
167. Nielsen, op. cit., pp.140 ff.
168. Helmuth Greinner, *Die oberste Wehrmachtführung* [The German Armed Forces Supreme Command] *1939–1941* (Wiesbaden, 1951), pp.312 ff.; Halder, op. cit., Vol.2, p.120 (1 October 1940); Rowehl, op. cit., pp.7 ff.
169. Nielsen, op. cit., p.143; Kesselring, op. cit., p.114; Kahn, *Hitler's Spies,* pp.447 ff.; Reinhardt, op. cit., p.20.
170. Robinson Ic of 25 November 1940, Sowjetrussland. Beurteilung der Luftwaffe [Soviet Russia. Assessment of the Air Force], in BA-MA OKM, Vsdr HR 969/PG 32969.
171. Kozevnikov, op. cit., p.27; Plocher, Vol.4/1, pp.268 ff; Rowehl, op. cit., p.9; BA-

MA MD RL 3/34, 1879; *Geschichte des Grossen Vaterlandischen Krieges*, Vol.1, p.562.

172. Colonel (ret.) Lothar von Heinemann, *Nachrichten über die russische Luftwaffe von 1940 bis etwa 1942* [Intelligence on the Soviet Air Force], 10, in BA-MA Lw 135; Schwabedissen, op. cit., pp.14 ff.; Nielsen, op. cit., p.148.

173. Plocher, op. cit., Vol.4/1, p.256; Nielsen, op. cit., p.142.

174. *Orientierungsheft (UdSSR)) unter besonderer Beruchsichtigung der Fliegertruppe und Flakartillerie sowie der Flugrüstungsindustrie in Rahmen der allgemeinen Wehrwirtschaftslage, Stand: 1.2.1941* [Orientation Manual (USSR) with special consideration of the air force, anti-aircraft artillery and aviation industry within the framework of the general economic situation on 1 February 1941], ObdL FüSt Ic/IV No.3500/41 g, in BA-MA Lw 107/67 (copy) pp.7 33, 37 f., 49, 52, 56, 59, 61. See also Schwabedissen, op. cit., pp.11–79, especially 79 ff.

175. Schwabedissen, op. cit., pp.21 ff. *Jahrbuch der deutschen Luftwaffe 1939*, pp.39 ff.; Hermann Franke (ed.), *Handbuch der neuzeitlichen Wehrwissenschaften* [Handbook of modern military sciences] Vol.3, Part 2: *Die Luftwaffe* (Berlin and Leipzig, 1939), p.400; Colonel (ret.) Schuettel, *Entwicklung und Beurteilung der russischen Luftwaffe bis zum Kriegsbeginn mit Sowjetrussland* [Development and Assessment of the Soviet Air Force until the beginning of the war against the Soviet Union], pp.26 ff., in BA-MA Lw 107/68.

176. Ibid., p.82. Plocher, op. cit., Vol.4/5, pp.742 ff., 747.

177. Schwabedissen, op. cit., pp.79 ff., 86; Nielsen, op. cit., pp.148 ff.; Plocher, op. cit. Vol.4/5, p.745 and Vol.4/9, p.198; Rieckhoff, op. cit., pp.250 ff.; Werner Baumbach, *Zu spät: Aufstieg und Untergang der deutschen Luftwaffe* (Munich, 1949), p.175; W.H. Tantum and E.J. Hoffschmidt (eds.), *Air Ministry: The Rise and Fall of the German Air Force (1933–1945)* (1948; reprint Old Greenwich, CT, 1969) (cited as *Air Ministry*), p.162.

178. Orientation Manual USSR, p.56, Schwabedissen, op. cit., pp.18 ff.; Halder, op. cit., Vol.2, pp.288 ff., 295.

179. Gerhard Hümmelchen, 'Die Luftstreitkräfte der UdSSR am 22. Juni 1941 im Spiegel der sowjetischen Kriegsliteratur', in *Wehrwissenschaftliche Rundschau, 20* (1970), p.331.

180. BA-MA RH 19 1/70.

181. Plocher, op. cit., Vol.4/1, pp.272 ff.

182. KTB (War Diary) I.Skl (1st Dept., Naval Ops Staff), in BA-MA RM 7/25 275. According to this the Luftwaffe Staff was quite confident despite an assumed three-to fourfold numerical superiority of the Red Air Force.

183. Hümmelchen, op. cit., pp.327, 330 ff.; ObdL FüSt Ic, Lagebericht (situation report) No.679 of 10 July 1941, in BA-MA RL 2 II/251.

184. Report Wag-SU-30/40 of 27 August 1943 gRs of the Speer Ministry (BA-MA Lw 106/13). According to Joachim Hoffmann, 'Die Sowjetunion bis zum Vorabend des deutschen Angriffs', in Horst Boog *et al.*, *Der Angriff auf die Sowjetunion*, Vol.4 of *Das Deutsche Reich und der Zweite Weltkrieg*, ed. by Militärgeschichtliches Forschungsamt (Stuttgart, 1983), p.75, the Soviets had produced 23,245 aircraft from 1938 to mid-1941.

185. For the strength of the German Air Force attacking the USSR see Horst Boog, 'Die Luftwaffe', in ibid., pp.312 ff.

186. GenSt GenQu 6. Abt No.3385/41 gk (IB of 24 June 1941, in BA-MA RL 2 III/736; see also BA-MA RL 2 III/713.

187. Note Generalluftzeugmeister to Reichsmarschall of 5 February 1941, in BA-MA MD Vol.65, p.7210.

188. Colonel Engineer Dietrich Schwencke, head of the Foreign Armaments Intelligence Department of the DGAA, in *Generalluftzeugmeister* conference of 21 July 1942 in BA-MA MD Vol.15, 1554. According to chart 42, *Geschichte des Zweiten Weltkrieges 1939–1945 in zwölf Bänden* [History of the Second World War in 12 volumes], ed. by an editors' committee, (Moscow, 1973), the Soviet Union produced 700 aircraft per month on average in the first half of 1941 and 1400 aircraft monthly on average in the

second half of 1941 and first half of 1942. According to the *Geschichte des Grossen Vaterländischen Krieges der Sowjetunion 1941/1945*, Vol.2, 430, the March 1942 production amounted to 1647 aircraft.

189. Plocher, op. cit., Vol.4/1, p.272.

190. Schwabedissen, op. cit., pp.86 ff.; Halder, op. cit., Vol.3, p.32 f. (entry of 1 July 1941) 'The Luftwaffe has considerably underestimated the strength of the enemy', and p.170 (11 August 1941). Hoffman von Waldau, op. cit., 3 and 15 July 1941; Irving, *Hitler*, pp.281, 303; Groehler, *Luftkrieg*, p.346; Papers Generaloberst Gunther Ruedel, BA-MA N 467/v.17.

192. Goebbels, *War Diary*, 29 September 1942, pp.432, 437.

193. Speech to the Gauleiters of 8 November 1943, in BA-MA MD Vol.63, 5866.

194. Conference of the Reichsmarschall with representatives of the aviation industry concerning problems of development, 13 September 1942, in BA-MA MD Vol.52, 5316.

195. Baumbach, op. cit., p.175.

196. *Der Prozess gegen die Hauptkriegsverbrecher vor dem Internationalen Militärgerischtshof* [International Military Tribunal] *Nürnberg, 14 November 1945–1 October 1946*, 42 vols. (Nuremberg, 1947–1949) (cited as IMT), Vol.9, pp.20, 96 ff., 234, 382–8, 476, 694, 718 f. Generaloberst a.D. Franz Halder in his book *Hitler als Feldherr* (Munich, 1949), p.21, confirms that Goering warned Hitler against the eastern campaign. Cf. Kesselring, op. cit., p.148; General der Flieger a.D. Josef Kammhuber, *Das Problem der Erringung der Luftherrschaft durch Gegenmassnahmen der Luftwaffe* [The Problem of Gaining Air Supremacy by Counter-Measures of the Luftwaffe], MGFA LW 12/1–5, Vol.12/3 pp.11 ff.; interview Kammhuber of 30 October 1968; Hillgruber, *Hitlers Strategie*, pp.396 ff.; Irving, *Tragödie*, pp.179 ff.; Irving, *Hitler*, p.186; papers of General der Flieger a.D. Hans-Georg von Seidel, p.45; Richard Suchenwirth, *Hermann Goering, Der Oberbefehlshaber der deutschen Luftwaffe*, MGFA Lw 101/3. pp.107–119; Richard Suchenwirth, *Historische Wendepunkte im Kriegseinsatz der deutschen Luftwaffe* [Historical Turning Points in Luftwaffe Operations of World War II], MGFA LW 35, pp.102 ff.; Plocher, op. cit., Vol.4/9, pp.20–42; Werner Bross, *Gespräche mit Hermann Goering* (Flensburg 1950), pp.26, 78ff.; Hildegard von Kotze (ed.) *Heeresadjutant bei Hitler 1938–1943. Aufzeichnungen des Majors Engel* (Stuttgart, 1974), entry of 15 September 1940: 'Both [Hitler and Goering] estimated Russian strength to be low'. Likewise Heinrich Koppenberg in his letter of 22 October 1957 to General der Flieger a.D. Paul Deichmann, BA-MA Lw 103/28.

197. State Secretary Paul Koerner in Suchenwirth, *Goering*, p.115; Galland, *Die Ersten und die Letzten*, p.134. Cf. *OKW War Diary*, Vol.1, pp.203, 258, 1018; Halder, op. cit., Vol.2, p.336.

198. Irving, *Tragödie*, p.180.

199. Walter Hewel, *Ambassador: Tagebuch [Diary] 1941*, in private possession, 29 May and 9 June 1941. Irving, *Hitler*, pp.266, 271, 278. Hillgruber, *Hitlers Strategie*, pp.218, 269, 367.

200. Irving, *Hitler*, pp.274 (14 June 1941); Galland, *Die Ersten und die Letzten*, pp.122 ff. Goering in fact seemed to be depressed according to Irving, *Tragödie*, p.187.

201. Hillgruber, *Hitlers Strategie*, pp.268 ff.; Irving, *Hitler*, pp.214 ff.; Reinhard, op. cit., p.25.

202. Wilhelm, Speidel, General der Flieger a.D., *Gedanken über den deutschen Generalstab*, MGFA MS No PO31a, Part 26/I, Landsberg am Lech, 20 January 1949, p.70. Letter Koppenberg to Deichmann, 22 October 1957, BA-MA Lw 103/28. Hammerstein, op. cit., p.121.

203. Irving, *Tragödie*, pp.178 ff., Plocher, op. cit., Vol.4/9, pp.35 ff.; IMT, Vol.9, pp.59, 96 ff.

204. Interview Wodarg of 21 March 1972, von Seidel, op. cit., pp.49 ff.; The *Chef der Luftwehr* [Chief of Defence Administration], who controlled the Air Administration Office in charge of clothing supply, wrote, when Milch claimed the credit for the timely supply of winter clothing for himself, on 2 February 1942: 'I don't know

anything about that. During the decisive months from January to July 1941 I have not heard of or seen him'. (Ruedel papers, BA-MAN 457/v. 17.).

205. Irving, *Tragödie*, pp.177, 188, 218; Karl-Heinz Ludwig, *Technik und Ingenieure im Dritten Reich* (Düsseldorf, 1974), p.42; Speer, op. cit., p.229; Reinhardt, op. cit., pp.283, 276 ff.

206. Milch in his speech before the Industry Council and the managers of the newly established Industrial Rings on 18 September 1941 in the Air Ministry, BA-MA Vol.53, 1155.

207. Lossberg, op. cit., p.127; Irving, *Hitler*, pp.287 ff.

208. Halder, *War Diary*, Vol.3, p.38 (3 July 1941) and 106 f. (23 July 1941; Suchenwirth, *Jeschonnek*, p.86.

209. Irving, *Hitler*, p.325: Jodl, on 8 October 1941, believed the war in the east was definitely won.

210. Letter State Secretary for Aviation and Inspector General of the Luftwaffe/General Staff No.675/41 gk of 15 October 1941 to Quartermaster General re Steigerung de Rustung (Increase of Armament Production), in BA-MA MD Vol.51, 467.

211. Milch in *Generalluftzeugemeister* conference of 27 May 1942, in BA-MA MD Vol.34, p.1728.

212. Milch in the development-conference of 7 August 1941, in BA-MA MD Vol.34, p.1728.

213. Milch in *Generalluftzeugmeister* conference of 20 August 1942, in BA-MA MD Vol.15, p.2050.

214. Milch in *Generalluftzeugmeister* conference of 27 October 1942, in BA-MA MD Vol.16, p.2940.

215. Milch in *Generalluftzeugmeister* conference of 19 July 1943 in BA-MA MD Vol.16, p.6075.

216. Milch in conference between State Secretary and *Generalluftzeugmeister* of 25 August 1943, in BA-MA MD Vol.30, p.415.

217. Milch, *Erinnerungen* (Nuremberg, 1947). Ms MGFA, pp.297 ff.

218. So Irving, *Tragödie*, p.180: 'Milch energetically voiced his opinion against the Russian campaign'.

219. The late Admiral Moessel, liaison officer of the navy to the Luftwaffe General Staff, in Plocher, op. cit., Vol.4/9, pp.26 ff.; Cf. Suchenwirth, *Jeschonnek*, p.790; Irving, *Tragödie*, p.188.

220. Ibid., p.188.

221. Rieckhoff, op. cit., pp.243 ff.; von Seidel, op. cit., p.27. Admiral Moessel in Plocher, op. cit., Vol.4/9, pp.38 ff.

222. Von Seidel, op. cit., p.27.

223. Ibid., p.45 f.; Plocher, op. cit., Vol.4/9, pp.38 ff.; IMT, Vol.9, p.209.

224. Plocher, op. cit., Vol.4/9, pp.40 ff.

225. Irving, *Hitler*, pp.213 ff., 770 ff.

226. Inspection report in: BA-MA RL 3/2245. See IMT, Vol.9, 95 Plocher, op. cit., Vol.4/1, pp.257 ff., 264; Nielsen, op. cit., pp.141 ff.; Irving, *Tragödie*, p.178; Irving, *Hitler*, pp.213 ff., 77 ff.; Groehler, *Luftkrieg*, p.291: Nicolaus von Below, Colonel (ret.), *Als Hitlers Adjutant 1937–1945* [Hitler's aide-de-camp], (Mainz, 1980), p.267.

227. Irving, *Tragödie*, p.178; Plocher, op. cit., Vol.4/1, pp.257–65, Vol.4/5, p.796; Rieckhoff, op. cit., pp.251 ff.; Statement by Milch of 28 July 1945, in BA-MA Lw 103/26; IMT Vol.9, p.95; Kesselring, op. cit., p.114; *Air Ministry*, p.162. According to Groehler, *Luftkrieg*, p.291, the inspection tour took place from 28 March to 17 April. While Rieckhoff, op. cit., pp.251 ff., and Baumbach, op. cit., pp.163 ff. – the latter on the basis of his own notes taken in Moscow in October 1940 – assert that the German air attaché in Moscow, Colonel Aschenbrenner, like General Koestring, warned against the military strength of the Soviets and against underestimating the solidarity of the Soviet state, the former Gauleiter of the NS-party administration district Halle-Merseburg, Jordan, maintains in his memoirs (Rudolf Jordan, *Erlebt und erlitten. Weg eines Gauleiters von München bis Moskau* (Leoni, 1971), pp.217 ff.) that Aschenbrenner had a very low opinion of the moral and military strength of the Soviets until the spring of 1941.

228. Statement of the former air attaché to Moscow after his return from there, in Plocher, op. cit., Vol.4/1, p.264. See also Nielsen, op. cit., pp.141 ff., who quotes Hitler's Luftwaffe aide-de-camp, Colonel von Below, with similar words. For more details of Luftwaffe intelligence assessment of the Soviet Air Force see Horst Boog, 'Die Beurteilung der sowjetischen Luftstreitkräfte 1930–1941' in Boog, Sowjetunion, 286–99.

229. Boog, Sowjetunion, pp.297 ff.; Schwabedissen, op. cit., p.128 f.; compare Asher Lee, The Soviet Air Force (London, 1952), and Raymond L. Garthoff, Die Sowjertarmee. Wesen und Lehre (Cologne, 1955).

230. Kozevnikov, op. cit., p.17; Von Hardesty, Red Phoenix. The Rise of Soviet Air Power, 1941–1945 (Washington, 1982), p.21.

231. Boog, Sowjetunion, p.689.

232. BA-MARW 4/v. 335–337. Nielsen, op. cit., pp.180 ff.; Hillgruber, Hitlers Strategie, pp.194 ff., 374 ff.; Boetticher, op. cit., pp.218–39; Wien, op. cit., p.287; Kahn, Hitler's Spies, pp.80 ff.; Alfred M. Beck. The Ambivalent Attaché. Friedrich von Boetticher in America 1933–1941 (Diss: Georgetown University; Washington D.C., August, 1977), pp.302, 212, 326, 329, points out that Boetticher's assessments of the USA were realistic in military matters but not as far as grand strategic matters and economic potentials were concerned.

233. Development conference of 30 October 1942, in BA-MA MD Vol.34, p.2347.

234. Interview Colonel Engineer (ret.) German Cornelius of 25 May 1970.

235. Luftrustungsvergleich Deutschland-Italien und Grossbritannien–USA 1939–1943 [Comparison of air armaments between Germany–Italy on the one hand and Great Britain–USA on the other] as of 1 July 1941, Part I, pp.6 ff., in Generalluftzeugmeister No.1123/41 gk of 30 August 1941, BA-MA E-2379.

236. Irving, Tragödie, p.194.

237. Craven and Cate, op. cit., Vol.6, pp.350–52, and Postan, op. cit., pp.484 ff. Rudolf Lusar, Die deutschen Waffen und Geheimwaffen des Zweiten Weltkrieges und ihre Weiterentwicklung, (Munich, 1971), p.171.

238. See note 235 above.

239. LwFüSt Ic of 7 June 1941, sgd. Schmid, in BA-MA MD vol.65, 7141.

240. Interview Wodarg of 18 April 1972.

241. LwFüSt Ic FrLwW No.32257/44 (B3); briefing note of 10 November 1944, in BA-MA RL 2/449.

242. Hillgruber, Hitlers Strategie, pp.196 ff., 224. Interview Colonel (ret) Nicolaus von Below of 25 January 1972, item 21.

243. Annex to personal letter of Fritz Siebel to Generalluftzeugmeister, Generaloberst Udet, of 7 October 1940, in BA-MA MD Vol.56, 2926–2933. See also Grabmann, op. cit., pp.219 ff.

244. Oral statement of Fritz Siebel after the war, undated, in BA-MA Lw 112/6.

245. This version is kept as a complete copy in the project von Rohden documents in BA-MA 4376–3091. The shortened version, which was sent by Admiral Lahs, Head of the Economic Group Aviation Industry and President of the Reich Association of the German Aviation Industry, to Director Mahle in Stuttgart on 24 December 1941 (Pr.312/41 La/Wp. Confidential!), was published in 1951 in the magazine Der Flieger (Munich: Luftfahrtverlag Walter Zuerl), pp.25–7, 55, 59, 102–4. See also Ludwig, op. cit., p.388.

246. Oral statement of Fritz Siebel after the war, without date, in BA-MA Lw 112/6. Accordingly State Secretary Paul Koerner witnessed this conference at Hitler's headquarters. Compare with a similar reaction of Hitler's in the summer of 1940, in Boetticher op. cit., p.219.; Nielsen op. cit., p.196; Koppenberg, too, the Director-General of the Junkers aircraft firm, was in despair in the autumn of 1941, because the leaders of the Reich did not take seriously his armaments comparison between Germany and the USA, which was very disadvantageous for the former (Speer, op. cit., p.198).

247. So General dr Flieger Hans-Georg von Seidel, op. cit., p.18.

248. Oral statement of Fritz Sieble, in BA-MA Lw 112/6; see also Nielsen, op. cit.,

pp.196 ff.
249. Osterkamp, op. cit., pp.376 ff.
250. Greiner, op. cit., p.391; Irving, *Hitler*, p.279.
251. Lossberg, op. cit., p.119 f.; Irving, *Hitler*, p.327.
252. Interview Nicolaus von Below of 25 January 1972, item 21.
253. Interview Eckard Christian of 24 June 1972, item 36.
254. Boetticher, op. cit., pp.235 ff.; also similar statement by General der Flieger a.D. Josef Kammhuber of 15 March 1956 about his conversation with Hitler in June 1943, in BA-MA Lw 135.
255. Boetticher, op. cit., pp.232 ff.
256. Nielsen, op. cit., p.198.
257. Generalleutnant Josef (Beppo) Schmid in Ansel, op. cit., pp.14 ff.; Goering said to Milch on 4 January 1943 that Hitler had told him the Americans were harmless. They could only make refrigerators and razor blades, but nothing else (Irving, *Tragödie*, p.251).
258. Ibid., p.334.
259. Interview Colonel (ret.) Hans Wolter of 6 June 1972.
260. Walter Schellenberg, *Memoiren*, ed. by Gita Petersen (Cologne, 1959), p.137. Under one of Schellenberg's reports Goering wrote 'Schellenberg is crazy' and ordered that none of these analyses of American war production should be forwarded to other staffs.
261. Statement Field Marshal Erhard Milch of 28 July 1945, in BA-MA Lw 103/36. Compare Baumbach, op. cit., p.63.
262. Milch in *Generalluftzeugmeister* conference of 20 October 1942, in BA-MA MD Vol.16, pp.2762 ff.
263. Irving, *Tragödie*, p.251.
264. Speer, op. cit., p.302.
265. Goering in *Generalluftzeugmeister* conference on development problems in the presence of representatives of the aviation industry on 13 September 1942, in BA-MA MD Vol.62, pp.5278, 5282 ff., and in the conference with the *Generalluftzeugmeister* and Industry Council of 14 October 1943, in BA-MA MD Vol.63, 6154 f.
266. Goering in the aircraft designer conference of 25 May 1944, in BA-MA MD Vol.64, p.6768.
267. Ansel, op. cit., pp.149 ff.
268. Boetticher, op. cit., pp.233 ff.; see also Suchenwirth, *Jeschonnek*, p.144.
269. BA-MA MD Vol.53, p.1156.
270. Development conference of 29 July 1942, in BA-MA MD Vol.34, p.1698.
271. *Generalluftzeugmeister* conference of 5 January 1943, in BA-MA MD Vol.18, p.3934 ff.; compare with MGFA, Milch Diaries, entry of 4 January 1943, and Irving, *Tragödie*, p.251.
272. *Reichsmarschall* conference of 28 October 1943, in BA-MA MD Vol.663, 6077 f.
273. Milch in conference of State Secretary, *Generalluftzeugmeister* and Speer Ministry of 27 October 1943, in BA-MA MD 31, 743.
274. Irving, *Tragödie*, p.454, footnote 19.
275. Wilfred von Oven, *Mit Göbbels bis zum Ende*, 2 vols. (Buenos Aires 1949 and 1950), Vol.2, p.78.
276. *Generalluftzeugmeister* conference of 20 August 1942 in BA-MA MD Vol.15, 1976. See also Milch, *Erinnerungen*, pp.297 ff.
277. Wilhelm Haenschkle, Generalleutnant a.D., 'Die Luftnachrichtentruppe 1944 im Westen', in *Wehrkunde*, IV, No.3 (March 1955).
278. Demonstrated by Hinsley's famous three-volume opus – see note 1 above.
279. See note 2 above.
280. Boog, *Luftwaffenführung*, pp.614 ff.
281. Gottschling, op. cit., Vol.2, p.3420. For German radio intelligence techniques and methods see also Fritz Trenkle, *Die deutschen Funkpeil-und -horchverfahren bis 1945. AEG/Telefunken* (Ulm, 1983) [German radio direction-finding and radio intelligence techniques and methods] and Fritz Trenkle, *Die deutschen Funkstörver-*

fahren bis 1945 (Ulm, 1982) [German radio jamming techniques].
282. Gottschling, op. cit., Vol.2, pp.63 ff., 75 ff.
283. Ibid., Vol.1, p.7.
284. Ibid., Vol.2, p.190.
285. Ibid., pp.255–78. See also Horst Boog, 'Ausweg in die Nacht. Die Luftschlacht über der Deutschen Bucht am 18.12.1939 und ihre Folge', in Luftwaffe No.9/1975, pp.6–28.
286. Gottschling, op. cit., Vol.2, pp.278, 288.
287. Ibid., pp.20a ff.
288. Ibid., pp.203 f., 207.
289. See note 286 above.
290. Gottschling, op. cit., Vol.2, pp.249 ff.
291. Ibid., pp.246 ff.
292. Cf. Webster-Frankland, op. cit., Vol.III, p.192, and Martin Middlebrook, *Die Nacht in der die Bomber starben* (Frankfurt and Berlin, 1975), pp.118 ff., 244–50.
293. See Craven and Cate, op. cit., Vol.II, pp.477–84; Gottschlng, op. cit., Vol.2, pp.472 ff. David Kahn, *The Codebreakers* (New York, 1968), p.464, attributes this success of the German Air Force Radio Intelligence Service merely to an intercept of a short message of the US 9th Air Force of 1 August 1943.
294. Gottschling, op. cit., Vol.2, pp.490 ff., 492 ff.
295. Ibid., p.166.
296. Ibid., pp.350 ff., 392.
297. Ibid., pp.318 ff., 388 ff.
298. Ibid., pp.317, 324, 390.
299. Ibid., pp.317 ff.
300. Ibid., pp.351, 407; Dr. Wolfram Freiherr von Richthofen, Generalfeldmarschall, *Tagebuch* (in private possession), pp.9, 11, 12, 14 November 1942; see also Manfred Kehrig, *Stalingrad. Analyse und Dokumentation einer Schlacht* (Stuttgart, 1974), pp.90–95, 101, 117.
301. Gottschling, op. cit., Vol.2, p.408.
302. Ibid., pp.169 ff., 404 f.
303. Ibid., pp.427 ff.
304. Ibid., pp.281 ff., 231. Trenkle, *Funkstörverfahren*, op. cit., pp.114 ff.
305. Gottschling, op. cit., Vol.2, pp.433 ff.; compare R.E. Gillman, *The Shiphunters* (London, 1976), pp.130 ff.
306. Boog, *Sowjetunion*, p.306.
307. Gottschling, op. cit., Vol.2, pp.234 ff.
308. Ibid., Vol.I, pp.306 ff.
309. Ibid., p.363 f.
310. Kahn, *Codebreakers*, p.461.
311. See also Kahn, *Hitler's Spies*, p.524.
312. Cf. Reinhard Gehlen, *Der Dienst, Erinnergungen 1941–1971* (Mainz-Wiesbaden, 1971), pp.42, 232, and Erich Sobik, 'Der G2 und die Aufklärung', in *Truppenpraxis* No.8 (1979), p.634.
313. Cf. Michael Howard, 'The High Command in Britain During the Second World War', in *Revue Internationale d'Histoire Militaire*, No.47 (1980), pp.60–71.
313. For this see Kahn, *Hitler's Spies*, pp.524, 527 ff.; Galland, *Die Ersten und die Letzten*, p.88, and Adolf Baeumker, *Ein Beitrag zur Geschichte der Führung der deutschen Luftfahrttechnik im ersten halben Jahrhundert 1900–1945* (Bad Godesberg, 1971), p.41.

A Comparative Analysis of RAF and Luftwaffe Intelligence in the Battle of Britain, 1940

SEBASTIAN COX

In analysing the performance of RAF and Luftwaffe intelligence in the Battle of Britain it is perhaps best to start by describing the organization of intelligence in the two opposing air arms, since this provides the key to understanding some of their shortcomings.

The Air Intelligence Branch of the Air Ministry was organized on a geographical basis whereby all material relating to a particular country was dealt with by a particular sub-section. Thus, AI3b was the sub-section that dealt with all information relating to Germany, including order of battle, aircraft, training and production. This geographically based structure was a relic of peacetime, when the origin of intelligence material, whether from open or clandestine sources, tended to relate to one particular country, and assessments were seldom required for more than one country at a time. For the first eight months of the war the geo-strategic situation remained relatively unchanged, but with the German offensive in the West, and the entry of Italy into the war, the situation was radically altered. The immediate crisis of the Battle of Britain and imminent invasion was obviously an inopportune moment for wholesale reorganization, but it is significant that once the threat had receded Air Intelligence underwent a long period of readjustment and reorganization between November 1940 and August 1941. The *de facto* disappearance of national frontiers in Europe and the increasing need to deal effectively with operational intelligence of the utmost urgency led directly to the abandonment of geographical divisions in the handling of intelligence in the war against Germany. Thus AI3b eventually became responsible for studying orders of battle and organization for all air forces in northern Europe, while other sub-sections performed similar roles for airfields, production and training. These changes also reflected the shift in relative importance between Sigint and photographic reconnaissance on the one hand, and published and clandestine sources on the other. The latter were of particular value in the pre-war period, but became relatively less so as the need for operational intelligence assumed priority. As will become clear, some of the failures of British intelligence during the Battle of Britain were organizational.[1]

Air Intelligence was, however, a separate Directorate within the Chief of the Air Staff's Department in the Air Ministry, and its Director was an Air Commodore equal in status to the Director of Plans. AI was thus able to produce independent assessments of aspects of the German war machine, which frequently criticized, implicitly or explicitly, the strategy of the Air Staff. Even when these appreciations were wide of the mark and influenced by pre-war doctrine and 'mirroring', there is no doubting the independence of the stance adopted.[2] Though some of the officers within AI at the start of the war were of moderate quality, good quality personnel were brought into the Directorate and intelligence officers were on the whole well regarded. Indeed, one of the strengths of AI was its ability to recruit from outside the Service in much the same way as Bletchley Park. In fact by the end of the war, of some 700 officers only 10, all in the rank of Group Captain or above, were regular officers.[3]

By contrast the intelligence service of the Luftwaffe did not enjoy separate status. The Air Intelligence Department, or 5th *Abteilung*, within the Luftwaffe General Staff was subordinated to the operations department. A similar structure pertained in the Luftflotten so that it was frequently the operations officers who prepared intelligence assessments, 'because the basis for all evaluations of the situation were the Luftwaffe's own operational intentions, objectives or missions'.[4] The intelligence officer might be consulted before such appreciations were prepared, but, as the position was held in low esteem, he frequently was not. Indeed the lowly status of Luftwaffe intelligence officers is well illustrated by the fact that they were regarded as 'maids of all work' and their duties included 'troop welfare, propaganda, and censorship'.[5] Equally indicative of the Luftwaffe's overall approach is the fact that 'in the Luftwaffe there were no representatives of the intelligence organisation stationed at units below the size of Fliegerkorps until 1944'.[6]

In addition, because of the political structure of the Third Reich, there was little co-ordination of intelligence in the British sense. Competing German intelligence bodies – and there were more than a dozen such agencies outside the armed services – were insular in their attitude to other parts of the intelligence community, because, as always in politics, knowledge was power. Intelligence from different sources thus came together only at the very highest level – Hitler – so that no organization such as the British Joint Intelligence Committee could exist because its members would have been surrendering knowledge, and with it political power, to rivals within the system. This attitude of insularity spread right down through the system, with competing departments jealously guarding their information, and resulted in information being disseminated largely vertically, and seldom horizontally. Since intelligence is a jigsaw in which a piece obtained, say, from radio intercepts can then be followed up by a POW interrogator, this was bound to weaken German intelligence. Thus, the Luftwaffe Signals and Cipher Intelligence Service was largely the personal fiefdom of the Chief of Luftwaffe Signals, General Martini,[7] and the friction and rivalry between this 3rd *Abteilung* of the Signals Service and the 5th *Abteilung* of the Luftwaffe General Staff led directly to erroneous assessments.

Insularity and empire-building, endemic in the Third Reich and encouraged by Hitler for political reasons, meant that, of some eight agencies collecting intelligence on air matters, only two were directly subordinated to the 5th *Abteilung*. On the technical side 'information on radar was evaluated by ten different agencies'.[8] With such a plethora of players in the field co-ordination would have been difficult even given goodwill, but the Nazi psychology of rivalry and mistrust inevitably permeated the entire organization of intelligence and prevented vital cross-fertilization between agencies. To take one example, the German POW interrogation organization was not subordinated to the 5th *Abteilung*, whereas RAF interrogation was conducted by a sub-section, AI1 (k), within the Intelligence Directorate. An interrogation report from AI1 (k) during the Battle of Britain would receive a wide distribution within the Air Ministry, and copies would be sent to operational commands and Naval and Military Intelligence automatically: altogether some forty copies would be produced. An item of particular interest to some organization would be copied to them, so that for example, a report on a new type of German tracer ammunition in July 1940 was copied to the Director of Armament Development in the Ministry of Aircraft Production.

As always in Nazi Germany, Hitler's personal attitude to a subject was of paramount importance in moulding the opinions of others. It comes as no surprise, therefore, that his personal dislike of unfavourable intelligence reports was shared by Goering and Jeschonnek.[9] The Head of the 5th *Abteilung* from 1938 was Major, later Colonel, 'Beppo' Schmid, who combined this duty for several years with that of working in Goering's ministerial office. He thus had ample opportunity to observe his master's prejudices at first hand, and as a shrewd and ambitious officer it is hardly surprising that he soon gained a reputation within the Luftwaffe for garnishing his reports to make them more palatable to Goering.[10]

II

After this brief outline of the organization of the rival intelligence directorates in mind we can consider the quality of the intelligence they produced, and the effect it had on the operational decisions made in the campaign. To take the British first there is no documentary evidence that intelligence affected British dispositions before the opening air battles in July. The basic infrastructure of Fighter Command had been laid down before the war and, once France fell, it was obvious that an attack was coming, and that it would be mounted from airfields extending from Brittany to Scandinavia. British air planners had in any case been postulating mass German air attacks since before the war, and Air Intelligence had tended to interpret any threatening German moves against the Low Countries as being part of a plan to seize airfields for an air assault on Britain, rather than an attempt to outflank the Maginot line and invade France. Thus Wing Commander Inglis of AI3 minuted on 2 May 1940:

> The invasion of Holland, which now looks imminent, will represent the first 'plank' in the northern encirclement of the British Isles, and will provide Germany with those air bases from which she may hope to neutralise our Air Force and Fleet as a preliminary to invasion.[11]

In an earlier minute of 2 February 1940 the same officer had written, of a report from Sweden, that Sweden and Norway would be invaded to act as a launching pad for air and seaborne assaults:

> If Germany finds herself forced to take the offensive the plan outlined ... fits in with Hitler's ambition – the overthrow of the British Empire, with the avoidance of a direct attack upon France.[12]

Air Intelligence's predisposition to interpret German strategy always in relation to air power was evident even after the German invasion of the West had begun. On 15 May 1940 Group Captain Elmhirst, head of the German section, wrote:

> We are of the opinion that the object of this advance is two-fold: (a) to occupy air bases in the Low Countries from which to attack England; (b) to enable Flak and Fighter Units to be established West of the Ruhr.
> When (a) and (b) are accomplished we consider that the whole weight of the GAF will be thrown against England. This may be followed by invasion.[13]

One doubts whether British military intelligence, or even the intelligence section of British Air Forces in France, saw things in quite the same light. The effect of these erroneous appreciations of German intentions was probably not very great. Although Air Intelligence suggested both the reinforcement of fighters in France and the bombing of targets in Germany, the limited extent to which these measures were undertaken would probably have been adopted in any case. The precariousness of the situation on the Continent does not, however, appear to have impinged on the consciousness of Air Intelligence as early as it might have done. In a minute of 3 June 1940 a suggestion by Wing Commander Inglis that fighter strength in France be further reinforced was endorsed by both the Deputy Director of the German section and the Director of Intelligence. This despite the fact that some two weeks earlier the War Cabinet had made its famous decision not to send further fighter reinforcements to France. An unknown hand, presumably that of a senior member of the Air Staff, annotated: '... I strongly deprecate the proposal to move our Fighter Squadrons to France in appreciable numbers'.[14]

Once France collapsed, of course, there could be little doubt over Germany's future intentions, and at least some of the lessons of German operations in France do seem to have been absorbed, since Air Intelligence predicted on 28 June that the opening of the German offensive against Britain would take the form of attacks on aerodromes by fighters and bombers. The first indications of the expected air offensive came from reconnaissance photographs of extensions to French runways, and low grade Sigint indicating the arrival of Luftwaffe bomber units in northern France. From the end of June Enigma intelligence on the improved states of serviceability and readiness in German bomber units, and the arrival of dive-bomber units on airfields across the English Channel, indicated that the period of grace while Luftwaffe units refitted after the French campaign was drawing to a close.[15]

Once the Battle started, which in British eyes means early July, intelligence contributed in two major areas: first in the provision of order of battle and organizational intelligence on the Luftwaffe, and secondly in more direct and immediate intelligence on Luftwaffe operations. Both firms of intelligence were heavily reliant on Sigint. German signals traffic was of four main types: high-grade cyphers encrypted by Enigma, low-grade W/T traffic, usually to and from aircraft, low-grade radio telephone traffic, and other signals traffic such as navigational beacons. Before the outbreak of war the RAF had set up an interception system consisting of one main interception station at Cheadle, and four subsidiary stations, and these had been intercepting and interpreting low-grade German W/T traffic since 1935. Luftwaffe signals security was relatively poor, and German bomber and transport aircraft used their unit markings as W/T call signs before the war, thus enabling the RAF radio intelligence service, or Y as it was known, to build up a reasonably accurate picture of German Air Force numbers and units. On the outbreak of war the codes were changed but, as so often in Sigint, the mass of knowledge already accumulated on units and airfields meant that by the end of 1939 most operational units had been re-identified. The increased amount of traffic intercepted in late June 1940 enabled Air Intelligence to build on its earlier solid base, and with its increased understanding of the organization and equipment of the German Air Force it made a very significant

adjustment in early July in its estimate of frontline strength. In June
Air Intelligence had estimated that the Luftwaffe disposed of 5,000
frontline aircraft, including 2,500 bombers capable of delivering 4,800
tons of bombs per day, and backed up by 7,000 aircraft in reserve. The
actual figures were approximately 2,000 frontline aircraft with 1,000 in
reserve.[16]

Professor Lindeman, Churchill's personal scientific adviser, was openly
sceptical of the Air Ministry's figures and said so at a meeting with Group
Captain Elmhirst on 5 July 1940. Lindeman queried in particular the
figure of 4,800 tons of bombs per day. The explanation given by Elmhirst
was:

> ... that this figure was based on 80 per cent of the German Bomber
> Force carrying full load and on a proportion of them making one or
> two sorties per day.
> Further it was explained that the figures was given with the following
> provisos –
> (a) the scale was for the initial day, and would diminish in
> accordance with unserviceability and casualties.
> (b) that this scale could only be achieved if Units were given a
> period of rest in order to maintain the maximum serviceability in
> squadrons.
> (c) that reserve crews were in readiness.
> (d) that a scale of one or more sorties per day might be maintained
> for the first week, but with diminishing numerical force.[17]

These caveats had not of course been given in the JIC paper, an example of
Air Intelligence continuing its pre-war tendency to make worst-case
assumptions. In the light of the improved intelligence from Enigma
Elmhirst revised his estimate of the Luftwaffe's likely capabilities on the
basis that the number of bombers available could be reduced to 50 per cent
averaging one sortie per day, which would give a bomblift of 1,800
tons. It is obvious from the comments which this minute engendered
that the Enigma intelligence was of excellent quality, the Director of
Intelligence referring to it as 'apparently sure evidence', and with
unconscious accuracy 'heaven-sent'.[18]

Equally interesting was the reaction of members of the Air Staff when
the revised estimate was circulated. Slessor, then Director of Plans,
wrote:

> I think the revised estimate is very much nearer the mark than
> anything we have had before. I have always felt that we were loading
> the scales unduly against ourselves [and the] JPC [Joint Planning
> Committee] commented, in that sense, on JIC's estimate of 4800.[19]

The Deputy Chief of Air Staff, Douglas, also minuted: 'I am quite prepared to accept your revised estimate, which I think is much more reasonable than the old one. I said at the time that I thought you had put the German effort too high.'[20]

This indicates quite clearly that Air Intelligence's estimates of German strength were not accepted uncritically within the Air Staff, any more than they were outside it. Nevertheless, the tendency was still to over-estimate German strength, both frontline and reserve, and thus to ascribe greater staying power to the Luftwaffe during the Battle than it actually had, even though the defences were claiming two to three times the true scale of German loss. It is true to say, however, that continued overestimation of German strength did not adversely affect Dowding's conduct of the Battle, since it would presumably have confirmed him in his conviction that maximum conservation of his exiguous resources was essential to victory. The only document giving direct evidence of a link between a piece of Enigma intelligence and a strategic decision by Dowding tends to confirm this view. This was in early September when Enigma detected the move of some 160 heavy bombers from Scandinavia into Belgium and France, together with considerable reinforcement of dive-bomber units in the same area. Keith Park, commanding the Fighter Group in South-East England, asked Dowding for reinforcements of from two to six fighter squadrons, some at forward bases. Dowding's response was to move one Hurricane night fighter squadron out of Park's 11 Group, and give him two further day fighter squadrons at Hendon and Debden, airfields which were sufficiently far from Luftwaffe bases to have suffered only sporadic attack. This was typical Dowding parsimony, given the increased scale of threat implied by the intelligence.[21] Such other changes in strategy as Dowding introduced, as for example in his scheme to keep 11 Group squadrons up to strength in pilots at the expense of squadrons in other Groups, were largely forced on him by his own losses and not through any intelligence input. Had Air Intelligence been underestimating, instead of overestimating, German strength it is of course possible that Dowding's strategy would have been adversely affected. Since Enigma intelligence did not give any indications of the scale of German losses, however, it could not be used by Dowding in any calculation of ultimate victory or defeat (Air Intelligence's estimates of German losses are dealt with below). Air Intelligence's continuing overestimation did lead to a fundamental misappreciation of German strategy during August. Air Intelligence believed that the Luftwaffe was holding back a large proportion of its long-range bomber force, which would be unleashed only after air superiority had been won. In fact, of course, the Luftwaffe was more or less fully committed to the Battle from mid-August. Again, this erroneous conclusion probably had little effect on British strategy other than to reinforce the central tenet of maximum conservation.[22]

This leads on to the vexed question of the extent to which Enigma intelligence was of operational value to Dowding. The official history of *British Intelligence in the Second World War* states categorically that 'the Enigma was of no help in forecasting shifts that occurred during the Battle in the GAF's methods and objectives'.[23] The reason was that the major strategic decisions were seldom transmitted by wireless. Thus, shifts in German strategy had to be deduced by Dowding and his Group Commanders purely from close observation of German operations, a skill at which they became remarkably adept. Occasional clues, such as odd references to Adler Tag, were too vague to indicate anything of value.[24]

At a tactical level, however, the official historians' view that Enigma gave very little assistance is perhaps more contentious:

> In the day-to-day fighting by giving notice of the time, the targets and the forces committed to individual raids, the Enigma provided an increasing amount of intelligence was sometimes obtained too late to be of operational value. Moreover, the GAF made last minute alterations of plan which were not disclosed in the decrypts, or were not disclosed in good time.[25]

This is true so far as it goes, and is perhaps a necessary corrective to the Winterbotham 'Ultra Won the Battle of Britain' school of thought. There is, however, at least some evidence to contradict the official historians' conclusion that Fighter Command received no advance warning of the pincer attacks against the north and south of England on 15 August 1940. The eminent British historian Ronald Lewin has stated, on the basis of decrypts available in the Public Record Office and on information from Group Captain Winterbotham, that Dowding knew, not only of the attacks on northern England by Luftflotte V, but also that the German plan involved a series of seven raids widely dispersed both geographically and chronologically.[26]

The issue is further complicated by contradictory evidence of exactly when Dowding was fully indoctrinated into the Ultra secret. According to Lewin, who appears to rely heavily on Winterbotham's memory, this took place in early August, when a Special Liaison Unit was set up in HQ Fighter Command.[27] However, Martin Gilbert, in his mammoth biography of Churchill, quotes a minute from the Prime Minister of 16 October asking that the Cs-in-C of Fighter and Bomber Commands be let in on the secret.[28] The latter would seem on the face of it a more reliable source than Group Captain Winterbotham's memory. A further indication is perhaps contained in the official history's comment that postponements of raids which were not decrypted, when Enigma had already given intelligence of the original date, led to the undermining of con-fidence in the source. It is difficult to see why the source should be undermined if its true nature were known.[29]

The official history does, however, make clear that organizational failings within Air Intelligence were a further contributory factor in reducing the value of Enigma's tactical intelligence. The exploitation of high-grade ciphers had never been expected to produce intelligence of tactical value, and it was initially passed to the section of Air Intelli-gence tasked with long-term assessments of German order of battle and organization. This section 'was not organised or staffed for the exploita-tion of operational intelligence. The result was a separation of the tactical information obtained from the high-grade and low-grade sources, the former occasionally revealing the GAF's orders and intentions, the latter reporting them as they were carried out, which prevented both sources from being used to the full during 1940'.[30] One might add that if, as Lewin claims, Dowding and Park were both indoctrinated into the secret of Enigma in early August, then the organizational shortcomings in the Air Intelligence Directorate would have been irrelevant, since strategic and tactical intelligence could have been synthesized by the two commanders themselves.

The exploitation of the low-grade sources was nevertheless efficient because the organization had from the start been designed to extract operationally valuable information. The RAF wireless interception service centred at Cheadle already had much experience of intercepting German W/T traffic, and they were able to put this to good use. The medium-frequency traffic of the German air traffic control service gave early warning of the departure of aircraft, and direction-finding often revealed the bases involved. The high-frequency traffic was generated by German bombers on operations, and the wireless discipline of these units was poor, enabling Cheadle to make frequent early and accurate guesses of the units taking part in a raid. At the same time the arrival of German fighter units in north-eastern France and the Low Countries meant that the radio telephone transmissions of the fighters came within interception range for the first time. The equipment to monitor these transmissions was already in place, although it would appear that initially nobody had remembered to provide German linguists to interpret it.[31] The radio discipline of the Luftwaffe fighter units was no better than that of the bombers, and vitally important operational information was intercepted. The interception units 'could, on occasion, determine where enemy aircraft were forming up for a raid outside radar's detection range, give the altitude of the aircraft', and indicate the type of aircraft in the formation.[32] Direct telephone lines were established between the interception units and the local Group and Sector headquarters, as well as with Fighter

Command, so that operationally important intelligence could be passed as rapidly as possible. The contribution of low-grade Sigint to the difficult task of assessing the enemy's intentions from the confused and conflicting radar tracks on the operations room table was obviously of great importance.

One area in which only tentative progress was made during the Battle was in the use of Sigint to help to establish the true rate of German losses. This is an area which has always been one of the most difficult for any air intelligence organization, yet at the same time one of the most important. The Falklands war demonstrated yet again that reliance on reconstructing air battles from eye-witness accounts after the event is fraught with difficulties. Air Intelligence, perhaps because of its relative inexperience in the field, was certainly too ready to accept RAF claims at face value. In the period 8 August to 16 August the defences claimed 501 enemy aircraft confirmed as destroyed, and a further 231 probably destroyed, when the actual scale of loss was only 283.[33] By the end of the Battle there were the first signs of doubt over the veracity of the claims. In a minute of 13 October Air Intelligence drew attention to the fact that anti-aircraft and fighter defences claimed 2,091 aircraft destroyed between 8 August and 2 October, but only 837 could definitely be identified as lost from wreckage or W/T intercepts, leaving a discrepancy of 1,254 aircraft.[34] The actual German loss for the period was 1,300 aircraft.[35] Instead of questioning the figures, however, Air Intelligence merely sought explanations for the discrepancy. The explanations concentrated on the shortcomings in sources, but at no time sought to question whether the defences were overclaiming, and there is no evidence to suggest that any action was taken over the discrepancy. This was to have serious consequences in 1941 when Fighter Command went over to the offensive, because instead of arriving at a realistic method of assessing claims based on analysing the real evidence of German losses available from the Battle of Britain, Fighter Command continued to accept exaggerated claims. As the air battles of 1941 took place over the Continent the problem of verifying such claims was far more difficult, and Fighter Command mistakenly believed it was winning a battle of attrition when it was in fact suffering severely.[36] Air Intelligence's minute of 13 October makes it clear that the first steps towards gleaning intelligence on losses of German multi-engined aircraft through W/T intercepts were made during the Battle of Britain, but there was apparently no comparable analysis of the R/T intercepts.[37] Here again, however, there is no evidence that such exaggerated claims had any adverse influence on Dowding's handling of the Battle. His assessment of the Luftwaffe's staying power probably owed more to his own analysis of German operations on a day-to-day basis than to any arithmetical calculation of losses.

If this was the slightly uneven performance of a British intelligence service which was not hamstrung by political in-fighting, it is hardly surprising that the Luftwaffe's intelligence performance was grossly inadequate. In a report of 2 May 1939 Schmid had concluded that the Western powers could not 'catch up with the major advance in the expansion of the air forces achieved by Germany during the next 1–2 years'.[38] Within a year British production was exceeding that of Germany by 50 per cent. Schmid went on to conclude that the democracies could only match Germany in the field of technical development of fighters, and that because of the lead time required the Western powers were two to three years behind in fighter aircraft and even further in bombers. Within a year again the Luftwaffe's pilots were to learn that the Spitfire was the equal of the Bf 109. Schmid also believed that the British defensive system was adequate only to defend London and that the rest of the country would be almost totally exposed to attack: this view was presumably based on Schmid's ignorance of British radar and a consequent calculation of defensive forces based on standing fighting patrols. The further conclusion that, because Britain was an island, the defenders' job was more difficult than the attackers' was again presumably based on the assumption that the only early warning available would be visual sighting of aircraft by ground observers. Schmid did, however, sound a warning note that the German lead in air armament might not be maintained indefinitely.[39]

The optimism in the Luftwaffe over the result of any air war with England was not general, however. General Felmy produced a report shortly after the outbreak of war which revealed many of the shortcomings in Luftwaffe force structure which were to prove decisive in the Battle of Britain. Predictably Goering and Jeschonnek castigated the report and its author, and on Hitler's orders he was relieved of his post on a pretext.[40] Several studies done on the comparative air armament position of Germany and the Western Powers during 1939 concluded that Germany was definitely in a superior position, but that this superiority would eventually begin to fade. These views, of course, were in accord with Hitler's general desire to settle matters with the Western Powers in the shortest possible time. In the aftermath of the Battle of France the state of euphoria in the German High Command led predictably to even more optimistic assessments, fed in part by French declarations that Britain and the RAF could not survive for long.[41]

The inadequacy of German intelligence is fully revealed in an appreciation prepared by the 5th *Abteilung* on 16 July 1940 right at the start of the Battle. A peculiarity of the report is that British strengths were identified as weaknesses and weaknesses as strengths. The report concluded that the British possessed approximately 900 fighters, an exaggeration of about 30 per cent, of which approximately 675 were serviceable, which was more accurate since Fighter Command had 622 serviceable aircraft. Schmid also characterized both Hurricanes and Spitfires as inferior to the Bf109. The Bf110 was considered superior to the Hurricane but inferior to skilfully handled Spitfires. This was almost certainly an example of Schmid garnishing an unpalatable truth for Goering who took great personal pride in the 110 units. The poor quality of the Hurricane and Spitfire had similarly been stressed by the Foreign Air Armament Department, probably for the same political reasons. The same Department may also have been responsible for the ridiculous assertion in Schmid's report that the Hampden was the best British bomber, when it was far and away the worst.[42]

The 5th *Abteilung* report was as inaccurate over production and personnel as it was over technical matters. The British aircraft industry was believed to be capable of producing between 180 and 300 fighters a month, but it was predicted to decrease rather than increase because of the effects of air attack and problems over raw materials. In fact production had started to accelerate in April, and averaged between 450 and 500 fighters between July and September, which partly explains the perplexity on the part of the Luftwaffe High Command at Fighter Command's continued ability to mount an effective defence when German calculations showed that it should have been destroyed. Schmid was also totally unaware of the massive effort put into repairing damaged aircraft by the Civilian Repair Organization. In its assessment of the RAF's personnel the report was just as inaccurate. The shortage of trained pilots was Dowding's Achilles' heel, and Fighter Command had *already* asked for pilots from other operational commands and from the Fleet Air Arm, yet German intelligence believed that 'there are no difficulties regarding the supply of men'. Most inaccurate of all, however, was the assessment of the RAF's command structure and organization, and it is worth quoting in full:

> The command at high level [i.e. Command/Air Staff] is inflexible in its organization and strategy. As formations are rigidly attached to their home bases, command at medium level [i.e. Group/station] suffers mainly from operations being controlled in most cases by officers no longer accustomed to flying (station commanders). Command at low level is generally energetic but lacks tactical skill.

Only the last statement contained a germ of truth. In fact the criticisms of the higher commanders could more accurately have been applied to the Luftwaffe than the RAF, since most station commanders flew actively and Keith Park regularly visited his units in his own Hurricane, and had himself flown over Dunkirk to view the air battle at first hand.[43]

Schmid's conclusions concerning the rigidity of the RAF organization were probably based on the interception of Fighter Command's HF radio telephone traffic by General Martini's 3rd *Abteilung*. The assumption, however, that close control of formations from the ground made the system inflexible was a costly error. Most incredible of all, perhaps, is the fact that nowhere in the report is any mention made of radar. General Martini's Signals Intelligence organization was certainly aware that the British possessed radar, and had flown radio intelligence gathering missions just before the outbreak of war, using the airship *Graf Zeppelin* to try to discover the frequencies. Either because internal rivalry had meant that the Signals Service had not told the 5th *Abteilung* of its existence, or because Schmid's department was bereft of technical expertise capable of appreciating its significance, the eyes of the British defence were ignored.

Unlike British intelligence, however, Luftwaffe intelligence did not improve and learn from its mistakes as the Battle progressed, but merely perpetuated them. Thus, having established through the activities of General Martini's monitoring service that radar information was used to control the fighters using radio telephone, Schmid concluded that his earlier appreciation of British inflexibility was fundamentally correct. In a circular to Luftflotten and Fliegerkorps dated 8 August he stated:

> As the British fighters are controlled from the ground by R/T their forces are tied to their respective ground stations and are thereby restricted in mobility ... Consequently the assembly of strong fighter forces at determined points and at short notice is not to be expected. A massed German attack on a target area can therefore count on the same conditions of light fighter opposition as in attacks on widely scattered targets.[44]

He concluded that mass attacks would swamp the system, whereas they were in fact easier to detect as they formed up over the Continent, and easier to track on their way to their targets, which made it easier to concentrate defending squadrons against them.

Martini's Signals Intelligence Service was apparently more efficient than Schmid's organization, but it failed to affect the Battle. It did detect British radar, and attempted some ineffectual jamming, but it was deceived into thinking that the bombing of radar stations which was undertaken early in the campaign was ineffective, by the British policy of continuing to transmit from damaged stations even when return signals could no longer be received. Reports from pilots indicating the apparent invulnerability of the lattice mast to blast damage led the Germans to conclude that the vitals of the radar stations were located in bombproof bunkers. In fact, several stations were put out of action, and had the attacks continued the defensive system would have been crippled. Martini's monitors should also have realized that RAF fighter squadrons were switched between Groups and Sectors as the situation demanded, and could be vectored on to raids some distance from their own bases. If this was detected the intelligence does not appear to have been passed to the 5th *Abteilung*. It may also have been due to the pinpointing of the sector airfields through D/F fixes of fighter R/T by Martini's monitors that German targeting of airfields improved and became far more selective during the last two weeks of August.[45]

These weaknesses in intelligence both mirrored and contributed to a fatal over-confidence throughout the German High Command. Hitler's own conviction that the British were weak and would capitulate and accept overtures for peace, either before or after a short air offensive, was bound to affect Luftwaffe thinking given the nature of the Third Reich. Goering himself considered that four days would be sufficient to defeat Fighter Command, and a month would complete the destruction of the RAF and the aircraft industry throughout Britain. This outlook led to serious delays in Luftwaffe operations during which time Fighter Command repaired some of the ravages of the French Campaign. Most Luftwaffe units had been rested, re-equipped, and redeployed to bases in northern France and the Low Countries by the third week in July, yet the Luftwaffe did not launch a concerted offensive until 13 August. Until the end of July the prevarication was largely Hitler's, but his patience with the British and his savouring of his victory in France were exhausted by 31 July when he had decreed an all-out assault. Poor weather played some part in further delays, but the Luftwaffe's planners seem to have lacked all sense of urgency, continuing with a series of planning conferences to settle aspects which should have been confirmed during the long interim after the victory in France, particularly as the first outline orders were issued a month before the real offensive opened. This attitude must have stemmed from the over-confidence of the High Command, an unfounded optimism which inaccurate intelligence did nothing to dispel.

These two interrelated factors of over-confidence and poor intelligence led to an ill-directed campaign, which breached a fundamental principle of war – the maintenance of the aim. The Luftwaffe appears never to have decided the aim which it was pursuing. Its attacks seem to have been aimed variously at defeating Fighter Command and attaining air superiority to facilitate the invasion; defeating the whole of the RAF and destroying the aircraft industry simultaneously, with the same object; the strategic bombardment of cities to break morale and force Fighter Command to commit all its resources to defending one vital target – London.

During July its attacks can be seen as a sensible attempt to exert pressure on Fighter Command and the Royal Navy while units were redeployed and the political leadership sought a political settlement. The attacks in mid-August were aimed primarily at coastal airfields and radar stations, but the selection of the former was indiscriminate, partly because of faulty intelligence,[46] and partly because the Luftwaffe, perhaps through over-confidence, attempted to attack every part of the RAF instead of aiming to achieve air superiority by concentrating on Fighter Command. The assessments of the results of these raids were also generally far too optimistic: thus Luftwaffe intelligence was claiming that eleven airfields had been permanently destroyed and twelve severely damaged by 17 August,[47] when in fact all RAF airfields were fully operational on that day. The attacks on the radar chain were abandoned as soon as they began to bear fruit. Only in the last week in August and the first week in September did the Luftwaffe concentrate systematically on a target system vital to the defence: the sector airfields of 11 Group. It is no coincidence that Fighter Command came closest to defeat in this period. Six of the seven sector airfields were extensively damaged, the telecommunications links to and from the operations blocks proving especially vulnerable.

At this point in the Battle the complete lack of reliable intelligence began to affect German strategy. The exaggerated claims of success against Fighter Command deceived some German commanders. In an assessment of 20 August German intelligence claimed 644 British aircraft destroyed in the period 12–19 August, when the true figure was only 141.[48] The following table gives a brief indication of the scale of Luftwaffe claims against the true scale of British aircraft losses during the crucial period of the Battle:[49]

Date	Luftwaffe Claim	RAF Actual Loss
24 Aug. 1940	57	20
26 Aug. 1940	63	29
28 Aug. 1940	40	14
1 Sept. 1940	52	13
3 Sept. 1940	61	14
7 Sept. 1940	93	25
15 Sept. 1940	78	29

The Luftwaffe was therefore claiming between three and four times the true rate of loss throughout the crucial period. The scale of loss being suffered by the Luftwaffe was itself giving cause for concern, and a conference of all the major Luftwaffe commanders was convened in The Hague in early September. The confusion over intelligence was such that Kesselring claimed that Fighter Command had been destroyed, while Sperrle claimed it had 1,000 aircraft.[50] Kesselring's view prevailed – presumably he did not consult his pilots! – and the centre of gravity of the Luftwaffe's attack was switched to London. Kesselring presumably regarded this as the *coup de grâce*, but it may be that some Luftwaffe commanders saw it as much in terms of reducing the rate of German casualties as of increasing those of Fighter Command.

The assault on London was apparently mounted partly in the belief that Fighter Command would be forced to commit all its strength including squadrons from the north, and that they could then be destroyed in a battle which would ensure air superiority and knock Britain out of the war at one stroke. Instead it effectively ensured that the Luftwaffe lost the daylight battle: first, it relieved the pressure on 11 Group's airfields, and enabled Fighter Command to patch up its sector stations and communications; and second, and just as important, it was a fatal miscalculation to believe that a greater number of fighter squadrons could be drawn into combat over London and destroyed.

The sector airfields were so vital to the defence that 11 Group had already committed all its resources to defending them, and had also drawn on reinforcements from neighbouring groups. In attacking London the Luftwaffe did not draw in more fighter squadrons, but instead allowed the RAF to concentrate its defending forces more fully, while simultaneously increasing the problems of the attacking formations. The German attacks on London by mass formations were easier to see and track both visually and by radar, and their intentions became obvious at a very much earlier stage. The attackers had to penetrate further inland to their target, and as a result provided greater opportunities for attack to the defending squadrons, particularly those from north of the Thames. The German fighters were now operating at the extremity of their range, and, because of the heavy losses suffered by the bomber formations earlier in the Battle, were ordered by Goering to stay closer to the bombers. As a result they became far less effective at shooting down RAF fighters. The Luftwaffe's change in strategy, which stemmed from faulty intelligence, and thus simultaneously allowed Fighter Command to recover its balance, made the defending squadrons more effective, and made its own attacks less effective in achieving its strategic aim by switching to a target system both less vulnerable and less vital.

III

Many of the conclusions which can be drawn from this analysis are familiar ones. Both intelligence services suffered from faults in organization, but in the British case these were simply relics from the pre-war era, when intelligence had not been geared to operational needs. The lessons were largely learned on the British side, and the intelligence organization was overhauled and placed on a sound basis which was capable of producing reliable intelligence. On the German side the organizational shortcomings were so intimately bound up with the political structure of the Third Reich that only a change in regime could have made any fundamental difference. The predilection for accepting only good news is as old as man, and it should be an accepted axiom of intelligence that you should not shoot the messenger. In a situation where the consequences of telling the truth could be so unpleasant it is hardly surprising that reports were doctored to suit the prejudices of those receiving them. Less understandable was the prejudice against intelligence shown by the military hierarchy, and the inadequate provision of intelligence officers at lower levels in the Luftwaffe. The failings of German intelligence can nearly all be traced to the nature of the intelligence organization that had been created.

British intelligence before the Battle did suffer from a tendency to interpret German strategy to fit into a preconceived mould – that any hostile move was designed to facilitate an air offensive against Britain – but since the RAF was not actively engaged for much of this period this did not affect matters very much. The dangerous suggestion that more fighters should be sent to France had already been resisted by the Chief of the Air Staff before the Cabinet, which had agreed to send no further reinforcements to the Continent, and there was little prospect of this policy being reversed. On the whole the errors made by Air Intelligence were of far less import than those of German intelligence, partly because they tended to reinforce an existing strategy which was fundamentally correct. Had there been a less determined government in power after the fall of France, however, the exaggeration of German strength might have had serious political consequences, although there is some evidence that the Air Staff were themselves inclined to question the estimates of Luftwaffe strength.

Both sides suffered from inaccurate intelligence on enemy losses, and neither RAF nor Luftwaffe intelligence developed a proper scepticism about the claims of pilots. In this case there is less excuse for the British, who had at least some of the tools for a proper analysis at hand, and seemed at one point to be about to make use of them, but chose for whatever reason not to do so. The effect was nevertheless far more serious for the Germans, as their shortcomings in this area were in part responsible for a change in strategy which considerably reduced the effectiveness of their offensive. There is no doubt, however, that there was a widespread feeling in the German High Command that a blow aimed directly at London would win the Battle even before the meeting at The Hague in early September. Dowding, a shrewd judge of the situation, had forecast in June that 'The nearness of London to German airfields will lose them the war'.[51] Had the Luftwaffe possessed a more efficient intelligence service these mistakes might have been avoided, but the low esteem in which all intelligence was held meant that the personal prejudices of the operational commanders would still probably have counted for more than the accuracy of the intelligence.

The obvious conclusion from this analysis is that the structure of the intelligence organization is perhaps equally as important as the quality of the sources, and that such structures are likely to mirror the bureaucratic forms of the relevant state. In the British case sources eventually came to dictate much of the organization of intelligence. Equally, one might conclude that poor intelligence does not automatically lead to poor strategy, but that it is more likely to do so in offensive air operations, where the need to direct the attack towards the weakest points is crucial, than in defensive ones where identifying the point of attack often devolves upon the operational commander rather than the intelligence organization.

NOTES

1. Air Ministry, Air Historical Branch Narrative – Air Intelligence.
2. PRO AIR 40/2321 Summary of Minutes of DDI3. See particularly the minutes on bombing policy in this file.
3. AHB, Air Intelligence Narrative.
4. Horst Boog, 'German Air Intelligence in World War II', Aerospace Historian, June 1986, p.122.
5. Ibid.
6. Derek Dempster and Derek Wood, The Narrow Margin (London, 1961), p.120.
7. Boog, op. cit., p.124.
8. Ibid.
9. Ibid., p.122.
10. Dempster and Wood, op. cit., p.101, and Boog, op. cit., p.122.
11. AIR 40/2321 Minute 22.
12. Ibid., Minute 25.
13. Ibid., Minute 43.
14. Ibid., Minute 102.
15. F.H. Hinsley with E.E. Thomas, C.G.G. Ransom and R.C. Knight, British Intelligence in the Second World War, Vol. 1 (London, 1979), pp.173–4.
16. Ibid.
17. AIR 40/2321, Minute 77.
18. Ibid.
19. Ibid.
20. Ibid.
21. PRO AIR 16/330 Reinforcement of Number 11 Group.
22. Air Ministry Daily Telegraphic Intelligence Summary, 20 Aug. 1940, Air Ministry Weekly Intelligence Summaries Nos. 51 and 52, 22 and 29 Aug. 1940.
23. Hinsley, op. cit., p.177–8.
24. Ibid., p.175.
25. Ibid., p.179.
26. Ronald Lewin, Ultra Goes To War (London, 1978), pp.84–7.
27. Ibid., p.85.
28. Martin Gilbert, Winston S. Churchill, Vol. VI (London, 1983), p.849.
29. Hinsley, op. cit., p.179.
30. Ibid.

31. Dempster and Wood, op. cit., pp.121–2.
32. Hinsley, op. cit., p.181.
33. AIR 40/2321, Minute 64.
34. Ibid., Minute 65.
35. Winston G. Ramsey (ed.), *The Battle of Britain Then and Now* (London, 1980), loss tables on p.707. This is the most comprehensive work on the difficult subject of comparative losses and has been used throughout this paper to give the best approximation of actual losses. These are almost certainly accurate for the British, but less so for the Germans because of gaps and inconsistencies in the records.
36. AHB Narrative: The Air Defence of Great Britain, Vol. IV, Pt. V, para. 120 and Appendix V(F).
37. AIR 40/2321 Minute 65. See also Hinsley, op. cit., Vol. II, pp.271–3.
38. Horst Boog, 'German Air Intelligence in the Second World War', see above, pp.355.
39. All references from Schmid's report of 2 May 1939 from Ibid., pp.355–7.
40. Ibid., p.359.
41. Dempster and Wood, op. cit., p.106.
42. Ibid., pp.106–7. The report is reproduced in full on pp.106–10. British serviceability states from Air Ministry War Room Daily Strength Return for 0900 hrs 15 July 1940.
43. Dempster and Wood, op. cit., p.109.
44. Ibid., p.113.
45. Ibid., p.116.
46. AHB Translation VII/59 – German Report (undated c. 1945?) 'A Study of British Air Defences'. In interpreting German strategy I have drawn heavily on Karl Klee, 'The Battle of Britain' in Hans-Adolf Jacobsen and Jürgen Rohwer, *Decisive Battles of World War II: the German View* (English translation London, 1965), pp.73–94.
47. Ibid.
48. Ibid., and Dempster and Wood, op. cit., p.115.
49. Figures for claims taken from AHB Translation R.353 of Luftwaffe Fuhrungstab 1c Lagerberichte [Situation Reports], actual loss figures from Ramsey, op. cit., p.707. Ibid., p.116.
50. Dempster and Wood, p.116. See also Kenneth Macksey, *Kesselring: the Making of the Luftwaffe* (London, 1978), pp.82–4.
51. Dempster and Wood, p.116.

Intelligence and Strategy:
Some Observations on the War in
the Mediterranean 1941–45

RALPH BENNETT

Can a correlation be established between the effectiveness of an army's performance and the quality of the intelligence supplied to its commander? It would seem obvious that there can (St. Thomas Aquinas might have begun like this, could he have been persuaded to extend his discussion of the just war[1] to include intelligence as well as deception), for otherwise an ignorant general is as good as a well informed one. But, following the method of the *Summa Theologica* St. Thomas would at once have objected that such a correlation would degrade strategy into mere reaction to known enemy intentions and preclude the seizing of the initiative, which is absurd. The truth, as so often, lies somewhere in the middle. There is such a correlation, but it can never be very close. The most prominent of several reasons for this is the need to leave room in the theory for considerations of policy and resources, space and time. To say this is not blindly to accept Clausewitz's disparagement: 'Most Intelligence is false', so that 'for lack of objective knowledge one has to trust to talent or to luck'[2] – a view which was no doubt scarcely an exaggeration in his time but one which Sigint has substantially discredited today – but rather to emphasize anew his best-known dictum of all: 'War is the continuation of policy by other means'. The policy of a state, or the policy mutually agreed between a state and its allies, will specify objectives to be sought. The presence or absence of the means to achieve them will be the first qualification, the first guideline to action; intelligence about the enemy comes next, but it can seldom or never dictate the objective. The single greatest decision of the Second World War – at any rate apart from the dropping of the atom bombs on Japan – was the 'Germany first' decision taken by Allied agreement at the Washington conference in December 1941, and that owed nothing to intelligence. The same holds good for Torch, the invasion of North Africa, which was the British Gymnast plan of the previous year turned through 180° to meet the new circumstances of the American alliance, and for the later invasions of Italy and France. Not even the choice of particular landing beaches in Sicily, at Salerno or in Normandy derived from knowledge of enemy locations, which could and did change long after plans for Husky,

Avalanche and Overlord were firmly settled. It might even be argued that the Baytown landing in the toe of Italy in September 1943 was conducted – though perhaps not planned – quite contrary to the available intelligence, for Ultra[3] had shown that all the major German troop formations had been withdrawn from the southern tip well before 8 Army's bombardment opened.[4]

There is another major obstacle to measuring the correlation between an army's effectiveness and the intelligence available to its commander. Clausewitz expressed it succinctly when he wrote that in battle 'the light of reason is refracted in a manner quite different from that which is normal in academic speculation'.[5] Writing in his study, perhaps long after the events he is describing, and possessing information which, however full, will almost always lack any record of the precise reason why a commander took a particular decision, the historian may miss the mark at which he aimed and fall unwitting victim to the hindsight he sought to avoid. The difference between the atmosphere of the study and the battlefield ensures that military history will sometimes err at critical moments and that any general principles it enunciates, including that of the relationship between Intelligence and action, must be regarded with caution. General principles distil only with reluctance from the mass of particulars in the Mediterranean theatre between 1942 and 1945 (with which alone this study is concerned); but hindsight, the perpetual foe of the historian, becomes an even greater menace than usual if it forbids all deductions from the past for the benefit of the future. In spite of the tremendous technological changes which the last 40 years have brought, the history of the Mediterranean theatre of war strongly suggests that there are still some lessons to be learned from it.

I

The story of British aid to Greece in the spring of 1941 strikingly demonstrates the primacy of policy over military intelligence. Chamberlain had pledged support for Greece in 1939; discussion about the form it should take accelerated in January 1941, when Ultra confirmed the existence of a Nazi threat to the Balkans, and became urgent with the formal Greek request for military assistance on 8 February. Meanwhile, in December and January O'Connor had driven the Italians out of Cyrenaica. If most of the troops which had gained this victory were now sent to Greece, would Cyrenaica be at once reconquered for the Axis by Rommel's embryonic Afrika Korps, which had landed at Tripoli on 14 February? The dilemma was serious and compromise impossible. In the circumstances of the time it was probably right to accept the risk of losing Cyrenaica for the sake of the moral gesture of aiding the threatened victim of aggression. But there is no evidence that the issue was ever considered in this seemingly obvious way. An extraordinary feature of the discussions which culminated in the landing of British troops in Greece on 7 March (they were driven out again at the end of April) was the complete disregard of military considerations, in particular the quite unfounded belief on the part of Wavell, the Commander-in-Chief, Middle East, that the flimsy remaining garrison would suffice to protect Cyrenaica. There was just enough intelligence (including a little Ultra; direct signalling to Cairo began in March) to alert him to the risks in both the Balkans and Cyrenaica, but he and Eden disregarded them in favour of the moral and political gesture even after Churchill had made it plain that his earlier ardour had cooled and that they were to decide in the light of the evidence they could assemble in Athens and Cairo. Military disaster on both fronts was far more the result of their bad judgement than of inadequate intelligence.

Almost immediately there followed an opposite but even more striking example of the correlation between Intelligence and Operations which particular circumstances can provoke. Because the assault on Crete was under the control of Fliegerkorps XI, which used one of the German Air Force Enigma keys (army Enigma was still baffling the cryptanalysts), Ultra revealed the whole German plan of operations two or three weeks before the first parachutists were dropped over Maleme airfield on 20 May. The reason why forewarned did not turn out to be forearmed was therefore not lack of intelligence. The garrison of Crete consisted of weary refugees from Greece. Wavell sent them no tanks (which could have wiped out the parachustists), their obsolete aircraft were either shot down or withdrawn from a combat they were bound to lose, and although more modern fighters were based in Egypt they lacked the range to operate over Crete. The battle was lost because the assailants could keep pouring in reinforcements to the airfield they managed to capture against stiff resistance but the defenders were unavoidably left to their own devices.

Crete is a peculiar case in other ways too. A few tanks and some modern aircraft might have given victory to the defence, and intelligence clearly indicated where they could best be used. But later experience was to show that the retention of Crete would have been strategic misadventure, because the island would have claimed more men and equipment to defend it than could be spared from the greater task in Libya. The nearly victorious defence of Crete so shook the German command, which had made much of the novel airborne method of attack in 1940, that its parachute divisions became no more than élite infantry, and Malta – a far greater prize than Crete – was never assaulted from the air. Policy and intelligence both pointed to the wrong objective; sheer chance delivered it to the British command unsought.

Intelligence and strategy began to come together for the first time in the summer and autumn of 1941. Rommel and Auchinleck, the two ground commanders in Libya, were both anxious to strike first, but each was beset by almost insoluble problems of supply. Helped by Ultra and the unexpected diversion of a large part of the Luftwaffe to the Russian front, the RAF quickly regained an ascendancy it seemed to have lost for good over Greece and Crete. For the next few months, British naval and air power made the short Axis supply route across the Mediterranean so hazardous that it had few advantages over the far longer route round the Cape of Good Hope which the British were compelled to use. Because of this Rommel had to put off his offensive so long that Auchinleck managed to strike the first blow in mid-November although (to Churchill's fury) he had insisted on waiting until he had accumulated what he regarded as sufficient strength. Incompetence on the battlefield by his subordinates unfortunately let him down, and the early success of Crusader in December had turned into disillusion and defeat by February 1942. But when in the previous October the Admiralty took the risk of basing Force K (two six-inch gun cruisers and two destroyers) on Malta to prey on enemy shipping, the Axis loss rate (already one-fifth of all cargoes loaded in Italy and Greece) rose to such heights that Hitler yielded to the arguments of Raeder (Commander-in-Chief of the German Navy) and Rommel, and reinforced the Mediterranean until a third of all operational U-boats were stationed there;[6] in the short term the pressure on Auchinleck was relieved and some respite even brought to the Battle of the Atlantic.

Despite these handicaps, in January 1942 Rommel recovered in a few days most of what it had taken Crusader six gruelling weeks to conquer, the U-Boats made the Mediterranean too dangerous for Force K, and Axis supply traffic flowed freely again. The tide was not to turn once more until the late summer. The autumn of 1941 had witnessed the first impact of intelligence on strategy in the Mediterranean theatre, but it had not affected the land campaign (Rommel's advance in January was largely attributable to the military intelligence staff's error in underestimating the number of his tanks) and it lasted only a few months. For the results which had been achieved then were made possible only by the Royal Navy's and the RAF's successful exploitation of the thousand or more Ultra signals conveying advance information about Axis shipping movements which were transmitted between June and October and by the knowledge, derived from the same source, that their efforts were causing signs of strain and even of panic to appear in the language used by the Axis supply staffs. Three out of four large liners were sunk on the only two crossings of the Mediterranean they made in August and September, for instance, and a cargo of petrol was sent to the bottom.[7] Ironically, this was just after

Hitler had ordered special protection for convoys because of rising
losses at sea, but it was not long before OKH was making a similar
demand in respect of artillery shipments.[8] Again, all seven ships in the
Duisburg convoy were sunk on 9 November,[9] to the Italians' consterna-
tion. Examples could be multiplied, but more valuable than any of them
was the growing body of Sigint evidence about the broad logistical
consequences of so many sinkings; it was possible, for instance, to
calculate that the Luftwaffe's reserves of aircraft fuel in Libya had sunk
from 4,000 tons in May 1941 to 3,000 in June, 1,400 in July and only 400 – a
mere tenth of what they had been five months earlier – in September, and
on the basis of known figures of daily consumption during the quiet
summer months to make an informed estimate of the length of time petrol
supplies would last when active operations began again.

As more Enigma keys (notably two used by the army, upon the inner
workings of which the decrypts had till now been silent) were broken
during the spring and summer of 1942, moreover, it gradually became
possible to maintain regular statistics of the petrol, ammunition, tanks
and rations Rommel could dispose of at the front, in stock at the main
depot outside Tripoli (the only deep-water port between Alexandria and
Tunis) several hundred miles to the rear, and at various intermediate
points along the Via Balbia which connected them. This was an immense
strategic advance; for the first time Ultra was really enabling us to 'look at
the cards in the enemy's hand' and to estimate with some accuracy
whether Rommel possessed the resources to carry through any large-scale
operation he might propose (the absence of any way of doing this had
caused several important decrypts to be misinterpreted the previous year)
or whether, on the contrary, his operations could be disrupted and his
plans stultified by intensifying the air and sea attacks on his supply line.

This new and happier state of affairs – which prevailed henceforth, with
only minor fluctuations, throughout the war in the Mediterranean – was
well illustrated during the two decisive battles of early autumn 1942. Since
this part of the story is already well known in outline, and since the pattern
of events repeats that sketched earlier, only a few of the outstanding
details need to be recalled here.

Without petrol, aircraft would be grounded and tanks immobilized; oil
tankers at sea were therefore the prime targets. An alarmist Panzer Army
Africa appreciation of 18 August[10] revealed that at the current rate of
consumption Rommel's petrol stocks would be exhausted by the 26th,
the date Ultra showed that he had just set for the opening of his
new offensive.[11] Thus the Commanders-in-Chief of the three services
(Alexander, Harwood and Tedder) and the new commander of 8 Army,
Montgomery, were just as well informed as the staff at OKW to which
Rommel had addressed his plans and disclosed the meagreness of his

resources, knew how thin was the thread by which Rommel's chances of success hung, and could calculate with some accuracy how many tankers it would be necessary to sink in order to bring his offensive to a standstill. Decrypts of the shipping programme for the next ten days and of the routes and sailing times of a number of individual vessels led to the sinking of at least ten tankers in the few days immediately before the Afrika Korps ran out of petrol under the Alam Halfa ridge on 1 September and was bombed so heavily that it had to retreat; it was even learned that the enforced halt was being attributed directly to the loss of two specified ships, the *San Andrea* and the *Abruzzi*.[12] The chaos into which the German supply system was falling became even more evident shortly before Alamein; by the third week in October Panzer Army could not even be described as living from hand to mouth for its petrol, so erratic and so subject to sudden delays had deliveries become. The devastating consequences of British knowledge of the complete tanker programme for 21–29 October (Alamein began on the 23rd)[13] were revealed almost at once in shortages[14] and confirmed after the war in Rommel's cry as three tankers went down in quick succession 'Now we are really up against it'.[15] The conclusion is plain: Montgomery and his fellow commanders went into battle confident that the enemy's resources were severely limited and that there could be no doubt which side could stand 'hard pounding' (in Wellington's famous phrase) the longest. Here at last the correlation between intelligence and operations was very close.

If Panzer Army Africa could be reduced so near to impotence by attacks on its supply routes why, it might be asked, were the attacks not stepped up enough to starve it to death altogether? It is difficult to give a wholly satisfactory answer. It is clear that Panzer Army was twice (in the autumns of 1941 and 1942) brought close to the point of extinction, yet each time it survived. One reason is that its commander's strongest suits were improvisation with slender means and boldness in taking risks; against the sluggish British command in 1941 and early 1942 his policy paid handsomely. Perhaps, too, some of the shortages were not as acute as they were made to appear. Ultra correctly reported what the German messages said, but it is a universal habit of quartermasters to exaggerate their difficulties in the hope of inducing their superiors to increase their next allocation to compensate; Rommel had occasion to rebuke his supply staffs for this practice only a few months later.[16] Security measures to protect the source are perhaps the most likely explanation. A few more tankers sunk – even the capitulation of Panzer Army Africa – would have been a poor exchange for the loss of Ultra; irresponsible use of it might easily have given rise to suspicions that Enigma had, against all the odds, been broken, and in consequence to its supersession by a new cipher which might have remained unreadable for the remainder of the war; the loss of

Ultra's help, which was at last beginning to be properly appreciated, in the Battle of the Atlantic or in the future Second Front in Europe to which all looked forward, would have been catastrophic. There does not seem to be any contemporary record or any discoverable recollection of complaints that Rommel's supplies were getting through too easily, and a phrase in Lieutenant-General Cunningham's attack plan for Crusader ('It is understood that the enemy supply situation cannot be interfered with to a much greater degree than at present')[17] may mean that any increase in air or naval action in the Mediterranean was thought likely to endanger the security of Ultra.

II

The marked advance in the operational use of Ultra by the autumn of 1942 was preceded, and in part caused, by an equally marked improvement in the handling of intelligence at both the production and the consumption end of the signals link between Bletchley and Egypt. Prominent among the shortcomings of the British Army in 1939 was its almost complete disregard of the value of intelligence, apart from the merely tactical information derivable from patrolling a static front line, and the consequent almost complete lack of intelligence officers in its ranks. The gap was hastily filled on the outbreak of war by recruitment mainly from the academic professions, with an admixture of men who had business and managerial experience. In the long run and on the whole, this improvised policy was a success, perhaps mainly because most of the recruits were young and willing, in the spirit of those years, to learn a new trade quickly. The ultimate success of this improvised policy has led to the belief (first widely propagated by Donald Maclachlan in *Room 39*[18] that amateurs make the best intelligence officers because they are not hidebound by inherited conventions and will rapidly grasp ideas which might remain hidden from men brought up in 'standard practice'. The argument is persuasive, but our experience suggests that it needs heavy qualification.

In spite of the undeniable similarities, the differences between the outlooks of the academic and of the intelligence officer proved at first an unforeseen handicap to efficiency. Both are of course accustomed to examining evidence with care. Yet one thinks in the long term, can always declare the evidence insufficient to base conclusions on, and will usually suffer no worse penalty for error than to have his theories rejected by his colleagues, while hours and even minutes matter to the wartime intelligence officer responsible for advising his general, for he must leave nothing, however scrappy, out of account if it might throw light on the enemy's plans; because lives may depend on his faithful presentation of the meaning of perhaps woefully incomplete information upon a matter of operational urgency. Looking back over our early signals in later life, I can see – what probably no one realized at the time – that to begin with we often failed to perceive all the implications of the texts in front of us. Untaught, we clearly did not at first grasp that (to invent a simple illustration) it was not enough to signal that the Afrika Korps was advancing on Tobruk at 1800 hours on a certain day if the German original entitled us additionally to state that according to Fliegerführer Afrika at 1800 hours it was advancing in that direction – for a Luftwaffe authority might not be correctly informed about army intentions (movement towards need not imply preparations for attack, but 'advancing on' seems to do so), and in any case Rommel might have changed his orders after Fliegerführer heard about them at six o'clock. Mercifully we learned fast – perhaps because we were amateurs – and the signals about Crete in May were better drafted than those about Rommel's movements in March, when the direct wireless link with Cairo was opened; but they still left something to be desired, and it was not until the summer of 1942 that all ambiguities were eliminated.

Our experience therefore tends to show that training is as important for the budding intelligence officer as for the infantryman or gunner, otherwise each generation must learn slowly and painfully from its own mistakes. This was very clearly demonstrated in the early stages of Torch. Neither the British nor the Americans had prepared an intelligence organization commensurate with the tasks ahead. American mistakes have received more publicity, because of Kasserine, but Anderson's 1 Army was in no better case, for its intelligence officers had not been given the chance to learn from their now far more experienced fellows in 8 Army. Not only does little or no attention seem to have been paid, during the first chaotic days of November and December 1942, to intelligence other than that which could be gained on the ground, but not even a rough sketch of the institutions required to collect, evaluate and disseminate anything like strategic intelligence appears to have existed, much less the personnel to man them.[19] When Sir David Hunt, then still a comparatively junior intelligence officer at GHQ Cairo, was sent over to Algiers in November 1942, he found that the (mainly British) Intelligence staff at AFHQ 'did not know what they ought to be doing and had learned a whole lot of wrong things they ought not to be doing'.[20]

The price for this unpreparedness was paid by American soldiers and a British intelligence officer. Kasserine – which was in reality no more than the last despairing throw by the losing side, intent on delaying its fate – did not disrupt Allied strategy and in historical perspective deserves recollection mainly for the lessons it taught, but it caused great dismay at the time. At different moments in February 1943 there were three different Axis plans of attack. The Ultra evidence about them was never conclusive and there were more gaps in it than usual; unhappily, one of the most teasing intelligence puzzles of the war confronted a very inexperienced intelligence staff. The result was a misreading of enemy intentions which prolonged beyond the danger-point a plausible but erroneous belief that the main attack would come through Fondouk rather than through the Faid pass; temporary disaster followed. Brigadier Mockler-Ferryman, Eisenhower's chief intelligence officer, has been accused of over-reliance on Ultra; his fault lay far more in forgetting (or, more probably, not possessing the experience to realize) that there were sometimes unexpected gaps in it and that an officer who had issued a given decrypted order might have changed his mind after issuing it, as Rommel in fact did on 18 February.[21]

Like Brigadier Shearer, who had miscounted Rommel's tanks because he disregarded Ultra clues and by so doing had facilitated the German reconquest of half Cyrenaica in January 1942, Mockler-Ferryman was dismissed for his mistake. Some sympathy may be felt for them both, for they were unfamiliar with the operational use of Ultra material, but the two cases underline the necessity for experience (or, when this is impossible, proper training) in the handling of a delicate source with peculiar characteristics. The refusal of Admiral Sir Dudley Pound to listen to the advice of officers who had long been accustomed to handling naval Ultra, to which Mr Beesly attributes Pound's unnecessary order for Convoy PQ 17 to scatter, offers a parallel; it also illustrates, more starkly than any single episode in the land campaigns, the supreme need to interpose the judgement of a proven intelligence officer between the raw material and a commander's operational orders. The qualities required for each can hardly be combined in a single man, for the previous experience, duties and responsibilities of the two are entirely different, but if in an emergency Operations takes decisions without previously weighing the opinion of Intelligence, disaster may be the result. This would no doubt have been the case in the western desert in 1941 if Auchinleck had not so stubbornly resisted when Churchill urged him on to premature attack on the basis of his own reading of isolated Ultra decrypts.

The momentary setback at Kasserine showed up defects in American battlefield command which were speedily corrected under Patton and Bradley. The shortcomings of Intelligence were rectified almost as quickly. Mockler-Ferryman's successor, Strong, was himself to make a comparable mistake over the German Ardennes offensive of December 1944, but during the next few months it became common for young American intelligence officers, destined to service Ultra in the field during Overlord, to be first introduced to their material by a period in Hut 3, where they worked alongside the rest of us, and then to be sent out on short attachments to Mediterranean commands where they saw Ultra in action; their 'Trip Reports'[22] are instructive, and their performance in Normandy showed how much they benefited from their period of acclimatization.

By the time they went on their travels, changes in personnel and organization in Hut 3 at Bletchley and in Cairo, which immeasurably improved the effectiveness of Ultra as an instrument of war, were already more than six months old. The transformation of what had been amateurs into professionals expert in an entirely novel technique had begun in the same months as the disaster at Tobruk and the ignominious retreat to Alamein in June and July 1942 and was bearing fruit by September. Tighter control and better drafting at home and a better understanding abroad of the potentialities of the source mercifully brought to an end a frustrating period during which good intelligence had seemed quite unable to stem the tide of defeat and the two halves of a common enterprise had seemed to be engaged in a dialogue of the deaf, perpetually doomed to misunderstand each other's needs and limitations. By the late summer of 1942 not only were the logistical studies already mentioned becoming a regular feature of the work but, even more important, the distant customer was beginning to comprehend the home supplier's problems and why he could not provide on demand everything the consumer wanted. The standing of Intelligence in the eyes of Operations was thus greatly enhanced shortly before the arrival on the scene of the first general really willing to listen to a well-prepared and well-presented intelligence briefing and – by way of an unlooked-for bonus – just before the decryption of the first message since Crete to give away the enemy's whole plan of attack in advance. The disclosure of Rommel's intentions in what became the battle of Alam Halfa had tremendous consequences not only for the reputation of Ultra but for the whole future conduct of ground operations in the West. It established Montgomery's reputation, in his own and the public's mind, as a general who won victories, and it showed hitherto often sceptical generals and air marshals what intelligence could do to help win battles.

When Montgomery took over command of 8 Army on 13 August he knew that Rommel was expected to renew his offensive in the near future, but he did not like the troop dispositions Auchinleck had made to meet it, particularly his failure to garrison the Alam Halfa ridge, the key to the whole defensive position, in strength. That same evening he asked Alexander for the newly-arrived 44 Division as a garrison, and was granted his request. Four days later a decrypt[23] revealed that Rommel hoped to unhinge the British defences by capturing the ridge and so breaking through to the Delta. Such complete and immediate proof of the correctness of his judgement so confirmed Montgomery's confidence in his own supreme military insight that he came later on to believe that he could never err, but it raised 8 Army's morale and self-reliance tremendously to find that their new commander could outwit the hitherto invincible Rommel. The happy co-operation of Intelligence and Operations established in the desert in August and September prevailed (apart from a brief interruption during the early months in Tunisia and occasional lapses thereafter) for the remainder of the war in both the Mediterranean and the western theatres. Finally, it is not altogether fanciful to suggest still wider repercussions of Alam Halfa's confirmation of Montgomery's belief in his own infallibility: without it, would he have been able to insist so firmly on the revision of the assault plans for Sicily and Normandy, a revision which increased their scale enough to prevent what might otherwise well have been the collapse of both landings in a welter of blood on the assault beaches?

III

The decision to invade Sicily after the fall of Tunis was not made on intelligence grounds, and Ultra contributed relatively little to the conduct of operations there. In the empty desert, both sides had relied almost exclusively on radio communications, so that there was much traffic to intercept. The contrast as the war moved into populated areas where land-lines existed or could be laid was first apparent when the volume of Enigma traffic dropped sharply as the Germans retreated into a narrow perimeter round Tunis and Bizerta, and it became progressively more marked in Sicily and Italy. In retrospect it is surprising that Sigint gathered so much useful information on European soil, but in June and July 1943 it was only too obvious that the number and location of Axis troops in Sicily were known with far less precision than had been the rule in Africa. For the first time too, another novel phenomenon provided compensation, and this came in the end to be of even greater value. To confuse and distract the enemy from what seemed the natural assumption that Sicily would be the Allies' next target (in fact, Hitler had always thought the Balkans more likely, and he remained of this opinion for many months yet), the Mincemeat ('The Man Who Never Was') deception sought to divert attention towards Sardinia and Greece. Other sources were able to report that the Spanish authorities had recovered the body of 'Major Martin', as they were intended to do, and that they had shown his 'despatches' to the Germans, but only Ultra could confirm the success of the deception through decrypts which revealed, for instance, that OKW had accepted the false information 'Major Martin' carried as genuine within a few days of receiving it, and that 1 Panzer Division (then being re-equipped in Brittany after suffering heavily in Russia) was moving to the

Peloponnese in May and June.[24] These were the first in a long series of signals showing the success of subsequent deception plans, culminating with Fortitude, which convinced the Germans that 'Army Group Patton' would land in the Pas de Calais in July 1944.[25]

In Italy deception plans frequently contributed to tactical successes; Ultra's assistance in revealing the enemy's delusions was never more welcome than when it confirmed that the secret transfer of 8 Army westwards across the Apennines for Diadem in May 1944 and back east again for Olive in August had remained undetected. Positive demonstration was achieved in August, with signals showing that Kesselring was keeping two of his best divisions (16 SS and 26 Panzer) on the wrong side of the Apennines,[26] so weakening his defences at the real danger-point. Rather more negative evidence had to suffice in May, but the occasion provides fascinating proof of the way Intelligence and Operations could work together. The basis of the Diadem plan was to bring 8 Army over to Cassino in order to ensure sufficient numerical superiority to effect the breakthrough which had hitherto eluded the Allies. If Kesselring discovered this, it would not be difficult for him to frustrate it in mountainous country which favoured the defence; it was therefore essential to find out whether or not he knew about it. It became clear from the early spring onwards that neither he nor OKH had the least idea what the Allies intended, so many possibilities did they air,[27] and even clearer that the depletion of Luftflotte 2 to strengthen the defences of France and Germany was depriving Kesselring of the chance to reconnoitre the Allies lines adequately. Regular air activity reports failed to throw up any evidence that 8 Army's movements had been noticed and, more significantly, revealed that (as was to happen again and again) Kesselring was doing nothing to counter a blow he evidently did not expect, for he was taking divisions away from the threatened sector to meet amphibious operations which existed only in the deception planners' minds. Their air superiority enabled the Allies almost to blind the Germans, thus emphasizing their advantage in the field of intelligence: they could observe the enemy's movements while denying him a sight of their own, and by reading his signals could discover what (if anything) his very occasional air reconnaissances had observed and what his own intentions were. A happier combination of Intelligence and Operations would be hard to imagine. It helped to make the surprise complete, and not for the first time emphasized the supreme value of Ultra in a period of preparation for the offensive.

Examples like these reinforce the argument of Professor Handel and others that surprise cannot be prevented,[28] but they add another dimension to it by indicating conditions in which the deceiver can discover whether his deceit has achieved its purpose, thus magnifying his

advantage. By so doing they demonstrate that Sigint and techniques
of intelligence-gathering have rendered invalid the theory (ultimately
derived from Clausewitz's doctrine that defence is the stronger form of
war and his belief that the 'right' method of defence – i.e. that in vogue in
his own day – had made reconnaissance impossible) that intelligence is less
necessary to the offence than to the defence.[29] Intelligence about the
enemy, though of course its content was completely different, was just as
important to Alexander's attack on the Gustav Line in 1944 as it was to
Montgomery's defence at Alam Halfa in 1942.

After these further 'puffs' for Ultra, it would be only right to admit that
the close co-operation between Intelligence and Operations broke down
momentarily over the evacuation of Sicily. On 14 July 1943, only four days
after the Husky landings, and a full month before the evacuation, Ultra
reported the appointment of Oberst Baade of 15 Panzer Division to
organize the all-round defence of the Straits of Messina in readiness
for a future evacuation, should this become necessary, the delivery of
extra flak for the purpose on Goering's personal order, and repeated
instructions, which were faithfully carried out, that everything portable
should be removed when the time came.[30] Standard accounts[31] rightly
stress the strength of the Straits defences, and the most recent of
them[32] insists that because of the heavy gunfire along both shores it was
impracticable to attack sea traffic. Nevertheless, it is strange that almost
to the end Alexander and Eisenhower believed that evacuation was not
imminent[33] and did not take urgent measures against it, although Ultra
reported on 1 August that a practice evacuation exercise would be held
that night and later that fuel was being laid in against 'coming heavy
demands on the ferry system';[34] moreover, a map had been captured
which showed that evacuation would follow the loss of Adrano, which fell
on 6 August, ten days before the last Axis troops left. The defence of
Festung Europa had been deprived of nearly a quarter of a million men by
the surrender on Cape Bon in May; another 50,000 could have been added
had the wholesale evacuation of Sicily been prevented.

IV

Two episodes during the Italian campaign suggest further reflections on
the relation between intelligence and strategy. The decision to invade the
mainland, taken at the 'Trident' conference in Washington at the end of
May 1943, depended for its execution and timing on an Italian surrender,
which was at first envisaged as a sequel to the invasion, not as preceding it.
In the event, the two coincided on 9 September. But while much thought,
some of it unavoidably hurried, had been given to the landings, far less was
directed towards trying to foresee what would follow them. It was vaguely

hoped that German resistance would crumble soon after Italian and that a march of liberation would speedily carry the Allies far up the peninsula. This joint hope concealed a growing divergence between British and American forecasts of the future, which later on became very sharp. American opinion was persuaded that the Germans would quietly retire northwards in good order, but the British were convinced that they would stubbornly dispute every inch of the way; the American view credited Hitler with acting rationally in accordance with sound strategy, the British with continuing his emotional refusal to yield ground unless compelled.

In these circumstances it was of the utmost importance to discover the truth as soon as possible. If Ultra was to do this, it might have to gain access to intelligence at a higher level than had been usual in the past, for the tried and tested method of reconstituting high-level decisions from evidence of their implementation lower down might not serve in this case. The task was executed satisfactorily in the end, but it was complicated by a period of uncharacteristic indecision on Hitler's part; he changed his mind several times and did not finally resolve his doubts until November.

German misgivings that Italy might be intending to break the Axis took shape on the morrow of von Arnim's surrender in Tunisia with Hitler's instruction to Rommel to assemble a skeleton staff and prepare to occupy northern Italy if the Italians defected. Ultra identified a 'Planning staff: Rommel' in Austria at once[35] but could not discover its functions until the first few days of August, when Army Group B, composed of three corps and seven or eight divisions, suddenly appeared under Rommel's command on the Austro-Italian frontier,[36] a more formidable force (it had almost 200 tanks, nearly half of them the new Panthers and Tigers) than had ever been at either his or Kesselring's disposal before. Army Group B's future task was defined as that of forming 'a self-contained strategic reserve in Upper Italy',[37] but as soon as it crossed the frontier on news of Avalanche and the Italian surrender the urgent need became that of determining whether it would remain as an army of occupation in Lombardy or move down to hold Rome and the south, with Rommel perhaps replacing Kesselring as theatre commander (unknown to the Allies, it was just this personal issue which Hitler was finding it so difficult to resolve) – or, indeed, as eventually turned out to be the answer, whether the 'strategic reserve' was merely being placed in a convenient central position in which it might intimidate the Italians for the moment and then be dispersed to meet the emergency which had been building up on the Russian front since the failure of the Zitadelle offensive in June.

The first hints that a stand was to be made south of Rome came just after Avalanche,[38] but were heavily qualified by an Army Group B report that it had reconnoitred an 'Apennine position' – it was almost identical with the future Gothic Line – north of Florence.[39] In fact, Hitler had taken a

provisional decision on 30 September, in order to gain time, to accept
Kesselring's view that it was practicable to hold on south of Rome at least
through the winter. The Army Group B report did not conflict with this
because it carried no implication of the contrary – that Rommel had
persuaded Hitler to economize forces by retiring to the mountainous
north at once. (Rommel had in fact tried to persuade the Führer but
failed.) Yet even the most obvious interpretation – that northern defences
were being reconnoitred as a precautionary measure – left the timing
obscure. This obscurity represented the truth – Hitler had already
designated the Apennine position as the final line of defence in Italy, but
had imposed no time-table for manning it – but it could only promote
further disagreement between the Allies. Both the obscurity and the
disagreement were, at this moment and for some time to come, the
product less of any defect of intelligence than of Hitler's indecision.

If it was still impossible to predict what the Germans would do in
the more distant future, the Ultra revelations forced an immediate
reappraisal of Allied short-term strategy. Alexander dated the birth of the
Italian campaign from the discovery that there would be serious resistance
south of Rome;[40] Churchill, who on 1 October had been planning to meet
him in Rome at the end of the month, predicted only a week later that
there would be bitter fighting before the city was captured.[41]

The implicit demand that Ultra should penetrate the secrets of the
Führerhauptquartier to solve an immediate strategic dilemma had thus
been satisfactorily met in the weeks before and after Avalanche, and new
territories had been opened up to inspection as well. There had been
practically no Enigma traffic from northern Italy until the arrival of Army
Group B there, and none at all from Slovenia, which soon became its
principal focus of interest; simply because Army Group B evidently found
it impossible to communicate by land-line with its subordinate formations
as they become scattered over a wide area to suppress 'guerrillas',
therefore, Allied knowledge of resistance movements in northern Yugo-
slavia was greatly extended just as the Balkans were beginning to figure
more prominently in, at any rate, the British scheme of things in the
months after the parachuting of the first British mission to Tito at the end
of May.

These developments emphasize another feature of wartime Sigint
which is presumably equally characteristic of its successor today: its
largely uncontrollable variability as a source of information. New keys,
for new authorities and/or new areas, might come unexpectedly into use
according to the exigencies of war or organizational fashions at the centre,
and since in 1943 there were still too few of the 'bombes' which did the
repetitive daily donkey-work of decryption to meet all requirements,
from the intelligence officer's point of view there was always a degree of

uncertainty and surprise about what each day's work might bring, in spite of the establishment of a system for deciding priorities. Considerable flexibility of mind was required of the Ultra intelligence staff from this time onwards, and in even greater measure among those whose duty it was to take strategic decisions in the basis of the information we provided. It seems reasonable to suppose that the same is true today.

This point can be illustrated from the Ultra intelligence of the summar of 1944. With the piercing of the Gustav Line at the end of May (it is perhaps worth pausing to note that, predictably, Ultra throws no light on Mark Clark's astonishing preference for capturing Rome instead of rounding up the greater part of the German armies in Italy), a general Allied advance began. It was known that fortifications were being constructed in the northern Apennines, but there 'had been nothing to indicate their state of readiness since April.[42] Alexander had already lost some of his best divisions to Overlord, and the debate whether he should be required to surrender more for the Anvil landing in the south of France was now raging. On 13 June, ten days after Rome fell, he was ordered to give up seven more divisions to Anvil (they included the French mountain troops which had performed such feats in Diadem and would be required to form the spearhead of an assault on the Gothic Line). Believing that if he were allowed to retain intact the force which had gained stunning victories in May he could keep Kesselring in the run, get into the Lombard plain quickly and perhaps even penetrate as far as Vienna (or, if the Combined Chiefs of staff preferred, into southern France by the land route through the Italian Riviera) before the winter, Alexander appealed against what he regarded as a cruel and short-sighted decision.

On the same 13 June, following the return from a fact-finding mission of General Warlimont, the deputy chief of the OKW Operations Staff, Hitler issued a new directive[43] about the war in Italy. The directive was intercepted and decrypted. Here was another example of Ultra responding to the need to penetrate to a higher level than it had customarily managed to reach save in exceptional cases like Hitler's 'Stand fast' order which threw into chaos Rommel's effort to save his army from destruction at Alamein. Hitler was now addressing himself to the same question that was preoccupying the Allied command – the imminence of the threat to Lombardy – but in doing so he gave away an important new piece of information. 'Allied entry into the Lombard plain would have incalculable military and political consequences,' he admitted, yet so far little had been done over a large part of the chosen line to erect defensive works to protect it, and many months would be required to complete them. Therefore Kesselring was to contest every inch of the way back up the peninsula, and meanwhile the 'common misconception' that a fortified Apennine position already existed as to be 'scotched once and for all'.

Alexander's apparently wild dream was here shown to have a firm
foundation in reality because his enemy feared that he would do exactly
what he in fact proposed to do, and the argument that General Marshall
was at the moment deploying against his scheme – that it was unnecessary
because the Germans were in any case about to retire voluntarily to the
Alps with the minimum of resistance – was completely refuted. Had it
been impossible to decrypt Hitler's directive at once, instead of a fortnight
later, the debates of the combined chiefs might have taken a different
turn. By the time it became available on 27 June, unfortunately, the
decision for Anvil had for all practical purposes been taken, and the five
more days before its formal promulgation were insufficient to reverse it,
so deeply enmeshed had it become in national and political issues.
Alexander lost so many more divisions that he was unable to force the
Gothic Line until April 1945; had he not been deprived of them, he might
well have advanced either up the Rhone Valley or to the Danube by the
end of the year. As soon as the landings took place in August Hitler
completely undermined the strategy upon which Anvil was based by
ordering Army Group G to retire at once to Dijon and beyond, so that not
a single division was diverted from Overlord to defend the south.

Among much else, this episode exemplifies the grounds of possible
conflict between intelligence and the politician. Churchill and Brooke,
the British CIGS, who needed no further proof that the Germans would
fight for every inch of Italian ground because they had already deduced it
from Hitler's previous behaviour, remained convinced that the decision
for Anvil was wrong,[44] but by July 1944 the United States controlled so
large a part of the Allies' resources that there was no gainsaying its leaders'
wishes, even had Roosevelt not been unavoidably bound to consider how
best to secure the votes which would give him a fourth term as President. It
may well be, however, that had intelligence been available earlier in the
debate Alexander might perhaps have been allowed to retain his army
intact and that he might then have breached the Gothic Line many months
sooner and have brought so much pressure to bear on the southern edge of
the Reich that the Nazi empire might have collapsed in the autumn of
1944. With hindsight this appears a more promising strategic prospect
than either Montgomery's 'pencil-like thrust' or Eisenhower's 'broad
front' after the contemporary Falaise Gap battle in the west; in no other
way, perhaps, could the war have been brought to an end in 1944.

V

The dispute over Anvil and the advance through central Italy was the
nearest the Ultra experience came to a topic which has been prominent in
recent American literature and was much discussed at a conference

at the Royal United Services Institution in December 1984: the risk of intelligence becoming debased and its sharp cutting edge blunted at the interface between the intelligence officer and his executive or political superior.

Various reasons are put forward to explain this risk. Because of the difference between the conditions of peace and war, the Ultra experience does not illuminate most of them at all brightly, but one at least rings familiar: the complaint that the advance of technology had so increased the volume of intercepted material that it swamps the absorptive capacity of the human mind and threatens to frustrate the whole purpose for which an intelligence service exists. The point that overload can paralyse thought and action was forcefully made 14 years ago in T.L. Hughes's article 'The Fate of Facts in the World of Men'[45] (the title alone sums up the central problem which every intelligence organization must face). At Bletchley Park the threat of overload made itself felt in 1943 and 1944, when a proportion of incoming raw material had to be discarded, once it had been scrutinized for urgent items, without going through the rest of the normal processes, lest it choke the channels of communication with details of only marginal value. The solution adopted then, in what can only have been a microcosm of the present problem, was the obvious one of delegating the authority to discard to specialist departments, to rely on their judgement, and to hope that this delegation of authority would not lead to 'empire building', the creation of 'private armies', or the squirrel-like hoarding of precious information in obscure corners where it would be overlooked.

The trust and the hope were justified in our case; no one allowed his attention to be distracted from the single aim of providing speedy and accurate information which could help to win the war. A similar single-mindedness of purpose cannot be expected today, because the stimulus is lacking. The discipline of regular and objective reporting up the successive steps in the hierarchy, and the inculcation from above of the sense of responsibility which then came unbidden, must be the substitute for it. This is of course no more than to conclude that a standard practice cannot be radically improved;[46] but it is also to arrive more emphatically than ever at another familiar conclusion: that 'men not measures' are the crucial element in the business of intelligence, where one of the ground rules is 'You never know where you may find the vital clue' and where a single individual's alertness and insight may be the *sine qua non* of success.

As already implied,from the single-mindedness of purpose mentioned above it followed that we were immune from a disease which is said to be common today: that of shaping the evidence to suit the real or imagined predilections of superiors. On the other hand, it guaranteed no protection against a more subtle poison. No intellectual investigation can be successfully pursued without a working hypothesis, an approximate idea of the object to be attained; the danger then arises that the approximate idea imperceptibly becomes a fixed preconception, a pattern into which unconsciously all newly discovered evidence is forced, with the corollary that anything which will not fit is cast aside. It is agreed on all hands[47] that this is the single chief source of error in intelligence work, supreme above all others because it steals up on its victim unawares and leads him by easy stages further and further from the truth. We were enabled to escape this form of error because we were not required to draw operational deductions from our material, only to report it meticulously. Our customers in the field were sometimes less fortunate: Kasserine and the Ardennes are well-known examples.

What of the intelligence officer's superior, the general or the politician, and the other aspect of the danger of 'experts without authority and authorities without expertise?[48] Many mistakes were made during the first two or three years of the war by field commanders professionally distrustful of intelligence and not properly indoctrinated about Ultra. Some generals who rose to prominence later – Patton and Montgomery, for instance – are commonly credited with listening attentively to intelligence briefings (though it is hard to see the signs of this in some of Montgomery's actions), others with reluctance or worse. Past experience should here have guided the practice of the present, but it seems doubtful whether it has done so sufficiently, in England at least. Thorough courses of instructions are required in order to ensure that as far as humanly possible operational decisions will not be taken at variance with the latest intelligence.[49] It is entirely a matter of speculation whether anything could have altered Bomber Command's conviction that it could by itself paralyse German industry and destroy German morale, but in the spring and summer of 1944 there was enough evidence from Italy[50] to question its views seriously, and maximum use should be made of this kind of example.

This is not to make the mistake, noticed at the beginning, of converting all action into reaction or to risk becoming too intelligence-minded. Historians of intelligence have a special duty not to allow their vision to be distorted by their interests and to bear constantly in mind that 'the decisive factor is always the capacity to make use of intelligence'.[51] They should therefore be the first to point out that the early years of the Second World War saw examples of operational mistakes which could have been avoided by a better understanding of the value and use of intelligence, and to warn against the dangers which would follow a repetition.

NOTES

This paper was originally presented at the US Army War College Conference on 'Intelligence and Military Operations', Carlisle Barracks, Pennsylvania, 22–25 April 1986. Copyright US Army War College Foundation. The views expressed in this article are those of the author and do not reflect the official policy or position of the Department of Defense or the US Government.

1. *Summa Theologica*, Secunda Secundae, Quaestio XL articulus. – Art. 3 permits deception on the ground that Joshua used it to capture the city of AI (Joshua viii, 1–22).
2. Carl von Clausewitz, *On War*, ed. and trans. Michael Howard and Peter Paret (Princeton, 1984), pp.117, 140.
3. This paper is based mainly on the Ultra signals derived from the decryption at Bletchley Park of the German *Wehrmacht* Enigma cipher. I was intimately involved there with assessing Ultra Intelligence and drafting the resulting signals from early in 1941 until the end of the war.
4. JPs 2851, 3127, 3134, 3145, 3192. Reference in this form are Ultra signals preserved in File DEFE 3 in the Public Record Office, Kew.
5. Clausewitz, p.113.
6. I.S.O. Playfair, *The Mediterranean and Middle East*, ii, p.281; iii, p.107. Stephen Roskill, *The War at Sea* (London, 1956), i, p.614.
7. OLs 936, 938, 954, 1125, 1149, 1192.
8. OLs 1227, 1322.
9. OL 1835.
10. MKA 2282.
11. MKAs 2094, 2095.
12. MKAs 2523, 2568, 2596, 2614, 2647, QTs 60, 136, 245, 256, 310, 331, 585, 604, 607, 658, 733, 758.
13. QTs 3712, 3785.
14. QTs 3868, 3915, 3973, 4077, 4119.
15. B.H. Liddell Hart (ed.), *The Rommel Papers* (New York, 1958), p.313.
16. QT 7058.
17. General Sir Claude Auchinleck, *Despatch*, p.374, in *Supplement to the London Gazette*, 15 January 1948.
18. Donald Maclachlan, *Room 39* (London, 1968).
19. F.H. Hinsley and others, *British Intelligence in the Second World War*, Vol. II (London, 1981), pp.499–500, 740–3.
20. Sir David Hunt, *A Don at War* (London, 1966), pp.147–51.
21. Hinsley, Vol. ii, pp.761–3, makes a half-hearted attempt to exonerate Mockler-Ferryman which does not accord with my reading of the evidence.
22. NSA. SRH-031.
23. MKAs 2094, 2095.
24. MLs 1955, 2400, 2513, 2733, 4439.
25. The Ultra evidence about this is sketched in my *Ultra in the West*, p.53.
26. XLs 6013, 6257, 8575, 8610, 9527.
27. KVs 192, 773, 930.
28. M.I. Handel, *Perception, Deception and Surprise* (Jerusalem, 1976) and 'Intelligence and The Problem of Strategic Surprise' in *Journal of Strategic Studies*, Vol. 7, No. 3 (1984), pp.229–81; Walter Laqueur, *World of Secrets* (London, 1985), pp.256–71.
29. Michael Handel, *Military Deception in Peace and War* (Jerusalem Papers on Peace Problems 38), p.35; Clausewitz, pp.309, 361.
30. MLs 7518, 7543, 7562, 7638, 7658, 7709, 8301, JPs 1024, 1027, 1111, 1370.
31. E.g. Playfair, op. cit., v, p.165, A.N. Garland and H.M. Smyth, *Sicily and the Surrender of Italy* (Washington, 1965), p.370.
32. John Terraine, *The Right of the Line* (London, 1985), p.579.
33. Playfair, op. cit., v, p.174, Garland and Smyth, op. cit., p.412, W.G.F. Jackson, *Alexander of Tunis as Military Commander* (London, 1971), p.225.

34. JP 357.
35. C 132, ML 2394.
36. JPs 37, 1383, 1487, 1512, 2261, 2911, 2952, 3080.
37. JP 2760.
38. JPs 5651, 6048, 6758.
39. JP 6915.
40. Alexander, *Memoirs*, ed. John North (London, 1962), p.117.
41. W.S. Churchill, *The Second World War* (London, 1951), v, pp.135, 194.
42. KV 1578, 4321, 5245.
43. KV 9843.
44. John Ehrman, *Grand Strategy* (London, 1956), v, p.356, Playfair, op. cit., vi/1, pp.313–35.
45. Foreign Policy Association, Headline Series No. 233, December 1976; compare Laqueur, p.315.
46. Laqueur (p.341) concedes the 'prosaic' nature of any likely improvements in intelligence procedure.
47. E.g. Hughes, p.10, R.K. Betts, 'Analysis, War and Decision. Why Intelligence Failures are Inevitable', in *World Politics*, Vol. 31, No. 1 (October 1978).
48. Hughes, p.13.
49. But it is not very reassuring to learn from Laqueur, p.321, note 15, that A. Cave Brown, *Bodyguard of Lies* (New York, 1976) is a set book in some American courses. General Sir David Fraser, *Alanbrooke* (London, 1982), and *And we shall Shock them* (London, 1983), repeatedly stresses the lessons of the past.
50. Ultra reports of the effects of Strangle, the attempt to cut the road and rail communications of Kesselring's armies in the summer of 1944 by bombing them, though not conclusive, were enough to cast doubts on the effectiveness of the policy. See also my article 'Intelligence and Strategy in World War II' in K.G. Robertson (ed.), *British and American Approaches to Intelligence* (London, 1987), and the evidence assembled in my *Ultra and Mediterranean Strategy* (London, 1989).
51. Laqueur, p.339.